The Sociology of Work

CONCEPTS AND CASES

The Sociology of Work

CONCEPTS AND CASES

Carol J. Auster

Franklin and Marshall College

PINE FORGE PRESS

Thousand Oaks, California
London ■ *New Delhi*

For information, address:

 Pine Forge Press
A Sage Publications Company
2455 Teller Road
Thousand Oaks, California 91320
Phone: (805) 499-4224
E-mail: sales@pfp.sagepub.com

Grateful acknowledgment is accorded to *The New York Times* for permission to quote from several articles, Copyright © 1993 by The New York Times Company, reprinted by permission.

Production: Publishing Support Services
Designer: Lisa S. Mirski
Typesetter: Publishing Support Services
Cover: Paula Shuhert and Graham Metcalfe
Production Manager: Rebecca Holland

Printed in the United States of America

96 97 98 99 10 9 8 7 6 5 4 3 2 1

Library of Congress Cataloging-in-Publication Data
Auster, Carol Jean.
        The sociology of work : concepts and cases / Carol J. Auster.
            p.   cm.
        Includes bibliographical references and index.
        ISBN 0-8039-9033-2 (p : alk. paper)
        1. Industrial sociology. 2. Industrial sociology--United States--
Case studies   I. Title.
        HD6955.A93   1996   95-20396
        306.3'6--dc20   CIP

For my parents

About the Author

Carol J. Auster is Associate Professor of Sociology at Franklin and Marshall College. She received her undergraduate degree from Colgate University and her M.A. and Ph.D. from Princeton University. In addition to teaching a course in work and occupations, she teaches the sociology of gender, research methods, and introductory sociology. She is currently conducting a longitudinal study of women and men in engineering and is co-investigator for a study of ethics in the academic profession.

About the Publisher

Pine Forge Press is a new educational publisher, dedicated to publishing innovative books and software throughout the social sciences. On this and any other of our publications, we welcome your comments and suggestions.

Please call or write to:

Pine Forge Press
A Sage Publications Company
2455 Teller Road
Thousand Oaks, California 91320
Phone: (805) 499-4224
Fax: (805) 499-7881
E-mail: sales@pfp.sagepub.com

Brief Contents

Detailed Contents

A fence, who deals in stolen goods, highlights the centrality of work and its rewards even for someone whose occupation is not mainstream.

2 Choosing an Occupation

3 Learning the Ropes

5 Bending the Rules

6 Combining Work and Family

7 The Future

Preface

With nearly every adult participating in the work force at some time in his or her life, one can certainly understand why students choose to take courses that focus on the sociology of work, occupations, and professions. Although such courses are often intended to fill curricular needs for sociology majors, they are also chosen by those who have little or no background in the discipline but who are willing to explore work and occupations in a sociological way. These students seem not only to want the sociological perspective on work, but they also presume that they will gain knowledge and perspective that will aid in understanding and managing their own occupational choices, day-to-day work, and career development. Ideally, these courses should be able to engage a variety of students, but that has been difficult to do with the types of books that have been available up until now.

In fact, I have been frustrated by the limited range of books available for teaching the sociology of work. In the past, the books have been of three types: comprehensive textbooks, which students often find impersonal, tedious, and lackluster; collections of articles or case studies that provide few, if any, conceptual or theoretical materials; and book-length monographs that tend to be narrowly focused, both theoretically and empirically. While the theoretical and conceptual material is necessary to provide a context for analysis, case studies not only give students an insightful glimpse into the real-life experiences of workers in a variety of settings, but they also provide a common set of experiences for all students to discuss, regardless of individual work backgrounds. Since I could not find a book that provided both, I found myself compiling long lists of readings to reach the appropriate balance. Eventually, the limitations of the existing types of books available and the insight, enthusiasm, and success with which my students analyzed case study materials led me to write this book.

By providing a book that integrates theory with interesting case studies, I believe I have provided the best of all worlds! The theoretical and conceptual frameworks provide the necessary background, while the details of the occupations, workers, and work settings described in the case studies can be used to judge the applicability and insight of the larger issues. This dialectic between the concepts and cases also seems to be the ideal way to improve students' critical thinking skills.

The book is divided into seven chapters, each of which covers a particular topic, such as occupational choice, workers' feelings about their work, or deviant occupational behavior. The first section of each chapter discribes current trends and highlights important concepts and theoretical perspectives relevant to the chapter's topic. (The reader will also find the most important concepts defined and referenced in the glossary/index at the end of the book.) The second section of each chapter comprises several case studies related to the topic in that chapter. I have featured the study questions at the beginning of the case studies, as these questions are often overlooked when they appear, as they do in most books, at the conclusion of an article or case study. In doing so, I hope to guide students' reading, urging them to consider the connections between the theoretical and conceptual materials and the case studies. For instance, before they read Case Study 3.1, "Serving Hamburgers and Selling Insurance," a question prompts students to compare the socialization of workers whose jobs require emotional labor, such as those working at McDonalds, to that of, say, construction workers, whose jobs demand pure physical labor.

Several other features of the case studies should help overcome some of the past limitations of other books. First by including case studies drawn from a variety of different types of work (e.g., managerial, clerical, semiskilled, unskilled) in the same chapter, I hope to eliminate some artificial differences that get imposed when textbooks treat each of those different types of work as though there are no common themes or commonalities between them.

Second, the nature of the ethnographic case studies should make the workers' feelings, attitudes, and behavior come alive for the reader. These concrete and dramatic readings allow students to see the implications of macro-scale concepts, characteristics, and changes on a variety of occupations and their incumbents. A range of occupations and issues are presented, such as why some garbage collectors happily choose that occupation, why longshoremen steal goods from ships, how male strippers are socialized to their occupation, how poultry process workers feel about their work, and how dual-career couples deal with their everyday work and family responsibilities.

I have woven case studies that reflect issues of gender, race, and ethnicity throughout the book rather than isolating them in their own separate section or chapter. This should help integrate these important issues into class discussions throughout the course. Other current issues that are discussed in the case studies include the growing service sector, technological advancement, and the global economy.

Because many of the case studies were originally written for a professional audience with heavily theoretical and research interests in mind, I have edited the case studies to increase their interest and relevance to students without losing the original scholarly flavor.

And while I have placed each case study in the chapter with the most relevance, my hope is that the multifaceted nature of many of the case studies will insert their discussion into other sections of the course. For example, while Kathleen Gerson's case study on women making choices about the role of work and family in their lives appears in the chapter on occupational choice, revisiting this case study in the discussion of the work and family chapter is also useful.

Finally, I hope you will share the enthusiasm of my own students for this book. They used a draft of the book in the most recent semester I taught the course, and they were excited to finally find a book that they could connect to their own lives. Provided with a conceptual lens through which they could view the experiences and feelings of workers in a variety of fields, students raved about the insight they gained into their own occupational choices, day-to-day work experience, and career development.

Acknowledgments

I would like to begin by thanking Steve Rutter at Pine Forge Press for his vision of what books in sociology should be and particularly for his encouragement of this project. I also thank the many students who have taken my course over the years, who, with their many questions, have added to the insight with which this book was written. I also appreciate the many useful suggestions that the reviewers provided in the early stages of this project:

Beverly Burris, *University of New Mexico*; Katharine Donato, *Louisiana State University*; Jay Rex Enoch, *Memphis State*; Tom Gerschick, *Illinois State University*; Kenneth J. Mietus, *Western Illinois University*; Robert Perrucci, *Purdue University*; James W. Shockey, *University of Arizona*; Barbara Stenross, *University of North Carolina*; Judith Stepan-Norris, *University of California-Irvine*; Joyce Tang, *University of Vermont*; John Walsh, *University of Illinois-Chicago*; and Steven Zehr, *Illinois Institute of Technology*.

I would like to express my appreciation to Becky Smith whose talents as a developmental editor enhanced the coherence of the book; Melissa Andrews for her fine copy editing; Vicki Moran for her patient ways, attention to detail, and persistence in keeping this book on schedule; and Rebecca Holland at Pine Forge for overseeing many stages of this book from beginning to end. I also thank Arlene Mimm for her patience and help with the process of obtaining the many copyright permissions needed to include the case studies in this book.

This section of acknowledgments is for my family, all of whom contributed to this book in one way or another. I am grateful to my parents who have been supportive and encouraging of my choices and endeavors throughout my life. My father, a sociologist, and my mother, an economist, both retired academics, supported this project by providing two more sets of eyes to proofread the manuscript. I also thank my sister, friend, and colleague, Ellen, and her husband, Steve, both social science academics, for providing me with interesting sources on a variety of topics. Although my cats Digger and Buck provided an appropriate level of distraction, Pie, my most clever and determined cat, was an inspiring daily companion as she sat purring in my lap and literally pinning me down to the task of writing this book. I also thank my daughters, Lauren and Lisa, now nearly 7 and 5, who provided encouragement for this project; they were so proud that their mother was writing a book. I am grateful to my husband, Neil, not only for his love, support, and encouragement, but also for his willingness to read every word of this book in its early stages and for pushing me to provide interesting and thought-provoking examples.

Finally, I thank the many workers who provided the details of their lives to the authors of the case studies included in this book. Without their willingness to share their views, a book combining conceptual materials with real life work experiences would not have been possible.

1 | Trends in Work

Because this book focuses on both work and occupations, it is important to begin by distinguishing between these two seemingly similar terms. Although work might include unpaid jobs and tasks done in the home, social scientists typically use an economic approach by considering only paid work. **Work** is the set of activities associated with performing one's paid occupation. For society, work provides goods and services to be purchased; for individuals, work provides the money to purchase those goods and services. Work can be producing or repairing a machine, creating a work of art, or providing services such as education, tax advice, or police protection.

Occupation is the position one holds or occupies, such as clerk, doctor, account executive, or garbage collector. In an organization, an individual's job title often reveals the occupation. If someone tells you that she is a surgical nurse, you can determine where that occupation places her in the larger societal hierarchy as well as in the hierarchy of her employing organization, the hospital.

Both the occupation and the environment in which a particular person holds that occupation define the actual work expected. Consider two friends who attended medical school together. Both specialize in pediatric medicine. One joins a pediatric practice in a wealthy suburb of Philadelphia. She is on call once every 5 weeks and treats patients who expect and can afford the latest diagnostic techniques and treatments. Her friend returns to his native city of Sarajevo in Bosnia. He treats patients who cannot afford even the most basic health care. His hours will be all his stamina will allow. Both hold the occupation of physician; but, by necessity, their daily goals and actual activities are quite different. In sum, work involves the actual activities that an individual carries out as a result of holding an occupation in a particular environment.

Importance of Occupational Position

Occupation is much more than just a classification; an individual's occupation shapes nearly every aspect of life. Occupational position has a greater impact on social class than any other variable. And social class is one of the strongest predictors of many other aspects of life.

First and foremost, occupation affects life expectancy largely through its relation to social class. The higher the social class, the longer the life expectancy. Occupation and social class can affect life expectancy in a variety of ways. First, occupation and social class are good predictors of health insurance coverage. Those with little or no health insurance and those with little income available for health care often have chronic illnesses—illnesses that could have been prevented by visiting a physician. Those chronic health conditions can lead to premature death. Second, occupations differ dramatically in their death rates as a result of occupational accidents. A miner or a taxi driver is much more likely to die on the job than an insurance salesperson or a child-care worker.

Besides life expectancy, social class is also highly correlated with many other important aspects of life. For example, divorce is more frequent in the lower classes. One cause of the high rate of divorce may be the economic instability introduced by lack of job opportunities, unstable income, or job loss. In addition, attitudes toward politics are affected by social class. The higher the social class, the more likely the individual is to vote in elections and identify with the Republican party, rather than the Democratic party.

The importance of occupation is evident even at parties and other social events. Those who don't know one another will ask, "What do you do?"—meaning "What do you do *for a living*?" The use of "for a living" emphasizes the importance of work in our society.

Also at issue is the value of work based on whether it's paid or unpaid. In our society, unpaid work is often devalued. For example, some full-time homemakers may describe themselves as "just a housewife," despite the fact that the work goes on 24 hours a day, 365 days a year with no planned retirement. The word *just* refers to the fact that the work is neither paid for by someone outside the home nor calculated as part of the Gross National Product (GNP), a presumed measure of a society's economic productivity. In fact, many think that there should be a way to calculate housework and child care as part of the GNP, since those tasks aid in society's productivity. The inclusion of the tasks of a homemaker in the GNP would result in a more accurate calculation because if someone in the home does not take care of these tasks, then someone outside the home is often paid to do them.

Similar to other social categories, such as gender, knowing an individual's occupation makes others feel they can more easily interact with that individual. For example, when you become a new patient at a dentist's office, you are asked to jot down your occupation on your chart along with your medical history. The dentist then uses your occupation as a guide to interaction with you and as a topic of conversation. Moreover, in movies and television programs, the occupations of the main characters are usually revealed and are often central to plot development. Presumably, this helps the audience better place and understand the characters.

As you have now seen, one's occupation has a dramatic impact on a variety of aspects of life. In Case Study 1.1, "Rewards of Fencing," Darrell Steffensmeier highlights the centrality of work and its rewards even for someone like Sam, who buys and sells stolen goods for a living.

Work and Leisure

If the actual activities associated with an occupation constitute work, then how do we define **leisure**? Are work and leisure always distinguishable from one another? At this point in your life, work and leisure may appear to be products of the choices an individual makes, changes, and makes again throughout life. However, the type of work you do along with your age, social class, and a variety of other important sociological variables can have a strong influence on the relationship between work and leisure and the choice of leisure activities. This section examines a number of perspectives on the relationship between work and leisure along with the effects of social characteristics on that relationship.

Characterizations of Work and Leisure

On the first day of class, my students and I develop a list of characteristics that describes work and another list that describes leisure. The list of words to describe work includes *time watching, schedule, hierarchy, something you have to do, tedious, dirty, physically hard, stifling, important, not challenging, paid, alienating, satisfying, responsibility, character building, obedient, mindless,* and *creative.* The list of terms to describe leisure includes *fun, relaxation, not stressful, quiet, release, one's own choice, exciting, slow-paced, satisfying, rewarding, self-fulfilling, more of oneself, freedom, family, relationships, not enough time, mindless,* and *creative.* As we look at the two lists, I ask the students why they describe work and leisure this way. We learn that the many negative characteristics these students use to describe work are related to the kinds of jobs they have typically held—minimum wage jobs, temporary jobs, jobs they hope do not become lifetime occupations. These same jobs, waiter or waitress, cereal box stuffer, short-order cook, are lifetime occupations for others, who might or might not use the same words to describe these jobs. Most of these students hope that they will have careers that encapsulate the best characteristics of a potential occupation. Most hope to find an occupation that is interesting and provides lifelong satisfaction, not a boring, tedious job that offers endless clock watching and profound relief when each day of work ends.

The words for leisure listed by the students in my class reflect activity that is fun, rewarding, and something to look forward to. The words also reflect control over how the time available for leisure will be used. If you were to estimate the amount of time available for leisure in a week, you could use the following calculations. There are 24 hours in a day and 7 days in a week. That gives you a total of 168 hours in a week. If 40 hours (8 hours a day for 5 days) a week are used for working, then the remaining 128 hours are available for nonwork and leisure activities. But, nonwork activities can be very time consuming. One nonwork activity is sleeping. If we assume that 56 hours a week are used for sleeping, then 72 hours are left over. But some of those 72 hours are taken up by other nonwork activities such as taking showers, mowing the lawn, cleaning the house, shopping for groceries, cooking meals, doing the laundry, getting the car fixed, and taking pets to the veterinarian.

What, then, is leisure? Leisure activities can range from riding a bicycle 60 miles on a Saturday morning to lying in a hammock and daydreaming. Leisure activities are potentially satisfying and pleasurable activities chosen to fill the time left over after work, sleep, and other obligatory nonwork activities are taken care of. How obligatory are these nonwork activities? While one person may take pleasure in mowing the lawn or taking care of landscaping, another may be adding these activities to the list of slightly unpleasant obligatory tasks of the week.

Relationship Between Work and Leisure

Social scientists have three general perspectives on the relationship between work and leisure. The first is the *spillover* or *holistic* (Murphy, 1975) perspective in which meaning and satisfaction are found in both work and leisure. The activities, friendships, and satisfaction that are a result of work spill over into leisure. In this optimistic view, the activities of work or the friendships developed at work are so satisfying that an individual carries them over into leisure time. For example, when I am reading *The New York Times,* not only am I reading it for pleasure, but also I am looking for articles relevant to the courses I teach and the research or writing I am doing. Thus, aspects of my work are spilling over into my leisure time. Critics argue that this view loses sight of what is distinctive and different about leisure.

Another view of the relationship between work and leisure is called the *dualistic* or *compensatory* perspective (Kelly, 1982). Those who support this perspective believe that work and leisure are quite separate. This more pessimistic view of work suggests that leisure activities are chosen to compensate for dissatisfaction with work. The middle manager who is not challenged by his or her desk job might skydive or ride a motorcycle on the weekend. Because of negative aspects of either the actual work or the work environment, individuals must seek satisfaction and fulfillment in leisure rather than work activities.

A more optimistic view of this perspective is that leisure activities are chosen to compensate for particular activities missing from work even though the work itself may be satisfying on other levels. An executive who finds her job challenging and rewarding, but mentally exhausting, might choose rock climbing or running as a leisure activity. This notion of compensatory activity could account for the high educational level and occupational prestige of the majority of runners in the New York City marathon. On the other hand, a construction worker who sweats and strains all day may choose billiards, bowling, or beer drinking with friends for his leisure hours. Critics argue that this dualistic/compensatory view assumes that work is innately unsatisfying and overlooks the possibility that work can be very satisfying. Those who support the dualistic view are more likely to focus on the activities of work and consider the two spheres as separate, even if not necessarily compensatory.

A third view, the *pluralistic* view (Kelly, 1982), suggests that satisfaction can be found on the job in both the relationships one forms with coworkers and the inherent nature of the work. This perspective also recognizes that some jobs may be too constrained by supervision or task repetition to be self-fulfilling (Kelly, 1993: 128). Thus, those supporting this view would argue that it is difficult to predict what people will choose and find satisfying in their leisure activities. Some of the potential meaning and satisfaction of work may be found in leisure as well. Learning a new skill, accepting a new challenge, expressing creativity, and practicing genuine charity can be a part of either work or leisure. One needs to find self-fulfillment somewhere. The pluralistic perspective implies that there are a variety of ways in which both work and leisure can be satisfying.

In Case Study 1.2, "The British Railway Worker as Compared with Architects," Graeme Salaman examines the work and leisure lives of British railway workers and architects. The comparison of these two occupational groups illustrates the need for more than one perspective on the relationship between work and leisure.

Impact of Social Characteristics

The relationship between work and leisure can be affected by a variety of social characteristics of the individual, including age, social class, and gender (Jackson, 1993).

First, one's age or stage in the life cycle can have a large impact on work and leisure. For preschool children, leisure is life, and even learning the alphabet may be a game. In later years, education may become an obligation, and the boundary between work and leisure begins to become evident. During the main working years, from 25 to 65 or 70 years of age, leisure time is the most limited, not only because so many hours are spent working, but also because more hours are spent washing the car, mowing the lawn, balancing the checkbook, and caring for children. Finally, in retirement, the number of hours for leisure increases again.

Social class, which is largely influenced by one's occupation, has an impact on the choice of leisure activities. Social class culture may cause individuals to believe that some activities are more interesting than others. Those of the upper classes would be more likely to play tennis or go to the opera. Bowling and country line dancing are more likely to be interests of the working class. Moreover, income has an impact on the possible choice of activities. A prominent surgeon can own a yacht and join a local yachting club. A laundry worker with the same love of sailing may be limited to renting a rowboat once in a while. Or a laundry worker may be working so many hours to make a living that there is no time for leisure. Thus, the amount of income derived from work may limit or expand the range of available leisure activities.

Gender can also have an impact on the choice of recreational activities. While both women and men may ski, play tennis, bowl, and watch television, other recreational activities are gender typed. Men are more likely to go to football games, and women are more likely to take quilting classes. Some women and men may seek out their co-workers for recreational activities. In Case Study 1.3, "Abnormal Intimacy: The Varying Work Networks of Chicana Cannery Workers," Patricia Zavella illustrates how both gender and ethnicity affect work and friendship networks among Chicana cannery workers.

Trends in Leisure

In her book *The Overworked American* (1991), Juliet Schor argues that Americans are working more hours than ever before as a result of both personal desires and economic conditions. Members of the working class may find they need two jobs in order to sustain their family's expenses. Retrenchment and downsizing have forced some employees to work long hours to make up for the lacuna left by laid-off workers. Young, achievement-oriented, urban professionals add hours to their work week to pursue higher rungs on the career ladder. Cutting-edge companies obligate their employees to show commitment to the company by working long hours and being available. That availability may include the willingness to participate in leisure activities, such as a golf game or boat cruise, with current or potential clients. Are these activities truly leisure activities when the company demands employees' attendance at such events? In addition, commuting to and from work may add more than 3 hours to an employee's already long work day. When couples return home, wives are more likely than husbands to put in a **second shift** (Hochschild, 1989), taking care of household tasks. Women, in particular, find themselves deprived of leisure.

Even when individuals have the time to pursue leisure activities, those activities may not turn out as they planned. Staffan Linder, the author of *The Harried Leisure Class* (1970), further argued that consumption has become a leisure activity. For example, although the goal of a family of boat enthusiasts is to spend time on the water in the boat, they end up harried as a result of reading information about boats to purchase, visiting many boat dealers, and finally purchasing a boat. Once they own the boat, they find they spend less time on the water and more time maintaining the boat than they expected.

The demands at work, the "second shift," and the purchases associated with some leisure activities all decrease the time available for activities of one's own choosing.

The Labor Force

Before we move on to the other chapters, I will introduce you to some of the official **labor force** statistics. We will examine how these statistics are calculated and review critiques of those calculations before we look at some current labor force trends.

Definitions

The **civilian labor force** comprises all the civilians in the noninstitutional population 16 years or over classified as "employed" or "unemployed" according to the following criteria: **Employed** civilians comprise (a) all civilians who, during the reference week, did work for pay or profit (minimum of an hour's work) or worked 15 hours or more as unpaid workers in a family enterprise, and (b) all civilians who were not working but who had jobs or businesses from which they were temporarily absent for noneconomic reasons (illness, weather conditions, vacation, labor-management dispute, etc.)

whether they were paid for time off or seeking other jobs. **Unemployed** persons comprise all civilians who had no employment during the reference week, who made specific efforts to find a job within the previous 4 weeks (such as applying directly to an employer, or to a public employment service, or checking with friends), and who were available for work during that week, except for temporary illness. Persons on layoff from a job or waiting to report to a new job within 30 days are also classified as unemployed if they were available for work. All other civilian persons, 16 years old and over, are "not in the labor force." The total labor force includes, in addition to the civilian, employed and unemployed members of the Armed forces stationed in the United States (U.S. Bureau of the Census, 1994: 392).

Some terms in this definition need to be further explained. The term *civilian labor force* is most often used in the presentation of labor force statistics. The noninstitutionalized population is composed of the individuals who are not in prison, a residential mental institution, a nursing home, or some other institution that would keep them from fully participating in the work force. The **reference week** is "the calendar week, Sunday through Saturday, which includes the 12th day of the month" (U.S. Department of Labor, 1995b: 137). The information about the civilian labor force is collected during the week that includes the 19th of the month and refers to work during the previous week, the reference week. Each month, the Bureau of Labor reports the labor force participation rate for the month that just ended. The labor force is composed of the employed and the unemployed, and the **labor force participation rate** is a ratio of the number of employed and unemployed persons by the above criteria to the number of people in the civilian noninstitutionalized population who are 16 years or older. In simpler terms, the labor force participation rate is the percent of people who are working or looking for work divided by the number of people eligible to work. If you multiply that number by 100, you will have the percent of people who are working or looking for work relative to those eligible to work.

Definitional Difficulties

If these definitions are used, a variety of people who contribute to our economy and society are excluded from the labor force. First, people who carry out productive activity, but not for direct pay, are excluded. For example, homemakers carrying out the tasks associated with household upkeep or child care are not counted. Second, children engaged in these activities are also not acknowledged. Third, some individuals, although not paid, contribute to society by helping others through volunteer organizations, but they are excluded from the labor force. Fourth, workers who are not employed and have not made efforts to find a job in the last 4 weeks, perhaps because they have lost hope of being hired, are not included. Fifth, individuals producing goods or providing services who do not acknowledge their work to the government are not counted. Individuals in this group could range from those engaged in illegal activities, such as selling drugs, to the teenager who babysits for his or her neighbor's child. Sixth, those who have illegal immigrant status may be working productively, but neither their presence nor their labor is acknowledged.

Another important statistic is the unemployment rate. As stated previously, an unemployed person is someone who did not have a job during that reference week but who was available and had looked for work in the past 4 weeks. The **unemployment rate** "represents the number unemployed as a percent of the [civilian] labor force" (U.S. Department of Labor, 1995d: 71). It is computed by dividing the number of unemployed people by the number of people in the labor force. This decimal number is then multiplied by 100 for the unemployment rate.

Although the unemployment rate reflects the overall state of the economy, the government has revamped the survey used to collect information to determine the rate of unemployment. The last major revision of the survey was in 1967, and the Labor Department has been aware for some time that the 1967 wording is not sensitive to many of the changes that have occurred in the last 30 years or so (Hershey, 1993; U.S. Department of Labor, 1994).

One result of the new survey is that more women are legitimately classified as unemployed. In the past, interviewers were told to tailor the questions to their respondent's "apparent situation" (U.S. Bureau of Labor, 1994: 17). Consequently, respondents were asked, "What were you doing most of last week (working, keeping house, going to school, or something else)?" In practice, men were usually asked about working, women were usually asked about keeping house, and teenagers were usually asked about going to school (Hershey, 1993: D-2). Because of this wording, some women were not counted as part of the labor force when they should have been counted as unemployed members of the labor force. In the new survey, "*everyone* is asked whether he or she did *any* work for pay" (17). As a consequence, the labor force participation rate increased somewhat more for women than for men. In addition, the unemployment rate increased slightly more for teenagers and workers 65 years and older than for those in other age groups (U.S. Department of Labor, 1994: 16).

On the other hand, one group that has never been included as part of the labor force is **discouraged workers.** These are workers who are interested in working, but who have not looked for a job in the past 4 weeks because they have lost hope of finding a job. Some social scientists argue that if discouraged workers were included as part of the labor force and counted as unemployed workers, we would then have a more accurate picture of unemployment, particularly among groups with few viable work options. Consequently, the U.S. Department of Labor now collects additional information on these workers and reports the data quarterly.

Current Labor Force Statistics

Knowledge of the current statistical trends with regard to the labor force participation rate and the unemployment rate should provide a broad perspective on U.S. workers, including variations by gender, age, and race.

What do you think the labor force participation rate is for men? Do you think that it is 95 percent, 85 percent, 75 percent, or 65 percent? The answer might surprise you—the labor force participation rate for men is typically around 75 percent. So, what are the other men doing? Some are full-time students and do not work, particularly those who are still in high school. Table 1.1 shows that the labor force participation rate for those 16 to 19 years of age is lower than that of any other age group except for those 65 years of age and older. Another group of men who are not part of the labor force are those who are retired; this is reflected in the decreasing labor force participation rates of men 55 and older. The third largest group are those who are either physically or mentally unable to work.

Now that you know the current labor force participation rate for men, do you think the current labor force participation rate for women is closer to 20 percent, 40 percent, 60 percent, or 80 percent? Overall, the current labor force participation rate for women is 58.7 percent, very close to 60 percent. Table 1.1 shows that the pattern of labor force participation by age for women is similar to that for men, reaching its highest levels for women between 20 and 54 years of age and decreasing for those 55 and older. In the years of peak employment, the labor force participation rate is somewhat lower for women than for men, which is due to some women's choice not to participate in the labor force. Nevertheless, 60.6 percent of married women currently work. Moreover, for married women with children 6 to 17

Table 1.1

Labor Force Participation Rates for Men and Women by Age

| | Gender | |
	Men	Women
Overall	74.9	58.7
16 to 19 years	50.8	49.5
20 to 24 years	82.1	70.0
25 to 34 years	93.0	74.0
35 to 44 years	92.8	77.5
45 to 54 years	89.1	74.9
55 to 64 years	66.8	49.3
65 years and over	16.8	8.6

Source: U.S. Department of Labor, 1995a: Table A-13.

years of age the labor force participation rate is 76.0 percent; for those with children under 6 years of age the rate is 61.7 percent; and for those with children 1 year or under the rate is 56.1 percent (U.S. Department of Labor, 1995c: Tables 15 and 48). Interestingly, the *Statistical Abstract of the United States,* a commonly used government resource book, does not include figures for men's labor force participation rate by the presence and age of children. In Chapter 6, we will look carefully at the relationship between work and family.

Another way to look at the role of women and men in the labor force is to consider the percent of all workers who are women. Currently, there are 132 million workers in the labor force. Of those, 60.6 million are women, and 71.4 million are men (U.S. Department of Labor, 1995b: Table A-2). This means that women make up 45.9 percent of individuals in the labor force and men make up 54.1 percent. This emphasizes the important contribution of both women and men to our economy.

Table 1.2 shows unemployment rates by age, gender, and race. While women and men of the same race have rather similar rates of unemployment, age and race have dramatic effects on the unemployment rate. For example, those under 25 years of age of every race have a higher unemployment rate than those who are older than 25 years of age. Even among the two youngest groups, there are differences by race. While the unemployment rate of whites 16 to 19 years of age is 17.6 percent for men, the unemployment rate for Hispanic men is 26.2 percent, and for black men the unemployment rate peaks at 40.2 percent. The unemployment rate for women in this age group is similar to that of the men of the same race. On the other hand, the unemployment rate for women 45 to 54 years of age is much more

Table 1.2

Percent of the Labor Force Unemployed by Gender, Race, and Age

	White		Hispanic		Black	
	Men	Women	Men	Women	Men	Women
16 to 19 years	17.6	14.6	26.2	26.3	40.2	37.5
20 to 24 years	9.5	7.8	12.6	14.1	23.0	20.8
25 to 34 years	6.2	5.7	8.9	9.9	12.3	12.9
35 to 44 years	5.0	4.7	8.8	9.6	10.5	8.6
45 to 54 years	4.6	4.3	8.8	8.3	8.1	5.8
55 to 64 years	4.7	3.9	8.4	7.2	9.0	5.2
65 years and over	2.9	3.0	9.5	1.9	5.6	3.8

Source: U.S. Bureau of the Census, 1994: Table 628.

similar across racial groups: 4.3 percent for whites, 8.3 percent for Hispanics, and 5.8 percent for blacks.

You have now seen how the social categories to which individuals belong can have a dramatic effect on their labor force participation and unemployment as reflected by the significant variations in labor force statistics by age, gender, and race.

Societal Trends

Four important societal trends are having a dramatic impact on work and occupations: women's increased labor force participation, technological advancement, growth of the service sector, and the global economy. In the future, these trends will continue to shape not only the overall occupational structure, but also the specific work activities in which individuals are engaged.

Women's Increased Labor Force Participation

Although for men the labor force participation rate has changed little over the last several decades, one of the most striking trends in the U.S. labor force of the last several decades has been the increased entrance of women into the work force. Table 1.3 shows how these figures have changed historically. Over the last several decades, one of the most dramatic differences in women's labor force participation has been among married women with children. For example, while the labor force participation rate for married women with children aged 6 to 17 was 39.0 percent in 1960, it is now 76.0 percent for that same group. Similarly, while the labor force participation rate was 18.6 percent for married women with children under age 6 in 1960, it is now 61.7 percent. Not surprisingly, the labor force participation for

Table 1.3

Labor Force Status of Women (1940–1994) by Marital Status and Age of Children

(women 14 years and over 1940–1960; 16 years and over thereafter)

	1940*	1950*	1960	1970	1980	1994
Single	48.1	50.5	44.1	53.0	61.5	65.1
Married	16.7	24.8	30.5	40.8	50.1	60.6
Widowed/divorced/separated	32.0	36.0	40.0	39.1	44.0	47.3
Married with any children	—	—	27.6	39.7	54.1	69.0
Married, children 6–17 only	—	—	39.0	49.2	61.7	76.0
Married, children under 6	—	—	18.6	30.3	45.1	61.7
Divorced with any children	—	—	—	74.8	78.2	80.1
Divorced, children 6–17 only	—	—	—	82.4	82.3	84.9
Divorced, children under 6	—	—	—	63.3	68.3	67.5

Sources: U.S. Bureau of the Census (1980, Table 668; 1994, Tables 626, 627); U.S. Department of Labor (1975, Table 15; 1980, Table 15; 1995c, Tables 1, 15).

women who are divorced, widowed, or separated has changed very little; whereas the rate was 40.0 percent in 1960, it is now 47.3 percent.

Technological Advancement

A second trend, particularly of the 1990s, is the dramatic change in technology, especially with regard to the transmission of information. Some categories of white-collar workers find that car phones, fax machines, voice mail, and electronic mail are all a part of everyday life. Quick transmittal of information has become a premium in many of today's businesses. Even on college campuses, faculty members communicate with one another by electronic mail. This may mean that two faculty members on campuses 2,000 miles apart may work jointly on an article they are writing by transmitting it electronically as each makes revisions. We explore the far-reaching consequences of technology throughout the book.

Growth of the Service Sector

A third dramatic change in work in the United States over the last century has been the result of shifts in the economy. In the early part of this century, our economy was predominantly devoted to the **primary sector.** Most workers were in jobs directly related to raw materials, including logging the forests, fishing the waters, and farming and mining the land. Later in the century, although some workers continued to work in the primary sector of the economy, an increasing number of workers became engaged in jobs in the **secondary sector**, also known as the industrial sector. That is, more workers were engaged in converting raw materials into manufactured products. In the industrial society, factories reigned as the secondary sector of the economy expanded. Now, social scientists describe our society as postindustrial with increasing numbers of workers employed in the **tertiary** or **service sector** of the economy. The significance of the expansion and dominance of the service sector of our economy is that rather than the production of goods being the main economic activity, the provision of services now dominates the economy. These services include providing insurance, educating children, and handling computer technology. The shift in dominance from the primary sector to the industrial sector and then to the service sector means that more people are engaged in white-collar jobs than ever before, although some of these white-collar jobs are low level. (In fact, some workers engaged in the manufacturing of products are better paid than those engaged in some of the lower level white-collar jobs.) One consequence of the growth of the service sector is that more **emotional labor** is used and needed than ever before (Hochschild, 1983). For example, flight attendants are taught to manage their emotions and use their skills to manage the emotions of others aboard a flight. The friendly smile is intended to create a pleasant atmosphere; however, the ultimate goal is more passengers and higher profits.

The Global Economy

A fourth trend is the increasing dependence and interdependence of the economy of one nation on the economy of others. The most common term used to describe this phenomenon is **global economy.** Through NAFTA (North American Free Trade Agreement), an agreement designed to remove tariff barriers between the United States, Canada, and Mexico, the United States explicitly acknowledges its interest in and dependence on the economies outside our borders. The intended consequence of NAFTA is a common market of North America.

The aforementioned societal trends—the increasing number of women in the work force, the increasing number of service occupations, the impact of technology on work, and the global economy—are evident throughout this book.

Plan of the Book

The first part of each chapter focuses on the important concepts and ideas that shape the current sociological thinking on the topic in that chapter. The second part of each chapter consists of several ethnographic selections that relate to the chapter topic. These case studies are intended to make the workers' feelings, attitudes, and behavior come alive for you, the reader. The case studies also provide you with the opportunity to critically evaluate the theoretical perspectives presented in the chapter. Moreover, issues of gender and race/ethnicity are addressed in the case studies and also serve as an underlying theme throughout the book. Because of the multifaceted nature of many of the case studies, I hope that you will think about them not only in the context of the chapter in which they appear, but also in the context of the topics of other chapters.

Chapter 1 looks at the relationship between work and leisure, labor force statistics, and four major trends affecting work. In Chapter 2, we look at occupational choice, the beginning of the process of joining the work force. You may think that individuals with the innate talent to do so can pursue their dream careers; however, individuals' options are strongly affected by societal forces. In Chapter 3, we look at occupational socialization, the process of learning the skills and norms peculiar to an occupation or an occupational environment. Chapter 4 explores how the work in particular occupations and occupational environments has an impact on workers' feelings of satisfaction, alienation, and stress. Although it is tempting to try to locate the cause of deviant occupational behavior entirely within the individual, Chapter 5 shows the extent to which the potential for deviant behavior is created by opportunities presented to those in the occupation and the degree to which those already in the occupation condemn or condone the behavior. Chapter 6 discusses the link between work and family by examining both the impact of work on family and the impact of family on work. We will better understand how individual family dilemmas are a result of larger organizational policies and societal forces. In Chapter 7, the final chapter, we focus on three issues: technological innovation, reengineering, and worker participation. We explore the controversies associated with each of these and the impact they have on the individual worker.

As you move through this book (and through life), you will find that an array of societal factors—age, gender, occupation, social class, race/ethnicity—shape individuals' choices. This important theme is repeated throughout this book. Although as individuals we often feel that we have many unconstrained choices or that society does not have much of an impact on us, the world of work (as well as every other aspect of social life) is largely affected by the people, organizations, and society around us.

REFERENCES AND SUGGESTED READINGS

Dandridge, Thomas C. 1988. "Work Ceremonies: Why Integrate Work and Play?" Pages 251–259 in *Inside Organizations,* edited by Michael Owen Jones, Michael Dane Moore, and Richard Christopher Snyder.

Hershey, Robert D. 1993. "Jobless Rate Underestimated, U.S. Says, Citing Survey Bias." *The New York Times,* November 17: A-1, D-2.

Hochschild, Arlie Russell. 1983. *The Managed Heart.* Berkeley: University of California Press.

Hochschild, Arlie Russell with Anne Machung. 1989. *The Second Shift.* NY: Viking.

Jackson, Edgar L. 1993. "Recognizing Patterns of Leisure Constraints: Results from Alternative Analyses." *Journal of Leisure Research* 25 (2): 129–149.

Kelly, John R. 1982. *Leisure.* Englewood Cliffs, NJ: Prentice-Hall.

Linder, Staffan B. 1970. *The Harried Leisure Class.* New York: Columbia University Press.

Murphy, James. 1975. *Recreation and Leisure Service.* Dubuque, IA: William C. Brown.

Rybczynski, Witold. 1991. *Waiting for the Weekend.* New York: Viking.

Schor, Juliet B. 1991. *The Overworked American: The Unexpected Decline of Leisure.* New York: Basic Books.

U.S. Bureau of the Census. 1980. *Statistical Abstract of the U.S.: 1980.* Washington, DC: U.S. Government Printing Office.

U.S. Bureau of the Census. 1994. *Statistical Abstract of the U.S.: 1994.* Washington, DC: U.S. Government Printing Office.

U.S. Department of Labor. 1975 (March), 1980 (March) *Marital and Family Characteristics of the Labor Force: Current Population Survey.* Washington DC: Bureau of Labor Statistics.

U.S. Department of Labor. 1994. *Employment and Earnings* 41 (February). Washington, DC: Bureau of Labor Statistics.

U.S. Department of Labor. 1995a. *Employment and Earnings* 42 (January). Washington, DC: Bureau of Labor Statistics.

U.S. Department of Labor. 1995b. *Employment and Earnings* 42 (February). Washington, DC: Bureau of Labor Statistics.

U.S. Department of Labor. 1995c. *Marital and Family Characteristics of the Labor Force from the March 1994 Current Population Survey.* (February). Washington, DC: Bureau of Labor Statistics.

U.S. Department of Labor. 1995d. *Monthly Labor Review* 118 (March). Washington, DC: Bureau of Labor Statistics.

Wheeler, Stanton. 1990. "Double Lives." Pages 141–148 in *The Nature of Work,* edited by Kai Erikson and Steven Peter Vallas. New Haven: Yale University Press.

Rewards of Fencing

Darrell Steffensmeier

CASE STUDY QUESTIONS

1. What does Sam feel is rewarding about his work?
2. How are these rewards similar to and different from what people engaged in more legitimate occupations might expect from their work?
3. What does Sam's description of his life tell us about the centrality of work?

In It For The Money

What do you mean, why did I do it? Because it was good money. I did it for the easy dollar. What you can buy cheap will have a bigger cut in it for you.

One important reason for Sam enjoying fencing is, understandably, the money. Sam is a businessman, and whether he trades legitimately or illegitimately, he is in business to make a profit. Stolen goods can be purchased more cheaply than legitimate goods so that Sam stands a chance of making a greater profit. Furthermore, with the kind of business that he runs (antiques, secondhand goods), Sam may earn his profit with less travail when buying stolen rather than legitimate merchandise.

Source: From *The Fence: In the Shadow of Two Worlds* by Darrell Steffensmeier, 1986, Boston: Rowman and Littlefield. Copyright 1986 by Rowman and Littlefield.

Say there's an ad in the paper, somebody wanting to sell eight pieces of wicker furniture. I'm gonna buy it legit, right? So I makes a call, then I drives out and checks it over. The guy wants so much but I don't want to pay that. So we haggle over price. Maybe we don't come to terms, so I got to call him back or make another trip out. That is a lot of time, a lot of bullshit, really. Here's the thing: if I run to the auctions, watch the ads in the paper of private sales, and that, I can buy pretty cheaply. But I got my time, the trip, and having to deal with some Joe Blow who is trying to jew me. Fuck it. You don't always make more on the warm stuff, many times you don't, but there's less hassle and haggling.

As an incentive for fencing stolen goods, money is important to Sam for more than just its potential for acquiring material possessions. As with the rest of us, Sam places great importance on the symbolic value of money for satisfying all sorts of diverse needs in our society. Thus, when Sam interprets his fencing involvement as money-motivated, he means several things. First, he enjoys what money can buy—the goods and services that can be bought with it. Second, he enjoys the process of making money—the feelings of satisfaction and well-being that come from turning a fast dollar. Third, Sam enjoys the peer recognition that comes both from having and making money, since money is associated with achievement and recognition or, conversely, of failure.

It is not surprising that at first glance Sam ascribes the overriding (and sometimes the sole) motivation for his fencing involvement to the desire for money. After all, with know-how and connections, fencing stolen goods can be very lucrative. And in our culture, the desire to make money is a highly acceptable and rational explanation both to oneself and to others of why one does what one does, especially when asked to explain involvement in a high-risk enterprise, be it legal or illegal. Nonetheless, at other times, and on closer inspection, Sam is also attracted to fencing by the social or non-economic rewards that inhere in expertise, prestige, power, a positive self-image, and a number of other job conditions he defines as desirable.

"Being Somebody"

Within the criminal community—where status is determined by one's skills, racket or hustle, financial success, reputation for being solid, and connections—being a large-scale dealer in stolen goods brings with it a certain amount of prestige and power. Fences are viewed as skillful, well-connected, and as making good money. They are also seen as having a respectable hustle or a preferred kind of criminal business in that fencing is dependable, yields a good profit, allows for considerable independence and control, and is reasonably legitimate because it is built around a regular business. Furthermore, while not all fences are pillars of integrity, Sam takes special pride in being somebody who is solid, and more generally, is recognized as "good people."

First, as a fence, Sam occupies a strategic position in the underworld. He is an important person to know, in the obvious sense that he is a middleman for the trafficking in stolen goods, but also because he is a source of contacts and a conduit of information on underworld activities. As Sam's fencing operation shifted into high gear, he found himself increasingly in demand—by thieves coming to peddle stolen wares, merchants wanting to purchase merchandise at below-wholesale prices, and store customers hoping to find what they need at bargain prices. Sam may play down the significance of how burglars and other thieves view him, but he enjoys the recognition and adulation he receives from many of them. For a few, Sam acts as an "old head" offering advice on theft techniques and the underworld code.

The whole thing was being noticed. That everybody knew me, knew who I was. People would come in the store, "Where's Sam? When's he coming back?" Just being recognized on the street, or going into a place to have coffee. Stopping at Casey's after the races on Fridays, buying drinks for the house—which was a way of keeping the thieves in my pocket but it was being a big shot, too. It's human nature to want that recognition, not so much that you're the center of attention, now, but that they look up to you, respect you for what you are. Take the thieves asking for advice, really they are looking up to you.

Second, fencing for Sam is a step up from burglary, even a step up from being a "good burglar."

It changed for me, when I got into dealing, put it that way. I was making more money, some more, anyway. But mainly I wasn't crawling in windows anymore, where I could get shot or whatever else. See, a thief is a thief, and the fence has higher status, more recognition, than a thief. It's a step up. Even your good thief is still a thief, although they can be very respected.

I considered myself a notch above even the good burglar. On a scale of one to ten, the fence is pretty high, especially if he's solid. Now, I wouldn't be as high as Angelo or Little Nicky 'cause they were in the rackets something big and had ties, but your fence is pretty high.

Third, to the extent that fencing is an outgrowth (and perhaps a culmination) of prior illegal and quasi-legitimate involvements, becoming a successful dealer not only is a "promotion" of sorts but also may bring about changes in the "kind of crowd that one hangs with." Being a fence meant that Sam belonged to a more élite class of underworld members, that he associated with more important people, and that he was a "heavy" in the local community. More than anything, perhaps, Sam cherished being identified with and rubbing shoulders with the local gang as well as being a member of the gambling club.

The gambling group meets almost weekly and is both a play and a business group. It is a place to go and relax, a place to have fun, and a refuge from the hard work of criminal enterprise. It also combines at least a little business with pleasure, in particular, by being a source of information or a place where members can find out something about each other's activities or inactivities. Mainly, however, the club does not so much consciously facilitate crime as it emphasizes the satisfying and rewarding payoffs associated with illicit livelihoods. The club provides a setting where members can "play" successful and self-assured criminals, displaying little difficulty and even less ambivalence in accepting that identity.

> I enjoyed the gambling. That I can honestly say. It was relaxation and a chance to find out about what is happening in town. But the whole thing was being noticed, too. That I was a pretty big person around town. A big shot, you might say. There's a recognition that comes from rubbing shoulders with Angelo, Little Nicky, and them. You're aware of that. See, I came up without nothing. Everything I got I worked for, got on my own. It was more or less important to me to be hanging with the better class of people.
> You're in with a different class of people when you're fencing, in with businessmen and that. A really different class of people. When you're into burglary, you're with guys that horse around, have fun, drink beer, go nightclubbing. Guys that mostly don't work.
> I considered myself higher than the thieves. They sold to me, some hung in my store. I might buy them dinner or drinks at Casey's. But as far as social, no. There were a couple I was friends with, but that was it. I wouldn't travel in their crowd. I was traveling with a different crowd. Don't get me wrong, there are some burglars out there that are good people, but it's different. Whole different crowd.
> With the fencing, your dealers are higher class. They're really businessmen and are into a higher racket. You're playing cards, maybe going to Vegas or Atlantic City, or you go out for dinner at a better class of place, have steak, mixed drinks. It's a whole different league.

Also, as a legitimate general merchandise dealer, Sam can, and indeed does, lay claim to the status of businessman, a fact which is indistinguishable from his sense of well-being and his place in the broader society. Sam not only recognizes the legitimacy and stable social identity that attaches to anyone who falls into the general classification of businessman, but also appreciates that what he does as a businessman-fence differs only minutely from that of legitimate members of his trade; that is, fencing itself is a business and requires valued attributes, such as hard work, marketing skills, and the ability to manage money. That Sam associates with and is on friendly terms with many legitimate businessmen, he interprets as further evidence of his acceptance in the local business community.

> I look at it this way, I was a businessman. That's the way I saw myself. That's the way others treated me. Even those that didn't do business with me in the hot stuff, respected me, accepted me for what I was, and I respected them. I would have coffee and that with them. They might stop at my store, I might stop at theirs.

Finally, an added sense of respectability and of being somebody derive from Sam's business in still another way. As a merchant who offers merchandise at "bargain" prices and who is sometimes generous in other ways, Sam can play the role of "Robin Hood."…(Both the Robin Hood role and Sam's friendly association with local businessmen also form a major part of Sam's rationale.)

> I did a lot of good, helped a lot of people. I had the best prices in town which helped a lot of poor people. They came to me like I was the last one on earth. There were many of them that put me up on a pedestal like you wouldn't believe, 'cause I gave them easy credit and everything. Same with some of the local merchants 'cause buying from me helped them get over the hump. And the Red Cross and Hope Rescue would come to me to help out this or that family. This was a very good feeling. Like I was the last one on earth they could turn to.

Excitement: Enjoying the Action

In comparison with most conventional occupations and daily routines, there is an element of excitement and sometimes even drama in being a dealer in stolen goods. The "action itself" of wheeling and dealing or "of being where the action is" represent one set of attractions for fences like Sam. Even the actual buying and selling of stolen goods represents a source of action and, although it may come to be viewed as a routine activity, there will be occasional deals that are so challenging or lucrative as to generate a sense of excitement. Likewise, while concerns about the police can be annoying—the sporadic searches and questioning, the episodic periods of surveillance—they tend to make life more dramatic for the fence than it is for persons engaged in legitimate business. Really good deals and fear of detection, while probably more exciting to the newcomer, can generate some drama even for an "old head" like Sam.

In a sense, fencing is a kind of "adventurous deviance" in which the uncertainty, the anxiety, the risks involved are an intrinsic source of pleasure. When kept at a manageable level, the risks may be viewed as excitement, challenge, or fun—as more or less pleasantly fearful, pleasantly anxious, pleasantly uncertain, pleasantly risky.

> Fencing is hard work, don't get me wrong, but I like the excitement of it. It was never boring, always something happening. That, and having to be on your toes all the time, 'cause you can get burned bad if you're not careful. It's not like a high but in a way it is. There's a thrill there. See, there's a risk in fencing—with the cops, with whether you can get rid of what you buy, is your back covered? To me, that risk was tension, but it was enjoyment, too. In different ways, there is a challenge in fencing that in truth I could say I liked.

In other respects, running a fencing business is for Sam a kind of "competitive play," a way of matching wits with others. One kind of play is to buy stolen goods cheaply, to sell them for a nice profit, and to have defeated the law and its agents in the process.

> It would tickle me pink. Say, the state cops were watching my store. I might get in one of my trucks, take off and they was following me, but see I wasn't carrying anything warm. I would take them on a big fox and goose chase, drive out into the country and everything.
>
> Or the different times the police searched my store, never found anything. I wouldn't rub it in to them, but it tickled me pink. See, by the time they hit me with a search, the stuff was long gone.

Another kind of play is to beat the system in a more general sense, to gain control and to manipulate one's environment, such as by covering one's back, by arranging sales outlets, or in general, by establishing the contacts for buying and selling stolen goods.

Beating the police is one thing, but you got to be beating the system all the way down the line. It's like a big chess game, really, 'cause you always got to think ahead about covering your back, keeping the thieves in your pocket, and making your contacts for unloading.

A third kind of rewarding play occurs when Sam competes directly with trade partners, for example, when he negotiates with thieves or buyers over prices. Hard bargaining and sharp trading in dealing with one's "economic foes" confirms a professional, businesslike self-conception. Sam enjoys "getting over" on thieves and out-hustling other dealers, exercises in which the give-and-take is typically friendly, but his biggest kick comes from beating somebody "who wanted to be more than he was."

> Just the dealing part itself. How should I say it? You enjoy that. Making the thief think you don't want what he's peddling when you do. With the other dealers, you would try like hell to beat him, and they're doing the same to you. Then, afterwards, you kid each other. See, it's mostly friendly.
>
> I don't know if I enjoyed beating people; it wasn't that so much. Now, if it was someone that thought he was a big shot, wanted to be more than he was, I meant to beat him bad. I can truthfully say, I got a bang out of that.

A fourth kind of competitive play is a type of confidence game in which Sam takes advantage of either the dishonesty or the gullibility of the "victim." This usually involves selling run-of-the-mill merchandise at inflated prices: (a) by allowing a merchant to believe the goods were stolen but are of high quality, or (b) by concocting a story for a customer about the origins or authenticity of a particular item of merchandise. In both instances, Sam plays on his reputation as someone who handles stolen goods and also on the cupidity, if not the stupidity, of the victim.

> I really got a bang out of this. Say I got a load of rugs that were seconds, which I bought dirt cheap, but bought them strictly legit. What I might do is call another dealer, or a place that handled rugs, let them know that some rugs had come my way, that they looked very good and that I was interested in dumping them, if I could get the right price. Let them read between the lines that they're warm.
>
> Many times, the guy would jump so fast that he would pay more than he'd have to if he bought them legit.
>
> The other thing is, a lot of your public wants a story. See, some of them surmised I was dealing in warm stuff, and I would play on that. Make up a story about how so-and-so was peddling this or that piece, and I decided to take a shot at it, that the guy was in a hurry and he didn't even know what he had. Then I'd show them a piece, say, maybe an old chair that would pass for an antique, how I found out later that the chair is very valuable, that it belonged to this or that person, had come out of a well-known home. Many times they would pay a big price just for a piece of junk. All the time, I'm laughing like hell cause it's really funny how the public can be fooled that way. Your public wants a story, and I would give them that.

Another source of excitement for Sam comes from involvement in action situations. Not only is Sam's store an action spot, but his position as a fence facilitated entry into the gambling club, gave him special acceptance at bars and other hangouts, and also provided him with the money to seek excitement in women or in gambling.

> There was always something happening at my shop. Never a dull moment. Casey's, on Friday nights after the car races, would really be hopping. I would stop there for a sandwich or maybe have a drink, and everybody knew me, knew who I was. But the gambling was may main enjoyment. It wasn't just the gambling, but sometimes the gang would bring in girls and that, too. And Louie and I would go to Vegas or into Atlantic City to gamble, to have a good time.

Finally, "being somebody" is itself a form of action. Whether it is flashing a roll of bills in paying a thief, buying drinks for the crowd at Casey's pub, playing cards or shooting dice with the gambling group, conducting a buying spree at one of the local auctions, or hobnobbing with Louie, Charlie, or other big shots in American City, being somebody is a means of self-expression and generates an element of excitement for Sam. He is accorded prestige not only because he has successfully accumulated possessions, but also because he displays the here and now value of dramatically making the scene—by "blowing money," for example.

> I made a lot of money, but I blew a lot, too. But I blew it the way I wanted. I had two Caddies, one for me and one for my wife [i.e., Becky], three trucks, a house, and everything. I could buy what I wanted, go where I wanted. I can truthfully say I liked being a big shot. Like going to Casey's and buying drinks for the house. Or the gambling, if I wanted to shoot for it, the money would be there on the table.

Sam's display before his peers is not entirely a matter of seeking status. Since by definition his criminal entrepreneurship is secret, the fence must somehow communicate his successes and competence to others if he wishes to develop and sustain the contacts he needs to continue operating. Nevertheless, Sam's tendency to flaunt his success was greater in the early phases of his fencing involvement, for with time he came to appreciate the advantages of remaining in the background.

> It was more in the beginning that I was trying to be a big shot. Later on I handled it better. I wasn't out front as much, was more content to stay in the background. But you have to be noticed too, make people aware; once I got rolling that wasn't as necessary.

Accomplishment: Sense of Mastery Over One's Life

Sam's success as a fence fostered in him a strong sense of being in charge of his own activities and behaviors, a satisfaction with his ability to take care of himself and to deal effectively with stress and decision-making. There is, on the one hand, the sense of mastery that comes from performing well at a demanding job, taking charge and acting decisively to tackle both the routine and happenstance problems that arise in a fencing business. There is also a broader sense of effectiveness at surviving as a fence over the long haul, a feat which also intertwines with Sam's success as a legitimate businessman (albeit, as Sam fully understands, a success at least partly based on illegal gains). No matter how it is achieved, success is still *success*—and solving the social and economic realities of a dealership in stolen property is hardly a minor achievement.

> There's a satisfaction in knowing you can do it, knowing you can handle whatever comes up. See, it was up to me, depended on me, rested on my shoulders to deal with this or that. The fencing is much more satisfying than just having a legit business which is pretty cut and dried. You have to really be on your toes with the fencing, much more on top of things. Not that the legit side wasn't satisfying but in a different way. 'Cause I was building up my store, investing what I was making from the fencing. I thought it was good business to do that. Made me feel like I was progressing.
>
> The fencing gave me a sense of myself, of knowing what I was capable of doing. I always felt I had business ability, a knack for the business end of things. Now I knew it. The fencing gave me a different outlook on life, on myself. I always felt I had leadership qualities. The fencing proved that to me.

There's a feeling of confidence I have of going into an area and out-doing the next guy. Whether it's the fencing or strictly with the legit, I feel I can do whatever needs to be done. 'Cause the fencing taught me how to make things happen, that to make it go I had to stay on top of things and get others to work with me.

Interest and Expertise

There are, as well, a number of job conditions associated with fencing that Sam defines as desirable. First, he attaches a kind of intrinsic or creative enjoyment to "the dealin', the coverin', and the gettin' over." When one has a skill (or a set of skills), finely honed and polished, one uses it and enjoys it. Like the surgeon, the auto mechanic, or the salesman who uses his training, Sam enjoys and takes considerable pride in his ability to "doctor" merchandise, to capitalize on his reputation as a fence by selling perfectly legitimate goods as if they were stolen, or to engage in sharp trading with a thief or another dealer. Moreover, because fencing offers considerable job variety, it elicits a kind of all-around test of one's talents or mettle. For Sam, fencing is a source of self-expression, a kind of creative functioning as a whole rather than as a segmental person.

> I don't know how to say it, but fencing involved all of me in a way that burglary and the legit business didn't. Fencing made me use all of my abilities, tested me for what I was made of. I liked that.

Independence

Second, not only is fencing interesting and challenging, but it allows one to make decisions about one's own working and other behaviors. Sam enjoys both the autonomy and the responsibility of running a fencing business—of being self-employed, of being his own boss, and of not having to work within the structured and dull atmosphere of routine employment.

Association—Friendship

Lastly, Sam's fencing involvement is also a *social* undertaking: it not only serves as the medium for the formation and ranking of social relationships in general, but it serves as the source of the majority of the satisfying relationships that he has. While dealing itself is an enjoyable activity, it is made even more so because it sustains a network of both business and social relations.

This associational side of fencing has many elements. They include customers who provide an opportunity for sociability and friendship where there is a tie-in between good relations and the completion of sales, the dual satisfaction of real enjoyment in his salesmanship together with awareness of its financial return.

> I got a kick out of the people that came in my shop, all different kinds and from all walks of life. Many times they're looking for a bargain and think they're real hustlers. It would be funny as hell 'cause you could really take them over the coals if you wanted to. And I always had lots of regulars, especially the poorer people 'cause they could buy cheap and the better-off ones checked over the antiques. I would rap with them, find out about their families and that. It was all very friendly and good for business, too. Very few people walked away without buying something.

Another social element of fencing includes congenial relations with employees, local businessmen, and the assorted group of hangers-on and semi-retired thieves who stop by or simply hang out at Sam's store. While Sam may sometimes complain about some of the regulars who always seem to be in his store, he generally enjoys their company and the recognition that comes from their personal following.

But probably most enjoyable and satisfying to Sam are the feelings of camaraderie and the business affiliation he experiences with some of the dealers, such as Louie, Woody or Scottie. In similar fashion, Sam's associations with some members of the local clique combine business with pleasure and also give him access to the fast life that is an established feature of this upper segment of the underworld. With them Sam partakes in a kind of shared thrill of breaking the law, and in the excitement, perhaps, of having unlimited amounts of money to spend.

Taken together, the rewards of dealing and the satisfying relationships and mutual obligations to thieves, to buyers, and to other dealers increasingly involve Sam in the social and business activities of dealing.

His life and identity are extensively shaped by fencing and his continued well-being, both financial and social are heavily dependent on it. Fencing is both a business and a way of life, and Sam's enjoyment of it is a process, built up by favorable definitions of the experience that he acquired from others and from the action itself. Once acclimated to the dealing lifestyle and community, and pushed on by both the guarantee of a good income and by resulting patterns of association and friendship, Sam acquires a strong taste for fencing, which becomes increasingly pleasant, desired, and sought after. This taste is multifaceted and includes attainment of success and recognition, the application of skills, the feelings of growth and the control over one's life, and involvement in one's work.

The British Railway Worker as Compared with Architects

Graeme Salaman

1. What kinds of leisure activities do the railwaymen and architects engage in? With whom do they engage in leisure activities?

2. To whom do the men employed in each occupation feel connected? How did they meet the men to whom they feel connected? To what extent has geographic mobility and the length of socialization to the occupation had an impact on these connections?

3. How strongly do the railwaymen and the architects identify with their occupational culture? Does this have an impact on their leisure activities?

4. To what extent do we find evidence for one or more of the three perspectives on work and leisure among the railwaymen and the architects?

The Railwaymen

Like the architects, the railwaymen in the sample had a well-developed occupational culture; 80.4 per cent of the sample thought that members of their occupation were different from other people, and 72.6 per cent thought they held attitudes in common. Not surprisingly the subject on which they dis-

Source: From *Community and Occupation: An Exploration of Work/Leisure Relationships* by Graeme Salaman, 1974, New York: Cambridge University Press. Reprinted by the permission of Cambridge University Press.

played this consensus was work. Among other things railwaymen stressed the skills that their work required, the "proper" orientation that it demanded and the sort of personality characteristics that were necessary to do the job well.

Railwaymen frequently stressed that their work required intelligence and learning. One driver said: "Being a driver is a lifelong apprenticeship, you're always learning. The job demands it." This point is repeated by another railwayman, not of our sample, who writes:

> We worked the heavy, dirty coal trains from the Fife pits to the yards....The work was very unromantic, but it called for a high degree of skill; that kind of skill and knowledge that could not be picked up from textbooks or learned in colleges, but could only be acquired by years of experience on the job.[1]

Many of the railwaymen mentioned that steam engines required a higher degree of skill than diesel; a number bitterly regretted the decline of steam power on the railways.

Many of the railwaymen mentioned the many rules and regulations, techniques, procedures, routes, etc., which must be learnt. A typical comment: "You've got to be on top of your work all the time, there's no time to stop and ask advice."

The railwaymen not only felt their jobs demanded a high degree of skill and expertise, they also valued these skills and abilities. Railwaymen who were particularly knowledgeable or skilled, senior men or those who had especially responsible jobs were regarded, within the community, as men of high prestige, as "real" railwaymen. The accumulation of work-based knowledge and information, the mastery of skills and techniques, was a valued activity among the railwaymen....[R]ailwaymen derive enjoyment from actually doing their work (although of course they are likely to experience frustration in as much as they are unable to do what they think they ought to be doing in the way that they ought to be doing it).

The railwaymen considered that certain personality characteristics were essential to the good railwayman: ability to accept responsibility was frequently mentioned. This, it was asserted, was because of the nature of railway work. One signalman said: "My work is a life and death business. I just can't throw out my mistakes and start again. I have to be right every time." The respondents felt that they *must* be thorough and conscientious, for "A sloppy job can kill people in this business."

A further work-based value held by the railwaymen, and one that is closely related to their valued sense of responsibility, is the emphasis they placed on a vocational, non-instrumental attitude towards work. Many of the railwaymen stressed that the good railwayman did not do his work just for his weekly wage; he did it because he took a pride in it, for the satisfaction of a job well done. A further element in this attitude towards work is the value railwaymen place on punctuality. Cottrell has discussed the value that American railwaymen place on punctuality, and his comments seem equally valid in this century.[2] Many of the respondents boasted that they had never been late for work, or missed a day's work. One of the railwaymen in the sample had just returned from an emergency visit to the dentist where he had had all his teeth extracted. The interview had to be postponed because his replies were unintelligible, but his wife emphasized that he would go to work that afternoon as usual. She said "He never misses a day's work, and he's never been late for work in his life." Her husband signalled his agreement.

The good railwayman then is always punctual, reliable and steady. But many respondents felt that some of the current recruits were below standard because they did not seem to value the things that the older man did. The newcomers were not concerned with technical knowledge, they were less responsible, they saw their work merely as a means of making money. As one driver put it, "It's the couldn't-care-less business these days."

The railwaymen not only had strong views about how their work *should* be done, they also had attitudes about the relationship between their occupation and the larger society. They felt they supplied an important (and, previously, a glamorous) social service. As with the architects, this service aspect, and the high level of skill and conscientiousness it demands, were used as the basis for demanding higher status for the occupation—or bemoaning its decline in status....

Associations: Convergence of Work and Non-Work Activities, Interests and Relationships

The most striking aspect of the convergence of work and non-work displayed by the architects and railwaymen—and frequently noted among members of other occupational communities—was the extent to which they choose their friends and associates from among their occupational colleagues—or some of them. It was argued, ...[earlier] that patterns of preferential association may differ: they may have a local or a cosmopolitan basis. This distinction was investigated with reference to the two occupational samples. (It was suggested that members of local communities would be friends with work-*mates:* members of cosmopolitan communities would be friendly with occupational colleagues who did not necessarily work with them.)

Respondents were asked to give the occupation of their five best friends.[3] Some respondents felt that they didn't have that many friends; and in such cases they were asked how many they did have. The results...show that 33.3 per cent of the railwaymen, as against 1.9 per cent of the architects, had less than five best friends. The railwaymen saw very definite and distinct differences between best friends and other associates, and invested the best-friend relationship with an almost sacred significance. Architects on the other hand had no difficulty in naming their five best friends....

Two points arise from [the data]; first, while 19.2 per cent of the architects had no architect best friends, these respondents did have other, non-architect best friends; but most of the railwaymen who had no railwaymen friends had *no best friends at all.* Secondly, 65.4 per cent of the architects and 70.6 per cent of the railwaymen had two or more best friends from their occupation. This incidence of preferential association is remarkably high, particularly when compared with most manual occupations but also when compared with high-status, middle-class occupations. Gerstl's figures, which display the variation in preferential association within high-status occupations, are set out in Table 1.

Respondents were actually asked the occupations of their five best friends, not how many were in the same occupation. This was done in order to avoid bias in their answers and also in order to obtain data on respondents' friendship patterns in their entirety. The most interesting additional information thus gained concern architects' friendship with people in related work....

TABLE 1

Inclusion of Colleagues Among Ten Best Friends by Occupation

Proportion of Colleagues	Admen	Dentists	Professors
Low	36%	80%	12%
High	64%	20%	88%
Total	100%	100%	100%
No. of cases	(25)	(25)	(25)

Proportion dichotomised at one-fourth. *Source:* Joel E. Gerstl, "Determinants of Occupational Community in High Status Occupations" (*The Sociological Quarterly*, vol. 2, p. 267). © 1961 by Midwest Sociology Society.

[The data] show that 61.5 per cent of the architects had at least one friend from a related occupation. Architects who work for building or construction firms, or for other types of non-architectural organizations, and architects who were private-practice principals, were more likely than architects who worked in private or authority offices to have friends from occupations related to architecture, and less likely to have friends from the occupation itself. This is most marked among private-practice principals, only 16.7 per cent of whom had two or more architect friends (as against 65.4 per cent of the sample as a whole), and is probably the result of the sort of competitor/colleague relationships in which they were involved. As one principal said: "You can't be too friendly with other architects because either you are envious of his business, or he's envious of yours."

Principals also have to spend a great deal of their time trying to drum up business, and so preferred not to waste their time with other architects who were not going to be of any use in this respect.

During the pilot interviews a number of respondents from both occupations stressed the distinction—for them—between "best friends" and "associates," or "acquaintances." It was clear that these terms described very different sorts of relationships and consequently, during the interview proper, respondents were asked who they met frequently. They were asked: "Do you meet other architects or railwaymen casually—at lunchtime, in the evening, or just in the street?" Eighty-one per cent of the architects and 76.5 per cent of the railwaymen said that they did meet their work or occupational colleagues "regularly" or "occasionally."

Architects who associated casually with their colleagues said that this association usually took place during their lunchtimes or in the evening after work. Railwaymen said that such association usually took place in the vicinity of their home. Many made remarks like the following:

> "You can't walk down the street without meeting another railwayman."

> "There's lots of railwaymen around here—you couldn't avoid them if you wanted to."

Railwaymen's friends from the same occupation were nearly always their work-mates (90.2 per cent) as defined earlier, but this was less true of architects, only 23.1 per cent of whose colleague friends were work-mates. These differences in patterns of preferential association between the two occupational samples reflect the differences in occupational reference group identification discussed earlier.

The different structures of the two occupational communities are related to the different patterns of intra-occupational mobility experienced by architects and railwaymen: 94.1 per cent of the railwaymen in the sample had always been in the type of railway work they were doing when they were interviewed, and 90.2 per cent had always worked for the Cambridge Depot. On the other hand the architects had experienced much greater occupational and geographical mobility; only 59.9 per cent had *always* been in the type of work they were in when they were interviewed, 23.1 per cent had spent *most* of their time in other sorts of architec-

tural work, and 25.0 per cent had spent some time working outside London. Many of the architects' occupational friendships were with people who had been work-mates in previous jobs, and, all in all, 69.2 per cent of the architects' architect friends were work-mates, or had been earlier.

These differences in the pattern of preferential association displayed by the members of the two occupational samples are the result of the differences in the causal mechanisms that are present in the two cases.... [Earlier] it was argued that whereas both samples were heavily involved in their work tasks and skills, and that this constituted a necessary determinant of respondents' motivation to associate with other members of their occupation, the samples differed with respect to the "second" determinant. In the case of the architects the other factor was that they were all involved in and committed to a professional value system and world view which derived from the profession as a whole and which the architects learnt about and accepted as they experienced their professional training and socialisation. As a result of this they identified with the occupation and profession as a whole, and in consequence their occupational friends were drawn from a much wider population (the whole occupation) than were the railwaymen's. Some evidence for this is supplied by the fact that nearly half (42.3 per cent) the architects' colleague friends were people they had met during their training period. Of course they had often also worked with them at some time later in their careers.

It is argued, then, that the fact that the architects' colleague friends were less frequently current (or even past) work-mates derives not only from the greater occupational mobility of architects, compared to railwaymen, but also from the fact that architects are exposed to a lengthy training and socialisation in a profession-wide architectural world-view and value system. As a result of this training experience and the value system itself they are likely to pick their colleague friends not merely from their work-mates, but from the profession as a whole.

In the case of the railwaymen, on the other hand, it is argued that, although motivated to associate with their colleagues, their work-based friendship choices are severely limited by the involvement in what were termed restrictive factors. The way their work was organised simply made it difficult if not impossible for them to get to know any colleagues other than those they met at work, or worked with. As a result their occupational community was local, i.e. made up of work-mates.

Because of the obvious importance of this suggested relationship between differences in the architects' and railwaymen's patterns of preferential association and the sorts of factors that are held to be determinants that are present in the two cases, it is necessary to consider the possibility that the differences in type of preferential association, indeed the classification of the two communities as local and cosmopolitan, is merely an artifact of the way in which the populations were selected and limited.

Clearly there are some differences between the two samples that could be held to be relevant. For example, the architects worked in numerous organisations and all the railwaymen worked for the same organization. Therefore it might be suggested that the railwaymen had many work-mates so it was easy to have work-mate friends, or indeed that all Cambridge railwaymen were work-mates for each other. It should be clear, however, that in terms of the way in which the concept work-mate is used in this study such suggestions are invalid. The railwaymen did not have many work-mates: they saw and interacted with relatively few people when they were at work, yet they limited their occupational friendship choices to these colleagues. The architects, of course, worked in offices and organisations of dif-

fering sizes, yet few worked on their own in the way that, say, a signalman or guard did.

Another possibility is that the differences between the two communities may stem from the residential habits of members of the two samples. Maybe architects live near other (non-work-mate) architects, and get to know them this way. This seems rather unlikely in London. But, as will be seen, it is the railwaymen who tend to live together, not the architects, and yet even so the railwaymen were friendly with railwaymen with whom they worked, rather than railwaymen who were neighbours, although sometimes these two roles coincided.

The Convergence of Work and Non-Work Activities and Interests

The convergence of friend and colleague relationships is one aspect—and the most important one—of a general convergence of work and non-work life which is a central feature of occupational communities. For members of occupational communities work is a "central life interest." Indeed in some cases the distinction between work and non-work is not a meaningful one. Respondents were asked a series of questions which were designed to elicit data on their non-work activities and interests. In the first of these they were offered four statements, each of which represented a sort of work/leisure relationship, and were asked to choose one which best reflected their own assessment of this relationship. Their answers are set out in Table 2.

This table illustrates that the majority of the respondents felt that work and non-work were positively connected in some way. And this connection is further illustrated by the fact that members of both samples were prepared and eager to think and talk about their work and their careers in their free time. Three-quarters of the architects said that they were neither able nor

TABLE 2

Assessment of the Relationship Between Work and Leisure

	Architects (*n* = 52)	Railwaymen (*n* = 51)
"I am so involved in my work that it is often hard to say where work ends and leisure begins."	38.5	—
"I put up with work largely because of the money, and need my leisure to recover from work."	—	3.9
"Leisure and family are more important to me than work. I try and forget all about it in my spare time."	1.9	15.7
"A man can only really enjoy his leisure time if he gets something other than just money out of his work."	59.6	80.4

willing to forget about their work in their free time. One said: "I can't stop thinking about work. This is not a nine to five job, you just can't cut it off, it's with you all the time." Another remarked: "If something is important to you and you are totally involved in it, how can you possibly forget about it merely because you leave the office?" The railwaymen too were very eager to talk about their work outside working hours. One railwayman's wife said:

> "It's railways, railways, railways with him. All railwaymen are like it, they just want to get together and talk railways. As though they didn't have enough. If you want to find out about the railways ask the wives. We're the ones who have had the railways all these years."

Not only did many of the respondents think and talk about their work during their non-work time, but many of them were also members of societies, clubs, and other types of voluntary association which were in some way connected with their work. Thirty-nine per cent of the railwaymen and 44.2 per cent of the architects were members of some sort of work-based voluntary organisation. All were active members. Architects were members of the following semi-professional bodies: the Town Planning Institute, the Architectural Association, the Architects in Industry group, and the Association of Official Architects. They were all members of the R.I.B.A. Seventy-five per cent had attended during the previous year. Railwaymen were members of the Railways social club or the labour club. The former was actually organised and run by British Railways Board, the latter was a well-known railwayman's haunt. All the railwaymen in the sample were members of one or another of the main railway unions. Nearly forty per cent had attended a meeting in the previous year.

Further indication of the convergence of respondents' work and non-work lives can be obtained from a study of their hobbies. Many had hobbies which reflected their work interest, or which derived in some way from their work or the meaning it had for them. Sixty-two per cent of the architects and 7.8 per cent of the railwaymen had work-connected hobbies, i.e. hobbies which reflected the man's interest in his work skills and tasks. Nineteen per cent of the architects said that their main hobby was their work. By this they meant both that they regarded their work as more than just a job, and that they spent some of their leisure time in architectural work of some sort—studying architecture and looking at buildings. Twenty-seven per cent had artistic hobbies such as sketching, sculpturing, or designing generally. A further 15.4 per cent had such interests as modernising and converting old houses.

Few railwaymen had hobbies which could be described as work-connected in this sense. But 76.47 per cent of the sample had hobbies which were connected with the community, in that the hobby was typical of members of the railwaymen's occupational community. The main hobby was gardening. Now an interest in gardening does not derive from involvement in work skills and tasks, but from involvement in the occupational group. A large number of the railwaymen in the sample were keen gardeners; they were eager to talk about their hobby, at length, with colleagues, friends and others. It is suggested that because of the popularity of this activity among the railwaymen the hobby can be seen as a characteristic of the occupational community. (Although there are certain features of gardening as a hobby that make it particularly suited to railwaymen.)

It is felt that this remarkable convergence of work and leisure interests and activities reflects the respondents' involvement in their work, noted [previously]....It is interesting that a large number of railwaymen had hobbies which they pursued with a remarkable intensity and within which they had achieved striking success. Some bred and raced pigeons, others made wine, a number were proficient automobile engineers, others played musical instruments, and so on. The railwaymen themselves frequently suggested that this was due to a sort of displacement process: in their leisure time railwaymen used neglected skills and aptitudes and fulfilled creative needs which they could not exploit at work but which their earlier work experiences had taught them to value and expect.

A final indicator of the close links that exist between the architects' and railwaymen's work and non-work lives is their preparedness to read about their work in their free time. Respondents were asked how many hours—in an average week—they spent in work-connected reading. Their answers are set out in Table 3.

TABLE 3

Number of Hours—In an Average Week—Spent in Work-connected Reading

Number of hours	Architects (n = 52) Percentage	Railwaymen (n = 51)
0	3.9	21.6
1	13.5	52.9
2	26.9	13.7
3	9.6	5.9
More than 3	46.2	5.9

The railwaymen's work-connected reading consisted of books of regulations, new appendices to the rules, and technical works on diesel engines. Many of them pointed out the need to read regularly and reread the rule books and instructions on the many types of diesel locomotives.

Architects tend to more general reading: journals, architectural history, etc.

On the basis of the data discussed in this chapter reference to the architects' and railwaymen's *occupational communities* is justified and in view of the different patterns of preferential association and occupational reference group affiliations there is reason to describe these communities as *local* and *cosmopolitan*. The two communities also differed in other ways. The railwaymen's occupational community displayed the characteristics of the "traditional community," i.e. definite geographical boundary, multiple role relationships and connected friendship networks.

It is not surprising that the architects' community was very much less geographically based than the railwaymen's. Although 73.1 per cent of the architects' friends lived and worked within the London area, 100 per cent of the railwaymen's colleague friends lived and worked in Cambridge. Similarly the architects were not located within any particular part of North West London, while many of the railwaymen lived within a particular part of Cambridge—Romsey Town.

This part of Cambridge served as a focal point for the railwaymen's occupational community.

A further difference is that railwaymen frequently had relatives and friends who were colleagues, and neighbours who were members of the same occupation as well. The architects' occupational community involved the convergence of friendship and colleague relationships, the railwaymen's community was characterised by multiple relationships: the same people met in a number of different roles—neighbour, relative, friend.[4] This was very uncommon among architects.

A final difference lies in the interconnection of friendship networks, and necessarily follows from the features of the two communities already described. Railwaymen's colleague friends were much more likely to know and be friendly with each other than were the architects'.

NOTES

1. Robert Bonnar, 'Negotiating at the Top', in Fraser (ed.). *Work Volume* 2, pp. 330–45, pp. 330–1.

2. W. F. Cottrell, *The Railroader* (Stanford University Press, 1940).

3. Occasionally this question caused difficulties, because of the emotional implications of the term "best friend" and the lack of general agreement about the meaning of the term. It is obviously a concept that many of the respondents had considered previously. When respondents had difficulty they were asked for the occupations of the five people they knew best outside their family. It was felt that some limit on numbers was necessary in order to be able to compare the responses. Other studies of friendship patterns had run into difficulties because the investigators did not know the total number of respondents' friends with whom they were dealing. See Mott *et al., Shift Work,* especially p. 21.

4. Some of the railwaymen came from families in which, as they would put it, "Railways are in the blood." Forty-one (41.2) per cent of the railwaymen had fathers who were, or still are, railwaymen. (Only 1.9 per cent of the architects had fathers in the profession.) Furthermore, 35.3 per cent of the railwaymen had grandfathers who had been railwaymen; and 82.4 per cent claimed that they had one or more other relatives who had once been, or still were, on the railways.

Abnormal Intimacy:
The Varying Work Networks of
Chicana Cannery Workers

Patricia Zavella

CASE STUDY QUESTIONS

1. What have been the assumptions about Chicana networks in the past? Are these assumptions supported by an examination of the primary basis of friendship and support for the cannery workers?

2. Work-related networks are said to vary between two poles. What characterizes work-related networks at each end of the continuum?

3. To what extent does the description of these work-related networks support any of the three perspectives on work and leisure?

4. What impact do the friendship networks have on the workplace or the workers' feelings about their work?

5. How does this study change what researchers should look for in future studies of Chicana support networks?

Introduction

Recent feminist research has greatly enhanced our understanding of women's networks in the past and present. We now examine the conditions that create variation

Source: This excerpt is reprinted from *Feminist Studies,* Volume II, number 3 (Fall 1985): 541–57, by permission of the publisher, *FEMINIST STUDIES,* Inc., c/o Women's Studies Program, University of Maryland, College Park, MD 20742.

in the structure and functioning of women's kin and social networks, conditions which allow women to cooperate with one another even in extreme instability, or which create conflict among women.[1] Further, the meaning provided by support networks of kin and friends varies by race and class. Middle-class white women of the nineteenth century found meaning, love, and support for community moral reform,[2] while working-class and impoverished black women also relied on network members for basic survival or to adapt to the new country after emigration.[3] And we have seen how women's networks have provided crucial means of support to political activists.[4]

At the same time, feminist labor historians have shown how women workers in a variety of occupational contexts create "work cultures"—shared understandings and practices—just as male workers do. Again, feminists emphasize that different conditions of work create variation in women's work culture. In the context of relative autonomy, sales clerks can create a "sisterhood" that inculcates new workers with lore and floor practices, and the occupational segregation of women sometimes creates great solidarity among female workers.[5]

We still know little about how these worlds of home and work intersect, however, and how networks affect women's consciousness. And because of still prevalent stereotypes, we have a limited view of the lives of some groups of women.

A constellation of stereotypes surrounds Chicanas—Mexican American women. The literature on Chicano support networks[6] emphasizes the importance of kin ties above all others: more so than Anglos or blacks, Chicanos are thought to maintain cohesive ties with their extensive kin through frequent visiting and the exchange of goods and labor. Chicanos are said to regard support for emotional problems from relatives—especially close kin—as superior to other sources. Further, Chicanos tend to migrate to areas where relatives reside in order to utilize kin resources.[7] An implication of this research is that friendship is not considered to play an important part in Chicano support networks; at least most writers ignore this aspect of networks. In fact, some go as far as to claim that relatives are the primary source of support *"because* of the relatively low reliance of Mexican Americans on other informal resources such as fictive kin, friends, neighbors and coworkers."[8]

This view of Chicanos as solely reliant on kin parallels one that perceives Chicanas as solely kinswomen—as living outside the world of paid labor.[9] Yet along with other women, Chicanas have been rapidly entering the labor force. In the decade between 1960 and 1970, relatively more married Chicanas entered the labor force nationally than their white and black counterparts.[10] By 1980, the proportion of Chicanas who worked was similar to that of all women.[11] Yet there are very few discussions of Chicanas' work cultures.[12]

In this article, I address the following interrelated questions concerning the networks of Chicana cannery workers: How are work networks structured and operated, and why are work friendships important to Chicana workers? I show how women's work culture—of which coworker networks

are an important manifestation—evolved within the context of canning production. My approach, however, goes beyond the factories and examines how women's work networks operate within women's private lives. I suggest that in order to understand the significance of and variation in women's work networks we must link the changing conditions of women's work with family changes. Further, working women develop a consciousness of their situation, or recognition of their collective circumstances as workers, by contrasting their work situations with their family situations. In this way, women's consciousness is "negotiated"—actively modified in response to their actual experiences on the job and within families.[13]

The research is based on fieldwork I did in 1977–78 in the Santa Clara Valley, the southeastern tip of the San Francisco Bay. The bulk of my data is in-depth, open-ended interviews with cannery workers conducted in their homes, some in Spanish. Informants were selected by "snowball sampling"— through contacts I established with cannery workers and labor activists. I interviewed a total of thirty-one workers, of whom fifteen were Chicanas. The mean age of my female informants is forty-six years, and the women had on the average sixteen years of plant seniority. Many of the women, however, had worked for as long as thirty years in the industry. Informants' names are fictitious. I also did participant observation in mainly public settings—informal social gatherings such as parties and barbecues. I was also a participant in a local union election campaign, which involved attending numerous meetings and support activities such as fundraisers. I was unable to secure a job in the canneries, so I made no on-the-job observations.[14]

Canning Production

Recruitment practices of canning firms are largely informal.[15] There is no hiring hall, and workers wait around outside company gates to be hired. When I was doing fieldwork, the overwhelming majority of job applicants were Chicanos and Mexicans. Women informants often went job hunting accompanied by female kin, particularly sisters, or were able to secure jobs with the help of relatives who were already employed in the cannery. These informal recruiting mechanisms have resulted in a predominantly Mexican American labor force in Santa Clara Valley canneries. Chicanos as a whole make up approximately 64 percent of the cannery work force; while Chicanas alone make up about 36 percent of the workers. In particular canneries, however, Chicanos comprise as much as 90 percent of the production work force.[16]

The cannery labor force is segregated by race and sex, and more recently even by age. The majority of the seasonal workers (who mainly work during summer months) are women, especially Chicanas. Various mechanisms such as a relatively closed internal labor market, women's lack of information about promotions, and sexual harassment by supervisors keep women in the lowest paying jobs. In addition, there are ethnic cleavages in the work force. Italian Americans and Portuguese Americans entered canneries in earlier periods and have now risen to supervisory positions. Thus Chicanas are concentrated in the lowest paying jobs (such as sorting) and are usually supervised by white ethnic women. As one moves up the job hierarchy, men—especially white ethnics—predominate.

Increasingly, canneries are relocating to rural areas closer to where the produce is grown. Therefore, the number of cannery jobs in the Santa Clara Valley is diminishing. As a result, cannery workers—especially seasonal ones—are becoming a middle-aged labor force as only those with high seniority are able to keep their jobs.

Canning production is geared to a continuous conveyor belt that moves raw produce through various stages as it is processed, canned, cooked, and cased for storage or shipment to market. Production is highly mechanized except for sorting operations which require the largest number of workers. The actual process of sorting is fast paced and tedious, and women workers are immobilized. Sorters examine the produce and place it in various chutes, depending on the size and condition. My informants repeatedly noted that "it doesn't take much brains to work in a cannery." But the constant motion of so much produce on the conveyor belt, the humidity from water baths, the din of crashing cans and cooking machinery, as well as the nauseating odors of rotten produce and chemicals (such as chlorine) used in processing, make the job both distasteful and demanding. Supervisors (or "floor ladies" as they are called) constantly walk around inspecting the work and pressure women to work rapidly and carefully. Sorters have little room to control the pace or techniques of work and are forced to make instantaneous decisions regarding the quality of produce.[17]

Work-based Networks

When women first obtain jobs in canneries they are not formally trained. They are immediately placed on the job and learn from watching coworkers, with on-the-job instruction from the supervisor. Talking with coworkers is prohibited, and mandatory ear-plugs make it difficult to converse anyway. Supervisors must shout their instructions in order to be heard above the racket. New workers are often overwhelmed and feel dizzy or nauseated, and coworkers advise new women to adjust their equilibrium to the movement of the conveyor belt by concentrating on individual pieces of produce. Coworkers teach new employees how to perform their jobs so that the work is easier. They also point out that keeping up with the fast pace is not possible, nor even necessary. Training and advice by coworkers are given surreptitiously or during breaks, because if women do not concentrate on their work they will be fired.

Other jobs such as check weigher allow more flexibility. A check weigher, for example, grabs a handful of spinach, places it in a can, and weighs it for the proper amount. Women who are experienced learn to gauge the proper weight with their hands and bypass the weighing operation. Because they are paid by the piece rate, this shortcut is critical in enabling women to make more money. Here, coworkers teach new workers how to perform the job more effectively, or even how to rig the counting devices.

Coworkers also initiate women into the formal authority structure. Lisa Hernandez noted: "It's a big soap opera at the cannery. You know who hangs around the bosses and who 'makes the cans.'" Gossip provides important information about who belongs to different cliques. Euleria Torrez laughed: "You always know something about everybody." It helps to know supervisors in particular because work assignments are granted informally.

Line work provides conditions in which women are able to cooperate with one another, and this makes the work itself more pleasant. Connie Garcia recalled that "we all got along, you have to when you work that kind of work. We used to sing, make jokes." Further, women could anticipate staying on the line with many coworkers for years to come. Lupe Collosi observed: "Usually people in the cannery are good-natured; people have no problems. They're all so used to working hard that they don't complain." Workers try to keep their differences in check because of the constant menace of supervisors and the fear of losing their jobs. Vicki Gutierrez noted: "I got along pretty good with everybody. I wanted a job so I made it a point." Luz Betancourt said: "If you want to be working, you can't be fighting." These statements are in stark contrast

with the competition and antagonisms among women workers when they were paid by the piece rate.[18] The hourly pay coupled with pressured working conditions allows women to establish camaraderie. But women's cooperation also helped managers by providing a trained work force.

Coworkers become an informal group—similar to the "sisterhood" of sales clerks that Susan Porter Benson discusses—which socializes women into the work culture. Yet these are not self-conscious groups. Most women claimed with disgust: "I trained myself," even though they had help, and did not view coworkers as constituting a group. The term "work-based networks" better characterizes these informal relationships with coworkers.

There are any number of work-based networks within a particular factory, and they tend to be composed of workers of the same gender and ethnic background. Sea-sonal workers tend to make friends with other temporary workers, while full-time workers (usually men) have their own networks. Women with relatives in the same plant have a ready-made training team that also includes them in socializing during breaks.

Lisa is a third-generation cannery worker. She described her first season on the job: "It's hard work, but I can't say I didn't enjoy it. Everywhere I looked I knew somebody, I had relatives to talk to. They baby me, give me cans.…" She also described her parents' participation in the work-based network: "My mom and my stepfather live in the same world, the cannery world, with all the *chismes* [gossip]. In the cannery you can see them sitting together talking with all my aunts and their friends." Other women initiated friendships with coworkers through the informal training process. Connie observed: "You get to know all these people. You have this intimacy because you work with them at least eight hours a day." Vicki believes that work friendships detract from the monotony of the job: "You get to know everybody's little problems. It's interesting." Another woman characterized work friendships in a more cynical manner: "You have this *abnormal* intimacy. You make friends with people who are totally different than you, just because you work together." Nevertheless, many women believed they would not have stayed on the job without the help of coworkers.

The ethnic cohesiveness of networks replicated and perpetuated the segregation of the work force. A Chicana informant characterized Mexican-white friendships: "It's weird as I see it." One hapless Portuguese American woman described her social isolation until she made friends with other Portuguese women: "I used to sit with some Mexican women but they would only speak in Spanish. I felt so left out! I think it's only courteous to speak English." When she started working on the line she received little help from her coworkers because she could not communicate with them. "I don't know a lot of people; in three months' time you don't get close. This Spanish lady who works across from me doesn't speak English. So all we do is say hello or goodbye and smile." Yet after only twelve years of work, this woman was promoted to swing shift floorlady, while her Spanish-speaking compatriots with greater seniority remained behind. Participation in work-based networks provided information about promotions, and the exclusion of Spanish-speaking women was one way in which Chicanas became victims of discrimination.

Women also sanctioned those who left line work and no longer socialized with network members. Connie eventually took on a "man's job": she became a full-time checking clerk supervising the loading of box cars. She missed the friendship of her former coworkers. "It just seems like everytime that someone gets an advancement, there's a lot of things said. Petty things, like 'she thinks she's too good because she does all this stuff.' A lot of it is just jealousy."

By working on the line, women were able to establish friendships with one another. Yet because of working conditions, relationships at work were difficult to sustain. During the peak of the season, workers are on the job six or seven days a week. With half-hour lunches and only two twelve-minute breaks, there was little time to socialize. Besides, women occasionally preferred a silent retreat from the commotion inside the factory: "Sometimes I need to be by myself for that half-hour" (Vicki).

With work that has little intrinsic value and short occasions to socialize with coworkers, one could expect that union involvement would add meaning to the job.[19] It was difficult for Chicano workers, however, to find meaningful participation in their union local. Northern California cannery workers are affiliated with the International Brotherhood of Teamsters. Generally, cannery workers are dissatisfied with the Teamsters union,[20] and my informants were no exception. Some of them had almost a decade of rank-and-file activism within the local and established alliances with other dissident caucuses in northern California. The dissatisfaction stemmed from what workers perceived as a general lack of representation and union democracy. In addition, there was ethnic antagonism between the Italian American Teamster officials and Chicano caucus members, with mutual name-calling and red-baiting on the part of some union leaders. Chicano activists wanted the union contract translated into Spanish and for the local to hold bilingual meetings (among other things), but the union leadership refused. There was even a short-lived "Teamsters for [Cesar] Chavez" movement by Chicano cannery workers in the early seventies when the United Farm Workers and the Teamsters were having a jurisdictional battle in the fields. The Teamsters union was not a source of organizational support for most Chicano cannery workers.

In sum, the general work context included oppressive working conditions and an uninterested or even antagonistic union. Women's work culture was not conducive to the development of meaningful relationships at work. Work-based networks enabled women to bear the difficult conditions of their jobs and added the dimension of solidarity with other workers. Yet women had to develop these relationships outside the job.

Work-related Networks

Work-related networks are expanded work-based networks that function outside the factories and whose members engage in social exchange. For the most part, work-related friendships began with only social motivations. Members frequently socialized with one another during the off-season (roughly from October through May). The women visited each other's homes, telephoned several times during the week, went shopping or out to lunch, or went out for drinks, all without their husbands. Connie elaborated on the difference between work-based and work-related networks. "I don't know how many times I remember telling a coworker that I became particularly fond of, 'Hey, I'll be sure to come and see you after the season.' I never made it because I have kids to raise, things to do, and I just never got around to it. And then there are others, like Elena, that you become so involved with and become very dear friends." But although women initiated activities with coworkers, once established, the networks also included husbands. Cannery workers occasionally got together as couples for parties, barbecues, short weekend trips, or even went on extended vacations together. Some of my informants organized large-scale activities in which a number of cannery worker couples and their kin and friends participated.

The structure of work-related networks varied between two poles. On one end were friendship networks composed entirely of coworkers. Regardless of whether they were recent immigrants from Mexico or third-generation Chicanas, women who had no kin residing in the area developed work friendship networks separately from kin networks. The opposite extreme was kin-dominant networks. These were composed almost entirely of cannery workers who were relatives. Often married couples met one another at the cannery. It was also common for women's children to work at least one season at the cannery before moving on to better jobs. Women in these situations usually had work-related networks in which kin predominated, and networks included members of their own nuclear families.

The presence of kin residing in the area who were also cannery workers, however, did not mean that kin and friendship networks coincided. Some women had numerous relatives working in canneries, and they developed extensive friendship networks that were integrated into kin networks. Other women developed friendship networks separately from kin networks that were largely made up of cannery workers. Women who did not consider their cannery worker relatives as being part of their friendship networks usually had different political values, other interests, and considered themselves to be marginal to cannery work culture. Other women had networks somewhere in the middle of the kin-dominant and friend-dominant types. Both their friends and kin were part of the work-related networks, but they differed in terms of whether the relatives and coworkers were largely separate or integrated. Of course, not every woman had large intense work friendship networks. One woman does not want to be "bugged" to socialize with coworkers: "We are friends while at work."

Although the networks varied in terms of the number of members, several were "close knit." This was because some of the women's friends were also *comadres* with one another; that is, they were ritual comothers who became fictive kin through Catholic baptismal rites.[21] Usually a woman chooses a friend and her spouse to sponsor a child at baptism with the intension of honoring them and solidifying the friendship. By selecting friends rather than kin to be *comadres*, Chicanas express their great affection and respect.[22] The presence of fictive kin who are coworkers blurs the distinction between friendship and kin networks, but adds to their cohesiveness. The women were key in maintaining communication, organizing activities, and keeping the networks active. A few women were core members, and they either organized get-togethers such as birthday parties, or were honored at special occasions such as wedding anniversaries.

Work-related networks also operated like kin networks and served as sources of exchange among members. In particular, network members were good sources of information regarding problems that arose from their work situation. Women found babysitters through their networks or learned from coworkers how to qualify for unemployment benefits or how to claim disability pay. Work friends were also sources of advice and emotional support. Women discussed work and personal problems, especially those concerning their children. Marital problems were important topics, and work friends provided a crucial source of support in women's struggles with their husbands. The standards of housekeeping and how much labor their husbands should contribute was one problem; another was whether the woman should return to work each season. About one-third of my informants' husbands did not want them to work at all. Informants frequently sought out a work friend when they just needed to talk, and greatly appreciated the support. Connie observed: "If I needed her she was there. When I get real down, she is my moral support. Everyone needs someone like that."

The context of work had other consequences for how work-related networks operated. The lack of job mobility and unwillingness of the union to meet the special needs of the Chicano work force spurred some informants into labor organizing.

Although only a handful of the informants were politically active, these women's friends and kin were often also involved in organizing. In some instances, work-related networks became politicized after they were well established as social networks. Connie and about twelve of her friends met frequently, and the conversation inevitably turned to the work situation. They began to devise ways to change working conditions. After the calloused rebuffs from male union officials, the women decided to organize women cannery workers themselves. They founded a women's caucus (which included black and white women) and filed a complaint with the Fair Employment Practices Commission. The women later became plaintiffs in a race and sex discrimination suit against California Processors Inc., which they eventually won. In addition, the women wrote articles for a cannery workers' newsletter, and one woman ran for president of the union. Her friends served as campaign manager and volunteers in a bitter election that was narrowly lost. The friendship network evolved into a militant organization.

Political activists' work friends became important in personal ways as well. Many of the women activists had conflicts with their husbands over their political involvement. Husbands complained that organizing took up too much time and that the women were neglecting their families. Indeed, one woman claimed that reluctant husbands were the biggest obstacles to organizing women workers. Some of these husbands either demanded that their wives stop organizing or that they restrict their activities to times that were convenient for their families. Several of the activists eventually divorced their spouses, partly because of their husbands' opposition to their political activism. Most of these women had attained better-paying jobs and were in a position to leave poor marriages. Work friendships served as a crucial means of support to those women who went through the painful process of divorce. One of these women claimed: "I don't know how I would have *survived* without my friends."

Other women intensified their relationships not only with network members, but also with spouses through their political activism. These women got involved with a dissident caucus whose membership was predominantly male. This caucus sponsored numerous activities: the members twice ran a slate of largely Chicano workers for union office and organized rallies, meetings, dances, and fundraisers. Through these activities, work networks became larger and more intense. Coworkers and *compadres*[23] were not only friends from work, but also political allies who shared all the frustrations and camaraderie of labor organizing.

Work-related networks also functioned in a politically conservative manner. Lisa, for example, avoided visiting her mother during the work season because the job harassment her mother received became increasingly difficult for Lisa to bear. She had advised her mother to talk with a lawyer and explore the possibility of legal action to stop the harassment, but Lisa's mother refused. Lisa believed that her mother would not seek legal redress because of the advice of an older sister married to a supervisor at the same plant where Lisa's mother worked. The aunt actively discouraged her sister from taking any action that might jeopardize her husband's position. None of the other relatives working at the plant opposed the aunt's advice, so Mrs. Hernandez continued working under stressful conditions. Lisa shrugged: "The cannery is a way of life. You live in it and thrive on it." Thus, work-related networks can serve

to pressure women into acquiescence to unfair working conditions.

Even if they were not politically involved, work friendships were meaningful to my informants. Especially as they reach middle age and their children have either left home or no longer require so much attention, women have more time and desire to socialize.[24] Because home responsibilities have lessened and financial obligations for their children are not as pressing, the meaning of a job has changed for these women. They feel isolated at home and long for social contact. They do not see housework as meaningful in its own right. Of course most women value a clean house, but staying home full-time and cleaning house produces little intrinsic reward. Rather, homemaking is described as "doing nothing" or "being lazy." If the children are gone, not only is there little housework to do, but also "housework will always be there"—it can be put off.

The women's need to socialize differed from their situations when they started working and their children were young.[25] Vicki explained: "I don't have to work anymore; we don't need the money. But if I stay home, all I'll do is watch TV and get fat. I don't have anything to do. There's not really much housework. No way! No way am I going to stay home! I'm going to go work. Plus the extra money is always helpful." Celia said: "You look forward to another season." Luz gave the rationale for continuing to work: "Why not? The kids are gone, there's nothing for me to do at home, and I like my job." Connie observed of her coworkers: "Most of the women my age [forty-four] who work in the industry, their kids are all grown. They've got grandkids already. So their life is just cannery. The people they associate with are cannery workers; they can't see beyond anything else that has to do with the cannery." The cannery provided women like these with an escape from the solitary nature of homemaking, and work-related networks became the focus of their social lives.

Women's longevity on the job allowed friendships to flourish and provided expectations that they would endure. Especially if they were *comadres*, women were fictive kin and could feel free to develop *confianza* (trust or familiarity, usually reserved for kin) with coworkers. Women whose networks only included friends often characterized the relationships in kinship terms: "I don't know what I'd do without her, she's been like a sister to me." Another woman said of her work-related network: "It's like a little happy family. You look forward to seeing one another." Clearly, friendship networks were serving needs that kin networks typically provide, and in many ways work-related networks became surrogate kin networks.

Conclusion

Clearly, work friendships provided a crucial means of support for Chicana cannery workers. Work-related friendships were a second source of advice and personal support, especially for those women past the active child-rearing phase. This information suggests that future studies of Chicano support networks must closely examine the various contexts in which people establish networks, in particular the situations in which women are confined to dead-end jobs. Although kin networks can continue to provide important material exchange and social support, long-term employment provides a context in which women factory workers can expand their social networks.

Further, women's work-based networks reflect contradictory and simultaneous processes occurring in the factories. On the one hand, women's work is considered unskilled, and little formal training is provided. Yet there are many skills, especially social ones that are necessary to work effectively, so women socialize with each other regarding shop floor practices....At the same time, although all women were in the same position as line workers, ethnic cleavages among the work force were reflected in exclusive work-based networks....Chicana cannery workers formed their own networks and usually did not include their white ethnic compatriots. Within the context of working on the line, Chicanas established solidarity with their Chicana coworkers and maintained conflictive relations with other non-Chicana women.

Women's consciousness reflects these contradictory processes. Friendships initiated on-the-job function to "humanize" the workplace, and the camaraderie women develop in this process becomes an important positive feature of the job. Ironically, women's solidarity sometimes encourages women to bear the negative aspects of their jobs. Women's criticisms of work conditions are blunted, for they see work friendships as a way to create a "family" at work and thus the whole situation seems better.

For those women who were actively trying to change working conditions, work-related networks are a potent organizing means. Work-related networks not only bring meaning to the workplace, but they also become a focal point of their private lives. In a sense, these women bring work home as work relationships infuse their home and social activities, and at times women's political involvement even takes precedence over relations with their own families.

The conditions under which women's networks evolve contain contradictory processes, and this creates variation in women's consciousness and in the construction of meaning about work.

NOTES

I want to thank Felipe Gonzales, Louise Lamphere, Micaela di Leonardo, Rayna Rapp, Judith Stacey, and an anonymous *Feminist*

Studies reviewer for their helpful comments on earlier versions of this paper.

1. Louise Lamphere, "Strategies, Cooperation, and Conflict among Women in Domestic Groups," in *Woman, Culture, and Society*, ed. Michelle Zimbalist Rosaldo and Louise Lamphere (Stanford: Stanford University Press, 1974); Suad Joseph, "Working-Class Women's Networks in a Sectarian State: A Political Paradox," *American Ethnologist* 10, no. 1 (1983): 1–22.

2. Carroll Smith-Rosenberg, "The Female World of Love and Ritual: Relations between Women in Nineteenth-Century America," *Signs* 1 (Autumn 1975): 1–29, reprinted in *A Heritage of Her Own: Toward a New Social History of American Women*, ed. Nancy F. Cott and Elizabeth H. Pleck (New York: Simon & Schuster, 1979); Nancy Cott, *The Bonds of Womanhood: "Woman's Sphere" in New England, 1780–1835* (New Haven: Yale University Press, 1977); Mary P. Ryan, "The Power of Women's Networks: A Case Study of Female Moral Reform in Antebellum America," *Feminist Studies* 5 (Spring 1979): 66–86; Jessie Bernard, *The Female World* (New York: Free Press, 1981).

3. Elizabeth Bott, *Family and Social Network* (London: Tavistock Publications, 1957); Louise Lamphere, Filomena M. Silva, and John P. Sousa, "Kin Networks and Family Strategies: Working-Class Portuguese Families in New England," in *The Versatility of Kinship*, ed. Linda S. Cordell and Stephen Beckerman (New York: Academic Press, 1980), 219–50; Carol Stack, *All Our Kin* (New York: Harper/Colophon Books, 1974); Carol Stack, "The Kindred of Viola Jackson," in *A Heritage of Her Own*.

4. Blanche Wiesen Cook, "Female Support Networks and Political Activism: Lillian Wald, Crystal Eastman, Emma Goldman," *Chrysalis*, no. 3 (1977): 43–61, reprinted in *A Heritage of Her Own*, 415–44; Temma Kaplan, "Female Consciousness and Collective Action: The Case of Barcelona, 1910–1918," in *Feminist Theory, A Critique of Ideology*, ed. Nannerl O. Keohane, Michelle Z. Rosaldo, and Barbara O. Gelpi (Chicago: University of Chicago Press, 1981), 55–76.

5. Susan Porter Benson, "'The Clerking Sisterhood': Rationalization and the Work Culture of Saleswomen in American Department Stores, 1890–1960," *Radical America* 12 (March–April 1978): 41–55; Susan Porter Benson, "'The Customers Ain't God': The Work Culture of Department Store Saleswomen, 1890–1940," in *Working-Class America: Essays on Labor, Community, and American Society*, ed. Michael H. Frisch and Daniel J. Walkowitz (Urbana: University of Illinois Press, 1983), 155–211; Barbara Melosh, *The "Physician's Hand": Work Culture and Conflict in American Nursing* (Philadelphia: Temple University Press, 1982).

6. Most of the literature on Chicano support networks does not explicitly focus on women's networks. The exceptions are Brett Williams, "The Trip Takes Us: Chicano Migrants on the Prairie" (Ph.D. diss., University of Illinois at Urbana-Champaign, 1975); and Roland M. Wagner and Diane M. Schaffer, "Social Networks and Survival Strategies: An Exploratory Study of Mexican American, Black, and Anglo Female Family Heads in San Jose, California," in *Twice a Minority: Mexican American Women*, ed. Margarita B. Melville (St. Louis: C.V. Mosby Co., 1980), 173–90. I suggest that such a focus would yield interesting results and would change our conceptions of how Chicano kin networks function. For example, interviews with young married Chicana electronics and apparel factory workers show that women not only valued their work friendships highly, but at times *preferred* discussing sensitive matters with friends rather than kin because friends were socially distant and would not get involved in the problems. See my paper "Support Networks of Young Chicana Workers" (presented at the Western Social Science Association Meetings, Albuquerque, New Mexico, April 1983).

7. Jean M. Gilbert, "Extended Family Integration among Second-Generation Mexican Americans," in *Family and Mental Health in the Mexican American Community*, ed. J. Manuel Carlos and Susan B. Keefe, Monograph no. 7 (Los Angeles: Spanish Speaking Mental Health Research Center, UCLA, 1978); Susan B. Keefe, Amado M. Padilla, and Manuel L. Carlos, "The Mexican American Extended Family as an Emotional Support System," in *Family and Mental Health in the Mexican American Community*, Monograph no. 7 (Los Angeles: Spanish Speaking Mental Health Research Center, UCLA, 1978); Susan B. Keefe, "Urbanization, Acculturation, and Extended Family Ties: Mexican Americans in Cities," *American Ethnologist* (Spring 1979): 349–65; Carolyn J. Matthiasson, "Coping in a New Environment: Mexican Americans in Milwaukee, Wisconsin," *Urban Anthropology* 3 (1974): 262–77; Wagner and Schaffer; Maxine Baca Zinn, "Urban Kinship and Midwest Chicano Families:

Evidence in Support of Revision," Special Issue on *La Familia, De Colores, Journal of Chicano Expression and Thought* 6, nos. 1–2 (1982): 85–98.

8. Keefe, Padilla, and Carlos, 148 (emphasis added).

9. Historically Chicanas have had lower labor force participation rates than Anglo or black women. Unfortunately, some writers have placed the cause of this phenomenon with women themselves—the lack of work commitment by Chicanas, which stems from traditional cultural values, is said to prevent Chicanas from becoming wage earners. For this view, see Elizabeth M. Almquist and Juanita L. Wehrle-Einhorn, "The Doubly Disadvantaged: Minority Women in the Labor Force," in *Women Working: Theories and Facts in Perspective,* ed. Ann H. Stromberg and Shirley Harkess (Palo Alto, Calif.: Mayfield Publishing Co., 1978), 63–88; Walter Fogel, *Mexican Americans in Southwest Labor Markets,* Advance Report no. 10 (Los Angeles: Mexican American Study Project, UCLA, 1965); Vernon M. Briggs, Jr., Walter Fogel, and Fred H. Schmidt, *The Chicano Worker* (Austin: University of Texas Press, 1977). For analyses that point to lower educational levels of Chicanas, a decline in traditional family values, or changes in labor markets as causes of Chicanas' recent *rise* in labor force participation rates, see, respectively: Denise Segura, "Labor Market Stratification: The Chicana Experience," *Berkeley Journal of Sociology* 29 (1984); Rosemary Santana Cooney, "Changing Labor Force Participation of Mexican American Wives: A Comparison with Anglos and Blacks," *Social Science Quarterly* 56, no. 2 (1975); and Patricia Zavella, "The Impact of 'Sun Belt Industrialization' on Chicanas," *Frontiers* 8 (Winter 1984): 21–27.

10. See Cooney.

11. The labor force participation rate for women over twenty years increased steadily. In 1971, 43 percent of all women worked; that figure grew to 52 percent in 1981. See U.S. Department of Labor, *Employment and Training Report of the President* (Washington, D.C.: GPO, 1982), 4. Chicanas (women of Mexican origin) had a labor force participation rate of 36 percent nationally in 1970. By 1980, 49 percent of all women of Spanish origin were in the labor force (statistics on Spanish-origin women were all that were available at the time of this writing). See U.S. Department of Commerce, Bureau of the Census, *United States Census of the Population, 1970: Persons of Spanish Origin,* PO (2)–10 (Washington, D.C.: GPO, 1973) and *Census of the*

Population, 1980: Provisional Estimates of Social, Economic, and Housing Characteristics, PHO801S1-1 (Washington, D.C.: GPO, 1982).

12. Although they do not explicitly use the term "work cultures," the following historical pieces provide rich descriptions of the work contexts of Chicana food processing and garment workers and mention the relationships women established with each other. See Vicki L. Ruiz, "UCAPAWA, Chicanas, and the California Food Processing Industry" (Ph.D. diss., Stanford University, 1982); Laurie Coyle, Gayle Hershatter, and Emily Honig, "Women at Farah: An Unfinished Story," in *Mexican Women in the United States, Struggles Past and Present,* ed. Magdalena Mora and Adelaida R. Del Castillo (Los Angeles: Chicano Studies Research Center Publications, UCLA, 1980), 117–44; Magdalena Mora, "The Tolteca Strike: Mexican Women and the Struggle for Union Representation," in *Mexican Immigrant Workers in the U.S.,* ed. Antonio Rios-Bustamante (Los Angeles: Chicano Studies Research Center Publications, UCLA, 1981), 111–18.

13. Sarah Eisenstein, *Give Us Bread but Give Us Roses: Working Women's Consciousness in the United States, 1890 to the First World War* (London: Routledge & Kegan Paul, 1983). Eisenstein's formulation also examines how women's consciousness develops in response to contrasting ideologies of women's "proper place" and the radical critiques from social movements, a discussion beyond the scope of this article. Also see Micaela di Leonardo, *The Varieties of Ethnic Experience: Kinship, Class, and Gender among California Italian-Americans* (Ithaca: Cornell University Press, 1984); Jane Collier, Michelle Z. Rosaldo, and Sylvia Yanagisako, "Is There a Family? New Anthropological Views," in *Rethinking the Family: Some Feminist Questions,* ed. Barrie Thorne and Marilyn Yalom (New York: Longman, 1982), 25–39; Rayna Rapp, "Family and Class in Contemporary America: Notes toward an Understanding of Ideology" *Science and Society* 42, no. 3 (1978): 278–300.

14. Because the sample is small and not randomly selected, the data should be seen as illustrating only some of the processes that occur in the lives of Chicana cannery workers.

15. For a full discussion of the canning industry, the structure of the workplace, and women's attitudes toward their jobs, see *Women's Work and Chicano Families,* esp. chaps. 3 and 5; also see Martin L. Brown, "A Historical Economic Analysis of the Wage Structure of the California

Fruit and Vegetable Canning Industry" (Ph.D. diss., University of California, Berkeley, 1981); Peter W. Philips, "Towards a New Theory of Wage Structures: The Evolution of Wages in the California Canneries—1870 to the Present" (Ph.D. diss., Stanford University , 1979).

16. See *Women's Work and Chicano Families.*

17. For an amusing description of the work process by a former employee, see Steve Turner, *Night Shift in a Pickle Factory* (San Pedro: Singlejack Books, 1980).

18. Under the piece rate system, competition among women workers centered on the position they had on the line. Women who stood at the front of the line were able to choose the best produce and make more money. Supervisors gave out line positions, and the fair ones rotated the workers. See Ruiz.

19. Robert Blauner, *Alienation and Freedom: The Factory Worker and His Industry* (Chicago: University of Chicago Press, 1964).

20. Brown.

21. Women can also become *comadres* when their children marry one another, or when they sponsor children at other Catholic rites such as First Holy Communion or Confirmation.

22. Manuel Carlos, "Traditional and Modern Forms of Compadrazgo among Mexicans and Mexican-Americans: A Survey of Continuities and Change" (Atti Del XL Congresso Internazionale Degli Americapis, Roma-Genova: Tilgher, 3–10 Settembre 1972).

23. *Compadres* can refer to cofathers only or can mean coparents.

24. Lillian B. Rubin's analysis criticizes the literature that portrays the "empty nest syndrome" in which middle-aged women are said to experience crisis after their children leave home. Rubin's informants found a new meaning in life after their children left home and took on careers, sought education, and enjoyed social relationships more. See *Women of a Certain Age: The Midlife Search for Self* (New York: Harper & Row, 1979).

25. For a full discussion of women's obligations during the earlier years in their marriages, see *Women, Work, and Chicano Families,* chaps. 4, 6.

2 | Choosing an Occupation

As a child you were asked, "What do you want to be when you grow up?" At the beginning of the semester, I ask my students to write down three seemingly realistic occupational choices and three occupational fantasies. The students' fantasies have included business tycoon, Broadway actress, president of the United States, motorcycle racer, owner/operator of a day-care center, and Peace Corps volunteer. Some of the realistic choices have included advertising executive, criminal rehabilitation worker, homemaker, and personnel manager. The occupational fantasy of one student is sometimes an occupational reality for another and vice versa. The students all have ideas about the sorts of occupations they would like and the limitations on their choices. The exercise clarifies the point that different people have different occupational options available to them.

This chapter explains how people make occupational choices and the influences on their choices. We begin by examining two different views on inequality: the functionalist and the conflict perspectives. Then we look at the process of choosing an occupation; we consider theories that focus on both individual and societal influences on occupational choice.

Occupation and Status

In the earliest societies, there was no occupational choice. Everyone participated in the tasks needed for the survival of the community. The division of labor was based largely on ascribed characteristics, such as sex and age. Hunting large animals or sea mammals, which required leaving the tribe or group for days at a time, was typically taken care of by men, whereas the daily gathering of roots and berries was more likely to be undertaken by women because of the task's proximity to the family compound.

With the domestication of both plants and animals came communities with a greater division of labor and more specialization.

Farriers put shoes on horses. Furriers made coats. Farmers grew food. Typically, an individual's occupation was inherited. A farmer's son became a farmer. A candy shop was handed down from parents to children.

The notion of occupational choice did not emerge until industrialization began to attract workers from farms and small towns to big cities where they sought jobs based on their skills. In this new labor market, it was more evident than in the past that society rewarded some occupations more than others, with greater prestige or money or both. Today, occupations requiring the most education generally provide the highest earnings. In addition, the jobs with the highest status generally (but not always) pay more than low-status jobs. The following sections discuss two perspectives on why some occupations are valued or rewarded more highly than others.

The Functionalist Perspective

Some social theorists argue that social **inequality**, the unequal distribution of rewards, is necessary for society (Davis and Moore, 1945). **Functionalists** believe that society must somehow distribute its members across the available occupations for the most effective use of talent. If all jobs were equally appealing and all members of the society were equally talented, then inequality would not be necessary. Because that is not the case, society needs to motivate the most talented individuals to make the sacrifices necessary to pursue the occupations that are most important to the society. For example, functionalists would argue that a premedical student looking into the future would not be likely to undertake college, four years of medical school beyond college, two years of residency, and perhaps additional training in a medical specialty unless he or she could foresee substantial rewards—in money and status—for the rest of his or her working life.

In many cases, the occupations that receive the greatest rewards are those that combine the greatest functional importance for society with the greatest need for talent and training. In a striking example, Coser (1990) describes how the functional importance of concentration camp prisoners' previous occupational skills dramatically affected their treatment and chances for survival. Those trained in medicine were likely to receive many privileges and the ultimate reward—the chance to remain alive. Because lawyers had no functional value in a place where all lived under a death sentence, their chances for survival were substantially reduced.

But, can the functionalist argument explain the rewards associated with each occupation? For example, why are teachers paid relatively little for their years of education? Why do we pay child-care workers, who nurture what we call our most cherished resource, little more than the minimum wage? Why are individual second-string professional male basketball players paid more than entire women's teams? Are money and external rewards the only motivators, or will the work itself draw talented people willing to live in modest circumstances? Perhaps some physicians wanted to be musicians. Are the talents needed for the most functionally important positions as scarce as Davis and Moore (1945) lead us to believe? If children of lower-class families were given the educational opportunities that typically go to other classes, more talent would be discovered. Tumin (1953) raises some of these issues in his analysis of the functionalist position.

The Conflict Perspective

Conflict theorists, who base their work on the ideas of Karl Marx, argue that those who already have power and privilege in a society will try to maintain their status. For example, the American Medical Association (AMA) has been reluctant to recognize midwifery, holistic medicine, and other fields outside the traditional hierarchy because they would challenge the AMA's control over people's health care. Generally, conflict theorists argue that inequality is not necessary but rather is a function of the tendency of powerful groups and classes to try to dominate the less powerful.

Marx further believed that individuals' positions are determined by their relationship to the mode of production. Either one is part of the **bourgeoisie**, the class that owns the factories or other means of production, or one is a part of the **proletariat**, those who have only their labor to offer. The bourgeoisie continue to maintain their superior status by oppressing the proletariat in the midst of a capitalist system that supports (indeed, relies on) this inequality. Conflict theorists argue that the inequality of occupational status and the inequitable distribution of rewards in a capitalist system interfere with the most effective societal structure.

The conflict perspective raises as many questions as the functionalist perspective does. For example, in the United States today, do we have two great classes? If not, why not? Do those in positions of power and privilege actually attempt to keep others out? To what extent is inequality necessary to the effective functioning of society? Both the functionalist and conflict perspectives present views on inequality and suggest the ways in which society may either enhance or limit the possible occupational choices for individuals.

The Process of Choosing an Occupation

Both the functionalist and conflict perspectives are based on the notion that society exerts an influence on people's choice of occupation; but, how do individuals learn about occupations and decide whether a certain choice is realistic or not? At the age of 5 or 6, children who are asked about their occupational aspirations often mention visible occupations that they know little about—firefighter, police officer, ballet dancer, or figure skater. As a child, I took several trips through national parks with my family. The result was that I wanted to be a naturalist. Little did I know that the training would include dissecting many of the animals I had grown so fond of. Similarly, my love for cats pulled me back from the harsh realities of veterinary medicine. My occupational interests at that time would better have been described as Professional Cat Cuddler.

By adulthood, however, people have more realistic occupational goals. Social scientists have proposed a variety of schemes for describing the shift from occupational fantasies to occupational realities, typically in the form of a number of developmental phases or stages through which the individual passes. Through this developmental process, individuals presumably become aware of their own capacities and needs, while simultaneously learning about the opportunities and limits placed on them by society. In one scheme, for example, children first pass through a period of fantasy (6 to 11 years of age) in which they cannot evaluate their aptitudes or abilities (Ginzberg et al., 1951). During this phase, children mention choices because the associated activities are thought to be pleasurable (61). For example, young children may think they want to become an astronaut, although they do not have any real idea of how astronauts spend their work days. Children get their ideas for these fantasies most often from parents, peers, teachers, and the mass media. During the second phase, the tentative period (12 to 17 years of age), the individuals evaluate certain potential routes for satisfaction by becoming increasingly aware of their own interests and capabilities and the constraints of the real world (73). During the final phase, the realistic period (18 years or older), the occupational decision becomes real. Abilities, needs, and values compete with actual opportunities in this **rational decision-making** process. Finally, a compromise is reached, and the choice is made (185). In Case Study 2.1, "The World of Work: Aspirations of the Hangers and Brothers," Jay MacLeod compares the occupational aspirations of two groups of male teenagers who live in a lower class housing project: the Brothers, a predominantly African American group, and the Hallway Hangers, who are predominantly white.

Another developmental theory of occupational choice includes six major stages and a variety of substages that lead to the evolution of a vocational self-concept throughout life (Super, 1953, 1957). An individual passes through the following stages: adolescent exploration; reality testing (transition from school to work); the floundering or trial process (trying on a self-concept); establishment (modifying and implementing the self-concept); the maintenance stage (preserving the self-concept); and years of decline (adjustment to a new self). Both internal factors such as intelligence, aptitudes, and interest, and external factors such as the reality of the working world play a role. Children may acquire values and beliefs from many sources of socialization such as parents, peers, and schools. In addition, social class may either enhance or limit perceived or actual opportunities for occupational success as you will soon discover.

Others attempting to explain occupational choice believe that the process is more **fortuitous**—that is, it is due to chance and circumstance (Katz and Martin, 1962). An individual drifts into an occupation rather than following a rational decision-making process. This could happen either because choice is constrained by the lack of opportunity or because an extraordinary opportunity presents itself. Half of the poultry processing workers, those who butcher fowl, interviewed in one study said that they "needed a job or money, or that there were, simply, no job choices" (Bryant and Perkins, 1982). An unanticipated occupational opportunity occurs when an army tank commander wins a writing contest that allows him to take over the army base's newspaper. Consequently, occupational choice may be less of a process than the rational decision-making theorists would have us believe and more a case of limited opportunity for some and serendipitous circumstances for others. Although one might think of a garbage collector as having made a fortuitous choice as a result of limited opportunities, in Case Study 2.2, "San Francisco Scavengers," Stewart Perry shows that this choice by one group of men was far from fortuitous.

Influences on Occupational Choice

A variety of factors narrow the range of realistic options for all of us. They include such individual factors as talent and motivation and such social factors as gender, race, social class, and even the level of technological and economic development of the society in which we live. The individual and social factors work together to ease entry into some occupations and increase the difficulty of entering others.

Individual Influences

When I ask students about their occupational fantasies and then ask why their fantasies are not realistic occupational choices, some tell me that they lack the innate talent to make a living in their dream job. Each of us is born with a set of innate talents. Yet, some of these innate talents may be more valued than others in a particular society at a particular time. In the earliest societies, agility, strength, and endurance were most valued for the two major occupational tasks: hunting animals and gathering small fruits and roots. Our society has shifted. Now the highly valued occupations typically require more brain than brawn. Of course, top jocks rely on physical talents to make millions; but, collectively, top business executives make billions because of their intellectual and social abilities.

Motivation is another individual constraint on occupational choice. Some of my students say that they do not pursue their fantasy occupation because they cannot have or do not want to have an occupation that requires so much time and dedication. The slim possibility of success in some occupations discourages other students. One in 10,000 high school heros ever makes the big leagues. The odds against becoming the next Garth Brooks are even higher. Another admits that the risk and danger prevent him from being a professional motorcycle racer. Some confess that their fantasy job—such as Peace Corps volunteer or missionary, which falls near the bottom of the income pyramid—would not repay their student loans. Our social structure has moved professional boxers and merger brokers to the top of an income pyramid that finds child-care workers and farm workers near the bottom. Many individuals simply prefer the greater rewards associated with jobs at the top of the pyramid.

A person's interests are also motivating factors. Would you want to spend your days working with people or things? Would you want to work at a desk, in a lab, in a library, or at a lectern in front of a large audience? Would you want to be landing in Dallas 30 minutes before your next meeting or spending most of your time in the same place? Would you want to spend most of your time talking to people who know as much as you do about your work? Or do you want to talk to people in a "teaching" capacity as a supervisor or in a persuasive capacity selling ideas or products? How creative and autonomous should your ideal job be? Do you want work that becomes your life or work that allows you to have a life of your own? Do you want to be in a field in which the knowledge is constantly changing or a field in which the knowledge is changing more slowly? Do you crave stability or thrive on chaos? Do you want to work with your hands? Will you work nights and weekends?

In their search for the right occupation, some will take a vocational interest test or career assessment survey. These tests measure interests, not ability or opportunity. The most well-known of these, the Strong-Campbell Interest Inventory, asks whether respondents like, are indifferent to, or dislike a variety of occupations; school subjects; activities (making a speech, sewing, discussing politics); amusements (golf, fishing, poetry, religious music); and day-to-day contact with particular types of people (high school students, babies, religious people). In the last two sections of the interest inventory, respondents are asked to indicate which of two matched activities they prefer (airline pilot versus airline ticket agent; thrilling, dangerous activities versus quieter, safer activities; having a few close friends versus having many acquaintances), and to indicate what kind of a person they are (win friends easily, have patience when teaching others, usually start activities of one's group). When respondents receive their results, their level of interest on six different scales (realistic, investigative, artistic, social, enterprising, and conventional) is shown along with the degree to which respondents' answers are similar to those in over 100 occupations. Respondents are then encouraged to follow up on those occupations with which they shared the greatest similarity of interest.

The talent of the individuals or their actual likelihood of being able to enter a particular field is not part of the assessment; it is a psychological test and a measure of interest only. Some have wondered whether it measures what it claims, since the original scale was developed on the basis of the answers of 100 satisfied individuals in each of the occupations included on the interest inventory. We do not know who those individuals were or at what stage of their career they were tested. Individuals who entered a field more recently might feel differently about it than those who have been in it a long time.

Much like the Strong-Campbell Interest Inventory, another approach to occupational choice depends on a classification of personality types and occupational environments (Holland, 1959, 1966, 1973). It recognizes that a person is born with an innate set of needs and talents, but as a result of socialization and life experiences develops preferred ways for dealing with the world. A person making an occupational choice searches for occupational environments that fit closely with the way in which he or she deals with the world.

The occupational classification of environments includes motoric (farmer, truck driver); intellectual (physicist, anthropologist); supportive (teacher, social worker); conforming (bank teller, secretary); persuasive (politician, manager); and aesthetic (musician, writer).

Several occupational environments are characterized by their masculinity or femininity. For example, motoric types are described as follows: "above all they wish to play masculine roles....Persons of this orientation are typified by their masculinity" (36). In contrast, those of the supportive orientation are "characterized as responsible, socially oriented, and accepting of feminine impulses and roles....Persons of this class are best typified as orally dependent in the sense of being verbal, feminine, and dependent" (37). The description of the aesthetic orientation also mentions femininity (37).

The classification of occupational types as masculine or feminine is problematic. Must a man be feminine to enter a supportive or aesthetic environment and a woman be masculine to enter a motoric environment? In fact, Holland admits that his theory "is based chiefly on studies of men and is probably less useful for understanding the behavior of women" (1966: 13). This theory, then, may not be useful in explaining why a woman would choose to enter engineering or why a man would choose nursing.

Social Influences

Theories of occupational choice based on individual influences obviously have some shortcomings. A more comprehensive description of factors influencing occupational choice was developed during the 1950s by Peter Blau, a sociologist, along with his colleagues in psychology and economics (Blau et al., 1956). Their basic premise is the following: "The social structure...has a dual significance for occupational choice. On the one hand, it influences the personality development of the choosers; on the other, it defines the socioeconomic conditions in which selection takes place" (533). The social structure includes the social stratification system, cultural values and norms, demographic characteristics, the type of economy, and technology.

Figure 2.1 shows the interaction of individual and social factors. The social structure underlies the development of both the individual choosing an occupation and the environment in which the choice is made. On the side of those choosing occupations, the model includes talent, personality, orientation to occupational life, occupational information, and qualifications. The conditions beyond the control of the individual include environmental conditions, historical change, and available occupational opportunities. The basic assumption is that an individual's choice is a compromise between occupational preferences and assessments of the marketplace. This model also allows us to see that the opportunities and constraints which lead to the choice of a particular occupation may differ for each individual. Lortie (1975), for example, found that there were several routes to the

Figure 2.1

Social Structural Model of Occupational Choice

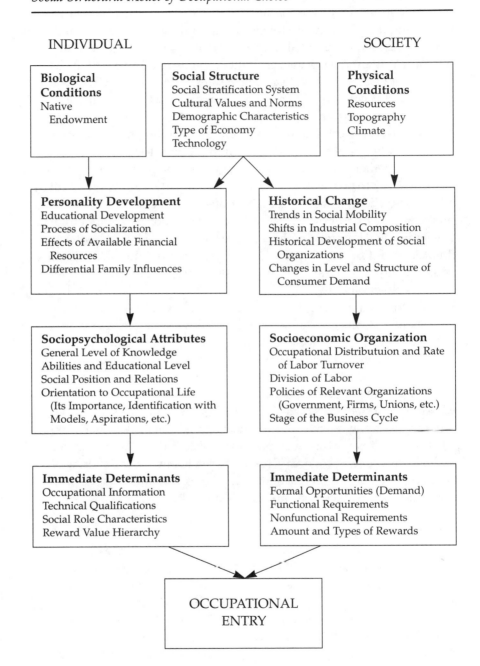

INDIVIDUAL   SOCIETY

Biological Conditions
Native
  Endowment

Social Structure
Social Stratification System
Cultural Values and Norms
Demographic Characteristics
Type of Economy
Technology

Physical Conditions
Resources
Topography
Climate

Personality Development
Educational Development
Process of Socialization
Effects of Available Financial
  Resources
Differential Family Influences

Historical Change
Trends in Social Mobility
Shifts in Industrial Composition
Historical Development of Social
  Organizations
Changes in Level and Structure of
  Consumer Demand

Sociopsychological Attributes
General Level of Knowledge
Abilities and Educational Level
Social Position and Relations
Orientation to Occupational Life
  (Its Importance, Identification with
  Models, Aspirations, etc.)

Socioeconomic Organization
Occupational Distributuion and Rate
  of Labor Turnover
Division of Labor
Policies of Relevant Organizations
  (Government, Firms, Unions, etc.)
Stage of the Business Cycle

Immediate Determinants
Occupational Information
Technical Qualifications
Social Role Characteristics
Reward Value Hierarchy

Immediate Determinants
Formal Opportunities (Demand)
Functional Requirements
Nonfunctional Requirements
Amount and Types of Rewards

OCCUPATIONAL
ENTRY

Source: Adapted from original, from "Occupational Choice" by Peter Blau, 1956,
Industrial and Labor Relations Review, 9, pp. 531–543. Reprinted with permission.

choice of schoolteaching. Some individuals were specifically attracted to teaching because they felt the occupation would provide characteristics they desired in an occupation: contact with children and young people, a chance to perform a service for society, the ability to continue in a school and learning setting, and a work schedule compatible with other priorities in life, such as family. Some left the business world and chose teaching because they perceived it as a more moral occupation. Others, however, chose schoolteaching as a result of constraints on their occupational choice. The economic constraints of some working class children caused them to attend state teachers' colleges even though their initial interest in teaching was low. During their time in college, they found themselves positively influenced by the emphasis on teacher training at such colleges. Still others who chose schoolteaching indicated that financial constraints prevented them from entering another occupation they preferred. One individual became a biology teacher because medical school was financially out of reach. In short, characteristics of both individuals and occupations have an impact on individuals' propensity to choose particular occupations.

When economists approach career choice, they emphasize individual factors such as tastes and talents coupled with such market factors as wages. They argue that occupational choice is a result of rational self-interest. Individuals evaluate aspects of occupations such as the wages and working conditions, and then choose the best option. Economists who support the human capital theory say that people "invest" in their education and training. Using this model, some economists argue that some women may decide an investment in education will not yield adequate returns because they plan to be absent from the market for several years to raise children. This example illustrates the influence of social constraints based on gender, but other constraints—race, social class, and societal development—also play a role.

Gender. Most major theories of occupational choice consider it to be a compromise between abilities, aptitudes, interests, and the access to particular occupations. At the same time, with some exceptions, the theories considered so far seem to underplay gender stereotypes as an influence on interests, trained abilities, and values and as a constraint on the range of occupations women and men may consider accessible. In part, this may be due to the societal context, the traditional 1950s and early 1960s, in which many of these theories were conceived. More often than not, these theories focused implicitly on the process of occupational choice for men without acknowledging how the process might be similar or different for women.

Nevertheless, a theory of occupational choice for women was also presented in the 1960s. Psathas (1968) argued that women take family priorities and preferences into account in the choice to work and in the choice of an occupation. Although this theory can be criticized for overemphasizing the differences between the factors which influence men's and women's choices, it highlighted the way in which societal expectations for women and men may affect their perceptions of their occupational options.

Even in the 1990s, societal expectations of women and men shape their occupational choice and the role of work in their lives. In Case Study 2.3, Maureen Connelly and Patricia Rhoton consider the role that gender role expectations play in choosing direct sales jobs, such as those provided by Mary Kay or Amway. In addition to the choice of a specific occupation, the place, more generally, of work and family in one's life can be affected by gender expectations. As you read the women's life histories in Case Study 2.4, "Alternative Paths in Adult Development," by Kathleen Gerson, you will see how these women's orientation towards work in general, which ultimately has an impact on their occupational choice, is affected by their own circumstances, their parents' employment, and gender expectations.

These expectations suggest that women should be nurturing, supportive, and maternal, while men should be strong, analytic, and driven. Many women and men choose occupations which seem congruent with societal expectations. Without acknowledging the consequences of gender expectations, it is difficult to explain the disproportionate representation of women and men in many ocupations. The **sex segregation** of the labor force means that there are many occupations in which there are many more men than women or women than men. Table 2.1 shows, for example, that while men account for over 90 percent of truck drivers, automobile mechanics, firefighters, engineers, and airplane pilots and navigators, women account for over 90 percent of the dental hygienists, secretaries, childcare workers, registered nurses, and prekindergarten and kindergarten teachers. Thus, women and men are overrepresented in occupations congruent with gender role stereotypes. Some refer to the female-dominated occupations as *pink-collar occupations* (Howe, 1977). If women are supposed to be nurturing and supportive, it is not surprising that occupations such as nursing are dominated by women, despite the fact that a nurse also needs to be physically strong to lift patients and think analytically to keep track of the condition of patients. On the other hand, in many occupations, women and men are making inroads into occupations previously dominated by the other gender. Nevertheless, early entrants to these occupations

Table 2.1

Percentages of Women and Men in Selected Occupations

	Percentage of Women	Percentage of Men
Dental hygienists	99.9	0.1
Secretaries	99.9	0.1
Child-care workers	97.3	0.7
Registered nurses	93.8	6.2
Teachers		
Prekindergarten and kindergarten	98.1	1.9
Elementary	85.6	14.4
Secondary	55.6	44.4
College and university	42.5	57.5
Lawyers	24.8	75.2
Physicians	22.3	77.7
Architects	16.8	83.2
Dentists	13.3	86.7
Clergy	11.1	88.9
Engineers	8.3	91.7
Truck drivers	4.5	95.5
Airplane pilots and navigators	2.6	97.4
Firefighters	2.1	97.9
Automobile mechanics	1.0	99.0

Source: U.S. Department of Labor, 1995a: Table 11.

were still overrepresented in fields congruent with stereotyped gender role expectations. For example, women physicians were overrepresented in pediatrics and psychiatry, both fields that require nurturing, support, and emotional labor. Women physicians are also overrepresented in public health, perhaps as a result of a desire for predictable hours that are more compatible with family responsibilities. Male nurses are overrepresented in administration and anesthesia (Auster, 1978), both of which are highly prestigious and well paid. Although some argue that the sex segregation of the labor force and choices of specialties within fields are the consequence of the differential socialization and resulting preferences of women and men, others argue that gatekeepers and coworkers make it very difficult for those who want to cross the sex lines. Interestingly, this is more of a problem for women than for men (Williams, 1992). For example, Floge and Merrill (1986) found that whereas men in nursing experienced an enhanced status as a result of their sex, women physicians reported they were treated as less than equals.

Angrist and Almquist (1975) propose an "enrichment" hypothesis to explain the choice of some women to enter male-dominated occupations. They argue that these women are a product of unusual positive factors, backgrounds, and experiences that result in a broadened perception of the female role and occupational options for themselves as women. Just as "normal" behavior is learned, so is "deviant" (here, statistically unusual) behavior. An extension of the notion of differential association (Sutherland and Cressey, 1966) would suggest that even if society is not supportive of nontraditional occupational choice, an individual may find personal support for his or her occupational choice among friends and family that would outweigh resistance by society as a whole. Women who enter engineering, for example, are not rebelling against those around them. In fact, they emerge from a supportive environment, an environment in which one-third of their fathers are engineers (Auster, 1984). Thus, the views of their significant others, even when they differ from those of society, are more important to their choice than all the discouraging words and images of conformity they may get from other agents of socialization.

Race. Like sex, the racial distribution across occupations is striking. African Americans make up about 12 percent of the population, yet they account for over 20 percent of social workers, cleaners and servants, prison guards, short-order cooks, nursing aides and attendants, and postal clerks. At the same time, less than 3 percent of managers in public relations and advertising, architects, geologists, dentists, dental hygienists, authors, airplane pilots, and bartenders are African American. Similar discrepancies and variations are apparent among other groups as well, particularly Hispanics and Asians. Table 2.2 shows the top occupations for blacks, Hispanics, Asians, and whites by sex.

The discrepancies in racial distribution across occupations have a complex explanation. For example, decades of discrimination have put many African Americans below the poverty line. As these children look to their future, their occupational realities are limited by their need to leave school to help support their families and by discrimination. Furthermore, whether perceived or actual, discrimination continues to limit occupational options.

Social Class. One of the most limiting influences on occupational choice is social class. Those of the highest social classes may find their aspirations and their actual occupational choices well matched if they have the innate talent for their dream occupation. For the lower social classes, the realities of limited resources, particularly the money to go to college, narrow the occupational possibilities. Although the talent necessary for the most rewarded occupations in our society may be found

Table 2.2

Top Occupations for Blacks, Hispanics, Asians, and Whites by Sex, 1990

Black Women		Black Men	
Total labor force	6,847,642	*Total labor force*	6,247,539
Cashier	346,359	Truck driver	342,492
Secretary	294,437	Janitor, cleaner	337,996
Elementary school teacher	257,434	Cook	194,282
Cook	192,660	Construction laborer	148,861
Janitor, cleaner	179,734	Guard	138,304
General office clerk	169,735	Assembler	136,189
Maid, "houseman"	162,870	Salaried manager, administrator, nec*	111,904
Registered nurse	157,515	Stock handler, bagger	92,378

Hispanic Women		Hispanic Men	
Total labor force	4,133,543	*Total labor force*	5,888,180
Secretary	219,115	Janitor, cleaner	255,573
Cashier	199,779	Truck driver	240,989
Janitor, cleaner	124,696	Farm worker	207,238
Sewing machine operator	123,539	Cook	191,390
Nurse's aide, orderly	123,131	Construction laborer	188,082
Elementary school teacher	104,645	Gardener, groundskeeper	151,017
Maid, "houseman"	103,022	Salaried manager, administrator, nec*	125,977
General office clerk	95,836	Assembler	123,232

Note: Blacks, Asians, and whites include people of Hispanic origin.
*The Census Bureau uses the abbreviation *nec* for miscellaneous occupations that are "not elsewhere classified."

Asian Women

Total labor force	1,684,082
Registered Nurse	80,494
Cashier	77,490
Secretary	62,929
Sewing machine operator	57,602
Accountant, auditer	49,971
Bookkeeper	43,741
Waitress	40,722
General office clerk	38,392

Asian Men

Total labor force	1,918,998
Salaried manager, administrator, nec*	85,999
Cook	80,976
Salaried sales supervisor, proprietor	56,068
Physician	45,483
Janitor, cleaner	39,322
Food service, lodging	38,685
Accountant	37,734
Cashier	36,479

White Women

Total labor force	45,826,627
Secretary	3,504,652
Elementary school teacher	2,038,535
Cashier	1,725,368
Bookkeeper	1,548,980
Registered nurse	1,517,912
Salaried manager, administrator, nec*	1,428,336
Sales, other commodities	1,066,418
Waitress	1,065,475

White Men

Total labor force	55,699,109
Salaried manager, administrator, nec*	3,107,913
Truck driver	2,231,097
Salaried sales, supervisor, proprietor	1,779,842
Carpenter	1,187,316
Janitor, cleaner	1,182,001
Sales representative, mining, manufacturing, wholesale	1,109,573
Supervisor, precision, production	930,804
Construction laborer	832,692

Note: Blacks, Asians, and whites include people of Hispanic origin.

*The Census Bureau uses the abbreviation *nec* for miscellaneous occupations that are "not elsewhere classified."

Source: Data from U.S. Bureau of the Census 1992a: Tables 1 and 2. Reprinted with permission from Reskin, Barbara and Irene Padavic. 1994. *Women and Men at Work.* Thousand Oaks, CA: Pine Forge Press.

in every social class, children who are products of the higher social classes are most able to develop their talents and pursue their dream careers. The higher the social class of the family, the more education their children are likely to attain. Children of the higher social classes are more likely to have parents, teachers, and peers unanimously supporting their efforts in school, and they score better on standardized tests. These tests place children in different educational tracks that lead to particular occupational futures. Once placed, children seldom change tracks. All of these forces result in better educational and occupational outcomes for those who start ahead in the game.

For the working class, the lack of occupational mobility among their family and peers perpetuates the notion that it is difficult to move up in the world. Nevertheless, many children of working-class origins are quite successful; but, upward social mobility does not come without costs.

Level of Societal Development. The level of technological and economic development of the society itself may also affect occupational choices. In an industrial or postindustrial society, the division of labor is very specialized. With the right talent, a person can have a career as a computer software engineer specializing in robotic welding controls, a microbiologist developing new microbes to destroy hazardous waste, or an astronaut training for years for a flight to Mars that may not happen in his or her lifetime. But, in Third World nations, the occupational options are more tied to what the land has to offer—farming, forestry, fishing, and mining. A factory built by an industrialized nation taking advantage of low-paid labor offers additional, although not always desirable, options in developing nations.

Conclusion

The question addressed by this chapter is whether individuals can make unconstrained occupational choices and pursue their dream careers. At this point, it should be obvious that occupational choice is constrained by both individual and societal factors. Do we expect a starving Somalian child to have the energy to consider occupational *choice*? Even when we disregard the 5-foot-tall basketball hopefuls and the potential surgeons who get dizzy at the sight of blood, we find compromise at every turn. Some have the talent to go to medical school, but not the money or social support. Others who have the money flunk biology. Whether the occupational choice process is best explained as a rational decision-making process or as the result of chance and circumstances, individuals are constrained by societal forces that have an impact on individual factors. Societal forces are part of the reason that a student seldom includes the same occupation on both the fantasy and realistic occupational choice list. As Mick Jagger said (in reference to an avocation rather than a vocation), "You can't always get what you want. But, if you try sometimes, you might find you get what you need" (Rolling Stones, 1969).

REFERENCES AND SUGGESTED READINGS

Angrist, Shirley S., and Elizabeth M. Almquist. 1975. *Careers and Contingencies.* Port Washington, NY: Kennikat.

Auster, Carol J. 1984. *Nontraditional Occupational Choice: A Comparative Study of Women and Men in Engineering.* Unpublished Ph.D. dissertation. Princeton University.

Auster, Donald. 1978. "Occupational Values of Male and Female Nursing Students." *Sociology of Work and Occupations* 5 (May): 209–233.

Blau, Peter et al. 1956. "Occupational Choice: A Conceptual Framework." *Industrial and Labor Relations Review* 9 (July): 531–543.

Bryant, Clifton D., and Kenneth B. Perkins. 1982. "Containing Work Disaffection." Pages 199–212 in *Varieties of Work,* edited by Phyllis L. Stewart and Muriel G. Cantor. Beverly Hills: Sage.

Coser, Lewis A. 1990. "Forced Labor in Concentration Camps." Pages 162–169 in *The Nature of Work,* edited by Kai Erikson and Steven Peter Vallas. New Haven: Yale University Press.

Davis, Kingsley, and Wilbert Moore. 1945. "Some Principles of Stratification." *American Sociological Review* 10 (2): 242–249.

Floge, Liliane, and Deborah M. Merrill. 1986. "Tokenism Reconsidered: Male Nurses and Female Physicians in a Hospital Setting." *Social Forces* 64 (4): 925–947.

Ginzberg, Eli et al. 1951. *Occupational Choice: An Approach to a General Theory.* New York: Columbia University Press.

Holland, J. L. 1959. "A Theory of Vocational Choice." *Journal of Counseling Psychology* 6 (1): 35–44.

Holland, J. L. 1966. *The Psychology of Vocational Choice.* Waltham, MA: Blaisdell.

Holland, J. L. 1973. *Making Vocational Choices: A Theory of Careers.* Englewood Cliffs, NJ: Prentice-Hall.

Howe, Louise Kapp. 1977. *Pink Collar Workers.* New York: Avon.

Katz, Fred E., and Harry W. Martin. 1962. "Career Choice Processes." *Social Forces* 41 (December): 149–154.

Lortie, Dan C. 1975. *Schoolteacher: A Sociological Study.* Chicago: University of Chicago Press.

Psathas, George. 1968. "Toward a Theory of Occupational Choice for Women." *Sociology and Social Research* 52 (2): 253–268.

Reskin, Barbara and Irene Padavic. 1994. *Women and Men at Work.* Thousand Oaks, CA: Pine Forge Press.

Rolling Stones. 1969. "You Can't Always Get What You Want," from the album entitled *Let it Bleed.*

Super, D. E. 1953. "A Theory of Vocational Development." *American Psychologist* 8: 185–190.

Super, D. E. 1957. *The Psychology of Careers: An Introduction to Vocational Development.* New York: Harper and Row.

Sutherland, Edwin H., and Donald Cressey. 1966. *Principles of Criminology.* Philadelphia: J. B. Lippincott.

Tumin, Melvin. 1953. "Some Principles of Stratification: A Critical Analysis." *American Sociological Review* 18 (4): 387–394.

U.S. Department of Labor. 1995a. *Employment and Earnings* 42 (January). Washington, DC: Bureau of Labor Statistics.

Wheeler, Stanton. 1990. "Double Lives." Pages 141–148 in *The Nature of Work,* edited by Kai Erikson and Steven Peter Vallas. New Haven: Yale University Press.

Williams, Christine L. 1989. *Gender Differences at Work: Women and Men in Nontraditional Occupations.* Berkeley: University of California Press.

Williams, Christine L. 1992. "The Glass Escalator: Hidden Advantages for Men in the 'Female' Professions." *Social Problems* 39: 253–267.

Young, Michael. 1959. *The Rise of Meritocracy.* New York: Random House.

The World of Work

Aspirations of the Hangers and Brothers

Jay MacLeod

CASE STUDY QUESTIONS

1. What occupational fantasies, if any, do the Brothers and the Hallway Hangers have? Where do these fantasies come from? To what degree are these only fantasies and why?

2. Would the Hallway Hangers be more likely to subscribe to a functionalist or conflict view of the world? Which perspective would make more sense to the Brothers?

3. The human capital approach that focuses on how people may invest in their education and training because they expect to reap occupational rewards. How well does this view explain the choices of the Hallway Hangers and the Brothers?

4. To what extent would you have expected the Hallway Hangers and the Brothers to have similar occupational aspirations? Why do you think they do not?

Like most old "projects" (as low-income public housing developments are known to their residents), Clarendon Heights is architecturally a world unto itself. Although

Source: Approximately 22 pages from *Ain't No Makin' It: Leveled Aspirations in a Low Income Neighborhood* by Jay MacLeod. Copyright © 1987 by WestviewPress. Reprinted by permission of WestviewPress.

smaller and less dilapidated than many urban housing developments, its plain brick buildings testify that cost efficiency was the overriding consideration in its construction.

Bordered on two sides by residential neighborhoods and on the other two by a shoe factory, a junkyard, and a large plot of industrial wasteland, Clarendon Heights consists of six large, squat, three-story buildings and one high rise. The architecture is imposing and severe; only the five chimneys atop each building break the harsh symmetry of the structures.

Even at its worst, however, Clarendon Heights is not a bad place to live compared to many inner-city housing developments. This relatively small development, set in a working-class neighborhood, should not be confused with the massive, scarred projects of the nation's largest cities. Nevertheless, the social fabric of Clarendon Heights is marked by problems generally asssociated with low-income housing developments. Approximately 65 percent of Clarendon Heights' residents are white, 25 percent are black, and 10 percent are other minorities. Few adult males live in Clarendon Heights; approximately 85 percent of the families are headed by single women. Although no precise figures are available, it is acknowledged by the City Housing Authority that significant numbers of tenants are second- and third-generation public housing residents. Social workers estimate that almost 70 percent of the families are on some additional form of public assistance. Overcrowding, unemployment, alcoholism, drug abuse, crime, and racism plague the community.

Although the general picture that emerges is dreary, its texture is richly varied. The male teenage world of Clarendon Heights is populated by two divergent peer groups. The first group, dubbed the Hallway Hangers because of the group's propensity for "hanging" in a particular hallway in the project, consists predominantly of white boys. Their characteristics and attitudes stand in marked contrast to the second group, which is composed almost exclusively of black youths who call themselves the Brothers. Surprisingly, the Brothers speak with relative optimism about their futures, while the Hallway Hangers are despondent about their prospects for social mobility.

Given that work determines one's social class, the perpetuation of class inequality requires that boys like the Hallway Hangers and the Brothers go on to jobs that are comparable in status to the occupations of their parents. Thus, the attitudes of these boys toward the world of work are critical to our understanding of social reproduction. In this [case study], their previous employment records, their general impressions of work, their aspirations and expectations, and their perceptions of the job opportunity structure are considered.

Before describing the boys' orientation toward work, I would like to make an analytical distinction between aspirations and expectations. Both involve assessments of one's desires, abilities, and the character of the opportunity structure. In articulating one's aspirations, an individual weighs his or her preferences more heavily; expecta-

tions are tempered by perceived capabilities and available opportunities. Aspirations are one's preferences relatively unsullied by anticipated constraints; expectations take these constraints squarely into account.[1]

The Hallway Hangers: Keeping a Lid on Hope

Conventional, middle-class orientations toward employment are inadequate to describe the Hallway Hangers' approach to work. The notion of a career, a set of jobs that are connected to one another in a logical progression, has little relevance to these boys. They are hesitant when asked about their aspirations and expectations. This hesitancy is not the result of indecision; rather it stems from the fact that these boys see little choice involved in getting a job. No matter how hard I pressed him, for instance, Jinks refused to articulate his aspirations: "I think you're kiddin' yourself to have any. We're just gonna take whatever we can get." Jinks is a perceptive boy, and his answer seems to be an accurate depiction of the situation. Beggars cannot be choosers, and these boys have nothing other than unskilled labor to offer on a credential-based job market.

It is difficult to gauge the aspirations of most of the Hallway Hangers. Perhaps at a younger age they had dreams for their futures. At ages sixteen, seventeen, and eighteen, however, their own job experiences as well as those of family members have contributed to a deeply entrenched cynicism about their futures. What is perceived as the cold, hard reality of the job market weighs very heavily on the Hallway Hangers; they believe their preferences will have almost no bearing on the work they actually will do. Their expectations are not merely tempered by perceptions of the opportunity structure; even their aspirations are crushed by their estimation of the job market. These generalizations may seem bold and rather extreme, but they do not lack ethnographic support.

The pessimism and uncertainty with which the Hallway Hangers view their futures emerge clearly when the boys are asked to speculate on what their lives will be like in twenty years.

(all in separate interviews)

Stoney: Hard to say. I could be dead tomorrow. Around here, you gotta take life day by day.

Boo-Boo: I dunno. I don't want to think about it. I'll think about it when it comes.

Frankie: I don't fucking know. Twenty years. I may be fucking dead. I live a day at a time. I'll probably be in the fucking pen.

Shorty: Twenty years? I'm gonna be in jail.

These responses are striking not only for the insecurity and despondency they reveal, but also because they do not include any mention of work. It is not that work is unimportant—for people as strapped for money as the Hallway Hangers are, work is crucial. Rather, these boys are indifferent to the issue of future employment. Work is a given; they all hope to hold jobs of one kind or another in order to support themselves and their families. But the Hallway Hangers…believe the character of work, at least all work in which they are likely to be involved, is essentially the same: boring, undifferentiated, and unrewarding. Thinking about their future jobs is a useless activity for the Hallway Hangers. What is there to think about?

For Steve and Jinks, although they do see themselves employed in twenty years, work is still of tangential importance.

JM: If you had to guess, what do you think you'll be doing twenty years from now?

(in separate interviews)

Steve: I don't fucking know. Working probably. Have my own pad, my own house. Bitches, kids. Fucking fridge full of brewskies. Fine wife, likes to get laid.

Jinks: Twenty years from now? Probably kicked back in my own apartment doing the same shit I'm doing now—getting high. I'll have a job, if I'm not in the service, if war don't break out, if I'm not dead. I just take one day at a time.

Although the Hallway Hangers expect to spend a good portion of their waking hours on the job, work is important to them not as an end in itself, but solely as a means to an end—money.

In probing the occupational aspirations and expectations of the Hallway Hangers, I finally was able to elicit from them some specific hopes. Although Shorty never mentions his expectations, the rest of the Hallway Hangers have responded to my prodding with some definite answers. The range of answers as well as how they change over time are as significant as the particular hopes each boy expresses.

Boo-Boo's orientation toward work is typical of the Hallway Hangers. He has held a number of jobs in the past, most of them in the summer. During his freshman year in high school Boo-Boo worked as a security guard at school for $2.50 an hour in order to make restitution for a stolen car he damaged. Boo-Boo also has worked on small-scale construction projects through a summer youth employment program called Just-A-Start, at a pipe manufacturing site, and as a clerk in a gift shop. Boo-Boo wants to be an automobile mechanic. Upon graduating from high school, he studied auto mechanics at a technical school on a scholarship. The only black student in his class, Boo-Boo was expelled early in his first term after racial antagonism erupted into a fight. Boo-Boo was not altogether disappointed, for he already was unhappy with what he considered the program's overly theoretical orientation. (Howard London found this kind of impatience typical of working-class students in the community college he studied.[2]) Boo-Boo wanted hands-on training, but "all's they were doing was telling me about how it's made, stuff like that." Boo-Boo currently is unemployed, but he recently had a chance for a job as a cook's helper. Although he was not hired, the event is significant nevertheless because prior to the job interview, Boo-Boo claimed that his ambition now was to work in a restaurant. Here we have an example of the primacy of the opportunity structure in determining the aspirations of the Hallway Hangers. One job opening in another field was so significant that the opening prompted Boo-Boo to redefine totally his aspirations.

In contrast to the rest of the Hallway Hangers who are already on the job market, Steve wants to stay in school for the two years required to get his diploma. Yet he has a similar attitude toward his future work as do the other youths. He quit his summer job with the Just-A-Start program and has no concrete occupational aspirations. As for expectations, he believes he might enlist in the air force after graduation but adds, "I dunno. I might just go up and see my uncle, do some fuckin' construction or something."

Many of these boys expect to enter military service. Jinks and Frankie mention it as an option; Stoney has tried to enlist, but without success. Although Jinks refuses to think in terms of aspirations, he will say what he expects to do after he finishes school.

JM: What are you gonna do when you get out?

Jinks: Go into the service, like everybody else. The navy.

JM: What about after that?

Jinks: After that, just get a job, live around here.

JM: Do you have any idea what job you wanna get?

Jinks: No. No particular job. Whatever I can get.

Jinks subsequently quit school. He had been working twenty hours a week making clothesracks in a factory with his brother. He left school with the understanding that he would be employed full-time, and he was mildly content with his situation: "I got a job. It ain't a good job, but other things will come along." Two weeks later, he was laid off. For the past three months he has been unemployed, hanging full-time in doorway #13.

Shorty has worked construction in the past and has held odd jobs such as shoveling snow. Shorty, an alcoholic, has trouble holding down a steady job, as he freely admits. He was enrolled in school until recently. Ordered by the court to a detoxification center, Shorty apparently managed to convince the judge that he had attended enough Alcoholics Anonymous meetings in the meantime to satisfy the court. He has not returned to school since, nor has he landed a job. Given that Shorty is often on the run from the police, he is too preoccupied with pressing everyday problems to give serious thought to his long-term future. It is not surprising that my ill-timed query about his occupational aspirations met with only an impatient glare.

Stoney is one of the few Hallway Hangers with a definite ambition. In fact, he aspires to a middle-class occupation—to own his own pizza shop. Although Stoney's goal is exceptionally high for a Hallway Hanger, ownership of one's own business, according to Ely Chinoy, is a common ambition for at least part of the blue-collar workforce.[3] Still, Stoney himself considers his aspiration unusually ambitious and is automatically defensive about his chances for success.

JM: What's your ambition?

Stoney: To *own* a store. One of these days I will. Watch. People might laugh at me now, but one of these days I will. It might be in fifty or sixty years. No, after a few years—if I'm about thirty years old, I can get a loan to get a store easy. Really. Get me some financial credit, buy me a little shop, work my way up.

Averse to both heavy manual work and "sitting behind a desk—I'd hate that," Stoney went straight to a local pizza establishment when he was put on a special work-study arrangement at school. He worked twenty-five hours per week, attending school in a special class from three to six in the afternoon. Stoney finally "got real sick and tired of school" and started working full-time, only to be fired soon thereafter. "I was working part-time anyway and I could work more if I wanted, so I told him [the boss] to put it up to thirty [hours per week] and I cut down my school more. Then I went up to forty. That's when I quit school. Then I got fired (*laughs*)."

Stoney can afford to laugh. In contrast to Jinks, he has a marketable skill—making pizza—and immediately found another job in a small pizza shop in a different part of town. He soon left that "gig," returning to his original job. Shortly thereafter, he was fired once again for "being mouthy." The very next day, he was hired by a third pizza shop. Stoney has worked there for the past seven months, earning $5.00 per hour under the table. He likes his boss, the small size of the operation, and the good wage.

A year ago, however, when Stoney was employed by the larger establishment, was working for a boss he did not like, and was making only slightly more than minimum wage, he tried to join the navy. "I wanted to get into the navy and travel for awhile. For two years, see the world, travel. I just found out real quick that they weren't gonna take me cuz of my drug record." Stoney was arrested last year for possession of mescaline. Although he could still have joined the army, he was not interested: "I don't want no bullshit army." According to Stoney, it is just as well that he was not accepted into the navy. "I like what I'm doing now, so I'll probably be here for awhile."

Like most of the Hallway Hangers, Slick already has held quite a few jobs. Between the ages of nine and thirteen Slick worked under the table in a supermarket that his uncle managed. He also has worked construction and as a clerk in a shoe store as well as odd jobs such as snow shoveling and minor landscaping. Slick quit school his junior year and began bagging groceries in another supermarket. "I just decided I had to put any kind of money away; whatever was available I would do, right? When I went down there (*pointing to doorway #13*), a lot of people would say, 'Well, fuck it; it's just bagging,' y'know? But you ain't gonna get no $20,000 a year job right off the streets anyway. You have to start somewhere, doin' somethin'.'"

Just the same, Slick could not take bagging groceries for long. He quit that job last June and enlisted in the army the next day. Slick really wanted to join the marines, but without a high school diploma, one must score exceptionally high on the standardized tests the marines administer to potential recruits. Slick missed by one point.

Once he was reconciled to entering the army, Slick was disappointed to find that without a high school diploma, he did not qualify for many of the benefits. Not one to accept a setback so easily, Slick did something about it. "I started talkin' about the bonuses and shit [with the recruiter], cuz I seen them on the paper up there, and I asked him. He said 'Well, you have to have your high school diploma.' So right across the street was the Somerville Adult Education Center." He enrolled in some classes at considerable cost but managed to have a bona fide diploma by midwinter. Although originally scheduled to report for service in October, Slick postponed his entry until late December when he expected to have his diploma.

By December, however, Slick had what he considered a better job lined up as a security guard at a local defense contracting firm the Hallway Hangers call "the weapons lab." Although he would not be able to start that job until mid-January, Slick somehow managed to cancel his enlistment. Shortly thereafter, however, his contact at the weapons lab was fired, and with him went Slick's prospective job. He currently is unemployed and, like Jinks, spends much of his time hanging at the Heights.

Despite these setbacks, Slick dreams of becoming a lawyer. Apparently, I was the first person to whom he voiced this hope. In a subsequent group interview in which five of the Hallway Hangers were discussing their plans for the future, an embarrassed Slick mentioned his aspiration in front of the group. The manner of this disclosure, which amounted to a confession, and the response of the group are instructive.

Slick: (sheepishly) I'm gonna be a lawyer.

(This response elicits surprise and whistles from the group.)

Chris: My boy ain't talkin' no petty cash.

Shorty: My boy wants to be a lawyer. He ain't even graduated from high school. Got himself a shit-ass diploma. Signed up for the army.

Frankie: I know. My boy bought his diploma and shit.

Slick himself is the first person to admit that he is not likely to achieve this goal, although his pride prevents him from expressing his reservations to the group. Slick, like Jinks and the rest of the Hallway Hangers, realizes that there is usually little room for choice in occupational decisions. "Well, *if I had the choice*, if I couldn't be a lawyer, I'd like to either do landscaping or construction (*my emphasis*)." Although his expectations are far different from his aspirations, Slick is the only Hallway Hanger who aspires to a professional career.

Like so many of the Hallway Hangers, Frankie's aspirations and expectations are in a constant state of flux. What follows are Frankie's comments on his occupational expectations on four separate occasions spanning a one-year period.

(2/22/83)

Frankie: I'm getting out [of school] this spring.

JM: What are you gonna do then? I mean for work.

Frankie: I don't fucking know. Probably work construction. That'll be good. I'll make like seventy-five bucks a day. Under the table. Sixty or seventy-five bucks a day. I could do that for the rest of my life. I get paid cash, every day. My brother sets it up for me.

(4/15/83)

JM: Have any idea what you'll be doing for work when you graduate, Frankie?

Frankie: I don't fucking know. If I can't get anything else, I'll just join the fucking service.

On May 13, 1983, the day he graduated, Frankie was feeling very strongly the sense of uncertainty surrounding his prospects for future employment.

Frankie: (unsolicited) I gotta get a job, any fucking job.

JM: What about the construction?

Frankie: Yeah, I can work with my brother, but that's under the table. Besides, he's in Bradford [state prison] now.

During the summer, when he was unemployed, Frankie was on the verge of joining the army. Finally, he landed a temporary job as a garbage collector for the city. He was laid off in November and since that time has been out of work.

In an in-depth interview in December, Frankie articulated a new occupational aspiration, which he presently nurtures. "My kind of job is like, y'know, I did a lot of construction. That's the kind of job like I want. What I want to do is save up some money and go to tractor trailer school and take heavy equipment. I don't wanna drive no eighteen wheeler, but I want to do heavy equipment like payloading. Hopefully, some day I can do it. I got to get up the cash first."

An aspiration to blue-collar work, such as this, is not easy to achieve. Coming up with the cash, Frankie realizes, is no easy task. In addition, even if he were able to get his heavy equipment license, there would be no guarantee that he will land the job he envisions. Frankie is aware of the problems; the scenario he foresees contains many "ifs." "If I do get my license, and say if I get a job with a construction company, I'll tell 'em I got my license, but I'm starting off as a laborer anyway. Gettin' in fuckin' holes, y'know. Then if higher jobs come up in it, I'd have a better chance than anyone, instead of them sending someone to school. Y'know, 'This kid already got his license, give him a couple of days to get back in the swing of things.'" Considering these contingencies, it is no wonder Frankie has yet to act on these hopes.

Whereas Frankie is lucid about his aspiration and how to achieve it, Chris is in doubt about his future. He never has held a steady job for any significant period of time and presently makes his money dealing drugs (mostly marijuana and cocaine) in the Clarendon Heights neighborhood. He works quite hard, actively seeking out customers and making himself available through the afternoon and evening hours. Because he is currently the sole major outlet of drugs for the teenagers of Clarendon Heights, Chris makes a good deal of money (about $150 per week). Although dealing pays well, the risks are high. He admits that the police seem to be watching him closely, and if he is convicted of another offense, he may well be sent away. The threat of violence from other kids trying to make a fast buck is an additional and sometimes greater risk, one brought home to Chris when he mentioned his occupational aspirations in a group interview.

Chris: I wanna sell cocaine, no lie. I wanna deal cocaine, be rich.

Slick: (*somewhat dubiously*) That's what he wants to do.

Chris: I'm just tellin' you the truth, man. That's what I'm s'posed to do, right man?

Slick: He's gonna get fuckin' blown away (*laughter*).

Frankie: I'll cuff off him a thousand dollars.

Like Frankie, who also used to make his money illegally (and still does to a lesser degree), Chris may weigh the risks and alter his aspirations, or he may take his chances and try to make a future out of selling drugs.

One cannot help but be struck by the modesty of the Hallway Hangers' hopes for the future. Only Slick aspires to a professional career; Stoney is the only other individual who aspires to a middle-class job. Refusing the risk of hope, the remainder adjust their occupational goals to the only jobs that they perceive to be available—unskilled manual work. Many expect to enter military service, not because they find it particularly appealing but because of the paucity of other opportunities. The concept of an aspiration is essentially alien to the Hallway Hangers. Most simply expect to take whatever they can get.

The Hallway Hangers are quite honest about their occupational expectations and aspirations, but it is not comforting to look closely at one's future when bleakness is its main characteristic. When free of the psychological complications inherent in considering one's own future, the Hallway Hangers predict even more inauspicious outcomes for the peer group in general.

JM: What sorts of jobs do you think the rest of the guys will have?

(all in separate interviews)

Stoney: Shitty jobs. Picking up trash, cleaning the streets. They won't get no good jobs.

Slick: Most of the kids around here, they're not gonna be more than janitors or, y'know, goin' by every day tryin' to get a buck. That's it...I'd say the success rate of this place is, of these people...about twenty percent, maybe fifteen.

Steve: I dunno. Probably hanging around here. I dunno. Shit jobs.

Jinks: I think most of them, when and if a war comes, they're all gone. In the service. Everyone's going. But for jobs—odds and ends jobs. Here and there. No good high-class jobs. I think they'll all end up working for the city, roofers, shit like that.

In Frankie's answer to the same question, we get a real feel for the deep sense of pessimism that dominates the Hallway Hangers' outlook on their future. Listening to him talk, one can detect a poignant fear for his own destiny.

Frankie: Well, some of them are gonna do okay, but, I dunno, some of them are just gonna fuck up. They'll just be doing odd jobs for the rest of their lives, y'know. Still be drinking, y'know; they'll drink themselves to death, what's some of 'em'll do. That's what I hope I don't do. Yeah, some of them are gonna drink themselves to death, but some of them, y'know, they're gonna smarten up. Get married, have some kids, have a decent job. Enough to live off anyways, to support a wife and kids. But some of them, they're gonna fuck up; they'll be just a junkie, a tramp. They'll be sitting out on the lawn for the rest of their life with their fucking bottle. Going to work every morning, getting laid off. Fucking, y'know, they're just gonna fuck up. That's what I hope I don't do. I'm trying not to anyways.

The definitions of aspirations and expectations given at the beginning of this [case study] suggest that an assessment of the opportunity structure and of one's capabilities impinge on one's preferences for the future. However, the portrait of the Hallway Hangers painted in these pages makes clear that "impinge" is not a strong enough word. But are the leveled aspirations and pessimistic expectations of the Hallway Hangers a result of strong negative assessments of their capabilities or of the opportunity structure?

This is not an easy question to answer. Doubtless, both factors come into play, but in the case of the Hallway Hangers, evaluation of the opportunity structure has the dominant role. Although in a discussion of why they do not succeed in school, the Hallway Hangers point to personal inadequacy ("We're all just fucking burnouts"; "We never did good anyways"), they look to outside forces as well. In general, they are confident of their own abilities.

(in a group interview)

JM: If you've got five kids up at the high school with all A's, now are you gonna be able to say that any of them are smarter than any of you?

Slick: (immediately) No.

JM: So how'd that happen?

Slick: Because they're smarter in some areas just like we're smarter in some areas. You put them out here, right? And you put us up where they're living—they won't be able to survive out here.

Shorty: But we'd be able to survive up there.

Frankie: See, what it is—they're smarter more academically because they're taught by teachers that teach academics.

JM: Not even streetwise, just academically, do you think you could be up where they are?

Frankie: Yeah.

Chris: Yeah.

Shorty: Yeah.

JM: When it comes down to it, you're just as smart?

Frankie: Yeah.

Slick: (matter-of-factly) We could be smarter.

Frankie: Definitely.

Chris: On the street, like.

Frankie: We're smart, we're smart, but we're just smart [inaudible]. It's fucking, y'know, we're just out to make money, man. I know if I ever went to fucking high school and college in a business cours....

Slick: And concentrated on studying...

Frankie: I know I could make it. I am a businessman.

JM: So all of you are sure that if you put out in school...

Frankie: Yeah! If I went into business, I would, yeah. If I had the fucking money to start out with like some of these fucking rich kids, I'd be a millionaire. Fucking right I would be.

Although these comments were influenced by the dynamics of the group interview, they jibe with the general sense of self-confidence the Hallway Hangers radiate and indicate that they do not have low perceptions of their own abilities.

If their assessments of their own abilities do not account for the low aspirations of the Hallway Hangers, we are left, by way of explanation, with their perceptions of the job opportunity structure. The dominant view in the United States is that American society is an open one that values and differentially rewards individuals on the basis of their merits. The Hallway Hangers question this view, for it runs against the grain of their neighbors' experiences, their families' experiences, and their own encounters with the labor market.

The Clarendon Heights community, as a public housing development, is by definition made up of individuals who do not hold even modestly remunerative jobs. A large majority are on additional forms of public assistance; many are unemployed. Like most old housing projects, Clarendon Heights tends to be a cloistered, insular neighborhood, isolated from the surrounding community. Although younger residents certainly have external points of reference, their horizons are nevertheless very narrow.

Their immediate world is composed almost entirely of people who have not "made it." To look around at a great variety of people—some lazy, some alcoholics, some energetic, some dedicated, some clever, some resourceful—and to realize all of them have been unsuccessful on the job market is powerful testimony against what is billed as an open society.

The second and much more intimate contact these boys have with the job market is through their families, whose occupational histories only can be viewed as sad and disillusioning by the Hallway Hangers. These are not people who are slothful or slow-witted; rather, they are generally industrious, intelligent, and very willing to work. With members of their families holding low-paying, unstable jobs or unable to find work at all, the Hallway Hangers are unlikely to view the job opportunity structure as an open one.

The third level of experience on which the Hallway Hangers draw is their own. These boys are not newcomers to the job market. As we have seen, all have held a variety of jobs. All except Steve are now on the job market year round, but only Stoney has a steady job. With the exceptions of Chris, who presently is satisfied with his success peddling drugs, and Steve, who is still in school, the Hallway Hangers are actively in search of decent work. Although they always seem to be following up on some promising lead, they are all unemployed. Furthermore, some who were counting on prospective employment have had their hopes dashed when it fell through. The work they have been able to secure typically has been in menial, dead-end jobs paying minimum wage.

Thus, their personal experience on the job market and the experiences of their family members and their neighbors have taught the Hallway Hangers that the job market does not necessarily reward talent or effort. Neither they nor their parents, older siblings, and friends have shared in the "spoils" of economic success. In short, the Hallway Hangers are under no illusions about the openness of the job opportunity structure. They are conscious, albeit vaguely, of a number of class-based obstacles to economic and social advancement. Slick, the most perceptive and articulate of the Hallway Hangers, points out particular barriers they must face.

Slick: Out here, there's not the opportunity to make money. That's how you get into stealin' and all that shit.

(in a separate interview)

Slick: That's why I went into the army—cuz there's no jobs out here right now for people that, y'know, live out here. You have to know somebody, right?

In discussing the problems of getting a job, both Slick and Shorty are vocal.

Slick: All right, to get a job, first of all, this is a handicap, out here. If you say you're from the projects or anywhere in this area, that can hurt you. Right off the bat: reputation.

Shorty: Is this dude gonna rip me off, is he…

Slick: Is he gonna stab me?

Shorty: Will he rip me off? Is he gonna set up the place to do a score or somethin'? I tried to get a couple of my buddies jobs at a place where I was working construction, but the guy says, "I don't want 'em if they're from there. I know you; you ain't a thief or nothing."

Frankie also points out the reservations prospective employers have about hiring people who live in Clarendon Heights. "A rich kid would have a better chance of getting a job than me, yeah. Me, from where I live, y'know, a high crime area, I was prob'ly crime-breaking myself, which they think your nice honest rich kid from a very respected family would never do."

Frankie also feels that he is discriminated against because of the reputation that attaches to him because of his brothers' illegal exploits. "Especially me, like I've had a few opportunities for a job, y'know. I didn't get it cuz of my name, because of my brothers, y'know. So I was deprived right there, bang. Y'know they said, 'No, no, no, we ain't havin' no Dougherty work for us.'" In a separate discussion, Frankie again makes this point. Arguing that he would have almost no chance to be hired as a fireman, despite ostensibly meritocratic hiring procedures, even if he scored very highly on the test, Frankie concludes, "Just cuz fuckin' where I'm from and what my name is."

The Hallway Hangers' belief that the opportunity structure is not open also emerges when we consider their responses to the question of whether they have the same chance as a middle- or upper-class boy to get a good job. The Hallway Hangers generally respond in the negative. When pushed to explain why, Jinks and Steve made these responses, which are typical.

(in separate interviews)

Jinks: Their parents got pull and shit.

Steve: Their fucking parents know people.

Considering the boys' employment experiences and those of their families, it is not surprising that the Hallway Hangers' view of the job market does not conform to the dominant belief in the openness of the opportunity structure. They see a job market where rewards are based not on meritocratic criteria, but on "who you know." If "connections" are the keys to success, the Hallway Hangers know that they are in trouble.

Aside from their assessment of the job opportunity structure, the Hallway Hangers are aware of other forces weighing on their futures. A general feeling of despondency pervades the group. As Slick puts it, "The younger kids have nothing to hope for." The Hallway Hangers often draw attention to specific incidents that support their general and vague feelings of hopelessness and of the futility of nurturing aspirations or high expectations. Tales of police brutality, of uncaring probation officers and callous judges, and of the "pull and hook-ups of the rich kids" all have a common theme, which Chris summarizes, "We don't get a fair shake and shit." Although they sometimes internalize the blame for their plight (Boo-Boo: "I just screwed up"; Chris: "I guess I just don't have what it takes"; Frankie: "We've just fucked up"), the Hallway Hangers also see, albeit in a vague and imprecise manner, a number of hurdles in their path to success with which others from higher social strata do not have to contend.

Insofar as contemporary conditions under capitalism can be conceptualized as a race by the many for relatively few positions of wealth and prestige, the low aspirations of the Hallway Hangers, more than anything else, seem to be a decision, conscious or unconscious, to withdraw from the running. The competition, they reason, is not a fair one when some people have an unobstructed lane. As Frankie maintains, the Hallway Hangers face numerous barriers: "It's a steeplechase, man. It's a motherfucking steeplechase." The Hallway Hangers respond in a way that suggest only a "sucker" would compete seriously under such conditions.

Chris's perspective seems a poignant, accurate description of the situation in which the Hallway Hangers find themselves.

Chris: I gotta get a job, any fucking job. Just a job. Make some decent money. If I could make a hundred bucks a week, I'd work. I just wanna get my mother out of the projects, that's all. But I'm fucking up in school. It ain't easy, Jay. I hang out there [in doorway #13] 'til about one o'clock every night. I never want to go to school. I'd much rather hang out and get high again. It's not that I'm dumb. You gimme thirty bucks today, and I'll give you one hundred tomorrow. I dunno. It's like I'm in a hole I can't get out of.

I guess I could get out, but it's hard as hell. It's fucked up.

The Brothers: Ready at the Starting Line

Just as the pessimism and uncertainty with which the Hallway Hangers view their futures emerges when we consider what they perceive their lives will be like in twenty years, so do the Brothers' long-term visions serve as a valuable backdrop to our discussion of their aspirations. The ethos of the Brothers' peer group is a positive one; they are not resigned to a bleak future but are hoping for a bright one. Nowhere does this optimism surface more clearly than in the Brothers' responses to the question of what they will be doing in twenty years. Note the centrality of work in their views of the future.

(all in separate interviews)

Super: I'll have a house, a nice car, no one bothering me. Won't have to take no hard time from no one. Yeah, I'll have a good job, too.

Juan: I'll have a regular house, y'know, with a yard and everything. I'll have a steady job, a good job. I'll be living the good life, the easy life.

Mike: I might have a wife, some kids. I might be holding down a regular business job like an old guy. I hope I'll be able to do a lot of skiing and stuff like that when I'm old.

Craig: I'll probably be having a good job on my hands, I think. Working in an office as an architect, y'know, with my own drawing board, doing my own stuff, or at least close to there.

James takes a comic look into his future without being prompted to do so. "The ones who work hard in school, eventually it's gonna pay off for them and everything, and they're gonna have a good job and a family and all that. Not me though! I'm gonna have *myself*. I'm gonna have some money. And a different girl every day. And a different car. And be like this (*poses with one arm around an imaginary girl and the other on a steering wheel)."*

The Brothers do not hesitate to name their occupational goals. Although some of the Brothers are unsure of their occupational aspirations, none seems to feel that nurturing an aspiration is a futile exercise. The Brothers have not resigned themselves to taking whatever they can get. Rather, they articulate specific occupational aspirations (although these often are subject to change and revision).

Like all the Brothers, Super has not had extensive experience on the job market; he only has worked at summer jobs. For the past three summers, he has worked for the city doing maintenance work in parks and school buildings through a CETA-sponsored summer youth employment program. During the last year, Super's occupational aspirations have fluctuated widely. His initial desire to become a doctor was met with laughter from his friends. Deterred by their mocking and by a realization of the schooling required to be a doctor, Super immediately decided that he would rather go into business: "Maybe I can own my own shop and shit." This aspiration, however, also was ridiculed. "Yeah, right," commented Mokey, "Super'll be pimping the girls, that kinda business." In private, however, Super still clings to the hope of becoming a doctor, although he cites work in the computer field as a more realistic hope. "Really, I don't know what I should do now. I'm kinda confused. First I said I wanna go into computers, right? Take up that or a doctor." The vagueness of Super's aspirations is important; once again, we get a glimpse of how little is known about the world of middle-class work, even for somebody who clearly aspires to it. Of one thing Super is certain: "I just know I wanna get a good job."

Although Super does not distinguish between what constitutes a good job and what does not, he does allude to criteria by which the quality of a job can be judged. First, a good job must not demand that one "work on your feet," a distinction, apparently, between white and blue collar work Second, a good job implies at least some authority in one's workplace, a point Super makes clearly, if in a disjointed manner. "Bosses—if you don't come on time, they yell at you and stuff like that. They want you to do work and not sit down and relax and stuff like that, y'know. I want to try and be a boss, y'know, tell people what to do. See, I don't always want people telling me what to do, y'know—the low rank. I wanna try to be with people in the high rank." Although Super does not know what occupation he would like to enter, he is certain that he wants a job that is relatively high up in a vaguely defined occupational hierarchy.

Mokey has not given as much thought to his occupational aspirations as have most of the Brothers. His contact with the job market has been minimal. His only job has been part-time janitorial work with his father. Mokey plans to attend college and does not envision working full-time until after graduation, several years from now.

JM: So what do you think you wanna do when you get out of school?

Mokey: I have no idea really.

JM: Don't think about it that much?

Mokey: Not really. Before, I wanted to be a motorcyclist, like motorcross. That was it.

JM: Didn't you tell me mechanic?

Mokey: And mechanic. That was when I wanted to be a motor mechanic. For motorcycles. I wanted to be a motorcross, that's what I wanted to be.

JM: How'd you decide on that?

Mokey: I seen a motorcycle race before and I've ridden a couple of minibikes before, and I just decided.

Usually, the aspirations of the Brothers reflect more thought than those Mokey articulates. Although his mother reports that he is interested in "general management, of his own or someone else's business," Mokey's aspirations are sketchy and contradictory.

In contrast to Mokey, James's aspirations are defined clearly. Since his eighth grade class visited the high school and James viewed the computer terminals, he has aspired to design video games. This is a goal to which James is strongly committed. His plans are well developed; he has even considered his prospective employers: Atari, Intelevision, or Colecovision. His enthusiasm for his foreseen occupation is unmatched by the other boys. "I like jobs that are fun and make money too. Like making computer games; it would be fun.... I want computers. I love computers. I fell in love with computers, so I know I want to do computers."

James is confident that he will achieve his occupational goal, despite the difficulty he has had finding any kind of summer employment. Last summer, after a two-month job search, James did maintenance work for the city recreation department. Paid and hired through the CETA job program, he spent the summer clearing parks and buildings.

The only boy whose plans are more definitively developed is Derek. Derek has never worked in his life; his summers have been spent traveling with a wealthy friend from Barnes Academy. Since he was a young boy, however, Derek has dreamed of joining the military. He wants to learn electronics and become a helicopter pilot, an aspiration Derek took a big step toward fulfilling by enlisting in the navy this past summer. He is on delayed entry until he receives his diploma this June; then he will report to basic training in July and will serve for six years.

Considering that the decision to enter the service is usually a last resort for most Heights teenagers, it is noteworthy that Derek aspires to a career in the navy, particularly given his success in high school and at Barnes Academy. Of all the Brothers and Hallway Hangers, he seems to have the best educational credentials and the best chance to move on to high-status employment. But Derek does explain his choice.

Derek: At first, they [his parents] wanted me to be a lawyer. Ever since I went to Barnes. But there's no way I could do that. I need a job that has action. I need to be active. I couldn't sit behind a desk all week to make a living; that wouldn't be right.

JM: What do you mean, it wouldn't be right?

Derek: I just couldn't do it. I like all the activities the navy has. And, y'know, sometimes I like to take orders. Carry them out. I don't want to just sit around.

This devaluation of white-collar work as inactive and boring, according to Paul Willis, is the main cultural innovation of the nonconformist lads that deters them from entering, or even trying to enter, white-collar work. This distaste for office work, which is bound up inextricably with the working-class culture's ideal of masculinity, serves to level the aspirations of the lads, thereby spurring them to work on the shop floor. A close examination of the Hallway Hangers and Brothers, however, reveals no such definitive cultural process at work, although we can detect traces of such an attitude among the Hallway Hangers (and with Derek). However, Super and his parents denigrate work that would require that he stand on his feet, a view shared by Juan.

Juan, whose previous employment record consists of a number of summertime jobs, aspires to be a cook. Like Super, he hopes to avoid manual work (a hope his father shares). "I like clean job, y'know, where you can keep yourself clean. That's what my father said. 'You should get a job where you can keep yourself clean.' I found out that the one that was better off for me was cooking. I like mechanic, but, no man, too rough for me."

Despite this aversion to auto mechanics, which Juan expressed last summer, he currently is seeking employment in precisely that area. The only Brother to have graduated from high school and thus currently on the job market, Juan has been unable to find work in food preparation. Although he retains his aspiration to be a cook because "it's fun; I like it," the unpleasant experience of unemployment for eight months has forced Juan to lower his expectations.

Craig, who like most of the Brothers has "never held a real job, just, y'know, summer jobs," hopes to be an architect. Craig has been a good artist since his earliest years and his father suggested that he consider architecture as a career. Craig has nurtured this aspiration since sixth grade and sees himself working for an architecture firm in the future. He adds, however, that if he is frustrated in his attempt to find employment in this field, he would like to be a computer operator or programmer.

This tendency to express contingency plans in case of failure is articulated fully by Mike. During the course of a year, Mike has revealed a hierarchy of aspirations and expectations. Mike's dream is to be a professional athlete: a wrestler, like his father, or a football player. He realizes this would come about only "if I get a big break." The occupational aspiration about which he talks the most is in the computer field, apparently a common aspiration for these boys because of the emphasis put upon the subject in high school. One step below that on his hierarchy of occupational preferences is more traditional blue-collar work, particularly as an electrician. Finally, he says, "If I don't make it in like, anything, if I flunk out or something, I'll probably join the service or something."

Like most of the Brothers, Mike is very concerned about the quality of his future employment. "Mostly," he comments, "I just wanna get ahead in life, get a good job." Specifically, he wants to avoid the dull, monotonous type of work he experienced last summer as a stock boy in a large hardware warehouse. "It's for fucking morons," he exclaims. Mike also has held a summer job in which he learned some carpentry skills doing weatherization work for the City Action to Save Heat project, another CETA program. He hated taking orders from a strict supervisor who, Mike recalls, "just sat on his fat ass all day anyway. Then again," he added upon reflection, "I wouldn't mind doing that."

Despite the Brothers' absorption with athletics and the status of professional sports in American culture, the Brothers have few illusions about the extent to which sports are a ticket to success. While their younger siblings speak incessantly about "making it in the pros," the Brothers no longer aspire seriously to a career in professional athletics. Only Mike and Craig see sports as a means to get a college education.

Although not all the Brothers aspire to professional or managerial work, all do have hopes for the future. The notion of a career makes sense when applied to their visions of future employment. They are committed to acting on their hopes, and although they realize that there is no guarantee that their dreams will come to fruition, they are not resigned to failure. In short, the Brothers are optimistic about their future employment, while the Hallway Hangers are deeply pessimistic about their prospective occupational roles.

In contrasting the Brothers and the Hallway Hangers, however, we must resist the temptation to define the two groups only in relation to one another. Certainly in comparison to the Hallway Hangers, the Brothers have high aspirations. To assert that the Brothers aspire to middle-class jobs while the Hallway Hangers do not, however, would be overly simplistic. In a society in which the achievement of a prestigious occupation is considered a valid goal for everyone, it is significant that a few of the Brothers have only modest goals.

The Brothers display none of the cockiness about their own capabilities that the Hallway Hangers exhibit. Instead, they attribute lack of success on the job market exclusively to personal inadequacy. This is particularly true when the Brothers speculate about the future jobs the Hallway Hangers and their own friends will have. According to the Brothers, the Hallway Hangers (in Super's words) "ain't gonna get nowhere," not because of the harshness of the job market but because they are personally lacking. The rest of the Brothers share this view.

JM: Some of those guys who hang with Frankie, they're actually pretty smart. They just don't channel that intelligence into school, it seems to me.

Craig: I call that stupid, man. That's what they are.

JM: I dunno.

Craig: Lazy.

(in a separate interview)

Super: They think they're so tough they don't have to do work. That don't make sense, really. You ain't gonna get nowhere; all's you gonna do is be back in the projects like your mother. Depend on your mother to give you money every week. You ain't gonna get a good job. As you get older, you'll think about that, y'know. It'll come to your mind. "Wow, I can't believe, I should've just went to school and got my education."

(in a separate interview)

Mokey: They all got attitude problems. They just don't got their shit together. Like Steve. They have to improve themselves.

In the eyes of the Brothers, the Hallway Hangers have attitude problems, are inca-

pable of considering their long-term future, and are lazy or stupid.

Because this evidence is tainted (no love is lost between the two peer groups), it is significant that the Brothers apply the same criteria in judging each other's chances to gain meaningful employment. James thinks Mokey is headed for a dead-end job because he is immature and undisciplined. He also blames Juan for currently being out of work. "Juan's outa school, and Juan does *not* have a job (*said with contempt*). Now that's some kind of a senior. When I'm a senior, I'm gonna have a job already. I can see if you're gonna go to college right when you get out of school, but Juan's not doin' nothin'. He's just stayin' home." Juan, in turn, thinks that Mokey and Super will have difficulty finding valuable work because of their attitudes. He predicts that Derek and Craig will be successful for the same reason.

These viewpoints are consistent with the dominant ideology in America; barriers to success are seen as personal rather than social. By attributing failure to personal inadequacy, the Brothers exonerate the opportunity structure. Indeed, it is amazing how often they affirm the openness of American society.

(all in separate interviews)

Derek: If you put your mind to it, if you want to make a future for yourself, there's no reason why you can't. It's a question of attitude.

Super: It's easy to do anything, as long as you set your mind to it, if you wanna do it. If you really want to do it, if you really want to be something. If you don't want to do it…you ain't gonna make it. I gotta get that through my mind: I wanna do it. I wanna be somethin'. I don't wanna be livin' in the projects the rest of my life.

Mokey: It's not like if they're rich they get picked [for a job]; it's just mattered by the knowledge of their mind.

Craig: If you work hard, it'll pay off in the end.

Mike: If you work hard, really put your mind to it, you can do it. You can make it.

This view of the opportunity structure as an essentially open one that rewards intelligence, effort, and ingenuity is shared by all the Brothers. Asked whether their chances of securing a remunerative job are as good as those of an upper-class boy from a wealthy district of the city, they all responded affirmatively. Not a single member of the Hallway Hangers, in contrast, affirms the openness of American society.

This affirmation of equality of opportunity is all the more astounding coming from a group of black, lower-class teenagers. Only Juan mentioned racial prejudice as a barrier to success, and this was a result of personal experience. Juan's mother was forced out of her job as a clerk in a neighborhood grocery store when some of the customers complained about the color of her skin. "Most of the time it depends on the boss, whether or not he has something against black. If they judge by the attitude, by the way they act, then that's it; there'll be an equal chance, but it's not usually that way."

Whereas the Hallway Hangers conclude that the opportunity structure is not open, the Brothers reach an entirely different, and contradictory, conclusion. Considering that both groups share neighbors and that the families of the boys have similar occupational histories, this discrepancy is all the more problematic. Indeed, we have uncovered quite a paradox. The peer group whose members must overcome racial as well as class barriers to success views the occupational opportunity structure as essentially open, whereas the white peer group views it as much more closed. The Brothers, whose objective life chances are probably lower than those of the Hallway Hangers, nevertheless hold positive attitudes toward the future, while the Hallway Hangers harbor feelings of hopelessness. To unravel this paradox is a challenge....

If the Hallway Hangers view their predicament as a race in which they, as members of the lower class, must jump a number of hurdles, while the rest of the pack can simply sprint, the Brothers see it as an even dash. The Hallway Hangers believe a strong finish, given their handicap, is out of the question and drop out of the race before it begins. They cannot understand why the Brothers compete seriously. Apparently, explains Slick, the Brothers do not see the hurdles. "It's a question of you wanna see it, and you don't wanna see it. They might not wanna see all the obstacles. In the long run, it'll hurt them. You hafta hear what's going on, or it's gonna hurt you later on."

The Brothers, for their part, are lined up at the start, unsure of their ability, but ready to run what they see as a fair race. They do not understand why the Hallway Hangers fail to take the competition seriously. It is, after all, the only game in town.

Derek: I don't know. I really don't. I guess they just don't realize what they have to do. It just doesn't get through to them. I dunno. I don't think anyone has really told them straight out what it takes to make it, to be a winner.

NOTES

1. Kenneth I. Spenner and David L. Featherman, "Achievement Ambitions," *Annual Review of Sociology* 4 (1978):376-378.

2. Howard B. London, *The Culture of a Community College* (New York: Praeger, 1978).

3. Ely Chinoy, *Automobile Workers and the American Dream* (Boston: Beacon Press, 1955).

San Francisco Scavengers

Stewart E. Perry

CASE STUDY QUESTIONS

1. Does a San Francisco garbage collector's occupational choice seem to be based more on rational decision making or on chance?
2. What attracts these garbage collectors to their work?

With all the problems and discontents in the work of the garbage collector, there are plenty of scavengers who will answer positively when you ask them, "What's good about this job?" They do not necessarily start off with the pay, although by San Francisco standards and even nationally the pay is good. In the West generally, skilled refuse workers are paid more, on the average, than anywhere else in the country—although the difference in pay from that of workers in the Northeast is not very great. And it was not until 1969 that the national average gross weekly pay of skilled workers in private companies (which almost always pay higher wages than public agencies, probably because of overtime) reached $190 per week, about what the Sunset partners were making in 1966. By 1974, Sunset pay had gone up considerably to about $18,000 a year, as compared to $10,000 in 1966. And in 1976, with

Source: "What's Good About This Job" (Chapter 7) from *San Francisco Scavengers: Dirty Work and the Pride of Ownership* by Stewart E. Perry, 1978, Berkeley: University of California Press. Reprinted with permission of the author.

regular overtime, a scavenger partner could make about $24,000, although without overtime it was perhaps about $21,000.

Yet, the pay is not necessarily what attracts a man into this work. Al Macari, a friendly guy I met working on a route in an upper-class neighborhood, who is himself the son of a scavenger, told me that his own son became a scavenger even though Al had pointed out that the pay was not as high as the son might make elsewhere. In one of my earliest interviews with Stefanelli, he agreed that the pay was not the main thing, although he told me he was trying to raise the pay so as to attract the best men possible. He knew that he himself, in his previous extra job as a life insurance salesman, could make more working full-time than the $10,000 he was getting then from Sunset and probably more than any raise that the men would be likely to vote him in the future. It was true that, for a working man, $10,000 in 1966 and $21,000 in 1976 was good pay, especially when so many people were out of work. But the pay was not the chief attraction, apparently. "I guess you have to go into the psychology of it," Lenny had said.

"The psychology of it" had a great many different aspects. One of these was what might be called the variety of the work, as unlikely as that may seem to the uninitiated. Ron told me: "Thing about this job is that you do different things." If he had taken the somewhat comparable job of pick-up man on a city street-cleaning crew, Ron said, he would "go crazy. That would be monotonous." The tasks on his route were varied enough to break the monotony of the work's routine—operating the blade, solving problems with customers, blanket work and can work, driving the truck, and so forth. But there was also a different kind of variety, the unexpected in the human events of the work day—like the burglar on that day with Freddie and his crew. When I met Freddie's young son working with his father in 1972, he told me that he had refused a nine-to-five job that paid more: "Staying in one place all day? Naw!"

Each route has its own possibilities; the early morning life varies from district to district. Yet, whatever the district, the scavenger comes to know a lot about the neighborhood. Life along his route takes on the quality of a continued story. You watch children growing up, older folks getting more timid, a house deteriorating, another being rehabilitated; and there is a certain stability to witnessing that sort of continuity and evolution. The garbageman can develop the same appreciation for his route that others develop for a soap opera or the familiar characters of a television sit-com. That kind of continuity can be reassuring in a world of change.

Also, as Everett Hughes has pointed out, alluding to Ray Gold's study of janitors, dirty work gives entry to the underside of life. One has access to special information that others do not. Even a respectable-looking house in a fine neighborhood does not hide the alcoholism that a garbageman can read into the number of liquor bottles he takes out. "*I* like to drink, but *still!*" And one morning in a nice neighborhood, a scavenger showed me a garage full of motorcycles—stolen. "You can buy 'em, if you want to. Other stuff too," he explained.

Of course, some routes are even more absorbing than others. Lenny told me about the route he had worked on for many years:

We had houses of prostitution; we had Lesbians; we had homosexuals, prostitutes, and streetwalkers. They just got all the publicity in the papers a while back, but that's been going on in that district for *years*. If the girls couldn't get a hotel room, they'd go right up in the park underneath a streetlight with some guy, and it's usually a Caucasian with a colored girl up there. You see these things going on in the morning.

I've seen people get shot; I've seen people get knifed. You don't see that in other neighborhoods. The garbageman is apt to see these things early in the morning.

I saved an apartment house from burning down; as a garbageman going down in the morning, I spotted a fire underneath the stairs. I went out and I called the fire department. I came back and put the fire out and got the people out of the house, and the irony of the whole thing was that the police and fire department chewed me out for not staying next to the fire box. It was right up at the corner, but I went back and put the fire out and got people out of bed in case they couldn't, and got a hose from the house next door and hooked it onto a place that I know where a faucet is because I always drank the water out of it, hooked it on and put the fire out. I got chewed out. I didn't expect a reward, but, Jeez, a "nice job" or something like that.

But I mean, these are the things you run into in the early hours. The prostitution, the murders, the knifing, and the stuff like that, you're more apt to find it in the lower-class neighborhoods than you are in the areas out there in the Sunset district or places like that. I mean, you could write a book on the things I've seen: naked women laying in the alleyways; guys with their head knocked off and laying in the street; stumbling over drunks in the early morning hours; finding dead babies in the garbage

My godfather went in looking for the light switch in one of these dark places, and there was a guy hanging himself right on the rafter next to the light cord. Things like this that you don't even read about in the paper are an everyday experience for the garbageman…That's what makes the job enjoyable—but not so much with my job now [as president]. Suppose you're running an IBM machine; it's monotonous. It's the same thing everyday, with very few exceptions. It's a monotonous job. Well, this job that I have now—I thought I'd never want to work in an office. I thought I'd be a garbageman all my life because every day there was something different; and I enjoy that differential. I mean you go to a job, and you never know what you're going to get. Basically, you're still picking up garbage, but you're finding things in the garbage. You find nudist books or something, you know? You see *all* that stuff there—there's always something doing.

A garbage worker once told me that at one particularly nice house where we picked up, he had been asked to save all the rubbish and turn it over to the FBI. Indeed, during a period of my own life when the FBI was paying a rather unnatural amount of attention to my own doings, because I happened to be a downstairs neighbor of Daniel Ellsberg, I discovered someone going through the trash at the house we both lived in. The stranger said he was a newspaperman, and maybe he was. In that same period, another stranger asked me for permission to take a sample of the refuse "for a study of ecology." The point is that garbage can have considerable interest under some circumstances.

Another part of "the psychology of it" was being able to set one's own pace. Freddie had said: "You are your own boss." A crew could work as fast or as leisurely as they wished. As I observed, they usually worked as swiftly as humanly possible—if only to go home early or, as Lenny told me from his own experience, to be in a bar waiting for another crew to come in and be able to say, "What's been keeping *you?*"

They scheduled their own breaks and as many different kinds of breaks as suited them and the strenuous pace of their work.

Indeed, even the breaks might be used to save some time, as I recorded in an observation in 1972:

> On the second beer break. Ernie and Freddie exchange and sort out the service complaint or request slips [that the driver brings from the office each morning] and decide what to do about them. Freddie explains to me, "They say, 'Oh, those garbagemen have it easy, stopping for a beer,' but we actually do some work while we stop, talking about customers, and things." I am sympathetic: "Of course." But Ernie raises his eyebrows, laughing. "Yeah, we work all right," he mocks.

Ernie refused to be too self-important about it, but they would have had to stop anyway to review the service slips, a chore that takes about five or ten minutes a day—which, incidentally, was another example of the variety in the work, the kind of thing that Ron was talking about.

Another special attraction of the work is what you can personally salvage for yourself. I was never out on a truck when one of the men did not at least pause to examine an item to consider whether it might be worth saving. Often it might be a good book, or perhaps a girly magazine, or a child's toy, or a busted radio ("Agh, no," said one man, reluctantly tossing a radio back into the hopper, "I've got too many of those things as it is"). Lenny remarked once:

> Another thing I enjoyed: you always found that if you want something, you'll find it in the garbage, eventually. It's hard to believe; but I mean, if it's something within reason. I wanted a brass rail from a bar one time, and I found one in [the trash from] a bar. I wanted a rubber life raft to go skin diving, and I found one. People throw away the damnedest things in the garbage. Maybe you've got no use for them, but you end up being a collector; you're bringing things home all the time.

A young scavenger, solicitous either of my moral well-being or perhaps my intellectual interests, once saved a seventeenth-century book of sermons for me. And I still prize a sheepskin rug that I retrieved in another city while out on the trucks one morning early. (As Lenny had predicted, since I had always wanted one, there it was!)

Incidentally, I found that my own pleasure in the deserted early mornings of a big city was no different from that of the scavengers. Being outdoors is a big advantage that even workers in less clement climates emphasized in our study of garbage collection in other cities. To be indoors all the time is a drag. In San Francisco, one scavenger who was "a real P.R. man," according to Lenny, was put in the new customer service office in the Sunset district; he could not stand if for long and asked to be put back on the trucks. Freddie felt the same way. "You're out in the open," he said. "Of course, this is all I *can* do now; but I would not like an office job." Yet, he himself was head of the Sunset customer relations committee because he was good on things like that, too. Of course, not all garbagemen are as fortunate as Sunset workers in the matter of outdoor work—and not only because of cold, rain, snow, or summer heat in other climates. Even the workers at the other San Francisco cooperative did not have it as easy as Sunset workers. Golden Gate Disposal Company scavengers have to do most of their work at night, when the traffic is lightest, because their districts are mostly commercial and downtown areas. So they do not have the pleasure of as much daylight work.

Any job is also made better by the relationships you have with your co-workers, the friendships you establish on the job. Garbage collection is no exception to this. But Sunset may have had an extra advantage here, too, in that many of the workers shared a common ethnic background and tradition. By historical accident and social oppression, other cities have also sequestered an ethnic group into the occupation; in such cases, it would seem that good morale and solidarity among the workers were engendered inadvertently, much like that among the Sunset scavengers. That was perhaps what was happening in the Memphis garbage workers' strike that Martin Luther King had come to encourage when he was assassinated. In San Francisco, certainly, the old country ties, transported there in a variety of forms, were singularly important. The Sunset company newsletter printed some of its articles both in English and Italian, and the articles often dealt with culturally specific matters—the mushroom-gathering exploits of a senior member, for example. And surely the values they shared—and the common fate of a disparaged social group—had made it possible "in the old days" to forego the intense competition in favor of cooperative sharing of the city routes.

The ethnic ties implied familial ties, and vice versa. In 1966, about half of the Sunset scavengers were somehow related to one another, according to Lenny's estimate. During the period of my study, the third generation (such as Al Macari's son or Freddie's son) was beginning to enter the company. In general, family relations are an important and rewarding part of life in the local working-class Italian-American community.

I have left until last what may be the most important reward of the job for the partners of the Sunset Scavenger Company: owning a share of the business. Their ownership is inextricably associated with a number of other things, including, of course, the ethnic and familial ties that so many of the men share. In the period that I have observed the company, the dollar value of stock in the company has appreciated considerably, but ownership had never before been particularly significant so far as monetary return is concerned. That is, the dividends on a partner's share have generally been modest (never as much as $900 in recent decades). In 1966, it was about $200; in 1973, it was $848; and in 1976, $500.

The dividends have always been welcome, especially as they are distributed at Christmas time, but the basic significance of owning a share is that, as Al Macari told his son, it is a permanent job. It is security.

If one only wanted security, however, that would be possible in a municipal job. In public refuse agencies, annual turnover, for whatever reason, is about 8.5 percent for skilled workers, as compared to 21.4 percent in private refuse companies. But, of course, the gross weekly wages of a public refuse worker are ordinarily lower than those of his counterpart in a private company. So the Sunset partner's job combines security with good pay, as compared to other refuse workers.

Again, however, what makes the job good is not merely the fact of ownership in these concrete ways, but, as Lenny told me in a tape-recorded interview, as we sat in his car outside his office one day to get away from the telephones:

A man always works for something...I guess—again, I'm not an expert—but in my own opinion, I feel that...a man walks through this yard here [at Sunset] and says, "I own a piece of this; this is mine." And it's pride of ownership, number one, that's really the governing factor. Of course, there's a lot of them like a bunch of old ladies, but on the other hand, thank God, the majority of the stockholders take pride in their company. It's theirs. *E cosa nostra*—it's our thing, it's ours....

But this [pride of ownership] is carried on through the family, basically, like you say. His father [*pointing to a man going by*] just retired at sixty-one, and he's got another brother that works for the company. I've been raised in the company. That guy there who's going by now, his father works over in the salvage department. I mean, you could just point these things out here all the way around the place, that they've been here

[by families]. Myself, I was raised in the business. I'm speaking for myself now. I loved it from—when I was old enough to count money, I collected garbage bills. Fred Fontana, the same thing. He was raised here.

I guess we all have a piece of it in our blood in one form or another. It's the people who have never had any connection with the garbage company that are the biggest problems in this company; they come in and they want the buck today and the hell with tomorrow. [But] some of us look for a future in the company and look back on their accomplishments. The old timers talk about "Gee, I remember when we had a horse and wagon," and "I remember when...I guess it's pride, I guess, just to summarize in one word—pride of ownership. It's an odd thing.

Lenny felt that times were changing, to the extent that it was necessary to provide much better pay. This was required just in order to attract outside people who would have the capacity to move into the more complicated administrative and technical tasks, but also to get those who might, because of family, have more of a reason to join Sunset. "How can you encourage them?" I asked.

Well, I can encourage them no. But we've got the problem of the dollar again. Most of the garbagemen want their sons to be something better than they were. That's just a normal way of life. They want them to be better than their father. They'll provide everything for them; they'll give them education. But I know that down deep in their hearts, they would like their sons to carry on the tradition of the company. There's no question about that. But I don't think they really get out and *push* it, because they say, "Well, Jeez, I broke *my* back all my life." But now, since they see the company starting to progress, and they see these new trucks [they have more pride in the business for their sons].

For example, we gave a new truck to this new guy, Tony Lucaro, the other day, [to try out], and if you took his *wife* away, he wouldn't feel so bad if you took that truck away! I'm going to have to buy it for 13,000 bucks, and the guy's going to crack up if we take that truck away from him. I mean we need it—It's not just a question of making him happy—it's a good buy, $13,000 for an $18,000 truck regularly. So we pick it up for $13,000, and the guy's just *so* happy about it. And [so] there's a situation where maybe the guy would want his son to come and take part in this....

To recruit the younger guys, we have to show their fathers, because the fathers are the ones who are going to tell them to go [into the company] or not to go. And the ones that we are getting now, their sons, are out for the dollar, to make a buck. Maybe they want to get married or they want some security for the future, and to do that, they buy a share, and they *do* acquire the security. Good God, how much security you've got in here once you've got a share in the company, if you do your job! Right now, what I feel is that it's been traditionally going along that the guys have had the pride that you're referring to, but I think it's going to get a lot better [with financial benefits as well]. Like today—three guys want to bring their sons down, they want to put them to work. [So even now] we have no trouble recruiting help. I just don't want to go overboard on it [by hiring too many people]. Because it's a question of economics now.

Five years later, I got firsthand knowledge of what Lenny meant, when I went out on the trucks again with Freddie and discovered that his 16-year-old son Danny was working alongside him. At the doughnut shop that morning, another crew, including Freddie's brother Pasquale, came in. For a while, Freddie and Pasquale kidded Danny about which boss scavenger he would work for, each pretending to top the other with hourly rate bids between $1.35 and $1.85 an hour. Then, according to my notes:

> Freddie told me, while Danny lounged listening, that he had told Danny, "If you don't want to go to school, work on the truck." He said, "I thought he'd want to go back to school, but no." I turned to Danny: "How long have you been on the truck?" "Since

April [eleven months]. My birthday I worked." Freddie couldn't believe it had been that long.

(Later:) In the cab of the truck, Freddie said to me: "I did not want to say it in front of him [Danny]: I'd rather he go to college, but what the hell, what else is he going to do? His father is a garbageman; his uncle; my father. What else is he going to do?"

On a break, waiting for the packer to return, I learned from Freddie that there were still four men on this packer because one was Danny, doing his apprenticeship. Freddie said: "The apprenticeship does not require a year, or maybe even six months, but being as he's pretty young, it's longer for him." It was then that I discovered from Freddie that Danny has been working for nothing! Since April, Freddie repeated. We were sitting in Ernie's pick-up truck, having a beer, waiting for Henry Rivera (the new driver) to return. Danny was on the truck bed, eating and drinking something else. Freddie told me that he had suggested that Danny work for a relative who operates a dental laboratory. Then he called Danny, who came around to the truck door. "Are you sure you don't want to work with [name]? You know he'd take you in. It's a good job, making false teeth. Good pay." Danny shook his head. "Naw, I don't want those nine-to-five hours. Staying in one place all day? Naw!" He went back to the truck bed. Freddie had tested it out again, and it was still true: his son wanted to be a garbageman. "What do you expect from someone who's sixteen?" he grinned at me. But he was thoughtful.

Later, I expressed my respect to Danny for his work and asked him when he thought he would be going on the payroll. "Pretty soon now. Couple weeks, anyway." He was very satisfied with his progress. Still later, I asked Freddie the same question. He answered, "Any day now. Whaddaya going to do? A baby. But now...." He shrugged his shoulders.

At one time in 1974, there were, according to Freddie's estimate, thirty or forty sons of shareholders working as helpers—that is, as non-partner workers. This family tradition would undoubtedly continue to be one of the strongest elements in the stability and service that Sunset represents for the city. People continue to pull out the garbage because their fathers did it before them; because their friends and other relatives make the company a familiar and welcoming place; because they develop significant personal relations with new co-workers over the years; because of the specific rewards of this kind of job (the open air, the self-determined pace, the salvageable items, the change and variety and human excitement of the customers and their environment);

because the pay is as good as their neighbors are getting and thus fulfills financial aspirations effectively; and, finally, because they own a part of the company, which means that they are more than workers and yet their jobs, as workers, are secure. It is no wonder, then, that the San Francisco scavengers ordinarily feel good about their work as garbage collectors and that that work is done superlatively most of the time. Their tasks, the dirty work as a whole, have been transformed by the social and economic relationships that make men proud of what they do for a living.

Women in Direct Sales: A Comparison of Mary Kay and Amway Sales Workers

Maureen Connelly and Patricia Rhoton

CASE STUDY QUESTIONS

1. Does a homemaker's decision to become a Mary Kay sales worker seem to be based more on rational decision making or on chance? How do women who become Amway sales representatives seem to make their occupational choice?

2. To what extent does the human capital perspective explain the choices of Mary Kay and Amway sales workers?

3. To what extent are women's and men's motivations to choose direct sales similar, and to what extent are they different?

Women who work in direct sales do not get involved as a result of a life-long dream to enter that field. Their entry could be explained more readily by the concept of "occupational drift" than "occupational choice." Working in direct sales is a "choice" heavily influenced by the fact that this is an occupation requiring little or no preparation or experience, no or few geographical restrictions, and in most cases a minimum amount of financial investment. Some contact with a direct sales organization seems to be almost a universal experience among adult American women—be it coerced par-

Source: Reprinted from *The Worth of Women's Work* by A. Statham, E. M. Miller, and H. O. Mauksch, 1988, by permission of the State University of New York Press.

ticipation in a neighbor's Tupperware party or merely occasional purchases from a local "Avon lady." For a significant number of women, however, this casual involvement leads to some formal affiliation. According to the Direct Selling Association (1984) the sales forces of these companies encompass approximately five million individuals, 80 percent of whom are women working part-time. The social science literature has directed scant attention to this phenomenon. Given the number of women estimated to be involved in this activity (four million), part-time direct sales work is clearly an important area of study.

This paper looks at the experience of women in direct sales, particularly women involved in two major sales organizations—Mary Kay Cosmetics and Amway Corporation. These two corporations were selected because their organizations and day to day operations seem to reflect differences between a "masculine" and "feminine" work culture. These differences appear in the structural aspects of these organizations as well as in the motivation for women's involvement. Analysis is based on participant observation of these organizations and their activities over a three-year period and a series of in-depth interviews with a sample of 20 women who had participated or were currently involved in Mary Kay or Amway.

Relevant Literature

The sociology literature has devoted little attention to the direct sales phenomenon. (See Green and D'Aiuts 1977, Taylor 1978 for the few existing studies.) Most discussions have appeared in business publications (e.g. Bage 1980, Coburn 1982, Koil 1981). The literature on similar occupations, for example, on self-employment, does not provide useful insights, particularly regarding women. This literature deals with the specific nature of self-employment; i.e., the characteristics of those who attempt to start their own business or the characteristics of those successful and nonsuccessful in their self-employment ventures (Daum 1984). Most of this research concentrates on men, limiting its relevance for women in direct sales. Other works in this area have either looked at the nature of direct sales organizations in general while concentrating on Tupperware specifically (Peven 1968) or looked at women historically in the more structured setting of retail sales in department stores (Benson 1983).

Sex differences in occupations have been neglected partly because of a reluctance in the social sciences to explore general sex differences, given the political impact of this scholarly work. The first major wave of social science research concerned with differences coincided with the rebirth of the women's movement in the 1960s. Research during that wave seemed either to downplay the existence of sex differences (see Maccoby and Jacklin 1974), or to argue for the socialized basis for observed differences. This wave of research aimed at distinguishing between biological sex, which for the most part are unalterable, and gender or sex roles, which are variable, socialized and therefore alterable.

Friedan's "second stage of the women's movement" (Friedan 1981) appears to parallel a comparable second stage of research and writing emerging in the 1980s. Exemplified in the work of Gilligan (1982), this research reexamines issues of sex differences. Rather than denying that any differences exist, it affirms a distinct women's culture, a distinct female experience. It deemphasizes questions of causality and argues for the legitimization of sex differences and the evaluation of the distinctly feminine.

Methodological Approach

Information on the two direct sales organizations under consideration here has been gathered in a number of ways. Participant observation with the Amway organization, the organization studied more extensively, included attendance at rallies or group meetings (24 within a 12 month period), reading Amway motivational literature, listening to tapes on a weekly basis and becoming involved in numerous discussions with Amway distributors. For comparative purposes, contact was also established with Mary Kay consultants. This contact consisted of attendance at Mary Kay parties, training meetings and regional gatherings.

During the summer of 1985, more formal interviews were undertaken. Twenty women (ten from each organization) were interviewed. Snow ball sampling procedures were used to generate interviews in Columbus, Ohio and Frostburg, Maryland (i.e., initial contacts were asked to provide names of two other potential interviewees). The instrument used was an open-ended questionnaire focusing on aspects of the women's motivation for participation; satisfaction and problems encountered; information detailing her life cycle stage and standard demographic data. Interviews were conducted in the women's home using tape recorders. Although written notes were made during the taping, the interviews were later transcribed for more detailed analysis. The discussions and analysis that follow incorporate responses from these interviews as well as material from the participant observations.

Two Major Direct Sales Organizations

Direct selling can be seen as "the marketing of products or services directly to a consumer, on a one-to-one or small group (party plan) basis" (July 1985: 1). Companies such as Shaklee, Avon, Tupperware, Fuller Brush, Home Interiors, Amway, and Mary Kay are examples of direct sales organizations currently operating in the United States and in some cases internationally. Mary Kay and Amway were chosen because of a number of similarities between the two. Both were formed by charismatic leaders who remain intimately involved in the current operation of the organization. Both are appropriately classified as multilevel marketing organizations in which the individual entrepreneur is both wholesaler and retailer. Both require that the worker engage in selling the corporation's products and recruiting other "salespersons." Both distribute products that are readily available locally considerably cheaper. Although the product lines carried by these two organizations are very different, both distribute products that are at the upper end of the scale in terms of price and quality. Mary Kay has a number of different products all related in some way to skin care or makeup. Amway started out with a single line of soaps, but now has a wide range of products such as water treatment systems, vitamins, safety equipment, satellite disks and a "personal shopper's catalog" similar but smaller than Sears' or J.C. Penney's.

Certain work is basic to all direct sales organizations—selling the company's products and recruiting others to do the same. Yet numerous and important differences exist between these two organizations. First, aspects of the reward system vary. Amway emphasizes cash incentives for both sales and recruitment. Successful movement up the Amway distributor ranks results in an increasing profit percentage. While this system exists as well in Mary Kay Cosmetics, emphasis is placed on nontransferable goods-in-kind as rewards. Success in Mary Kay is motivated by incentives of furs, jewelry, and cars which the company gives to successful consultants.

Structural links between the individual and the corporation also differ. Amway emphasizes a rigid hierarchical structure, and a distributor's link to the corporation is mediated by various levels. Bookkeeping on product sales and distribution of profit checks and other routine aspects of Amway "work" are routed through the upline sponsors or downline recruits. Distributors are counseled to be cognizant of the hierarchical structure even in disclosing their personal frustrations as Amway Distributors. Frustrations and complaints are never to be shared with subordinates downline; rather, the distributor is instructed to take problems upline and to share successes downline. The first direct contact the individual has with the corporation beyond filing the initial application does not occur until the person reaches the status of direct distributor—a position obtained with monthly sales of $7,000 plus and achieved by relatively few in the distributor ranks. In contrast, consultants in Mary Kay have a more direct and unmediated link to the corporation. Admittedly, a hierarchical structure exists in Mary Kay. Subordinate to each consultant are those they have recruited—termed "offspring." Yet routine aspects of the work, such as orders, are not routed through the hierarchical structure but carried out by each individual consultant, who is directly linked to the company.

While both organizations strongly support the ideal of the traditional family, the two differ in the way that a woman functions within the organizational structure. Women working in Amway are most often involved initially by their spouse. A traditional division of labor exists and is perpetuated within the Amway family, with the wife performing the secretarial and bookkeeping functions in the home while the husband goes out and shows the plan and sponsors new recruits. The value system emphasizes achievement and success as traditionally defined by how much money an individual is making. In contrast, Mary Kay seems to reflect a uniquely feminine work experience. Spouses of consultants have peripheral involvement in their wives' work. There is also a great deal of emphasis placed on nurturance and support, which coexists and even dominates the emphasis on success.

Getting Involved in Direct Sales

Reasons for engaging in direct sales are varied. Women often seek this essentially part time employment for its convenience. They can make extra money, perform most of their work at home, structure the work day, and fit the work into the confines of their existing life and its associated constraints.

The route to involvement varies in the two organizations. Mary Kay consultants make their own choice to become involved. Although they may have been encouraged to participate by family or friends, particularly if these are Mary Kay consultants, their decisions have not been precipitated by their husbands. In contrast, in Amway the husband in the family is usually the first person approached as a potential recruit.

The Amway woman is more often than not unmotivated to participate. She usually does not share her husband's vision of immediate and dramatic financial success. Rather, she often anticipates the extra work of their involvement—the products that need to be transported and the paperwork that needs to be completed and transmitted. When women are motivated initially to join Amway, it is often for reasons other than the expected financial gain. For example, the wife may see this work as a way of improving the family's and the couple's relationship. She thinks she can become involved in her husband's work in a way not possible in his traditional job. Amway can be seen as a way of improving her relationship with her husband, as something they can "share together."

Additional motivators for participation are evident in the company's suggestions for appealing to potential recruits. Amway emphasizes the "democratic" nature of participation: no individual can buy into the Amway corporation—movement up the hierarchy must be earned. Furthermore, Amway equalizes traditional social class advantages: formal education is not a prerequisite for success. Anyone can be successful so long as they follow the plan and work hard. Mary Kay stresses the concept of flextime; young mothers can stay home with their children during the day and schedule their parties at night, while mothers with older children can schedule their parties during the day and be home when the children return from school.

The Work of Direct Sales

Some physical labor is involved in the selling of both organizations' products, but the two companies vary in the amount of physical labor required. This difference is related not only to the type of product sold but also to the organization's procedures for distributing products and processing paperwork. Physical labor is more intense in the Amway organization: the product comes in larger quantities and larger containers, and distributors must pick up their orders at the home of the upline distributor. The order is broken down as downline distributors arrive to pick up their portions of the consolidated order, and this pattern is repeated until the product is delivered to a consumer. Within Amway "families," a standard pattern of division of labor exists in which these tasks are relegated to the wife. Mary Kay has a more "refined" approach to product distribution: orders are smaller in bulk and are delivered by UPS to each consultants' home. The physical labor consists of unloading the smaller size boxes and taking them to individual customers.

The distribution of the products is, however, only a minor aspect of the labor involved in selling. Getting people to use the products encompasses emotional and mental labor and impression management. Both companies purposefully socialize their workers for these various activities. In Mary Kay consultants are instructed to offer potential customers a "free facial" as a vehicle for introducing the product line. These facials can be performed on an individual basis or in a group party setting. Regardless of the setting, the facials are carefully structured— consultants are trained to introduce each product in a precise and standard fashion. Once a product has been purchased consultants are advised in ways to maintain contact with the consumer and encourage continued consumption. For example, they are advised to send each customer a birthday card and to allow the person a product discount as a birthday present.

The selling of Mary Kay products is couched in a nurturance ideology. At meetings for current and potential consultants, the altruistic nature of their work is often emphasized. Selling Mary Kay is defined as important work since "you are helping other women become more beautiful."

In discussing the work of selling in the Amway organization, it is important to distinguish between the official company position and that articulated by various "groups" within the Amway organization. The term "group" refers to large organizational structures which have emerged around key people within the organization. Technically, all direct distributors have their own groups as soon as they sponsor someone. Their group consists of persons they have sponsored directly and the people that their recruits have sponsored. While all distributors can have their own groups, some are considerably more active than others. An indication of the size and the prominence of a particular direct distributor and the resultant group is whether or not the group is referred to by that direct distributor's name.

The official position of the Amway Company regarding selling and recruitment is quite similar to that of Mary Kay. Distributors are to perform two major tasks, selling products and recruiting other members into the organization. Furthermore, distributors are encouraged to sell their products by demonstrating the product's use. As with Mary Kay, the person is instructed to do so using a structured presentation, either before individual potential customers or groups of customers.

Some of the more prominent groups within the Amway organization, however, deemphasize selling to customers. Rather they suggest that Amway work consists of merely recruiting other families who will consume approximately $100.00 worth of Amway products per month. Instead of selling products the recruit only has to sell the idea of selling the idea.

Furthermore, Amway distributors are encouraged to become the ultimate Amway consumers: members of some groups are encouraged to purge themselves of all "poison products" from their homes—i.e., those not available through Amway. Distributors often point with pride to their attire reassuring their potential recruits that all items on their body are available from the Amway catalog. "If Amway doesn't sell it you don't need it." Sponsoring or recruiting other members is the second major task in multilevel direct sales organizations. All such organizations encourage their members to recruit other members, and they provide monetary incentives for doing so. In each organization, the sponsor receives a proportion of the sales generated by recruits.

Amway and Mary Kay differ, however, in some important aspects of this recruitment.

The two organizations seem to differ in how sponsorship relates to the hierarchical structure of the sales force. Lineage and hierarchy appear to be reinforced in the Amway organization. "Downline" and "upline" are omnipresent in the Amway vocabulary. The organization reinforces this hierarchy in its incentive operation: if the recruit's immediate sponsor should drop out of the organization, their percentage of the recruit's sales goes to that sponsor's sponsor. No similar mechanism exists in Mary Kay; there, when a consultant drops out of the company, the 3 percent portion of recruit's sales reverts to the parent organization.

In Mary Kay, a nurturance theme seems to be reflected in sponsorship and the language used to describe aspects of it. Individuals sponsored are called "offspring" —a marked contrast to the term "downline" used in Amway. Should a Mary Kay consultant be geographically distant from her sponsor, the emotional support and training provided by this relationship can be acquired from a surrogate. In such a situation, the "offspring" gets "adopted" by a consultant working in the same geographic area. This geographically proximate consultant receives no monetary compensation for "adopting." However, a strong norm encourages her to provide the same services and support to her adopted offspring as to her own offspring, whose sales she directly profits from. This policy is in marked contrast to the Amway procedure, in which reliance is put solely on the upline person. Regardless of geographic distance, the sponsor is required to perform the training and motivational function. This expectation applies even to the mechanics of the product distribution. A distributor, for example, even at a great geographic distance, must still channel their downline's orders, if necessary, mailing the products down line. The Amway organization has a mechanism for switching groups, but the procedure is formal in nature and rarely used. A distributor can switch to a geographically proximate group only with the agreement of all parties involved. Since this switch will result in the termination of the original sponsor's percentage of the recruit's sales, there is little incentive for the sponsor to agree to this arrangement.

Furthermore, the members in the two organizations differ in their emphasis on the sponsorship function and, seemingly, their degree of comfort with this activity. We have seen that in some Amway groups, sponsorship is presented as the only work involved in participation and as work entailing very little labor. Although the Amway corporation itself repeatedly warns against using this "chain letter" approach in the presentation of the plan the strength and regularity of such warnings are evidence of the frequency of such patterns.

At Mary Kay meetings, sponsorship is down-played. Recruiting other women is mentioned, yet the fact that a person financially profits from such activity is not emphasized. A number of women we interviewed talked of sponsorship as the "least attractive" aspect of their experience. One individual has been working as a Mary Kay consultant for four years. Throughout the interview, she outgoingly discussed how Mary Kay "changed her life." Yet, when talking of recruitment of others she became uncomfortable, shy, hesitant and said "I guess I need to work on that...but I don't know...somehow I don't feel right asking other people to join," and was unable to articulate why she was uncomfortable recruiting others. She has four "offspring," and talked at length of the satisfaction she got working with them—and yet, she hesitated to recruit and viewed herself as "needing to work on this." In hearing women like her talk of recruitment, we felt their hesitancy was tied to unarticulated issues of exploitation, and somehow recruiting others and financially profiting from their recruits' work seemed unnatural and not quite right.

A final aspect of sponsorship is what could be termed the secondary market aspect of this activity. Both Mary Kay and Amway make a multitude of training and facilitating products available to the recruit. The products range from motivational tapes and books to a computer designed for the direct sales home office. These products, designed to enhance the recruit's success as a direct sales worker, are consumed by the sales force, and they need them solely because of their involvement in Mary Kay and Amway. The two companies differ in the extensiveness of this secondary market and its relationship to the sponsorship activity.

Mary Kay's secondary market products are fewer in number and are purchased directly from the parent company. An Amway distributor is exposed to a much larger array of motivational products and these are often retailed by the distributor's group as well as by the company. Certain Amway groups produce and market their own motivational materials. For example, one such group distributes for purchase by its downline a motivational "book of the month," "tape of the week," and "rally of the quarter." The upline in this group profits then not only from their downline's sales of Amway products, but also from the downline's consumption of the motivational aids.

Impression Management

Impression management occurs throughout both of these organizations. Each encourages conformity to an organizational dress code coupled with a positive attitude and outlook on life. Subtly, each seems to justify these behavioral and attitudinal presentations of self in light of other aspects of the organization's ideology.

Mary Kay stresses that the well-groomed woman never leaves her house without being "made up." "Looking Good and Feeling Great" is a term used by various consultants to summarize this norm. In her autobiography, the organization's founder, Mary Kay, articulates the justifications for and functions of this activity. Positing a link between outward experience and emotional state, she writes "A tremendous change comes over a woman when she's looking good and knows it. A woman's psychology is such that when she looks attractive, she becomes more confident" (Ash 1981, 129). Cultivation of a consultant's grooming is then encouraged not merely as a vehicle for advertising the company's products, but as a technique for promoting the growth of the women involved. Like the dissonance theorists, Mary Kay posits the need to change behavior first, with the idea that internal changes will automatically follow. She describes, for example, a consultant who initially struggled with her sales. The woman was encouraged to buy a new dress and then almost immediately increased her sales. "The secret was that at long last she was confident that she looked good. And, with her new self confidence, she was able to project more enthusiasm and conviction in her presentation" (Ash 1981, 130).

A similar justification is given for the organization's emphasis on a positive outlook. "Mary Kay Enthusiasm" and the idea "You Can Do It" are keynotes in the presentation of self. Again the emphasis is on the ramifications these ideas have for the women involved. "For me, the most meaningful thing about the growth of Mary Kay Cosmetics has been seeing so many women achieve. All of us here thrive on helping instill in other women the `You can do it' spirit. So many women just don't know how great they really are. They come to us all vogue on the outside and vague on the inside. It's so rewarding to watch them develop and grow" (Ash 1981, 8). Thus impression management in Mary Kay is tied to personal growth as well as being a tool for the sale of the products.

Amway also has a dress code for its distributors. Men are expected to wear suits and ties; women are expected to wear dresses, heels and makeup. Sports jackets on men and pants on women are viewed as not adequately conveying the Amway image—one of a professional albeit an at-home entrepreneur. Concurrent with this code of dress, distributors are expected to convey a positive and enthusiastic attitude when dealing with the world. Uplines, for example, will coach recruits on the appropriate response to the inquiry "How are things going?" Amway distributors are instructed to respond with a "Great, never been better" and to do so with conviction and enthusiasm. In some of the Amway interviews, the women involved expressed their initial discomfort with this policy. One distributor described her distrust and perception of it as being "phony." "It's not normal to be that 'up' all the time." Distributors are instructed never to reveal their doubts and concerns to those below them in the organization, "Never say anything negative downline." Rather, if feeling less than enthusiastic and great, the recruit is to bring these concerns upline.

Division of Work Time Within Direct Sales

For most of the women interviewed, work in direct sales organizations is essentially a part time activity. Asking them to articulate how they divided their time, for example, how many hours they devoted to attending rallies and meetings, seemed a fruitless activity. They were often stunned by this question, would struggle with it for a while and then would almost lament "I can't really say…,That's so difficult to answer."

There are a number of explanations for this difficulty. Often, the total amount of time devoted to the direct sales organization fluctuated during their phases of involvement. "Are you talking about the time I spend now or when I first joined or when I was most into Amway?" one woman asked. Furthermore, one of the prime motivators these women often had for being involved in direct sales is the very irregularity of the time allocation and the possibility of their controlling their own allocation. In contrast to traditional nine-to-five jobs, direct sales can be "fitted" into the day and other rhythms of life. One successful Mary Kay distributor, for example, varies her schedule seasonally. A golf enthusiast, she works more than full time during the colder months of the year. During the summer, she takes a vacation from Mary Kay. Other distributors and consultants "fit" their work into the demands of their family life and other employment if they are already in an employment situation. The Mary Kay organization specifically states that Mary Kay work should be subordinate to family demands—"God first, family second, career third" (Ash 1981, 56). In discussing her own experience with other direct sales work, Ash writes:

> …One of the nicest things about my flexible hours was that I could always be home to give my tender loving care if one of the children was ill. There was very little I ever let interfere with my work—except my family. Employers need to understand that these are a woman's priorities. I've seen women with nine-to-five jobs come to work when they had a very sick child at home. In my opinion, their employers would have been better off to tell them to stay at home and take care of the child. There's no way a mother can keep her mind on her work when she's worried about a sick child (1981, 60).

The Pleasure of Direct Sales

Motivation for seeking particular employment is related to, but not synonomous with, the pleasures of the work. Often when selecting a type of work, motivation comes from the anticipated pleasures of the work, from what the person discerns as its pleasures. At times, however, the pleasures of work are emergent phenomena—almost unexpected by-products of the employment. In our interviews, we asked for both the reasons for choosing direct sales as well as what the interviewee saw as "the most attractive aspects" of her work. Often, the women interviewed linked these two. They referred back to their motivation when addressing the pleasures. Yet at times, the question regarding pleasures elicited very different information. One woman, for example, talked of the impact Mary Kay work has on her children. Since becoming involved in direct sales, she sees her family as being affected by the company's "You Can Do It!" philosophy. Thus, she described her children as becoming more positive, confident and enthusiastic as a result of her work.

Not only was a range of pleasures articulated, but they often differed from those articulated by the organizations. The Amway organization, for example, in its motivational tapes and rallies, emphasizes the pleasure of new found wealth. A typical plan presentation found in some Amway groups starts by asking the potential recruits to fantasize their dream home or vacation. Commenting on the gestalt of an Amway rally, 60 Minutes concluded "What they are really selling is—the hope of getting rich beyond your wildest dreams" (1983, 2). Some of the Amway women interviewed mentioned that this idea of making "easy money" was one of their initial reasons for getting involved. Those who dropped out of Amway often linked their dissatisfaction to their failure to achieve this dream of unlimited and easy wealth. Most of the women detailed pleasures often not addressed by the Amway organization. For example, they met friends through the rallies and meetings, they got to spend some time traveling with their husbands without their children, or they came in contact with a group of people who "looked together." Interestingly,

one theme promoted by sponsors and at rallies was never mentioned by the women we interviewed. Amway is often touted as a means of getting free from the clock—the successful distributor gets to "throw the alarm clock out," often in the midst of a celebration specifically for that purpose. Yet, none of the women interviewed mentioned this, even those who have worked or were working in more traditional and time structured employment. Perhaps this is a pleasure or a theme more suited to the male Amway recruits. Perhaps women, particularly those encumbered by the demands of child care, cannot fathom a life in which work-related demands are ever entirely restricted to certain times of the day.

Mary Kay similarly attempts to attract with a vision of material success. Furs, jewelry, and the ultimate, a pink Cadillac, are pleasures to be reaped by the successful consultants. Some of the women interviewed mentioned that working for Mary Kay resulted in "things I'd probably never buy for myself." However, the theme most addressed in the interviews was the flexibility they had with respect to the time afforded by their work—"I can fit Mary Kay in."

The Problems in Direct Sales

In a similar vein, in our interviews, we asked the women to articulate the "least attractive aspects" of their work. As one might expect, more problems were addressed by those who had aborted or curtailed their involvement prior to our interviews. Former Amway women seemed more bitter in their discussions. They often saw the problems they experienced as externally caused and linked to some deception by sponsors and the Amway corporation. One woman, for example, focused on the effort involved to be successful. She initiated involvement, thinking that it would entail very little time, and dropped out when she realized "more time was needed." Others complained that they discovered that they weren't making enough money. When their dream for unlimited wealth was not realized, they became disenchanted with the work.

In our Mary Kay interviews, the women more often talked of their own personal problems in executing the work. A number discussed their problems recruiting, their reluctance to approach friends or family, or their fears and anxieties regarding "cold bookings" (approaching complete strangers).

These problems seem to be both intrinsic and extrinsic to the work per se. Sales and recruitment by their very nature entail some imposition upon others. Mary Kay women, as previously stated, often addressed this and their difficulty in doing so. When asked to speculate on what types of people are more successful in direct sales, they often described people who were more aggressive than they. Amway complaints often were extrinsic to the work per se—the previously discussed discrepancy between their promised "easy money" and the reality of their commission checks.

Our analysis also suggests that there are problems in the rules and roles of the organization. Within the direct sales normative structure, a paradox exists. The worker is viewed as free, an independent, at-home entrepreneur. Yet within both organizations, workers experience extensive normative constraints. Codes of dress and set routines for presentation of products and recruitment of other members are restrictions on one's freedom. Although these structures can aid in making the transition into sales, they also limit the worker's options.

A model of the perfect family unit is fostered by some of the more successful Amway groups. Their rallies and tapes presented the specialization of functions within the family unit as a requisite for success. The husband in such a family functioned in the public arena—charged with the tasks of pre-

senting the plan and recruiting others. The wife in such a family functioned in the background. Ever supportive, she performed the "clerical" aspects of the work—did the bookkeeping, and moved the products through the various distributor channels. Although it was agreed that singles can do it too, the suggested route to success consistently portrayed this ideal family unit.

In Mary Kay, this traditional division of labor does not exist. This organization recruits women, not family units. Although at the yearly meetings there are some activities for Mary Kay husbands, the organization has minimal expectations regarding their actual participation. At best, the husband is expected to be emotionally supportive of his wife's work. He may babysit the children while she does facials and encourage her involvement, but rarely does he participate in the work itself.

Solving the Problems in Direct Sales

A variety of coping mechanisms exist for solving the problems extrinsic and intrinsic to this work. Getting out or "sneaking out" of the organization appears to be the dominant solution used by individuals as a response to problems. Becoming involved in direct sales, in contrast to other forms of work, often entails minimal investment from the individual. One does not undergo a formal education as training for this work, and setting up the business can be done with a minimal monetary investment. Ergo, when confronted by problems, a relatively easy solution exists in getting out—deciding to no longer be a direct sales worker. Mechling, for example, estimates that three out of four Amway sales distributors quit after the first year (1980, 462). This was the strategy used by almost half of the women we interviewed. Some severed their ties to the organization. Some "snuck out," maintaining a nominal affiliation, but viewing themselves as no longer "working" in direct sales. One woman, for example, described herself as now merely being "a good customer." She maintains her official affiliation as an option for her retirement years.

Criticism of direct sales organizations often focuses on former members who have large inventories which cannot be returned to the company. This is a function of inventory loading—a practice in which the direct sales entrepreneur is coerced into purchasing large quantities of products in order to qualify for certain incentives. A recent court case in California (Barlett versus Patterson, et al.) addressed such an occurrence. The plaintiffs charged that their Amway upline coerced them into purchasing over $50,000 in products to qualify for the status of "direct distributor" (Juth 1985, 16). None of the women we interviewed had this experience.

Aside from this coping mechanism, our interviewees did not directly address the issue of their coping strategies. However, we thought that coping mechanisms were reflected in their discussions. Lack of success, for example, is often coped with in one of two ways. Some women blamed the parent organization and deemed themselves as having been misled when they were originally recruited. Some of the elements that seemed most attractive in the beginning were ultimately blamed for failure. Workers are afforded unlimited flexibility in the amount of time devoted to their work, yet this flexibility and the fact that the worker determines it seems to relieve the organization from responsibility for individual failure. Success is often, even by the workers, equated with effort. If the recruit is not doing well—not making the fortune one had come to anticipate—failure to do so is often attributed to not putting in enough time. Such internalization of responsibility and blame seems to be reflected in their analyses regarding success. They seem to believe that if only they had been more aggressive or

invested more effort they might have realized their dream.

Conflicts Between Direct Sales and Other Aspects of the Woman's Life

Our interviews and observations suggest that in contrast to other types of work, direct sales is less likely to create problems in other spheres. By its very nature, this work can be fit into one's existing life demands and constraints. In fact, given the ideology of both Mary Kay and Amway—that family is important—women in direct sales were unlikely to say that they experienced conflicting role demands. Women in Mary Kay, for example, often quote the organization's prioritization—God first, family second, Mary Kay third—when asked to address this issue. They often described how legitimate it is in Mary Kay to cite family obligations as a reason for not doing some Mary Kay work.

A few of the women we interviewed described some conflict with their extended family and friends. These conflicts revolved not around the issue of competing demands but rather around the perceived legitimacy of their work. Thus, they described their family as being critical of the direct sales organization and not supportive of their work. One respondent said she would never forget what her mother said when she got into Mary Kay, "You have a college degree and you're peddling lipstick!" Such conflicts seemed to be dealt with by avoidance. The women talked of avoiding the issue—not mentioning the organization and their involvement when interacting with these individuals.

The Realities of Direct Sales from an Economic Standpoint

While prescribed recruitment material tells the recruiter to stress the positive aspect of self-employment, it has little to say about the start-up costs involved in establishing such a business. Costs involved in purchasing special telephone equipment such as an answering machine or a device to record phone conversations can be considerable. Even if the recruit decides to start out with just the basics, not investing in office and storage equipment, there are still numerous items as product handouts, samples, customer gifts, and supplemental literature. All of these items are designed to bring the products to potential purchaser's attention and to keep the products in their minds. However the cost of these items has to be taken out of whatever profit is made by the individual doing the direct selling.

Money is made in two ways in a direct sales organization. First the difference between what the worker pays for the product and what the worker sells the product for is profit; however, this amount is affected by a number of factors. Each organization has built-in incentives to increase the volume of products sold so the more product that the individual purchases from the company the less the products cost. This practice can have serious consequences for the recruits of an individual who is trying to build volume quickly since they may encourage their recruits to purchase a large inventory irrespective of the recruit's ability to sell.

Purchased inventory can be an incentive to a recruit in the sense that the large amounts of money tied up in inventory can certainly motivate one to do some selling. However, if the recruit decides that he or she no longer wants to be involved in the organization it may be awkward to return the products. Some women seem to feel that it is easier to withdraw from the organization if they do not try to return the products they have purchased. In some cases this is because the products have some use to the individual—some can be used by the house-

hold, some can be given away as gifts or some can be sold either at cost or at a loss. Others are left with larger quantities of products that they cannot use or feel comfortable trying to sell. Since both organizations have a very liberal return policy it seems that the reason individuals end up with large unsold inventories of goods is not the actual difficulties of returning the goods but the difficulty of facing their sponsor and announcing their intention to quit. In order to avoid this, it becomes easier to keep the inventory and so avoid any confrontation.

In both organizations there is a financial advantage to be gained in a situation in which the sponsor has a number of recruits who make regular sales to a small group of individuals. This advantage occurs because the recruit who sells the item to a customer absorbs the cost of the sale and yet may make only a 3 percent or 6 percent bonus or profit on the transaction because their overall volume is below a certain level. If the sponsor has enough volume to be at a higher profit level then the difference in profit percentage goes to the sponsor, rewarding the sponsor for the time, energy, and money spent on training and motivating recruits.

From the company's perspective there are a number of advantages in using this type of sales personnel. First, the company invests absolutely no money in the salesperson until that individual has risen far enough in the organization to have already made a firm commitment to the company itself. If the individual does not make any sales, the company is under no obligation to give any money to the salesperson. Nor does the company have to worry about such costly and/or time-consuming items as pension plans, social security taxes, unemployment compensation, workman's compensation or health plans. This is different from a situation where the salesperson works on a draw until their sales are high enough to work for straight commission.

Also, each recruit provides his or her own warehouse space, office, office help, supplies, typewriters, phones, file cabinets, shelving and photocopying equipment. They purchase the forms needed to do the paperwork that the company requires, from the company itself. In actuality these companies have two related lines, one involving the sale of the actual products and a secondary business of selling sales and motivational support material to the salesperson. This material can be used either to make the sales process easier or more professional or keep the level of interest and effort high.

Noneconomic Returns from Participation in Direct Sales

The heart of the direct sales organization is the distribution system. This system itself has many advantages for the distributor. Its basic appeal lies in the ready made support network of individuals who are not going to make any money unless the new recruit succeeds in selling the product at some level. Unless the person sponsored either buys the product for their own use or sells the product to others, no money changes hands. Thus sponsors will make a concerted effort to help their recruits to the very best of their ability. In many cases the training period is a pleasant time of constructive dreaming of what if, of goal setting, meeting new people, sharing new experiences, and in some cases traveling to new places.

This participation in direct sales can also precipitate a change with respect to the women's entry or reentry into other parts of the labor force. One woman who is a makeup and wardrobe consultant became involved in Mary Kay as a side to her existing business. Others found outside jobs when they realized that they were not making enough money through their sales work. Some went into direct sales when they could not find a job they wanted in their geo-

graphic area. The most successful Mary Kay woman interviewed had left a job that she had begun to dislike intensely.

Conclusions: Direct Sales and a Female Work Culture

The primary analysis of direct sales presented here suggests a number of themes related to larger issues relevant to women and work: integration of work and family, a distinct female work culture or experience, and exploitation of women workers.

Traditionally women more than men confront the need to balance work with family or home responsibility. Women who are employed outside the home often do a "double day." While these women allocate fewer hours daily or weekly to household responsibility than do full time homemakers, they spend more time on these tasks than do their spouses. Blumstein and Schwartz, for example, conclude from their study of American couples, "working women...still do the vast bulk of [housework]" (1983, 145). Furthermore, they see women interweaving their work and family concerns; wives allow their relationships to affect their jobs and their jobs to affect their relationships (1983, 155). For example, when women select their place of employment they often use criteria that reflect their family responsibility. They choose a particular job because it is convenient to the house, daycare, or their children's school.

Direct sales work then seems almost ideally suited to the interweaving of work and family. The ideology of direct sales companies often espouses consideration of family concerns and, if anything, allows family responsibility to override work. The flexible hours of direct sales pragmatically facilitate this balancing of work and family.

The idea that women have a distinct culture, a mode of experiencing, that distinguishes them from men is the thesis advocated by Gilligan (1982) and others. Gilligan suggests that relationships are primary considerations for women, that female solutions to moral problems, for example, tend to emphasize the ethics of care, human attachment, and the resolution of conflict through communication and cooperation. That this distinct culture might be reflected in the world of work seems plausible and seems to integrate numerous findings and speculations regarding women and their work....The low status of the teaching, nursing, and social work professions which women have historically dominated, all emphasize nurturance and helping.

The idea of a distinctive female work culture and perhaps a distinctive female work experience have been present throughout our analysis. It is our thesis that Mary Kay is different from Amway in some important ways, and that these differences reflect a female work culture. A number of aspects of Mary Kay work seem to echo this culture: the theme of nurturance; the less rigid hierarchical structure; the ambivalence regarding exploitation; and the nature of the reward system.

Nurturance, caring for others, appears as a dominant theme in Mary Kay work. The work itself is touted as nurturing—"You are helping other women become more beautiful." Caring for and helping others was mentioned or alluded to so frequently that an uninformed observer might have concluded that the usual Mary Kay meeting was a meeting for social workers or others in the "helping" professions. Not only is nurturance emphasized in the relationship with customers, it also permeates the organizational's internal relationships. The terminology of "offspring" and "adopters" symbolically conveys a maternal and nurturing relationship, particularly when these terms are compared to their Amway equivalent, "downline." That adopting exists as a viable alternative to overcome problems of geographical distance likewise suggests the importance of support within the organization.

The nurturing aspect of the company's founder is also emphasized. A highlight of the yearly meeting in Dallas is the invitation to Mary Kay's home. During this visit to her residence, consultants are given cookies that she has baked herself in her own kitchen.

Similarly, this theme of nurturance is reinforced by the lack of hierarchical structure in Mary Kay. Amway emphasizes one's position within a hierarchical chain of command even in the routine work of placing orders. In contrast, Mary Kay emphasizes a closer link between each consultant and the parent organization. Meetings are held on the basis of geographic proximity rather than a chain of command.

Perhaps here our analysis is on more tentative and speculative ground, but we think that exploitation of others is less acceptable within the Mary Kay world. As we have seen, a number of the Mary Kay consultants talked about their hesitancy in recruiting others. While they realized that this activity was important and necessary for success, they experienced difficulty doing so. Consistently, they were unable to articulate the reasons surrounding this difficulty. At times, they merely said it "didn't feel right" to them. Given that some of these women are quite comfortable with other aspects of their direct sales work—meeting customers and giving facials to groups of strangers, we thought that their hesitancy reflected something other than their self-perceived lack of aggression.

Finally, the nature of the reward structure in Mary Kay seems more compatible with a traditional female experience. Rewards and incentives in the organization often are in the form of nontransferable goods. Cash incentives exist, but these are not emphasized to the extent that they are in Amway. Meetings do not symbolically display the checks received by successful consultants. Reference is made to money, how much one can earn in Mary Kay, but such references are more fleeting and veiled. Rather, the incentives and rewards touted are the luxury items "given" away by Mary Kay. The bumble bee pins, furs, jewelry, and cars are often the motivators — the "prizes" received for performance. Thus, working for Mary Kay seems to reinforce the wage structure of a traditional homemaker role.

In contrast the typical scenario presented on Amway motivational tapes illustrates a far different sequence of events. There the enthusiatic husband brings his reluctant and often antagonistic wife into the "family" of Amway work. Although the husband's motivation is not the focus of concern in this paper, the prominent place given to money in the motivational literature suggests that for them the freedom of choice afforded by the money that will be made is a large part of the attraction. The promise is access to the good life—luxurious housing, expensive cars, and exotic vacations—all while freed from the constraints of traditional employment. Furthermore, this work allows for the participation of the spouse in the earning process without interfering with her primary function as homemaker.

Direct sales in general, whether performed by females or males, is a grey area in the labor force. As a means of making money, there seems to be a wide range of success. Only three of the women involved made enough money in direct sales to consider it the equivalent of a full time source of income, yet the majority of the women interviewed on the whole were more positive about their experiences than we expected that they would be. In the majority of the interviews, the women or household either lost money or made very little in terms of what they had expected to make originally. Yet in most cases they either continued to use the products or continued to sell the products to friends, relatives and neighbors even though they were not making a large amount of money by doing so. Most of them focused on the growth that they had experienced on a personal level. Their experiences had resulted in their feeling better about their lives, their spouses, or themselves. Even the women who expressed some bitterness (always those involved in Amway, never those involved in Mary Kay) found more positive than negative things to say about their experiences. It may be that in direct sales organizations the product is only a vehicle for the social interaction that takes place, and the financial losses that occur are not very important in terms of what the participants perceive themselves to have gained. As one respondent said, "It's the women in it, they are very good people."

REFERENCES

Ash, M.K. 1981. *Mary Kay*. New York: Barnes and Noble Books.

Benson, S.P. 1983. "The customers ain't God': The work culture of department-store saleswomen, 1890–1940," In *Working Class America: Essays on Labor, Community, and American Society*, edited by M.H. Frisch and D.J. Walkowitz, Urbana, Illinois: University of Illinois Press.

Bage, T.J. 1980. "Selling to farmers," *Advertising Age* 51 (November): S4–S5.

Blumstein, P. and P. Schwartz. 1983. *American Couples.* New York: William Morrow.

Coburn, M.F. 1982. "Direct's sleeker sell," *Advertising Age* 53 (March 1): M18.

Daum, M. 1984. *Correlates and Consequences of Salaried and Self-Employment in Middle and Late-Life.* Brookdale Center on Aging: New York.

Freidan, B. 1981. *The Second Stage.* New York: Summit.

Galginaitis, C. 1980. "What do farmers think?" *Advertising Age* 51 (November 24): 55–57.

Galluccio, N. and A. Lappen. 1979. "Avon calling…with acquisition still on her mind," *Forbes* 123 (April 16): 142–45.

Gilligan, C. 1982. *In a Different Voice.* Cambridge, Massachusetts: Harvard University.

Green, J. and F. D'Aiuts. 1977. "A case study of economic distribution via social networks," *Human Organization* 36 (Fall): 309–15.

Koil, M. 1981. "Racing the competition," *Advertising Age* 52 (May 4): S14–S15.

Jobin, J. 1982. "Direct sales," *Women's Day* 45 (May 18): 20–25, 143.

Juth, C. 1985. "Structural factors creating and maintaining illegal and deviant behavior in direct sales organization: A case study of Amway Corporation." Paper presented at the 80th Annual Meeting of the American Sociological Association, August 26–30, Washington, D.C.

McElena, J.K. 1978. "Motivate distributors by tickling competitive nerve!" *Advertising Age* 49 (October 16): 2–6.

Maccoby, C. and N. Jacklin. 1974. *The Psychology of Sex Differences.* Stanford, California: Stanford University Press.

Maxa, R. 1977. *Dare to be Great.* New York: William Morrow.

Mechling, T. 1980. "Patriotism, capitalism and positive thinking," *Commonweal* 29 (August 29): 459–62.

Peven, D.E. 1968. "The use of religious revival technique to indoctrinate persons: The home-party sales organization," *Sociological Quarterly* 9 (Winter): 97–106.

Richmond, E. 1975. "On the road to riches," *Harpers Magazine* 250 (February): 12.

Rubin, L. 1983. *Intimate Strangers.* New York: Harper and Row.

Rudnitsky, H. 1981. "The flight of the bumblebee." *Forbes* 127 (June 22): 104–06.

Taylor, R. 1978. "Marilyn's friends and Rita's customers: A study of party-selling as play and work," *The Sociological Review* 26 (August): 573–94.

60 Minutes. 1983. "Soap and Hope." Volume XV, Number 17 as broadcast over the CBS Television Network Sunday, January 9, 7:30–8:30 EST: 2–7.

Wedemyer, D. 1975. "There's a tupperware party starting every 10 seconds…" *Ms.* 4 (August): 71–4, 82–5.

Alternative Paths in Adult Development

Kathleen Gerson

CASE STUDY QUESTIONS

1. To what extent are these women's initial orientation toward and final decisions about work, marriage, and children influenced by the social class and employment patterns of their parents?

2. To what extent are these women influenced by their own circumstances regardless of their background?

3. Which women were most likely to choose the role of full-time homemaker? Which women were most likely to combine the two? Which women pursued a work-oriented life?

4. To what extent did the women's initial choices correspond to their later decisions? For those whose later decisions matched their initial choices, what motivated their continuing loyalty to the original decision? For those who changed their minds, what factors transformed their choices? How much are the women affected by the types of occupations they believed were available to them?

5. What themes in the descriptions of these women's life histories typify the decisions of many women? What aspects of these women's lives vary from the lives of other women? To what extent do you think these

women's lives represent the lives of women in the 1990s?

6. To what extent do women and men take the same factors into acount when they think about choosing an occupation? To what extent do societal expectations of women and men expand and limit their choices?

Despite the rising number of women who appear to be breaking from former patterns, those who constitute this strategic generation have not made uniform choices. This group displays a varied range of responses to the structural dilemmas facing all women. Indeed, the experiences encountered by women of all generations may be found to some degree within its ranks.

Many have embraced the patterns of their predecessors; they have married, borne children, and settled down to full-time mothering; they have worked outside the home only intermittently, if at all. Yet a sizeable number of women have departed from this "traditional" path. These women have postponed, and even foresworn, motherhood; they have developed ties to the workplace that resemble the committed, permanent pattern once reserved for men; and they have rejected the domestic path that places children, family, and home above all else. In short, they have moved through their young adult years in markedly different ways from earlier generations. There have always been some women who fit this emerging pattern, but

Source: From *Hard Choices: How Women Decide About Work, Career, and Motherhood* by Kathleen Gerson, 1985, Berkeley: University of California Press. Copyright © 1985 by The Regents of the University of California.

today their numbers are growing on a scale never seen before.

Consider, for example, the diverse paths taken by the following women drawn from the larger group interviewed in this study:

Laura grew up in a "typical" middle-class family. Her father, a middle-level manager for a large utilities company, was happy in his work and able to support his wife and three children with ease. Her mother never worked for pay, devoting herself instead to caring for her family and managing their comfortable suburban home.

Laura never gave much thought to the future when she was young; she always "just assumed" that she would become a wife and mother much like her mother before her. Because there were ample financial resources, she also planned for college. She looked upon this period as a chance to train for a profession, such as teaching or nursing, that would mesh with homemaking. College would also provide the perfect setting, she reasoned, for meeting a man who would support her domestic aspirations.

For Laura, things turned out much as she expected. After two years of post–high school training, she went to work as a nurse. She met her husband, Steve, on the job, and two years later they were married. Because her work did not offer the pay or advancement opportunities that Steve enjoyed as a physician, she began to look forward to trading the long, late hours of nursing for what she imagined would be the more rewarding work of parenting. Because Steve's income rose rapidly, she did not feel financially obligated to remain at a job that had grown tedious. She soon became pregnant and withdrew from the workplace.

Since the birth of her first child, Laura has stayed home with few, if any, regrets. Although she plans to return to work part-time when her two children are older, she states firmly that her family "will always come first." She also resents the undertones of disapproval she senses when she tells inquirers that being a mother is her "career."

Joanne's childhood was not filled with the same advantages as Laura's, but she did grow up with similar expectations. As a repairman, her father struggled to make ends meet. Her mother nevertheless did not work outside the home until Joanne was in the eighth grade. Both parents agreed that the children should have a full-time mother, even if this arrangement entailed forgoing material luxuries. Despite their limited finances, they hoped Joanne would attend college to prepare herself for a "better life" than either of them had achieved.

Joanne, however, did not share her parents' aspirations. She was more interested in dating than in schoolwork and was not inspired by her part-time job as a waitress in a fast-food chain. Thus, when she became pregnant at seventeen, she did not greet this news with disappointment or panic. Instead, much to her parents' chagrin, she married her high school boyfriend and settled down to full-time mothering.

Two children, several sales jobs, and ten years later, Joanne still prefers domesticity to her other options. She occasionally feels social and financial pressure to forsake her domestic commitments for paid work. However, her husband earns enough money as a mechanic to "make ends meet." And every time she searches the want ads, she remembers how much she disliked the few temporary jobs she has held over the years. She then promptly turns her attention back to her children and her home. She is even considering having another child.

These two life histories illustrate the *traditional model* of female development in which an adult woman chooses the domestic life for which she prepared emotionally and practically as a child. Although they have disparate social backgrounds, Laura and Joanne share a similar life course trajectory. For each, adult life went according to plan. Neither experienced a substantial change in life goals or emotional priorities as she moved into and through adulthood. Both were also insulated from events that might have caused them to veer off their expected life paths: They were neither pushed out of the home by economic necessity or marital instability nor pulled into the workplace by expanding opportunities. They thus remained committed to the domestic path they assumed was a woman's proper place. In its essentials, these life histories fit well the traditional model of female domesticity that gained momentum during the late nineteenth and twentieth centuries and reached a peak during the post–World War II period.

In contrast, consider the life paths of Elizabeth and Jane:

Elizabeth, like Laura, grew up in a traditional, comfortable, middle-class home. As a lawyer, her father took great pride in supporting his family in style. Indeed, he vetoed the few attempts his wife made to find work outside the home, arguing that children need their mother at home and her working would reflect badly upon both parents. Similarly, he expected his daughter to go to college not to prepare for an occupation, but rather to find a suitable mate. Adopting the messages she received, Elizabeth grew up believing a woman's place is in the home.

Elizabeth, the dutiful daughter, thus married a young engineer soon after college graduation. Within a few years, however, the marriage began to sour. Before she could fully assimilate the implications of her situation, she was divorced and out on her own for the first time in her life. Desperate for a paycheck, she wandered into an employment agency looking for a job, any job. They placed her in a small company, where she started as a receptionist and office manager. She quickly made herself indispensable and over a period of about five years worked her way up the organization to her present position of executive vice-president.

Elizabeth is now in her mid-thirties, and there appear to be few limits on how high she can rise. Rearing a child could, of course, conflict with her career goals. There is little chance that motherhood will interfere with her work, however, for she has foresworn marriage forever and probably childbearing as well. Despite her childhood expectations, home and family just do not fit with the commitments she has developed as an adult. As she looks back over this chain of events, she wonders how she could have come so far from where she began.

Like Laura, Joanne, and Elizabeth, Jane also assumed when she was growing up that she would marry, have many children, and live "happily ever after," just as her parents before her. Her father, a Southern European immigrant, worked day and night to support his large family. Her mother clung tightly to the "old country" ways, which included loyalty to her husband and an almost total devotion to her children. Jane harbored a hidden desire to go to college, but her father opposed such pursuits for women and could not have underwritten the expense in any case.

Jane worked for a short time after high school as a filing clerk. She married two years later and was pregnant within six months of the ceremony.

Shortly after the birth of her daughter, however, she became bored and dissatisfied. Taking care of a baby was not the ultimate fulfillment she had anticipated. Instead, she found motherhood to be a decidedly mixed experience—alternately rewarding and frustrating, joyful and depressing. Although she was reluctant to admit these feelings to herself or others, a growing sense of emptiness plus the need for additional household income spurred her to look for a paid job.

Thus, to keep herself busy and help with the family finances, she took a job as a bank teller. She expected this situation to be temporary, but the appropriate time to leave work never arrived. Her husband, Frank, could not seem to "make it" as a salesman working on commission, and his income consistently fell short of their needs. As time passed, the marriage began to falter. Frank's work difficulties, coupled with his growing desire to have another child, left Jane feeling that she might be happier without Frank than with him.

Just when it seemed that the marriage had become unbearable, Jane's boss offered her a promotion into management, including higher pay, increased responsibility, and more respect from peers and co-workers. The bank was facing affirmative action pressures and had responded by initiating a program designed to advance women who lacked college degrees. Jane was initially worried about the increased pressures the new job would entail, but she was also eager to move ahead. Not coincidentally, she also divorced Frank.

Today, Jane is dedicated to her job, aspires to upper-level management, and has no plans to expand her family beyond her only child. She is convinced, moreover, that her daughter is better off because she left the bulk of child care to someone else who enjoyed the work more than did she.

These lives illustrate an emerging and increasingly common pattern among both middle-class and working-class women that involves *rising work aspirations* and *ambivalence toward motherhood.* Elizabeth and Jane grew up wanting much the same things in life as Laura and Joanne, but adult experiences intervened to push them off their expected life courses. Despite their contrasting class backgrounds, both Elizabeth and Jane experienced similar constraints and opportunities as adults. Not only did their early marriages deteriorate over time, but unanticipated work advancement opportunities also opened to both. Growing work ambitions and a diminishing interest in mothering thus eventually replaced their early domestic aspirations. These examples illustrate the developmental path taken by an increasing proportion of women from both the middle and working classes who grew up believing in the "feminine mystique," only to find that adult life offered a very different set of alternatives.

The next four lives begin from notably different starting points than the first four stories. First, there are the cases of Gail and Mary:

Gail was not attracted to motherhood as a child, but rather hoped to avoid it. Her mother had relinquished a promising career as an artist to raise three children and never seemed to recover from this sacrifice. As her children grew, Gail's mother slipped deeper into depression and frustration.

Gail's father, in contrast, seemed to thrive on both his work and his children. As a successful businessman who had pulled himself out of poverty after the Depression, he encouraged his children, all girls, to aim for whatever they wanted in life. It is not altogether surprising, therefore, that for as long as she could remember Gail wanted to be a lawyer. She knew this was an unusual desire for a girl, but the prohibition against it only fueled her determination.

In major respects, Gail has not waivered from her early plans. She went to college, graduated in the top third of her class, and entered law school, where she was surprised to find that over 30 percent of her classmates were women. After receiving her law degree, she joined a small law firm and was eventually made a partner. Throughout this period, she never found the time or felt the inclination to marry or have a child.

Now secure in her career, Gail has begun to view children as an option she can afford to consider. Time is running out, however, and no partner is in sight. There have been a few serious relationships with men, but they have all ended badly. She is fast losing confidence that she will find a suitable partner for the joint enterprise of child rearing and has reluctantly concluded that an exclusive commitment to one person for life may not be possible anymore. Because having a child outside of marriage seems unfair to herself and the child, the chances are high that she will never have children. She acknowledges this probability with mild regret.

Mary, like Gail, yearned from an early age for a life beyond the boundaries of home, children, and family. As the oldest of six children in a strict Catholic family, she had few illusions about the constant, often thankless task of rearing children. Her father worked hard as an electrician to keep his children clothed and fed. Her mother also worked hard cooking, washing, cleaning, and generally making sure her numerous children stayed out of trouble. Although Mary remembers her mother as devoted to her duties, she also remembers never wanting to follow her example. Her mother's life seemed stifling, and children seemed more a burden than a fulfillment.

Although she harbored vague ambitions for the independence work could offer, she married within a year of high school graduation. She now admits her primary motivation was to escape her parents' home and the confining atmosphere of her family. Unlike many of her friends, however, she did not rush into motherhood, but instead went to work for a mid-sized corporation.

The work was frustrating at first, but every time she quit, she found staying home was worse. From time to time, she considered starting a family; but both she and her husband had become dependent on her income, and she still viewed children as something she was supposed to but did not want. Rather than getting pregnant, she took a series of clerical jobs. Eventually her persistence paid off, and in her late twenties, she was promoted into the lower level of management at a major corporation.

Today Mary is just past thirty. She is more committed to work than ever and still has strong misgivings about becoming a mother, but she also feels the biological clock ticking away. Her husband, who loves young children, is growing impatient to have a child of his own. Mary is beginning to fear that never having a child might condemn her to loneliness later in life. She has recently decided that having one child might be the perfect compromise. With one child, she reasons, she can pursue her growing work ambitions without sacrificing completely the pleasures of building a family.

Despite their divergent class and family backgrounds, neither Gail nor Mary found domesticity an appealing option. Even as children, they viewed motherhood apprehensively and hoped for something different out of life. Although Gail formed clear career goals early in childhood and Mary's goals remained vague well into her twenties, both

saw children as a potentially dangerous obstacle to achieving other desired life endeavors. For these women, mothering did not represent the ultimate fulfillment to which they could happily devote their lives; rather, it threatened to be a trap they wished to avoid.

Like Laura and Joanne, Gail and Mary realized their early life goals and did not substantially change direction over the course of their lives. Because their goals were different from those of traditional women, however, Gail's and Mary's lives developed in a different direction: out of the home, away from motherhood, and toward committed work ties. These women met a set of circumstances in adulthood that enabled them to travel a *nontraditional path*. Their original occupational aspirations were supported by the people and institutions they encountered as adults.

In an earlier historical period, these women would have been more likely to have succumbed to the pressures to foreswear career ambitions in favor of childbearing. Today, however, women's social environment is more likely to nurture their work aspirations. Similarly, women today who experience deeply felt ambivalence toward mothering are less likely to repress, deny, or ignore these misgivings than they were in the past, when the sanctions against antimaternal feelings were strong.

The next two women shared Gail's and Mary's high work ambitions and early apprehensions about parenthood. Unlike Gail and Mary, however, they did not meet felicitous circumstances in adulthood that supported these early goals. They thus experienced a marked change of life direction as they turned toward home and children over time:

> Susan grew up in a middle-class home, but it was not a happy one. Her parents, who eventually divorced, fought often. Her father worked for an airline and was absent from

their home much of the time. Her mother, whom she remembers fondly, worked part-time as a door-to-door saleswoman and occasionally took Susan on these outings. The money her mother received from this intermittent work helped the family over occasional economic rough spots. With her husband generally gone, Susan's mother doted on her two children and wished for them the education and opportunities she never received.

Susan shared her mother's hopes and earned a scholarship to college. She attended college with optimism, but a number of factors ultimately thwarted her career ambitions. First, she met and married John in her senior year. His education required her economic support as well as her attention to the household tasks. Because his career needs collided with hers, she dropped her plans for a business degree and earned a teaching credential instead. She did not particularly like the idea of working with children, but a teaching degree on the primary school level could be earned quickly and promised her job security—or so she thought.

As it turned out, she had a difficult time finding a job and eventually settled for preschool teaching. Despite the low salary, economic constraints have kept her in teaching ever since. She has, not surprisingly, grown steadily weary of the demanding work and lack of chances for advancement.

In contrast, John is beginning to make progress in his architectural career and has begun to complain that he wants more of her attention directed to their life together. Susan can now depend on John for financial support; so she plans to resign and start a family. Ironically, she now looks forward to motherhood as her best chance to escape from the world of children that defines her job.

Vicki's childhood was marked by difficulty. Her father supported his wife and four children on a janitor's salary. Her mother provided little in the way of emotional or economic help, for she was in and out of mental hospitals throughout many of Vicki's early years.

Vicki was never especially oriented toward motherhood. Instead, since she was old enough to know who the police were, she wanted to be a policewoman. She was attracted to the excitement of life on the streets, to the physical and mental challenge. An exciting career also offered the hope of leaving behind her parents' poor existence.

Forced to take the best job she could find after high school, Vicki became a secretary-clerk. She also took the qualifying exam for police work and passed with high marks. No jobs were available, however, and she returned to her desk job, still hoping for "bigger things."

In the meantime, she met and married Joe. Joe's job as a construction worker required that they move a lot. Vicki found herself changing jobs often for the sake of Joe's "career." Once she even turned down the chance to advance because Joe's work came first. She ultimately grew to hate working, for it usually involved taking orders from bosses she did not respect.

Joe also began to pressure her to have children. Children were very important to Joe, for he had been orphaned and wanted to give his children the love he never received. Vicki viewed children as a burden she could do without, but Joe even threatened to leave her if they did not start a family soon. She decided that losing Joe was too heavy a price to pay for her fears and became pregnant in her late twenties.

After the birth of her first child, Vicki discovered that staying home to rear a child was more rewarding than her succession of boring, dead-end jobs. By her mid-thirties, she was a full-time mother of two.

Today she has given up hope of becoming a policewoman, but in return for this sacrifice she feels she has gained the secure home life she never knew as a child. She occasionally considers taking a part-time job, but she hopes she will never have to return to the full-time work she grew to abhor. She worries that, if something ever happened to Joe or the marriage, she would be forced out of the home again.

Susan and Vicki represent a fourth pattern for women that has probably long been in existence but only recently recognized: a woman who harbors deep-seated ambivalence toward mothering and domesticity but over time experiences *falling work aspirations* and begins to see *the home as a haven*. As children, neither Susan nor Vicki identified with the ideal of feminine domesticity, but as adults, they did not meet the supportive environment that greeted Gail and Mary. They ventured into the workplace with high hopes, only to find thwarted opportunities and stifling experiences. In time, work became burdensome, not fulfilling, to these women. They also came to perceive work as a threat to securing the intimacy and support they depended on at home.

Susan and Vicki thus ultimately concluded that mothering was preferable to the frustration of paid work and that it also promised to cement a cherished relationship at home. Despite their early work ambitions and persistent ambivalence toward child rearing, they eventually opted for domesticity over strong work ties.

These two women may seem out of step with their age peers who have found a more supportive environment for rising work aspirations, but they represent a growing group forced into jobs and occupations they find stultifying in order to earn a living. These women also resemble men who find themselves in jobs they would prefer to leave, except for one important difference: Men can weigh the relative costs of remaining in an unsatisfying job versus finding a new one, but few men enjoy the traditional, although shrinking, female option of trading paid work for domestic work. This group of women ultimately reaches occupational roadblocks that lead them to view domestic pastures as greener.

These two examples also demonstrate three important aspects of female development. Many women choose motherhood not to fulfill deep-seated emotional needs, but rather as the best option among a number of unappealing alternatives. Second, an apparent lack of ambition may actually be a well-founded concern for preserving a stable private life. Finally, the erosion of the domestic option, although no loss to women like Gail and Mary who secure work that is rewarding, is perceived as an understandable threat to women like Susan and Vicki who find work a dead-end street. Unlike most men, many women have traditionally had the option *not* to earn a paycheck. As this option erodes, some women's gains are inevitably offset by others' losses.

Each of these eight life histories illustrates the powerful, interactive link between women's work and family decisions. As a group, they also illustrate the varied paths women negotiate through adulthood. Although these are only eight cases amid considerable diversity, they demonstrate four general patterns that a woman's life course can assume, whether she was born into the working or the middle class.

These four patterns are based on two especially important dimensions around which distinct groups of women form. First, women differ in their early expectations about the goals they plan to pursue as adults. Exposed to a diverse, complex set of experiences as children, women, like men, develop a variety of conscious and unconscious aspirations long before they are able to test these wishes as adults. For some, these early images take the shape of well-formed plans in which the future appears as certain as the past. For others, these goals are more amorphous, assuming the form of vague hopes that may or may not be realized.

However misty or clear, these early desires form the baseline for adult life. Some plan to build their lives around the traditional feminine commitments to home, husband, and children; these women expect their own lives to resemble the domestic model that has been so prevalent in the recent past. Others view marriage and motherhood with trepidation and aspire to the less traditionally feminine pursuits of work advancement. Because their numbers have been few in the past, members of this latter group may be less convinced that their life choices are guaranteed than are those who start with domestic aspirations. Their lack of certainty, however, in no way diminishes the power of their feelings. The aspirations that women take into adulthood may thus center around domestic or occupational goals.

Once established, these early orientations are subjected to the real constraints and opportunities encountered in adulthood, the second dimension that distinguishes groups of women from each other. The social circumstances adults confront can support or undermine their original goals. Initial goals can prove viable, leading one down a life path wholly consistent with early expectations, or these early plans can ultimately turn out to be uninviting or even impossible, encouraging or perhaps requiring individual change. Unexpected events can lead adults to reevaluate their past assumptions and reorient themselves toward the future. Thus, pathways through adulthood may either follow or diverge from one's beginning baseline.

People differ in the extent to which they are exposed to change-inducing experiences. They consequently vary in the degree to which change characterizes their developmental path. When the pace of historical change is slow, most people are insulated from events that might shake up their views of the world or their proper place in it. Under these circumstances, most people tend to assume that their lives are preordained and rooted in the natural order of things. Even during periods of accelerated social change, many are able to move stably through life without veering significantly from an expected path.

Periods of rapid change increase the likelihood of exposure to triggering events that promote and sometimes force individual change. At these times, people who might otherwise assume that the order of their lives is given find that they must undergo personal change in order to adapt to changing social circumstances. These people experience turning points when they abandon old assumptions and confront new possibilities....

Each group can be distinguished by its initial orientation toward work and family (determined primarily by early childhood experiences) and the subsequent experience of stability or change in adulthood. Some of those who began adulthood wanting to become mothers and homemakers stayed on the domestic path; others veered away from the private sphere and into the workplace. Among those who entered adulthood ambivalent toward motherhood and aspiring for workplace accomplishments, some remained on this...path, and others moved toward domesticity over time. Those whose initial life plans did not change enjoyed supportive circumstances that sheltered them from challenges to their goals or from enticements to new directions. In contrast, unexpected obstacles or opportunities faced those who did change as they moved through the early stages of adulthood....

To understand the subtle revolution, we must determine why women born into the same historical period and confronting similar life cycle deadlines make different choices and orient themselves toward different goals as their lives proceed.

3 | Learning the Ropes

Whereas cats and canaries learn their life's work in a matter of weeks, human beings spend many years going through the long process of socialization, learning the culture of the society of which we are a part. This culture includes the norms, values, and beliefs that shape the physical, mental, and social skills expected of those who want to play a full role in society. Throughout childhood, an unknowing infant is transformed into a fully functioning social being through the process of primary socialization. In contrast, occupational socialization begins in childhood but occurs primarily in adulthood. The process of learning the ropes of a particular occupational culture—the skills, knowledge, norms, values, and beliefs—is known as **occupational socialization**. Although occupational socialization has much in common with primary socialization, it is much more focused on the learning of a particular role, the occupational role.

The Process of Occupational Socialization

Some individuals prepare for work in an occupation long before they actually enter the occupation. Once an individual enters an occupation, the process of learning the ropes includes not only gaining the knowledge and skills necessary to function in the occupation but also understanding the culture of the occupation and the culture of the immediate work environment.

Anticipatory Socialization

Socialization to particular jobs, professions, and responsibilities often occurs before people actually take on those roles. **Anticipatory socialization** is the sociological term for this phenomenon, which occurs both in a work context and in everyday life.

Consider how children learn to become parents. Most of them play at being parents long before they are actually called on to fill the role. This anticipatory socialization helps them learn about the role, although they cannot understand its full complexity unless they, as adults, actually choose to become parents. Similarly, when children pretend to be firefighters, farmers, or fry cooks, they may come to understand a bit about the role expected of them if they were to enter that occupation or something similar.

Anticipatory socialization for occupations continues into adulthood. In the medical field, for example, the premedical programs and summer internships in hospitals and physicians' offices constitute anticipatory socialization for aspiring doctors. Summer jobs, training programs, and apprenticeships offer anticipatory socialization in other occupations as well.

Formal and Informal Learning

Occupational socialization can be formal or informal. The formal aspects of some occupational roles can be learned in a matter of hours. A waiter or a waitress in a small restaurant can begin work within an hour of hiring; however, many of the informal norms and expectations of the employer, the other waiters and waitresses, and the customers may take days or weeks to learn and understand. Of course, many jobs require an even longer period of formal and informal learning. A student beginning medical school may find himself or herself immersed in the learning process for many years—throughout medical school, internships, and one or more residencies. At every step in the process—from premedical undergraduate coursework to medical school—the aspiring physician will be confronted with both formal and informal norms that need to be mastered. In Case Study 3.1, "Serving Hamburgers and Selling Insurance: Gender, Work, and Identity in Interactive Service Jobs," Robin Leidner explores both the formal and informal training that is part of learning to be effective at these two quite different service occupations. Leidner also shows how gendered expectations affect the training for jobs in service industries.

The process of learning and practicing the norms of a job applies as much to changing jobs within a company as it does to beginning a new job or profession. Even changing positions in the same company may require a dramatic change in behavior, including readjustment of relationships with others.

Although individuals may learn about their profession through formal training, other aspects of learning a profession can be more ephemeral. For example, mentor–protégé relationships can develop in any occupation but are most likely to develop in the professions. In ancient mythology, Mentor was a "wise and faithful teacher and counselor...a friend and teacher to whom Odysseus entrusted his son while he embarked on his legendary journeys" (Auster, 1984:142). Protégé, a derivative of the French word that means "to protect," refers to someone whose career is guided by a more experienced person, usually someone with more clout. While the mentor offers his or her knowledge of the real world of such fields as sociology, business, or law, the protégé offers the mentor the possibility of vicarious satisfaction when the protégé is successful. The mentor may also reap the rewards of working closely with and personally socializing a neophyte in the profession. Difficulties in some mentor–protégé relationships may occur as the protégé breaks away from the influence of the mentor—difficulties not unlike those between parents and young adults. Moreover, the mentor–protégé relationship is vulnerable because it is made up of only two people. Despite these possible problems, a mentor–protégé relationship can be one of the most important and rewarding relationships each may find in the course of his or her career.

Occupational Status and Socialization

One aspect of an occupation that has an especially significant impact on the type and length of socialization is the value society places on the occupation. Although some occupations attempt to professionalize, some risk deprofessionalization as a result of broad-reaching social forces.

Occupations Versus Professions

One measure of an occupation's status is the extent to which the occupation is considered a profession. Although you might think that the process of deciding whether an occupation is a profession would simply be based on whether the occupation is highly valued by society, it is not that easy. It is more useful to think of an occupation/profession continuum based on a set of criteria, which we will discuss. We will see that some occupations have all of the characteristics of a profession and should clearly be labeled as such, others may have some characteristics but not others, and a third group of occupations may not meet any of the criteria. For example, there may be some debate in your class about the extent to which teaching is a profession, but most would agree that teaching is more of a profession than factory work.

In medicine, the most prestigious occupation is that of physician. Despite delineations in prestige among physicians in different specialties, physicians have more power and prestige than others in the medical field such as nurse practitioners, physicians' assistants, nurses, midwives, and clerical staff. However, physicians' assistants and nurse practitioners may perform routine exams, make diagnoses, and fill the role of the physician. Whereas the physicians are considered professionals, the clerical staff are not, and those in other occupations are between the two ends of the continuum.

Some sociologists do not concern themselves with the occupation/profession continuum because they believe that the defining characteristics are vague, making classification difficult. However, for many others, the concept is valuable because occupational status affects our lives in many ways and because the professions have significant power in our society. Thus, sociologists have put some thought into what constitutes a profession.

Sociological Definitions

There are a number of ways to determine the degree to which an occupation is a profession, and sociologists have focused on a variety of aspects of the occupations to make this determination. For example, Greenwood (1957) uses five criteria to define a profession.

1. A profession must have a *systematic body of theory*. This means that abstract concepts describe the phenomena that are at the center of the professional's interest. A learned skill is not the sole equipment that a professional brings to his or her work. A complex theoretical knowledge behind the skills is required for professional practice. Moreover, some of those who are actually in the occupation should be doing research to further contribute to the knowledge in the field. A chemist uses a body of theoretical knowledge about the normal interactions of atomic particles to develop new plastics and to make suggestions for recycling existing plastics.

2. An occupation that is considered a profession should be regarded by the general public as having *professional authority* over the knowledge and skills in that field. The notion here is that clients surrender themselves to those who have professional authority and follow the professional's advice. For example, the first advice an attorney gives an arrested felon is "Be quiet." When the arrested felon transfers his or her authority to represent himself or herself to an attorney, the arrested felon recognizes the attorney's training and practice.

3. A profession must have the *sanction of the community*. One cannot use the title of that profession without the appropriate or required training. In addition, those in the profession should have a certain monopoly over the skills and knowledge associated with that profession. Although an individual may master the body of knowledge needed to treat patients, to practice medicine legally

requires the sanction of the professional community in the form of a medical degree and state licensing.

4. A profession must have a regulative *code of ethics*. The code of ethics could be devised by the professional association, by the employer, or as part of the initiation to the profession. The code of ethics defines appropriate and inappropriate behavior for those in the profession and how knowledge is shared among those in the profession. In my position as a sociologist, I adhere to a number of ethics codes. The American Sociological Association has a code of ethics that defines what my relationship should be with students and colleagues. It also provides guidelines for appropriate conduct in research. If I did not adhere to the code of ethics, I could face penalties that might end my career as a sociologist. In addition, my college has a code of ethics that sets its own limits on the behavior appropriate for a professor. Again, if I do not adhere to the appropriate conduct, action can be taken against me up to and including dismissal from my position.

5. A *professional culture* distinguishes professions from occupations. Similar to other subcultures, the professional culture has a language, symbols, and norms of its own. When a vice-president of advertising says to her colleague, "We want to be in the vertical books because the horizontal books won't get the demographics we're after," her colleague, because of his socialization to the professional culture, knows that this means their client should advertise only in specialized magazines because general interest magazines won't reach the buyers of interest. In addition, adherence to the professional culture implies a career and a lifelong commitment to the work that goes far beyond the actual working hours.

A Legal Application of Sociological Definitions. A sociological definition of profession may seem useful, but it is only one of the ways of classifying occupations. People in our society do not automatically apply Greenwood's criteria. In the example that follows, it seemed that a court of law was going to be called on to determine whether a particular occupation was a profession or not.

In 1968, Clyde and Mary Stumpf sold some lots of land in Pennsylvania to a developer. In their document of sale, they imposed the following restrictions:

> The premises hereby conveyed shall be used for residential purposes only, and no store, tavern, or other public, commercial or industrial business shall at any time be maintained thereon. The prohibition, how-

ever, shall not restrict the maintenance of *quiet, professional offices on the premises* [italics mine] provided the same are established as a part of the dwelling or other structure erected and maintained on said premises in accordance with the approved plans and specifications hereinabove required.

In 1983, Lester and Ruth Ann Carnathan wanted to open a beauty shop in their home in the development. They went before the local zoning board about signs and parking spaces, and ended up as defendants in County Court. Several of the residents of the development claimed that a beauty shop did not constitute a "quiet, professional office." The Carnathans maintained that their beauty shop was well within the definition.

I was asked to appear before the judge as an expert witness to decide if the work in this beauty shop was a profession or not. To do this, I reviewed the statutory and regulatory documents concerning cosmetology for the state of Pennsylvania. The Department of State set forth regulations about what had to be in the beauty shop and about how to run the shop, including concerns about sterilization and required equipment. The statutes also included the requirements one needed to perform cosmetology in Pennsylvania. I'll share what I learned, and then you can decide whether you think cosmetology is a profession or not.

In Pennsylvania, one must be licensed in order to practice cosmetology. To be licensed, one must have a certificate. To take the exam for certification, one must (1) be 16 years of age and of good moral character; (2) have completed a 10th grade education or its equivalent (for those 35 years of age or older and for veterans the educational requirement is waived); and (3) have completed 1,250 hours at a registered school of beauty culture, served as an apprentice for 3 years in a licensed beauty shop, or spent 24 months as an operator in another state. To enroll in beauty culture school, one must have completed the ninth grade and be of "good moral character." To teach beauty culture, one must have an operator's license, be 18 years of age, have completed the 12th grade or its equivalent, and have received 500 hours (about 13 weeks) of specialized training in addition to that needed to qualify for the operator's license. In the textbook used in beauty school at that time, three pages were devoted to ethics.

If the case hinged on the notion of the quiet professional offices, with the emphasis on *professional,* what would you have decided about cosmetology? Given the kinds of attributes that Greenwood (1957) and other sociologists use to determine a profession, to what extent do you think cosmetology fits with that scheme?

The degree of debate about this among students in my Work and Occupations class varies from year to year. Sometimes, the class feels strongly that cosmetology is not a profession. These students claim that those practicing cosmetology have little interest in the theoretical knowledge, particularly as it relates to chemical hair treatments, such as coloring, curling, or straightening. Chemists working in the research and development departments of top hair care companies focus on this work. Others in the class say that their hairdresser knows a lot about those chemicals. In retort, other students point out that these products are also sold over the counter at the drug store and that anyone can use chemicals that give results similar to those provided by a hairdresser. Others argue that some of the chemicals are available only to those who are licensed cosmetologists.

What do you think the verdict was in the Carnathan case? Unfortunately, for our goal of defining what a profession is, the judge ruled on an entirely different basis. He explained that a citizen of Pennsylvania has the right to do whatever he or she wants to with his or her own property when it does not interfere with the rights of others. When restrictions such as those in the original deed are ambiguous, that right is maintained. Although the decision did not resolve the issue of whether cosmetology was a profession or not, the decision did make clear that the Carnathans had a right to run a beauty shop in their home.

The Professions

Whether an occupation is a profession or not may have a significant impact on the process of socialization. A brief history of the position of physicians helps illustrate this. At the beginning of the 19th century, doctors were regarded as much less useful than ministers of churches. Doctors spent much less time in training and were paid less. They had a cure rate of about one patient in four—the same rate of cure they had since Hippocrates devised the physicians' oath, and nearly the same cure rate as not seeing a doctor at all. By the end of the 19th century, the cure rate of doctors was up dramatically, and their formal training had become longer and more specialized. The general reputation of doctors also grew as did the status of their occupation. Today, every doctor from general practitioner to neurosurgeon faces a longer training and socialization process than those who enter the ministry. Doctors can be sure they will be paid much better than most ministers and will be considered more useful by society—even by most of those who attend religious services. To a great extent, the **professionalization** of doctors' work, which required more formal credentialing, is what made society change its mind about the value of the occupation.

The Struggle to Professionalize.   Because of the prestige and power associated with the professions, workers in many occupations try to professionalize their occupation. By gaining a monopoly over a particular set of skills, knowledge, and service, they attain status and prestige. Most attempts to professionalize encounter resistance. Occupations that are already professions and that are closely aligned with those in the aspiring occupation often seek to maintain their current status and close the gates to the aspiring occupations.

The socialization of health care professionals provides a good example of how different occupational groups compete for professional status. At the top, aspiring physicians enter medical school with a college degree. At the end of 4 years of medical school, which includes supervised practice, they must pass a licensing exam. Moreover, they often pursue additional years of residency in specialized areas, such as general surgery, ophthalmology, or emergency medicine. Although there is some variation by state, nurse practitioners (also called nurse clinicians) must be registered nurses with a bachelor's degree in nursing, hold a master's degree as a nurse practitioner, and be certified. Licensed practical nurses (LPNs) do not need a bachelor's degree, although they must be licensed. Nursing aides and orderlies have even fewer requirements for training and certification. Nursing associations have tried to change the requirements for becoming a nurse to further enhance the position of registered nurses and nurse practitioners in the hierarchy of medical occupations (Glazer, 1991). They have tried to make a bachelor of science degree in nursing a requirement for licensing, have encouraged limited training of LPNs and aides, and have further sought to limit the tasks performed by the latter two groups. Registered nurses and nurse practitioners thus are seeking to professionalize at the expense of LPNs and nursing aides. The lower class women and women of color who are overrepresented in these less powerful occupational groups are then even further disadvantaged (Glazer, 1991). Because those who lack social status have a difficult time challenging those of higher status, the occupational socialization of LPNs and nursing aides is often dictated by those in dominant social categories. In the same way, medical licensing boards (which are dominated by doctors) and physician associations have encouraged policies that help doctors maintain their profession position.

Nurse practitioners also engage in turf battles with physicians' assistants (PAs). Unlike nurse practitioners, PAs have a wide variety of backgrounds. Some entering PA training may be registered nurses, but others hold an associate's or bachelor's degree that can be in any field. PAs must then complete a 2-year physicians' assistant certification program and be supervised by a physician in his or her work. The physicians' assistant programs were developed after the Vietnam War to take advantage of the experience of the medics who treated severely wounded soldiers in combat, but who, after the war, had no job in which they could use their experience. Nurse practitioner programs were seen as an extension of the existing registered nurse programs. We still find that PAs are often in acute care, specializing in cardiothoracic surgery or emergency care. Nurse practitioners are more likely to be found caring for patients with chronic problems. Despite these patterns, PAs and nurse practitioners are found in a wide variety of similar and overlapping areas in medicine. Thus, the two frequently battle over status and prestige.

Socialization into the Professions. As you have seen, the process of professionalization involves gaining a monopoly over a particular set of skills, knowledge, and service. One means of increasing the status of an occupation is to further credential the group with increased education, training, licensing, and certification. In fact, our society seems to have a great desire to require more credentials of employees (Collins, 1979). The first consequence of this for those who are in the profession or aspiring to it is more work and more sacrifice. The socialization process for many professions is formal and admittedly more lengthy than it would be if the occupation were not a profession. Some of that training is useful for performance in the occupation, but other aspects of the training and socialization appear to be part of the process of initiation to a prestigious profession. In Case Study 3.2, "One L," Scott Turow describes his experiences as a first-year law student. The intimidating nature of the culture of the law school classroom interaction and his overly competitive peers leave the author confused and scared at the end of his first day of class.

The emphasis on credentialing may actually leave the neophyte practitioner without many of the skills needed to function day to day as a lawyer, professor, physician, or veterinarian. For example, the final credential most often needed to teach at the college level is that of a Ph.D. Thus, much of the graduate training of your professors focused on the accumulation of knowledge and the preparation to be researchers. The central requirement of a Ph.D. is a thesis or dissertation, which must demonstrate that the aspiring professor is able to pursue a lengthy research project independently. The written product that results from this project must meet with the approval of a faculty committee. This committee is not designed to evaluate the candidate as a teacher. Despite holding the credential (the Ph.D.), many faculty starting their first full-fledged college-level teaching position are unprepared to teach classes. They might have been teaching assistants during their graduate school career—a position that typically requires holding student discussion groups, helping with the writing and grading of exams and other assignments, and giving only an occasional original lecture. New faculty members are expected to develop their own courses including choosing the readings and preparing their own classes and lecture materials. Graduate programs typically offer little formal training in teaching.

The transition from graduate student to professor is often abrupt in every field from astronomy to zoology. Even Doctors of Education who may have devoted their time in graduate school to the study of administration become experts in that aspect of education but are no more prepared to face a classroom of students than is a physicist who spent most of her graduate career studying in an underground particle accelerator laboratory. Graduate programs in some disciplines are taking actions to help ease the transition from graduate student to professor. In some sociology programs, these actions include a required component of graduate training that specifically focuses on teaching. Other sociology programs formally introduce the business of counseling and consulting to those who choose clinical and applied sociology.

Training in other professions is also expanding to include practical and personal aspects of professional work, bringing the training more in line with the work that will later be expected of the professional. For example, the Cornell University veterinary school recently changed its training program. First-year veterinary students now have contact with their future patients—the animals. In the past, this experience was available only to third- and fourth-year veterinary medicine students.

In Case Study 3.3, "The Fate of Idealism in Medical School," Howard Becker and Blanche Geer examine aspiring physicians' progress through medical school. Although students have an idealistic view of medicine when they begin medical school, the training they receive often does not fit with their expectations. Students often feel that their socialization in medical school—the formal training— is irrelevant to the training to become a doctor. Many medical students feel that the informal socialization, such as learning from their peers and interacting with patients, is better preparation for their lives as doctors. In this respect, they are much like aspiring professors and veterinarians, as well as many other professionals.

In summary, professionalization appears to go hand in hand with longer and more formal socialization. Socialization to the professions tends to be longer than that of other occupations and places more emphasis on formal requirements and credentialing. At the same time, many new professionals, armed with considerable technical skill and knowledge, are unprepared to deal with the requirements of their everyday work life. The result is that university or department administrators are working to institute requirements that cause the formal socialization to the occupation to be more in line with what will later be expected of the professional.

Deprofessionalization. At the same time that those in some occupations are trying to professionalize further, there are strong forces that are deprofessionalizing the professions. Rothman (1984) summarizes seven forces toward deprofessionalization in his consideration of the place of lawyers in the United States.

- *Narrowing of the competence gap.* If those in the professions are supposed to have an expertise that others do not, what happens if the average educational level of a population increases? Or, perhaps more important, what happens when people's general knowledge and competence in a particular area, the specialty of the professional, increase? In addition, the "routinization of expert knowledge," such as the inexpensive computer programs that one can use to write a will or draw up a divorce decree, narrows the competence gap. With regard to health and medical issues, too, many people are more informed than ever before. For example, a runner finishes a race with a pain in her heel. Other runners tell her she has a bone spur. She confirms this diagnosis with two self-help medical books and then goes to the podiatrist recommended by her friends without consulting the family doctor. At the podiatrist's office, she says, "I have a bone spur. What's the best thing to do about that?" This woman and other avid athletes like her view doctors more as resources than authorities. In addition, more individuals seek a second opinion. Although the second opinion often results in confirmation of the first diagnosis or treatment, it puts the expertise of the first professional in question. Similarly, the televised trial of O. J. Simpson, accused of a double homicide, has brought the public closer to and further informed them of intricate court proceedings.

- *Specialization within particular professions.* Specialization may threaten the professional status. Although increasing specialization would at first seem to enhance professional status because of the greater in-depth knowledge of the specialist, it interferes with the group solidarity or community expected among those sharing the same profession.

- *Competition among those in a particular profession.* Competition detracts from the professional status. This competition can take the form of advertising, such as that in which particular personal injury lawyers have engaged. When lawyers advertise recovery of damages, they trade the dispassionate authority image of an officer of the court for one of a "hired gun" whose sole aim is the good of the client—even if that good has no connection with fairness or justice. Two scientists in the same field race to complete an experiment so that they can be credited with discovery rather than working together to achieve even greater heights of knowledge. Although this conduct may raise the status of that individual, it lowers the image of the profession.

- *Inadequate policing of others in the profession.* The failure of licensing and certification boards to punish the members of the profession, even when offenses are clear, are made public, and include conduct universally acknowledged as wrong, further calls the occupation's professional status into question. In Pennsylvania, a state supreme court judge was recently indicted on multiple charges of prescription drug fraud. He was taking illegal doses of narcotics and getting the pills by using friends' names on the prescriptions. The judge was removed from the bench but continued to receive full pay and benefits for months. He may never be disbarred.

- *Encroachment from allied professions.* Accountants, bankers, tax consultants, and realtors often do tasks that the field of law had sole propriety of in the past. This means that law, for example, no longer has a monopoly over provision of these services, and that detracts from professional status.

- *Organizational employment.* An increasing number of professionals—lawyers, physicians, sociologists—are employed by large organizations and companies. Their loyalties tend to shift from the profession to the employer. For example, lawyers who choose government employment find that their "individual independence, initiative, and judgement may be circumscribed by organizational priorities and a bureaucratic structure that stresses centralized authority and standardized procedures" (Rothman, 1984: 196). In his book *The McDonaldization of Society*, Ritzer describes a heart surgeon "who performs delicate open-heart surgery in a 'heart surgery factory' that operates 'with the precision of an assembly line'" (1993: 52). He also points to the expansion of hospitals, medical conglomerates, chains, health maintenance organizations, third-party payers, and government in the lives of physicians (54). Although autonomy has been an important identifier of those in the professions in the past, employment in large organizations may place increasing limits on this autonomy in the future.

■ *Shifting demographics.* In the past, the professions were dominated by white males. Now, an increasing number of women and minorities have gained access to the professions, a trend we examined in Chapter 2. The newer groups may bring different views concerning the role that the profession should play in policy issues. This diversity may interfere with professional status as it "contrasts with earlier perceptions of a homogenous professional community" (Heinz et al., 1982; Rothman, 1984).

Although social scientists appear to agree on the forces at work in our society such as increasing bureaucratization, they disagree about the impact of these forces on the position of the professions. Some sociologists argue that these forces do not necessarily detract from professional status (Anleu, 1992). Instead, they constitute new ways of achieving power and monopoly. For example, increasing organizational employment and specialization have allowed lawyers to exert control on medicine, science, and finance far beyond their traditional role. Anleu also argues that large firms, although admittedly more bureaucratic, offer lawyers more choices of specialty and deal with some of the largest, most controversial, and most complex legal issues (1992: 191). Thus, lawyers gain even more power and control and the concomitant prestige associated with this. Lawyers (and other professionals) will continue to control the process by which lawyers become lawyers because they control the certification and socialization processes.

Workplace Influences on Socialization

Learning the ropes of a new occupational position may seem to be a personal and individualized process. Based on their own personality, individuals will make choices about how they adopt some of the occupational expectations. However, many other aspects of socialization are shaped by factors outside the individual. The process of socialization is affected, as you have seen, by the value society places on that occupation as a profession. The process of socialization is also affected by a variety of aspects of the workplace, including the risk or danger associated with work in the occupation, the place of the occupation in a particular organization, and the diversity of individuals in that occupation in the workplace.

Job Characteristics

Characteristics of the work itself influence the process of socialization. For example, the danger associated with the work in particular occupations influences the way people become socialized. In Case Study 3.4, "Learning Real Feelings: A Study of High Steel Ironworkers' Reactions to Fear and Danger," which is about workers who assemble the skeletons of tall buildings, Jack Haas offers an interesting perspective on socialization to that job arising from his experience as a participant-observer. This case study enlightens us about the role of physical danger—and perhaps other job characteristics—in the process of occupational socialization.

Type of Organization

The type of organization in which a person works is another important influence on socialization. It determines much of what the worker must learn to be a functioning person in the occupation. A work organization may be one of three types:

- Publicly held, such as IBM, Xerox, and Ford, which issue stock (and therefore ownership) to the public.
- Privately held, including anything from an individually owned house-painting business to a large partnership employing hundreds of people.
- Nonprofit, including colleges and universities, every level of government, and every organized religious group.

The work environment, and therefore the socialization process, differs widely among these three because their corporate goals, or reasons for existing as an organization or a corporation, are different. Publicly held corporations must first and foremost make a profit for their shareholders. If they do other good things in this process, that is a benefit to us all; but their main business is to make money for their owners, the shareholders. Privately held companies also exist for the profit of the owner or owners, but the owner is obliged to no one to make a profit. Nonprofit corporations are guided by an intangible goal other than profit, such as the education of students. Because the goal of a nonprofit organization is, in general, harder to define than that of a profit-making corporation, socialization is guided by the mission statement. Note that socialization in any type of workplace can be guided by the quirks of the management or owners as well as the overall mission.

Let's look at what it means to be socialized to the same job in each of the three types of occupational settings. Three college friends, JoAnne, Jeff, and Jill, get jobs as public relations assistants. JoAnne works for Procter & Gamble (the detergent company), a publicly held corporation; Jeff is hired by a large Philadelphia architectural firm, a privately held business; and Jill works for a hospital with a regional trauma center, a nonprofit organization.

JoAnne is hired by Procter & Gamble because she can write well and talk confidently to reporters about products. Her supervisor encourages her to learn everything she can about detergents and differences among various brands. In her first days on the job, JoAnne writes press releases about a new no-phosphate detergent. Within 6 months her story idea about environmentally responsible detergent is picked up by *Woman's Day* magazine. JoAnne learns that anything that increases sales and the visibility of Procter & Gamble earns praise from her supervisor, praise that informs her of the goals to which she needs to be socialized. Within a year she earns a bonus and a staff position, rewards that make clear that she has been well socialized to the goals of this profit corporation: gaining visibility and increasing sales. Although a number of aspects of her socialization could be true of any well-managed organization, a publicly held company would seem to be more accountable. The presence of stockholders and the singular goal of profit cause such companies to develop clear policies and criteria for job performance.

Jeff, employed by the privately owned architectural firm, takes pointers from JoAnne and goes for national coverage of a design innovation in air conditioning his firm pioneered. Although Jeff was doing what he was trained to do and his efforts were well received, he felt he was missing something. This was partially due to the autonomy of Jeff's job and the relative lack of supervision and socialization. After 6 months, Jeff's supervisor told him he was doing a great job and then let him know, indirectly, that the owner's real goal was to get his picture on the cover of *Architectural Digest*. Jeff took the hint, dropped every other idea he had, and started working on the editor of *Architectural Digest*. It took almost 2 years and caused the neglect of opportunities that could have generated more business for the firm. But, Jeff's success depended on knowing and pursuing the real goal of the owner, not taking the traditional route. The relative lack of supervision is not necessarily endemic to privately held companies, but the lack of accountability to outsiders means the owner can continue his business practices without the fear of being fired. An owner loses his job only at the point at which he chooses, unless he finds it necessary to file for bankruptcy.

At the hospital, Jill jumped into her work. She talked with surgical nurses, laundry workers, accounting assistants—anyone who could give her stories about the selfless dedication of the hospital staff. She worked up her ideas, presented them to her boss, and waited while he made an appointment to talk to his boss, who wanted to see what the fund raiser thought, who wanted to know what the president thought. She was sometimes invited to meetings in which her ideas were considered by up to a dozen staff members. These ad hoc committees killed more ideas than they kept. After almost a year of frustration, she found that upper management wanted to be recognized and applauded for the trauma center. The rest of the hospital was of secondary concern. Jill still suffered the committee approval of her ideas, but she was much happier and more productive when she figured out that her superiors wanted to emphasize a larger mission to serve the community.

In each of these three cases, the new employee had to learn not only the formal and stated goals of the organization, but also the real and often informal goals. The goal of JoAnne's organization was to maximize profit. The goal of Jeff's was to gratify the organization's owner. And the goal of Jill's was to maximize community perceptions of the organization's ability to achieve its service mission through a participatory decision-making process.

Dynamics of Tokenism

The proportion of individuals of a certain gender, racial, or ethnic group in an occupation may also have an impact on the process of occupational socialization. In *Men and Women of the Corporation*, Rosabeth Kanter (1977) writes about the dynamics of disproportionate representation in a large corporation she calls Indsco. She writes about skewed groups in which the ratio of men to women is 85 to 15. Kanter describes how those in the minority become tokens, regardless of whether the token is defined by gender, race, ethnicity, or another visible social category. Although the women hired at Indsco were meant to represent the company's commitment to gender equality, they were treated differently from the majority in many ways, including how they were socialized to their occupation and to the organization. The women executives' socialization was made potentially more difficult by three dynamics of majority/token situations:

- *Heightened visibility.* The women found that others were watching them more carefully. As tokens, they were more noticeable. They were paraded in front of clients, and the spotlight was on them. Although this could potentially be helpful when these women had successes, it also made many more people aware of blunders committed by a neophyte in the early stages of socialization to a new position. Moreover, some men resented the heightened visibility of the women when they were successful.

- *Boundary heightening.* The presence of only a few tokens made the dominants more aware of these tokens. At Indsco, when men were around token women, there were sometimes exaggerated displays of aggression and potency, incidents of sexual innuendos, and prowess-oriented war stories (223). This boundary heightening often led to the exclusion of women from some of the informal socialization available to their male colleagues.

- *Role encapsulation.* Women at Indsco seemed to get cast into one of four stereotyped roles: the mother, the one the men told their private troubles to with the expectation of being comforted; the seductress, the one who needed to be protected by a powerful male who would keep others away; the pet, the one who was taken along to meetings and who was expected to admire male displays; and the iron maiden, the one who would not mold herself into the other roles. Being cast into any of these limiting roles made it less possible for these women executives to bring their own personality to their work effectiveness. Moreover, it meant that rather than using time for informal socialization, the male colleagues were engaged in conversations that fit with the woman's expected role. For example, if she was cast as the mother, she would be more likely to hear about their problems at home than how to produce the most appropriate information for the next meeting with a client. As an iron maiden, she was often left to fend for herself, not privy to the helpful information provided in the process of informal socialization.

Kanter's framework can be extended to other occupations as well. For instance, in Case Study 3.5, "Equal Versus Equitable Treatment: Policewomen and Patrol Work," Susan Martin describes how the occupational socialization of policewomen differs somewhat from that of policemen. The difference is due to a combination of both tokenism and gender. In Case Study 3.6, "Becoming a Male Stripper: Recruitment, Socialization, and Ideological Development," Paula Dressel and David Petersen describe how men, as tokens, are socialized as male strippers, an occupational position more often filled by women. One difference in this situation, however, is that those in the minority, the men, do not typically work in the same place as the women. In addition, it is an occupational role that many consider deviant. The authors tell us that "because of minimal anticipatory socialization the dancers' first performances generated uncertainty and anxiety" (346). Does anticipatory socialization in general make a difference, or is it the actual time in an occupational position that makes a difference? Think of jobs that you have held and the ones in which you were most nervous in the beginning.

Although Kanter describes the dynamics for women as tokens at Indsco, she argues that these dynamics emerge in any workplace situation where individuals with a socially visible characteristic constitute a small minority of the workers. The dynamics of tokenism, with its consequences for socialization, can occur whether the socially visible characteristic is race, ethnicity, age, religion, sexual orientation, or physical disability.

Societal Influences on Socialization

We have just seen how occupational socialization can be affected by a variety of aspects of the workplace and working environment. Occupational socialization can also be influenced by larger societal trends such as the level of technology associated with the occupation, the type of economy, and the development of the global economy.

Technological Advancement

Those entering even the most mundane occupations have the potential to bring more technological expertise to their work than ever before. Typically, older and more experienced workers socialize their younger and less experienced colleagues to the norms of the occupational and organizational culture. *Reverse socialization* refers to the situation where those who are younger play a large role in socializing those who are older. The increasing use of computers and other technology means that often special trainers from outside the organization or those who have been most recently trained find themselves in the position of training and thus socializing older or longer term employees of an organization to the latest technology. For example, many stockbrokers are learning about new software packages from recent college graduates whose job it is to fly around the country and retrain these long-time securities traders. Although some stockbrokers are excited about the new technology, others strongly connected to paper trading slips reluctantly participate in the mandatory training sessions.

Some argue that technology has had the effect of requiring less from the worker, a declining level of skill. This is referred to as **deskilling**. In deskilling, socialization to the formal aspects of the job declines, but the socialization to the work culture and the ways of dealing with a mostly automated job may become more important. Since deskilling may be linked to alienation, we will return to this topic in Chapter 4 on workers' feelings and again in Chapter 7.

Growth of the Service Sector

Our society has been transformed from that of an agricultural economy, to a largely industrial economy, to our current service economy. In a service economy, more corporations than ever before are in the business of providing services, rather than manufactured goods, to their customers. Because of this, more jobs require the employee to interact not only with coworkers, but also with the clients or customers to whom the services are being provided. Hochschild (1983), in her book *The Managed Heart*, provides examples of workers who must now engage in *emotion work*. That is, part of their job is to provide their clients or customers with a particular feeling. Providing customers with such feelings also requires that the employees control their own emotions, portraying only emotions appropriate to the circumstance. This required control of emotions and appropriate emotional responses must be learned as part of the process of occupational socialization. Hochschild explains, for example, how airline flight attendants are trained to control their own feelings in order to create feelings of security and comfort in their passengers. For example, in the midst of a turbulent flight, the attendants must reassure passengers of their safety. Also, flight attendants must treat even obnoxious passengers with courtesy and politeness.

The Global Economy

The globalization of the economy also has an impact on socialization. Although many employees may remain provincial in their outlook, white-collar workers increasingly find themselves learning the language and culture of other countries in which their company does business. The problem of interacting and negotiating across cultures is examined in the *Sloan Management Review*, a prestigious business journal. In "Negotiating with 'Romans'" Weiss (1994a, 1994b) explains how to interact with those from other cultures, cautioning that the expectations for outsiders may be different from those for insiders. Weiss also points out that one needs to both reflect on the negotiating style of one's own culture and be cognizant of the negotiating style of the other party's culture to avoid misunderstandings in the negotiation process. Thus, one consequence of the global economy is that the process of socialization requires additional emphasis on how to interact with others from a variety of cultural backgrounds. For example, American managers who run factories in another culture need to learn to communicate their expectations to their employees in a language that can be understood both literally and figuratively.

Conclusion

Although it may have at first appeared that the process of being socialized to an occupation was largely a function of individual choice or the particular choice of the individuals in the immediate work environment who may be formally or informally "in charge" of the socialization process, this chapter points to a variety of aspects of the occupations that have an impact on the content of the process of socialization. For physicians and many other high-status white-collar professionals, the high degree of necessary skills and knowledge along with the occupation's professional status has a tremendous impact on the process of socialization. The effects of technological advancement, the service economy, and globalization also influence the way in which individuals are socialized to their occupations. Other factors, such as the risk associated with the occupation, described by the high steel workers, can have a dramatic impact on the actions, ideologies, and ultimately the emotions associated with dangerous work. Thus, although individual choice is a factor, a variety of characteristics of the occupation itself and a variety of societal changes also influence occupations and ultimately occupational socialization.

REFERENCES AND SUGGESTED READINGS

Anleu, Sharyn L. Roach. 1992. "The Legal Profession in the United States and Australia: Deprofessionalization or Reorganization." *Work and Occupations* 19 (2): 184–204.

Auster, Donald. 1984. "Mentors and Protégés: Power-Dependent Dyads." *Sociological Inquiry* 54 (Spring): 142–153.

Collins, Randall. 1979. *The Credential Society.* New York: Academic Press.

Glazer, Nona Y. 1991. "Between a Rock and a Hard Place: Women's Professional Organizations in Nursing and Class, Racial, and Ethnic Inequalities." *Gender and Society* 5 (3): 351–372.

Greenwood, Ernest 1957. "Attributes of a Profession." *Social Work* 2 (July): 45–55.

Heinz, John P., and Edward O. Laumann. 1982. *Chicago Lawyers: The Social Structure of the Bar*. New York: Russell Sage.

Hochschild, Arlie. 1983. *The Managed Heart*. Berkeley: University of California Press.

Kanter, Rosabeth. 1977. *Men and Women of the Corporation*. New York: Basic Books.

Riemer, Jeffrey W. 1979. *Hard Hats: The World of Construction Workers*. Beverly Hills: Sage.

Ritzer, George. 1993. *The McDonaldization of Society*. Newbury Park, CA: Pine Forge Press.

Rothman, Robert A. 1984. "Deprofessionalization: The Case of Law in America." *Work and Occupations* 11 (2): 183–206.

Weiss, Stephen. 1994a. "Negotiating with 'Romans'—Part 1. *Sloan Management Review* 35 (2): 51–61.

Weiss, Stephen. 1994b. "Negotiating with 'Romans'—Part 2. *Sloan Management Review* 35 (3): 85–99.

Serving Hamburgers and Selling Insurance:

Gender, Work, and Identity
in Interactive Service Jobs

Robin Leidner

CASE STUDY QUESTIONS

1. As you look at serving hamburgers and selling insurance, what do you learn about the work of individuals engaged in these two occupations?

2. How does the gendered nature of the expectations affect the formal and informal socialization process? How explicit are supervisors' expectations?

3. How does the process of being socialized to emotional labor differ from the process of being socialized to physical labor?

4. What are the consequences of learning the proper emotions for feelings about work?

All workers look for ways to reconcile the work they do with an identity they can accept, either by interpreting the work positively or by discounting the importance of the work as a basis of identity....

Author's Note: I would like to thank Carol A. Heimer, Arthur L. Stinchcombe, Arlene Kaplan Daniels, Sam Kaplan, Judith Lorber, and the *Gender & Society* reviewers for their help and suggestions.

Source: From *Gender and Society*, Vol. 5, No. 2, 1991, pp. 154–177. Reprinted by permission of Sage Publications, Inc.

Interactive service jobs have several distinctive features that make them especially revealing for investigation of the interrelation of work, gender, and identity. These jobs differ from other types of work in that the distinctions among product, work process, and worker are blurred or nonexistent, since the quality of the interaction may itself be part of the service offered (Hochschild 1983). In many kinds of interactive service work, workers' identities are therefore not incidental to the work but are an integral part of it. Interactive jobs make use of workers' looks, personalities, and emotions, as well as their physical and intellectual capacities, sometimes forcing them to manipulate their identities more self-consciously than do workers in other kinds of jobs. The types of relations with service recipients structured by the jobs may also force workers to revise taken-for-granted moral precepts about personal interaction. Workers who feel that they owe others sincerity, individual consideration, nonmanipulativeness, or simply full attention may find that they cannot be the sort of people they want to be and still do their jobs adequately (Hochschild 1983). While a variety of distancing strategies and rationalizations are possible (Rollins 1985), it may be difficult for interactive service workers to separate themselves from the identities implied by their jobs (Leidner 1988).

When interactive work is routinized, workers' interactions are directly controlled by employers, who may use scripting, uniforms, rules about proper demeanor and appearance, and even far-reaching attempts at psychological reorientation to standardize service encounters. The interactions are expressly designed to achieve a certain tone (friendliness, urgency) and a certain end (a sale, a favorable impression, a decision). Analysis of how employers try to combine the proper interactive elements to achieve the desired effects can make visible the processes by which meaning, control, and identity are ordinarily created through interaction in all kinds of settings. Workers' and service recipients' acceptance or rejection of the terms of the standardized interactions and their efforts to tailor the prescribed roles and routines to suit their own purposes are similarly revealing about the extent to which people sustain beliefs about who they are through how they treat others and are treated by them.

Gender is necessarily implicated in the design and enactment of service interactions....

[S]cripts can embody assumptions about proper gendered behavior in fairly obvious ways. To do such jobs as intended, workers must "do gender" in a particular way (Berk 1985b; West and Zimmerman 1987). Even where the gender component is less obvious, workers in all kinds of jobs need to consider how their work relates to their own identities, including their gender identities. Whether workers take pride in the work itself or see it as stigmatizing, whether they work harder than is required or put in the least effort they can get away with, and whether they identify themselves with the job or seek self-definition elsewhere are related not just to job tasks and working conditions but to the extent that the jobs can be interpreted as honorable, worthwhile, and suitable for persons of their gender (Ouellet 1986).

This process of interpretation may be unusually salient and unusually open to analysis in routinized interactive service work. In such jobs, a convincing performance is important, and so employers are concerned about the degree to which workers enact their roles with conviction. The employers may therefore participate in reconciling workers' selves with the identities demanded by the work by providing positive interpretations of the work role or psychic strategies for dealing with its potentially unpleasant or demeaning aspects. In short, employers of interactive service workers may be unusually open in their attempts to channel workers' attitudes and manipulate workers' identities....

I conducted fieldwork at McDonald's and at Combined Insurance Company of America. At McDonald's, my research centered on the food servers who dealt directly with the public (*window crew*, in McDonald's parlance), and at Combined Insurance, I studied life insurance agents. These jobs were not strictly gender segregated, but they were held predominantly by either men or women, influencing how workers, employers, and customers thought about the jobs. Most, but not all, of McDonald's window crew were young women, and almost all of Combined Insurance's agents were men. Their gender attributes were not essential to their jobs. In fact, both jobs can be gender typed in the opposite direction—in its early years, McDonald's hired only men (Boas and Chain 1976), and in Japan, door-to-door insurance sales is a woman's job (*Life Insurance Business in Japan*, 1987/88).

Workers in both jobs tried to make sense of de facto job segregation by gender, interpreting their jobs as congruent with proper gender enactment. Examination of these two jobs and of how workers thought about them highlights a central paradox in the construction of gender: The considerable flexibility of notions of proper gender enactment does not undermine the appearance of inevitability and naturalness that continues to support the division of labor by gender. Although the work of the insurance agents required many of the same kinds of interactive behavior as the McDonald's job, including behavior that would ordinarily be considered feminine, the agents were able to interpret the work as suitable only for men. They did so by emphasizing aspects of their job that required "manly" attributes and by thinking about their interactive work in terms of control rather than deference. Their interpretation suggests not only the plasticity of gender idioms but the asymmetry of those idioms: Defining work as masculine has a different meaning for men workers than defining work as feminine has for women workers.

Because interactive service work by definition involves nonemployees in the work process, the implications of the gender constructions of the routines extend beyond the workers. When service jobs are done predominantly by men or predominantly by women, the gender segregation provides confirming "evidence" to the public that men and women have different natures and capabilities. This appearance is especially ironic when employers, treating their workers' selves as fairly malleable, reshape the self-presentations and interactional styles of the service workers. A brief account of my fieldwork and of the routinization of the two jobs precedes further discussion of how work, gender, and identity are enmeshed in these jobs.

Routinized Interactions

My data were gathered from participant observation and interviewing. I attended classes at McDonald's management training center, Hamburger University, in June 1986, and spoke with "professors" and trainees there. I conducted research at a local McDonald's franchise from May through November 1986, going through orientation and window-crew training, working on the window, interviewing window workers and managers, and hanging around the crew room to observe and talk with workers. At Combined Insurance, I went through the two-week training for life insurance agents in January 1987. Between January and March, I interviewed trainees and managers and spent one-and-a-half weeks in the field with a sales team, observing sales calls and talking to agents. Since insurance agents must be licensed and bonded, I did not actually sell insurance myself. I also conducted follow-up interviews with Combined Insurance managers in the summer of 1989. The workers and managers with whom I worked at both companies were aware that I was conducting research.

These two jobs were similar in a number of ways. Both were filled, by and large, with young, inexperienced workers, and both had extremely high rates of employee turnover. Neither job is held in high esteem by the public, which affected both customers' treatment of workers and the workers' willingness to embrace their roles (see Zelizer 1979, on the low prestige of life insurance agents). The companies, however, took training very seriously, and they carried the routinization of service interactions very far indeed. McDonald's and Combined Insurance each tried to exercise extensive control over their workers' presentation of themselves. However, they went about this task differently and placed different sorts of demands on their workers' psyches. The differences largely have to do with the kinds of relations that the companies established between workers and customers and are related to the gender typing of the work.

McDonald's

McDonald's has been a model of standardization for many kinds of service businesses, and its success, based upon the replication of standard procedures, has been truly phenomenal. The goal is to provide the same quality of food and service every day at every McDonald's, and the company tries to leave nothing to chance. Individual franchisees have considerable leeway in some matters, including labor practices, but they are held to strict standards when it comes to the McDonald's basics of QSC—quality, service, and cleanliness.

At the McDonald's where I worked, all of the workers were hired at the minimum wage of $3.35. There were no fringe benefits and no guarantee of hours of work. As is typical at McDonald's, most men worked on the grill, and most women worked serving customers—about three-quarters of the window workers were women. About 80 percent of the restaurant's employees were Black, though Blacks were a minority of the city's population. Few of the workers were older than their early 20s, but most were out of high school—65 percent of my sample were 18 or over. The clientele, in contrast, was quite diverse in class, race, age, and gender.

The window workers were taught their jobs in a few hours and were fully trained in a couple of days. The job involved carrying out the "Six Steps of Window Service," an unvarying routine for taking and delivering orders. The modern cash registers used at this McDonald's made it unnecessary for window workers to remember prices or to know how to calculate change. The machines also reminded workers to "suggestive sell": For example, if someone ordered a Big Mac, french fries, and a shake, the cash register's buttons for apple pies, ice cream, and cookies would light up, to remind the worker to suggest dessert. (Garson [1988] provides a scathing view of McDonald's routinization and computeriza-

tion.) These workers were closely supervised, not only by McDonald's managers, but also by customers, whose constant presence exerted pressure to be diligent and speedy.

The workers wore uniforms provided by McDonald's and were supposed to look clean-cut and wholesome—for instance, a young man with a pierced ear had to wear a Band-Aid on his earlobe. The lack of control workers had over their self-presentations was brought home clearly when a special promotion of Shanghai McNuggets began, and window workers were forced to wear big Chinese peasant hats made of Styrofoam, which most felt made them look ridiculous.

Workers were told to be themselves on the job, but they were also told to be cheerful and polite at all times. Crew people were often reprimanded for not smiling. Almost all of the workers I interviewed said that most customers were pleasant to deal with, but the minority of rude or unreasonable customers had a disproportionate impact. Enduring customers' behavior, no matter how obnoxious, was a basic part of the job. Unfortunately for the workers, they completely lacked what Hochschild calls a "status shield" (1983, 163). Some customers who might have managed to be polite to higher-status workers seemed to have no compunction at all about snarling at McDonald's employees. The window crew could not escape from angry customers by leaving, and they were not allowed to argue or make smart-alecky remarks. Their only legitimate responses to rudeness or angry outbursts from customers were to control their anger, apologize, try to correct the problem, and in extreme cases, ask a manager to handle it.

The major task for the workers was to serve, and their major psychic task was to control or suppress the self. Workers were required to be nice to one person after another in a way that was necessarily unindividualized and to keep their tempers no matter how they were treated. What McDonald's demanded of its workers was a stripped-down interactive style, with some *pseudo-gemeinschaft* thrown in. The workers were supposed to be efficient, courteous, and friendly, but in short bursts and within a very narrow range. While they were told to be themselves, there was obviously not much range for self-expression.

Combined Insurance

Combined Insurance placed very different sorts of demands on its workers. The company's business is based on door-to-door sales in rural areas and small towns, and its profits depend on a high volume of sales of relatively inexpensive policies. Combined Insurance was founded in the 1920s by W. Clement Stone, and its agents still use many of the sales and self-conditioning techniques that he developed when he started out in the business—*The Success System That Never Fails* (Stone 1962). Almost all of the company's life insurance agents are men, most are white, and most are young—all of the members of the sales team I studied were in their early twenties. The prospects I called on with the agents were all white, about equally men and women, and quite varied in age.

The agents' initial training was more extensive than the McDonald's workers', involving two weeks of lectures, script memorization, and role playing. During sales school, trainees were taught what to say and do in almost hilarious detail. They memorized scripts for the basic sales presentations, for Rebuttals 1 through 5, corresponding to Objections 1 through 5, and for Interruption-stoppers. They were taught exactly how to stand while waiting for a door to be opened, how to position themselves and the potential customers (known as "prospects"), when to make and break eye contact, how to deliver the Standard Joke, and so on. A lot of class time was spent chanting the scripts in unison and rehears-

ing proper body movements, as well as in practicing responses to be used in various sales situations.

The trainer underlined the possibility of success through standardization with stories of foreign-born agents who succeeded even before they could speak English—they allegedly learned their sales presentations phonetically. It might seem that the message of these stories was that a parrot could succeed in this job, but in fact, the trainer argued that personal characteristics were vitally important to success, and the most important of these was a Positive Mental Attitude—what Stone called PMA. While McDonald's merely instructed workers to smile and behave pleasantly to customers, Combined Insurance tried to affect its employees' psyches quite fundamentally—to inculcate optimism, determination, enthusiasm, and confidence and to destroy habits of negative thinking. The trainees were taught that through proper self-conditioning, they could learn to suppress negative thoughts altogether. The message for agents was somewhat paradoxical: You should do everything exactly the way we tell you to, but success depends on your strength of character.[1]

While McDonald's workers' main task was to serve people who had already chosen to do business with McDonald's, Combined Insurance's agents had to sell, to take prospects and turn them into customers. The agents' job was to establish rapport quickly with the people they called on (by "warming up the prospect"), to go through the basic sales presentation, to counter any objections raised by the prospects, and to persuade them to buy as much life insurance as possible. Naturally, most of the people they called on were strongly motivated to prevent them from going through this sequence, so their task was not easy. Since the agents' incomes were entirely based on commission, and their desire to handle their interactions successfully was of course very great, the detailed instructions for proper behavior provided by the company did not seem to strike them as ludicrous or intrusive.

Because the agents worked on their own, rather than in a central workplace, and because their interactions with customers could be much longer and cover a broader range than those of McDonald's workers, the agents were called on to use much more of their selves than the window workers were. They had to motivate themselves and keep up their enthusiasm, and they had to respond appropriately to a wide variety of situations, adjusting their behavior to suit the problems presented by each prospect. Although their basic routine was unvaried, they needed to be chameleon-like to a certain extent and adapt to circumstances. They were, like the McDonald's workers, required to control themselves, but their focus was always on controlling the prospect and the interaction. Virtually every detail of their routines was designed to help them do just that.

Doing Gender While Doing the Job

Although their jobs were largely segregated by gender, McDonald's and Combined Insurance workers interacted with both men and women as customers or prospects. Neither company suggested significantly different approaches to men and women service recipients; the Combined Insurance trainer recommended slightly varied techniques for persuading men and women to buy policies without first consulting their spouses. While the gender of the service recipient might well have influenced how the workers experienced their interactions, I did not find consistent patterns of variation in workers' behavior along this dimension.

At McDonald's, most of the window crew took the division of labor by gender for granted and did not seem to feel any need to account for it. Since there were no differences in the pay or prestige of window and

grill work, and since there were exceptions to the pattern of gender segregation, few workers considered the division of labor by gender unfair.[2] When I asked the workers why they thought that there were more women than men working the window, about two-thirds of the 23 respondents said that they did not know, with about half offering a guess based on stereotypes about proper gender roles, whether or not they thought the stereotype was justified. About one-quarter of the sample, however, stated explicitly that they disapproved of the division of labor by gender, and three women said that they had asked a manager about it. The store's manager told me that women were typically assigned to start work on the window because "more females have an aversion to grill." Two of the window workers, however (both Black men), thought that men might have an aversion to window because that job required swallowing one's pride and accepting abuse calmly:

Theo: [More women than men work window] because women are afraid of getting burned [on the grill], and men are afraid of getting aggravated and going over the counter and smacking someone.

Alphonse: I found the men who work here on window have a real quick temper. You know, all of them. And women can take a lot more. They deal with a lot of things, you know.

Although I never heard the masculinity of the few male window workers impugned, it was commonly taken for granted that men were naturally more explosive than women and would find it more difficult to accept abuse without answering back. The male window workers were usually able to reconcile themselves to swallowing insults, as the women were, either by dissociating themselves from their role or by telling themselves that by keeping their tempers they were proving themselves superior to the rude customers. Refusing to become riled when provoked is consistent with "the cool pose," which Majors says Black men use to "fight to preserve their dignity, pride, respect and masculinity" by enacting an imperviousness to hurt (1989, 86). Thus, while the job did not allow workers to try to get the better of opponents, its demands were not seen as irreconcilable with enacting masculinity. However, no workers argued that men's capacity to tolerate abuse made them especially well-suited to the job, and the Black men quoted above made the opposite argument. Moreover, the job requirements of smiling and otherwise demonstrating deference are not in keeping with the cool pose. Those committed to that stance might well find such behavior demeaning, especially in interactions with white customers or those of higher status.

Other explanations given by workers of the predominance of women on window crew included assertions that women were more interested in dealing with people, that women "were more presentable" and looked better on window, that their nimble fingers suited them to working the registers, and that customers were more likely to find them trustworthy. Several of the workers who offered such stereotyped responses indicated that they did not believe that the stereotypes were sufficient justification for the predominance of women on the window crew.

It might easily have been argued that men were unsuited to work on the grill—cooking, after all, is usually considered women's work. As the work was understood at McDonald's, however, cooking presented no challenge to masculinity. Serving customers, which involved adopting an ingratiating manner, taking orders from anyone who chose to give them, and holding one's tongue when insulted, was more difficult to conceive as congruent with the proper enactment of manliness. Thus, while the crew people did not argue that window work was especially expressive of femininity, most found it unremarkable that women predominated in that job.

The work of Combined Insurance's agents, in contrast, was defined as properly manly, even though the job presented interactive imperatives that are generally identified with femininity, along with some stereotypically masculine elements. The life insurance sales force was almost entirely composed of men, and the agents on the sales team I observed felt strongly that women would be unlikely to succeed in the job.[3] Moreover, the 22-year-old manager of this sales team told me bluntly (without my having raised the question) that he "would never hire a woman."[4] Since some aspects of the agents' job required skills that are not generally considered manly, the agents' understanding of the job as demanding masculine attributes meant that these skills had to be reinterpreted or de-emphasized....

Thus the glad-handing insincerity required of many sorts of businessmen may seem effete and demeaning to working-class men. The job of salesman, which is on the lower end of the white-collar hierarchy, would seem especially degrading from this point of view. Since success is largely dependent on ingratiating oneself with customers, playing up to others is an essential part of the agent's job, rather than just a demand of the social milieu. Salesmen must swallow insults, treat even social inferiors with deference, and keep smiling.

These aspects of the sales job were quite pronounced for Combined Insurance's life agents. The warming-up-the-prospect phase of the routine called for agents to figure out what topics might interest the prospects and display a flattering enthusiasm for those topics and for the prospects' accomplishments. Agents had to be willing to disguise their true feelings and to seem to accept the prospect's view of the world in order to ingratiate themselves. It was crucial that they not lose their tempers with prospects but remain polite and respectful at all times. Like most salespeople, they had to try to change prospective customers' minds while never seeming to argue with them and to stay pleasant even when rudely dismissed.

The skills required for establishing and maintaining rapport—drawing people out, bolstering their egos, displaying interest in their interests, and carefully monitoring one's own behavior so as not to offend—are usually considered womanly arts. In analyses of a small sample of conversations, Fishman (1978) found that women had to do much more interactive work than men simply to sustain dialogues; men largely took for granted that their conversational attempts would succeed in engaging their partner's interest. Judging only by these interactive demands of insurance sales work, it would seem that women are especially well suited to be agents. We might even expect that the association of ingratiating conversational tactics with women would lead men to view the extensive interactive work required of salespeople as degrading, since it requires that they assume the role of the interactive inferior who must constantly negotiate permission to proceed. Given the additional attack on personal autonomy implicit in Combined Insurance's programming of employees to follow scripts, it would seem to be difficult for men to combine successful enactment of the role of Combined Insurance agent with the successful enactment of gender.

On the contrary, Combined Insurance's trainers and agents interpreted the agent's job as demanding manly attributes. They assigned a heroic character to the job, framing interactions with customers as contests of will. To succeed, they emphasized, required determination, aggressiveness, persistence, and stoicism. These claims were accurate, but qualities in which women excel, including sensitivity to nuance and verbal dexterity, were also important for success. While the sales training did include tips on building such skills, determination and aggressiveness were treated as the deci-

sive factors for career success. It was through this need for toughness that the work was construed as manly.[5]

Of course it was quite true that considerable determination, self-motivation, and persistence were required to do this job. The agents had to make numerous sales calls every day, despite the knowledge that many people would be far from glad to see them. They had to keep making calls, even after meeting with repeated rejection and sometimes hostility. And in sales interactions, they had to stick to their objectives even when prospects displayed reluctance to continue the conversation, as most did. Some agents and managers believed that women were unlikely to meet these job demands because they are too sensitive, too unaggressive, and not able to withstand repeated rejection. Josh, one of the agents, claimed, "Most girls don't have what it takes. They don't have that killer instinct." Josh had, however, recruited a woman he knew to join Combined's sales force. "She does have [the killer instinct], if I can bring it out," he said. Ralph, the sales manager, also acknowledged that there might be some exceptional women who could do the job. He amended his statement that he would never hire a woman by saying, "Only if she had a kind of bitchy attitude." "A biker woman" is the kind he meant, he said, "someone hardcore." Obviously, he did not believe it was possible to combine the traits necessary for success as an agent with femininity.[6]...

This emphasis on aggression, domination, and danger is only one possible construction of sales work. Biggart (1989) and Connelly and Rhoton (1988) discuss in detail the very different ways that direct sales organizations that rely on a female labor force characterize sales work. These organizations, some of which are hugely successful, emphasize nurturance, helpfulness, and service both in relations with customers and among salespeople. Combined Insurance's training also encouraged agents to think of themselves as providing a service to prospective customers, largely in order to overcome trainees' reluctance to impose on others, and some of the agents I spoke with did use the service ideology to counter demeaning images of insurance sales as high-pressure hucksterism. For the most part, however, the agents emphasized the more "manly" dimensions of the work, though there is ample evidence that women can succeed in life insurance sales. For example, Thomas (1990) notes that after the Equitable Life Assurance Society made a commitment to recruiting and supporting women agents, the company's saleswomen outperformed salesmen in sales and commissions.

While most agents would not feel the need, on a daily basis, to construct an explanation for why there were so few women selling life insurance for their company, they did need to construct an interpretation of their work as honorable and fitting for a man if they were to maintain their positive attitudes and do well at their jobs, which required much more self-motivation than did McDonald's jobs. The element of competition, the battle of wills implicit in their interactions with customers, seemed to be a major factor that allowed the agents to interpret their work as manly. Virtually every step of the interaction was understood as a challenge to be met—getting in the door, making the prospect relax and warm up, being allowed to start the presentation, getting through the presentation despite interruptions, overcoming prospects' objections and actually making the sale, and perhaps even increasing the size of the sale. Since many prospects did their best to prevent the agents from continuing, going through these steps did not simply represent following a prescribed routine; it was experienced by agents as proof of their skill and victories of their wills. Each sales call seemed an uphill battle, as the interac-

tions took place on the prospects' turf and prospects always had the option of telling the agent to leave.

The spirit of jousting was especially clear in some of the techniques taught for closing sales. As the trainer explained "The Assumptive Close," the agents were supposed to "challenge customers"; it was up to the prospects to object if they did not want to go along with the sales. The routine allowed agents to limit the customers' options without seeming to do so, to let prospects believe that they were making decisions while the agents remained in control of the interaction. The pattern bears some resemblance to the seduction of an initially unwilling partner, and the satisfaction that the agents took in "winning" such encounters is perhaps similar to the satisfaction some men take in thinking of sexual encounters as conquests. The agents seemed to approach sales interactions with men in much the same spirit as those with women, however, though they often adjusted their presentation of self to suit a particular prospect's gender, age, and manner—subtly flirtatious, respectfully deferential, or efficient and businesslike.

This sort of manipulation of interactions required a peculiar combination of sensitivity to other people and callousness. The agent had to figure out which approach would work best at any given moment and avoid seeming cold or aggressive but still disregard the customers' stated wishes. The required mix of deference and ruthlessness was well illustrated in an exchange that took place during a sales-team training session. The agents were discussing how to deal with interruptions during a presentation: One of their superiors had advised ignoring them altogether, but the "training module" stated that it was insulting to fail to acknowledge a prospect's comment. When the sales manager instructed, "You have to let them know that you heard them," one of the agents finished the sentence for him: "and that you don't give a shit."...

If following a script could be given a manly cast when it involved asserting one's will through controlling an interaction, it was more difficult to do so when the interactions did not go the agents' way. Refusals were such a routine part of the job, however, that agents could accept most of them as inevitable, not a result of lack of skill or determination. In sales school, the trainers emphasized that not everyone was going to buy—some people really do not need or cannot afford the product; some are just close-minded and would not listen to any salesperson. A greater challenge to the agent's definition of himself was presented by customers who were actively hostile. Some people were angry at being interrupted; some had a grievance against the company; some became furious if they felt that they were being manipulated. In any case, it was not unusual for agents to meet with loud insults, condescending sneers, and slammed doors. To accept this sort of treatment passively could certainly be seen as unmanly. However, the agents were expected to keep their cool, refrain from rudeness, and leave graciously. Some agents did tell me, with glee, of instances when they shouted obscenities once they got out the door, in response to particularly outrageous treatment from a customer. For the most part, however, passive acceptance of ill-treatment was reconciled with manly honor by defining it as maintaining one's control and one's positive attitude, a strategy similar to that used by male and female McDonald's workers. In this view, screaming back at a customer would not be considered standing up for yourself but letting the customer get the better of you, "letting them blow your attitude." Agents proved themselves to be above combative and insulting customers by maintaining their dignity and holding on to their self-

concepts as winners, not by sinking to the customers' level.

Other attributes of the job, not directly connected with job routinization, also contributed to the salesmen's ability to define their jobs as compatible with properly enacting gender. The most important of these were the sense of independence agents felt and their belief that they could earn as much as they were worth. Within the limits of their work assignments, agents could set their own schedules, behave as they chose, and work only as hard as they felt like. Because of the importance of self-motivation to success, those who did well could feel justifiably proud, and those lacking in motivation could appreciate the freedom from pressure. The agents thus felt that their jobs provided some of the benefits of self-employment. They could live with the knowledge that many people looked down on them, put up with insults, endure futile days of failure, and still maintain a sense that their work was compatible with manliness and social honor, as long as there was the possibility of "making it big."

Discussion

...Workers at both McDonald's and Combined Insurance were expected to adjust their moods and demeanors to the demands of their jobs and to learn to handle customers in ways that might be very different from their ordinary styles of interaction. To some extent, workers in both jobs had to take on the role of interactive inferior, adjusting themselves to the styles and apparent preferences of their customers. They were supposed to paste on smiles when they did not feel like smiling and to behave cheerfully and deferentially to people of every status and with every attitude. The workers were not permitted to respond to rudeness in kind but had to try to remain pleasant even in the face of insult.

This sort of behavior is usually associated with femininity, but in fact the two jobs were interpreted quite differently. At McDonald's, many workers and managers considered it natural, even self-evident, that women were best suited to deal with customers. At Combined Insurance, women were generally seen as ill equipped to handle such work. The insurance agents were able to define their job as masculine by emphasizing those aspects of the work that require "manly" traits (control and self-direction) and by reinterpreting some of the more "feminine" job requirements in ways that were not degrading. McDonald's workers' superiors emphasized that the crew's role was to serve, and attempts by window workers to assert their wills in interactions with customers were strongly discouraged. Combined Insurance's agents, on the other hand, were taught that their job was to establish and maintain control in interactions with prospects. They were told that they control their own destinies and were urged to cultivate the qualities of aggressiveness, persistence, and belief in themselves. While success might require that they take on a deferential manner, it was seen as a matter of skill in manipulating situations, not as servility, and therefore was not taken to be inconsistent with manliness. Similarly, accepting abuse calmly was interpreted as a refusal to let someone else dictate the terms of the interaction, not as a loss of control. This conceptualization of the work as an arena for enacting masculinity allowed the agents to accept working conditions that might otherwise have been seen as unacceptably frustrating and demeaning....

NOTES

1. Combined Insurance has recently made changes in its life insurance products and sales techniques. Agents are now taught a more interactive sales routine ("needs selling") for a policy that can be tailored to suit customers' circumstances, allowing the agents somewhat greater flexibility. The company's largest division, which sells accident insurance, continues to follow Stone's original techniques closely. Positive Mental Attitude training is still stressed for all agents.

2. The job of "host," however, was viewed as less prestigious by some workers. That polite job title referred to those whose main responsibilities were to empty the trash and keep the lobby, windows, bathrooms, and dining areas clean. When one woman took this job, I heard two women window workers express their disapproval; they felt that "girls" should not have to do the dirty work of handling garbage.

3. I learned, in fact, that the two other women in my training class had lasted, respectively, only one day and three weeks in the field. Managers interviewed in 1989 reported that the number of women agents had increased since the new selling system was introduced, though women were still a small minority of the sales force. Reduced travel demands were one reason given for the job's increasing attractiveness to women. See also note 5.

4. The higher-level managers I interviewed did not endorse these discriminatory views, and some commented on the many successful women in the insurance industry. See Thomas (1990) for a discussion of the growth of women's employment in insurance sales. She shows that by 1980, women were 25 percent of U.S. insurance agents.

5. Some managers believe that the new needs-selling approach is better suited to women agents because it requires a less domineering stance and allows women to draw on their understanding of families' needs.

6. Similarly, Williams (1989, 32) reports a backlash against women in the military among male soldiers during World War II. She argues that military men claimed that women soldiers must be unfeminine because the men did not want to accept the alternative explanation for the women's presence—that military service is not inherently masculine.

REFERENCES

Acker, Joan. 1990. Hierarchies, jobs, bodies: A theory of gendered organizations. *Gender & Society* 4:139–58.

Beechey, Veronica. 1988. Rethinking the definition of work: Gender and work. In *Feminization of the labor force: Paradoxes and promises*, edited by Jane Jenson, Elisabeth Hagen, and Ceallaigh Reddy. New York: Oxford University Press.

Benson, Susan Porter. 1986. *Counter cultures: Saleswomen, managers, and customers in American department stores, 1890–1940*. Urbana: University of Illinois Press.

Berk, Sarah Fenstermaker. 1985a. *The gender factory: The apportionment of work in American households*. New York: Plenum.

_____. 1985b. Women's work and the production of gender. Paper presented at the annual meeting of the American Sociological Association, Washington, DC.

Biggart, Nicole. 1989. *Charismatic capitalism: Direct selling organizations in America*. Chicago: University of Chicago Press.

Boas, Max, and Steve Chain. 1976. *Big Mac: The unauthorized story of McDonald's*. New York: Mentor, New American Library.

Chodorow, Nancy. 1978. *The reproduction of mothering: Psychoanalysis and the sociology of gender*. Berkeley: University of California Press.

Cockburn, Cynthia. 1983. *Brothers: Male dominance and technological change*. London: Pluto.

_____. 1985. *Machinery of dominance: Women, men and technical know-how*. London: Pluto.

Connelly, Maureen, and Patricia Rhoton. 1988. Women in direct sales: A comparison of Mary Kay and Amway sales workers. In *The worth of women's work: A qualitative synthesis*, edited by Anne Statham, Eleanor M. Miller, and Hans O. Mauksch. Albany: State University of New York Press.

Fishman, Pamela M. 1978. Interaction: The work women do. *Social Problems* 25:397–406.

Frye, Marilyn. 1983. Sexism. In *The politics of reality*. Trumansberg, NY: Crossing Press.

Garfinkel, Harold. 1967. *Studies in ethnomethodology*. Englewood Cliffs, NJ: Prentice-Hall.

Garson, Barbara. 1988. *The electronic sweatshop*. New York: Simon & Schuster.

Goffman, Erving. 1977. The arrangements between the sexes. *Theory and Society* 4:301–31.

Gray, Stan. 1987. Sharing the shop floor. In *Beyond patriarchy: Essays by men on pleasure, power, and change*, edited by Michael Kaufman. Toronto: Oxford University Press.

Halle, David. 1984. *America's working man*. Chicago: University of Chicago Press.

Hochschild, Arlie Russell. 1983. *The managed heart: Commercialization of human feeling*. Berkeley: University of California Press.

Hughes, Everett C. [1951] 1984. Work and self. In *The sociological eye*. New Brunswick, NJ: Transaction.

Kanter, Rosabeth Moss. 1977. *Men and women of the corporation*. New York: Basic Books.

Kessler, Suzanne J., and Wendy McKenna. 1978. *Gender: An ethnomethodological approach*. Chicago: University of Chicago Press.

Lally-Benedetto, Corinne. 1985. Women and the tone of the body: An analysis of a figure salon. Paper presented at the annual meeting of the Midwest Sociological Society, St. Louis, MO.

Leidner, Robin, 1988. Working on people: The routinization of interactive service work. Ph.D. diss., Northwestern University, Evanston, IL.

Life insurance business in Japan. 1987/88. Tokyo: Life Assurance Association of Japan.

Majors, Richard. 1989. Cool pose: The proud signature of Black survival. In *Men's lives*, edited by Michael S. Kimmel and Michael A. Messner. New York: Macmillan.

Melosh, Barbara. 1982. *"The physician's hand": Work culture and conflict in American nursing*. Philadelphia: Temple University Press.

Milkman, Ruth. 1987. *Gender at work: The dynamics of job segregation by sex during World War II*. Urbana: University of Illinois Press.

Ouellet, Lawrence J. 1986. Work, commitment, and effort: Truck drivers and trucking in small, non-union, West coast trucking companies. Ph.D. diss., Northwestern University, Evanston, IL.

Personick, Valerie A. 1987. Industry output and employment through the end of the century. *Monthly Labor Review* 10 (September): 30–45.

Reverby, Susan M. 1987. *Ordered to care: The dilemma of American nursing, 1850–1945*. Cambridge: Cambridge University Press.

Rollins, Judith. 1985. *Between women: Domestics and their employers*. Philadelphia: Temple University Press.

Schroedel, Jean Reith. 1985. *Alone in a crowd: Women in the trades tell their stories*. Philadelphia: Temple University Press.

Sennett, Richard, and Jonathan Cobb. 1972. *The hidden injuries of class*. New York: Knopf.

Silvestri, George T., and John M. Lukasiewic. 1987. A look at occupational employment trends to the year 2000. *Monthly Labor Review* 10 (September): 46–63.

Spradley, James P., and Brenda J. Mann. 1975. *The cocktail waitress: Woman's work in a man's world*. New York: Wiley.

Steinem, Gloria. 1983. I was a Playboy bunny. In *Outrageous acts and everyday rebellions*. New York: Holt, Rinehart & Winston.

Stone, W. Clement. 1962. *The success system that never fails*. Englewood Cliffs, NJ: Prentice-Hall.

Swerdlow, Marian. 1989. Men's accommodations to women entering a nontraditional occupation: A case of rapid transit operatives. *Gender & Society* 3:373–87.

Thomas, Barbara J. 1990. Women's gains in insurance sales: Increased supply, uncertain demand. In *Job queues, gender queues: Women's movement into male occupations*, edited by Barbara Reskin and Patricia Roos. Philadelphia: Temple University Press.

West, Candace, and Don Zimmerman. 1987. Doing gender. *Gender & Society* 1:125–51.

Whyte, William F. 1962. When workers and customers meet. In *Man, work, and society*, edited by Sigmund Nosow and William H. Form. New York: Basic Books.

Williams, Christine. 1989. *Gender differences at work: Women and men in nontraditional occupations*. Berkeley: University of California Press.

Willis, Paul. 1977. *Learning to labor: How working class kids get working class jobs*. New York: Columbia University Press.

Zelizer, Viviana A. Rotman. 1979. *Morals and markets: The development of life insurance in the United States*. New York: Columbia University Press.

One L

Scott Turow

CASE STUDY QUESTIONS

1. What factors do you feel contribute to the competitiveness of law school students?

2. Think about how various types of lawyers spend their time—meeting the corporate executives, negotiating with other lawyers, interviewing alleged criminals, helping families, reading law books, writing briefs, and appearing in court. To what extent does the law school classroom experience prepare students for these tasks?

3. What kinds of assumptions are made about the practice of law in the choice by law school faculty to create the classroom atmosphere in the way that they do? To what extent do you feel the role of tradition plays a role in faculty members' choice to create a particular classroom atmosphere? Do you think that men and women students would feel similarly about the classroom atmosphere?

4. What impact does the manner in which one is socialized to a profession have on those aspiring to be a part of that profession?

Just a note before I leave for school.

Today is the start of regular classes. We will now commence "normal" law school life. The 2Ls [2nd year law students] and 3Ls [3rd year law students] will be present and

the section will begin the schedule we'll be on for much of the year. This semester we'll have Contracts, Civil Procedure, Criminal Law, and Torts. The latter two courses last only one term and they'll be the subjects on which we'll take our first exams in January. Second semester, Contracts and Civil Pro continue, Property will be added and we'll each be allowed to choose an elective.

We've been warned that today's classes—Criminal and Contracts—will not seem much like Legal Methods. The courses we begin now are considered the traditional stuff of law school, analytical matter, rather than mere how-to. Unlike Methods, these courses will be graded, and they'll be taught by professors, not teaching fellows. The classes will be made up of the whole 140-person section instead of a small group. And, most ominous to me, the instruction will be by the noted "Socratic method."

In a way I'm looking forward to Socratic instruction. I've heard so much about it since I applied to law school—it will at least be interesting to see what it's like.

The general run of student reaction is most succinctly expressed in a comment I heard from David this summer, the day he showed me around the law school. He was kind of mimicking a tour guide, whining out facts and names as he took me from building to building. When we reached Langdell, he stood on the steps and lifted his hand toword the columns and the famous names of the law cut into the granite border beneath the roof.

"This is Langdell Hall," he said, "The biggest building on the law school campus. It contains four large classrooms and, on the upper floors, the Harvard Law School library, the largest law school library in the world.

"The building is named for the late Christopher Columbus Langdell, who was dean of Harvard Law School in the late nineteenth century. Dean Langdell is best known as the inventor of the Socratic method."

David lowered his hand and looked sincerely at the building.

"May he rot in hell, " David said.

The Socratic method is without question one of the things which makes legal education—particularly the first year, when Socraticism is most extensively used—distinct from what students are accustomed to elsewhere. While I was teaching it was always assumed that there was no hope of holding a class discussion with a group larger than thirty. When numbers got that high, the only means of communication was lecture. But Socratism is, in a way, an attempt to lead a discussion with the entire class of 140.

Generally, Socratic discussion begins when a student—I'll call him Jones—is selected without warning by the professor and asked a question. Traditionally, Jones will be asked to "state the case," that is, to provide an oral rendition of the information normally contained in a case brief. Once Jones has responded, the professor—as Socrates did with his students—will question Jones about what he has said, pressing him to make his answers clearer. If Jones says that the judge found that the contract had been breached, the professor will ask what specific provision of the contract had been violated and in what manner. The discussion will proceed that way, with the issues narrowing. At some point, Jones may be unable to answer. The professor can

either select another student at random, or—more commonly—call on those who've raised their hands. The substitutes may continue the discussion of the case with the professor, or simply answer what Jones could not, the professor then resuming his interrogation of Jones.

Professors' classroom procedures differ so widely that this description cannot be called typical. Some professors never ask for a statement of the case, commencing discussion with a narrower question instead. Some interrogate students for thirty seconds—others leave them on the hot seat for the entire class. A few professors never do any more than ask questions, disdaining any direct statements. Most, however, use a student's response as the starting point for a brief lecture on a given topic before returning to more questioning.

However employed, the Socratic method is often criticized. Ralph Nader has called it "the game only one can play," and there have been generations of students who, like David, have wished curses on Dean Langdell. The peer pressures which Peter Geocaris described to my Methods group during orientation often make getting called on an uncomfortable experience. You are in front of 140 people whom you respect, and you would like them to think well of you.

Despite student pain and protest, most law professors, including those who are liberal—even radical—on other issues in legal education, defend the Socratic method. They feel that Socratic instruction offers the best means of training students to speak in the law's unfamiliar language, and also of acquainting them with the layered, inquiring style of analysis which is a prominent part of thinking like a lawyer.

For me, the primary feeling at the start was one of incredible exposure. Whatever its faults or virtues, the Socratic method depends on a tacit license to violate a subtle rule of public behavior. When groups are too large for any semblance of intimacy, we usually think of them as being divided by role. The speaker speaks and, in the name of order, the audience listens—passive, anonymous, remote. In using the Socratic method, professors are informing students that what would normally be a safe personal space is likely at any moment to be invaded.

That feeling might well have made me more attentive in class, but it also left me quite agitated when I went for the first time to take my place in Criminal Law, that day last September. It was a little after 9:00 A.M. and I hunted down the rows to find my seat. At most law schools, Harvard among them, class seats are assigned in advance. The allotment is random and there is a different seat for each course. Every student's seat number is recorded on a diagram of the classroom which professors normally have before them at all times. Many professors cut students' pictures out of the first-year students' handbook and place them on the chart as well. Students are more easily recognized when called on, and they are also prevented from sitting in the back of the class, out of their assigned seats, a practice called "backbenching."

Seat assignment is a requirement of the Socratic method. The seating chart allows professors to select students freely throughout the classroom for questioning, rather than awaiting volunteers. I understood the rationale, but still I chafed. I was twenty-six years old, a grown-up, and here I was being told exactly where to place my fanny come 9:10 A.M. And beyond that remained the disquieting thought of getting called on, and, even worse, the paralyzing little possibility, no matter how remote, that I might be the initial victim. Ineptness could make me a legend. "Remember Turow? Mann called on him and he passed out cold." I was giddy and ill at ease when I finally took my seat.

As it happened, there was no need for great concern. Professor Mann spent the period making introductory remarks. He called on no one and I'm certain we were all grateful.

About 9:12 he mumbled to himself, "I think we should start." Then he looked at the ceiling and began to speak. He was a man near sixty, quite meticulous, with a large pomp of white hair and a still, humorless face. He wore a pin-striped suit. As he talked, he moved back and forth, somewhat stiffly, behind the podium.

I had not listened to Professor Mann long before I recognized that he was not a great teacher. Given what Peter had said, that was no surprise. It was not any secret that every section was planned so that the distribution of teaching talent between them was relatively equal, which usually meant that each would have its good teachers and bad. Like other academic institutions, Harvard Law School does not place sole premium on teaching ability in developing a faculty.

The men and women who are professors of HLS have proved their brilliance many times. In just a few days, I had seen that they were treated as lofty, superior beings, the students plainly in awe of their intelligence and especially of their achievements. Most of the HLS professors are themselves graduates of the law school. Wherever they were educated, virtually all were members of the Law Review, and most also ranked at the very tops of their classes. Many were law clerks to members of the U.S. Supreme Court, a very high honor. After graduation, nearly all practiced law for some time, often with great success, and a number have interrupted their teaching careers at points to take on prominent positions in government—assistant cabinet secretaries, presidential advisors, high-ranking bureaucrats. But the capacity for legal scholarship—the ability to speculate about and research the law—remains a primary criterion for hiring faculty, and publication is indispensable. Bertram Mann, I'd been told, had written a wealth of well-regarded studies on victimless crimes—prostitution, narcotics use, gambling—and after the first hour I became certain that his best efforts with the law were there.

I had been told that he taught as if he were talking to himself; that proved to be a telling description. Now and then he would twist himself around and look at us, as if to make sure that he still had an audience; then he would stare back at the the ceiling and continue. His comments were only vaguely tied to each other and every remark seemed offhand.

"Of course, I want you to be prepared each day," he said at one point, "very well prepared. As if this were a tutorial, me and you, me and each one of you. But of course"—he shot out a hand, glancing down momentarily from the acoustical tiles—"of course if you're not prepared occasionally, now and then, why you should come to class anyway; no need to say away. If it's one of those days, well, then, just say it—just say, 'I'm unprepared'—and I'll give you another chance, in a day or two—soon after that. No need to worry."

He paced, nodding now and then to himself. Eventually he began talking about the course. He said that Criminal Law would be unique in many ways. It was the only course that would concentrate expressly on the relationship beweeen government and private citizens. And he also said that it would be the single class in which we would do close reading of statutes as well as cases. Much of our time would be spent on the Model Penal Code, a criminal statute drafted in the '60s by the American Law Institute, a group of legal scholars, and since adopted by a number of states.

I found Terry Nazarrio after class. He asked me what I thought about Mann and I told him you couldn't win them all.

"Seemed like a nice dude, at least," Terry said. "The thing about not being prepared?"

I agreed.

We had half an hour before our first meeting with Rudolph Perini in Contracts.

Terry said he wanted to buy a book in the meantime and I volunteered to go with him. I had bought all mine the week before, but I wanted to get a look at the Lawbook Thrift Shop, where he was heading—a store in the law school where used books are bought and sold.

I'd had lunch with Terry on Thursday and had gotten to know him better. The route he'd taken to law school was a lot different than most everybody else's. He was near my age—twenty-five—but he'd finished college only the preceding June. After high school, by his own account, he'd been a "bum," hanging around the tracks, but at twenty he'd gotten married, borrowed the money to open a store selling stereos, and started college at night. He prospered. His wife gave birth to twin boys; he opened a second store and hired people to run both stores while he transferred to the college's day division, where he did phenomenally well. Last December, a large chain had offered him too much money for his stores, for him to turn down.

"We had enough," he told me, "to live good for three, four years. I figured we could do anything—go to Europe, move to California and lay on the beach. But hell, man, I *like* school; I get off on that stuff. I didn't see the odds in grad school. I mean, there're no jobs there and I wanted to be able to do something besides run a store when I finished. So I decided to go to law school. After I aced the LSAT, I said, Hey, try Harvard, you're as good as anybody else. And bingo! Donna's parents, mine—man, they think there's something almost wrong, that they let me in."

He laughed as he told the story. He was tough, proud, ferociously independent, bright with that incredible city quickness. I admired him.

The Lawbook Thrift Shop was crowded when we arrived. It is run by the wife of one of the law students out of a small office in Austin Hall and it was full of 2Ls and 3Ls hunting course books on their first day back. I told Terry I'd wait outside.

I should say a word or two about law books, since they are plainly the focus of so much of a law student's attention. There are three general categories. The first are the casebooks, the thousand-page volumes out of which class assignments are regularly made. The cases in the book are usually edited and have been selected for their importance in the development in given areas of the law. In the second category, a kind of academic purgatory, are the "hornbooks," brief treatises produced by well-known legal scholars which summarize leading cases and which provide general descriptions of the doctrines in the field. Professors discourage hornbook reading by beginning students. They fear that hornbook consultation will limit a 1L's ability to deduce the law himself from the cases and also that it will decrease a student's interest in class, since the hornbooks often analyze the daily material in much the same way that the professors do themselves. In the final category, the nether world well beneath academic respectability, are the myriad study aids, commercially prepared casebook and course and subject-matter outlines, and other kinds of digests. The best-known series is the Gilbert Law Summaries. Although law students have gotten by for generations with the aid of these and other prepared outlines, there are members of the faculty who claim to have never heard the word "Gilbert's" from a student's lips. Before I started, I myself was somewhat incredulous that students would buy a course guide rather than prepare it themselves. It seemed to border on plagiarism.

Whatever category, two generalizations about law books usually hold true. They are quite large—I'd already had to invest in a big orange knapsack to haul all of them around. And they are expensive. The casebooks are especially dear, $16 to $25 when bought new, the prices probably inflated because the publishers recognize that casebooks are required reading and have to be purchased. Faculty agitation for lower prices would probably do little good and in any event is unlikely, since the professors are most often the editors or authors of the books they assign. In all but one of my first-year classes, the required casebook had been produced by either that professor or another member of the HLS faculty. Used-book exchanges like the Lawbook Thrift Shop are the only means students have to lessen costs.

Terry emerged with a heavy green book which he showed me at once. "Got that yet?"

I examined the title page. It was a Contracts hornbook, written, as was our casebook, by Gregory Baldridge and Rudolph Perini.

"Two buddies of mine say that the dude's whole course is in there," Terry told me.

"He wrote a hornbook, huh?" I asked, still fingering the cover.

"'Wrote a hornbook?' Hey man, this guy *is* Contracts—he is *the* authority. That is *the* hornbook."

"I thought profs say don't read hornbooks for a while."

"That's what they say, man—that's not what people do. At least, that's what I hear."

I shrugged and handed him the book back. But I worried. How did I know what was right? I felt my faith should be in the professors, but I didn't want to fall behind my classmates, either.

"I'll wait," I said.

"Your choice," Terry answered.

"I want to see how bad Perini really is, first."

He nodded and we went off together toward the classroom in Austin where we would both find out.

Most law school classrooms are arranged in roughly the same way. Broken usually by two aisles, concentric semicircles of seats and desks issue back from the podium, resulting in a kind of amphitheater. In Pound, where we had met Mann, the newly constructed classrooms had been built with remarkable compactness. But in Austin the rooms were ancient and enormous. The seats and desks were in rows of yellowed oak, tiered steeply toward the rear. At its highest, the classroom was nearly forty feet, with long, heavy curtains on the windows and dark portraits of English judges, dressed in their wigs and robes, hanging in gilt frames high on the wall. It was an awesome setting, especially when its effect was combined with the stories we had all heard about Perini. There was a tone of tense humor in the conversations around me, most voices somewhat hushed. As I headed for my seat, I overheard a number of people say, "I don't want it to be me," referring to whom Perini would call on.

I introduced myself to the men sitting on either side of me. One was a former marine from Ohio, the other a kid named Don, just out of the University of Texas. The three of us gossiped about Perini, exchanging what little information we knew. Don said that Perini was a Texan. He had graduated from the University of Texas Law School, but he had been a professor at HLS for twenty years. Only in the late '60s had he interrupted his teaching, when he had briefly been some kind of counsellor to Nixon.

It was already a few minutes after ten, the hour when we were supposed to start. The class was assembled and almost everyone was in his seat. Don asked me what Perini looked like.

"I don't know," I answered. "No idea."

Greg, the ex-marine on the other side, said, "Just take a look."

Perini moved slowly down the tiers toward the lectern. He held his head up and he was without expression. My first thought was that he looked softer than I'd expected. He was around six feet, but pudgy and a little awkward. Although the day was warm, he wore a black three-piece suit. He held the book and the seating chart under his arm.

The room was totally silent by the time he reached the lectern. He slapped the book down on the desk beneath. He still had not smiled.

"This is Contracts," he said. "Section Two, in case any of you are a little uncertain about where you are." He smiled then, stiffly. "I have a few introductory comments and then we'll be going on to the cases I asked you to look at for today. First, however, I want to lay out the ground rules on which this class will run, so that there will be *no* confusion in the future."

He spoke with elaborate slowness, emphasis on each word. His accent was distinctly southern.

Perini picked up the casebook in one hand.

"The text for this class is *Selected Cases in the Law of Contracts*. The editors are Baldridge and"—Perini lifted a hand to weight the silence—"et cetera." He smiled again, without parting his lips. Around the room a few people snickered. Then he said, "Needless to mention, I hope you bought it new," and got his first outright laugh.

"We will proceed through the book case by case," Perini told us. "Now and then we may skip a case or two. In that event, I'll inform you in advance, or you will find a notice on the bulletin boards. You should stay three cases ahead, each day."

Between the desk on which the lectern sat and the students in the front row, there was a narrow area, a kind of small proscenium. Perini began to pace there slowly, his hands behind his back. I watched him as he came toward our side of the room, staring up harshly at the faces around him. He looked past fifty, coarse-skinned and dark. He was half-bald, but his black hair was styled carefully. There was a grim set to his mouth and eyes.

"This class will deal with the law of obligations, of bargains, commercial dealings, the law of promises," Perini said. "It is the hardest course you will take all year. Contracts has traditionally been the field of law of the most renowned intellectual complexity. Most of the greatest legal commentators of the past century have been Contracts scholars: Williston, Corbin, Fuller, Llewellyn, Baldridge—" He lifted his hand as he had done before. "Et cetera," he said again and smiled broadly for the first time. Most people laughed. One or two applauded. Perini waited before he began pacing again.

"Some of your classmates may find the Property course in the spring the hardest course *they* take. But you will not feel that way, because you will be taking Contracts with me. I am not"—he looked up—"an easy person."

"I expect you to be here *every* day. And I expect you to sit where the registrar has assigned you. On the so-called back benches, I should see only those persons who are visiting us seeking a momentary glimpse of something morbid." Laughter again from a few places.

"I expect you to be very well prepared, *every* day. I want to be absolutely clear on that. I have *never* heard the word 'pass.' I do not know what 'unprepared' means. Now and then, of course, there are personal problems—we all have them at times—which make full preparation impossible. If that is the case, then I want a written note to be handed to my secretary at least *two* hours before class. You can find her on the second floor of the Faculty Office Building in room two eighty-one."

I wrote it all down in my notebook: "No absence. No pass. No unprepared. Note to sec'ty 2 hrs. b-4 class, FOB 281."

Holy Christ, I thought.

As expected, Perini told us to read nothing aside from class assignments for the first few months—not even "a certain hornbook" we might have heard of. For the present, he assured us, we would have our hands full. Then he described the course in some detail. In that discussion too, Perini maintained that tone of barely veiled menace. We may have been Phi Beta Kappas and valedictorians, but this was Harvard Law School now—things would not be easy.

There were moments when I was certain that Perini was only half serious. There was such obvious showmanship in all of this, the deliberateness of the gestures, the archness of his smile. It was almost a parody of the legendary tough professor, of the Perini of rumor. But if it was an act, it was one which he was determined would be compelling. He revealed no more than a trace of irony and there were often moments, as when he had looked up at us, that he seemed full of steel.

As he went on describing the subjects with which we would soon be dealing—offer, acceptance, interpretation; the list was extensive—I began to think that, like Mann, he would let the hour slip away. No one would be called and we'd all be safe for one more day. But at six or seven minutes to twelve he returned to the lectern and looked down at the seating chart.

"Let's see if we can cover a *little* ground today." Perini took a pencil from his pocket and pointed it at the chart. It might as well have been a pistol. Please, no, I thought.

"Mr. Karlin!" Perini cried sharply.

Nearby, I heard a tremendous thud. Five or six seats from me a man was scrambling to grab hold of the books that had been piled before him, two or three of which had now hit the floor. That, I was sure, was Karlin who had jolted when he heard his name called. He was a heavyset man, pale, with black eyeglasses. He was wearing a yarmulke. His eyes, as he struggled with his books, were quick with fright, and at once I felt terribly sorry for him and guilty at my own relief.

"Mr. Karlin," Perini said, ambling toward my side of the room, "why don't you tell us about the case of *Hurley* v. *Eddingfield*?"

Karlin already had his notebook open. His voice was quavering.

"Plaintiff's intestate," he began. He got no further.

"What does *that* mean?" Perini cried from across the room. He began marching fiercely up the aisle toward Karlin. "In-*tes*-tate," he said, "in-*tes*-tate. What is that? Something to do with the *stomach?* Is this an anatomy class, Mr. Karlin?" Perini's voice had become shrill with a note of open mockery and at the last word people burst out laughing, louder than at anything Perini had said before.

He was only five or six feet from Karlin now. Karlin stared up at him and blinked and finally said, "No."

"No, I didn't think so," Perini said. "What if the word was 'testate'? What would that be? Would we have moved from the stomach"—Perini waved a hand and there was more loud laughter when he leeringly asked his question—"*else*where?"

"I think," Karlin said weakly, "that if the word was 'testate' it would mean he had a will."

"And 'intestate' that he didn't have a will. I see." Perini wagged his head. "And who is this 'he,' Mr. Karlin?"

Karlin was silent. He shifted in his seat as Perini stared at him. Hands had shot up across the room. Perini called rapidly on two or three people who gave various names— Hurley, Eddingfield, the plaintiff. Finally someone said that the case didn't say.

"The case doesn't *say!*" Perini cried, marching down the aisle. "The case does *not say*. Read the case. *Read* the case! *Carefully!*" He bent with each word, pointing a finger at the class. He stared fiercely into the crowd of students in the center of the room, then looked back at Karlin. "Do we really care who 'he' is, Mr. Karlin?"

"Care?"

"Does it make any *difference* to the outcome of the case?"

"I don't think so."

"Why not?"

"Because he's dead."

"He's *dead!*" Perini shouted. "Well, that's a load off of our minds. But there's one problem then, Mr. Karlin. If he's dead, how did he file a *law*suit?"

Karlin's face was still tight with fear, but he seemed to be gathering himself.

"I thought it was the administrator who brought the suit."

"Ah!" said Perini, "the ad*mini*strator. And what's an administrator? One of those types over in the Faculty Building?"

It went on that way for a few more minutes, Perini striding through the room, shouting and pointing as he battered Karlin with questions, Karlin doing his best to provide answers. A little after noon Perini suddenly announced that we would continue tomorrow. Then he strode from the classroom with the seating chart beneath his arm. In his wake the class exploded into chatter.

I sat stunned. Men and women crowded around Karlin to congratulate him. He had done well, better, it seemed, than even Perini had expected. At one point the professor had asked where Karlin was getting all the definitions he was methodically reciting. I knew Karlin had done far better than I could have, a realization which upset me, given all the work I had done preparing for the class. I hadn't asked myself who was suing. I knew what 'intestate' meant, but not 'testate,' and was hardly confident I could have made the jump while under that kind of pressure. I didn't even want to think about the time it would be my turn to face Perini.

And as much as all of that, I was bothered by the mood which had taken hold of the room. The exorbitance of Perini's manner had seemed to release a sort of twisted energy. Why had people laughed like that? I wondered. It wasn't all good-natured. It wasn't really laughter *with* Karlin. I had felt it too, a sort of giddiness, when Perini made his mocking inquiries. And why had people raised their hands so eagerly, stretching out of their seats as they sought to be called on? When Socratic instruction had been described for me, I had been somewhat incredulous that students would dash in so boldly to correct each other's errors. But if I hadn't been quite as scared I might have raised my hand myself. What the hell went on here? I was thoroughly confused, the more so because despite my reservations the truth was that I had been gripped, even thrilled, by the class. Perini, for all the melodrama and intimidation, had been magnificent, electric, in full possession of himself and the students. The points he'd made had had a wonderful clarity and directness. He was, as claimed, an exceptional teacher.

As I headed out, Karlin, still surrounded by well-wishers, was also on his way from the classroom. I reached him to pat him on the back, but I had no chance to speak with him as he went off in the swirl of admiring classmates. A man, and a woman I'd met, a tall blonde who had gone to Radcliffe, Karen

Sondergard, had stayed behind. I asked them about Karlin.

"He's a rabbi," Karen said, "or else he trained for it. He was at Yeshiva in New York."

"He did quite a job," I said.

"He should have," the man told me. "He said he read Perini's hornbook over the summer."

I stared for an instant, then told the guy that he was kidding.

"That's what he said," the man insisted. "I heard him say so." Karen confirmed that.

Nazarrio came up then and I had the man tell Terry what he had said about Karlin.

"Over the *summer,*" I repeated.

Terry glanced at me, probably suppressing 'I told you so,' then shook his head.

"Folks around here sure don't fool around," he said.

We all laughed and the four of us went off together for lunch. Afterward, I went back to the Lawbook Thrift Shop. I wasn't sure if it made me feel better or worse when I bought Perini's hornbook.

The Fate of Idealism in Medical School

Howard S. Becker and Blanche Geer

CASE STUDY QUESTIONS

1. When aspiring doctors begin their medical training, what do they think will help them to become good doctors?

2. Does their socialization help students keep their cynicism about their education separate from their idealistic beliefs? Is students' idealism destroyed forever by their medical school training, or does the idealism emerge again at a later time?

3. What frustrations do medical students encounter when they finally have contact with patients?

4. If there is a gap between the formal training and what a medical student needs to know to become a good doctor, what is the purpose of the type of medical school training that is provided? Do you think the gap is a consequence of the fact that physicians are in an occupation that is at the far end of the occupation/profession continuum?

It makes some difference in a man's [woman's] performance of his work whether he [she] believes wholeheartedly in what he [she] is doing or feels that in important respects it is a fraud, whether he [she] feels convinced that it is a good thing or believes that it is not really of much use after all. The distinction we are making is the one people

Source: "The Fate of Idealism in Medical School," Howard S. Becker and Blanche Geer, 1958, *American Sociological Review,* Vol. 23, pp. 50–56.

have in mind when they refer, for example, to their calling as a "noble profession" on the one hand or a "racket" on the other. In the one case they idealistically proclaim that their work is all that it claims on the surface to be; in the other they cynically concede that it is first and foremost a way of making a living and that its surface pretensions are just that and nothing more. Presumably, different modes of behavior are associated with these perspectives when wholeheartedly embraced. The cynic cuts corners with a feeling of inevitability while the idealist goes down fighting. *The Blackboard Jungle* and *Not as a Stranger* are only the most recent in a long tradition of fictional portrayals of the importance of this aspect of a man's adjustment to his work.

Professional schools often receive a major share of the blame for producing this kind of cynicism—and none more than the medical school. The idealistic young freshman changes into a tough, hardened, unfeeling doctor; or so the popular view has it. Teachers of medicine sometimes rephrase the distinction between the clinical and pre-clinical years into one between the "cynical" and "pre-cynical" years. Psychological research supports this view, presenting attitude surveys which show medical students year by year scoring lower on "idealism" and higher on "cynicism."[1] Typically, this cynicism is seen as developing in response to the shattering of ideals consequent on coming face-to-face with the realities of professional practice.

In this [case study], we attempt to describe the kind of idealism that characterizes the medical freshmen and to trace both the development of cynicism and the vicissitudes of that idealism in the course of the four years of medical training. Our main themes are that though they develop cynical feelings in specific situations directly associated with their medical school experience, the medical students never lose their original idealism about the practice of medicine; that the growth of both cynicism and idealism are not simply developments, but are instead complex transformations; and that the very notions "idealism" and "cynicism" need further analysis, and must be seen as situational in their expressions rather than as stable traits possessed by individuals in greater or lesser degree. Finally, we see the greater portion of these feelings as being collective rather than individual phenomena.

Our discussion is based on a study we are now conducting at a state medical school,[2] in which we have carried on participant observation with students of all four years in all of the courses and clinical work to which they are exposed. We joined the students in their activities in school and after school and watched them at work in labs, on the hospital wards, and in the clinic. Often spending as much as a month with a small group of from five to fifteen students assigned to a particular activity, we came to know them well and were able to gather information in informal interviews and by overhearing the ordinary daily conversation of the group.[3] In the course of our observation and interviewing we have gathered much information on the subject of idealism. Of necessity, we shall have to present the very briefest statement of our findings with little or no supporting evidence.[4] The problem of idealism is, of course, many-faceted and complex and we have dealt with it in a simplified way, describing only some of its grosser features.[5]

The Freshmen

The medical students enter school with what we may think of as the idealistic notion, implicit in lay culture, that the practice of medicine is a wonderful thing and that they are going to devote their lives to service to mankind. They believe that medicine is made up of a great body of well-established facts that they will be taught from the first day on and that these facts will be of immediate practical use to them as physicians. They enter school expecting to work industriously and expecting that if they work hard enough they will be able to master this body of fact and thus become good doctors.

In several ways the first year of medical school does not live up to their expectations. They are disillusioned when they find they will not be near patients at all, that the first year will be just like another year of college. In fact, some feel that it is not even as good as college because their work in certain areas is not as thorough as courses in the same fields in undergraduate school. They come to think that their courses (with the exception of anatomy) are not worth much because, in the first place, the faculty (being Ph.D.'s) know nothing about the practice of medicine, and, in the second place, the subject matter itself is irrelevant, or as the students say, "ancient history."

The freshmen are further disillusioned when the faculty tells them in a variety of ways that there is more to medicine than they can possibly learn. They realize it may be impossible for them to learn all they need to know in order to practice medicine properly. Their disillusionment becomes more profound when they discover that this statement of the faculty is literally true.[6] Experience in trying to master the details of the anatomy of the extremities convinces them that they cannot do so in the time they have. Their expectation of hard work is not disappointed; they put in an eight-hour day of classes and laboratories, and study four or five hours a night and most of the weekend as well.

Some of the students, the brightest, continue to attempt to learn it all, but succeed only in getting more and more worried about their work. The majority decide that, since they can't learn it all, they must select from among all the facts presented to them those they will attempt to learn. There are two ways of making this selection. On the one hand, the student may decide on the basis of his own uninformed notions about the nature of medical practice that many facts are not important, since they relate to things which seldom come up in the actual practice of medicine; therefore, he reasons, it is useless to learn them. On the other hand, the student can decide that the important thing is to pass his examinations and, therefore, that the important facts are those which are likely to be asked on an examination; he uses this as a basis for selecting both facts to memorize and courses for intensive study. For example, the work in physiology is dismissed on both of these grounds, being considered neither relevant to the facts of medical life nor important in terms of the amount of time the faculty devotes to it and the number of examinations in the subject.

A student may use either or both of these bases of selection at the beginning of the year, before many tests have been given. But after a few tests have been taken, the student makes "what the faculty wants" the chief basis of his selection of what to learn, for he now has a better idea of what this is and also has become aware that it is possible to fail examinations and that he therefore must learn the expectations of the faculty if he wishes to stay in school. The fact that one group of students, that with the highest prestige in the class, took this view early and did well on examinations was decisive in swinging the whole class around to this position. The students were equally influenced to become "test-wise" by the fact that, although they had all been in the upper range in their colleges, the class average on the first examination was frighteningly low.

In becoming test-wise, the students begin to develop systems for discovering the faculty wishes and learning them. These systems are both methods for studying their texts and short-cuts that can be taken in laboratory work. For instance, they begin to select facts for memorization by looking over the files of old examinations maintained in each of the medical fraternity houses. They share tip-offs from the lectures and offhand remarks of the faculty as to what will be on the examinations. In anatomy, they agree not to bother to dissect out subcutaneous nerves, reasoning that it is both difficult and time-consuming and the information can be secured from books with less effort. The interaction involved in the development of such systems and short-cuts helps to create a social group of a class which had previously been only an aggregation of smaller and less organized groups.

In this medical school, the students learn in this way to distinguish between the activities of the first year and their original view that everything that happens to them in medical school will be important. Thus they become cynical about the value of their activities in the first year. They feel that the real thing—learning which will help them to help mankind—has been postponed, perhaps until the second year, or perhaps even farther, at which time they will be able again to act on idealistic premises. They believe that what they do in their later years in school under supervision will be about the same thing they will do, as physicians, on their own; the first year had disappointed this expectation.

There is one matter, however, about which the students are not disappointed during the first year: the so-called trauma of dealing with the cadaver. But this experience, rather than producing cynicism, reinforces the student's attachment to his idealistic view of medicine by making him feel that he is experiencing at least some of the necessary unpleasantness of the doctor. Such difficulties, however, do not loom as large for the student as those of solving the problem of just what the faculty wants.

On this and other points, a working consensus develops in the new consolidated group about the interpretation of their experience in medical school and its norms of conduct. This consensus, which we call *student culture*,[7] focuses their attention almost completely on their day-to-day activities in school and obscures or sidetracks their earlier idealistic preoccupations. Cynicism, griping, and minor cheating become endemic, but the cynicism is specific to the educational situation, to the first year, and to only parts of it. Thus the students keep their cynicism separate from their idealistic feelings and by postponement protect their belief that medicine is a wonderful thing, that their school is a fine one, and that they will become good doctors.

Later Years

The sophomore year does not differ greatly from the freshman year. Both the work load and anxiety over examinations probably increase. Though they begin some medical activities, as in their attendance at autopsies and particularly in their introductory course in physical diagnosis, most of what they do continues to repeat the pattern of the college science curriculum. Their attention still centers on the problem of getting through school by doing well in examinations.

During the third and fourth, or clinical years, teaching takes a new form. In place of lectures and laboratories, the students' work now consists of the study of actual patients admitted to the hospital or seen in the clinic. Each patient who enters the hospital is assigned to a student who interviews him about his illnesses, past and present, and performs a physical examination. He writes this up for the patient's chart, and appends the diagnosis and the treatment that he would use were he allowed actually to treat the patient. During conferences with faculty physicians, often held at the patient's bedside, the student is quizzed about items of his report and called upon to defend them or to explain their significance. Most of the teaching in the clinical years is of this order.

Contact with patients brings a new set of circumstances with which the student must deal. He no longer feels the great pressure created by tests, for he is told by the faculty, and this is confirmed by his daily experience, that examinations are now less important. His problems now become those of coping with a steady stream of patients in a way that will please the staff man under whom he is working, and of handling what is sometimes a tremendous load of clinical work so as to allow himself time for studying diseases and treatments that interest him and for play and family life.

The students earlier have expected that once they reach the clinical years they will be able to realize their idealistic ambitions to help people and to learn those things immediately useful in aiding people who are ill. But they find themselves working to understand cases as medical problems rather than working to help the sick and memorizing the relevant available facts so that these can be produced immediately for a questioning staff man. When they make ward rounds with a faculty member they are likely to be quizzed about any of the seemingly countless facts possibly related to the condition of the patient for whom they are "caring."

Observers speak of the cynicism that overtakes the student and the lack of concern for his patients as human beings. This change does take place, but it is not produced solely by "the anxiety brought about by the presence of death and suffering."[8]

The student becomes preoccupied with the technical aspects of the cases with which he deals because the faculty requires him to do so. He is questioned about so many technical details that he must spend most of his time learning them.

The frustrations created by his position in the teaching hospital further divert the student from idealistic concerns. He finds himself low man in a hierarchy based on clinical experience, so that he is allowed very little of the medical responsibility he would like to assume. Because of his lack of experience, he cannot write orders, and he receives permission to perform medical and surgical procedures (if at all) at a rate he considers far too slow. He usually must content himself with "mere" vicarious participation in the drama of danger, life, and death that he sees as the core of medical practice. The student culture accents these difficulties so that events (and especially those involving patients) are interpreted and reacted to as they push him toward or hold him back from further participation in this drama. He does not think in terms the layman might use.

As a result of the increasingly technical emphasis of his thinking the student appears cynical to the non-medical outsider, though from his own point of view he is simply seeing what is "really important." Instead of reacting with the layman's horror and sympathy for the patient to the sight of a cancerous organ that has been surgically removed, the student is more likely to regret that he was not allowed to close the incision at the completion of the operation, and to rue the hours that he must spend searching in the fatty flesh for the lymph nodes that will reveal how far the disease has spread. As in other lines of work, he drops lay attitudes for those more relevant to the way the event affects someone in his position.

This is not to say that the students lose their original idealism. When issues of idealism are openly raised in a situation they define as appropriate, they respond as they might have when they were freshmen. But the influence of the student culture is such that questions which might bring forth this idealism are not brought up. Students are often assigned patients for examination and follow-up whose conditions might be expected to provoke idealistic crises. Students discuss such patients, however, with reference to the problems they create for the *student*. Patients with terminal diseases who are a long time dying, and patients with chronic diseases who show little change from week to week, are more likely to be viewed as creating extra work without extra compensation in knowledge or the opportunity to practice new skills than as examples of illness which raise questions about euthanasia. Such cases require the student to spend time every day checking on progress which he feels will probably not take place and to write long "progress" notes in the patient's chart although little progress has occurred.

This apparent cynicism is a collective matter. Group activities are built around this kind of workaday perspective, constraining the students in two ways. First, they do not openly express the lay idealistic notions they may hold, for their culture does not sanction such expression; second, they are less likely to have thoughts of this deviant kind when they are engaged in group activity. The collective nature of this "cynicism" is indicated by the fact that students become more openly idealistic whenever they are removed from the influence of student culture—when they are alone with a sociologist as they near the finish of school and sense the approaching end of student life, for example, or when they are isolated from their classmates and therefore are less influenced by this culture.[9]

They still feel, as advanced students, though much less so than before, that school is irrelevant to actual medical practice. Many of their tasks, like running laboratory tests on patients newly admitted to the hospital or examining surgical specimens in the pathology laboratory, seem to them to have nothing to do with their visions of their future activity as doctors. As in their freshman year, they believe that perhaps they must obtain the knowledge they will need in spite of the school. They still conceive of medicine as a huge body of proven facts, but no longer believe that they will ever be able to master it all. They now say that they are going to try to apply the solution of the practicing M.D. to their own dilemma: learn a few things that they are interested in very well and know enough about other things to pass examinations while in school and, later on in practice, to know to which specialist to send difficult patients.

Their original medical idealism reasserts itself as the end of school approaches. Seniors show more interest than students in earlier years in serious ethical dilemmas of the kind they expect to face in practice. They have become aware of ethical problems laymen often see as crucial for the physician—whether it is right to keep patients with fatal diseases alive as long as possible, or what should be done if an influential patient demands an abortion—and worry about them. As they near graduation and student culture begins to break down as the soon-to-be doctors are about to go their separate ways, these questions are more and more openly discussed.

While in school, they have added to their earlier idealism a new and peculiarly professional idealism. Even though they know that few doctors live up to the standards they have been taught, they intend always to examine their patients thoroughly and to give treatment based on firm diagnosis rather than merely to relieve symptoms. This expansion and transformation of idealism appear most explicitly in their considerations of alternative careers, concerning both specialization and the kind of arrangements to be made for setting up practice. Many of their hypothetical choices aim at making it possible for them to be the kind of doctors their original idealism pictured. Many seniors consider specialty training so that they will be able to work in a limited field in which it will be more nearly possible to know all there is to know, thus avoiding the necessity of dealing in a more ignorant way with the wider range of problems general practice would present. In the same manner, they think of schemes to establish partnerships or other arrangements making it easier to avoid a work load which would prevent them from giving each patient the thorough examination and care they now see as ideal.

In other words, as school comes to an end, the cynicism specific to the school situation also comes to an end and their original and more general idealism about medicine comes to the fore again, though within a framework of more realistic alternatives. Their idealism is now more informed although no less selfless.

Discussion

We have used the words "idealism" and "cynicism" loosely in our description of the changeable state of mind of the medical student, playing on ambiguities we can now attempt to clear up. Retaining a core of common meaning, the dictionary definition, in our reference to the person's belief in the worth of his activity and the claims made for it, we have seen that this is not a generalized trait of the students we studied but rather an attitude which varies greatly, depending on the particular activity the worth of which is questioned and the situation in which the attitude is expressed.

This variability of the idealistic attitude suggests that in using such an element of personal perspective in sociological analysis one should not treat it as homogeneous but should make a determined search for subtypes which may arise under different conditions and have differing consequences.

Such subtypes presumably can be constructed along many dimensions. There might, for instance, be consistent variations in the medical students' idealism through the four years of school that are related to their social class backgrounds. We have stressed in this report the subtypes that can be constructed according to variations in the object of the idealistic attitude and variations in the audience the person has in mind when he adopts the attitude. The medical students can be viewed as both idealistic and cynical, depending on whether one has in mind their view of their school activities or the future they envision for themselves as doctors. Further, they might take one or another of these positions depending on whether their implied audience is made up of other students, their instructors, or the lay public.

A final complication arises because cynicism and idealism are not merely attributes of the actor, but are as dependent on the person doing the attributing as they are on the qualities of the individual to whom they are attributed.[10] Though the student may see his own disregard of the unique personal troubles of a particular patient as proper scientific objectivity, the layman may view this objectivity as heartless cynicism.[11]

Having made these analytic distinctions, we can now summarize the transformations of these characteristics as we have seen them occurring among medical students. Some of the students' determined idealism at the outset is reaction against the lay notion, of which they are uncomfortably aware, that doctors are money-hungry cynics; they counter this with an idealism of similar lay origin stressing the doctor's devotion to service. But this idealism soon meets a setback, as students find that it will not be relevant for a while, since medical school has, it seems, little relation to the practice of medicine, as they see it. As it has not been refuted, but only shown to be temporarily beside the point, the students "agree" to set this ideal-

ism aside in favor of a realistic approach to the problem of getting through school. This approach, which we have labeled as the cynicism specific to the school experience, serves as protection for the earlier grandiose feelings about medicine by postponing their exposure to reality to a distant future. As that future approaches near the end of the four years and its possible mistreatment of their ideals moves closer, the students again worry about maintaining their integrity, this time in actual medical practice. They use some of the knowledge they have gained to plan careers which, it is hoped, can best bring their ideals to realization.

We can put this in propositional form by saying that when a man's ideals are challenged by outsiders and then further strained by reality, he may salvage them by postponing their application to a future time when conditions are expected to be more propitious.

NOTES

1. Leonard D. Eron, "Effect of Medical Education on Medical Students," *Journal of Medical Education*, 10 (October, 1955), pp. 559–556.

2. This study is sponsored by Community Studies, Inc., of Kansas City, Missouri, and is being carried on at the University of Kansas Medical School, to whose dean, staff, and students we are indebted for their wholehearted cooperation. Professor Everett C. Hughes of the University of Chicago is director of the project.

3. The technique of participant observation has not been fully systematized, but some approaches to this have been made. See, for example, Florence R. Kluckhohn, "The Participant Observer Technique in Small Communities," *American Journal of Sociology*, 45 (November, 1940), pp. 331–343; Arthur Vidich, "Participant Observation and the Collection and Interpretation of Data," *ibid.*, 60 (January, 1955), pp. 354–360; William Foote Whyte, "Observational Field-Work Methods," in Maria Jahoda, Morton Deutsch, and Stuart W. Cook

(editors), *Research Methods in the Social Sciences,* New York: Dryden Press, 1951, II, pp. 393–514; and *Street Corner Society* (Enlarged edition), Chicago: University of Chicago Press, 1955, pp. 279–358; Rosalie Hankey Wax, "Twelve Years Later: An Analysis of Field Experience," *American Journal of Sociology,* 63 (September, 1957), pp. 133–142; Morris S. Schwartz and Charlotte Green Schwartz, "Problems in Participant Observation," 60 (January, 1955), pp. 343–353; and Howard S. Becker and Blanche Geer, "Participant Observation and Interviewing: A Comparison," *Human Organization* (forthcoming). The last item represents the first of a projected series of papers attempting to make explicit the operations involved in this method. For a short description of some techniques used in this study, see Howard S. Becker, "Interviewing Medical Students," *American Journal of Sociology,* 62 (September, 1956), pp. 199–201.

4. A fuller analysis and presentation of evidence will be contained in a volume on this study now being prepared by the authors in collaboration with Everett C. Hughes and Anselm L. Strauss.

5. Renee Fox has shown how complex one aspect of this whole subject is in her analysis of the way medical students at Cornell become aware of and adjust to both their own failure to master all available knowledge and the gaps in current knowledge in many fields. See her "Training for Uncertainty," in Robert K. Merton, George G. Reader, and Patricia L. Kendall (eds.), *The Student Physician: Introductory Studies in the Sociology of Medical Education,* Cambridge: Harvard University Press, 1957, pp. 207–241.

6. Compare Fox' description of student reaction to this problem at Cornell (*op. cit.,* pp. 209–221).

7. The concept of student culture is analyzed in some detail in Howard S. Becker and Blanche Geer, "Student Culture in Medical School," *Harvard Educational Review* (forthcoming).

8. Dana L. Farnsworth, "Some Observations on the Attitudes and Motivations of the Harvard Medical Student," *Harvard Medical Alumni Bulletin,* January, 1956, p. 34.

9. See the discussion in Howard S. Becker, "Interviewing Medical Students," *op. cit.*

10. See Philip Selznick's related discussion of fanaticism in *TVA and the Grass Roots,* Berkeley: University of California Press, 1953, pp. 205–213.

11. George Orwell gives the layman's side in his essay, "How the Poor Die" in *Shooting an Elephant and Other Essays,* London: Secker and Warburg, 1950, pp. 18–32.

Learning Real Feelings

A Study of High Steel Ironworkers' Reactions to Fear and Danger

Jack Haas

CASE STUDY QUESTIONS

1. In his first days on the job, the author admitted being very scared as he worked many stories from the ground. The other workers showed no fear at all. What could account for this discrepancy?

2. If a worker typically hides his fears, what function does that serve for the worker and for his fellow workers? When, if ever, were fears shown? Why?

3. How does the sociological concept of "definition of the situation" figure into describing the feelings and actions of the high steel workers?

4. How and why do workers test other workers? Do workers take any precautions to try to lessen the actual dangers of their jobs? Why or why not?

Author's Note: I am indebted to Blanche Geer and Howard S. Becker for their assistance in helping teach me how to do research and how to think sociologically. Thanks to Berkeley Fleming for his editorial suggestions. Thanks also to the local union and contractors' association for permission to do the research. My gratitude and sincere thanks to the ironworkers of this study for their cooperation and friendship.

Source: From *Sociology of Work and Occupations*, Vol. 4, No. 2, 1977, pp. 147–170. Reprinted by permission from Sage Publications, Inc.

Sidewalk observers watch in a mixture of respect and awe as, high above the ground, hardhat construction workers perform their dangerous ballet. They watch silently as the high steel ironworkers maneuver into place the tinker-toy-like sections of steel that form the skeletal framework of today's high buildings and bridges. High above the workmen, cranes dangle steel beams that must be caught and fixed into place; far below loom enormous chasms of empty space. These workers are protected from certain death only by their skill in balancing on slender beams, a skill threatened by swirls of weather and wind. One cannot but ask how, when faced with such danger, the high steel ironworkers can so casually ignore the perils of his occupation? The confidence and quickness of the workers is bewildering to onlookers who well note the hazards that beset such an occupation; how can these men walk the emerging structures with such confident aplomb? Are we considering brave men, or are these workers foolhardy, challenged by the very nature of their occupation; alternatively, does the answer to the enigma lie in the fact that these men are innately gifted, specially trained, or culturally conditioned so as to enable them to remain calm in the face of such danger? Questions like this are raised in the observer's mind because he cannot relate to the workers' situation; to most of us, such displays, such defiance of risk and the certain consequences of error are inexplicable.

In this [case study] I shall describe how high steel ironworkers feel and act toward the dangers inherent in their occupation. I shall explore the seemingly inconceivable attitude and behavior of the workers by a juxtaposition of my own reactions when exposed to the same dangers. I will describe how I came to understand the high steel ironworkers' perspectives toward fear and danger. I found myself (in spite of myself) beginning more and more to act as they did. As I came to know these men they admitted to sharing my fear-laden assessment of their occupational situation. We came to share a definition of the situation, a situation they had developed a perspective[1] for dealing with that I had yet to learn.

During the nine months of observation of the construction of a 21 story office building I was a participant observer in a variety of work and recreational settings. I observed union activities, participated in a formal training program for ironworker apprentices, and ate and drank with them. I focused upon the apprentices and attempted to understand the processes by which they were socialized.[2]

The analysis of the data takes two forms. First, the natural history of the research is described as I came to learn the attitude of the workers toward their perilous work. I found that the ironworkers' perspective toward danger was not revealed in their words or actions, but remained an important, although not overtly communicated, part of their everyday methods of coping with their occupational situation. Workers were expected to act in ways which would convince others that they were not afraid. Second, I describe how ironworkers act out their implicitly accepted perspective about danger, and how, through a variety of mechanisms, both individual and collective, they manage to maintain a control of with whom

and when they work. The element of danger depends on the trust they are able to afford their fellow workers, the nature and predictability of the weather, the location of their work activity on the emerging structure, and the risks their particular specialty requires.

A Natural History of My First Days in the Field

My traumatic introduction to the work day realities of high steel ironworking came the day the construction superintendent passed me through the construction gate, gave me a hard hat, and wished me good luck. Directly ahead were five incomplete levels of an emerging 21 story office building. From my vantage point I observed a variety of workers engaged in the construction process. The most visible and immediately impressive group of workers were those on the upper level who were putting steel beams into place. These were the ironworkers I had come to participate with and observe. This chilling reality filled me with an almost overwhelming anxiety. I began to experience a trepidation that far exceeded any usual observer anxiety encountered in the first days of field research. It was the first time I felt this since attempting to gain entree to do a study of apprenticeship training. I watched the men at the top, the precariousness of their position, and the risks of first-hand observation were profoundly obvious. It was with fearful anticipation that I moved toward the job site.

I had anticipated this day but never so directly and profoundly. I had taken out a $50,000 accident policy to protect my family—just in case. I had not told my wife about the research. She found out when a fellow graduate student blurted it out at a party. I protected her and hid my true feelings from my colleagues. Long before the research started I had expected to convince parties to the agreement that I do the research, by writing a letter forgiving them any liability. In these ways I prepared. But as I looked up, I knew I was not prepared for this. These were the people I had come to study and they were up there, and as I watched them I was dumbfounded and awe-struck by their aplomb. They "ran the iron" with seeming abandon. It was apparent from the ground that workers moving so confidently across and up and down beams were unafraid.

There I stood, with work shoes, levis, work shirt, and a borrowed hardhat, in controlled terror. I noticed two apprentices at the ground level getting out of a trailer van. My strategy had been to locate those apprentices I had met two days previously at an apprentice welding class and follow them on the job.

I yelled to them:

"Hi, how are you doing?"
    An apprentice says, "What's up?"
    I told him that I had just got on the job, and that I would like to follow some of the guys around.

By this time another fellow, Bob, came up behind us. We stood and talked for a while.
    I said,

"I just saw the superintendent of Slippery Structural Steel. I had to see them before I could get on the job. How are things up there?
    "Safe enough?" he answers, "Yeh, it's all right, they've got planking all over. Why don't you come up with us? We'll show you around."
    "Fine, let's go." Believe me, what follows were tense moments. We walked past workmen putting rods in and setting concrete foundations to a ladder.

Tom, using only one hand, while carrying welding rods on his shoulder, went up ahead of me on the ladder and climbed to the second level of the building. The ladder was some 20 feet high; tied securely at top and bottom. I climbed up behind Tom, my apprehension growing in direct proportion to my height above the ground. It appeared that large sections between the girders were planked, but others were not. Many places were exposed and one had to be extremely careful with his footing. Scared but "poised," I carefully and exactly followed Tom. A large quantity of cable was apparent, most of it running diagonally from beam to beam. I followed up another ladder to more planking and over to a planked work area.

This was my introduction to "running the iron," a traumatic experience I somehow survived. In retrospect it was a critical first step in my understanding of how ironworkers perceived and reacted to danger. Needless to say, it was a most important beginning for developing rapport with the ironworkers. I was an outsider beginning to meet their career-long challenge. I earned some credibility as a person who could begin to appreciate and empathize with the problems of their work situation.

For the first few weeks I was very scared. On the steel (or as I now know "iron") I was cautious, but not too visibly. I knew I was on stage. We were all on stage and I was concerned about developing rapport and not being defined and mocked as the weak deviant. But, I was really scared. I was afraid but trying not to show it. They were boisterous, boastful, and continually demonstrating, by their actions, a lack of intimidation about the same situation of which I was most apprehensive. The discrepancy between my personal reactions to "running the iron" and their unified and contrary reaction to the same situation raised the first important question of the research—why did they act this way?[3] I thought it possibly a difference between them and me (never a matter of genetics, culture, or the Mohawk Indian stereotype, but more likely a matter of experience). I had been told before I went on the steel that ironworkers were in fact a very different and unique group of workers.[4]

The actions of ironworkers from the very first day were quite disconcerting; my feeling was one of great fear, yet their actions belied this approach. I felt, and this proved correct, that in order to establish rapport with these workers I would have to demonstrate a certain willingness to participate in the situation and indicate that I could, and would, accommodate myself.

The discrepancy between my feelings and the lack of meaning of their unusually confident behavior raised a question in my mind; was I attempting to interpret their actions according to my relevance structure? I had assumed that, sharing the same experience, we would have the same feelings about it; their actions, however, suggested we were not defining the situation similarly, and, in fact, they had overlooked what was, in my assessment of the situation, frightening. This perplexing discrepancy between the meaning of their behavior and my own definition of the situation led me to attempt to understand why their behavior would be appropriate to such a situation.

Schutz (1967: 174-175) describes three different approaches for understanding the motives of others. The observer can search his memory for similar actions and can assume his motive for such an action holds true for another's actions. If this approach is unsuccessful, the observer can resort to what he knows about the person's behavior and deduce his motive. Finally, if he lacks information about the person he is observing, he can ask him whether one or another motive would be furthered by the act in question. In this situation, I was not able to compare actions in my past with those I observed, nor did I know much about those I was observing except what I had been told by the contractors' representative. The third approach, of attributing different motives, was immediately relevant, but not immediately obvious to me.

In questioning their behavior, I asked myself whether it could be possible that these workers had gained an immunity to fear because of their constant exposure to dangerous situations. It seemed plausible. The more I walked the high steel, to some degree, the more confident and assured I became. This was relative. Whenever I went up on the steel, fear was a strong emotion but there were peaks and valleys depending on what I was on, and where. If ironworkers' actions belied any indications of fear, I suspected they might, nevertheless, talk about it and also about ways of handling it. I was disappointed. They did not talk about being afraid, although they did talk a great deal about danger.

This questioning process was essentially a process where on the basis of my own experience and perceptions I was attempting to understand the actions of others and to a point it didn't make sense until I realized, I was doing what they were doing. I was tempted in this sense to reconcile my reactions with the reactions of others. The consistency of ironworker actions on the high steel and their total lack of discussion about fear (a problem I considered paramount), led me to suspect that they had developed a shared perspective for dealing with the problem of which these particular actions were a part. This was a perspective I was beginning to learn, as I came to realize I was acting like they were.

Shared Perspective: The Disavowal of Fear

I had developed a perspective: fear was a reaction to walking the steel, but it was controlled when running the iron. Either ironworkers were immune to the fear of heights and danger, or as I had, they hid their fears when they went up on the steel. Was this perspective peculiar to me or was it one shared by the workers also?

The working hypothesis was that fear was part of their definition of the situation, and that the collective way they dealt with the problem was to treat it as if it did not exist. Individual workers concealed fear from each other. Collectively these reactions produce a situation of pluralistic ignorance (Schank, 1932: 102, 130-131; Mayer and Rosenblatt, 1975) in which each worker tended to think he was more frightened than coworkers who convincingly controlled their fears. To test this hypothesis is difficult, particularly if workers feel reluctant to talk about their fear—their reticence, both confirms the hypothesis and denies the testing of the hypothesis.

Faced with this methodological problem, the provisional explanation was that workers cannot express their fears, because such expression would raise doubts of their trustworthiness. In a work situation, where the actions of one can affect the safety and lives of others, workers must inspire trust and confidence. Showing fear is exactly contrary to the development of this kind of trust.

One hint that workers did indeed have the perspective that I was beginning to develop, was their discussion about workers who were afraid. They were extremely critical of such workers, and part of their criticism was that they added to the danger of the situation.

While working near the top of the emerging office building, a journeyman ironworker reveals the problem a fearful worker presents. I say:

> "I guess you have to watch out for the other fellow."
>
> Abe answers, "That's right, most of these guys know what they're doing, but you get some of the fucking apprentices, like that guy over there (he points to Roy) who's scared up here, and you have really got to watch yourself, because you don't know what the hell they're liable to do."

The journeyman points out that a worker who is afraid has to be watched. He warns me that a worker who acts afraid is unpredictable. This instruction helps me to learn

his perspective about fear. The process of developing shared beliefs and actions about a problem was expressed even more clearly by a journeyman teacher at the apprentice class. He warns apprentices about assumed trust of their coworkers by saying:

> "There's one thing I want you guys to remember, because in so many ways your life depends upon not doing things in a stupid way. Think out what you're going to do beforehand. Make sure that the guy that you're working with knows what the hell he's doing too.
>
> There's no sense working with a dummy, because you can never trust them, you've always got to watch out for them and you're not learning a damn thing. If something's been done by another guy, say he's hung a float for you, or done this or done that for you, and you've got to get out on it, you're a damned fool if you don't check it yourself. Now I don't say this is always the case, if you work with someone, say you're paired up with a guy and you've been working with him for awhile and you know him well, and you can trust him and he's no dummy, then you don't have to be that thorough. But if you come on a new job, you are doing the most foolish thing that you could ever do by not making sure."

In this quote, one may perceive the process by which a group (apprentices) come to learn this shared perspective. Apprentices are told the importance of guarding themselves against untrustworthy workers. They are told how to act by thinking out what they are going to do and making sure that their coworkers do too. Later, the instructor presents a number of possible situations. Each situation is interpreted for the apprentices and the proper action for each situation is described. Interpreting situations and actions for others is part of the process of sharing this perspective about fear and threatening coworkers.

Oftentimes a group will develop a special language or argot that focuses on special problems or experiences that the group might face. During the research, I was struck by the vivid phrases ironworkers used to describe actions that revealed fear. The phrases ironworkers used are "to coon it," "to seagull it," or "to cradle it." Cooning it or cradling it (it being the steel beam) involves walking on all fours across the steel, or holding onto the steel while traversing it. Seagulling refers to walking the steel with arms outstretched, as in flight, to provide balance. These phrases are only used criticizing the actions of others.

The importance of this relationship of personal danger to the actions of work associates is reflected in the following conversation with a journeyman ironworker:

High up on the steel, I look down and say to the journeyman,
"Pretty scary up here, eh?"
The journeyman responds,
"It really isn't that bad, just depends on who you're working with. If you're working with a guy that knows what the hell he's doing up here, it's safe as can be. It's only when you get a guy that doesn't know what's going on that you have to watch out."

A fearful or unknowing worker adds a measure of unpredictability to the work situation and makes it potentially even more dangerous. One who is afraid cannot be trusted to act correctly; he may act rashly, being concerned about his own protection or unsure about how to respond. The worker who is afraid may, moreover, neglect or avoid his responsibilities, and, as a consequence, endanger others. One who reveals his fear cannot be trusted to put his responsibility to others in priority to his emotions.

Considering this, it is obvious that one of the crucial tests one must pass to gain acceptance by his ironworker colleagues is to manage his impressions and to hide his fear. Workers act confidently on the steel and do not express their fears because to do

so would damage their prospects for gaining the confidence of others and acceptance as a colleague. Their reputation and employability depends upon being defined as trustworthy.

Fear is taken for granted in that it is not talked about or revealed. It is, however, a personal reaction that ironworkers feel. Worker fear is hidden, controlled, and privately lived. Beyond that, there is little one can do about it. A journeyman at the union hall describes what can be done and, given that, how one must accept danger and fear without allowing it to control or adversely affect his behavior.

"I think it [danger] is something you realize as soon as you step foot on it [the steel]. It is a dangerous situation or at least it can be made so. So in a sense you take every precaution you can, and make the job as safe as you can. And then you don't worry about it. You really don't worry about it. I know that sounds funny with you, but no one is going to make it that sits there and stands there and worries about it all day. You recognize it and you respect it, but you don't let it get to you."

The journeyman explains how each ironworker must deal with this reality. Workers take all the precautions possible. After doing so, they must attempt to submerge their feelings and go about their job.

The journeyman's closing statement is instructive. It is important that the worker doesn't allow his fear to bother him and, hence we might assume, his colleagues. Workers must act as if there was nothing to fear. Hughes (1958: 90–91) makes this same point when he says:

It is also to be expected that those who are subject to the same work risks will compose a collective rationale which they whistle to one another to keep up their courage, and they will build up collective defenses against the lay world....These rationales and defenses contain a logic that is somewhat like that of insurance, in that they tend to spread the risk psychologically (by saying that it might happen to anyone), morally, and financially.

The collective "whistle" suggests Goffman's (1959) dramaturgical analogy of front and backstage behavior—workers maintain a front of confidence and lack of fear before their audience. In this case, the audience is composed of fellow workers, and consequently there are few backstage areas where their front breaks down. One such backstage area was in private conversation with the observer. Alone and in my confidence, workers would tell me of their fear.

Verifying this perspective—that ironworkers deliberately pretend to be unafraid—was a continuing research interest. Ironworkers I observed throughout the research acted almost with disdain to the dangers surrounding them. As a way of proving themselves to their work fellows, many seemed deliberately to flaunt the situation by taking risks—they showed off by volunteering for the most dangerous work activity, as a way of demonstrating their trustworthiness and enhancing their reputations. The very few who acted afraid were treated as deviants, threats, and objects of ridicule to be driven out of ironworking before they allowed their fear to disrupt the shared perspective.

There were only two occasions where advertently or inadvertently ironworkers revealed their fear-laden feelings. The confessions that were made to me privately and personally were most important. These confessions were made when some ironworkers came to trust me as one who would not betray their confidence to fellow workers. Many of them wanted to quit ironworking but they were hopelessly bound into a network of relationships and a career that was difficult if not impossible to terminate. Leaving ironworking would be tantamount to admitting they were afraid, and that would mean total expulsion from a way of life they had become bound and committed to, despite its anxiety provoking consequences.

The most touching example I encountered was when a highly regarded Indian ironworker literally begged me to open university doors to a new career. We both agreed, in a boozy and emotional stupor, that he could not because his whole life, particularly his honored status among ironworkers and reservation Indians, would be forever altered. Competing with his young brother on the high steel, he knew he was pushing the limits. It was only a matter of time before that competition, and the veneer of fearlessness, would be shattered by one or the other's fall.

The other graphic breakdown of front which corroborates the underlying but conscious suppression of fear is when a worker falls "in the hole" and is killed. Although I fortunately never directly experienced such a situation, an Indian journeyman recounted his first dramatic confrontation with the underlying reality. He says:

"I remember one time when a guy fell in the hole. He hit his head on a piece of steel on the way down, so he was killed instantly. Well anyways, this has an effect on you. Most of times you stop work and quit for the day. I didn't feel too bad. I guess death has got to hit closer to home, like if your brother or father gets it. Maybe, I was too new then, but anyways the older guys up there just froze. They wouldn't move, and they wouldn't come off the iron. I had to go up there and bring them down one by one, and some guys were so scared I had to bring them down almost by carrying them."

When a worker falls and is killed, ironworkers leave the job. They go drinking and reminisce about their lost colleague. The next day, seemingly adjusted once more to the dangers, they return to work.

The above story indicates how their managed impressions and assumed behavior were dramatically confronted. The accident and loss of a colleague stimulates a reevaluation of the worker's socially constructed reality. Contrary to the way they were expected to act and the behavior supposedly consonant with their definition of the situation was the fact there was much to fear. It is not difficult to understand their complete breakdown of front. They are reminded— in the most personally affecting way—there is much to be afraid of.

Testing Fellow Workers

Although one should conceal fear, workers do agree that the relativity of danger allows a worker to define for himself situations which are too dangerous. Part of their perspective about fear is the recognition that workers should protect themselves and others from situations which increase their common danger. One way to do this is to test the trustworthiness of their fellow workers.

Workers recognize that running the iron is a managed performance and may not reflect one's true feelings. It is important for workers to know whether a confident front (Goffman, 1959) will break down in a crisis. Workers believe it is important to know as much as possible about the trustworthiness of fellow workers in all sorts of situations, and they test this by binging, a process similar to styles of interaction observed in black ghetto youth (Kochman, 1969), white lower-class gang members (Miller et al., 1961), hospital personnel (Goffman, 1951: 122), and perhaps as Berne (1964) suggests, North Americans in general. These studies indicate the many purposes of this form of interaction. Hughes (1945: 356) points out an important use of binging in testing newcomers when he comments:

> To be sure that a new fellow will not misunderstand requires a sparring match of social gestures. The zealot who turns the sparring match into a real battle, who takes a friendly

initiation too seriously, is not likely to be trusted with the lighter sort of comment on one's work or with doubts and misgivings; nor can he learn those parts of the working code which are communicated only by hint and gesture....In order that men may communicate freely and confidently, they must be able to take a good deal of each other's sentiments for granted.

In the following quotation, a journeyman, three apprentices, and I engage in a sparring match, on top of an emerging 21 story building. Abe, the journeyman says:

> "These fucking apprentices don't know their ass from a hole in the ground."
> The journeyman turns to me and says,
> "I hope you don't think these guys are representative of the whole apprenticeship. They're pretty sad lot."
> Joining in with the kidding, I say,
> "Yeh, I've noticed that."
> Bud, an apprentice, adds,
> "Don't listen to him. He's just a fucking Indian."
> The journeyman responds,
> "Yeh, and he's a fucking nigger."
> Abe yells down to the apprentice below,
> "What the fuck are you doing down there, playing with yourself? For Christ's sake get up here and bring that machine up here with you."

The example demonstrates how repartee tests relationships and exchanges information. The style is characteristically earthy, there is little regard for amenities, and the jibes seem deliberately provocative—a verbal challenge. In a dangerous work situation where we expect workers to try to ease conflict, we find deliberate provocation. An Indian journeyman sums up the importance of this form of interaction as he and I drink beer in a bar:

> "You see, I don't get upset often. And when I do I forget right after. You've got to figure, if you're going to work with the guy, you can't hold something against him, because he

could kill you and you could kill him. You forget fast when you're in this business. What you do is try to see what the guy is made of, because if he gets agitated, and wants to fight over something like this, then you don't know what he's going to do up on the steel if something goes wrong. A lot of times you're responsible for that other guy up there and you can either make him or break him."

Workers use binging to test trustworthiness and self-control—will a man keep cool when subjected to such personal abuse? If he loses his poise, it indicates he may lose control in other threatening situations, e.g., high above the ground. If he takes such kidding too seriously, he may carry a grudge into a situation where revenge could be easy. Binging also conveys information about expected relationships among participants; relationships characterized by constant redefinition, indicated by subtle cues from the participants. Such interaction permits the apprentice to experiment by binging back in anticipation of a favorable response, which shows journeymen consider him acceptable.

The one-sided nature of binging between journeymen and apprentices was apparent throughout the study. New apprentices are called "punks," and their role involves carrying out the most demeaning tasks and the acceptance of the deliberate castigation of veteran workers.

On the top of the building, I talked with a journeyman about his constant kidding of new apprentices, I say,

"Looks like you were busting Jerry, the fire-watch, the other day."

Abe, the journeyman, answers, "That's all right, I used to take it even worse than that. You see, I started pretty young. I used to work summers at this, and they had me doing all sorts of punking, and everyone was on my ass, all the time. I remember one summer, I carried bolts around, and that's all. I got so fucking sick of looking at those

bolts, I was about ready to go out of my nut. If I took it these guys can take it. You've got to take it and dish it right back."

This journeyman makes it clear that binging is an institutionalized part of the apprentice's career; it is an initiation all must pass through before acceptance as a peer who can "dish it right back." The process is used by ironworkers to test the trustworthiness and loyalty of coworkers, and apprentices are most subject to it. The mechanism is used to test the self-control of coworkers; ironworkers believe it is useful in measuring a man's ability to handle himself in a dangerous situation. Ironworkers also believe that an apprentice's willingness to accept disparaging and hostile attacks on his person provides predictable evidence that he will commit himself to the interests of the group, over and above any self-interests.

Worker Autonomy to Reduce Danger

In an attempt to reduce the threats to their safety, ironworkers try to control factors they perceive that add to their danger. Such factors include superiors who have little regard for worker safety and unsafe weather conditions. Ironworkers try to limit the effects of both.

It is not difficult to imagine the kind of havoc the wind can play in the high, open areas where ironworkers frequently work. The wind complicates the worker's problem of keeping his balance on steel beams, which range in width from four to 12 inches. The wind is particularly dangerous when workers are carrying equipment across the steel. For example, the heavy wooden "floats" of plywood, on which the welders sit or stand, act as sails when caught by the wind and workers must take special care not to be blown off the beams. Two workers are usually required to carry a float. In a strong wind they will drag the float across the steel. They carry the float away from the wind, then if a sudden breeze stirs up the float does not push them off for they can let it give and reduce the sail effect. If the wind blows very hard, they can drop the float, grab the ropes, and sit or stand on them while the platform swings free in space. Their other alternative is to drop the float completely, endangering workers below—a last and rarely considered option.

Workers frequently were observed telling stories about unusual and extremely dangerous working situations. The following is an example of a story about the wind told by an ironworker journeyman to other journeymen, three apprentices, and myself:

> "I remember when I was on this job putting this bridge over the seaway, and this stupid son-of-a-bitch is up there on the bridge and he had his hat on backwards, so this wind comes and lifts the peak up and the hat starts flying off his head. So this guy comes and reaches up with both hands and grabs his hat and goes overboard with it. I mean this fucking guy should have known better and let the goddamned hat drop. So there he is falling down through the air about 100 feet still holding on to the goddamned helmet. And then you look down below and there he is swimming and he still has one hand on that goddamned helmet. I don't know how stupid guys can be."

The journeyman warns the others of the problem that the wind presents and suggests that they ensure their safety first, and then worry about their clothing or equipment. In addition to the wind, snow, sleet, rain, and ice reduce the workers' visibility and/or make the steel beams and wood planking slippery. Walking the iron is difficult enough without these added imponderables.

Work, however, continues despite difficult weather; snow is shoveled off the steel beams and wood planking and ice is melted from the beams by a portable heater. During the winter, workers dress as warmly as possible and carry on the work activity. The weather is always a problem because it affects not only workers' safety but also their wages. The values of money and safety are sometimes in conflict. The worker is paid by the contractor for showing up in the morning, whether he works or not. If the weather is too inclement, he is paid two hours "show up time." Oftentimes, there is a difference of opinion between the workers and the foreman as to whether work should continue. Sometimes the workers want to work to increase their wages, and the foreman tells them to take the day off; other times the workers feel the weather has made working too dangerous, but the foreman believes the work should go on. The following discussion by a group of apprentices at the apprentice class indicates some of the problems the weather presents.

Nine apprentices stand around talking about their work week.

Dick says, "How many hours you guys get? I got forty again this week."

(Bill) "Twenty-eight hours, can you imagine that? Friday we came in and we worked up there in that fucking blizzard until quarter of ten and then the blizzard starts to stop and then they tell us to go home. That pisses me off. I mean I'm willing to work, I say fuck the weather. You know what they have me do, they go and give me a broom and have me go out and sweep the beams off so the welders can go out there. Friday was a bastard, you couldn't even coon it to get out there. Tell 'em Roy."

(Roy) "Well I only got twenty-two hours. They put you up there and you work your show-up time and then things start to clear up and they tell you to go home. You see, you get all these guys from Connecticut. We haven't worked a Friday in the last five weeks. Fucking guys are all getting an early start home, so they tell us to get off."

(John) "I only had twenty hours. I didn't even get in Wednesday. Did you work Wednesday, Bill?"

(Bill) "Damned right, about froze my balls, but I got in four hours until lunchtime.

You know that welder, Joe Walker? Christ he was hanging out in the front of the building. What do you think of this Ralph (teacher-journeyman)? There he is on the goddamned float and the wind's blowing like hell and it's cold as hell up there and the float is banging away up there. So he's got to hold on to the steel with one hand to keep the float from banging away, and try welding with the other. So he just said 'fuck it' and got off of it, and went down to the Cartel (bar) and got himself some brews."

(Dick) "I don't know about you guys. All the decking crew got their forty hours in this week. All the rodmen were down there working. Structural guys, they always drag up. What's the matter with you guys, can't you take it up there?"

(Bill) "Oh, fuck you. You go up there and walk around in that shit. Goddamn wind's blowing so hard and it's snowing and you can't see your foot in front of you. It's all right, you guys are down on the bottom. That stuff was starting to freeze on Friday. It's all right if it's slushy. I mean it's slushy. I mean it's still not good, but it's not as bad as when that stuff is freezing up on you. Then you're really on your ass."

These comments point out the varied definitions of safe working conditions. Under ordinary conditions workers are expected to handle their fears and accept the problem of danger. In unusual conditions workers decide for themselves whether or not to work. There are, however, other considerations which they may take into account in defining the situation. Some of the factors which influence their decision are the loss of pay, leaving early, and determining how their action will affect the ability of their coworkers to continue working.

At the end of the apprentices' discussion, an apprentice (Bill) indicates that the problem of danger is a relative one. He commented, "It's all right if it's slushy….It's not as bad as when the stuff is freezing up on you." Some kinds of foul weather are more dangerous than others, and some places and jobs on the steel structure are more dangerous than the others. For example, the tops and sides of the structure are more dangerous than the center and lower areas of the building. The top is more dangerous because it is higher; the sides because there is nothing to break a fall.

The relativity of danger in ironworkers' thinking sometimes leads to different interpretations of the situation. Some workers may choose to leave work while others may stay. The important point is the collective support given to workers to choose freely, excepting occasions when their refusal to work affects the group. If the group is burdened by a member's decision to "drag up," he is criticized; otherwise, his action is not rebuked.

In the next example, an apprentice describes how the decision to work or not to work is made.

> At the apprentice class one apprentice says to the rest of the group, including myself, "I will always go up and take a look at what it is like….I usually go up like I did Wednesday, when it was 26° below—I went up there and went all the way to the eighth floor and looked around and it was too cold. So, I came back down."

It is the apprentice who goes up to the floor where he will be working and who checks out for himself the working conditions; his decision not to work is an independent one, not relying on the judgments of others. The decision to work or not may be a group one; when a decision is made to thwart the foreman or contractor's usurpation of their autonomy the group will then invariably act together. On one occasion I followed Ray (apprentice) up to the top level which was almost completely planked. Because of the planking, this floor had accumulated between two or three inches of hardpacked snow. It was quite slippery and treacherous because of open spaces and planking that was insecurely based.

Ray said:

"Most of the guys aren't in today, they all took off.

"You mean they came in earlier?" I asked.

"Yeh, but Bill didn't come in," Ray answers.

I asked,

"Who decides whether they're to leave?"

Ray responds,

"They do. Mac (the foreman) asked a couple of them to go and shovel snow and they said 'no' and took off."

In this example, the foreman directs the workers to shovel snow; the group chooses not to, and the men leave the job. Other workers remain free to decide for themselves whether or not to work. The perspective of worker autonomy is enacted and reinforced.

Conclusion

The processes of social control I have described—testing and controlling fellow workers and maintaining and enhancing individual and collective control over the work setting—are processes characteristic of occupations where danger is a perceived worker problem. The careful surveillance and testing of colleagues, particularly newcomers, the controlled actions belying any fear, and the unified efforts to increase worker autonomy are sociologically relevant outcomes in situations where workers face extreme danger. The processes ironworkers have derived for controlling and directing the behavior of apprentices, as well as journeymen, in many ways parallel those described of pipeline construction workers (Graves, 1958), lumberjacks (Haynes, 1945), miners (Gouldner, 1954; Lucas, 1969), combat personnel (Grinker and Spiegel, 1963; Stouffer, 1949; Weiss, 1967), and ghetto social workers (Mayer and Rosenblatt, 1975).

In dangerous occupations participants are described as engaging in a great deal of horseplay, joking and banter, or, as I refer to it—binging. This form of interaction supports worker efforts to maintain control of their work environment and to evolve rigorous sets of expectations about appropriate behavior and shared worker attributes. This suggests that the perception of danger leads to very similar processes and expectations in very disparate occupational groups. The single characteristic they all share is their perception of danger; this perception produces a set of perspectives around the problem of danger that is rigorously and continuously enforced.

The workers' attempt to increase control over their work environment and lessen the dangers is the second and related theme of this [case study]. This perspective emphasizes the ironworkers' commitment to increasing worker autonomy and thus a control over their environment. They strive to maintain control by collectively supporting individual and group decisions to judge for themselves safe and unsafe working conditions. They support the actions of fellow workers who decide whether or not to work in inclement weather. Fellow workers accept or reject the judgments of work superiors who may not give precedence to ironworkers' considerations and who could consequently pose a threat to their personal and collective security. Workers who perceive physical danger develop mechanisms to control their reactions and the reactions of others. Individually and collectively they struggle to enhance the security of their situation. Symbolic or real threats bind workers together in an effort to protect themselves. Part of the defense, however, lies in controlling one's personal trepidations and insecurities and maintaining an appearance of fearlessness.

These reactions, I believe, are characteristic of many groups and are only more obvious and dramatic in the observation of high steel ironworkers. Behind the calculated performances and fronts of much social activity is the underlying insecurity and threat of failure. These fears are contained and controlled, because to do otherwise is to admit personal failure and to face ridicule or ostracism.

NOTES

1. The concept perspective is taken from Becker et al. (1961) and refers to a set of beliefs and actions an individual or group has towards a perceived problem. In this case the perspective is a shared or group one, which has developed out of the interactions ironworkers have about their mutually defined problem.

2. After each observation I dictated in as complete a form as possible all that I had seen and heard in the course of the observation. These near verbatim dictations were typed in full as field notes and later coded and categorized and serve as the basis of this analysis.

3. An important point is that as a stranger to the situation I did not share the expectations of others. This estrangement on my part made the actions of others more profound and dramatic. See Garfinkel (1957: 37), where he points out that such estrangement is helpful for bringing into view the background expectancies of the participants. See also Simmel (1950: 405), where he makes the point that the stranger role carries with it a certain objectivity, i.e., he is not committed to the "unique ingredients and peculiar tendencies of the group."

4. During the interview phase of the study, when the decision to study ironworkers had not yet been reached, respondents provided me with a preliminary set of expectations which affected my thinking. Having had no experience or contact with ironworkers, their comments provided me with a framework of understanding about ironworkers even though subsequently they were found to be incorrect or exaggerated.

In this example, the contractor's representative tells me about Indian ironworkers:

> You know they're the damndest ironworkers (Indians). I don't care what you say,

they can go out Saturday night and get a real toot and Monday morning have the jumping jeepers. But, by gosh, you get them up there and they're not afraid of anything.

This statement by the contractor's representative suggests that Indians are unafraid and that there is indeed something to fear, a very important point for me.

5. The term "binging" was, I believe, first used and described by Roethlisberger and Dickson (1934). They describe workers binging each other by punching others on the shoulder. This action served as a means of social control, a warning to the worker that he had exceeded the work group's informally agreed upon standard of production.

REFERENCES

Becker, H. S., B. Geer, A. Strauss, and E. Hughes (1961) *Boys in White*. Chicago: Univ. of Chicago Press.

Berne E. (1964) *Games People Play*. New York: Grove.

Garfinkel, H. (1957) *Studies in Ethnomethodology*. Englewood Cliffs, N.J.: Prentice-Hall.

Goffman, E. (1959) *Presentation of Self in Everyday Life*. New York: Doubleday Anchor.

———. (1951) *Encounters*. Indianapolis Ind.: Bobbs-Merrill.

Gouldner, A. (1954) *Patterns of Industrial Bureaucracy*. New York: Free Press.

Graves, B. (1958) "'Breaking out': an apprenticeship system among pipeline construction workers." *Human Organization* 17 (Fall): 9–13.

Grinker, R. R. and J. P. Spiegel (1963) *Men Under Stress*. Philadelphia: Blakerston Co.

Haas, J. (1974) "The stages of the high steel ironworker apprentice career." *Soc. Q.* 15 (Winter): 93–108.

———. (1972) "Binging: educational control among high steel ironworkers." *Amer. Behavioral Scientist* 16 (September/October): 27–34.

Haynes, N. (1945) "Taming the lumberjack." *Amer. Soc. Rev.* 10 (April): 217–225.

Hughes, E.C. (1958) *Men and Their Work*. New York: Free Press.

———. (1945) "Dilemmas and contradictions of status." *Amer. J. of Sociology* 5 (March): 353–359.

Kochman, T. (1969) "'Rapping' in the black ghetto." *Transaction* 6 (February) 26–34.

Lucas, R. (1969) *Men in Crisis, A Study of Mine Disaster.* New York: Basic Books.

Mayer, J. E. and A. Rosenblatt (1975) "Encounters with danger: Social workers in the ghetto." *Sociology of Work and Occupations* 2 (August): 227–245.

Miller, W. B., H. Geertz, and H. S. G. Cutter (1961) "Aggression in a boy's street-corner gang." *Psychiatry* 24 (November): 283–298.

Roethlisberger, F. L. and W. J. Dickson (1934) *Management and the Worker.* Boston: Harvard University Graduate School of Business Administration.

Schanck, R. L. (1932) "A study of a community and its groups and institutions conceived of as behaviors of individuals." *Psychiatry Monographs* 43, 2.

Shutz, A. (1967) *The Phenomenology of the Social World* [trans. by George Walsh and Frederick Lehnert]. Evanston, Ill.: Northwestern Univ. Press.

Simmel, G. (1950) *The Sociology of Georg Simmel* [trans. and ed. by Kurt H. Wolff]. New York: Free Press.

Stouffer, S. (1949) *The American Soldier: Combat and its Aftermath,* II. Princeton, N.J.: Princeton Univ. Press.

Weiss, M. (1967) "Rebirth in the airborne." *Transaction* 4 (May): 23–26.

Equal Versus Equitable Treatment

Policewomen and Patrol Work

Susan E. Martin

CASE STUDY QUESTIONS

1. If certain aspects of socialization appear to be distinctly linked with masculine culture, what will women do to indicate their commitment and socialization to the informal culture?

2. What are the difficulties of being properly socialized to an occupational culture when one is a token?

3. What negative impact could the dynamics of tokenism have on those being socialized to an occuption? Are there any advantages to being the token with regard to the process of socialization?

...Of particular interest are the differential impacts of organizational policies regarding the socialization of new officers and the distribution of assignments to male and female officers that make "breaking and entering" into police work more difficult for a woman than for a man....

It is the women who are expected to assimilate into the policemen's world, on the men's terms, and to change to overcome handicaps arising from their prior experi-

Source: From *Varieties of Work* (pp. 101–121), edited by Phyllis E. Stewart and Muriel G. Cantor, 1982, Thousand Oaks, CA: Sage Publications. Reprinted by permission of Sage Publications, Inc.

ence, the attitudes of male co-workers, existing informal channels of power and opportunity within the department, and departmental policies....

The work and work culture handicap women in two ways. The fiction of military discipline and the emphasis on rare instances of the need to physically control others lead to the belief that women are inappropriate for the job, thereby affecting their recruitment, training, and promotional opportunities. The informal power structure, based on close personal ties, makes it difficult for an outsider to gain the acceptance or sponsorship necessary for "success" and advancement.

Organizational Policy Dilemmas

The policies of work organizations have a major impact on the way new employees perform their occupational roles. The organization selects and trains workers and is responsible for creating the environment and opportunities which enable them to learn and perform their work. It *can* establish effective training patterns, actively seek to limit discrimination against and harassment of minority or "token" workers, ensure opportunities for mobility and power for all workers, open channels for redress of grievances, and adopt policies that vigorously address problems that arise, or it may fail to do so.

The training and placement of female officers in assignments which affect subsequent opportunities for mobility, achievement, and autonomy pose particularly difficult problems for a police department. How can it provide equality of opportunity and meet the needs of both male and female officers? Treating a woman as "just another officer," in fact, is treating her like a man and puts a woman, who is likely to be physically smaller and have been socialized differently, at a disadvantage. But singling women out for "special" treatment leads to difficulties: it heightens their visibility, often implies "inferiority," and leads to resentment of double standards by male co-workers, which may retard acceptance of women as officers.

The findings reported in this [case study] are based on a study of a single department—the Metropolitan Police Department of Washington, D.C. (MPDC)—but the dilemmas are common to the approximately 15,000 police and sheriff's departments around the nation.[1] Because the MPDC has voluntarily introduced a large number of policewomen into patrol work, the barriers faced by the women in this department are likely to be fewer and smaller than those in departments that have resisted the introduction of women.

Socialization

Becoming a police officer is a gradual process, through which an individual is socialized into the attitudes, values, skills, and knowledge that are part of the job. The process has several stages: anticipatory socialization, including recruitment; formal training in the police academy; the period of certification for street patrol during the first few months an officer is assigned to a district; and the final "metamorphosis," which generally occurs by the sixth month of street experience (Van Maanen, 1975).

Anticipatory Socialization

The process by which an individual "tries on" a role and/or adopts the values of a group to which he or she does not yet belong is termed anticipatory socialization. It eases adjustment into a new group by permitting imaginative (although sometimes erroneous) rehearsal of the activities, responsibilities, and problems of membership, thus easing the future "reality shock."

The anticipatory socialization of women to police work tends to be shorter and less intense than that of male officers. Boys are more likely to play "cops and robbers" than girls. As teenagers, boys usually spend more time than girls thinking about a career and their occupational options, including police work. Many boys fantasize about acts of bravery, heroism, and physical combat. For young males, actual and media police heroes provide role models which were virtually unavailable to young girls until the mid-1970s.

Prior work experience also better prepares men than women for police work. More than a quarter of the men, but none of the women, in my sample had previously served in the military, thereby gaining experience with military discipline, the chain of command, and the definition of themselves as "men's men." Other male recruits came from jobs traditionally viewed as men's work such as construction and truck driving, through which they acquired the values of blue collar men. Most of the women, on the other hand, were recruited from the white collar world of the female office worker.

Recruitment policies of police departments have traditionally selected as officers men whose views of their own masculinity identified them as possessing "the mark of affinity" (Gray, 1975) that enabled them to "fit" into the informal social world of the police. The mark of affinity standard, or conception of masculinity, served to disqualify women from consideration for police patrol work. Female recruits were selected according to different informal and formal standards.[2] When women were integrated into police patrol, recruiters faced a dilemma with respect to standards for female recruits. As yet, no comparably clear standard for women has emerged since, by definition, women do not "fit" existing standards, and neither their conceptions of masculinity nor femininity are an appropriate test of their acceptability for policing. Instead, the department has relied heavily on a self-selection process to eliminate the most inappropriate potential female recruits and has accepted a more heterogeneous group of female than male officers.

The males and females who enter the police academy have different amounts of anticipatory socialization and work experience which, as will be shown, give the male recruit an early advantage that tends to be magnified rather than reduced when it is simply ignored.

The Training Academy

Formal socialization to police work begins at the training academy. New officers in the MPDC spend about four months at the academy prior to assignment to a district. There they receive formal instruction on the D.C. Crime Code and the law of arrest, departmental regulations and procedures, the communications system, community relations, court and judicial procedures, general patrol techniques, first aid, the use of weapons (including firearms), and self-defense. The rookies participate in a physical training program and must pass physical, driving, firearms, and written tests before graduation. Beyond the formal curriculum, recruits are exposed to the covert curriculum that emphasizes actual police standards and values, paramilitary discipline, and the importance of group solidarity. Training is geared to providing newcomers with a new identity as members of the police fraternity. Like basic training in the military, the training is a rite of passage, designed to break down civilian attitudes and behavior patterns and replace them with new perspectives and habits, including the sense of group membership and loyalty.

Prior life experiences benefit male and handicap female recruits in several ways. Boys are encouraged to defend themselves physically (or face the stigma of being labeled a "sissy"). Girls, particularly those socialized to be "little ladies," acquire skills in verbal manipulation, but learn not to be physically assertive. Instead, in the face of physical threat, they are encouraged to turn to a protector (usually a parent, teacher, or brother), use tears, or demand respect for themselves as "ladies." In interacting with males, girls have learned to follow rather than lead, to suggest rather than command, to manipulate politely rather than confront directly or risk insulting another. While each of these behaviors can be useful at times on police patrol…police officers cannot rely on these devices and patrol effectively. They cannot turn to protectors; they must protect others from danger or violence, by coercive action if necessary.

Because guns and cars are regarded as symbols of masculinity, more teenage boys than girls have tinkered with cars and learned to use a firearm. These prior experiences make acquisition of the driving and shooting skills in the academy easier and more rapidly acquired by male recruits.

Prior athletic and body building activities magnify the physical differences between males and females that again give male recruits an advantage. Experience on the playing field introduces participants into elements found in the police subculture: controlled use of violence, the ability to endure pain, willingness to inflict it on others, an emphasis on teamwork and a group effort, and uniform behavior (Gray, 1975). Few of the female recruits to police work have participated in team contact sports. This is due to the limited number of sports for which there have been girls' teams, and the fact that popularity and prestige for teenage girls do not emanate from being an athlete, but from being the leader of those cheering for the boys' teams or having a boyfriend who is a sports hero. Smallness and delicacy rather than size and strength are esteemed for girls. Thus, adolescent social values and activities magnify differences in physical development during adolescence, increasing the differences between the sexes in such a way that women entering the police academy are at a disadvantage they must be helped to overcome.

Both physical training (p.t.) and the formal and informal classroom curriculum affect the effectiveness of subsequent role performance of both male and female officers. There was near unanimity among officers that the academic aspects of the academy training are unbiased, due largely to the individualized module system of instruction and testing. The content of the curriculum and the informal "lessons" taught by instructors, however, do foster inequality in a number of subtle ways. The focus is on the physical, violent, and dangerous crime-fighting aspects of the work, and the need for a "manly" response to threats rather than on human relations in difficult circumstances. This emphasis on the coercive rather than the interpersonal skills necessary in police work heightens the men's belief that women are inappropriate as officers, and fails to call attention to or build on skills in which women generally surpass men. When scout cars were racially integrated, the department initiated a training program for all officers that addressed the prevailing prejudices, myths, and stereotypes, and gave officers an opportunity to deal with their feelings about the changes that were thrust on them. A unit on race relations remains in the training curriculum. No analogous effort to address tensions and misunderstandings was made when sex integration occurred. Yet men and women

are socialized differently, live in different cultural worlds (Bernard 1978, 1981), perceive life differently, and often fail to recognize gaps in understanding and communication that occur.

The problems arising in physical education and training pose the most visible dilemma for the police department. Should they maintain a single training qualification standard for men and women, who are physically different in size and strength (on the average)? If so, what should it be so as to be equitable to both? Initially, the department had a single standard for the academy physical training; p.t. requirements subsequently were altered so that women do modified push-ups, fewer pull-ups, and are allowed more time to complete the obstacle course than the men. P.t. requirements are problematic because it is not clear just how much physical training is really necessary to prepare officers for their work and what are valid, job-related measures of fitness and physical skills.

Physical fitness tests have had a long history as a mechanism for screening out women and others as "unfit" for police work. The academy p.t. program probably has been more useful as a hazing mechanism to create solidarity among those suffering the rigors of the training than as a way of ensuring fitness for patrol officers because, in the MPDC, officers are not required to maintain their fitness.[3]

The MPDC physical training program divides the women with respect to what standards are appropriate, how existing standards were actually applied at the academy, and how women should cope with the requirements. Some believe the standards are too high and not job-related, and that it is acceptable for women to seek exemptions. For example, one woman stated:

> They wanted us to do men's style push-ups. That's ridiculous! J___ wanted to compete with the men but we couldn't, so it didn't bother me not to keep up.... We weren't

physically able to do what was required of us.

Other women are determined to meet all requirements and compete with the men. They bitterly resent the efforts of other women to seek lower standards and respond to the exemptions given to some women by feeling obliged to become standard bearers and "overachievers" to prove to others that "all women aren't like that." One woman observed that all recruits had to run a mile a day. Many women protested that they could not keep the pace and were permitted to run far behind. She and three other women in her class "refused to accept different standards for women....I felt that if I could do it, and I was smoking a pack a day, there was no reason any other woman couldn't keep up with me." Another asserted:

> Some women tried to be treated differently in p.t. That pissed me off because it reflected on me. I tried to keep up with the men. I can't run but I kept trying. The other women were angry at me because they wanted an excuse for not trying and didn't want any woman to excel because they'd lose their excuse.

The exemptions granted by male instructors to some women had several negative consequences for the women as a group. The women who were simply "passed on" by instructors unable or unwilling to deal with the women's manipulative efforts were generally less well-prepared for the realities of street patrol. Furthermore, they had failed to learn the lessons of group loyalty and suffering in silence as part of the initiation ritual, which undermined the men's confidence in the ability of the women to adhere to the norms of the department. The instructors who may have believed that they were helping the women in fact perpetuated the women's reliance on traditional female behavior, employed a double standard, and fostered a division among the women over

appropriate occupational role attitudes and behaviors. By permitting some women to be "different," they subtly fostered the male officers' existing resentment of policewomen as a group because of the high visibility of the relatively few female recruits and the men's tendency to negatively label the token women, particularly when they displayed behavior characteristic of their existing stereotypic image.

The tension and communication problems between men and women, and the division among the women were exacerbated by self-defense exercises. When exercising with a woman, were the men merely preparing the women for the realities of street fighting, or were they being particularly rough as a way of embarrassing and hurting their female partners? Were some women complaining about normal or excessive treatment? The "truth" is impossible to determine (and probably varied under different individual circumstances), but the outcome was clear: divisiveness rather than a sense of group solidarity and shared toughness that other recruits got from the police academy (Harris, 1973; Van Maanen, 1975) and an undermining of men's (already limited) confidence in the ability of women to provide adequate backup.

Certification and Street Patrol

Upon completion of academy training, rookies are assigned to a district in which they undergo an apprenticeship period known as certification. During this period, usually lasting 8 to 14 weeks, rookies learn to adapt to the "reality shock" of the street and the informal norms and procedures by which policing is actually done. As their bodies are adjusting to the rigors of shift work and irregular hours, and their families are adapting to mid-week days off and job-related tensions that often get brought home, they are learning the geography of the district and how to handle situations on the street, as well as how to survive in the department ("don't make waves") and evade certain rules. They may work exclusively with one training officer or "float" among different scout cars and experienced officers.

The initial months of street patrol are very important because during this period an officer "makes" a reputation that follows him or her through his or her career, and cycles of motivation and success or of discouragement and failure are set in motion. Officers viewed as showing good judgment, "heart," and initiative are encouraged, win the trust of trainers and peers, and are provided with support and tips on "tricks of the trade." Rookies who are too retiring, who do not follow the norms, or who get reputations as complainers or troublemakers, get labeled "not police material" and are not likely to get adequate instruction. Those who seek to avoid making mistakes by being passive get reputations as unreliable, stupid, or disinterested, and others are unwilling to trust or confide in them.

Assignments and instruction during certification affect opportunities for learning and gaining self-confidence. Insufficient instruction, limited opportunities to take action, and the feeling that one is the victim of discrimination (whether real or not) are likely to lead to ego-protective indifference and demotivation for most officers. Conversely, "good" assignments are viewed as a reward for performance and encourage those with these opportunities to take further initiative.

Most of the men interviewed in my study were positive about their initial training experiences. Most were pleased to find that they got little hazing, and after an initial period of watching and asking questions "found" their own style. None reported being told to remain in a scout car when difficult situations arose, although several were critical of training officers who taught them little. Several who were shy noted that initially they had gotten insufficient instruction and feedback on their performance and had

been viewed by others as disinterested. One male officer, whose certification period had been extended (a sign of initial failure), explained:

> I'm sh]nd wouldn't speak out or say I wanted to handle a situation....I waited for instructions; they waited for my questions....Now I know a lot better. I missed a lot of things because I wasn't exposed to them.

Other men who may have had similar initial difficulties probably were less forthcoming because such problems are signs of "unmanly" (i.e., passive) behavior and discussion of them is a further indication of "unmanliness."

The obstacles faced by all rookies on entering street patrol were compounded for the initial policewomen assigned to patrol by the largely unfriendly reception they received from male officers. The most blatant discriminatory practices and harassment have been eliminated, but female officers still must overcome the obstacles posed by smaller stature, unfamiliarity with street life, the negative attitudes of male co-workers and supervisors, "performance pressures" emanating from visibility, and a double standard of behavior and evaluation.

The evaluation of the initial phase of the Policewomen on Patrol program (Bloch and Anderson, 1974: 11) reported that departmental guidelines for the integration of policewomen were "reasonably well observed during the first 6 to 8 months of the program." Several of the "experimental" policewomen, however, noted that women often did not receive the same on-the-job instruction as male officers, that their assignments were changed in the course of a tour of duty, and that a few "favored" women were assigned to the station, while the majority were left to "sink or swim" on the street with little instruction and assistance from partners, who tended to be hostile. One woman reported:

I was certified when the sergeant came in, handed me a piece of paper and said "sign this." I had been in the district about two months but had never ridden in a training car and did not know the streets....The men who came into the district went into training cars... but I wasn't put into a training car or instructed—ever. Yet I was certified because they handed me a piece of paper....I had to learn the hard way—through mistakes—but when I made a mistake they'd come down on me just as hard regardless of whether they'd trained me or not.

At the time, she and others like her feared complaining to their supervisors, many of whom were responsible for the discriminatory treatment. She noted:

> In those days...you didn't dare question or say anything...there was no union, no EEO officer....Oh, you could say what you wanted, but who would investigate? ...Besides, I didn't say anything about lots of situations because I couldn't afford any kind of labels; not as a chicken, not as a complainer or crybaby, or anything.

Adjusting to street patrol poses a greater hurdle for rookie women than men, since it represents more of a leap into the unknown for the former. Many girls have been sheltered from street life, kept protectively close to home away from danger and violence. On entering patrol, they find themselves in unfamiliar "tough" neighborhoods, exercising newly acquired authority, and expected to control sometimes unruly citizens. While this responsibility is both frightening and exciting to most officers, it is less familiar and, in some cases, may be overwhelming to female officers.

In the face of a threatening new situation, cultural norms dictate different behavior for men and women. Men are expected to hide their fear; they may not whine or say "I'm scared" to a superior. Those that do not remain silent, master their emotions, and take action face humiliation for failure to "act like a man." Women are permitted a greater range of self-expression and are encouraged to be helpless. They are expected to show fear, and are permitted to whine, cry, or seek exemptions from situations felt to be too difficult or threatening, since "they're only girls." Whereas men learn to act and women to avoid, a police officer, by definition, cannot refuse to act out of fear, although some do. The job requires the officer to deal with situations others cannot cope with on their own. For most policewomen (and some policemen), this means learning new patterns of behavior to perform their job well.

Two contradictory sets of expectations may confuse new policewomen and increase their difficulties in learning new work-related behaviors. On the one hand, they face strong performance pressure due to their high visibility. The women's work is closely scrutinized, and their shortcomings are widely reported within the district and viewed as the failure of all women. At the same time they feel pressured to act as exemplars and meet higher performance standards, they are protected, expected to act as subordinates of the men and to fail as officers. One woman observed:

> If you're a man and a police officer it's accepted that you can do the job. Nobody's watching to see if you can....But if you're a woman, everybody's watching to see how brave you are, how commanding you can be and how well you can take charge of a situation. You have to prove to the citizens you're a police officer when you take over a scene and you have to do twice as much to prove to your partner and official that you can handle the job.

At the same time, many men encourage passivity and prefer incompetent female partners. Few are so explicit as one man who stated:

> I don't think it's a woman's place [to be on patrol]. I've been taught that women should be treated as queens and I try to treat any

woman who rides with me as a queen. Anything we come upon, I take the aggressive initiative. In most cases it's almost mandatory that I do so....Females usually shun being aggressive.

Thus a self-fulfilling prophecy is set in motion. By treating the policewoman like a "queen," she sits back, acting like a queen—and thereby performs inadequately as a police officer, "proving" her inappropriateness for the job. Her behavior reinforces his treating her according to a double standard of expectations for male and female partners.

The competent women, who do not sit back and act like queens, do not avoid problems even though, as several noted, the men do not know how to deal with them and feel threatened by women who reject the double standard. Incompetence is tolerated because it is familiar and, while making the work more difficult, preserves the man's sense of male superiority and dominance. By acting assertively, like a police officer, the policewoman fails to act like a "lady"; men do not know how to deal with or evaluate such women and often pin negative labels, including "bitch" and "lesbian," on those who fail to conform to traditional female stereotypes.

The women of the MPDC studied their reception in the district and responded to the performance pressures and double standard in different ways. Some felt they were coddled and protected, and resented this; others acknowledged the double standard and either welcomed or were unable to overcome it. A few asserted that they were subjected to tougher rather than sheltered treatment, but dealt with it by redoubled effort and resolve to "make it." Others subjected to similar pressure appear to have transferred out of patrol or to have left police work. One "experimental" woman explained that she was able to overcome the performance pressures of the initial entry period by adopting the attitude "I'm going to make it regardless," overconformity to the rules, and gaining the support of a "super gung ho" officer with whom she was assigned to work. From the beginning, "anything he got involved in, I got involved in, 100 percent." This won his confidence and support, which "was like getting the Pope's blessing." Other similarly assertive women were frustrated by what they viewed as "coddling" by male partners and co-workers. One woman repeatedly told male officers not to ride in on her assignments unless she requested assistance; several others transferred to scooter squad, where they could work more independently and develop their own cases.

Other women were more accepting and even appreciative of male protective behavior and did not seek to alter patterns of interaction. The situation of one woman whose probationary year evaluation stated that she was "hesitant to take aggressive action" may have been typical. She attributed her behavior to the reluctance of many male partners to permit her to assume a more active police role. In fact, when they appeared on the scene of a fight, one partner told her to remain in the scout car (which she did). Determined to improve her negative probationary evaluation, she has made an effort, when working with a veteran male, "to get out of the car first and take aggressive action before he does"; despite her effort, however, the men continue to regard her as pleasant but far too unassertive an officer. For this young black woman and many others like her, the difficulties in overcoming behavior patterns "natural" for a woman are compounded by norms regulating relations with respect to age and race....

Permanent Assignments and Promotions

...Women's gravitation to inside jobs may result both from a push to remove them from assignments where they are most likely to jeopardize the safety of themselves and others, and a pull toward assignments that are more compatible with sex role norms and family life (since most involve regular daytime hours). Because the work is more routine, policewomen with such assignments are less subject to intense supervision and harassment by co-workers than those on patrol. At the same time, they have less opportunity to "disappear" for several hours on the job, to make decisions that affect the life and liberty of citizens, and to win informal prestige and likely future assignment in the "mainstream" of police work.

Throughout the department, policewomen tend to be overrepresented in the administrative, community relations, and youth service units and on the sex squad (which handles rape cases), and to be underrepresented in criminal investigation (except sex squad), traffic, and special operations units. As of 1978, there were no women in canine units or the robbery squad. In these two cases, women applicants were told they could not handle the assignments: in canine because the dogs were too big, and in robbery because the work involved dangerous confrontations with violent criminals.

Women are also underrepresented in supervisory positions for several reasons. First, their newness and the length-of-service requirements limit the number of women eligible for promotion. Second, their aspirations tend to be more limited: a number of the women, particularly those who have sought and obtained assignments with regular daytime hours, are reluctant to return to street patrol and shift work (to which new sergeants are assigned) and to face the discomforts of supervising policemen, many of whom are strongly opposed to female officers. Third, the informal system of influence and sponsorship limits the likelihood that a woman, excluded from most of the drinking and social activities of the men, will gain the support of a powerful official and be perceived by others as "appropriate" for promotion.

In sum, the opportunities for mobility within the department most readily available to policewomen tend to be those that move them back into low prestige duties traditionally regarded as appropriate for females: working with women, children, and typewriters. Many policewomen readily accept these avenues for mobility both for the reasons that policemen do—regular working hours compatible with further education and family life—and as a means of reducing the stresses arising as a result of male opposition to their presence, which are greater for women on patrol than for those in most other assignments due to the uncertain nature of the work and the demand that patrol officers "fit" in the work group. To avoid similar but intensified stresses, policewomen often limit their aspirations and efforts to gain promotions.

The Impacts of Assignments and Training: Differential Opportunities and Cycles of Success and Failure

Patrol officers face a "reality shock" when they begin street patrol. They must master their fears and learn skills that enable them to take control in situations. Initial success in dealing with paperwork, supervisors, and, most importantly, citizens on the street, leads to greater self-confidence, more willingness to take control, and widening opportunities for testing and using their developing patrol skills. Individuals who do not have or take opportunities to develop and use these skills (whether due to inadequate instruction, overprotection by partners, or limited assignments) are likely to be hesitant to take action and fail to behave appropriately. Because an incompetent officer is a danger both to him- or herself and to other officers, many veterans are anxious to get such an officer off the street or to minimize his or her opportunity to take action, thereby perpetuating the cycle of incompetence.

Several young women who did not appear to be "police material" on entry into the district, for example, were frequently assigned to quiet foot beats and scout cars with more assertive male partners with whom they acted in an "appropriately" subordinate manner. Feeling that they were victims of departmental discrimination, they developed "do nothing" attitudes. For example, one stated:

> I'm not gung ho. I just do what I have to.... I get disgusted when I get my assignments...Others with less time in the section [the ostensible criterion governing assignments] get to ride [in scout cars] more often than I do....so I'm not going to break my neck, especially when I don't have a radio [on a foot beat]....I'm not that strong and...I'm not going to drag myself to a call box.

This woman does not seek to make arrests, takes little initiative, feels little need to be assertive, and, uncertain about her ability to manage dangerous situations on the street, avoids them. Her performance and attitude have contributed to the view that she is not a promising officer and to her reputation as a complainer. She is caught in the cycle of demotivation and failure that makes it highly unlikely that she will obtain the detective assignment she desires.

Self-confidence and willingness to face the unknown are not sex-linked attributes. But patterns of prior and job-related socialization and the differential expectations of male and female rookies affect the ways they adapt to their new jobs. Without actively trying to overcome the unassertiveness of many women and the protectiveness of the men, the department's policies are likely to permit the realization of a self-fulfilling prophecy. Presumed to be unable to handle many situations, women are given either fewer opportunities and less encouragement to prove themselves on the street or else excessive praise and attention for what, to a male officer, would be a routine activity,

indicating a double standard of expectations. Without the opportunities to learn to act decisively and confidently, female officers "prove" their unsuitability for patrol. Overprotected and underinstructed, many continue in traditionally female ways rather than adapting their on-the-job behavior. One female sergeant observed:

> I saw women crying I didn't even know had tears crying. I guess they knew that crying wouldn't do any good with me whereas with the men they knew it might do some good....Society has reared men to be protectors of women....[When] women come and say, "I want to do the job equally but I'm scared"...the men are not conditioned or trained to say, "you have to do it."...Some of the men fear sending a woman out because they think, "suppose she gets hurt, am I to blame?"

This situation stems less from individual shortcomings or from deliberate discrimination than from continuation of learned social behavior patterns and the department's failure to try to alter them.

Conclusion: Organizational Policy, Structural Barriers, and Equity Versus Equality of Treatment

The entry of women into police work raises difficult questions for departments related to the training and socialization of officers and the distribution of assignments in a way that provides equality of opportunity, adopts an even-handed policy, and meets the needs of both male and female officers and the department. While the MPDC took an important first step by accepting a substantial number of women for patrol and vigorously prohibiting sex discrimination during their first few months on the job, it has not taken further action, expecting time and experience alone to lead to women's assimilation. While harassment and open resistance to policewomen has greatly diminished, wide differences in the opportunities, power, and numbers of women and men in the department still greatly handicap the female officer.

Can departmental policies be altered to reduce structural barriers without producing greater inequities? Short-term policies, including greater emphasis in training and retraining courses in communication skills and human relations, including consideration of the ways certain behaviors of both sexes perpetuate sex-typed behaviors and more frequent assignment of women to work alone and together hold some promise. Longer-term, broader changes, however, are required if policewomen are to have the same opportunities and work autonomy as their male counterparts. Some changes, such as reconsideration of the nature of the police role, modification of training to prepare officers for it, and increases in the number of female officers and female supervisors, thus reducing the problems that stem from their token status, are squarely the responsibility of the department. At the same time, organizational changes must be accompanied by altered cultural values and interpersonal patterns of behavior that replace the "male only" ethos of the police world with a heterosexual basis for solidarity among male and female officers.

NOTES

1. To understand the problems and coping strategies of a new group of women in an occupation traditionally limited to men, I undertook a participant-observation and interview study of patrol officers in a single patrol district in Washington, D.C. Approximately 30 out of about 400 officers in the district were women. I joined the Metropolitan Police Reserve Corps, a volunteer citizens' organization, received limited training, a uniform barely distinguishable from that of sworn officers, was assigned to a district of my choice, and was able to attend roll call and patrol with officers not assigned a partner for their tour of duty. During nine months I worked all three shifts on all days of the week with approximately 50 officers, including 8 policewomen. During the last three months I interviewed 28 policewomen, 27 male officers, and 15 officials from the observation district, as well as several key informants related to the department's policewomen program. The interviews averaged 1 1/2 to 2 hours in length....

2. The physical size requirements were lower, but the educational standards tended to be higher for the women officers, who were expected to display interest and skill in providing social services to women and children.

3. The only fitness test is an annual weight check to ensure that the officer has not exceeded the departmental weight maximum. Officers over the weight maximum lose their eligibility for promotion and may be punished in terms of assignments until they lose the excess weight.

REFERENCES

Bernard, Jessie. 1978. "Models for the relationship between the world of women and the world of men." Pp. 219–338 in L. Kreisberg (ed.), *Research in Social Movements, Conflict, and Change: An Annual Compilation of Research.* Vol. 1. Greenwich, CT: JAI Press.

Bernard, Jessie. 1981. *The Female World.* New York: The Free Press

Bloch, Peter B., and Deborah Anderson. 1974. *Policewomen on Patrol: Final Report: Methodology, Tables, and Measurement Instruments.* Washington, DC: Urban Institute.

Gray, Thomas C. 1975. "Selecting for a police subculture." Pp. 45–46 in J. H. Skolnick and T. C. Gray (eds.), *Police in America.* Boston: Little Brown.

Harris, Richard N. 1973. *The Police Academy: An Inside View.* New York: John Wiley.

Van Maanen, John. 1975. "Police socialization: A longitudinal examination of job attitudes in an urban police department." *Administrative Science Quarterly* 20 (June): 207–228.

Becoming a Male Stripper

Recruitment, Socialization, and Ideological Development

Paula L. Dressel and David M. Petersen

CASE STUDY QUESTIONS

1. How does the fact that male and female strippers work in different places affect the socialization process? Does the fact that this occupation is "deviant" have any impact on the socialization process?

2. How does one become socialized to the role of male stripper? Do experienced strippers formally train the new ones?

3. Does a new stripper need to learn any ethical standards to behave appropriately with the audience and with coworkers? Does one have to bring any particular skills to the job? How do strippers learn the norms for interaction with those in the audience?

4. How does the socialization or even anticipatory socialization of male strippers differ from that of female strippers?

5. What kind of ideology and justifications are developed by strippers to overcome the negative images society has of their occupation?

Authors' Note: The authors wish to thank Charles H. McCaghy for his helpful comments on an earlier version of this article.

Source: From *Work and Occupations*, Vol. 9, No. 3 (August), 1982, pp. 387–406. Reprinted by permission from Sage Publications, Inc.

In the past decade social scientists have charted the terrain of the work world of female strippers (Skipper and McCaghy, 1970, 1978; McCaghy and Skipper, 1972; Salutin, 1971; Boles and Garbin, 1974a, 1974b, 1974c) and kindred working women (Ames et al., 1970; Verlarde and Warlick, 1973; Carey et al., 1974; Verlarde, 1975; Bryant and Palmer, 1974; Hong and Duff, 1977). However, it has been only in the past few years that changes in certain cultural themes in American society regarding gender roles have provided the opportunity structure for males to become strippers. Only quite recently, therefore, have male strippers become the subject of systematic investigation (Prehn, 1981; Petersen and Dressel, forthcoming)....

The primary purpose of this article is to describe several occupational issues related to this nontraditional work for men. Our reference to this work as nontraditional reflects the fact that it is work previously not engaged in by men and also that it is deviant work (Miller, 1978). Our intention here is to concentrate on the individual dynamics of becoming a male stripper. Specifically, we will discuss (a) the situational contingencies affecting how males are recruited to stripping, (b) the socialization process they undergo, and (c) the outcome of socialization, which is the development of ideologies regarding the occupation of stripping. A secondary purpose is to put our findings in perspective by comparing and contrasting our findings with those on females involved in stripping. We will highlight similarities and differences which exist in this form of deviant entertainment which involves public exposure of one's body to members of the other sex.

Research Design

Sources of Data

The primary source of data for this analysis is intensive team interviews with regular strippers at a male strip show in a southern metropolitan area. Our concern was to identify and interview those dancers who might view their work as an occupation, if only part-time. Of the many males who had stripped at the club over the two years during which it had been in operation, a great number performed for no more than a single night. Therefore only those persons who had performed regularly for at least a two-month period were considered for interviews. Of the sixteen persons who met our criterion, interviews were successfully completed with fourteen of these subjects.[1] Interviews averaged about two hours in length and were conducted either in the home of the dancer, the authors' offices, or a quiet public place.

Other slices of data (Glaser and Strauss, 1967) which represent secondary sources of corroboration for this analysis include (a) eight months of observation at the club featuring the dancers interviewed, (b) informal conversations with workers at the same club, (c) more limited observations and informal conversations at five other clubs in the same state and two clubs in other states (one in a neighboring southern state and one in the West), and (d) newspaper and maga-

zine articles and transcripts of television talk shows.

The Research Setting

We provide here a very brief description of the male strip show and its performances to place this article in perspective. The setting, functions, and type of interactions occurring in this nightclub have been described in detail elsewhere (Petersen and Dressel, forthcoming).

The club where the interviewees performed offers the only male strip show in the central city and is located on a main thorough-fare in an uptown area about five miles from the central business district. The format of the show includes production numbers, individual acts, and a show finale called "table topping." During the course of an evening at least three elaborately costumed, choreographed production numbers in which stripping does not occur will be performed by three or four of the regular dancers. Interspersed between these production numbers are an average of eight or nine individual dance numbers during which the dancers strip down to small G-strings. Total nudity does not occur at the club. The appearances, costumes, and performance techniques of the dancers varied considerably. For example, there is quite a variety of dress among the dancers ranging from ordinary street clothes to elaborate costumes coordinated to the dancer's choice of music (e.g., a Superman costume, complete with cape, for the song of the same name). Physical contact between dancers and audience members is an expected and integral part of the show. The typical sequence is one in which a customer approaches a dancer of her choice offering a tip, after which physical contact is initiated by one or the other, including kissing and fondling. The show's finale ("table topping") consists of all dancers leaving the stage area and performing simultaneously on the tabletops where the customers are seated.

The audience at the club is exclusively female and appears to represent a diversity of women with regard to age, background, appearance, and reasons for attendance. However, during the course of the study the audience as well as the dancers were predominantly white. On any given night the audience includes housewives, students, secretaries, school teachers, and other professionals, ranging in age from eighteen into their sixties. Generally, the audience numbers from 100 to 150, many of whom have been at the club for at least an hour before showtime because of the limited seating available.

Recruitment of Males to Stripping

A recurrent finding in the sociology of work across varied occupations—particularly deviant occupations—is that people are more likely to use informal than formal means of obtaining a job (Ritzer, 1977; Miller, 1978).[2] The typical informal channels of recruitment are through family, friends, and acquaintances. In addition, the deviance literature documents that career entry for most workers is gradual; they drift into their work as a result of activity of a nonwork nature, although they may assess the line of work based on the advantages the work appears to offer (Miller, 1978). Our findings on recruitment to male stripping are generally consistent with this literature.

Becoming a male stripper for most of our interviewees was not a carefully and deliberately planned occupational move on their part. Rather, ten of the fourteen dancers reported that, instead of initiating the idea themselves, various friends and relatives originally suggested to them the possibility that they become strippers. One stripper described the casual nature of his recruitment experience in the following way:

I knew some female strippers from the south side of town, and they suggested that I do it. They talked about who did it and the money, and I figured I would give it a try. I started the first night, and I didn't even audition.

In fact, in two of these ten cases a specific occurrence which precipitated their entry into stripping was a dare from a friend. As one of these two dancers commented, "I heard about it from a girl I was dating. I did it as a goof. She dared me and kept egging me on." The significant others who introduced the idea of stripping to our respondents included a cousin who worked in a band at the club, female friends who worked as strippers, girlfriends, females who had attended the male strip show, and male friends who already worked as strippers. Thus, the decision for the males to enter a nontraditional occupation was prompted and supported by significant persons who had some form of contact with or knowledge about the show already, either as individuals who themselves were in the entertainment business or as individuals who frequented that form of entertainment.

Three of the remaining dancers we interviewed came to stripping through their own initiative. Two had read or heard about the show through club advertisements in the mass media and decided to audition. The third had previously been a stripper in another city and had merely relocated. The final respondent had been frequenting the club after the strip show in order to meet women, caught glimpses of the show, and decided to try it for himself after being approached by the head dancer.

It is reasonable to argue, however, that many men who possess dancing skills, are reasonably attractive, and who hear about the male strip show through various media or who are prodded to become a stripper by a friend or relative will not be moved to audition for the job. Indeed, our research revealed several inducements of the job which appeared to attract our interviewees toward this form of work.

The foremost incentive of stripping for males is the money earned during the performance. A majority of the strippers we interviewed mentioned this theme as their primary reward for being a stripper. Although several dancers held full-time jobs during the day ranging from hairdresser to aerospace engineer, at some time during their experience as strippers a majority of the interviewees depended on stripping for their main or only source of income. In fact, once they discovered that stripping could be a lucrative endeavor and that holding a full-time job in the daytime along with part-time work at night was exhausting, some chose to leave the day jobs for stripping. The range of income for dancers is quite variable. Under $30 for an evening's work is generally considered to be a bad night, with $100 to $150 considered to be a good night. For a number of dancers the importance of their income derives both from the amount and from the fact that it is easy to avoid reporting it as taxable income. As one respondent noted, "You get money right then, that night, no taxes, and take it with you."

Many of the males we interviewed were also attracted to stripping because of the lifestyle advantages this type of work offers. These include easy work and short hours. In stripping they felt they could make at least as much money in fewer working hours than in more traditional jobs, thereby having more time to themselves. One stripper summarized this theme:

> What other kind of job can you walk around, talk, joke, and drink, and be working [at the same time]? I actually do no more than forty minutes total labor a night, about $2.50 per minute. I come home more often than not at night with $100.

Additional lifestyle advantages became apparent to strippers once they were on the job. A number of strippers reported the added reward of receiving gifts and favors from members of the audience in addition to the regular tips. Gifts and favors included cash, jewelry, wardrobes, transportation, and entertainment. Moreover, a few dancers described themselves as "being kept."

Another inducement of stripping reported by our interviewees is the excitement inherent in entertainment work, or, in the words of one of our respondents, "the thrill of being an entertainer." In addition to this facet of the work serving as a recruitment inducement, our respondents frequently remarked that audience response was an important source of job satisfaction. The response of the audience is, in the words of one, "a good build-up mentally." A second dancer commented: "I enjoy applause. That's my self-praise. It makes me know I'm doing good making someone happy." Even those dancers who described themselves as gay reported that audience response was important to them. A 27-year-old homosexual respondent stated: "For an aging man who is gay, it's an ego trip. It's hundreds of women screaming and loving every minute of it. It's really something!" Finally, for dancers whose self-image prior to stripping had been somewhat low, the audience response proves gratifying and helps them overcome shyness and insecurity.

A fourth incentive of stripping is that the job allows dancers a ready means of meeting women. While this theme is reported by a number of dancers as being important for recruitment, all of the heterosexual dancers verbalized it as a significant fringe benefit of the job. Interaction with audience members at the club provides abundant opportunities for strippers to make social contact with women. This benefit is exemplified in the following remarks from one dancer:

> Socially I can pick out any girl I like and go out with her after the show or on a subsequent night. That is a definite advantage. I don't like to go to singles bars—it's too

uptight. [At the strip club] I have the pick of the girls. [They] see me as something more than a regular guy—I'm on stage. Some act like groupies....It seems almost bizarre to me—I'm no Valentino.

Contacts established at the club between dancers and customers were reported frequently to result in sexual activity. Indeed, one dancer stated succinctly that a benefit of the job is that he had "more lay than I could handle." Even without initiative on the part of the dancers, female customers often made requests for or offers of sexual favors. The strippers reported that receiving propositions is part of the nature of the business and that some customers have expectations of paying for the sexual services of men. One dancer expressed the view that paying for sex was part of the mystique of the sexual encounter for some women: "A lot do it for the excitement of being able to pay for it...I used to say it's free, but they wanted to pay."

The majority of our respondents reported that while stripping as an occupation had a great number of benefits and that they were satisfied with the job, they did not view it as a vocation in which they would remain for a considerable period of time, and definitely did not view it as their lifetime career. Nevertheless, a final incentive of stripping as an occupation is the belief by a few strippers that this form of work might enable them to launch an entertainment career. It is their hope that the showmanship and talent they demonstrate as a stripper will be discovered and that they will receive national recognition. For these respondents stripping represents a first step in one's career ladder as an entertainer.

The literature on female strippers reflects both similarities with and differences from male strippers with regard to the situational contingencies that contribute to becoming a stripper. A major similarity between male and female stripping is the role of informal recruitment agents in one's entry into the occupation. In both cases these agents were individuals who already had knowledge about or connections with persons involved in this deviant form of entertainment. In addition, there are certain perceived rewards of the occupation of stripping that are viewed as attractive inducements for both males and females. These include easy economic gain, lifestyle advantages (e.g., easy work, short hours), the excitement of entertainment work, and the initiation of a career in entertainment (Boles and Garbin, 1974b, 1974c; Skipper and McCaghy, 1970, 1978; McCaghy and Skipper, 1972; Carey, Petersen, and Sharpe, 1974).

A major difference which exists between male and female stripping is that women apparently do not become strippers for social or sexual outlet. Our research indicates that male strippers not only perceive of such outlet as a positive inducement for becoming a stripper but also report these contacts as a significant fringe benefit of the job (see also Roebuck and Frese, 1976). Although females are not drawn to stripping for this purpose, the literature on female stripping details the nature of on-the-job contacts with male customers. These include the opportunity for and engagement in prostitution as well as the complex relationships between the stripper and her audience, which include the moral rejection of audience members by the strippers (Boles and Garbin, 1974b, 1974c; Skipper and McCaghy, 1970, 1978; McCaghy and Skipper, 1972; Salutin, 1971).

At least two situational contingencies regarding recruitment to stripping are not present for males but are consistently reported as being important for the likelihood of women becoming strippers. One difference between male and female strippers is that the experience of a major personal crisis (typically a financial crisis) by the latter is a usual precipitating factor in becoming a stripper. The majority of female strippers studied entered stripping at a time either when they had divorced, when their present jobs no longer provided them adequate income, or when they were without other means of support. The choice of stripping was made with the knowledge that a greater amount of money could be made by stripping than these women could make in more legitimate occupations (Skipper and McCaghy, 1970, 1978; Boles and Garbin, 1974b, 1974c). None of the male strippers we interviewed was impelled to take up stripping through a crisis situation.

Another difference in factors in recruitment to stripping for males vs. females is the female's greater likelihood of having been involved in previous jobs which required some display of the body. Research studies report that the majority of female strippers had worked as go-go girls, barmaids, waitresses, dancers, or models prior to stripping for a living (Boles and Garbin, 1974b, 1974c; Skipper and McCaghy, 1970, 1978). In contrast, only one of our male strippers had previous work experience which required substantial body display, that as a nude model for art classes.

Socialization to the Stripper Role

Socialization to an occupation can occur through both formal and informal processes. Formal training tends to characterize the professional, semiprofessional, and managerial occupations, although informa7 41 :M1 processes do play an important part. In less prestigious and especially in the deviant occupations there is minimal formal training; the skills and information required are relatively simple and straightforward, and most socialization occurs on the job. In stripping the content of socialization ranges from the acquisition of work skills to the development of a code of ethics guiding work-related behavior, including organizational requirements and interactions with other strippers and members of the audience (Ritzer, 1977;

Miller, 1978). In this section we will discuss the processes of anticipatory socialization as well as on-the-job socialization for males who become involved in stripping.

Because male stripping is a relatively new phenomenon and because most male strip clubs prohibit men from being in the audience, our interviewees had only vague expectations about what the stripper role entails. What preliminary knowledge they did have was derived from their attendance at female strip shows, their friendships with female strippers, information from girlfriends, sisters, and female coworkers who had attended a male strip show, or the brief glimpses the men themselves had had of male strippers.

Prejob socialization experiences among our strippers were extremely limited. None of the interviewees had received professional training in dancing or related fields such as music. In addition, previous employment in some other facet of entertainment work was limited to one dancer who had past experience as a singer and dancer as well as a stripper in nightclubs. One other dancer, however, although self-taught in dancing, was skillful enough to have had previous work experience as an instructor in a dance studio.

For the rest of our dancers a strong avocational interest in dancing existed, and they reported frequent attendance at night clubs and discotheques. The typical presocialization experiences are exemplified in the comments of one respondent:

> Most of the stuff is things I've learned in discos. I watch people all the time; that's how I've learned. I've never had any training. I started watching American Bandstand. That's how I first learned to dance.

Because of minimal anticipatory socialization the dancers' first performances generated uncertainty and anxiety. A number of respondents reported being taken to the club by a friend to inquire about the possibility of becoming a stripper. Instead, it was a typical occurrence that they were asked to dance that same night without even auditioning. The comments of one dancer illustrate the nature of first night experiences:

I figured I'd have to be completely drunk to do it. I can remember everything—the music, my dress, everything. I was nervous as I could be. I had one glass of vodka on the rocks and when I came off [the stage], I needed another. I wore what I wore down to the club. [Another dancer] handed me a G-string. I did two singles [dance numbers] and table-topped. I guess I made about $30 that night.

The nature of these dancers' initial stripping experiences was not uncommon: They did not expect to dance that first night, they were not prepared with costume or G-string, and they required alcohol to loosen themselves up in order to get on the stage and remove their clothes. However, since the first performances were rewarding in terms of money and audience response, our strippers appeared for work on subsequent nights.

As is the case with other deviant occupations, male stripping provides no formal on-the-job socialization. Rather, what is available in the way of socialization ranges from informal training or advice in the development of skills to providing information in casual conversation on an occupational code of ethics. A major form of socialization is simply watching other dancers and learning from them. The other means of on-the-job socialization is that of direct advice from other dancers.

To be a successful stripper one must acquire certain work skills, techniques, and tricks of the trade. As we have already noted, although strippers have not had formal training in dance, they do enter the occupation with a certain level of dance skills. Our dancers report that they are expected to be fairly self-reliant in terms of

dance skills. Nevertheless, some informal socialization does occur, as they also indicate that they spend considerable time watching others perform to pick up cues and that they occasionally ask other dancers for advice about specific moves.[3]

Another area in which dancers are expected by their coworkers to be relatively self-sufficient is that of the selection of specific costumes, music, and gimmicks. Those strippers who used costumes were apparently socialized to the idea of the use of costumes and gimmicks and the coordination of these with music by noticing their success when utilized by other dancers. Beyond the general idea of coordination, however, dancers were expected to develop the specific content of their costumes, music, and gimmicks on their own and not to imitate other dancers.

The acquisition of certain other work skills occurs for the neophyte stripper almost entirely on the job under the tutelage of the experienced dancers. Through informal conversations, and in a more limited way through observations, new strippers learn about the appropriate way to remove one's clothes, how to wear a G-string properly, and various tips about grooming and other factors in presenting oneself to the audience. Although not trying to eschew the provocative nature of the act, it is important to male strippers to get down to the G-string as quickly as possible. Since tipping almost universally occurs by the customer placing money in the dancer's G-string, it is in the dancer's financial interest to maximize the time during his performance that he is accessible for tips. An essential part of the stripper's act includes proper placement of the G-string so that exposure of his genitals does not occur accidentally while he is dancing. In addition, strippers are cautioned to hold their G-strings in place when receiving tips. Dancers are also socialized to the need for maximizing their attractiveness to the audience and for maintaining the manifest heterosexuality of the show (Petersen and Dressel, forthcoming). To do this, they learn to employ a number of specific techniques to enhance their desirability to audience members including using makeup to diminish the glare of the lights against their features, trimming what they felt was excessive body hair, keeping in shape physically, and establishing eye contact with as many audience members as possible to break down social distance.

Besides acquiring job skills, a stripper must learn a certain occupational code of ethics. Although the code is not formalized, it provides dancers with guidelines regarding their relationships to the work organization, to the customers, and to fellow dancers. With regard to the code as it governs strippers in the work organization, expectations include reporting for work on time; being alert to when one's individual performance is scheduled; not bringing women or glassware into the dressing room; keeping one's genitals covered at all times and not touching that area during the performance; and not mingling with the audience during the course of the show. The latter norm was important to protect dancers from charges of solicitation.

Norms relative to interaction with the audience are directed to manipulating the audience to the dancer's advantage and to ways of maintaining physical distance between the dancer and his audience. With regard to the former, dancers learn from one another who the good and the bad tippers are. It is also important for a dancer after receiving his tip to know how to initiate physical contact with an audience member in a manner which prevents the customer from feeling shortchanged but which allows him to move quickly to other audience members to maximize his tips. In addition, it was thought detrimental to potential club attendance for a dancer to date more than one female from the same group who attended the show. Among the norms regarding the maintenance of physical distance are that dancers should not allow audience members to touch their genitals, that they should not "feel girls up," and that they should not have sex with customers on the premises.

Several norms pertain to strippers' interactions with fellow dancers. The most important of these norms centered around the stripper's act. One was not to use another dancer's gimmick or duplicate another stripper's costume. Moreover, it was acknowledged that certain songs "belonged" to particular dancers and that another dancer could not use the same song for his routine without permission from the original user. Finally, there was the understanding that strippers should not discuss their own or other dancers' sexual preferences with anyone in the audience.

In comparing our data to the literature on female strippers, we again find both similarities and differences between their respective socialization experiences. In terms of anticipatory socialization females are more likely to have prejob experiences and skills relevant to stripping. In addition, female strippers are more likely to receive extensive formal training in stripping on the job.[4] The one similarity in terms of socialization between male and female strippers is that of informal indoctrination to work skills and occupational ethics following employment.

As noted, unlike their male counterparts female strippers are likely to have broader experiences of anticipatory socialization for their work. First, it has already been mentioned under the section on recruitment that female strippers have held previous jobs in the area of entertainment, many of which require some measure of body display. Second, the majority of female strippers report that they have had professional training in dance or music. Third, it is not uncommon for some women to have an agent who prepares them for future employment as a stripper (Boles and Garbin, 1974c; McCaghy and Skipper, 1972).

Experience with formal on-the-job training is exclusive to female strippers (mostly feature dancers). These women receive considerable training by individuals whose job is specifically to train strippers prior to their performance before an audience. This training entails the learning of basic dance steps, the development of an appropriate act, and the utilization of a trademark or gimmick (Boles and Garbin, 1974c). In contrast, male strippers have no formal training on the job.

As is the case with deviant occupations, socialization occurs largely through informal means following occupational entry. Both male and female strippers must acquire certain work skills and must learn their occupational code of ethics, including guidelines for relationships with the employing organization, the audience, and other strippers. Comparison of the available data for both male and female strippers suggests that their respective work requires many of the same skills and that their codes of ethics cover many of the same issues (Salutin, 1971; McCaghy and Skipper, 1972; Boles and Garbin, 1974c).

The Development of Ideologies

Many occupations are characterized by worldviews that make them distinct from other occupations. An important element in an occupational worldview is its ideological aspect, or a coherent perspective passed on through the socialization process that details the nature of the relationship between the occupation and its members with other types of work as well as with the larger society (Ritzer, 1977). Deviant occupations are identified (Ritzer, 1977; Miller, 1978) as having ideologies which may not accurately conform to established fact but which the occupational members believe nevertheless. Occupational ideologies are important in helping members of deviant occupations handle problems which they encounter in their work. In addition, they function to justify the occupational activities of those in nontraditional work.

Goode (1978) maintains that the end product of socialization into deviant behavior is an actor's attempt to normalize what he does. Thus, it is not surprising that male strippers will develop ideologies which serve to legitimate their unconventional behavior.

Our respondents feel that the larger society views male stripping in a negative light. They believe that people who have not seen a show perceive it to be "crude" and "cheap." The fact that the strippers were working in the Bible Belt where "do-gooders think you're going to hell" heightened their belief of the likelihood of negative feelings on the part of the public about male stripping. The men also viewed part of the public as ambivalent, if not hypocritical, about male strip shows. On the one hand they suspect that some men are envious of their role and that women who come to the show enjoy it. On the other hand, they maintain that both of these groups are reluctant to admit such attitudes.

In light of the possibility of public disapproval of male strippers our interviewees offered four primary justifications for their work (Sykes and Matza, 1957; Scott and Lyman, 1968). The first is that the existence of male strip shows represents a form of equal rights for women and that it is appropriate that females should be allowed an outlet similar to what men have had for a long time. The response from one stripper as to why women patronize the club was typical: "They want to experience something they haven't seen before. They want to see something they've been denied and have their rights like men." The second justification is that the club offers a secure environment for women to act in ways which would be considered inappropriate for them elsewhere. According to one stripper, the club allows women "to come in without someone trying to pick them up and breathing down their necks." Another dancer summarized: "They can act different around all other women. They can act themselves without any restrictions. They can do what they feel, oblivious to everything." The third justification offered by our male strippers is that they provide sexual outlet for women who do not have men available, for whatever reason, and that they provide sexual diversity for those women who do have a regular male partner. Several dancers noted that the act of kissing a man after extended periods without heterosexual contact is an exciting possibility for many customers. One dancer related an incident in support of this claim:

> At the end of the show Wednesday, some poor woman ogled me. She told me I'm the first man she's kissed in fifteen years. But she didn't know how to kiss—she'd never been around. It didn't do anything to me to have that physical contact; it was what was in her eyes, like [getting] a toy at Christmas.

The fourth justification is that male stripping is a form of commercial entertainment that people would find "interesting," "entertaining," "unique," "enjoyable," and acceptable if they would attend a show. Indeed, one stripper noted regarding people he had encountered who had seen the show: "Anybody I've come in contact with has always thought it's fantastic, but they're educated and hip." Another dancer put it this way: "It's a nightclub act, not just a strip joint. We don't always take our clothes off.... It's entertainment."

While our dancers have clearly developed justifications to normalize their behavior, our data reveal that they have not yet reached a state of being where the role of stripper is incorporated into their identities (Goode, 1978). Consequently, in the presentation of self to others, few of them acknowledge introducing themselves as strippers to new acquaintances. Rather, they will usually indi-

cate that they are an "entertainer" or a "dancer" or a "nightclub worker," or use their day line of work in introductions. One stripper stated that in general he preferred the term "dancer" over stripper because "dancing is the important thing to me, not taking my clothes off." But he added, "Telling [people] I'm a dancer is a softer blow."

In addition, a number of male strippers are reluctant to announce or try to avoid announcing their line of work to others who know them, particularly to family members. Keeping the job secret from one's parents is a foremost consideration for many of those dancers whose families reside in the immediate metropolitan area. One mother when aware of the fact that her son was stripping, told him never to come around to her place of employment again. The remarks of another stripper highlight the gap between his perceptions of stripping and what he believes his colleagues at school might think of him:

> I don't think there's anything at all to be ashamed of. I think it's just the opposite— something exciting you're doing....I go to this professional school, and that's the only thing I'm really uptight about. I've heard from some people that there's talk on campus that there's a male stripper among us, and they equate it with a male prostitute.

Because male and female stripping are deviant occupations, we would expect both groups of strippers to perceive that they have a negative societal image, to develop justifications to normalize their work, and to develop certain strategies of impression management in interaction with others. Comparison of our data with the literature on female strippers does indeed indicate that male and female strippers believe that the public holds negative stereotypes about them (Salutin, 1971; Boles and Garbin, 1974c; Skipper and McCaghy, 1978).

With regard to attempts to normalize their negative societal images, male and female strippers employ justification techniques, the content of which varies between the groups. Similarities in ideology revolve around the claims of the entertainment and sexual service functions provided by both male and female strippers. The literature on female stripping identifies an additional justification, that of educational instruction and information for the female patrons in attendance at strip shows. Some female strippers report being approached by women seeking advice on becoming seductive or sexy (Boles and Garbin, 1974c; Salutin, 1971). The differences for males identified by our data are their utilization of the justifications of the strip club's allowing women equal rights and a secure sex-segregated setting.

Finally, despite their development of such ideologies to normalize their work, both male and female strippers report strategies for impression management with new acquaintances and significant others. Just as we have reported for male strippers, some female strippers conceal their occupation from family members and when meeting new people call themselves entertainers, dancers, or singers rather than strippers. Moreover, the literature indicates that they use the additional strategies of reporting false occupations and wearing conservative dress and little or no makeup in public as means of avoiding stigmatization (Boles and Garbin, 1974c; McCaghy and Skipper, 1978).

Summary

Male strippers as deviant workers differ from traditional workers only with respect to the stigma imposed on their line of work by the larger society, not the fact that their work is categorically different from other occupations. Like all workers in modern American society, male strippers are concerned with making a living. In pursuing their work role in entertainment, as in the case with individuals employed in the semi-professions, the professions, the crafts, and

so on, they must undergo common processes in terms of recruitment and socialization to the occupation and the development of work ideologies and identities. In this article we have explored the nontraditional occupation of male stripping in terms of these issues. In addition, we have provided comparison and contrast between our findings and the existing literature on females involved in stripping.

NOTES

1. Admittedly, the number of respondents from whom data were obtained is small. However, comparable studies of female strippers have also used limited samples [Boles and Garbin (1974a, 1974b, 1974c), N = 51; Skipper and McCaghy (1970; 1978), and McCaghy and Skipper (1972), N = 35; and Salutin (1971), N = 20], while the absolute number of potential respondents was much larger than those available for the purposes of this [case study].

2. Previous research on female strippers has examined selected physical, social and psychological characteristics as possible predisposing factors affecting occupational choice among women who become strippers (Boles and Garbin, 1974c; Skipper and McCaghy, 1970). Consequently, we have examined such characteristics as age, race, religious affiliation, marital status, educational background, place of birth, occupational history, family social class, and sexual orientation. Consistent with the literature on female stripping, no conclusions seemed appropriate concerning patterns of personal-social characteristics which might have led our respondents to seek stripping as an occupational endeavor.

3. One exception to this description applies to those dancers who participate in production numbers. Those three or four regular dancers who are a part of this feature of the show are paid extra compensation in addition to tips from the audience and meet on a regular basis outside the club to plan and practice their choreographed numbers.

4. Careful formal training prior to stripping tends to be characteristic primarily of feature dancers in contrast to touring strippers or house girls (Boles and Garbin, 1974c; Skipper and McCaghy, 1978).

REFERENCES

Ames, R. G., S. W. Brown, and N. L. Weiner (1970) "Breakfast with topless barmaids," pp. 35–52 in J. D. Douglas (ed.) Observations of Deviance. New York: Random House.

Boles, J. and A. P. Garbin(1974a) "The strip club and stripper-customer patterns of interaction." Sociology and Social Research 58: 136–144.

___ (1974b) "The choice of stripping for a living." Sociology of Work and Occupations 1: 110-123.

___ (1974c) "Stripping for a living: an occupational study of the night club stripper," pp. 312–335 in C. D. Bryant (ed.) Deviant Behavior: Occupational and Organizational Bases. Chicago: Rand McNally.

Bryant, C. D. and C. E. Palmer (1975) "Massage parlors and 'hand whores': some sociological observations." J. of Sex Research 11: 227–241.

Carey, S. H., R. A. Peterson, and L. K. Sharpe (1974) "A study of recruitment and socialization in two deviant female occupations." Soc. Symposium 11: 11–24.

Glaser, B. G. and A. L. Strauss (1967) The Discovery of Grounded Theory. Chicago: Aldine.

Goode, E. (1978) Deviant Behavior: An Interactionist Approach. Englewood Cliffs, NJ: Prentice-Hall.

Hong, L. K. and R. W. Duff (1977) "Becoming a taxi dancer." Sociology of Work and Occupations 4: 327–342.

McCaghy, C. H. and J. K. Skipper, Jr. (1972) "Stripping: Anatomy of a deviant life style," pp. 362–373 in S. D. Feldman and G. W. Thielbar (eds.) Life Styles: Diversity in American Society. Boston: Little, Brown.

Miller, G. (1978) Odd Jobs: The World of Deviant Work. Englewood Cliffs, NJ: Prentice-Hall.

Petersen, D. M. and P. L. Dressel (forthcoming) "Equal time for women: Social notes on the male strip show." Urban Life.

Prehn, J. W. (1981) "Invasion of the male strippers: Role realignment in a small-town strip club." Presented at the meeting of the Popular Culture Association, Cincinnati, Ohio.

Ritzer, G. (1977) Working: Conflict and Change. Englewood Cliffs, NJ: Prentice-Hall.

Roebuck, J. B. and W. Frese (1976) "The after-hours club: An illegal social organization and its client system." Urban Life 5: 131–164.

Salutin, M. (1971) "Stripper morality." Trans-Action 8: 12–22.

Scott, M., and S. Lyman (1968) "Accounts." Am. Soc. Rev. 33: 46–62.

Skipper, J. K., Jr. and C. H. McCaghy (1970) "Stripteasers: The anatomy and career contingencies of a deviant occupation." Social Problems 17: 391–404.

___ (1978) "Teasing, flashing, and visual sex: Stripping for a living," pp. 171–193 in J. M. Henslin and E. Sagarin (eds.) The Sociology of Sex. New York: Schocken.

Sykes, G. M. and D. Matza (1957) "Techniques of neutralization: A theory of delinquency." Am. J. of Sociology 22: 664–670.

Verlarde, A. J. (1975) "Becoming prostituted." British J. of Criminology 15: 251–263.

Verlarde, A. J. and M. Warlick (1973) "Massage parlors: The sensuality business." Society 11: 63–74.

4 | Feelings About Work

As discussed in Chapter 1, work is central to the identity and lives of many individuals. Because occupational status is typically a major determinant of social class, your occupation affects nearly every aspect of life—from who your friends are to the length of your life. Moreover, since full-time workers generally spend at least 40 hours a week doing their work, how they feel about their work may have repercussions for how they feel about themselves.

Social scientists have explored many feelings about work, including work motivation, satisfaction, alienation, stress, and burnout. Motivation refers to the amount of excitement and interest a worker feels toward his or her work. Work **satisfaction** and work **alienation** are at different ends of the same continuum, representing positive and negative feelings about work, respectively. Of course, even in the seemingly most satisfying jobs, workers often find some less satisfying aspects, just as workers in seemingly alienating jobs may find some satisfying aspects to their work. **Work stress** refers to physical, mental, or emotional tension or strain that results from work. When high levels of stress are prolonged and overpowering, and a worker loses the ability to function in his or her position, this individual is suffering from **burnout**.

Many sociologists argue that these feelings about work are intricately linked: For example, high worker satisfaction has a positive impact on motivation to work and commitment to other workers and the employer, which ultimately results in increased productivity. Other sociologists are less sure of the link between these feelings.

Although workers' feelings about their work may be attributed in part to psychological differences among individuals, attitudes toward work both shape and can be shaped by the occupational environment in which the work is performed as well as the management practices and formal structure of the employing organization. Moreover, larger societal forces have an impact on a variety of aspects of workers' jobs that may then affect their feelings about their work.

In this chapter, we explore a variety of workers' feelings about their work in an attempt to better understand the individual, organizational, and societal influences that shape these feelings. We move from theories that are more psychological and focus on the individual, to theories related to the occupational environment and organizational structure, and finally to theories that emphasize the societal structure.

Individual Influences

What motivates workers, particularly those in jobs that are seemingly not interesting or challenging? If you were a manager, how would you come to understand the motivation of the many different kinds of workers you might supervise? Are there psychological differences among individuals that may affect their attitudes about their work? Over the last several decades, psychologists have developed theories related to the individual's need to develop fulfilling skills and talents.

Psychological Needs Hierarchy

Abraham Maslow, a noted psychologist, describes a hierarchy of human needs (1943, 1954, 1970). As you read the following list, keep in mind that these needs may have an impact on individuals' work motivation in an organization.

- The physiological need for food and water is at the base of Maslow's hierarchy.
- The second level is composed of safety needs, including security, stability, and freedom from pain.
- The third level is that of belonging and love needs.
- The fourth level is esteem, including the need for self-respect and respect from others.
- The fifth and highest order need is the need for self-actualization or self-fulfillment— the need to feel that one has reached his or her potential.

Although Maslow acknowledges that the hierarchy of needs may vary from one individual to another, he believes that the lower level physical and physiological needs must be fulfilled before an individual develops motivation to fulfill higher order needs. An individual in need of food, water, and shelter will not be motivated to fulfill higher order needs. Sociological factors may, however, shift the need hierarchy. A sociologist taking the life-span development approach might argue that this hierarchy of needs differs depending on one's stage in the life cycle. A woman employed as an executive for 20 years may expect self-actualization from her work. A single mother who is similarly employed as an executive may be most interested in the financial security of the position. The cohort of women and men who were children during the economic depression of the 1930s may find security a stronger need than others who did not suffer such deprivation. On the other hand, this hierarchy of needs may help explain why some workers are motivated to do their work well, while others doing the same job are not.

The salaries of loading dock workers employed by the one of the largest trucking companies in the United States are controlled by a contract between the union and company management. As a result, dock workers do not receive raises or other formal rewards as a result of how quickly they work; they receive raises only as the union gains salary increases. On every shift of about 80 workers, there are about 10 "bill killers" or "freight hogs"—extremely productive workers. I spoke with bill killers who said they worked hard because they had always worked hard. The job fulfilled their basic needs for sustenance and safety. Their families and friends provided love and belonging. For these men, working at the acceptable union pace, a slower pace, would contradict their fourth-level needs for self-esteem. For them, mediocrity would injure their self-image. For some of the dock workers, the third-level need for acceptance by their union brothers, which caused them to work at a slower pace, blocked the route to fulfilling needs for esteem and self-actualization, the fourth- and fifth-level needs. With regard to self-actualization, the bill killers included men who were very involved in their church, ran farms and other businesses after work, and did free-lance writing. For the bill killers, dock work met the first four levels of need, so that they were free to pursue self-actualization outside their primary employment.

Maslow believes that his hierarchy holds for all individuals. But, does his hierarchy apply cross-nationally? Everyone in every culture needs food and shelter. Yet, what constitutes self-actualization in one culture or even subculture may be very different from that for another culture or subculture. With the global economy, an awareness is needed of what constitutes self-actualization for different cultures. Profit may be the only goal of a manager from one culture. Producing consensus may be the first priority of a manager from another culture. Thus, even the interpretation and use of Maslow's theory is influenced by culture, a social force.

The Discrepancy Gap

Some theorists (Katzell, 1964; Porter, 1961) believe that the degree of alienation and satisfaction a worker experiences is directly related to the worker's expectations of the job. Alienation can represent the discrepancy or gap between the expectation and the experience of a particular job. For example, many students rush to beach resorts to get jobs as waiters and waitresses for the summer. I have never heard a student describe the upcoming experience as a beach resort waiter or waitress in a way that led me to believe that students expected to find that the job would bring them self-actualization. Their low expectations for self-actualization and their high degree of camaraderie with coworkers seem to mitigate the potentially alienating aspects of their job. On the other hand, it is clear that students expected to work long, hard hours and to make lots of money, particularly in tips. Maslow might argue that the recreational hours spent with many other students in a similar situation may help with the third-order need, the need for belongingness.

Influence of the Occupational Environment

We now move from theories that focus predominantly on the individual to those that look at the impact of the occupational environment on individuals' feelings about their work. In this section, we look at the impact of the formal job characteristics and informal reward structures on workers' feelings, and we explore how modern industry has affected specific job characteristics and also how the occupational environment affects workers' feelings of stress.

Formal Job Characteristics and Informal Reward Structures

While workers' feelings about their job may be affected by a hierarchy of needs, various characteristics of the job itself may have an even more important influence on work satisfaction and motivation. Hackman and Oldham (1976) argue that a set of core job dimensions affect critical psychological states, which in turn affect work satisfaction, motivation, and performance. There are five core dimensions of work.

- The first is *skill variety*, the extent to which the activities associated with the work challenge the worker's many abilities and skills.

- The second is *task identity*, the extent to which the worker sees the job or work from start to finish.

- The third dimension is *task significance.* This addresses the extent to which a worker feels that his or her work is significant, important, and useful to society and other people.

- The fourth dimension, *autonomy,* emphasizes the extent to which the worker experiences freedom and independence with regard to decision making, responsibility, and the work itself.

- The fifth and final dimension is that of *feedback,* the frequency with which workers receive information about how well they are doing their jobs.

These job dimensions affect critical psychological states such as the experienced meaningfulness of the work, the experienced outcomes of the work, and the knowledge of the actual result of the work activities.

We now turn to consideration of the possible difference between the formal and informal structure in the workplace, particularly as it relates to rewards. I previously mentioned that the formal structure for the loading dock workers is controlled by a contract between the union and company management. As a result, dock workers receive raises only as the union gains salary increases. Nevertheless, the company's reputation and revenues are affected by the rate at which the dock workers unload trucks ("strip"), move freight ("run"), and reload ("stack") the freight into other trucks. But, the company cannot offer formal incentives to these workers for increased productivity, that is, stripping, running, and stacking freight more quickly. In addition, the workers are governed by a strict set of rules, including not being allowed to read in the bathrooms and not being allowed to speak with other workers for more than 2 minutes. Foremen, whose job it is to direct these men, are rewarded if productivity increases. They may not physically participate in the freight-moving process; however, they may only direct others.

Several characteristics typify the job of a dock worker. First, except for physical strength and endurance, it requires minimal skills. Second, when one shift ends, a truck is simply left for those on the next shift to finish stripping or stacking. The focus is predominantly on stripping and stacking a particular truck, and the dock workers seldom look beyond that truck to recognize the significance of their work. The workers make few decisions about how their work is carried out, and the rules for behavior in the workplace are rigid. And finally, the foremen give very little, if any, feedback to the workers about either the quality or quantity of their work. Even the choice of men to lay off is affected by seniority, not by productivity. Using Hackman and Oldham's model, one would expect the motivation, productivity, and satisfaction of the dock workers to be quite low given the job characteristics I described. However, there are mitigating factors that make the job less alienating for some than for others.

As mentioned previously, on every shift of workers, there are a few bill killers or freight hogs, who are extremely productive workers. These workers are courted by the foremen. Given the formal reward structure described above, what motivates these men to be so productive? The answer lies in the informal structure that exists along with the formal structure. Although the bill killers and freight hogs have a marginal status and are often ostracized by their fellow dock workers, they have discovered an informal reward structure that works to their satisfaction. With the exception of task significance, the work of the bill killers and freight hogs would rate more highly on core job dimensions than the work of the typical dock worker. For example, the foremen give the bill killers and the freight hogs much more autonomy and control over the work and allow more bending and breaking of the rules because the foremen need the higher productivity levels for their own advancement. Bill killers and freight hogs do receive feedback on their work. They report being thanked at the end of the shift for good work and often find themselves being offered coffee or cigarettes by the foremen during the shift. The foreman occasionally leaves it to the bill killer to decide whether he would like a runner for the shift. In addition, because they work so quickly, the bill killers and freight hogs are more likely to see the stripping and stacking of an entire truck come to a close, thus increasing task identity.

The bill killers and freight hogs receive neither monetary nor promotional rewards for their work; yet, they continue to be extremely productive. In addition, because of their autonomy, power, and rule breaking, they are not necessarily good employees; but, they are good workers. Given the limited control foremen have because of union work rules, the bill killers and freight hogs offer them the best chance to "make their numbers" for each shift. In contrast, the typical dock worker is a good employee but not necessarily a highly productive one. In short, one cannot adequately account for particular levels of productivity and satisfaction by examining only the formal reward structure; one must also look at the informal rewards that may either parallel or contradict the formal reward structure.

Impact of Modern Industry

Blauner (1964) accepts the notion that there are alienating forces in modern industry, but he emphasizes how the individual worker feels as a result of the immediately alienating aspects of the work environment in which employees work. He argues that workers feel alienated in a variety of ways.

- First, workers feel *powerless* over the more immediate working conditions. Workers often cannot control the noise, temperature, or lighting level of their work environment.

- A second dimension of alienation is that of *meaninglessness.* As the division of labor increases and workers become more specialized, their tasks become so small that workers lose sight of how their task contributes to the final product. A machine tool operator drills cylinder head castings but never sees an automotive engine, let alone a finished car.

- Third, workers feel an increasing sense of *isolation,* as though they are not connected to a community.

- Fourth, workers feel *self-estranged.* Work activities that many employees engage in are not self-expressive or creative. A McDonald's worker is told not only what to wear and how to do the job, but also what to say and how to say it to customers.

It is clear that a variety of factors may have an impact on workers' feelings about their work.

Causes of Stress

Although job stress may increase as a result of factors outside the workplace, such as those related to family, we will focus on workplace factors affecting job stress. Some social scientists have focused more on the causes of stress for blue-collar workers (Shostak, 1980), while others identify the causes of white-collar stress (Pines, 1982). I believe, however, that the sources of stress are similar for both.

One source of stress is *compensation.* Many male blue-collar workers may see their salary as a reflection of their adequacy as a provider. Others fear that inflation will make their salary increase only a reflection of the increase in the cost of living and not a real gain. In addition, union workers know that their compensation gains do not signal that their work was meritorious, because their compensation increases result from gains for all workers (Shostak, 1980).

Occupational *health and safety hazards* (Shostak, 1980) present another source of stress. In Chapter 3, we saw the kinds of adaptations that high steel ironworkers made in response to the very dangerous work that they do. We saw that part of the process of informal socialization was learning to deal with the fears associated with such work.

Even when the workplace is not dangerous, *unpleasant conditions* are an additional source of stress (Shostak, 1980). Blue-collar workers may find their work noisy, dirty, hot, or cold. Walking past a pounding jackhammer is unpleasant. Imagine feeling the vibration and hearing the noise all day long. Working on the grounds crew on your college's campus may be fairly pleasant when the task is to mow a lawn in 70-degree weather. But, that job can become stressful and unpleasant when you are part of the emergency snow removal crew on the roof of a college building in danger of collapse. Or think of the dock workers I described. The loading dock has a roof, but neither walls nor doors. Snow, sleet, rain, and extremes of heat and cold are a regular part of this "inside" job. In white-collar environments, factors ranging from the architectural design to work space, noise, and the flexibility to change the work space may cause stress (Pines, 1982).

Another source of stress is that of *potential job loss*. Anxiety about job loss is high among many blue-collar and white-collar workers as a result of changing economic conditions and corporate downsizing. It is not the actual demand for workers in a field that makes the difference, but rather the demand relative to the supply of workers available.

Relations with others are another potential source of stress (Shostak, 1980; Pines, 1982). Although social interaction with others, including coworkers, can be very rewarding, it can also be a source of stress if tensions arise or some workers are excluded from the informal social activity. In terms of customers or clients, both the number and the severity of the problems or the intensity of the encounters can make a difference. In addition, relations with supervisors or bosses may involve some stress. The loading dock workers are forced to follow rules about how long to talk with one another. Other blue-collar environments are often rife with rules about everything from where to park to when to chew gum. Rules and regulations perceived as inhibiting job performance or personal freedom can cause stress. Seemingly meaningless paperwork and overloaded communications systems cause stress that builds every day. And stress can be further increased by a supervisor's pressure to improve productivity. Such stress can be overwhelming if appropriate feedback, rewards, and support are not received.

Lack of autonomy and a *lack of variety* can contribute to stress (Pines, 1982). Where autonomy and variety are high, one would expect less stress unless the individual is suffering from work overload. The degree of autonomy should correspond to the individual's abilities and the resources available to carry out the task. Similarly, while monotony on the job can be a source of stress, too much variety can result in overload. Overload can also result from too little time to complete the necessary work.

Burnout arises when the stress level becomes so high that the worker does not function appropriately in his or her occupational position. Although individuals have a different capacity for stress, the characteristics of the occupational environment put the worker in a situation that is likely to induce stress. In Case Study 4.1, "Sources of Burnout," Cary Cherniss shows how the occupational environment of two social workers had an impact on their differential ability to cope with the demands of their work.

As you read all of the case studies in this chapter, you should consider the extent to which these sources of stress are present in their work environments. More important, this discussion should alert you to potential sources of stress in an occupation that you may be considering. If you are already experiencing job-related stress, it may be helpful to know that the source of the stress may not be in the individual, but in the nature of the occupational environment. Moreover, there is an assumption that stress impedes work satisfaction, and that this ultimately affects worker productivity. The knowledge of that causal connection should cause corporate executives to consider strategies that might reduce stress and alienation.

Influence of Organizational Structure and Management Practices

In this section we examine the formal aspects of the work environment. We address the impact of the organizational structure and consciously chosen management practices on workers' feelings about their work.

Bureaucracy

Max Weber's analysis of bureaucracy defines work in this field (Gerth and Mills, 1946). He identifies characteristics that typically distinguish bureaucratic organizations from other social organizations.

- First, tasks are typically specialized, having a distinct division of labor.

- Second, within bureaucratic organizations, there is typically a hierarchy of authority that makes clear who is supervising whom, how information should travel from one level to another in the hierarchy, and who has power over whom.

- Third, there are written rules that define the way in which the bureaucracy will be governed. These written rules and procedures describe the hierarchical structure as well as the division of labor.

- Fourth, Weber characterized bureaucratic organizations as being rational and objective in their decision making. Impersonal, business-based relationships among employees of an organization should help keep employees from basing their decisions on personal relationships or subjective criteria.

- The fifth characteristic of bureaucracy is technical competency. Weber assumed that positions in a bureaucracy would be filled on the basis of technical competence, rather than favoritism, nepotism, or other less objective criteria. Evaluations and the subsequent promotions would also be made on the basis of objective criteria.

Weber's model was intended to be an ideal type, a model against which organizations could be measured. That is not to say that Weber thought organizations should meet these criteria; instead, he believed these characteristics would be typical of bureaucracies.

Questions about the reality of bureaucracies need to be raised. To what extent does Weber's characterization fit with the bureaucratic organizations of which you have been a part? For example, did relationships among workers and between workers and supervisors remain impersonal, or did personal relationships develop as a result of individuals working together? Was the real power in the organization a reflection of the individual's place in the organizational hierarchy, or did individuals intentionally and unintentionally attain power that did not necessarily reflect their formal position in the organization? The answers to these questions may indicate that although Weber's ideal type of bureaucracy reflects the formal structure of some organizations, it does not take into account the informal structure that inevitably emerges alongside the formal structure (Krackhardt and Hanson, 1993).

Although Weber thought that many organizations were either already bureaucratic or headed in that direction, he did not wholeheartedly support that move. On the one hand, Weber thought that the bureaucratic model he described might be the most efficient way to run an organization. On the other hand, he feared that this same bureaucratic organization could be dehumanizing for its members. For example, he was concerned that the increasing specialization of tasks and fragmentation of work would reduce the individuality and creativity that employees could bring to their jobs, increasing the potentially alienating aspects of work. Moreover, he believed the call for impersonal and formal relationships between coworkers might rob workers of an important component of sharing organizational membership with others, the possibility of friendship and personal ties, and thus reduce possible sources of work satisfaction.

Scientific Management

Although Weber feared some of the consequences of the bureaucracy he characterized, Frederick Taylor relished the idea of such efficiency and proposed a model of management to match. First and foremost, the scientific model of management proposed by Taylor emphasized human beings as economic beings. Taylor presumed that the most basic motivator was economic, particularly in the form of pay. Karl Marx's description of the consequences of capitalism and the theory of scientific management share one thing: They view the worker as an economic being. Marx hoped that the *proletariat* (those who have only their labor to sell) would recognize that they were being oppressed by the *bourgeoisie* (those who own the factories and means of production) and a revolution would follow. (See also the discussion of the conflict perspective in Chapter 2.) Taylor hoped for a revolution in the way that management thought about workers and the process of production. Companies were to commit themselves to scientific determination of the optimal way to increase productivity and profit; management and labor were two quite distinct functions; and workers must be provided with a financial reward or incentive to perform their job the best way possible based on external control.

Under scientific management, the tension and antagonism between management and labor was expected to cease. Together management and labor would recognize that high productivity would be in the best interest of both. High productivity would result in surplus, which would lead to increased profit for the manufacturer and increased wages for workers. Fundamental to the notion of scientific management is that both management and workers recognize that individual opinions and judgment must be replaced by scientific investigation and knowledge. Scientific investigation would be used to determine the most efficient and productive way to accomplish work. This scientific investigation typically resulted in the workers' tasks becoming increasingly specific. Although the label *scientific* implies openness to all verifiable ideas, the assumption was that workers would be most efficient when the complexity of their tasks was reduced.

The positive idea behind scientific management was to move away from nepotism. In the past, workers were often paid and received jobs on the basis of how well a supervisor knew their relatives. Now tasks would be free from bias and judgment and could simply be accomplished in the most efficient way possible. The principles of scientific management indicated that workers could be paid enough to keep motivation and productivity high, regardless of the potentially alienating nature of the work. The message to managers was clear: Make decisions on a scientific, objective, and rational basis. Although scientific management and efficiency made sense on paper, Taylor and others could not have anticipated the extent to which workers became demotivated by the boring and tedious nature of their work. Factory workers found their work dehumanizing. This is not surprising, since scientific management encouraged managers to treat workers as robots, programming each for an efficient, repetitive task. In Case Study 4.2, "'Banana Time': Job Satisfaction and Informal Interaction," Donald Roy shows how the repetitive nature of the work of the machine operators caused them to try to bring some humanity back to their alienating work.

The Human Relations Approach

Despite the positive projections associated with scientific management, Elton Mayo showed that there was more to worker motivation than money (Mayo, 1933, 1945; Roethlisberger and Dickson, 1939; Whitehead, 1938). Mayo's studies of motivation took place between 1929 and 1932 at the Western Electric Company's Hawthorne plant in Chicago. For example, Mayo found that when illumination of the work area was increased, worker productivity increased. At first, he believed that the brighter lighting itself improved workers' attitude and ultimately their productivity. But, later in the study it was found that worker productivity also increased when illumination of the work area was decreased. Eventually, researchers had to conclude there was only a spurious relationship between the illumination and worker productivity. Instead, they concluded that the attention the workers received caused the increased productivity. That is why research methodologists refer to a situation where the research itself has an impact on the results as the Hawthorne effect. The Hawthorne studies pointed to the need for new theories of management—

theories that were not based solely on the notion of the worker as primarily an economic being.

The human relations model had a different focus. Whereas those supporting scientific management had focused on the worker as an economic being, those supporting the human relations model emphasized people as social beings. Many aspects of work beyond money play a large role in the level of worker motivation. The findings of the Hawthorne studies indicated that the attention workers receive affects their level of motivation. Moreover, the informal structure in the workplace plays an important role in workers' perception of their work, and relationships at work are not based purely on economic connections. Friendships do emerge, and individuals gain power as a result of relationships that develop outside the mandated authority structure. In Case Study 4.3, "Containing Work Disaffection: The Poultry Processing Worker," Clifton Bryant and Kenneth Perkins point to the positive impact of relations with coworkers.

Human relations theorists recognized that informal norms that emerge as a result of personal relationships within groups have an impact on workers' perception of their work, including their feelings of motivation, satisfaction, and alienation. The message to managers was clear: Focus on interpersonal and small-group behavior to enhance worker productivity.

In the previous chapter we saw that high steel ironworkers, who work high in the air on the frameworks of buildings, learn to cope with the danger of their job through the process of informal socialization. The dangerous nature of their work environment forces workers to cope with the possibility of serious injury. The physical environment can affect workers' feelings in other ways, too. Those who work in a harsh environment together often form close bonds with their coworkers. Common burdens and mutual dependence are the fertile soil from which strong friendships grow. Deep-pit miners, combat soldiers, and arctic explorers find compensation for deprivation and danger in friendships that last a lifetime.

An article in *The New York Times* describes the work of "sandhogs," those who dig tunnels for vehicles, subways, and bridge foundations. They talk of "boring obscurely into spaces of the earth never seen, hundreds of feet below the waters and walkers and cars and trains of the city...we go where nobody has ever gone" (Fisher, 1993: A-45). They are described as some of the closest of union members. One sandhog remarked, "You'll never find a tighter bunch of men than you'll find around here" (Fisher, 1993: A-45). The perils of this job mold and nurture the commitment these men have for one another.

Danger does not always foster professional loyalty or commitment to coworkers. Race car driving, one of the most dangerous and competitive sports in the world, is as likely to elicit hatred among team members as loyalty and friendship. In the top forms of the sport, such as Formula One and Indy Car racing, two-car teams are notorious for causing life-long enmity among top drivers. In recent years, top drivers have stipulated that they will not drive for a two-car team unless the other driver is not a top-ranked competitor. In addition to danger, shared hardships—not million-dollar salaries—are necessary to form the relationships common among soldiers and sandhogs. Competition between drivers overrides their shared experience of danger because when the race is over, even drivers who finished midfield are surrounded by fans trailing them to postrace parties and private planes.

Influence of Society

As we discussed previously, some social scientists have focused on individual psychological differences and specific aspects of the occupational environment and organizational structure. We now look at the influence of society more generally by focusing on the economic system and the impact of societal stereotypes.

The Economic System

Rather than focusing on the organizational structure of the employing organization, Marx (1844) clearly locates the cause of workers' feelings of *alienation* toward their work in society's economic structure ([1844] Tucker, 1972: 57–67). Marx, in his classic statement on the relationship between work and workers' feelings about their work, describes alienation as a consequence of one particular type of economic structure: capitalism. He argues that when the bourgeoisie own the means of production and reap all the benefits of the work of the proletariat or laborers, alienation is inevitable. The bourgeoisie encourage the proletariat to work harder and become more productive; but, the proletariat realize that the profits of their additional efforts go only to the bourgeoisie. As the proletariat work harder and longer, the bourgeoisie accumulate more wealth from their exploitation of the workers. Workers can accumulate capital only by offering their labor, while the bourgeoisie benefit from the work of others. Marx sees worker alienation as an obvious result.

- First, the worker is alienated from the material objects that he or she produces. Although workers may attempt to inject creativity in the making of these products, they realize that their work promotes the interests of the capitalists. The workers become alienated from these material objects as they realize that the energy and effort they put forth yields rewards only for those who own the means of production.

- Second, workers become alienated from the act of production itself. They find themselves in jobs with little inherent satisfaction because they must somehow earn a living. They earn wages only through their labor. Work is only a means to an end. And as machinery further dominates workers' lives, they become even more alienated from the production process.

- A third type of alienation is innately linked to the two already described. Workers increasingly repress their self-expression because capitalism robs them of satisfaction from the product and the production process. The workers lose their desire to put forth special effort in their work.

- Finally, human beings become alienated from other human beings. Relationships between individuals are transformed into a market relationship; the owners buy the work they need without regard to the individual worker.

In addition to the type of economic system, the state of the economy or even the number of jobs in a particular field can have an impact on workers' feelings about their work and themselves. Unemployment can be financially and emotionally devastating for both blue-collar and white-collar workers. In Case Study 4.4, "The Hollywood Actor: Occupational Culture, Career, and Adaptation in a Buyers' Market Industry," Norman Friedman examines the impact of repeated rejection on actors' and actresses' feelings about their work. He describes the emotional adaptations they make to deal with the consequences of the high supply of actors and actresses relative to the demand.

Impact of Societal Stereotypes

We have already looked at the sex segregation of the work force, how gender stereotypes affect occupational choice, and how gender stereotypes can affect occupational socialization, particularly when the individual is a token. Here, we look more carefully at the impact of societal stereotypes and bias at the organizational level. Whether or not bias is based on employers' or supervisors' overt hostility, it is clear that stereotypes contribute to the difficulties of a variety of groups, including women and racial and ethnic minorities.

Glass Ceiling. Although women have achieved the titles of president or chief operating officer of such billion-dollar companies as Mattel, Pepsi-Cola of North America, Saks Fifth Avenue, Maxwell House Coffee, and The Seagram Beverage Group (Dobrzynski, 1995), this is unusual. Many women and minorities encounter a glass ceiling as they try to climb the organizational hierarchy. The U.S. Department of Labor uses **glass ceiling** to refer "to those artificial barriers based on attitudinal or organizational bias that prevent qualified individuals from advancing upward in their organization to management-level positions" (U.S. Department of Labor, 1991: 1) and reaching their full potential. More often than not, glass ceiling is used to refer to barriers to women and minorities. In some organizations, the glass ceiling may be so low that mobility is nearly impossible. Catherine Berheide (1992) calls this the "sticky floor." One African American woman said she faces a "cement ceiling," since historically, African American women and men have fared worse in promotions than other groups. Some women ministers refer to the barriers to mobility in church hierarchies as the "stained glass ceiling."

As workers climb the organizational hierarchy, those desiring promotions would expect to be promoted to those positions based on their talents and work performance. Although glass ceiling is now a popular metaphor, it needs to be demystified (Auster, 1993). First the notion of the *glass* ceiling implies that we cannot see this ceiling until it is reached. But, the "*glass* ceiling is not transparent. It is visible and apparent, particularly to those who experience it" (Auster, 1993: 49). Individuals are quite aware of the biases against them in an organization. Because the biases are often noticeable from the moment employment begins, those who are the focus of such bias may try to develop strategies early in their employment to deal with the glass ceiling.

Auster (1993) points out that the glass *ceiling* "is not one ceiling nor a wall in one spot. It is gender bias. It occurs all the time and takes many forms" (48). So far, we have focused on gender bias, but these ideas can be extended to racial, ethnic, or even age bias. The bias against women, members of racial and ethnic groups, homosexuals and lesbians, and people with physical disabilities results from stereotypes that lead to the unequal treatment of those in these groups. The bias could also be against those who are of a token age group or those who are disabled. Although the actions that perpetuate the glass ceiling are a result of stereotypes of groups, the actions can be intentional or unintentional. But, categorical bias means that evaluations of the accomplishments and behaviors of individuals in these categories are diminished by the fact that they belong to these categories.

The term *glass wall* refers to situations where entire divisions of a company are dominated by one sex. Criticism can be leveled against this terminology, since again the glass is not transparent, but readily apparent to those subjected to the segregation and the wall is always there, not just there as one moves closer to the margins of the occupations.

To deal with the increasing number of glass ceiling complaints, the Glass Ceiling Commission was created as a part of the Civil Rights Act of 1991. The commission studies the kinds of barriers that women and minorities encounter as they attempt to move up in their organizational hierarchies. The topics the commission has explored have included harassment, the lack of family-friendly workplace policies, and the impact of stereotyping on recruitment practices, promotions, and pay increases.

In the context of this chapter, we need to ask how recognition of the limited mobility imposed by the glass ceiling affects different categories of workers' feelings about their jobs. Do you think these workers are more alienated than other workers? How do those who are affected by the glass ceiling perceive their supervisors and the employing organization? And how might this affect workers' productivity and their commitment to their employing organization?

Tokenism. The glass ceiling is one indication of the ways in which bias can carry over into the workplace and affect workers' feelings about their work. In the previous chapter, we described tokenism and the impact it can have on the process of socialization. Although Kanter's (1977) argument is based on the notion that women are treated as they are at Indsco because of their status as tokens at the management level, Zimmer (1988) argues that to understand the position of the token, one must also look beyond the ratio in an organization. One must consider the societal power and status of the group of which the token is a part. In Case Study 4.5, "Tokenism Reconsidered: Male Nurses and Female Physicians in a Hospital Setting," Liliane Floge and Deborah Merrill test this proposition by considering male nurses and female physicians in the same hospital setting.

Sexual Harassment. Sexual harassment is an all too common aspect of the social environment at the workplace. There are many definitions of sexual harassment. In my school's *College Life Manual,*

(1995–1996), the definition of **sexual harassment,** which is based on the Equal Opportunity Commission (EEOC) Guidelines issued in 1980, is as follows: "Deliberate or repeated unsolicited sexual advances; requests for sexual favors; or verbal comments, gestures, or physical contact which are unwelcome constitute sexual harassment when (1) submission to such conduct is made either explicitly or implicitly a term or condition of academic status or employment; (2) submission to or rejection of such conduct by an individual is the basis for evaluations of academic performance or employment decisions; (3) such conduct has the purpose or effect of substantially interfering with academic or work performance or creating an intimidating, hostile, or offensive living or working environment; or (4) such conduct threatens an individual's emotional well-being" (39).

This particular definition and the instituted policy are designed to cover sexual harassment among the many categories of individuals that make up the college community: students, faculty, administration, and staff. Yet, many elements of this definition typify those used by others in various companies and organizations. The definition covers a wide variety of behaviors and other actions, and it is linked to work performance whether academic or as an employee. Another common thread in current definitions is the notion of a "hostile" working environment. A *hostile* environment is one that can be perceived or is perceived as abusive, humiliating, degrading, intimidating, or uncomfortable in a way that discourages the worker from remaining on the job or interferes with work performance or career advancement.

Although either women or men can be victims of sexual harassment, it is more typically women who are harassed. In part, this is a consequence of men's power over women in many working circumstances. With regard to both men and women, what impact do you think sexual harassment has on workers' feelings about their work, their coworkers, and employing organization?

Although the great frequency with which sexual harassment takes place and the relatively low frequency of those formally reporting sexual harassment would make one pessimistic about the future, other evidence promises more optimism. "A unanimous 1993 ruling by the U.S. Supreme Court (*Teresa Harris* v. *Forklift Systems*) now gives workers a basis for claiming sexual harassment without having to prove that they have suffered psychological damage. Forcing employers to examine how workplace environments foster sexual harassment and holding them accountable is a major step forward" (Reskin and Padavic, 1994: 175). In addition, more organizations than ever before have written policies concerning sexual harassment.

Employing organizations will need to take a harder look at these issues as they lose valuable employees or as employees become less productive because of sexual harassment.

Conclusion

In this chapter, we examined a variety of perspectives and factors that affect workers' feelings about their work. We saw how job characteristics, managment practices, and relationships with coworkers can affect workers' feelings of satisfaction, alienation, and stress. We also examined how the type of economic system as well as the impact of societal stereotypes, particularly for gender and race, can affect the work environment and career ladders, which ultimately shape workers' feelings about their company, their coworkers, and their work. This chapter uses workers' feelings about their work to further elaborate the central theme of this book: that organizational and societal structures play a tremendous role in workers' perceptions of their work environment, their work, and themselves.

REFERENCES AND SUGGESTED READINGS

Auster, Ellen R. 1993. "Demystifying the Glass Ceiling: Organizational and Interpersonal Dynamics of Gender Bias." *Business and the Contemporary World* 5 (Summer): 47–68.

Baridon, Andrea P., and David R. Eyler. 1994. *Working Together: The New Rules and Realities for Managing Men and Women at Work.* New York: McGraw-Hill.

Berheide, Catherine. 1992. "Women Still 'Stuck' in Low-Level Jobs." *Women in Public Services: A Bulletin for the Center for Women in Government* 3 (Fall).

Blauner, Robert. 1964. *Alienation and Freedom.* Chicago: University of Chicago Press.

Burawoy, Michael. 1979. *Manufacturing Consent.* Chicago: University of Chicago Press.

Dobrzynski, Judith H. 1995. "Way Beyond the Glass Ceiling." *The New York Times,* May 11: D-1, D-6.

Erikson, Kai. 1990. "On Work and Alienation." Pages 19–35 in *The Nature of Work,* edited by Kai Erikson and Steven Peter Vallas. New Haven: Yale University Press.

Feldman, Richard, and Michael Betzold, eds. 1988. *End of the Line: Autoworkers and the American Dream.* New York: Weidenfeld and Nicolson.

Fisher, Ian. 1993. "Tunneling into a World of Danger." *The New York Times,* November 28: A-45, A-48.

College Life Manual. 1995–1996. Lancaster, PA: Franklin and Marshall College.

Garson, Barbara. 1994. *All the Livelong Day.* New York: Penguin Books.

Gerth, H. H. and C. Wright Mills. 1946. *From Max Weber: Essays in Sociology.* New York: Oxford University Press.

Hackman, J. Richard, and Greg R. Oldham. 1976. "Motivation Through the Design of Work: Test of a Theory." *Organizational Behavior and Human Performance* 16: 250–279.

Hamper, Ben. 1991. *Rivethead: Tales from the Assembly Line.* New York: Warner Books.

Kanter, Rosabeth. 1977. *Men and Women of the Corporation.* New York: Basic Books.

Katzell, R. A. 1964. "Personal Values, Job Satisfaction, and Job Behavior." In *Man in a World of Work,* edited by H. Borow. Boston: Houghton Mifflin.

Krackhardt, David, and Jeffrey Hanson. 1993. "Informal Networks: The Company Behind the Chart." *Harvard Business Review* 71 (July-August: 104–111.

Leidner, Robin. 1993. *Fast Food, Fast Talk: Service Work and the Routinization of Everyday Life.* Berkeley: University of California Press.

Maslow, Abraham H. 1943. "A Theory of Human Motivation." *Psychological Review* 50: 370–396.

Maslow, Abraham H. 1954. *Motivation and Personality.* New York: Harper and Row.

Maslow, Abraham H. 1970. *Motivation and Personality* (2nd ed.). New York: Harper and Row.

Mayo, Elton. 1933. *The Human Problems of Industrial Civilization.* New York: Macmillan.

Mayo, Elton. 1945. *The Social Problems of an Industrial Civilization.* Cambridge, MA: Harvard Graduate School of Business.

Paine, Whiton Stewart. 1982. *Job Stress and Burnout.* Newbury Park, CA: Sage.

Pennsylvania Commission for Women. 1993. *Sexual Harrassment on the Job: A Guide for Managers and Employees.* Harrisburg, PA.

Pines, Ayala M. 1982. "Changing Organizations: Is a Work Environment Without Burnout an Impossible Goal?" Pp. 189–211 in *Job Stress and Burnout: Research, Theory, and Intervention Perspectives,* edited by Whiton Stewart Paine. Beverly Hills: Sage.

Porter, L. W. 1961. "A Study of Perceived Need Satisfactions in Bottom and Middle Managment Jobs." *Journal of Applied Psychology* 45: 1–10.

Reskin, Barbara, and Irene Padavic. 1994. *Women and Men at Work.* Thousand Oaks, CA: Pine Forge Press.

Roethlisberger, F. J., and William Dickson. 1939. *Management and the Worker.* Cambridge, MA: Harvard University Press.

Shostak, Arthur B. 1980. *Blue-Collar Stress.* Reading, MA: Addison-Wesley.

Taylor, Frederick W. 1912. Hearings Before the Special Committee of the House of Representatives to Investigate Taylor and Other Systems of Shop Management. January 25th, pp. 1387–89. (Found in *Management Classics,* Michael T. Matteson and John M. Ivancevich. Plano, TX: Business Publications, Inc., 1986, pp. 3–6.)

Taylor, Frederick W. 1947. *Scientific Management.* New York: Harper and Row.

Tucker, Robert C. 1972. *The Marx–Engels Reader.* New York: W. W. Norton.

U.S. Department of Labor. 1991. *A Report on the Glass Ceiling Initiative.* Washington, DC.

Whitehead, T. North. 1938. *The Industrial Worker.* Cambridge, MA: Harvard University Press.

Williams, Christine L. 1989. *Gender Differences at Work: Women and Men in Nontraditional Occupations.* Berkeley: University of California Press.

Zimmer, Lynn. 1988. "Tokenism and Women in the Workplace: The Limits of a Gender-Neutral Theory." *Social Problems* 35 (February): 64–77.

Sources of Burnout

Two Case Studies

Cary Cherniss

CASE STUDY QUESTIONS

1. How would you describe the relative stress level of each of the two social workers, Karen and Diane? Was the difference due to their personalities or to a variety of aspects of their work environment?

2. How well do the factors that may contribute to stress described in this chapter explain the situation of these two women? To what extent are the factors that cause burnout in this study applicable to the work of those in other fields or in other organizations?

3. If you had the resources and power, what would you do to reduce the stress level for these two women? What organizational factors might constrain you from introducing the changes you would desire?

In searching for sources of burnout in a human service setting, there is a tendency to focus on a single level of analysis. For some, that level is the individual; they ask, "What kind of person is most likely to burn out?" For others, the investigation focuses on the organizational level. Here, the central question becomes, "In what kind of job, in what

Source: From *Staff Burnout: Job Stress in the Human Services* (pp. 63–77) by Cary Cherniss, 1980, Thousand Oaks, CA: Sage Publications. Reprinted by permission of Sage Publications, Inc.

kind of organization, is burnout most prevalent?" Or, to put the question in a slightly different form, "What are the characteristics of jobs and organizations that contribute to or prevent burnout?" Finally, there are a few who emphasize the societal or cultural level of analysis. Their central question always is, "What aspects of our society contribute to burnout in human service occupations?"

Obviously, one can find sources of burnout at each of these three levels: societal, organizational, and individual. In fact, an adequate treatment of the problem must address each of these levels and recognize their interrelationships.

There are two reasons for beginning with the organizational level. First, differences in jobs and organizations probably are more powerful sources of burnout than are differences in individuals. Some support for this proposition comes from a study of burnout in child abuse programs, a study which assessed the relative contribution to burnout of various factors (Berkeley Planning Associates, 1977). The researchers found that "organizational climate variables" such as leadership behavior, communication, and clarity of goals were more significant than individual demographic variables such as sex and educational level. Of course, one study does not prove the proposition. However, any human service professional who has worked in both a large, custodial, bureaucratically enmeshed state mental hospital and a small, relatively autonomous, progressive clinic serving a primarily young, attractive, verbal, and well-educated client population will probably appreciate the enormous difference that organizational factors can make. Although I know of no research on the subject, it seems safe to predict that organizational burnout in the large state hospital would be higher than in the small, progressive clinic. There are many settings in the human services that seem to be structured for burnout.

However, there is a second reason for focusing first on the job and organization: It is ultimately easier to reduce the incidence and severity of burnout by intervening at this level. This statement might seem odd to those who have been frustrated in their attempts to change a human service organization. However, changing individuals is not easy, either. One clearly confronts the same problems of internal resistance and lack of control over critical contingencies when attempting to change either individuals or settings. And those who have tried to find and hire the "right kind" of individual for a human service job will recognize that our knowledge and ability to make an impact at this point also will be limited.

Individual behavior is strongly influenced by the social setting. We usually can change a person's attitudes and feelings more easily by changing the structure of his or her roles than by working directly with the person. Of course, we must first gain the power to change or create the organization's role structure. However, once we are able to do this, we are in a much better position to reduce the incidence of burnout. For instance, it is easier to reduce "role conflict" (an organizational-level source of burnout) than to change an adult's "locus of control" from external to internal (an individual-level source of burnout). Furthermore, for the amount of time and skill necessary to modify one person's locus of control, one could reduce role conflict for a large number of people. In other words, interventions at the organizational level not only tend to be more effective, but they also have the potential for affecting more individuals for the same resources.

Many of the factors in a work setting that contribute to job stress and burnout are revealed by comparing and contrasting actual experiences. In fact, much can be learned by studying the work situations of mental health professionals who differ in their degree of burnout. A particularly good comparison is provided by two social workers who participated in a study of burnout in new professionals (Cherniss, 1980a). These two individuals were similar in numerous respects; however, one became burned out after only nine months in her job while the other became increasingly involved, committed, and enthusiastic about her work during that period.

Both of these individuals had received masters' degrees in social work within the last year. Both were women in their mid-thirties who had been married but were now divorced. Both worked with client populations that traditionally have been less successful candidates for treatment in the human services (the mentally retarded and alcoholics). Both began their jobs with great anticipation and a sense of purpose. Despite these similarities, only one showed signs of burnout during the first year of work.

A Stressful Work Setting

The person who burned out, whom I shall call Karen Mikelson, worked in a large state institution for the retarded. Most of her time, however, was spent in a distant county where she supervised the community placements of retarded clients who had been discharged from the institution. The remaining time she worked at the institution where she was responsible for a number of clients who were still institutionalized.

The first important source of stress in Karen's job was the clientele. She had worked with the retarded before, but these previous experiences involved an "educable" population. In her current job, she worked with a "lower functioning" group, people who were expected to learn very little, people who were dependent and could not even take care of their physical needs. For these clients, the goal was simply to ensure that their physical needs were being met. The emphasis was on maintenance, not rehabilitation. Although Karen did not complain specifically about this aspect of her job, she was deprived of an important source of gratification, meaning, and stimulation in work: There were apparently few opportunities for experiencing a sense of efficacy or utilizing the skills she had developed during her training.

Matters were made even worse by the case load. Karen was responsible for the supervision of over 90 clients spread over a two-county area, as well as 50 inpatients still awaiting discharge from the institution. She said that she was frustrated because all of her time was consumed by crises that needed immediate attention (such as a client who suddenly needed a new placement within 48 hours). The heavy case load prevented her from helping home operators improve their management practices. The reactive crisis orientation allowed little time to work with individual clients or help develop new community resources. Thus, the size of her case load, as well as the type of client with whom she worked, prevented Karen from feeling she was efficient; she often felt as though she were just "treading water."

Another major source of stress for Karen was organizational conflict and lack of support within the institution. Karen was one of six social workers employed by this institution. Together, they constituted the social services department. In this medically oriented setting, the social services department was one of the smallest and most marginal. According to Karen, the department was really not "accepted" within the institution. The work they did was neither valued nor understood by other staff. In fact, Karen believed that many staff thought the social workers were merely "transportation aides." At one point she summed up this source of stress in her work: "You just don't get support for breaking your neck out in the community."

Relations among the various departments were strained. Competition, jealousy, and rivalry characterized their interactions. Karen said that the one thing social workers had in common was their defense against a "common enemy." Cooperation and collaboration between different staff groups was actually discouraged. For instance, a proposed orientation group for new residents was vetoed by the department heads involved because the group was to be co-led by a nursing aide and a social worker. Such collaboration was regarded as "unwise."

Thus, the intergroup conflict within the institution and the social service department's marginal and precarious position gave rise to an emphasis on caution and a distaste for innovation and creativity. There developed a rigid, restrictive set of norms designed to ensure that staff would not further weaken the department's position in the institution. According to Karen, her director's attitude was, "Don't rock the boat. Don't confront the issues here. Don't make waves."

Although this attitude may have been an appropriate one given the department's marginal position within the institution, Karen found it intolerable. She said that she was just "not like that at all." Her style was to confront problems, not cover them up. Initially, Karen attempted to change the restrictive, bureaucratic climate of her department. She spoke up at staff meetings. She challenged policies that seemed to serve trivial bureaucratic purposes at the expense of clients. Unfortunately, Karen's co-workers were unwilling to support her attempts to change things. She was labeled the "pushy, aggressive, malcontent" in the group. Once this occurred, people just "tuned out" whenever she said anything critical. They stopped listening to what she said, and she lost what little influence she might have had. Consequently, her frustration increased still further. She came to believe that she could have no impact on the system, that it was hopeless. She coped by withdrawing. She avoided the institution and spent as much time in the community as possible.

However, even in the community, Karen was still a state employee, and decisions made at the state level further contributed to her sense of frustration and powerlessness. She said that the state's priorities concerning after-care planning kept changing without notice or reason. After this happened a few times, she could not become enthusiastic about, or strongly committed to, any particular programmatic thrust; for there was always the sense that it would only be temporary.

Karen also received little help or support for her efforts to cope with this confusing and demanding work situation. When she started her job, she received no formal orientation to the complex environment in which she would be working. She was told simply to spend the first week reading through a set of rules and procedures that were meaningless to her at that point. True to form, there *was* a formal, two-week orientation program—five months after she had begun her job! (In the interests of bureaucratic efficiency, the orientation program was delayed until there was an "adequate" number of new employees to participate in it.) Needless to say, this orientation program was not very useful by the time Karen participated in it.

Another potential source of support—supervision—became another source of conflict and strain. Initially, Karen had two supervisors: the director of social work and the supervising social worker. These two individuals differed in their views, frequently argued with one another, and avoided interaction with each other whenever possible to avoid further conflict. Consequently, they often gave Karen conflicting messages. Fortunately, the director resigned six months after Karen began the job, eliminating this source of conflict. However, until the decision concerning his replacement was finally made, this uncertainty was yet another source of tension for Karen and her co-workers.

Even when the supervision issue was resolved and Karen only had one primary supervisor, she continued to receive conflicting messages. On the one hand, her supervisor seemed to tell her, "Go out and do the job, you're competent. I trust you." But then Karen would come back a few days later, and her supervisor would say, "What's going on? What are you doing out there? I want to know everything that you do before you do it."

Karen usually received no supervision at all. Much of the time her supervisor was not available for consultation. Supervision meetings would be scheduled and then canceled at the last moment. When Karen and her supervisor did meet, her supervisor simply provided her with administrative information. Her supervisor seemed to be uninterested in and/or unable [sic] of giving Karen the kind of ongoing emotional support and technical assistance that could increase her effectiveness in her work. Again, the primary concern in supervision seemed to be that Karen do nothing that might "rock the boat."

Karen also did not receive much support from her peers. She said that there was little "informal sharing" among the social work staff. Because they supervised placements in different counties, they only came together as a group when staff meetings were scheduled. Days could go by without their paths crossing. When they did come together for staff meetings, the structure of those meetings prevented them from engaging in a genuine exchange of ideas and discussion of professional issues. The director set the tone for the meetings; the tone was formal, businesslike, and bureaucratic. The director used the meetings to communicate information concerning administrative rules, changes in policies, and so on. The director controlled the content and flow of the meeting. The message that Karen and the others received was that this was the "director's meeting," and the director wanted to use the meeting only to tell staff what they should be doing. Emotional support, mutual problem-solving, and professional learning and growth clearly were not part of the agenda.

No work situation is totally negative, and there were two aspects of Karen's that were positive. First, there were professionals in other agencies in the county to which she was assigned who became an important source of support. Other social workers employed by the local CMHC, the schools, and the Department of Social Services frequently worked with Karen because of mutual clients or programs. She had developed close, positive relationships with several of these colleagues, and their acceptance and support helped Karen cope with the problems she faced back at the institution.

The second positive feature in Karen's job was the high degree of autonomy. Karen found that she could modify her role in significant ways without her superiors' knowing or interfering. For instance, if she wanted to deemphasize client contact and direct her energies instead into program development, she could do so. This high degree of autonomy seemed to be the one benefit of the lack of supervision.

Thus, despite some positive aspects, Karen's job generally was filled with stress, frustration, and disappointment. Consequently, her energy and commitment gradually declined over time. At first, she had "big ups and downs": One week she would be depressed and feel that everything was hopeless; two weeks later she would feel ready to try to change the situation to make things better. Eventually, Karen settled into a "survival" mentality. Her agitation and dissatisfaction lessened as she resigned herself to the situation and learned to "live with it." However, she felt a sense of stagnation, as though she were just marking time. She said that she was "looking out" for other job possibilities, but the work situation no longer seemed so bad that she wanted to look actively for another. Karen was more aware than ever that many other jobs could be as bad or worse than this one, and she was conscious of the stresses associated with adjusting to a new job, even a good one. At least in her present job she had come to feel "comfortable."

In her last interview, Karen summed up these feelings—the feelings of burnout—in this way:

I don't know what my "agenda" is now. I think my agenda right now is just plain survival and perseverance until something else comes along. Yeah, I guess I've concluded that I'm not totally happy in this situation, but I'm not really ready to invest too much to change it. I will just go along at the moment, do what I can where I like to do it, until something else comes along. I keep my ears open as far as other job possibilities; so in a very limited way I'm looking for something else. But it's not bad enough to make me really look. I now have the sense that things here are just stagnant, that what's happening is going to continue to happen and that I'm not getting a real challenge. And I need challenge to be able to grow more. So if I really want to grow, professionally, I've got to get into a different situation....But there's comfort in this job that holds me back from looking for something else.

(Interviewer: What are the comforts?)

The fact that I know what's expected of me. I can do the job. I know the people. I'm beginning to know the ropes, and job changing means having to learn whole new expectations again, maybe getting into things that I don't know about. And that's kind of scary....I guess the job's become comfortable, and I really don't like facing that fact. Somehow, just the connotation of being comfortable with the job...I don't like that and I don't know why.

A Contrasting Example

The case of clinical social worker Diane Peterson presents a very different picture. Despite some initial difficulties, her job was stimulating and fulfilling. She found strong supports in the job and from the people she worked with. Consequently, at the point in time when Karen Mikelson was feeling emotionally detached and stagnant, Diane Peterson felt exhilarated and fulfilled. Unlike Karen, Diane looked ahead to a future filled with exciting new possibilities.

Diane Peterson worked in a new, federally funded alcoholism program. The program was relatively small: three other master's-level professionals hired shortly before Diane, and six nonprofessional therapists, most of whom were ex-alcoholics. There were three primary activities associated with Diane's job: individual and group therapy with alcoholics; public education, primarily through lecturing; and consultation and training for other mental health professionals.

The clients with whom she worked directly were not always the most rewarding. In this sense, they had much in common with the mentally retarded clients with whom Karen Mikelson worked. Diane said that many of her clients initially were resistant to treatment, especially those who had been referred by the courts for drunk driving and were going through the program merely to avoid a stiffer sentence. However, working with these clients ultimately proved to be rewarding for several reasons.

First, Diane believed that despite their initial resistance, many of her clients ultimately responded to the lectures and other parts of their program. Second, compared with Karen Mikelson's retarded clients, Diane's functioned at a higher level. They were self-sufficient and many were intelligent, verbal, and capable of self-reflection and insight. Consequently, Diane was able to use her clinical skills and techniques with them, and at some level they usually responded. A third important factor was her case load: there was no pressure for this special federally funded program to take any more clients than they wished to. Consequently, Diane and all of the other workers carried relatively light case loads. The expectation was that a worker would take clients as she felt she needed them.

Despite these many positive aspects of the work with clients, Diane observed that it could be demoralizing to work with alcoholics in treatment all day, every day. Fortunately, the variety built into her job prevented this from occurring. Besides working directly with clients, Diane worked with family members, employers, and other agencies and professionals. She also could mix individual treatment with family and group therapy, lectures and educational presentations, and staff development and consultation. Combined with this variety was an unusually high degree of autonomy: The workers in her agency were able to modify their roles so that they did the things they felt most comfortable doing. Thus, one worker might do more one-to-one counseling and therapy, while another might do more group work or lecturing. Staff were encouraged to expand their roles and competencies, but they were allowed to do so at a rate they felt comfortable with.

Perhaps the most important factor that made this job unusually rewarding was the strong emphasis placed on the personal and professional growth of the staff. It began with orientation. When Diane was hired, she was told, "We know you're probably not ready to start seeing clients right away. There are several things you'll want to learn first." In other words, there was explicit recognition that receiving a professional degree was just the *beginning* of her professional development. During her first two months on the job, Diane worked part-time. She did not have a case load. She was sent to an intensive, week-long training program, during which she attended numerous seminars and lectures and, most important, observed treatment being done by others. When she returned from this week of training, she sat in on interviews conducted by other therapists. When she felt ready, she began seeing clients on her own. She said that this orientation was extremely useful, and she lamented that her training in graduate school had not been nearly so good.

Even after her formal orientation ended, Diane continued to participate in training experiences. All of the staff were encouraged to attend outside workshops and to share what they learned with the others when they returned. Only three months after she began working at the agency, Diane was given permission to enter a year-long training program in alcoholism treatment that required her to be away from her job three days each month. She found the program invaluable and said that it was the "biggest fringe benefit of the job."

This support for professional growth and development for the staff seemed to be part of a more basic attitude of the agency's administration. Diane tried to sum it up when she described her work setting as a "people-oriented" agency. What she meant was that her supervisor and other administrators seemed to be sensitive to and concerned about the emotional and intellectual well-being of their staff, and they trusted the staff and assumed that their commitment to the work was strong and sincere. The emphasis was placed on support rather than control. For example, Diane's supervisor rec-

ognized that "time-outs" were necessary in the kind of work she did. Thus, there were no raised eyebrows when Diane had no meetings scheduled for one or two hours at a time. Also, when Diane requested a week off only three months after she had begun her job, the request was granted. The implicit message seemed to be, "You know what is best for you. You will work as hard as you can without our breathing down your neck because you are a dedicated professional." Diane thought that this policy on the part of the administration probably made her and most of the other staff work harder than they would have if the supervision had been less supportive and more controlling and bureaucratic.

This "people-oriented" approach to supervision probably contributed to the high level of sharing and support that characterized relations among the staff. Diane stated that the atmosphere in the office was positive. The staff trusted and respected each other. No one seemed to feel that others were not pulling their weight; no one felt exploited or rejected. Staff members were willing to do things that were not explicitly part of their formal job description; for instance, the professional staff answered the telephones for the secretaries when the secretaries were too busy with other pressing work. Diane summed it up when she described the agency as a "comfortable place to be, a fun place."

Diane was especially close to two other workers in the agency who were hired when she was, and these colleagues were an important source of support. The structure of their jobs allowed them to see each other two or three times each week and all day on Thursdays. They came to know and like each other during the week of training they went through together shortly after being hired. Diane said that they backed each other up "all the time." For instance, if one could not do a lecture she had promised to do, another would do it for her.

Diane recognized that there was much potential for conflict between the professional and paraprofessional clinicians. However, she claimed that in this agency, the professionals uniformly respected the ability of the paraprofessional workers. Everyone seemed to believe that both the professional and paraprofessional had something valuable and unique to offer to alcoholism treatment. Diane observed that there was much mutual give-and-take among the two groups at the agency, and this further contributed to the positive social atmosphere, the collegiality and support that characterized staff interactions.

Just as Karen Mikelson's job was not all negative, so Diane Peterson's was not all positive. One major source of stress and difficulty was a misunderstanding initially concerning the nature of her role. Staff at a family counseling agency where she was supposed to spend part of each week thought she would start sooner than she did. This agency also began using her as a crisis worker which was inconsistent with the way that her supervisor in the alcoholism agency wanted her to function. Diane also had difficulty in getting staff at the family counseling agency to attend the training sessions on alcoholism that she offered. Fortunately, the directors of the two agencies finally met with Diane and worked out the differences in their conceptions of her role. When this role conflict was resolved, much tension was relieved.

The second shortcoming of her job was not so easily rectified. Diane had been hired under a federal grant, and problems in the administration of the grant and the application for refunding made her job precarious. This lack of job security was a major source of stress for Diane, as she had no control over the situation. The decision ultimately would be made in Washington, and it apparently would depend on political and bureaucratic considerations that Diane and others at the agency could not control, pre-

dict, or even fully comprehend. Diane said that this uncertainty concerning refunding and the status of her job was a major source of anxiety for her and several other workers.

Fortunately, the support that staff in this unusual work setting received from each other and from the organization helped them cope with the pressures and uncertainties that could not be prevented. Consequently, after eight months, Diane was more committed and enthusiastic about her work than she had been when she had started. In fact, at one point she contrasted her work role with her role as a mother: As a mother, she felt that she gave and gave, getting nothing in return. But in her work, she believed that she constantly got something in return. She said that she enjoyed her job "immensely." She had become "fascinated" by the problem of alcoholism and wanted to stay and make a career in the field. In our last interview, she summed up her involvement as follows:

> One has to start realizing, "Am I going to make this a 9–5 job, or am I prepared to give an awful lot more of myself?" I'm really seeing now that my hobby is my job. It involves reading more and just being involved more. This is a whole way of life. It's not just a job. I read journals in the bathtub. In bed I read the newest pamphlet that just came out on alcoholism. I guess I enjoy it. It's not like school. I often feel that I'm doing this because I want to, not because I have to.

What Made the Difference?

In considering these two work experiences, it is difficult to imagine two responses to work in the human services that could be more different. Karen Mikelson seemed to epitomize the frustrated, discouraged, demoralized individual whose efforts to improve her work situation are constantly stymied and who eventually settles into an acceptable but stagnating situation. Diane Peterson, on the other hand, represents an unusually positive response to work. She began with little background or interest in the field of alcoholism, and after eight months in a fulfilling job she had decided to make the field her career. What factors seem to account for the difference in these two reactions?

There seemed to be several differences in the work situations that could account for the differences in these workers' reactions, many of which related to *a sense of impact and control* over one's work situation. Karen Mikelson worked in a large, state-operated facility. Many of the rules and policies were set by bureaucrats sitting in offices at the state capital. As a social worker, Karen was part of a particularly marginal and powerless group within the setting. The institution was bureaucratic in the classical sense: there were numerous detailed rules and regulations defining what one could and could not do, and supervisory personnel regarded many of those rules as important and inviolable. Karen's supervision, especially during her first months on the job, was close and controlling. She was expected to discuss many of the things she did with her supervisor.

On the other hand, Diane Peterson worked in a relatively small, independent agency. The agency was dependent on the federal government for its funding, and this imposed certain restrictions; but it was much more autonomous than the state-run facility for which Karen Mikelson worked. The agency's "locus of control" was much greater in Diane's case. Also, as a social worker, Diane was part of the highest status group within the setting, and the power structure of her agency was informal and collegial rather than formal and bureaucratic. There were few rigid rules and restrictions imposed on the workers by a mistrustful and controlling administration.

These differences in the nature of organizational and individual power were perhaps best demonstrated by the way in which disturbing role conflicts were handled. Both Diane and Karen received conflicting role messages initially. However, in Diane's situation, the two role senders who created the conflict responded to her complaints, met, and resolved the conflict. In contrast, Karen felt helpless in her attempts to resolve the conflict. The two role senders refused to discuss their differences, and the conflict ultimately was resolved only when one of the parties quit.

The differences in *clientele and case loads* also influenced the relative sense of impact and control experienced by these two mental health workers. Karen Mikelson had a large case load comprised of clients who were functioning at low levels. Consequently, she believed there was little she could do to improve their functioning. Diane Peterson not only had a small case load, but she controlled its size. Her clients generally functioned at a higher level than did Karen's. This difference in the clientele not only provided Diane with a greater sense of impact and efficacy; it also allowed her to use her clinical skills to a much greater extent. The verbal, intelligent client living in an intact family allowed her to do "real" treatment. Her role was more consistent with her professional identity.

The two work settings also differed in the opportunities they provided for *learning new skills and perspectives.* There was a strong emphasis on training and professional development in Diane's agency that was totally lacking in Karen's institution. The differences in the orientation each received typified this more general difference in institutional priorities. Diane's setting also encouraged *experimentation and innovation* to a much greater degree. In fact, Diane worked in a *setting that was new* and part of a field that was beginning to grow in popularity. After many years of neglect, alcoholism was receiving new support from the government and the mental health professions. Diane's agency represented the new ideas that were guiding work in the area.

Consequently, Diane saw herself as part of a new and exciting "crusade," full of hopes and possibilities. The future was bright for her field and the kind of work her agency did. Karen Mikelson, on the other hand, worked in an old, established setting that was generally regarded as obsolete. There was a growing belief that the large institution for the retarded had been a mistake. The primary objective now was to get clients out of the institution and close it down as soon as possible. Maintaining enthusiasm and commitment to one's work in such a setting clearly was difficult.

Relations with co-workers was the last area in which there were important differences. The level of interpersonal and intergroup conflict was much lower in Diane's setting. Staff generally regarded one another with trust and respect. There were more opportunities for supportive interaction among the staff. They were less isolated from one another physically as well as psychologically. Not surprisingly, Diane came to feel that she could rely on her co-workers for help if she needed it. In Karen's setting, the only thing that united the social work staff was their sense of a "common enemy" in their medically dominated setting.

Thus, despite many similarities in their training and personal backgrounds, these two human service professionals differed in their response to their work; and there were numerous differences in the work settings that contributed to the difference in response. Although personality structure, knowledge, and skill may have played a role, the work setting seemed to be crucial. This analysis of two actual work experiences suggests some of the factors that influence job stress and burnout more generally in the human services.

"Banana Time":
Job Satisfaction and Informal Interaction

Donald F. Roy*

...Since the operatives were engaged in work which involved the repetition of very simple operations over an extra-long work-day, six days a week, they were faced with the problem of dealing with a formidable "beast of monotony." Revelation of how the group utilized its resources to combat that "beast" should merit the attention of those who are seeking solution to the practical problem of job satisfaction, or employee morale...

My account of how one group of machine operators kept from "going nuts" in a situation of monotonous work activity attempts to lay bare the tissues of interaction which made up the content of their adjustment. The talking, fun, and fooling which

*Dr. Roy is in the Department of Sociology, Duke University, Durham, North Carolina.

Source: Reproduced by permission of the Society for Applied Anthropology from *Human Organization*, 18, 1959, pp. 158–168.

provided solution to the elemental problem of "psychological survival"...

My fellow operatives and I spent our long days of simple repetitive work in relative isolation from other employees of the factory. Our line of machines was sealed off from other work areas of the plant by the four walls of the clicking room. The one door of this room was usually closed. Even when it was kept open, during periods of hot weather, the consequences were not social; it opened on an uninhabited storage room of the shipping department. Not even the sounds of work activity going on elsewhere in the factory carried to this isolated work place. There were occasional contacts with "outside" employees, usually on matters connected with the work; but, with the exception of the daily calls of one fellow who came to pick up finished materials for the next step in processing, such visits were sporadic and infrequent.

Moreover, face-to-face contact with members of the managerial hierarchy were few and far between. No one bearing the title of foreman ever came around. The only company official who showed himself more than once during the two-month observation period was the plant superintendent. Evidently overloaded with supervisory duties and production problems which kept him busy elsewhere, he managed to pay his respects every week or two. His visits were in the nature of short, businesslike, but friendly exchanges. Otherwise he confined his observable communications with the group to occasional utilization of a public address system. During the two-month period, the company president and the chief chemist paid one friendly call apiece. One man, who may or may not have been of managerial status, was seen on various occasions lurking about in a manner which excited suspicion. Although no observable consequences accrued from the peculiar visitations of this silent fellow, it was assumed that he was some sort of efficiency expert, and he was referred to as "The Snooper."

As far as our work group was concerned, this was truly a situation of laissez-faire management. There was no interference from staff experts, no hounding by time-study engineers or personnel men hot on the scent of efficiency or good human relations. Nor were there any signs of industrial democracy in the form of safety, recreational, or production committees. There was an international union, and there was a highly publicized union-management cooperation program; but actual interactional processes of cooperation were carried on somewhere beyond my range of observation and without participation of members of my work group. Furthermore, these union-management get-togethers had no determinable connection with the problem of "toughing out" a twelve-hour day of monotonous work.

Our work group was thus not only abandoned to its own resources for creating job satisfaction, but left without that basic reservoir of ill-will toward management which can sometimes be counted on to stimulate the development of interesting activities to occupy hand and brain. Lacking was the challenge of intergroup conflict, that perennial source of creative experience to fill the otherwise empty hours of meaningless work routine.[1]

The clicking machines were housed in a room approximately thirty by twenty-four feet. They were four in number, set in a row, and so arranged along one wall that the busy operator could, merely by raising his head from his work, freshen his reveries with a glance through one of three large barred windows. To the rear of one of the end machines sat a long cutting table; here the operators cut up rolls of plastic materials into small sheets manageable for further processing at the clickers. Behind the machine at the opposite end of the line sat another table which was intermittently the work station of a female employee who performed sundry scissors operations of a more intricate nature on raincoat parts. Boxed in on all sides by shelves and stocks of materials, this latter locus of work appeared a cell within a cell....

Introduction to the new job, with its relatively simple machine skills and work routines, was accomplished with what proved to be, in my experience, an all-time minimum of job training. The clicking machine assigned to me was situated at one end of the row. Here the superintendent and one of the operators gave a few brief demonstrations, accompanied by bits of advice which included a warning to keep hands clear of the descending hammer. After a short practice period, at the end of which the superintendent expressed satisfaction with progress and potentialities, I was left to develop my learning curve with no other supervision than that afforded by members of the work group. Further advice and assistance did come, from time to time, from my fellow operatives, sometimes upon request, sometimes unsolicited.

The Work Group

Absorbed at first in three related goals of improving my clicking skill, increasing my rate of output, and keeping my left hand unclicked, I paid little attention to my fellow operatives save to observe that they were friendly, middle-aged, foreign-born, full of advice, and very talkative. Their names, according to the way they addressed each other, were George, Ike, and Sammy.[2] George, a stocky fellow in his late fifties, operated the machine at the opposite end of the line; he, I later discovered, had emigrated in early youth from a country in Southeastern Europe. Ike, stationed at George's left, was tall, slender, in his early fifties, and Jewish; he had come from Eastern Europe in his youth. Sammy, number three man in the line, and my neighbor, was heavy set, in his late fifties, and Jewish; he had escaped from a country in Eastern Europe just before Hitler's legions had moved in. All three men had been downwardly mobile as to occupation in recent years. George and Sammy had been proprietors of small businesses; the former had been "wiped out" when his uninsured establishment burned down; the latter had been entrepreneuring on a small scale before he left all behind him to flee the Germans. According to his account, Ike had left a highly skilled trade which he had practiced for years in Chicago.

I discovered also that the clicker line represented a ranking system in descending order from George to myself. George not only had top seniority for the group, but functioned as a sort of leadman. His superior status was marked in the fact that he received five cents more per hour than the other clickermen, put in the longest workday, made daily contact, outside the workroom, with the superintendent on work matters which concerned the entire line, and communicated to the rest of us the directives which he received. The narrow margin of superordination was seen in the fact that directives were always relayed in the superintendent's name; they were on the order of, "You'd better let that go now, and get on the green. Joe says they're running low on the fifth floor," or, "Joe says he wants two boxes

of the 3-die today." The narrow margin was also seen in the fact that the superintendent would communicate directly with his operatives over the public address system; and, on occasion, Ike or Sammy would leave the workroom to confer with him for decisions or advice in regard to work orders.

Ike was next to George in seniority, then Sammy. I was, of course, low man on the totem pole. Other indices to status differentiation lay in informal interaction, to be described later.

With one exception, job status tended to be matched by length of workday. George worked a thirteen-hour day, from 7 a.m. to 8:30 a.m. Ike worked eleven hours, from 7 a. m. to 6:30 p.m.; occasionally he worked until 7 or 7:30 for an eleven and a half- or a twelve-hour day. Sammy put in a nine-hour day, from 8 a.m. to 5:30 p.m. My twelve hours spanned from 8 a.m. to 8:30 p.m. We had a half hour for lunch, from 12 to 12:30.

The female who worked at the secluded table behind George's machine put in a regular plant-wide eight-hour shift from 8 to 4:30. Two women held this job during the period of my employment; Mable was succeeded by Baby. Both were Negroes, and in their late twenties.

A fifth clicker operator, an Arabian *emigré* called Boo, worked a night shift by himself. He usually arrived about 7 p.m. to take over Ike's machine.

The Work

It was evident to me, before my first workday drew to a weary close, that my clicking career was going to be a grim process of fighting the clock, the particular timepiece in this situation being an old-fashioned alarm clock which ticked away on a shelf near George's machine. I had struggled through many dreary rounds with the minutes and hours during the various phases of my industrial experience, but never had I been confronted with such a dismal combination of working conditions as the extra-long workday, the infinitesimal cerebral excitation, and the extreme limitation of physical movement. The contrast with a recent stint in the California oil fields was striking. This was no eight-hour day of racing hither and yon over desert and foothills with a rollicking crew of "roustabouts" on a variety of repair missions at oil wells, pipe lines, and storage tanks. Here there were no afternoon dallyings to search the sands for horned toads, tarantulas, and rattlesnakes, or to climb old wooden derricks for raven's nests, with an eye out, of course, for the tell-tale streak of dust in the distance which gave ample warning of the approach of the boss. This was standing all day in one spot beside three old codgers in a dingy room looking out through barred windows at the bare walls of a brick warehouse, leg movements largely restricted to the shifting of body weight from one foot to the other, hand and arm movements confined, for the most part, to a simple repetitive sequence of place the die,—punch the clicker,—place the die,—punch the clicker, and intellectual activity reduced to computing the hours to quitting time. It is true that from time to time a fresh stack of sheets would have to be substituted for the clicked-out old one; but the stack would have been prepared by someone else, and the exchange would be only a minute or two in the making. Now and then a box of finished work would have to be moved back out of the way, and an empty box brought up; but the moving back and the bringing up involved only a step or two. And there was the half hour for lunch, and occasional trips to the lavatory or the drinking fountain to break up the day into digestible parts. But after each momentary respite, hammer and die were moving again: click,—move die,—click,—move die....

The next day was the same: the monotony of the work, the tired legs and sore feet and thoughts of quitting.

The Game of Work

In discussing the factory operative's struggle to "cling to the remnants of joy in work," Henri de Man makes the general observations that "it is psychologically impossible to deprive any kind of work of all its positive emotional elements," that the worker will find *some* meaning in any activity assigned to him, a "certain scope for initiative which can satisfy after a fashion the instinct for play and the creative impulse," that "even in the Taylor system there is found luxury of self-determination."[3] De Man cites the case of one worker who wrapped 13,000 incandescent bulbs a day; she found her outlet for creative impulse, her self-determination, her meaning in work by varying her wrapping movements a little from time to time.[4]

So did I search for *some* meaning in my continuous mincing of plastic sheets into small ovals, fingers, and trapezoids. The richness of possibility for creative expression previously discovered in my experience with the "Taylor system"[5] did not reveal itself here. There was no piecework, so no piecework game. There was no conflict with management, so no war game. But, like the light bulb wrapper, I did find a "certain scope for initiative," and out of this slight freedom to vary activity, I developed a game of work....

Thus the game of work might be described as a continuous sequence of short-range production goals with achievement rewards in the form of activity change....

But a hasty conclusion that I was having lots of fun playing my clicking game should be avoided. These games were not as interesting in the experiencing as they might seem to be from the telling. Emotional tone of the activity was low, and intellectual currents weak. Such rewards as scraping the block or "getting to do the blue ones" were not very exciting, and the stretches of repetitive movement involved in achieving them were long enough to permit lapses into obsessive reverie. Henri de Man speaks of "clinging to the remnants of joy in work," and this situation represented just that. How tenacious the clinging was, how long I could have "stuck it out" with my remnants, was never determined. Before the first week was out this adjustment to the work situation was complicated by other developments. The game of work continued, but in a different context. Its influence became decidedly subordinated to, if not completely overshadowed by, another source of job satisfaction.

Informal Social Activity of the Work Group: Times and Themes

The change came about when I began to take serious note of the social activity going on around me; my attentiveness to this activity came with growing involvement in it. What I heard at first, before I started to listen, was a stream of disconnected bits of communication which did not make much sense. Foreign accents were strong and referents were not joined to coherent contexts of meaning. It was just "jabbering." What I saw at first, before I began to observe, was occasional flurries of horseplay so simple and unvarying in pattern and so childish in quality that they made no strong bid for attention. For example, Ike would regularly switch off the power at Sammy's machine whenever Sammy made a trip to the lavatory or the drinking fountain. Correlatively, Sammy invariably fell victim to the plot by making an attempt to operate his clicking hammer after returning to the shop. And, as the simple pattern went, this blind stumbling into the trap was always followed by indignation and reproach from Sammy, smirking satisfaction from Ike, and mild paternal scolding from George. My interest in this procedure was at first confined to wondering when Ike would weary of his tedious joke or when Sammy would learn to check his power switch before trying the hammer.

But, as I began to pay closer attention, as I began to develop familiarity with the communication system, the disconnected became connected, the nonsense made sense, the obscure became clear, and silly actually funny....

Times

This emerging awareness of structure and meaning included recognition that the long day's grind was broken by interruptions of a kind other than the formally instituted or idiosyncratically developed disjunctions in work routine previously described. These additional interruptions appeared in daily repetition in an ordered series of informal interactions. They were, in part, but only in part and in very rough comparison, similar to those common fractures of the production process known as the coffee break, the coke break, and the cigarette break. Their distinction lay in frequency of occurrence and in brevity. As phases of the daily series, they occurred almost hourly, and so short were they in duration that they disrupted work activity only slightly. Their significance lay not so much in their function as rest pauses, although it cannot be denied that physical refreshment was involved. Nor did their chief importance lie in the accentuation of progress points in the passage of time, although they could perform that function far more strikingly than the hour hand on the dull face of George's alarm clock. If the daily series of interruptions be likened to a clock, then the comparison might best be made with a special kind of cuckoo clock, one with a cuckoo which can provide variation in its announcements and can create such an interest in them that the intervening minutes become filled with intellectual content. The major significance of the interactional interruptions lay in such a carryover of interest. The physical interplay which momentarily halted work activity would initiate verbal exchanges and thought processes to occupy group members until the next interruption. The group interactions thus not only marked off the time; they gave it content and hurried it along.

Most of the breaks in the daily series were designated as "times" in the parlance of the clicker operators, and they featured the consumption of food or drink of one sort or another. There was coffee time, peach time, banana time, fish time, coke time, and, of course, lunch time. Other interruptions, which formed part of the series but were not verbally recognized as times, were window time, pickup time, and the staggered quitting times of Sammy and Ike. These latter unnamed times did not involve the partaking of refreshments.

My attention was first drawn to this times business during my first week of employment when I was encouraged to join in the sharing of two peaches. It was Sammy who provided the peaches; he drew them from his lunch box after making the announcement, "Peach time!" On this first occasion I refused the proffered fruit, but thereafter regularly consumed my half peach. Sammy continued to provide the peaches and to make the "Peach time!" announcement, although there were days when Ike would remind him that it was peach time, urging him to hurry up with the mid-morning snack. Ike invariably complained about the quality of the fruit, and his complaints fed the fires of continued banter between peach donor and critical recipient. I did find the fruit a bit on the scrubby side but felt, before I achieved insight into the function of peach time, that Ike was showing poor manners by looking a gift horse in the mouth. I wondered why Sammy continued to share his peaches with such an ingrate.

Banana time followed peach time by approximately an hour. Sammy again provided the refreshments, namely, one banana. There was, however, no four-way sharing of Sammy's banana. Ike would gulp it down by himself after surreptitiously extracting it from Sammy's lunch box, kept on a shelf behind Sammy's work station. Each morning, after making the snatch, Ike would call out, "Banana time!" and proceed to down his prize while Sammy made futile protests and denunciations. George would join in with mild remonstrances, sometimes scolding Sammy for making so much fuss. The banana was one which Sammy brought for his own consumption at lunch time; he never did get to eat his banana, but kept bringing one for his lunch. At first this daily theft startled and amazed me. Then I grew to look forward to the daily seizure and the verbal interaction which followed.

Window time came next. It followed banana time as a regular consequence of Ike's castigation by the indignant Sammy. After "taking" repeated references to himself as a person badly lacking in morality and character, Ike would 'finally" retaliate by opening the window which faced Sammy's machine, to let the "cold air" blow in on Sammy. The slandering which would, in its echolalic repetition, wear down Ike's patience and forbearance usually took the form of the invidious comparison: "George is a good daddy! Ike is a bad man! A very bad man!" Opening the window would take a little time to accomplish and would involve a great deal of verbal interplay between Ike and Sammy, both before and after the event. Ike would threaten, make feints toward the window, then finally open it. Sammy would protest, argue, and make claims that the air blowing in on him would give him a cold; he would eventually have to leave his machine to close the window. Sometimes the weather was slightly chilly, and the draft from the window unpleasant; but cool or hot, windy or still, window time arrived each day. (I assume that it was originally a cold season development.) George's part in this interplay, in spite of the "good daddy" laudations, was to encourage Ike in his window work. He would stress the tonic values of fresh air and chide Sammy for his unappreciativeness.

Following window time came lunch time, a formally designated half-hour for the midday repast and rest break. At this time, informal interaction would feature exchanges between Ike and George. The former would start eating his lunch a few minutes before noon, and the latter, in his role as straw boss, would censure him for malobservance of the rules. Ike's off-beat luncheon usually involved a previous tampering with George's alarm clock. Ike would set the clock ahead a few minutes in order to maintain his eating schedule without detection, and George would discover these small daylight saving changes....

Pickup time, fish time, and coke time came in the afternoon. I name it pickup time to represent the official visit of the man who made daily calls to cart away boxes of clicked materials. The arrival of the pickup man, a Negro, was always a noisy one, like the arrival of a daily passenger train in an isolated small town. Interaction attained a quick peak of intensity to crowd into a few minutes all communications, necessary and otherwise. Exchanges invariably included loud depreciations by the pickup man of the amount of work accomplished in the clicking department during the preceding twenty-four hours. Such scoffing would be on the order of "Is that all you've got done? What do you boys do all day?" These devaluations would be countered with allusions to the "soft job" enjoyed by the pickup man. During the course of the exchanges news items would be dropped, some of serious import, such as reports of accomplished or impending layoffs in the various plants of the company, or of gains or losses in orders for company products. Most of the news items, however, involved bits of information on plant employees told in a light vein. Information relayed by the clicker operators was usually told about each other, mainly in the form of summaries of the most recent

kidding sequences. Some of this material was repetitive, carried over from day to day. Sammy would be the butt of most of this newscasting, although he would make occasional counter-reports on Ike and George....

About mid-afternoon came fish time. George and Ike would stop work for a few minutes to consume some sort of pickled fish which Ike provided. Neither Sammy nor I partook of this nourishment, nor were we invited. For this omission I was grateful; the fish, brought in a newspaper and with head and tail intact, produced a reverse effect on my appetite. George and Ike seemed to share a great liking for fish. Each Friday night, as a regular ritual, they would enjoy a fish dinner together at a nearby restaurant. On these nights Ike would work unitl 8:30 and leave the plant with George.

Coke time came late in the afternoon, and was an occasion for total participation. The four of us took turns in buying the drinks and in making the trip for them to a fourth floor vending machine....

Themes

To put flesh, so to speak, on this interactional frame of "times," my work group had developed various "themes" of verbal interplay which had become standardized in their repetition. These topics of conversation ranged in quality from an extreme of nonsensical chatter to another extreme of serious discourse. Unlike the times, these themes flowed one into the other in no particular sequence of predictability. Serious conversation could suddenly melt into horseplay, and vice versa. In the middle of a serious discussion on the high cost of living, Ike might drop a weight behind the easily startled Sammy, or hit him over the head with a dusty paper sack. Interaction would immediately drop to a low comedy exchange of slaps, threats, guffaws, and disapprobations which would invariably include a ten-minute echolalia of "Ike is a bad man, a bad man a very bad man! George is a good daddy, a very fine man!" Or, on the other hand, a stream of such invidious comparisons as followed a surreptitious switching-off of Sammy's machine by the playful Ike might merge suddenly into a discussion of the pros and cons of saving for one's funeral.

"Kidding themes" were usually started by George or Ike, and Sammy was usually the butt of the joke....

The "poom poom" theme was one that caused no sting. It would come up several times a day to be enjoyed as unbarbed fun by the three older clicker operators. Ike was usually the one to raise the question, "How many times you go poom poom last night?" The person questioned usually replied with claims of being "too old for poom poom." If this theme did develop a goat, it was I. When it was pointed out that I was a younger man, this provided further grist for the poom poom mill. I soon grew weary of this poom poom business, so dear to the hearts of the three old satyrs, and, knowing where the conversation would inevitably lead, winced whenever Ike brought up the subject....

Another kidding theme which developed out of serious discussion could be labelled "helping Danelly find a cheaper apartment." It became known to the group that Danelly had a pending housing problem, that he would need new quarters for his family when the permanent resident of his temporary summer dwelling returned from a vacation. This information engendered at first a great deal of sympathetic concern and, of course, advice on apartment hunting. Development into a kidding theme was immediately related to previous exchanges between Ike and George on the quality of their respective dwelling areas. Ike lived in "Lawndale," and George dwelt in the "Woodlawn" area. The new pattern featured the reading aloud of bogus "apartment for rent" ads in newspapers which were brought into the shop. Studying his paper at lunchtime, George would call out, "Here's an apartment for you, Danelly! Five rooms, stove heat, $20 a month, Lawndale Avenue!" Later, Ike would read from his paper, "Here's one! Six rooms, stove heat, dirt floor. $18.50 a month! At 55th and Woodlawn." Bantering would then go on in regard to the quality of housing or population in the two areas. The search for an apartment for Danelly was not successful.

Serious themes included the relating of major misfortunes suffered in the past by group members. George referred again and again to the loss, by fire, of his business establishment. Ike's chief complaints centered around a chronically ill wife who had undergone various operations and periods of hospital care. Ike spoke with discouragement of the expenses attendant upon hiring a housekeeper for himself and his children; he referred with disappointment and disgust to a teen-age son, an inept lad who "couldn't even fix his own lunch. He couldn't even make himself a sandwich!" Sammy's reminiscences centered on the loss of a flourishing business when he had to flee Europe ahead of Nazi invasion.

But all serious topics were not tales of woe. One favorite serious theme which was optimistic in tone could be called either "Danelly's future" or "getting Danelly a better job." It was known that I had been attending "college," the magic door to opportunity, although my specific course of study remained somewhat obscure. Suggestions poured forth on good lines of work to get into, and these suggestions were backed with accounts of friends, and friends of friends, who had made good via the academic route. My answer to the expected question, "Why are you working here?" always stressed the "lots of overtime" feature, and this explanation seemed to suffice for short-range goals.

There was one theme of especially solemn import, the "professor theme." This theme might also be termed "George's daughter's marriage theme"; for the recent marriage of George's only child was inextricably bound up with George's connection with higher learning. The daughter had married the son of a professor who instructed in one of the local colleges. This professor theme was not in the strictest sense a conversation piece; when the subject came up, George did all the talking. The two Jewish operatives remained silent as they listened with deep respect, if not actual awe, to George's accounts of the Big Wedding which, including the wedding pictures, entailed an expense of $1,000. It was monologue, but there was listening, there was communication, the sacred communication of a temple, when George told of going for Sunday afternoon walks on the Midway with the professor, or of joining the professor for a Sunday dinner. Whenever he spoke of the professor, his daughter, the wedding, or even of the new son-in-law, who remained for the most part in the background, a sort of incidental like the wedding cake, George was complete master of the interaction. His manner, in speaking to the rank-and-file of clicker operators, was indeed that of master deigning to notice his underlings. I came to the conclusion that it was the professor connection, not the straw-boss-ship or the extra nickel an hour, which provided the fount of George's superior status in the group....

So initial discouragement with the meagerness of social interaction I now recognized as due to lack of observation. The interaction was there, in constant flow. It captured attention and held interest to make the long days pass. The twelve hours of "click,—move die,—click,—move die" became as easy to endure as eight hours of varied activity in the oil fields or eight hours of playing the piecework game in a machine shop. The "beast of boredom" was gentled to the harmlessness of a kitten....

Conclusions

...[I]n regard to possible practical application to problems of industrial management, these observations seem to support the generally accepted notion that one key source of job satisfaction lies in the informal interaction shared by members of a work group. In the clicking-room situation the spontaneous development of a patterned combination of horseplay, serious conversation, and frequent sharing of food and drink reduced the monotony of simple, repetitive operations to the point where a regular schedule of long work days became livable. This kind of group interplay may be termed "consumatory" in the sense indicated by Dewey, when he makes a basic distinction between "instrumental" and "consumatory" communication.[6] The enjoyment of communication "for its own sake" as "mere sociabilities," as "free, aimless social intercourse," brings job satisfaction, at least job endurance, to work situations largely bereft of creative experience.

In regard to another managerial concern, employee productivity, any appraisal of the influence of group interaction upon clicking-room output could be no more than roughly impressionistic. I obtained no evidence to warrant a claim that banana time, or any of its accompaniments in consumatory interaction, boosted production. To the contrary, my diary recordings express an occasional perplexity in the form of "How does this company manage to stay in business?" However, I did not obtain sufficient evidence to indicate that, under the prevailing conditions of laissez-faire management, the output of our group would have been more impressive if the playful cavorting of three middle-aged gentlemen about the barred windows had never been. As far as achievement of managerial goals is concerned, the most that could be suggested is that leavening the deadly boredom of individualized work routines with a concurrent flow of group festivities had a negative effect on turnover. I left the group, with sad reluctance, under the pressure of strong urgings to accept a research fellowship which would involve no factory toil. My fellow clickers stayed with their machines to carry on their labors in the spirit of banana time....

NOTES

1. Donald F. Roy, "Work Satisfaction and Social Reward in Quota Achievement: An Analysis of Piecework Incentive," *American Sociological Review,* XVIII (October, 1953), 507–514.

2. All names used are fictitious.

3. Henri de Man, *The Psychology of Socialism,* Henry Holt and Company, New York, 1927, pp. 80–81.

4. Ibid., p. 81.

5. Roy, *op. cit.*

6. John Dewey, Experience and Nature, Open Court Publishing Co., Chicago, 1923, pp. 202–206.

Containing Work Disaffection

The Poultry Processing Worker

Clifton D. Bryant and Kenneth B. Perkins

CASE STUDY QUESTIONS

1. Do the harsh conditions of the poultry processing workers draw the workers together or pull them apart? What other factors seem to have an impact on the level of cohesion?

2. What makes the work of the poultry processing workers much more satisfying to them than the objective conditions of their work environment might suggest?

3. To what extent do the theories of alienation presented so far seem to explain the workers' feelings about their work, the other workers, and, more generally, their employment situation?

The sociology of work and occupations has been relatively silent on the subject of rural industries and nonagricultural work systems. Industry, however, has located in rural areas, and some of these enterprises have distinctively rural characteristics and are largely integral to the rural context. Poultry processing plants are particularly notable examples. The work forces of such plants are

Source: "Containing Work Disaffection: The Poultry Processing Worker," Clifton D. Bryant and Kenneth B. Perkins from *Varieties of Work*, Phyllis L. Stewart and Muriel G. Cantor, eds., 1982, pp. 199–212. Permission granted by Sage Publications, Inc.

frequently rural and agricultural in origin. Agricultural work is largely self-paced and self-directed, affording a large measure of job autonomy, whereas industrial processing work activities are usually directed by the speed of the line, severely restricting the parameters of job autonomy for the workers. Poultry processing plants have the mechanical characteristics of urban industry, but also have a malodorous atmosphere, uncomfortable temperatures and humidity, and involve aesthetically offensive work. Beyond this, poultry processing employment carries an element of social stigma and is sometimes the butt of humor, as witness the ubiquitous "chicken plucker" jokes and comedy sketches.

Given the marked departure in job autonomy from agricultural to industrial work and the added disagreeable working conditions attendant upon industrial contexts such as poultry processing, there was reason to believe that workers in poultry plants would exhibit especially severe manifestations of frustration, discontentment, and work dissatisfaction in reaction to what were seemingly extraordinary disaffective working and job conditions. A rural industry with assembly line work, employing a labor force of agricultural origin, and one that incorporates an inordinate degree of "dirty work" (i.e., work that is culturally defined as aesthetically distasteful, physically uncomfortable, or psychologically repugnant), poultry processing represents an unusual work situation with seemingly constituent unsatisfactory working conditions, disaffection, and worker morale problems.[1] This study was an attempt to explore such disagreeable work and the means by which poultry processing employees accommodate themselves to the intrinsic dimensions of their job and to the constituent working conditions, as well as to examine the processes of morale maintenance and the mechanisms used in coping with such work.

Surprisingly, the study revealed that poultry processing employees managed to identify effective means of accommodating themselves to their employment, demonstrating a relatively high degree of satisfaction with their work, and sustaining morale through a widespread network of social interaction both on and off the job. To appropriately understand this phenomenon, some familiarization with rural industry in general, and the nature of poultry processing work in particular, is indicated. The subsequent discussion will address the industrial components of poultry processing and the attendant work role of employees before turning to an examination of the individuals who work in these plants, their careers, and the means by which they socially adjust to such disaffective work.

The Poultry Industry in the United States

Food processing represents one of the major sectors of the manufacturing industry within the United States. Approximately 15 percent of the value of all manufactured or processed products is as food products, and approximately 9 percent of all employees in manufacturing are directly involved in food processing industries and receive a similar percentage of all manufacturing wages. Within the food processing industry, 26 percent of all food products is meat and 19 percent of its employees are engaged in work related to meat processing, while 27 percent are engaged in poultry processing activities. The poultry industry in the United States is responsible for bringing over *10 billion pounds* of edible birds per year to the marketplace.

With the advent of widespread refrigeration, air conditioning, modern packaging techniques, and supermarket merchandising arrangements, mass production poultry slaughtering and dressing has become economically and technologically feasible. In the first two decades after World War II, poultry processing plants were very labor intensive, and there was only a minimal mechanized component to the process. Subsequently, however, poultry processing plants have become increasingly automated as new techniques have been developed. This has resulted in fewer but larger and more highly mechanized poultry processing plants, some of which are capable of slaughtering and processing as many as 50,000 turkeys or 150,000 chickens in a single day. ...This decrease in the number of plants appears to be due to the closing down of the smaller, less mechanized plants, so that today greater production outputs are coming from fewer, but more modernized, plants. Just under one-half of the nation's poultry dressing plants are located in the South. Approximately one-quarter are located in the north-central or midwestern states, with the rest just about equally divided between the Northeast and the West. The preponderance of these plants are located in small towns and rural areas.

The poultry processing industry is composed of two basic sectors. The first, poultry and egg production, is primarily involved in growing poultry and egg-gathering. The second sector of poultry processing begins with the live bird, slaughters it, then dresses and prepares it for marketing. Poultry processing establishments may also engage in what is called "further processing"—cooking, canning, smoking, freezing, and dehydrating. (The present study is concerned exclusively with the poultry processing sector of the industry.)

Poultry Processing as Rural Industry

The poultry processing industry would appear to qualify as an authentic rural industry. Rural industries are technologically advanced production systems originating and subsequently located in rural areas. They are also frequently compatible with the ethos and routine of the local community and its citizens. Although many corporations locate their subsidiary plants in small towns or even in open country, they generally continue to reflect the urban industry model. Much of the work force may be imported or transferred from urban areas. Suppliers and raw materials may well be obtained from urban industrial sources. Thus, raw materials, work force, process, product, and even the culture of the plant itself may well have an urban progenesis. The true rural industry, such as poultry processing, is largely integral to the rural context and therefore differs substantially in these respects.

Since the mid-twentieth century, when technology and science combined with agriculture to create the modern mass-produced chicken, the poultry industry has, in most instances, effected as an industrial model a "six-stage, vertically coordinated operation, with the family farmer as only one link in the chain" (Talbot, 1978). The various components of the industry are systematically linked and are generally located in rural areas or small towns, and the industry is, accordingly, integrated with the farm. The work force is generally local and thus rural, often even into the supervisory levels.

Poultry processing, although it is highly mechanized, basically derives from a rural process, originally involving all handwork. In contrast to urban industries, poultry processing can claim raw materials, work force, process, product, predominate value systems, and plant culture as being of rural origin and orientation. The rurality of poultry processing has significant social import for both the assimilation of the work role as well as for the manner in which the dissaffective nature of such work is addressed.

The Research Site and the Data Base

Data for this research were obtained from the work force of two poultry processing plants located in the Shenandoah area of Virginia.[2] The first of the plants, for purposes of anomymity, is labeled "Valley Farm Plant," largely processes chickens, and is located just outside a small town in a rural area of the state. The plant employs a total of 490 workers, all of whom work one daytime shift. The workers at this plant come from a rather wide area of the rural countryside surrounding the plant location.

The second plant, given the pseudonym "Central Town Plant," is located just outside the major population center of the area in a bordering small town and draws its employees from this circumscribed area. This plant employs a total of 1200 workers on two shifts. (To control for this difference, only workers from the daytime shift were included in the sample.) The characteristics of the workers in this plant, however, did not appear to differ from those at the Valley Farm Plant. The management at Central Town Plant takes a somewhat more distant and impersonal attitude toward its employees than is the case at Valley Farm and this, coupled with its location and larger size, makes it appear much more removed from its rural base than is actually the case. The plants included in this study were two of the 100 largest such operations in the nation.

Central Town Plant is the largest turkey dressing plant in the nation.

In addition to extensive observation of the work process in the two plants, and a number of probing interviews with plant officials, in-depth interviews were conducted with a random sample of 60 production workers from each of the two plants. Most of these interviews were conducted in the homes of the workers. The overall study focused on five job parameters of the poultry processing industry: the organization of the work force in the work setting; the personal and background characteristics of the work force; career patterns of the work force; job satisfaction; and the individual and social effects of work in the plant on the workers.

"Fowl Work and Offal Activity:" Poultry Processing as Dirty Disassembly

Poultry processing is a highly rationalized industrial technique that involves a series of well-defined tasks. It is an extremely efficient and productive process. As one of the interviewed workers characterized it, "You don't throw nothing away but the cackle." Poultry processing differs from most manufacturing work, however, in that it does not incorporate an assembly effort but rather involves an inherently dirty disassembly process. In contrast to a certain neatness of solidity of auto parts, fowl bleed, excrete, and otherwise emit odorous fluids and semi-solids. A poultry processing factory can, in effect, be conceptualized as an assembly plant running in reverse, accomplishing to disassemble dead, feathery, bleeding chicken and turkey carcasses.

Poultry must be handled, initially, as live birds. Workers (almost inevitably male because of the weight handled) must snatch live birds from cages unloaded from tractor trailer trucks and hang them, upside down, on shackles attached to moving conveyor lines. The "hanging" job may even involve 30-40 pound turkeys. The "hangers" are subjected to wing battering by the dirty, squawking birds who not infrequently urinate and/or defecate on the workers handling them. As the flopping, noisy birds move down the line, they undergo an electric shock intended to relax all muscles for a thorough bleeding after the throat is cut. This step also results in additional execretory discharges from the birds. All five senses of the workers are assaulted. One "hanger" who was interviewed revealed that, on weekends, he took six to eight showers trying to rid himself of the stench.

After being shocked, the birds are slaughtered by having their throats cut, either by hand with a knife or by a machine with a worker standing by to kill birds where the machine fails to do so. As with all workers who are involved in "dirty work," there is the incipient problem of social stigma and low self-esteem resulting from such an identify. Poultry processing workers are aware of the potential social image of their "dirty work," but attempt to ignore it. One female from the "killing room" explained it this way:

> You go out there and tell a lady in a store that you back up a killing machine and she will say, "Oh, what's that," and tenses her face up. But that don't bother me none.

After killing, the carcasses move along the line and are dipped in scalding water, then taken through a device with rubber fingers to remove the feathers, after which a "pinner" removes any remaining feathers. In the next phase of the dressing process, the birds move along the line into the eviscerating department, where another set of activities occurs. Here, through successive steps, the employees disembowel the birds, removing their viscera. The eviscerating department employs the largest number of workers.

Within the third department, cooling and chilling, the carcass is dipped into ice-chilled water to reduce the temperature. Workers in this department are responsible for keeping the cooling tanks supplied with ice. In the next department, workers are employed who separate the poultry products according to gross size and/or inspect the carcasses for grading purposes. After sizing and grading, the carcass moves to the department employing the second largest number of workers, where the cutting, boiling, and trimming is accomplished. Here the bird is prepared for packaging, either as a whole bird or as clusters of pieces. The employees in the packaging department then package the dressed poultry. From here, the product moves to be weighed and either stored or routed and loaded for shipping. Further processing, the final department, converts meat into quick food dinners, pies, sandwich meat, and the like.

Poultry processing of necessity involves the commodious use of water, and thus there is an inevitably high degree of dampness and frequency of standing water constituent to this industrial process. The water used may have to be scalding, to remove feathers, or near-freezing, in order to cool the carcasses of the birds. Extreme temperatures are, accordingly, encountered. Thus, employees may have to work in damp, cold, or hot rooms, literally standing in water (and sometimes blood, such as in the "killing room"), handle blood, gore, offal, and visceral organs and materials. In short, the sights, sounds, smells, and tactile sensations associated with their work appear to be aesthetically distasteful, if not repugnant.

Poultry processing work is not without hazard as well. Working with boning knives and equipment such as the "lung gun," that sucks the air sacs and lungs out of the scalded carcasses, the employees sometimes experience minor injuries, and also complain about dermatological problems from the water and poultry body fluids.

The Social Profile and Career

Unlike poultry dressing plants in other parts of the country, the two plants in this study employed a labor force that was almost exclusively white. The production line work force at both plants was made up of approximately 75 percent females. The predominantly female force apparently resulted from the fact that the plants were located in rural areas, and traditionally the male population has been heavily involved in agriculturally related work. Also, the salary level in the poultry processing industry is relatively low and men, having greater opportunities in the job market, presumably seek higher paying jobs. In addition, it appeared that because of the traditional pattern of female employment and because of the nature of the work, preparing poultry for eventual consumption, work in poultry dressing plants had come to be defined primarily (though not exclusively) as "women's work."

Although the workers were distributed throughout all age ranges, there are relatively fewer workers between the ages of 31 and 40 than there are under 30 or between the ages of 41 and 50. This pattern holds for both the male and female employees. Presumably, the females feel the need to contribute to the family finances in the early years of marriage, drop out of the work force during their husbands' more economically productive years, and go back to work after their children have left home.

Of the total sample, 57 percent never received a high school degree, and a sizable proportion of this group (one-third) never went beyond the eighth grade. The educational achievements of the women surpassed those of the men, in that almost two-thirds of the men had never received a high school degree as compared to only slightly more than one-half of the women. Upwards of one-third of the men never went beyond the eighth grade, as compared with only 15 percent of the women. The workers who did not complete high school indicated that they had dropped out to go to work or because they didn't like school. Women, in addition, mentioned that they had dropped out of school to get married. Some of the workers had dropped out of school in order to help out their families. Given their educational backgrounds, their occupational horizons had been definitely limited—something the workers clearly perceived themselves. The workers, with their substandard educational background, were following the tradition of their parents. Of those respondents who were able to report on their parents' educational level, 85 percent reported that their mothers, and 92 percent their fathers, had less than a high school degree.

Of particular interest is the fact that a fairly substantial number of the parents had also had occupations in the poultry dressing industry. In all, 19 percent of the fathers and 43 percent of the working mothers (13 percent of all mothers) had worked in poultry dressing plants. Poultry dressing, then, represents a two-generational work pattern for a good number of these workers. For those workers from families where farming was the basic means of livelihood, work in a poultry dressing plant would seem to represent the first step away from farming. Given the nature of the work, this step may represent one much more amenable than, say, work in other types of industrial enterprises. For women from farming backgrounds, work in poultry dressing may be perceived as essentially the same type of work done by their mothers. And for those whose parents worked in poultry dressing, this type of industrial work represented something about which they had some knowledge and, perhaps, that they could feel comfortable going into. For the rest of the workers, whose parents were primarily in semi-skilled and skilled occupations, poultry processing work represented a continuation, for the most part, of the occupational level of their parents.

A rather large number of the spouses (32 percent) also worked in the poultry dressing industry (42 percent of the male workers' wives and 29 percent of the female workers' husbands). Work in the poultry plant appears not infrequently to be a family affair. Husbands, wives, parents, in-laws, and children often work in the same plant, as do many of the respondents' friends. As will be indicated later, such an arrangement appears to have a positive influence upon work satisfaction, and tends to extend the rural ambience into the work place.

Career

The workers studied had enjoyed only minimal work ambitions. When asked about their particular work ambition when younger, 25 percent of the males and 37 percent of the females responded that they had had no particular occupational aspirations. Of the males, not a single one had held professional aspirations when younger, and only one mentioned a white collar occupation. One-quarter of the males specified that they had hoped to be mechanics. The rest of the males (38 percent) mentioned a variety of vocational pursuits that could only appropriately be categorized as "Other" (these included pursuits ranging from professional baseball to contracting). The females had apparently held higher ambitions. Almost one-half had entertained professional, semi-professional (including nursing and teaching), and white collar occupational aspirations. Only 8 percent had planned to be a housewife and the others, in general, had hoped for various kinds of service occupations such as being an airline stewardess or beautician.

When asked why they originally came to work at the poultry dressing plants, approximately half of the workers interviewed could give no reason other than they needed a job or the money, or that there were, simply, no other job choices. Approximately one-quarter of the respondents said they came to work because of friends or relatives working there, and another 16 percent mentioned convenience or location as leading them to come to work at the plants. Only 19 percent mentioned a positive feature about the job (the fact that it was full-time, paid better, or was preferable to what they were doing before) as being important to their coming to work at the plants. When asked outright if they had had a choice in coming to work at the plant, almost 40 percent of the total sample said no. Some 46 percent of the females, as compared to 18 percent of the males, indicated that they had had no choice. When asked if they felt they would still be working at the poultry dressing plants in the future, 75 percent indicated that they thought they would be. However, only slightly over 40 percent indicated that this would be because of free choice.

In general, the workers were realistic about their job qualifications and their prospects in the labor market, and were also quite fatalistic (that abiding characteristic of all rural persons) in their assessment of employment possibilities. The inevitable can be more pleasant, however, if meaningful social interaction is available. As this one female employee succinctly expressed it:

> Well, I guess in a way it is about as good as you gonna find for the education because the one thing about it is its mostly women there working. I'd say it's a pretty good place. There is a lot of women who work there and you are bound to find someone you can be friends with, and you have time to be sociable and get to know (them). Some other place you might not have time.

The largest percentage category of number of years worked in the plants for the total sample was 5 to 10 years, with the median for males being 5 years and that for females 7 years. The range of years worked was 1 to 35 years, with 3 to 5 years and over 15 representing the second largest percent-

age categories. The findings also indicated a good deal of movement out of and back into the plant work forces. Some 13 percent of the workers stated they had left work and then come back. Of the total sample, 8 percent had left and come back two or more times.

Job Autonomy and Containment of Disaffection

The discussion thus far has pointed to the unmistakable problematic character of poultry processing work. From the lack of alternative job opportunities and the low educational level of the workers to the messy nature of the work, poultry processing presents itself as a difficult job to which to accommodate oneself. The point to be developed in this final section is that poultry workers did, in fact, express positive aspects about the work: 60 percent of the respondents said they were either "generally satisfied" or "completely satisfied" with their job; 63 percent reported that they would choose that same job again; and, when comparing their job to the worst and best of all possible jobs they could think of, *81% gave a rank of 5 or better on a scale of 0 to 10* (with 10 symbolic of the "ideal" job).

When probed about the rationale for their expressions of work satisfaction, the interviewees were inclined to mention factors such as "co-worker relations," "management relations," "treatment by management," or "liking that kind of work or activities" as the major reasons. Human relations concerns appear to be generally more important than other kinds of considerations in terms of job satisfaction. As one worker, for example, phrased it when asked what she particularly liked about her job:

> The people, I think, more than anything— that I work with. That really helps out. I mean if you are working with somebody that you like. I just—I just like that kind of work.

Yet another replied to the same question:

It's the company I work for I guess. They have always treated me good and everything.

When the workers were further queried about the things that they particularly liked about their job, approximately 40 percent of all the respondents listed "people" or "co-worker relations" as the thing they liked most about the job.

Additional insights concerning work satisfaction were gained from examining the workers' approach to job autonomy via the traditional sex role division of labor, and their sense of occupational community, which functioned to insulate them from the harsher and more disagreeable parameters of their work role.

The Sexual Division of Labor

There was a very pronounced, implicit, sexual division of labor evident in the plants. In the departments requiring a considerable degree of physical strength, such as in the hanging and killing rooms, and in the shipping and storage rooms where the processed birds had to be stacked and loaded, men frequently had the jobs. Males also had most of the foreman and supervisory positions. Although some males were scattered along the processing line, these were activities that were for the most part carried out by females. Of these line activities, four were identified as "women's jobs": eviscerating, cutting and trimming, boning, and packaging. The employees explained the segregation of activities into "men's jobs" and "women's jobs" by offering several different reasons. In regard to the "men's jobs," it was stated that men were required to do them because of strength requirements. In addition, respondents, both male and female, noted that it wasn't the place of women to be doing these jobs because, simply, they were "men's jobs." In discussing the "women's jobs" the major response given was that men

could do these jobs, but should be doing, and were needed to do, other things—presumably picking and hanging, and weighing and shipping. Another reason given was that these were "women's jobs" because they involved something women normally knew how to do and would ordinarily be doing in their roles as housekeepers—the preparation of meats for cooking and consumption.

From the standpoint of the male employees, the sexual segregation of work activities seems to be a compensating factor in facilitating their toleration for disaffective work. Sexual differentiation in work assignments serves as a major mechanism by which the male employees can maintain their sense of masculinity. Positioned in jobs that are primarily closed to females and of a higher status serves to offset the ego threats and anxieties, and to compensate males. For the most part, having specific jobs in the plant that are sex-classified as masculine work makes it possible for the male workers to accommodate themselves to low status, low paid, and uncomfortable work. Importantly, the men are able to perform their "male" jobs in such a way that they are able to structure a considerable degree of job autonomy into their work role. In some departments, for example, men who are not as tied to the pace of the line as the women workers will stand and wait until a fairly large number of packages are finished and then route them for weighing or box them. In this way they retain a degree of individual control over the actual way in which they perform their jobs.

Although some of the women workers did complain about the inequitability of work roles that grew out of the sexual stereotyping of certain jobs in the plant, the sexual division of labor seems also to operate to make the female employees more content with their work. While many see themselves as doing the messier and more difficult jobs, as compared to the men, they are able to accept that because of the fact that it is "women's work." Just as a housewife might see her own responsibilities as being perhaps more demanding and exhausting than those of her spouse, but accepting such a division of labor as natural, so too do the female workers reconcile themselves to the more demanding, difficult, and seemingly more disagreeable types of work. In one sense, there is a kind of pride in the fact that "women's work" is often more difficult and that female workers are more stoic than males in performing the harder jobs. As one female worker put it in describing the plant jobs that women tend to get:

> Take a man, he won't stick to some of those harder jobs like craw pullin'. A man will stick his finger in there and gets a sore finger and walks the floor all night long—he will quit that job, he won't stick to it.

Occupational Community

The study vividly demonstrated that the physical activity of the job was secondary to interactional dimensions. Poultry processing workers know each other, go to church together, and visit in each other's homes, from time to time date and marry one another, and are seldom other than friends. The working relationship is the mainstay of their social existence as employees.

The most intriguing finding was that, in the plants studied, there was the presence of an occupational community. Workers participated in an occupational community which functioned not only to insulate them in a "cloak of mechanical solidarity," as it were, but also provided margins for a gregarious and sympathetic curiosity and concern about one another. One worker described this sympathetic concern:

> Last year I had cobalt. I had about 70 meters [sic] of radiation. I was off my job from the first of March to the very last day of May. I was able to talk to my nurse at the plant. She

was very encouraging. April Fools' Day I went to take my cobalt and I come back home. My friends down there called me and asked me to come down. If you've ever had a call on April Fools' Day, you wonder what it's all about. And I got down there and they said, "Good Morning," and there sat a huge table of the most delicious lookin' cakes there are. Those girls raffled those cakes off and made me pretty near four-hundred dollars in money to help me plus give me a beautiful cake. The thoughts of that beautiful cake…

The literature on occupational communities contains various overlapping definitions of the concept. It has been suggested, primarily by Blauner (1964), and later Salaman (1974), that occupational communities are characterized by a "convergence of work and self," the presence of an occupationally based reference group, and off-hour socialization among workers, along with the emergence of positive social sentiments. The poultry processors' occupational community exhibited these characteristics to a significant degree, even the convergence of work and identity. The emergence of their occupational community was a case of an already existing network of relationship moving into the workplace, but their cohesiveness, to a great extent, could be understood as an effort to protect themselves from the imposition of stigma due to the dirty-work component of their labor. This protection was accomplished by banding together as a group, which could translate objective disaffection into a "collective representation" in the Durkheimian sense; that is, poultry processing employment as a requirement for group membership and the attendant gratifying social interaction.

Within any occupational community there is a degree of mechanical solidarity. There is a pressure to be like everyone else, at least to some tolerable degree defined by the group. In this case, the typification of being a poultry processing worker, along with a few other basic themes (e.g., religious preference and community of residence), was the benchmark for social interaction. In more Durkheimian terms, the "social resemblances" facilitated social interaction, dating, and marriage among the workers, and largely precluded interaction with outsiders and strangers. This attraction and concern for one another exemplified by the April Fools' Day cake raffle would seem to be a vivid operationalization of Durkheim's original conception of mechanical solidarity. The interface of work and friendship is indicated in the following comment from an employee:

> Nobody else likes that job [cutting the oil sac on the tail of the carcass]. I don't know why. They have a hard time gettin' anybody to stay at it. I like it though. I like it because I get to work with Donnie...she is my best friend. We double up and let each other go out whenever we want to.

Conclusions

Aesthetic concerns or physical annoyances such as odors, heat, dampness, and the like were apparently only minimally disaffective. Workers frequently expressed the belief that cutting chickens or using knives was something women would do at home, and therefore there was no reason to dislike such activities in a job. Where job dissatisfaction was evident, it seemed to stem largely from the pressure of speed and tempo on the line, in the case of women, and from managerial pressure in the case of male workers. Workers seemed particularly sensitive to such things as the speed of the line and the managerial posture toward workers. Some workers complained of their "nerves," or their jobs "getting to them" if the work tempo was too fast or if they sensed undue pressure from their supervisors.

One might anticipate that killing, plucking, and eviscerating poultry carcasses all week long would be at least sufficiently dis-

affective as to spoil the workers' appetite for chicken. Not so! The plants give the workers a discount price on dressed chicken, once a week, and on Friday afternoon (discount price day) they literally line up to take advantage of the offer. The workers are even able to structure both a craftsmanship and religious rationalization into their work, which lets them accept it as both challenging and fulfilling. As one female employee who worked as a killer detailed it:

> It is just as I said a while ago—you stop and look at the bird. It's such a simple little thing to make that little cut. You don't have to stand there and think about I'm killing this man or I'm burning this man or something like that. You're helping—you're doing like I just said...You are preparing a piece of delicious meat. I've been there so long—I know how to do it to the best of my ability and I try to do it to the best of my ability. I believe He puts the food here for us to eat, and I believe He meant for us to process it and eat it.

She went on to say with pride:

> No, I kinda look to my work as a thrill. I want to go to work.

...The findings would seem to suggest that even in the instance of the seemingly most unpleasant work situations, there are compensatory circumstances and mechanisms. In the instance of these poultry processing employees, the male workers hold jobs that are appropriate to their sex role, enjoy relatively good salary levels, occupy work statuses higher than the female workers, and see their jobs as both secure and a mark of work attainment in excess of their educational capability.

The women enjoy the sociability of interaction with fellow workers, view their job as activities which were not unlike what they might naturally perform as part of household duties, enjoy the advantages of additional family income, see working as preferable to staying home alone, and conceivably, given the fact of their husband's low educational-aspirational level, may well see work in the plant with its opportunity for interaction as a satisfactory means of compensation for a relatively mundane marital relationship.

From an urban perspective, work in a poultry dressing plant is viewed as basically unappealing and disaffective work. This is apparently not the case, however, inasmuch as there are a number of ameliorating circumstances and operative conditions in the work setting which tend to compensate for the seemingly disagreeable nature of the job. Poultry work is a traditional type of work in the area, and in some cases workers have parents, friends, and relatives who work in the industry. The social-interactional opportunities, among other factors, are a sufficient tradeoff for the messy work, and a means of containing the attendant work disaffection. In view of this, and the rural context, such work is apparently not viewed as especially unpleasant. As one worker summed it up, "I like to work with chickens."

NOTES

1. The literature on industrial morale problems and work disaffection is voluminous, but for one classic statement see Eli Chinoy, *Automobile Workers and the American Dream* (New York: Doubleday, 1955). See also Harvey Swados "The Myth of the Happy Worker," in *A Radical's America* (New York: Atlantic-Little Brown, 1957). For more recent overviews of industrial ennui see Robert L. Kahn, "The Meaning of Work," in *The Worker in the New Industrial Environment* (Ann Arbor: Foundation for Research on Human Behavior, 1967); also Harold L. Sheppard and Niel Q. Herrick, *Where Have All the Robots Gone? Worker Dissatisfaction in the '70's* (New York: The Press, 1972).

2. For a detailed report on this research process, see Clifton D. Bryant et al., *Work and Career in Poultry Processing: A Pilot Study of Morale and Disaffection in a Rural Industry* (Blacksburg, VA: Virginia Polytechnic Institute and State University, 1980.

REFERENCES

Blauner, Robert. 1964. *Alienation and Freedom*. Chicago: University of Chicago.

Durkheim, Emile. 1947 [1893]. *The Division of Labor in Society*. (George Simpson, trans.) Glencoe, IL: Free Press.

Salaman, Graeme. 1974. *Community and Occupation*. London: Cambridge University Press.

Talbot, Ross B. 1978. *The Chicken War: An International Trade Conflict Between the United States and the European Economic Community, 1961–64*. Ames, IA: Iowa State University Press.

The Hollywood Actor

Occupational Culture, Career, and Adaptation in a Buyers' Market Industry

Norman L. Friedman

CASE STUDY QUESTIONS

1. How do actors and actresses who audition feel when they are repeatedly rejected? How do actors and actresses cope with this common dynamic?

2. What happens to their commitment to the occupation as they audition and are rejected? How would Maslow explain their continuing motivation?

3. How would Blauner describe the possibilities for their alienation? What other kinds of occupations are affected similarly by the market forces?

4. What insights does this case study provide about the effect of economic conditions on an individual's motivation and commitment to work after long periods of unemployment? Would those in some fields be affected differently than those in other fields?

This [case study] considers some aspects of the occupational culture, career, and adaptation of the Hollywood actor in films, television shows, and television commercials. Emphasis is placed on: (1) the larger indus-

Source: From *Current Research on Occupations and Professions,* Vol. 5, 73–89, 1990. Reprinted by permission from JAI Press Inc., Greenwich, Connecticut, and London, England.

trial context and the cultural aspirations and norms of actors within it; (2) the career strategies and redefinitions of actors including the work done by some as "extra" performers; and (3) the adaptations of actors to frequent job search and rejection, with special focus on the case of auditioning for television commercials.

Method

In mid-1977 the study began. A university sociologist, I decided to do research on Hollywood actors and their role-sets mainly through participant observation. More specifically, I attempted to "become" an actor myself as the research approach, and tried gradually to inject myself into and become part of the Hollywood actor community....

During the period from 1977–1986 I made and kept participant observation field-notes about the various settings and interactions. I interacted, in the "natural" course of my participant observer career as an actor, with hundreds of actors, casting directors, agents, producers, directors, and advertisers. I also supplemented and cross-checked that observational data through immersion in the "specialty literature" of the field:

actors' casting publications such as *Drama-Logue* and *Casting Call,* trade papers such as *Daily Variety* and *Hollywood Reporter,* and "how to" advice books and manuals for actors.[1] This paper combines a general descriptive analysis of the occupational and cultural sociology of the actor with some more particular depictions of some of my own career and adaptation activities....

Impossible Dreams and Cultural Prescriptions in a Buyers' Market Industry

A Buyers' Market Industry

...[A]spiring film and television actors search for jobs and success in the context of a huge pool of actors available for a very limited amount of acting work. The vast majority of would-be film and television actors, therefore, remains unemployed and underemployed, spending most of its time searching for jobs rather than working at them (Peters and Cantor 1982, pp. 53–64). Yet many remain steadfast in the face of job search adversity, rejection, and failure, dreaming of ultimate success because:

> there is always the possibility for a person to begin with virtually no capital or credentials and to become ultimately successful. It is this feature of the occupation which probably explains the remarkable persistence of many aspiring actors in the face of deprivation and compromise (Peters and Cantor 1982, p. 65).

My research uncovered a similar situational milieu for Hollywood actors that might be called a "buyers' market" industry. Here the "buyers" of actors' services (casting directors, producers, directors, advertisers, and others) have an unlimited supply of actor "sellers" to select from for their productions. In the face of this, actor unemployment and underemployment are rampant and widespread. Only a tiny percentage earns a satisfactory-to-high full-time income from acting. Viewed from this perspective of the aspirant and even the more experienced actor, the situation for employment often seems too highly competitive at best and almost impossible at worst. This is seen as a very "difficult-to-make-it-in" occupation (acting) and industry (the production of films, television shows, and commercials). It is most definitely a buyers' market industry in regard to actor/sellers. As one casting director remarked to actors in a workshop: "In this town it's easier to win the state lottery than to get a part on a show."

Impossible Dreams

Nevertheless, for most actors their practically "impossible dreams" of success, fame, and fortune persist. Hopes are maintained, in the culture, by the perpetuation of "success stories" about the fortunate few who against these great odds have done everything from making a satisfactory full-time living as an actor to striking it big as a "star." These fortunate few constitute less than 5% of all Hollywood actors.

But it is true that some have broken through the obstacles to "make it" in this buyers' market industry. Such (exceptional) success stories are shared in interactions among actors as well as written about in the actors casting publications such as *Drama-Logue* and *Casting Call.* The latter publication, for instance, in one such story alerted readers to "the fact that an unknown actor can make several thousand dollars on a 'scale' commercial on residuals." And in another issue, it was pointed out that: "If you click in this business, even in a small way, you will make more money in the course of a year than most of the lawyers you know."

Cultural Prescriptions

A major initial part of dealing with the difficulties of a buyers' market industry is for the actor to become socialized into and to internalize the various normative cultural prescriptions that have evolved over the years in this setting. These prescriptions help to lend encouragement and foster steadfastness in the face of potential and actual adversities. They are shared in interaction among actors and between actors and other members of their role-sets (agents, coaches, casting directors, producers, directors, advertisers). They also appear repeatedly in the specialty literature of the occupation and industry in directives, guidelines, stories, and interviews with the powerful and/or successful. They are present in comments, sayings, phrases, and slogans, as well as manifested in the actual behavioral adaptations by many actors to the difficulties and imperatives of their job searches and work experiences.

The most common cultural prescriptions are sayings that urge career staying power in the face of adversities:

Hang in there!

Remember, perseverance and persistence.

It's just a matter of time.

Others emphasize the strength of individual determination:

How badly do you want it?—You've got to want it very badly!

Other sayings implore the actor to forget the competition:

Don't count the numbers of unemployed— there is *only you!*

There's no one else like you.

Another cultural prescription is that to get ahead, an actor needs "breaks" and also "luck." Since some actors have succeeded with little talent or skill, it appears to many others that chance "breaks" and "luck" played a big part in their successes. Perhaps they happened to be "in the right place at the right time." A variation in the "luck" theme is the idea that the actor must:

Make your own luck.

Be ready for luck.

He/she must be well trained and experienced in acting ("pay your dues") so that when the lucky break or breaks come, he/she is ready to handle them. Luck and breaks have been important themes in American culture generally, as well as in various occupations. Luck and breaks *do* seem to be important factors and contingencies in individual economic success (Jencks 1979, pp. 306–311), and may be even more stressed and operative in occupations such as acting that are in difficult buyers' market industries.

Career Strategies and Redefinitions

In spite of learning encouraging cultural prescriptions, the novice actor's path is still almost invariably blocked by actual experiences of non-selection and/or under-selection for jobs. Because of the labor oversupply and the intense competition for scarce jobs, there is a tendency for actors to stress the need continually to forge career strategies and career redefinitions in the course of career events and contingencies, in order to try to "beat" the odds against success.

Career Strategies

The discussion here of career strategies goes beyond the strategic efforts and choices that are made in common by all actors in the attempt to build up and surmount the hurdles of their careers: having pictures made and resumes written, obtaining acting training and experience, getting into unions, acquiring and changing talent agents, sending out promotional mailings, and making contacts in the field. It considers a few additional special career strategies engaged in by many actors.

Among these special career strategies that reflect the dogged determination of most actors to succeed is the fairly common tendency to "lie on resumes." The culture frequently openly urges them to do so. The openness of this, as a result of an "anything that gets your foot in the door is worth it" means/end justification, probably means that the incidence of resume lying is higher in acting than in most other occupations, but others usually do not openly encourage it or treat it as lightly as actors do. Perhaps it is highest in the most competitive buyers' market industries generally. One actor even indicated that she took an acting workshop that taught students how to lie on resumes more effectively and accurately in regard to statement of credits, dates, and productions.

Since 1982, another special strategy for many actors is to attend workshops about "cold reading" for auditions given by many casting directors.[2] These workshops, according to the rules of the Casting Society of America (C.S.A.), the casting directors association, are "neither a promise nor guarantee of employment." Nevertheless, they provide relatively new and/or unestablished actors an opportunity to meet casting directors who they might not otherwise more conventionally meet (through the actors' agents). Actors then hope to be remembered at a later time by the casters and brought in for a job interview. Additional benefits are that students find out each caster's procedures, pet peeves, and opinions about the casting situation. Benefits to the casting directors are meeting new actors and gaining additional income....

Doing Extra Work

One special career strategy engaged in by many new actors is to do "extra" work as an "atmosphere" or "background" nonspeaker player. Such work—especially as a non-union minimum-wage extra, rather than as a unionized higher-wage Screen Extras Guild (SEG) or American Federation of Television and Radio Artists (AFTRA) extra—is often the only kind of acting-related work that is more readily available and accessible ini-

tially to the actor until "better" acting jobs might materialize. Extra work at least places the actor "around" what he/she wants (films, television shows, commercials) and enables him/her to observe how productions are made, but he/she is in a very low status level capacity. For the actor who aspires to "better" things, extra work constitutes life at the bottom of the occupational hierarchy of acting.

For such actors, after the initial novelty wears off, extra work becomes "alienating," at least on the alienation dimensions (Blauner 1964; Seeman 1959) of "powerlessness" and "self-estrangement." As to powerlessness, the actor quickly realizes how little authority, autonomy, and status—none—he/she has on set or on location. And the work also quickly becomes self-estranging, that is, monotonous and boring, with great stretches of waiting around while the "real" actors and others carry forth. (Interestingly, it is not so "meaningless" or "isolating" as to alienation dimensions, since actors realize they are a necessary part of a collaborative film effort, and they do have extensive contact with other workers, at least other extras). Also, they soon discover that they are not only of low status as extras, but also are invisible "nonpersons" (Goffman 1959, pp. 151–153), as the assistant director (films) or stage manager (television) yells to the nameless extras:

> Atmosphere!
>
> Hey, you: get over here!
>
> People—don't speak to the principals!

There are further differences in the degree of alienation in extra work according to union affiliation and setting. In general, union extra work is less alienating than non-union, and AFTRA extra work on taped shows in comfortable studios (situation comedies and soap operas) is less alienating than SEG extra work in films and television dramas at outdoor locations.

Thus extra work overall becomes generally demoralizing for those would-be actors who aspire to better and higher acting jobs. As one remarked: "You're *close* to what you want to do, but *you're* not doing it." Also, actors fear that if they only do extra work for too long, it might become too difficult to leave and reroute their careers into more regular actor channels. To be sure, there are other types of extras, for whom extra work *is* a more acceptable and gratifying form of work. These include: (1) former actors who have given up struggling for better things, who have settled in as long-term career (usually union) extras: "We opted to eat regularly"; (2) students, housewives, retired persons, and the unemployed, who are doing (usually nonunion) extra work as an interesting part-time and/or temporary source of income.

To be certain, once the actor does get better things, such as principal speaking-roles in films and television, it is quite striking what the differences in treatment and status are....

Career Redefinitions

The search for jobs and success as an actor in a buyers' market industry becomes emotionally engulfing. Actors need not only to consider and devise specific career strategies and ploys, but also tend over time frequently to make more general career redefinitions in regard to career developments and contingencies. Particularly when career experiences do not go well for a long period of time, this usually prompts a rethinking of the questions: "Where am I and where am I heading?"

One aspect of career redefinitions is the cultural belief among many actors that they ought to set a "time limit" for success. They should give themselves a deadline date by which to achieve relative success, and if they do not, they should leave the occupation. Most hang on and do not leave, or keep revising their time limit onward and hope for the best, or stay at it indefinitely in spite of relative failure. Also problematic is that the belief does not specify exactly how long a time limit should be. It is understood in the culture that an actor needs to "pay your dues," but for how long? Individual career responses vary from a few months to a lifetime.

On a more formal level, some in the role-set (other actors, agents, managers, and so forth) advise actors to have a whole "plan of action" or at least a "five-year plan" about their careers. Actors, it is urged, should see themselves as a sort of business in which they themselves are the product that should be carefully and effectively designed, marketed, and sold to potential buyers. Most actors do not plan their careers in such a formal and systematic business-like way, but develop more informal and nondeliberate thinking about and rethinking of their career progress. Thus, interestingly, although actors have their own formally recommended normative "timetables" (Roth 1963)—in encouragements to set time limits or frame time-limited plans of action—informally they tend more often to ignore than to follow them.

Each actor's informal career formulations and redefinitions over time differ, according to their own personal circumstances and needs....Ups and downs. Highs and lows. Such was the promise and plight of a Hollywood actor's career.

Adaptation: Catering, Energizing, Cushioning

Both searching for jobs (and success) and coping with rejection (and failure) are ever present facts of life for actors. Certain aspects of both are discussed in this section in general and in relation to the "extreme" case of the would-be and actual actor in television commercials. (This is a more extreme case within an already relatively extreme buyers' market industry.)

The subworld of auditioning for major roles in television commercials is "extreme" in the sense that most actors who are active in both being considered for commercials and in being considered for movie and television parts go out much more *frequently* on auditions for commercials. Even more than for other actors: "Most of our work is looking for work." And success can be rewarding. Sixty cents of every dollar earned by Screen Actors Guild members comes from commercials.

In commercials, frequent auditioning becomes a way-of-life. Commercial auditions usually have competitive "cattle-calls" (bringing in a large number of actors) for the first interview. Then a fortunate few attend a "callback" interview for final selection or rejection.

The actor therefore lives a life of pre-audition anticipation, wondering how he/she did at the audition and sometimes at a callback for a second interview, then wondering if he/she has gotten the commercial, and feeling elated if he/she has but rejected when he/she almost always has not. Thus there are the occasional ups and frequent downs and occasional highs and frequent lows of success or failure in securing the job, and they occur much more frequently in the commercials field than in the theatrical field.

The actor in general, and more extremely for success in commercials, tends to adapt to these circumstances of constant search and rejection by catering, energizing, and cushioning. He/she carefully has to "cater" to the desires and expectations of the buyers in this buyers' market industry. He/she has to "energize" before and during auditions (and performances) in order to attempt to put the best and most enthusiastic face forward to buyers. And he/she has to "cushion" these activities with beliefs and rationales about rejection and failure, if and when the efforts are unsuccessful.

Catering

"Catering" to producers, directors, casting directors, and advertisers develops from a number of imperatives. These buyers are operating in a very expensive industry, in regard to production costs. They also do not want their offices to be invaded by hordes of uninvited actors. They therefore expect and demand that the actors they see, hire, and re-hire will be polite and courteous, prompt, calm and poised, confident, and not "make any waves" or trouble at the audition or on the set or on location. At auditions actors should:

Get in, get on, and get out.

Do it and leave.

And they should not make direct phone calls to casters; only their agents may do so. They should not be offensive or abrasive. Because of the oversupply of actors, buyers demand and receive this kind of deferential behavior. (Some celebrity actors who are "problems" are sometimes more tolerated, of course, but this is not the case with rank-and-file actors.) As Peters and Cantor (1982, p. 56) have observed, most actors have little control over their work.

Actors, in turn, tend to try to cater to the above demands. They say "thank you" to buyers at auditions and at work and after jobs, much more than it is said in most other occupations. They do so orally and in writing. They strive to be nice, cooperative, and cheerful, even under difficult filming or taping circumstances. At casting directors' workshops, they applaud when the casting director is introduced to the group by the coordinator. Buyers, in turn, refer to some actors as "real professionals," by which they usually mean those actors who are polite and courteous, calm and poised, prompt, confident, nontroublemakers, and who "know their lines" and do not need endless "takes" of scenes on the set or on location. "Professional" means those qualities as much or more than it means that actors are highly skilled in the craft of acting itself. Actors who do not compliantly cater to buyers often find themselves replaced by those who do.

Energizing

"Energizing" refers to the high level of energy actors are expected to produce, exhibit, and maintain at auditions and performances. Actors have to be "up." They are expected not to appear tired, worried, or indifferent. They have to work hard, even under adverse or pressured conditions. They are supposed to act like that hour or day in an audition or work setting is the most important event in their lives. The audition casting director or on set/location director sometimes then directs actors to "bring it down" or "give me more" or "have more fun with it," in regard to energy expended on characterization, but the high energy level is expected to be in ready reserve for variations.

Specific suggestions as to how to energize are shared in various actor settings. For instance, there was this suggestion to me and other students from a television commercials workshop teacher as to how to energize before entering the commercial casting office door: say aloud to yourself, at a rising energy level, "Wa-wa-wa-wuuuu!! Wa-wa-wa-wuuuu!! Wa-wa-wa-wuuuu!!" She indicated that most commercials casting directors prefer and are more impressed by "tap dancers", that is, live-wire (but not troublesome or abrasive) actors who are "up" and "on" the moment they enter the casting office.

At the audition or on-the-set, actors sometimes defuse external or internal energy-tension by mockingly deprecating the written popular art contents of their material. For example, a soap opera actor commented, after flubbing a line: "Well, it sure ain't Shakespeare!" And two different commercial auditioners, one after having to gobble up a pizza and the other after having to simulate a car motor warming up as he drinks a morning cup of coffee at a convenience store, remarked: "And for this I spent three years at the Royal Academy of Dramatic Art!" At a commercial audition requiring actors to hold their breath and make big cheeks, one actor said, "What would my drama coach say about this?" Another actor replied, "He'd probably wish he was here." Such comments are quite common, especially around commercials, situation comedy television shows, and soap operas, and at least in part as energy-related tension reducers.

At the commercial auditions, tensions and mild anxieties arise in regard to the challenge of instantly getting into a 30–60 second character, often in role and plot situations that are of the comedically "absurd" or "off-the-wall" types. Such commercial auditions that I attended included: a character with a catatonic look preparing barbeque charcoals; a jogger falling into a ditch; a singing razor blade; a conehead-type creature in the year 2094; a scoutmaster extolling "an ice cream you can trust"; a man reacting to a pay telephone that literally eats up all of his coins; a husband slurping soup while his wife rattles on; a "refrigerator man" (half human, half refrigerator), that (who) puts a juice product into itself (himself); a man who acts like a carpet fiber; and so forth.

Another aspect of energizing is that successful actors need to possess the tenacity to keep pushing for jobs, to keep up their persistence and perseverance. This tenacity requires energy and effort. It is a difficult task, though, because the actor needs to not become so aggressive or abrasive as to anger or irritate the casting director buyers. He/she has to become and be—as actors and their role-sets put it—"a polite pest" or "considerate in persistence" or a "subtle nudge." This involves politeness in in-person managed impressions and extensive use of mailings (about credits and appearances) for self-promotion rather than making annoying phone calls. Ideally it involves these contradictory efforts somehow to tenaciously but "pleasantly" promote and market himself/herself.

Cushioning

"Cushioning" refers to the fact that since most auditions do not secure the job, the actor is subsequently confronted with a sense of rejection and loss, which needs to be eased or cushioned. (Or, indeed, the sense of rejection and need for cushioning in many cases is derived from not even being important enough or successful enough in a career to even be submitted for and sent out on auditions by an agent.) The notion here of "cushioning" is similar to Goffman's (1952, pp. 451–463) idea of "cooling out" oneself as adaptation to failure. Cushioning, though, refers more to a special kind of milder coping definitions devised for a continuing set of less severe or crisis-like rejections that are a more conventionally routinized and institutionalized part of an occupation's cultural/adaptational usages.

From experiences, interactions, and socialization into and internalization of cultural prescriptions, actors voice a number of cultural sayings that attempt to cushion and cope with potential or actual rejection. These are used by all sorts of actors, and especially by the more frequent commercials auditioners.

1. One major cushioning approach is to *downplay* and *deflect from* the current or past audition in favor of other emphases:

   > Look ahead, never backward.
   >
   > Do it and forget it.

   In other words, actors advise themselves to downplay and deflect from thoughts and activities about the audition: go on to the next thing, or nonchalantly view the audition as something he/she happens to have done today in-between museum-going and an acting class.

2. A second major cushioning approach is to *depersonalize* the rejection experience. In this type actors tell themselves:

   > Don't take it personally. They just needed another *type*.
   >
   > They didn't *reject* me. They just didn't select me.
   >
   > There's a difference.
   >
   > They're not rejecting *me*; they're rejecting something that they're looking for.

3. Another major cushioning approach mixes *self-confidence* with the realities of the *probabilities* of the situation and the actor tells himself/herself that:

   > I can do it as well or better than anyone else, but I probably won't get it.
   >
   > It might as well be *me—somebody's* got to get it—but chances are it won't be me.

   Or, as to just self-confidence—"*They* are *wrong* not to choose me. My time will come!" Or, as to probability ("the law of averages") mixed with fatalism:

   > It just isn't meant to be this time.
   >
   > I'm going to get the jobs that I'm supposed to get, and other people are going to get the jobs that they're supposed to get.

4. Another cushioning approach argues that the actor needs to *learn from failures*:

   > Failure is a just a step away from success.
   >
   > When you've failed, you've learned something.
   >
   > The only way to tell you've failed is if you haven't tried.

5. A fifth approach suggests that the actor should *count your blessings*. The actor

emphasizes that his/her trials and tribulations are minor, compared with the miseries and sufferings of many other people in the world. As one actor urged others to count their blessings:

I say stop wallowing in self-pity that you're not going to make it. Who said life's going to be easy? Nobody asked you to become an actor. Sad but true, nobody wants to hear your problems. If you get emotional and think that life is over for you, take a trip to the Children's Orthopedic Hospital in downtown L.A., right off the Harbor freeway, and go in there and say, "I'd like to be a volunteer for a couple of days a week." Take a walk through those wards and then come out of there and tell me how unfortunate your life has been.

Thus there are five adaptive approaches to cushioning and coping with rejection and failure: downplay and deflection, depersonalization, self-confidence in the face of probabilities, learn from failure, and count your blessings. But frequently they do not seem to work well or work well enough in regard to the ever-presence of rejection and failure. Nevertheless, they are still used extensively by actors as cushioning devices for and attempted reliefs from the harsh realities associated with the difficult search for jobs and success in a buyers' market industry.

Summary and Conclusion

Hollywood actors operate within a buyers' market industry that utilizes their services for films, television shows, and commercials. Despite the difficulties of getting scarce jobs and succeeding in a buyers' market industry, actors are driven by the feeling that even seemingly impossible dreams do come true for a fortunate few. They are also sustained by the normative cultural prescriptions in their occupation and industry that encourage persistence and perseverance, and they hope for "luck" and "breaks."

The realities of the difficulties, however, prompt the use of various special career strategies, such as lying on resumes and attending casting directors' workshops to promote and ingratiate themselves. Some temporarily do extra work, but for mobile and determined actors this eventually proves to be alienating in terms of powerlessness and self-estrangement, and humiliating in terms of being treated as a "nonperson." Frequent career redefinitions also occur over time, as actors informally review and evaluate their career progress. Few seem to set an exact "time limit" for success, though they might be culturally urged to, or to design a formal "plan of action," which the culture also urges. Informal career redefinitions, especially in contemplating and dealing with career non-success, are often emotionally painful, stressful, and depressing.

The imperatives of searching for jobs and coping with rejection in a buyers' market industry necessitate special responses and adaptations. These adaptive modes are: catering, energizing, and cushioning. They involve catering to buyers with an emphasis on politeness, deference, promptness, cooperation, cheer, and niceness. Energizing of efforts is needed before and during auditions and work, and involves alterness, enthusiasm, hard work, and (pleasant) tenacity in pursuit of objectives. Cushioning of rejection and failure experiences involves dealing with and managing them through downplaying and deflecting, depersonalizing, showing self-confidence and being aware of probabilities, learning from failure, and counting your blessings. All three adaptations are especially prominent among actors who constantly and frequently audition for commercials.

The above social system model of one occupation's culture, careers, and adaptations would seem generally to be similar to other occupations that operate in buyers' market industries. This might not only include similar arts and crafts workers (Peterson and Ryan 1983)—such as musicians, writers, and painters—but possibly other occupations as well.[3]...

NOTES

1. For further discussion of the "covert" and other aspects and strategies of the methodology, see Friedman (1990).

2. Although this paper will discuss "auditions" and the process of "auditioning," auditions in Hollywood are actually called casting "interviews."

3. For an especially insightful and elaborate analysis that links industrial market factors with individual careers in a related arts field, see Faulkner (1983). Also see Becker (1982).

REFERENCES

Becker, H.S. 1982. *Art Worlds*. Berkeley, CA: University of California Press.

Becker, H.S., and B. Geer. 1960. "Participant Observation: The Analysis of Qualitative Field Data." Pp. 267–289 in *Human Organization Research: Field Relations and Techniques*, edited by R.N. Adams and J.J. Preiss. Homewood, IL: Dorsey.

Blauner, R. 1964. *Alienation and Freedom*. Chicago: University of Chicago Press.

Faulkner, R. 1983. *Music on Demand: Composers and Careers in the Hollywood Film Industry*. New Brunswick, NJ: Transaction.

Friedman, N.L. 1990. "Conventional Covert Ethnographic Research by a Worker: Considerations from Studies Conducted as a Substitute Teacher, Hollywood Actor, and Religious School Supervisor." In *Studies in Qualitative Methodology*. Vol. 2: *Reflections on Field Experience*, edited by R.G. Burgess. Greenwich: JAI Press.

Goffman, E. 1952. "On Cooling the Mark Out: Some Aspects of Adaptation to Failure." *Psychiatry* 15: 451–463.

_____ 1959. *The Presentation of Self in Everyday Life*. Garden City, NY: Doubleday.

Jencks, C. 1979. *Who Gets Ahead? The Determinants of Economic Success in America*. New York: Basic Books.

Peters, A.K., and M.G. Cantor. 1982. "Screen Acting as Work." Pp. 53–58 in *Individuals in Mass Media Organizations: Creativity and Constraint*, edited by J.S. Ettema and C. Whitney. Beverly Hills: Sage.

Peterson, R.A., and J. Ryan. 1983. "Success, Failure, and Anomie in Arts and Crafts Work: Breaking into Commercial Country Songwriting." Pp. 301–323 in *Research in the Sociology of Work: A Research Annual*, Vol. 1, edited by I.H. Simpson and R.L. Simpson. Greenwich: JAI Press.

Roth, J. 1963. *Timetables: Structuring the Passage of Time in Hospital Treatment and Other Careers*. Indianapolis: Bobbs-Merrill.

Seeman, M. 1959. "On the Meaning of Alienation." *American Sociological Review* 24: 783–791.

Tokenism Reconsidered: Male Nurses and Female Physicians in a Hospital Setting*

Liliane Floge and Deborah M. Merrill

CASE STUDY QUESTIONS

1. To what extent did the women physicians and male nurses experience the dynamics that Kanter associates with tokenism?

2. Was the consequence of tokenism positive or negative for the women physicians and male nurses?

3. How did the patients they served view the women physicians relative to male physicians and the male nurses relative to the female nurses?

4. Did the gender-typing of the occupation play a role in the consequences of the tokenism? Did the ranking of the gender in society play a role in the consequences of the tokenism?

*This is a revised version of a paper presented at the 1985 American Sociological Association meetings. The data were collected by Deborah Merrill with funding provided by a Bowdoin College Surdna Foundation Fellowship. We thank the staff and administration of the two hospitals for making this research possible. The comments of Stephen Crawford, Susan Bell, Margaret Clark, Craig McEwen, Francis Portnoy, Roberta Tansman-Jacobs, and two anonymous referees are gratefully acknowledged. Our thanks also to Jean Lee and Julie Hodgkins for their skillful typing.

Source: Reprinted from *Social Forces* (Vol. 64. No. 4, June, 1986). Copyright © The University of North Carolina Press.

5. To what extent do you feel that the women physicians' and male nurses' feelings about their work were affected by the dynamics of tokenism?

...The purpose of the present [case study] is to examine how gender as a status characteristic interacts with the effects of tokenism in one organization, the hospital. The existence of small numbers of male nurses and female physicians working in the same hospitals permits us to examine male tokens in an occupation stereotyped as female and female tokens in an occupation stereotyped as male. First we examine whether the three perceptual tendencies described by Kanter occur for both types of tokens and whether the responses to these tendencies by the male tokens are the same as those of the female tokens. Second, we examine Kanter's suggestion that the content of these interactions may differ when males rather than females are the tokens. Finally, it is our aim to discover how some of these processes work at the face-to-face level. We assume that the expectations of all the actors involved in these interactions will differ according to the gender status of the token. Thus we examine whether the specific and general expectations (states) associated with males will result in mostly positive outcomes of the tokenism processes for male nurses while the expectations associated with females lead to more negative outcomes for female physicians. We suspect that it is the process resulting from heightened visibility, contrast and assimilation that help male nurses advance more rapidly in their careers.

Methods

The medical personnel in two Northeastern hospitals were observed and interviewed during the summer of 1983. The hospitals were relatively small—fewer than 100 beds—but each had both male and female tokens, male nurses and female physicians. One hospital had 147 nurses and 47 physicians; the other hospital had 88 nurses and 30 physicians. In each hospital, the head administrator was contacted and asked if the researcher could observe personnel in the hospital for a project on organizational behavior. All personnel were informed of the researcher's pending arrival.

Data Collection

In each of the hospitals, 3 units were the focus of observation. The researcher sat behind the nurse's station and watched people. In addition, time was spent in the cafeterias, doctors' lounges, nurses' lounges, and medical records area. At both sites there was free access to all areas of the hospital. The researcher stayed in the hospitals for 5 to 6 hours each shift for all 3 shifts, 6 or 7 days a week—for about 540 hours of observation. Because of the extensive length of time spent in the hospitals and the access to all of their areas, many events were observed that might not have been without this freedom; the researcher often stayed at the hospital until late into the morning, sometimes taking naps in the doctors' lounges. As a result of this, personnel could be observed at all times of their working day; physicians were observed both at their prime in the morning and when they were awakened late at night. Most of the researcher's meals were eaten in the hospitals in the nurses' lounges and in the cafeterias. During the observation periods most of the nurses and doctors chatted with the researcher; the male nurses were eager to engage in conversations about being a "male nurse." Five physicians also were accompanied while they were making their rounds.

Interviews were conducted with hospital personnel after the observations were concluded. Twenty-six interviews were held in one hospital, 18 interviews in the other. All the token nurses and physicians were interviewed: 7 male nurses and 3 female physicians. The other personnel interviewed were those who had the most contact with the tokens, including their supervisors, the directors of nursing, and other nurses and doctors. The interviews consisted of questions about the respondents' work histories and career plans; their perceptions of differences between the tokens and the dominant group; how the tokens interact with, and if they are excluded from, the dominant group; and whether there are gender role expectations for the tokens.

There were some discrepancies between what was observed and what respondents stated during their interviews. Answers the tokens themselves gave were most consistent with what was observed. For instance, it was observed that male nurses were more often asked to lift than were female nurses. Male nurses verified this observation during interviews while several other staff members said that male nurses were not asked to do more lifting than female nurses. Also the answers given by nurses regarding the behavior of physicians matched our observations more often than did their answers about other nurses, and vice versa. However, most interview replies were consistent with the observations.

Measurement

Our first goal was to determine whether the three perceptual responses to tokenism—

heightened visibility, contrast, and assimilation—occurred in the hospitals. To measure visibility, the observer looked for ways in which the token might stand out from the dominant groups. For example, did people looking for help notice the token before they noticed his or her peers. The proximity of the client to staff members was noted and visibility was counted only when members of the dominant group were around and it was equally likely that a client could ask a token or dominant group member for help. In addition, distinctions clients made toward the tokens, such as referring to them as "the male nurse" or "the female physician," were noted.

Contrast, or the exaggeration of the token's differences, was measured by the degree to which the token was excluded from the conversations of the dominant group. Staff members were asked with whom they were close friends to see which social networks the token was included in most often. As a final indication of the degree of exclusion, staff members were asked for their perceptions of whether the token was excluded from the dominant group's social networks.

In order to measure assimilation or the expectation of stereotypical behaviors by the token, examples of the dominant group asking the token to behave stereotypically were noted. For instance, did female nurses ask male nurses to assume leadership roles? Did male physicians expect female physicians to handle petty details?

The Setting

In both hospitals, the 3 work shifts vary enormously in their activities. The 7:00 A.M. to 3:00 P.M. shift is quite hectic, for this is when most physicians give their orders, laboratory and x-rays are done, and visitors are present. The 3:00 P.M. to 11:00 P.M. shift concentrates mainly on medicating the patients and helping them to fall asleep. Some physi-

cians, respiratory therapists, and visitors are around. The 11:00 P.M. to 7:00 A.M. shift concentrates on medicating the patients and seeing that they are comfortable through the night....

Findings

Perceptual Tendencies

Through both observation and interviewing we confirmed the presence in both hospitals of all three perceptual tendencies described by Kanter, heightened visibility, contrast, and assimilation, for both male nurses and female physicians. The male nurses were more visible than their female counterparts. Several nurses reported, and it was also observed, that nurses, supervisors, physicians, and often patients' families were aware of the male nurses' names, the units and shifts they worked, and even aspects of their personal lives. By contrast, many fewer people knew the names of the female nurses. For instance, during an in-service educational seminar the female nurses all had to introduce themselves. Persons searching for a nurse would tend to gravitate toward the male nurse. One time a plumber, and in another instance, a family member, went around the nurses' desk and past several female nurses to ask a male nurse a question that any of the nurses could have answered: the plumber asked permission to go into a room and the family member asked where a patient was staying. In addition, one of the male nurses said that when a patient is brought up from X-ray, the orderly will inform him that the patient is back, even though it is not his patient. This was confirmed by observations.

The gender of the male tokens was also quite noticeable. For example, it was observed, and several people commented, that staff members and patients would refer to the men as "the, my, or our male nurse." The majority (20) of the nurses and physicians interviewed in one hospital knew the number of male nurses in the hospital, but did not know the number of female nurses.

There was also evidence that female physicians were more noticeable than male physicians. New nurses did not have to ask the names of female physicians although they did ask the names of male physicians. Staff members were aware of the female consulting physicians' names and aspects of one of the female physicians' personal life although they mentioned fewer of the male consulting physicians and fewer details of the men's lives.

Like the gender of male nurses, the gender of female physicians was also very noticeable. During the interviews more than half of the physicians and nurses mentioned the number of female physicians they had and their specialties before they were asked questions about female physicians. Numerous instances of people referring to the "lady doctor" or the "female physician" were observed. In one instance it was emphasized that a woman was the head of the department.

The second perceptual tendency associated with tokenism, contrast, occurs when the dominant group members exaggerate their similarities with one another and their differences with the token group. The predicted result is that the token is excluded from the dominant group's social networks. Observations indicated that the typical conversations of female nurses revolved around "female" topics. The nurses in one unit talked about baby and bridal showers, their dates, finding a man, dirty jokes, their husbands' sexual habits and sexual needs, and various aspects of the female menstrual cycle. Conversations in the other units centered around their experiences giving birth and raising children (including breastfeeding), boyfriends' and husbands' habits, and clothing and haircuts. Male nurses were not included in these conversations and the

female nurses made no attempts to include them. Only once were two female nurses observed to change their topic of conversation when a male nurse was present. Female nurses usually directed their comments to other female nurses or women, especially if the comment was of a female nature. It was only when the female nurses were not discussing such female-oriented subjects that male nurses were included, although there were several (three) instances in which men were not included even in gender-neutral conversations. When asked if they were included in the female nurses' conversations, a typical response from a male nurse was "I'm sure there are conversations I'm not included in—girls have their little girl talk sessions." Most male nurses (5) said they chose not to be included in some conversations. For instance, after listening for a few minutes to the conversation of two nurses who were discussing their boyfriends, one male nurse walked off and stood by himself.

There were many social events in which male nurses were not included. One hospital had a female nurses' softball team. Several male and female nurses said that male nurses are not invited to lingerie parties, tupperware parties, and houseware parties; yet these were the only parties that the nurses had. In one hospital, only one of the 13 nurses named a male nurse as her closest friend in the hospital. Two male nurses said that they did not have a closest friend and two named female nurses (although the feeling was not reciprocated). In the other hospital, only one female charge nurse mentioned a male charge nurse as her closest friend.

There were several examples of the male nurses' differences being exaggerated. In both hospitals, two supervisors referred to the nurses as "the girls." In all of the units there were women's magazines lying around such as *Good Housekeeping* and

Woman's Day along with Avon books and order forms. In addition, the female nurses referred to each other by pet names such as "Rockin Rita" or "Donna Baby," while they called one of the male nurses "sexy."

However, the evidence indicates that male nurses are not totally excluded from female nurses' social networks and conversations. The male nurses would talk with the female nurses about their outside lives: mortgages, vacations, their divorce experiences, daily activities, family members, and the foods they eat. The male nurses were sometimes aware of the female nurses' conditions: two asked how their co-workers were feeling after they had been ill. Just as the female nurses would often touch each other, several times female nurses were observed touching a male nurse (and another mockingly strangling him) and vice versa.

Direct observation and comments made during interviews yielded very different findings from those obtained when staff members were specifically asked if men are excluded from female nurses' social networks. In one hospital, 17 of 21 staff members said that male nurses are not excluded, yet three male nurses mentioned specific conversations from which they were excluded. In the other hospital, only one of 10 female nurses said male nurses might be excluded from female nurses' social networks. Two of the male nurses said that women do not talk about dating and "woman" things, indicating either their exclusion from female nurses' conversations, or a denial of their context.

Female physicians also experienced exclusion from the dominants' social networks. For example, all the female physicians were excluded from an all-male club in which the head administrators of the hospitals, other male physicians, and local lawyers and businessmen belonged. Although the male physicians stated that most of their socializing was with other physicians, only one of the female physicians said she socialized with male physicians, and this was usually with her partner, a male physician. Two of the women said they had declined social invitations from male physicians, so it is not clear to what extent their exclusion from male social networks was involuntary. The lack of social ties outside the hospital was repeated within the hospital. Male physicians frequently arrived at, and departed from, the hospital together, and usually ate together in the hospital cafeteria. While male physicians would greet each other and exchange social amenities, perhaps casually teasing each other about losing weight or going sailing, female physicians were never observed in any casual discussions with other physicians. Several times a female physician was observed in close proximity to male physicians who did not even acknowledge her presence. Despite their social isolation the female physicians believed that they were included in the pertinent medical conversations with their hospital colleagues.

Assimilation, the third perceptual tendency, refers to the assignment of gender-specific traits to a token. There are many indications of male nurses' experiencing assimilation. The majority of both male and female nurses in both hospitals said that male nurses are more frequently assigned lifting tasks and/or are better at lifting. Observations at the hospitals confirm that female nurses ask male nurses to do more lifting. Moreover, one man frequently asked to lift was of shorter than average stature, shorter than many of the women requesting him to lift. Leadership is another characteristic attributed to men. Seven of 16 staff members and 2 of 11 nurses said that male nurses are given leadership roles. Although 3 female nurses said that male nurses in their hospitals are not assigned leadership characteristics because they do not have the ability to be leaders, they thought this was atypical of most male nurses. (Three of these male nurses were still general nurses and not in a position to assume a leadership role.)

Although respondents said otherwise, several instances were observed in which male nurses were inappropriately assigned leadership roles. A supervisor said that female R.N.s will often give the position of charge nurse to a male R.N. even if women have been assigned the position. Male nurses also took on more responsibilities. For example, one of the male nurses took over the responsibility of arbitrating interpersonal relations. During a unit meeting and then later with two other nurses, he told his female counterparts that they should be more direct with one another.

There were other ways in which male nurses were perceived as having gender-specific traits. When asked if male nurses perform the job differently than female nurses the following responses were frequently given: they're not as well-organized; they're stubborn; they're not as well-adjusted and experience conflict more; they're more knowledgeable about physical functions of the body and the technical aspects of the job than are women, who are caught up in the psychological aspects; and patients are less likely to use foul language around them or "swing" at them. In addition, 3 of the male nurses and several staff members said that other people think the male nurses are gay. This was as true for the married nurses as the single ones. All of the male nurses said that people ask them why they did not go to medical school. Male nurses are often taken for physicians, but never for nurses' aides or orderlies. This occurred in spite of the different apparel worn by physicians and nurses: physicians wore civilian clothes while nurses, both male and female, wore white uniforms. The assimilation of male nurses into male status was symbolically displayed in one depart-

ment by the arrangement of their mail boxes: the male nurses' slot was placed closest to that of the male physicians' and administrators', and away from the nurses', including the nursing supervisor.

In addition to male nurses' being assigned stereotypically male characteristics, there is also evidence that female physicians are assigned stereotypically female traits. Whether unconsciously done or not, both full-time female physicians in the hospitals were given pink identification tags to put on their charts rather than less "feminine" colors like blue or yellow which were given to the men. When the female physicians were irritable or cranky, it was assumed to be because they were female. For instance, one of the unit supervisors said that during a staff meeting, one of the male physicians said to another male physician about a female physician, "Boy, is she in a bitchy mood; she must be having her period." Several other nurses (3) felt that one female physician might sometimes be cranky because she was also a mother and had many responsibilities at home.

When asked during the interviews whether any female attributes are assigned to the female physicians the following characteristics were mentioned: more upset when the patient went "bad," tender, empathetic, temperamental, and lenient with the patient. In addition, one male nurse said that female physicians are called "sweet" while male physicians are thought to "know their stuff." Two female physicians felt that male physicians are used to women in the nursing role and don't like female physicians to give orders nor do they like to ask their female colleagues for consultations. One physician also added that male physicians tease her about the softness and maternal approach she takes towards her patients.

We see that all three perceptual tendencies that result from tokenism were present in the hospitals. Not only were male and female tokens more noticeable as individuals, but their gender was also quite noticeable. The bulk of the evidence shows that male nurses were excluded from female nurses' social networks, especially when the conversations or social events were female-oriented. Female physicians, in turn, were excluded from their dominant group's social networks. They were also thought to be more moody and emotional than male physicians. In contrast, the evidence indicates that assimilation resulted in male nurses' being assigned leadership characteristics by their co-workers. Having established that the three perceptual tendencies occur for both types of tokens, we turn to the effects of gender as a status characteristic. How do the dynamics of token interaction differ for males and females?

Gender Differences in Tokenism Dynamics

Heightened Visiblity

We have seen above that increased visibility exists for both male and female tokens in our hospital settings. Kanter has pointed out that increased visibility can result in greater notice being taken of both the mistakes and the accomplishments of tokens. One way in which the effects of visibility might differ for males and females would be if the accomplishments of male tokens are more noticed while the mistakes of female tokens are more noticed. Such outcomes for male nurses might explain their greater occupational mobility. The evidence on this point is unclear: the interview data indicate little one way or the other. Only a few respondents believed that a male nurse's mistakes are noticed more than a female nurse's, while only one (female) nurse felt that a male nurse's accomplishments are noticed more. According to one physician, most of the physicians in the hospital were aware of a recent Letter of Praise received by a male nurse, while they were unaware that the

same recognition had been previously given to a female nurse. On the other hand, one male nurse said that he was afraid to complain because it would draw attention to him and he didn't want to be seen as a troublemaker. In the case of female physicians, only a few respondents felt that either a female physician's mistakes or her accomplishments are noticed more than those of male physicians.

The observations were also equivocal. Several instances were observed in which mistakes made by male nurses were noticed and repeatedly commented on. One incident is particularly striking. A supervisor told other nurses that a patient had complained about a male nurse. Later, two separate groups of nurses (both groups including one male nurse) in another unit were heard discussing how this male nurse had "badgered" patients and how a physician had complained about him. On the other hand, not once during the observation period were any mistakes by female nurses discussed by the staff. It is hard to imagine that none were made; it is more likely that they weren't observed or noticed. As for physicians, several instances were observed in which the female physician's mistakes or presumed mistakes were noticed and discussed by the staff. In one instance, one of the nurses said to another nurse, "Does it seem odd that Dr. X ordered ____ for John Doe? I'm not sure that that's right." Another nurse assured her it was correct; however, the nurse still questioned the doctor about the orders she had given. In another instance, two nurses were irritated that a female physician finished writing an order in mid-sentence. Two ward secretaries then discussed how the physician's handwriting changed when she was tired. Thus our evidence indicates a tendency by peers, subordinates, and supervisors to notice the mistakes of both male and female tokens more than those of dominant group members, but does not suggest any clear differences by gender.

Contrast and Boundary Maintenance

Turning now to the interaction processes associated with contrast, we consider whether these will help a male token in his career while hindering a female token in hers. How does the exclusion of male nurses from female nurses' social networks affect the former's other interactions? The evidence indicates that male nurses more frequently associate with male physicians and that their interactions are more equalitarian. Many respondents, including all but one of the male nurses, felt it was easier for male physicians to treat male nurses as their equals, on both a personal and professional level. Both the interviews and observation data confirm this. The physicians often joked with male nurses, and went out of their way to say "hello" and make conversation. Male physicians frequently sat down with male nurses at the nurses' table and asked them about their cars or leisure activities. Physicians treated male nurses more as co-workers and less as subordinates. For example, they never asked male nurses to get coffee for them or give patients a bedpan, tasks that were frequently requested of female nurses. All agreed that physicians do not talk down as much to male nurses as to female nurses and that male nurses are more likely to say "I really don't like being treated like that," or "You're being a jackass." One of the male nurses said that he socializes more with physicians than nurses: two physicians often cook with him; he runs and goes on trips with physicians, and he has lunch with them.

The fact that male nurses are not involved in all of the conversations of female nurses means that they lose some information. This might hurt them in their careers; it would seem important to know what is happening in the hospital. In one instance, two of the male nurses did not realize that the unit they worked in had been reduced by two beds while the female nurses on duty were aware of the change. Male nurses might also be hurt by not being friends with the director of nursing and the ward secretaries. The latter have a great deal of control in scheduling laboratory work and x-rays and calling physicians. However, the top administrators in nursing said that it is important to be distant from the nurses when in an administrative position and many were not friends with the staff nurses. Perhaps, then, it is beneficial for male nurses to be excluded from female nurses' social networks. This would make it easier for them to serve in administrative positions.

But does male nurses' greater degree of association with physicians help them in their careers? If physicians play a major role in determining the nurses' promotions, it will. On the other hand, if the director of nursing solely determines nursing promotions, it is not clear whether greater contact with physicians is helpful. In fact, physicians were found to have a very strong indirect effect in determining nurses' positions in the hospital, both in promoting and demoting nurses. In one instance, a male nurse was told that he would have to change his behavior or leave the hospital after a physician had complained about him. In another instance, a male nurse was awarded a notice of outstanding achievement by the medical director of his unit.

Like the male nurses, the female physicians were close to other staff members of their gender, in this case, the female nurses. This was confirmed by interviews and observations. The female obstetrician seemed particularly close to the nurses with whom she worked. The obstetrical nurses would often talk about female-related issues: their husbands, bathing suits, and their husbands' sexual needs. They also brought in their children to visit quite often and had pictures of each other on the wall. The female physician seemed quite comfortable with the nurses. She would put her hand on the nurses' shoulders; bring in produce for them from her garden; call the nurses by their nicknames or "hon"; and ask advice about how to get a spot out of her dress. She also treated the women as professional equals with statements like, "Why don't we do this?" The closeness of the nurses to this female physician is evident from the fact that the nurses were creating a "friendship quilt" for the physician, who would soon be leaving the hospital. The female physician herself agreed that she was better able to communicate with the nurses and have "girl talk" and said that she confided in her closest friend, a female nurse, about personal issues.

However, some respondents felt that female physicians are not closer to nurses but rather simply do not "fit anywhere." These respondents indicated that nurses were quite critical of one female physician who "barked orders" and did not develop a sense of camaraderie. A typical comment from the female physicians was that the nurses "see you as one of them" and that rather than playing handmaiden as they do with the male physicians, they expect the female physicians to "wait on themselves."

Does this greater association with nurses hurt the careers of female physicians? There are indications that the male physicians feel the female physicians side with the nurses. If this is true, the males might feel betrayed by the female physician and have less trust in her. This would probably affect the number of consultations and referrals the woman received. Male physicians will have less respect for someone who associates with subordinates—nurses—and again will be less likely to ask for a consultation. Does exclusion from the male physicians' social networks hurt the woman physician's career? Only a few people felt that it would, including one physician who believed that exclusion from the all-male club did hurt her career because physicians tend to make referrals and consultations on the basis of friendship. In fact, research has shown the importance of social networks for the advancement of physicians' careers (Freidson), especially female physicians' careers (Lorber).

The Assimilation Process

Turning now to the gender-specific effects of the assimilation process, we examined whether the general expectation states associated with males meant male nurses were seen as better workers. First, we found that male physicians thought male nurses were more competent than female nurses. For example, one male nurse stated that physicians do not check up on him as much to make sure that he is doing things correctly—they trust him more. This greater degree of trust in male nurses was confirmed by a female nurse who said that physicians give telephone orders to a male nurse for procedures that they come in to deliver personally to her. Female nurses also accepted the male nurses' opinions without hesitation or question. One nurse, who soon will be going into private practice with a physician, believed he was selected, and would receive a wage close to that of a female nurse who had worked with the physician for 5 years, because he is a man. "It's easier for a man to trust another man." He also said that he will be given more responsibilities than the female nurse even though she had more experience.

Furthermore, it appears that male nurses do not have to play the doctor–nurse game the way female nurses do (Stein). While female nurses must appear passive whenever they make recommendations to physicians, this does not seem to be the case for male nurses. We found that male nurses were more likely to voice their opinions than female nurses and to have their opinions accepted by male physicians. One typical example was a male nurse saying to a physician, "You'll find that _____." Several male nurses made suggestions during supervisors' conversations without being asked, and interrupted supervisors who were telling a story, to finish telling the story themselves. It was also common to hear a physician asking a male nurse for his opinion. In addition, one male nurse recalled a time when a female nurse was called a "bitch" after she pointed out a male physician's mistake to him, while the male nurse was thanked and told to change the medication when the same physician repeated the same mistake at a later time. Only one instance was observed in which a male nurse was denounced for taking the initiative. It was believed that the nurse had overstepped his bounds when writing his nurse's note and had made judgments only a physician can make.

There were many instances in which male nurses asked for and/or were given additional responsibility and authority. For instance, a supervisor mentioned that male R.N.s delegate more bedside nursing to L.P.N.s and aides, and do more charting and paperwork than female R.N.s. All of the male nurses and the majority of female nurses and supervisors felt that more is expected of male nurses: L.P.N.s expect them to know more; they are given charge and supervisory positions more often than women. Two nurses said that this occurs because male nurses are more confident and leader-like. One male nurse felt that men are funneled into management positions because people in the hospital are psychologically geared towards taking orders from men. Several nurses (including a director of nursing) felt that male nurses are more administrative-minded, want to get ahead, and are more aggressive and better workers.

Staff members also said that patients view male nurses as having more authority. For instance, it was stated that belligerent patients respond better to a male voice. As well as investing a male voice with notions of greater authority, staff members said that patients trust a man more. They believed this was true because unconscious patients supposedly respond better to a male voice.

Admiration of male nurses, however, was not unanimous. Several people mentioned that male physicians do not like male nurses and will make comments like, "Oh, you're working tonight" or condescending statements like, "Bobby will do a good job for me tonight, won't you Bobby?" In addition, several administrators felt that male nurses are disorganized and sloppy.

In looking at female physicians, the evidence is mixed as to whether women are hurt by assumptions that they possess "female" traits. Regarding the physician–physician interaction first, only 6 people (including one female physician) felt that female physicians are not given as many referrals or consultations by male physicians as men are because females are seen as less competent. However, one female physician felt that she was consulted only because she had been in practice a long time. All respondents in one hospital agreed that the female physician who was the chief of department was at a severe disadvantage in her position because of her gender. The physician herself felt that the male physicians did not listen to her and that other chiefs have been able to obtain departmental approval more easily. Other staff members who had attended department meetings said that the male physicians brush her ideas aside and do what they want; that they outtalk her and listen to her later only because they have to. It was also reported that she often backs down because she is not aggressive enough and cannot get her ideas adopted. In addition, she ends up with committee assignments that the men do not want. Their attitude is, "Let _____ do it, she likes to do those things. Let her do it, she's a woman." Likewise, one situation was observed in which a male physician bullied and tried to intimidate the female chief of department to approve a proposal he favored. Later it was confirmed in the interviews that this often happens.

When we asked about the attitudes of male physicians towards female physicians, a frequent response was that male physicians do not like to see a woman giving orders; they prefer to see the woman in the nursing role. One female physician added that male physicians feel threatened by women doctors. Comments have been made to her, such as "Not many of you women around but you're starting to wield a lot of power." Many male physicians seemed to assume that a female physician would not "do her share" around the hospital.

As concerns physician–nurse relationships, evidence is mixed as to how nurses respond to female physicians. Several instances were observed in which a female nurse questioned what a female physician was doing. As to the way nurses react when a physician is being aggressive, a typical comment was that the nurses will say "She's acting like some crazy man. It's not feminine; ladies shouldn't act like that," or "She's another woman. She should respect nurses." However, when a male is being too aggressive, nurses will say "boys will be boys." However, few people (7) actually said that nurses are more upset when a female physician is being abrasive than when a man is being abrasive. In addition, a few nurses mentioned that female physicians are more helpful because they pick up after themselves. Several people made the statement during their interviews that female physicians are more compassionate with patients and experience more camaraderie with female patients.

We found many differences between male and female tokens in the dynamics of token interaction. Gender and gender expectations, however, did not appear to heighten visibility. The mistakes of both male and female tokens were noticed more than the mistakes of the dominant group's members.

Moreover, we did not find strong indications that heightened visibility increases the attention given to the accomplishments of male nurses any more than it does the accomplishments of female physicians. The effects of contrast and assimilation, however, differed for male and female tokens. Male nurses interacted much more and in a much more equal manner with male physicians than did female nurses, while female physicians associated more with female nurses and treated them in a more equalitarian manner than did male physicians. There was evidence that the former relationships aided nurses in their careers while the effects of the latter relationships on physicians' careers are less clear, but unlikely to be particularly beneficial.

Finally, we examined whether gender affects the assimilation process. Kanter's concept of assimilation seems to be a specific case of the more general conditions explicated by expectation states theory. The token situation appears to intensify the use of status characteristics rather than individual characteristics by the dominant actors and others who interact with the token. We found that the assignment of stereotypical male characteristics to male tokens had different consequences for them than the assignment of stereotypical female characteristics to female tokens. Our findings indicate that the assimilation process results in peers, supervisors, and patients assigning to male nurses several male-status characteristics, such as authority, greater competence, and leadership, which should favorably influence their careers. Although nursing is seen as a "female occupation" for which female characteristics are appropriate, expectation states associated with males caused male nurses to be seen as better workers. Lack of some specific expectation states associated with females, such as nurturance, proved no hindrance to promotion to supervisory positions, where such qualities are considered less important. On the other hand, the female physicians appear to be caught in the type of double bind that Kanter found: either they are not considered as competent as males, or, if they act in a competent and authoritative manner, they are seen as threatening to their peers and unfeminine by both subordinates and peers.

Discussion

Our research findings...combined with those of other tokenism studies, lead us to consider two issues: the first dealing with a need for greater specification of Kanter's tokenism hypotheses, the second being the use of expectation states theory to provide a link between individualistic and structural explanantions for sex differences in occupational achievement. First, we note that although the direct effects of tokenism as manifested in the three perceptual tendencies are seemingly pervasive for many types of tokens, the consequences of these changed perceptions may vary greatly not only according to the status of the token but also in response to various organizational and occupational variables. Although boundary heightening and contrast may occur in most token situations, the consequences for a token's career will vary in different organizations and for different occupations, depending on: the importance of the peer group for job performance; the availability of other group interactions; the importance of supervisors and subordinates to occupational achievement; and the composition of the subordinate and supervisory groups.

The more collegial relationships which female physicians enjoy with female nurses may facilitate their work performance, but appear to create even more distance between them and their male colleagues. As Freidson has noted, the peer network is a source of referrals for the majority of medical special-ties, in particular the more prestigious ones such as surgery. There are some physicians, however, who can depend primarily on lay referrals and whose isolation from the colleague community will not be as detrimental to their private practice as it is for those who depend on colleague referrals (Freidson). Thus, if women physicians are excluded from colleague networks they will be able to practice, but only in a limited number of client-dependent fields. Colleague networks however, provide physicians with a variety of other career-enhancing opportunities besides referrals (Lorber). Thus, such isolated physicians may attain financial success but they will not be able to gain the professional recognition that makes for medical success (Twaddle and Hessler).

In the case of nursing, the social network of peers does not seem very important for job performance or upward mobility. For male nurses, exclusion from their peer group facilitates their association with male physicians, who may have as much influence on their upward mobility as their direct supervisors. The gender composition of supervisory groups may be as important as token status within a peer group. As Gans (b) has pointed out, the shift in gender composition that occurs during a nurse's career is such that females are numerical dominants until they reach departmental directorships, at which time their organizational peers are men and they become tokens in their work groups. The reverse is the case for male nurses.

This shift in gender composition for nurses highlights an organizational factor mentioned by Gutek and Morasch which needs to be examined when studying the effects of tokenism: the sex ratios of the work role-set. This sex ratio, which reflects those persons regularly encountered and associated with on the job—whether they are in the same job—is not necessarily the same as the occupational sex ratio. The work peers of nursing directors are not other nursing directors but rather other hospital administrators and physicians (mostly males). For female physicians, upward mobility to department head will not diminish token status as it will for male nurses. Thus the consequences of career mobility for the sex ratios of work role-sets need to be examined for each occupation and organizational setting when studying the effects of tokenism on occupational achievement.

Both individual explanations, including socialization, and structural explanations, such as Kanter's theory of proportions, have been used to explain sex differences in occupational achievement. The findings indicating gender differences in the effects of tokenism help to link socialization arguments and structural arguments. Kanter's theory of proportional rarity, as well as the other structural explanations for individual behavior which she discusses in her work about Indsco, provide a useful antidote to explanations of gender differences in achievement and behavior based on differential male–female socialization. Most socialization arguments examine only one side of socialization: how we learn to behave differently as men and women. Expectation states theory encourages us to focus on the other half of the socialization process: the learned expectations regarding the behavior (as well as attitudes and capabilities) of categories of persons. Individuals who belong to a category, as well as those who do not, acquire these expectations.

We learn to expect certain characteristics (specific and/or diffuse) of males and certain characteristics of females. Moreover, sex is a diffuse characteristics such that the status of males is associated with a larger number of favorable traits than are attributed to females (Berger et al.; Lockheed and Hall). The degree to which any individual actually possesses these characteristics is less important than the fact that they are expected.

(Indeed, studies that have tried to measure actual sex differences in ability and behavior have found only minimal differences; see for example, Teitelbaum). It is these expectations that affect the tokenism processes in a gender specific manner.

The diffuse expectation states associated with each sex make a particularly strong impact on the assimilation process that occurs in token situations. We have seen how individual male nurses are assumed to have leadership characteristics, to be competent, knowledgeable, physically strong, etc. Their assimilation into the "male status" does not in this situation lead to disadvantages in their occupational achievement. Although expectation states for females also exist, female nurses are the numerically dominant group and as such their individual differences are not hidden by the assimilation process. Thus, female nurses are more likely to be treated according to their individual characteristics than are male nurses.

The process of boundary heightening or contrast also rests on expectation states associated with the token status. Just as Kanter (a) found that males excluded women from their discussions because of expectations that females are not interested in sports or dirty jokes, female nurses excluded men from their discussions because of expectations that males are not interested in baby showers or menstruation difficulties. In turn, members of the token group expect that they are not welcome in such discussion groups, regardless of their interest in the specific topics.

Thus the power of tokenism is that the three perceptual tendencies it elicits strengthen the influence of status characteristics over individual characteristics by increasing the importance of expectation states. Although our own evidence concerns sex as a status characteristic, the findings of others suggest that other status characteristics such as race will have similar effects

(Dworkin et al.). When studying the influence of tokenism dynamics on occupational achievement, the status characteristics of the token and dominant groups need to be taken into consideration, as well as occupational and organizational characteristics.

NOTE

1. We use the term "dominant" to indicate the numerically dominant group or its members, in accordance with Kanter's usage which she explains as follows, "the numerically dominant types also control the group and its culture in enough ways to be labeled "dominants" (b,208).

REFERENCES

Berger, J., S. J. Rosenholtz, and M. Zelditch. 1980. "Status Organizing Processes." *Annual Review of Sociology* 6: 479–508.

Crocker, J., and K. M. McGraw. 1984. "What's Good for the Goose Is Not Good for the Gander: Solo Status as an Obstacle to Occupational Achievement for Males and Females." *American Behavioral Scientist* 27(3): 357–69.

Dworkin, A. G., J. S. Chafetz, and R. Dworkin. 1986. "The Effects of Tokenism on Work Alienation Among Urban Public School Teachers." *Work and Occupations* (in press).

Freidson, Eliot. 1970. *Profession of Medicine: A Study of the Sociology of Applied Knowledge.* Harper & Row.

Gans, Janet E. a:1983. Sex Differences in Tokens' Career Attainment. Paper presented at the meeting of the Society for the Study of Social Problems.

_____. b: 1983. "Explaining Gender Differences in Nurses' Career Attainment." Unpublished manuscript.

Gutek, B. A., and B. Morasch. 1982. "Sex-Ratios, Sex-Role Spillover, and Sexual Harassment of Women at Work." *Journal of Social Issues* 38(1): 55–71.

Izraeli, D. N. 1983. "Sex Effects or Structural Effects? An Empirical Test of Kanter's Theory of Proportions." *Social Forces* 62 (September): 153–65.

Kanter, Rosabeth M. a:1977. *Men and Women of the Corporation.* Basic Books.

_____. b: 1977. "Some Effects of Proportions on Group Life: Skewed Sex Ratios and Responses to Token Women." *American Journal of Sociology* 82(5):965–90.

Lockheed, M., and K. P. Hall. 1976. "Conceptualizing Sex as a Status Character-istic: Applications to Leadership Training Strategies." *Journal of Social Issues* 32(3): 111–24.

Lorber, Judith. 1984. *Women Physicians: Careers, Status, and Power.* Tavistock.

Macke, A. S. 1981. "Token Men and Women: A Note on the Salience of Sex and Occupation Among Professionals and Semi-professionals." *Sociology of Work and Occupations* 8(1): 25–38.

South, S. J., C. M. Bonjean, W. Mackham, and J. Corder. 1982. "Social Structure and Intergroup Interaction: Men and Women of the Federal Bureaucracy." *American Sociological Review* 47(5): 587–99.

Spangler, E., M. Gordon, and R. Pipkin. 1978. "Token Women: An Empirical Test of Kanter's Hypothesis." *American Journal of Sociology* 84:160-70.

Stein, L. 1967. "The Doctor–Nurse Game." *Archives of General Psychiatry* 16: 699–703.

Teitelbaum, Michael S. 1976. *Sex Differences: Social and Biological Perspectives.* Anchor.

Twaddle, Andrew C., and Richard M. Hessler. 1977. *A Sociology of Health.* Mosby.

Yoder, J. D., J. Adams, and H. Prince. 1983. "The Price of a Token." *Journal of Political and Military Sociology* 11(2): 325–37.

5 | Bending the Rules

Why would a longshoreman unloading a ship take a few cases of wine home for the family? Why would a taxi driver learn how to work the meter so that his take from a day's work was higher than it should be? Why does a police officer use a gun when the public might think it was inappropriate? Why does a college basketball coach recruit top players with cars and cash? Why does a personnel director want to hire illegal aliens to work in the plant? All of the behaviors in these situations can be described as bending the rules. All of the behaviors also can be characterized as deviant. But why and by whom?

Definitions of Deviance

When we think of deviance as it applies to society at large, we typically think of behavior of which others strongly disapprove. Does it matter who disapproves of the behavior? I think it does. **Deviance** is behavior that violates important social norms or expectations. *Deviant behavior*, therefore, is behavior viewed negatively by a large percentage of our society. Note that deviant behavior is not simply statistically rare or unusual behavior. If it was statistically rare behavior, then being president of the United States would be deviant behavior. It must be behavior that violates significant social norms or values.

Vague as this definition sounds, it gives us a starting point for the consideration of deviant occupational behavior. Although we could examine those in illegal occupations, in this chapter the focus is on individuals employed in legitimate occupations and the ways in which they might break workplace or societal norms. There are five categories of deviant occupational behavior.

- The first category includes workers in legitimate occupations who engage in illegal behavior—behavior that breaks written local, state, or federal laws. This would describe the stockbroker who legitimately gets insider information, but then uses that information to buy stock for herself and makes thousands of dollars, thereby defrauding legitimate investors.

- The second category includes workers who break the formal rules of their occupation or of the organization that employs them. For example, in some privately held companies, a worker can be fired for simply discussing his or her salary or bonus with other employees. In contrast, the salaries of government employees are available to the public.

- The third category includes workers in legitimate occupations who engage in legal but unethical behavior. For instance, a professor assigns a graduate student to analyze all of the data generated by a study of promotions in an insurance company. The student writes up the results in appropriate manuscript form to hand in as a term paper. The professor then revises the paper, removes the graduate student's name, and sends the manuscript out for possible publication in a journal as her own work.

- The fourth category includes workers who break the informal, unwritten norms of their occupation, norms that may be peculiar to their occupation in a particular setting. At a local trucking company, there are unwritten, informal rules about when a dock worker who is moving freight from one truck to another needs a forklift. The understanding among the workers is that anything under 50 pounds or so can be moved with the use of a hand cart and that the motorized forklifts should be saved for heavier items, particularly since there is a shortage of forklifts on the loading dock. Dock workers using the forklift to lift lighter boxes are called "motorhogs" and derided by their coworkers for violating the informal rules.

- The fifth category includes behavior that is illegal, unethical, or not in line with company rules, but that is very much a part of the expectations of coworkers. Some business people may feel they need to pad their expense accounts so that they can laugh with their peers about a 10-dollar reimbursement for a small bottle of sparkling water.

In this chapter, we look at a variety of deviant occupational behaviors. Regardless of whether workers violate the laws of society, the rules of their profession, or the norms of their workplace, these violations constitute an important aspect of work behavior.

Explanations of Deviant Behavior

A variety of general theories have been proposed to explain deviance, the violation of important social norms. The theories tend to be biological, social psychological, or sociological. To a certain extent, these general theories help us explain occupational deviance.

Biological Explanations

The earliest theories advanced to explain deviance were biological. In 1876, Caesare Lombroso (Lombroso-Ferrero, 1911), an Italian physician, developed what he believed was a biological explanation for deviance and criminality. After studying individuals in prison, Lombroso concluded that deviants had a special set of physical characteristics, including abnormal skulls, low foreheads, large jaws, and long arms. He believed that these individuals were a throwback to more primitive human beings. He thought that little could be done to change those individuals, since deviance and criminality were predominantly biological. Unfortunately for Lombroso, his methods were flawed. He studied only people in prison and was, therefore, lacking a control group. In the early 20th century, Charles Goring (1913), a British physician, studied both criminals and noncriminals and found no physical differences between the two populations.

Two other partially biological theories have also been proposed. Using a popular classification of body types, Sheldon and Eleanor Glueck (1950) proposed a hypothesis about deviance and criminality. The three body types are the mesomorph, strong and muscular; the ectomorph, thin and wiry; and the endomorph, fat and round (Sheldon, Hartl, and McDermott, 1949). The Gluecks studied two groups of young men, 500 juvenile delinquents and 500 nondelinquents, to see if body type had any influence on deviance. The findings indicated that although mesomorphs were a part of both populations, they were more prevalent among the juvenile delinquent population. The Gluecks did not conclude that body type, as a biological influence, was the sole determinant of juvenile delinquency, but rather that body type in combination with societal expectations may have led to these results. If you need to choose a peer to fight for you, a mesomorph is likely to be a better fighter than someone with one of the other two body types. Similarly, a strong and agile mesomorph friend would be a better bet for a second-floor burglary than would a huffing and wheezing endomorph. In short, biological aspects in combination with societal expectations may contribute to some groups being more likely to engage in certain deviant activities than others.

The XYY chromosome syndrome has also been blamed for deviant behavior, particularly violent behavior (Jacobs, Brinton, and Melville, 1965). Normal males have an XY chromosomal combination, whereas normal females have an XX chromosomal combination. Some researchers hypothesized that an additional Y (male) chromosome predisposed such males to deviance. However, later studies indicated that XYY men were not typically imprisoned for violent crimes. Further research suggested that XYY men were overrepresented in prison because lower intelligence is often associated with the XYY chromosome syndrome. Employment can also play a role. Because of their lower intelligence, XYY men have a more difficult time finding a decent job. As a result, they are more likely to do something like shoplift for food and clothes. Their lower intelligence also makes it more likely that they will get caught.

Some researchers are still exploring a genetic approach or another biological basis to criminal and deviant behavior. In the meantime, it seems that the largest role biology can play is connected to its interaction with societal influences. After all, even someone with a biological predisposition to grow tall will not do so if he or she is malnourished. Here, even with innate biological traits or genetic predispositions that would lead to deviance, the individual would become deviant only in certain types of surrounding social conditions. Thus, the major shortcoming of biological theories is that they are extremely narrow and omit the norms and expectations of other people, organizations, and society.

Sociological Explanations

Sociological theories of deviance take into account the ways in which our behavior is shaped by other people, organizations, and society. Three such theories—differential association, structural strain, and labeling—have been particularly popular explanations.

Differential Association. One of the most well-known sociological explanations of deviance is Edwin Sutherland's (1924) theory of **differential association**. He reminds us that the socialization process and interaction with others teach us to conform to societal norms. However, he points out that socialization through interaction with others who do not conform to societal expectations can lead to deviance. In other words, deviance is learned and transmitted in a way similar to other aspects of culture. I think of this theory as the "bad kids on the block" theory. If one associates with those who engage in deviant behavior, then that socialization is more likely to lead to deviant behavior by the individual being socialized. And the stronger one's relationship is to those who engage in deviant acts, the more likely one is to engage in deviant acts.

For example, let's look at the boxer who knows he will never make it in the big time. The only way a third-rate boxer can stay a boxer is to "take a dive," intentionally losing a match to advance the career of another pugilist. Because the socialization to the boxing culture is strong, a boxer is willing to engage in an illegal and unethical act that is encouraged by his employer and accepted by some of his peers. His alternative is to leave boxing.

In Case Study 5.1, "Institutionalized Stealing Among Big-City Taxi-Drivers," Edmund Vaz provides another example of how differential association leads to occupational deviance. Taxi drivers learn the specifics of how to steal from coworkers, and those who do not conform to the norms of this occupational subculture are sanctioned.

Although differential association may help explain a great deal of deviant behavior, it does not explain many acts of deviance that people try to hide from family and friends. It also doesn't tell us how certain acts are defined as deviant or not. It does, however, point to the relative aspect of deviance. What is deviant in mainstream culture can be the norm for those within a subculture, especially an occupational subculture.

Structural Strain. A second sociological approach to deviance falls into the general category of *structural strain* theories. Structural strain theories locate the cause of deviance in the social structure and highlight the potential strain between the expectations of society and the accepted means available for meeting these expectations.

The most well-known structural strain theory is that of Robert Merton. Merton (1968) classifies individuals on the basis of the extent to which they adhere to or reject acceptable cultural goals and means.

- *Conformists* are *not* deviant; they adhere to acceptable cultural goals and seek to fulfill them through acceptable cultural means. A woman who starts her own real estate business as a way of attaining wealth would be an example of a conformist. Her goal is in line with society's expectations, and her means are acceptable. On the other hand, deviants adopt unacceptable goals, unacceptable means, or both.

- *Innovators* accept the traditional goals for success, but use unacceptable means to achieve these goals. This reasoning is often used to explain the deviance of individuals who want to work hard and be successful but whose lack of education and opportunity leaves them without employment that yields what they need. They then seek alternative means for achieving success by engaging in illegal acts such as selling drugs, burglarizing homes, or stealing cars. In the midst of a legitimate occupation, the innovator may be the embezzler.

- *Ritualists* are unable to achieve traditional success because they lose sight of their goals and instead become overly focused on the means for achieving them. An emergency room admissions clerk who persists in asking questions about an incoming patient's insurance company when the patient is bleeding from a stab wound is a ritualist. The stabbing victim cannot respond coherently, but the ritualist sees only forms to fill out (the means), not the person who needs help (the goal).

- The *retreatist's* response to failed expectations is to abandon both the acceptable goals and the acceptable means for achieving these goals. Many homeless people fit the classification of the retreatist. In occupational terms, these may be discouraged workers who have given up hope of finding employment and, therefore, give up on society's goals for traditional success.

- *Rebels* reject society's acceptable goals and means and instead substitute their own alternative goals and means, which they may promote through religious or political activities. David Koresh, with his goal of setting aside an area of Texas as the Kingdom of God, created a cult to help him achieve his goal. The goals were not achieved, as both he and his dream disappeared in fire and ashes.

Although Merton's theory has the virtue of locating the predominant cause of deviance in the social structure, it suffers from several shortcomings. For example, it does not explain why many of the disadvantaged do not turn to deviance. It also does not acknowledge individual interpretations of success. While one worker may find her $30,000 annual salary acceptable, another may feel he must augment the same level of income with unconventional, unacceptable means.

Labeling. A third sociological approach to explaining deviance is **labeling theory.** In one of the first formulations, Howard Becker (1966) argued that deviant behavior is "behavior that people so label." Conflict theorists would point out that individuals or groups with power in society are the ones who do the labeling because they have the power to determine what constitutes deviant behavior. For example, the deviant behavior of one generation may be conforming behavior for the next generation. The acceptable behavior of the previous generation may be unacceptable to the current generation. For example, as we have become more sensitized to the issue of sexual harassment, this generation is rejecting behavior that was acceptable and perhaps even expected two decades ago.

Labeling theory implies relativity in deviance. If deviance is relative and determined by those in power, what is the place of the worker? Should a worker conform to the official company rules because the company ultimately has the power to retain or fire the worker? Or should the worker conform to the norms of coworkers, which may differ from company policy, in order to make day-to-day work life more comfortable? In Case Study 5.2, "The Portland Longshoreman: Work Culture," William Pilcher points to this relativity of deviance. His subjects pilfer cargo from the ships they load and unload, but they do not consider this stealing.

The labeling perspective on deviance is also influenced by the symbolic interactionist framework, which focuses on how our interactions with others shape our behavior. The idea is that conformity can be encouraged by labeling deviant behavior that violates the norms. Deviant behavior is that so labeled by others. However, not all deviant acts fall prey to labeling. **Primary deviance** (Lemert, 1951) is behavior that breaks norms but is often temporary or easily concealed. If this primary deviance is discovered, **secondary deviance** occurs when the individual is labeled by others as deviant.

Here's an example. A sergeant in the army in charge of a firing range is responsible for every piece of ammunition for as many as 300 soldiers. The sergeant signs papers verifying that she has accounted for more than 50,000 rounds of ammunition. She, just like every other sergeant, is formally acknowledging that she knows where every single round of ammunition is, but she, just like every other sergeant, knows that nobody can account for every single bullet. When the sergeant signs the papers accounting for the ammunition, she is therefore engaging in primary deviance. One day in the midst of an argument, a soldier from that unit shoots his former girlfriend's lover, using ammunition he stole from the firing range. The stolen ammunition is traced to papers the sergeant signed. Although the sergeant lost track of only one bullet in 50,000, she is immediately labeled a deviant. After a hearing, she is reduced to the enlisted ranks and can no longer go to the club on base where sergeants socialize. She must make new friends among the troops she was ordering around the week before. Although the former sergeant's peers have done the same thing, they have not been labeled deviant because no crime was ever the result of their actions. Once she was caught, found guilty, and demoted, she was labeled as deviant by others, a sign of secondary deviance. Labeling theorists argue that she will come to think of herself as deviant and that this stigma will affect her later behavior.

Labeling theory has the virtue of acknowledging the role of those in power to define what is deviant. It has the further virtue of explaining the ways in which individuals are viewed by others and may come to view themselves as deviant. This theory does not, however, tell us what types of people are likely to engage in deviant acts. In other words, it doesn't directly explain how the organizational or societal structure itself may affect individuals, nor does it illuminate how the individual makes a decision about whether or not to engage in deviant acts.

Influences on Occupational Deviance

The general explanations for deviance apply to people at work as much as to people in their other social roles. However, those who study the sociology of work have noted some additional explanations for occupational deviance. Workers are subject to individual social psychological influences, workplace influences, and societal influences.

Social Psychological Influences

In his book *Corporate Violence*, Stuart Hills (1987) provides a number of explanations for occupational deviance. Among them are several that result from the interaction between individuals' personalities and company norms. Many workers internalize the rationalizations that their company and peers provide, and this allows them to choose deviant behavior over their own moral standards. These rationalizations neutralize the guilt of engaging in activities considered deviant by the general public. For example, the plant manager of a battery company knows that if the company spent the money necessary to comply with federal regulations, it would have to shut down. The manager feels that preserving his job and the jobs of others is the most important goal. Thus, he shuts from his mind the effects of lead contamination on a neighboring soccer field.

Because big companies employ hundreds of specialized workers, any particular individual is responsible for only a very small part of the process or services provided. The size and complexity of most organizations result in a *denial of responsibility* by the individual, which serves to neutralize guilt. Each worker has formal responsibility for a small part of the process and little control over other parts of the process. Because they have little control, they also feel they have little responsibility for others' deviant activities.

In an attempt to neutralize guilt, workers or business owners may engage in *denial of injury* and *denial of the victim.* Workers or managers who are responsible for dangerous products and dangers to their own workers rationalize by saying to themselves, "It was just an unfortunate accident." Or workers may come to believe that the victim is to blame and that tragedy is not a consequence of their actions. This would describe the situation of a plant manager at a chemical company who dumped arsenic into a nearby pond before such dumping was federally regulated. From his office window, the plant manager could see the pond was dying; but, he continued to believe he could leave this problem to nature. The arsenic in the pond then began leeching into the water table. Until the plant was shut down and the plant manager was arrested, he continued to tell himself that because the dumping had not been regulated, he could deny the cumulative effects.

Corporate executives may also *condemn the condemner,* claiming that the government is trying to enforce rules or laws that are unjust or not proven by empirical evidence. In a class action suit on the part of flight attendants and family members against cigarette makers and tobacco companies, plaintiffs contend that "exposure to cigarette smoke in flight causes their illnesses and deaths" (Janofsky, 1993: D-1). In a deposition, a lawyer representing the flight attendants asks the president and chief executive of Philip Morris U.S.A. whether cigarette smoke causes cancer. The executive replies, "To my knowledge, it's not been proven that cigarette smoking causes cancer" (D-8). The chairman of another cigarette company is later asked some questions about secondhand smoke, and he denies any knowledge of the subject. The lawyer says, "And I assume you don't have any knowledge on the subject." The executive responds, "I have no knowledge." Lawyer: "And no interest in acquiring any knowledge?" Executive: "That is correct." Lawyer: "As I understand your position generally, that kind of issue is going to be someone else's battle, and you're going to do your thing, as long as it is legal to do it." Executive: "That is correct." Lawyer: "And make as much money as you can while you're doing it." Executive: "I am a businessman." The executives deny the empirical research and are unwilling to consider any information that might interfere with potential profits.

Faceless customers are not the only ones who might become victims of a company's practices; sometimes the company's own employees are victims. In Case Study 5.3, "Crimes Against Health and Safety: Murder in the Workplace," Nancy Frank illustrates the effect of a number of social psychological influences in one company. A Polish immigrant who could not read English was hired by a firm to recycle x-ray plates in a cyanide solution. The executives' justifications for their deviant behavior and its tragic results are quite striking.

Workplace Influences

Clifton Bryant (1974), in the introduction to his book on deviant occupational behavior, discusses three aspects of work life that contribute to occupation-deviance: the work culture, opportunity structure, and occupation-related stress. These three elements have pervasive effects on individual behavior.

Work Culture. In his discussion of *work culture,* Bryant (1974) reinforces the idea that occupational subcultures have their own norms and values. As we have seen in the examples of the taxi drivers and the longshoremen, the work culture defines the boundaries of conformity. Work cultures also provide the rationalizations that workers need in order to continue to engage in deviant activities. Work culture defines the informal ways in which workers deal with clients or customers or with the boredom or strain associated with their job. For example, artists working for an advertising agency must bill all of their time, including breaks, to one client or another. As new artists are socialized to coworker norms, they learn that they should bill "dead time" to the million-dollar-a-year client where the charges will not be obvious, rather than to the client with the small budget.

Work culture also defines the accepted pace of work. Working too slowly—or even too quickly—may be deviant. My father, who later became a sociologist, tells a story of his work for the Empire Brush Company as a teenager. In 1941, he made 25 cents an hour during the night shift dipping brushes in paint. One night, a foreman asked my father and another teenager if they would like to spend their shift working the machine that put the wire bristles into the brushes. It took two workers to operate the machine, and each would be paid a penny for each completed brush. My father and his friend worked furiously to see how many brushes they could make. At the end of the shift, exhausted, they loaded 600 brushes into a large cardboard box and presumed they had each earned 6 dollars, triple their usual pay. The next night, the foreman told them the boss wanted to see them. In harsh language, the boss announced that he wanted only 200 brushes made each night. The boss told them that he ought to fire them and that he would never let them near that machine again. This example shows that even when behavior is legal, ethical, and in line with the Protestant work ethic, the behavior may still be labeled deviant because of the organizational or occupational subculture of which one is a part.

The *goal of profit*, a prominent feature of many work cultures, may also foster deviance. The profit motive is powerful enough to override ethical considerations (Hills, 1987). The place of profit as the highest goal filters down to workers when their performance is measured not in terms of social good, but rather in terms of production goals or sales quotas. Managers and then other workers feel pressure to choose between their personal values and their company's expectations (Jackall, 1988). In an automotive plant with production quota pressures, the manager adds a second shift of welding, but does not add another inspector. With twice as many welds being made over two shifts, the inspector cannot possibly inspect all the welds that he should. Decreased inspection increases apparent productivity, leaving bad welds to be discovered by unsuspecting customers. Once again, the work culture leads to occupational deviance.

In a recent case brought against the Denny's restaurant chain, the goal of profit played a major role in the resulting discrimination toward African American customers (Kohn, 1994). One target of lost revenues were "walkouts," customers who eat and leave without paying their bill. Some managers encouraged and pressured their employers to require prepayment and minimum purchases from African American customers, who were targeted as a group with high walkouts. In August 1994, a federal judge issued approval of a $54.4 million settlement for a class action suit filed by some of the many who experienced discrimination. Analysts of the Denny's case conclude that the goal of profit motivated the restaurant managers to encourage or at least condone the discriminatory acts.

The pressure toward success and profit pushes many individuals to make illegal and unethical choices. To reduce the incentive to engage in deviant acts, either the value placed on social good must be increased or the negative consequences of engaging in deviant actions must be both more visible and more drastic. But, organizational exposure of occupational deviance is rare. Companies hide their white-collar criminals for fear of the press finding out about corruption within a company. A company may let an embezzler keep her reputation and even some of the stolen money in return for her silence because disclosing the theft of a half-million dollars may cause the company's stock to drop ten times that amount. To do what is best for the shareholders, the company does a disservice to the community. Of course, these actions eventually become known within the company. The effect on potential whistleblowers is chilling. They wonder, "Why should I risk my job and relationship with coworkers when the result is almost no penalty for the thief?" Thus, secrecy may help short-term profits, but it encourages future deviance. The line between acceptable and unacceptable blurs when flagrant deviance goes unpunished.

You can see the effect of a success-oriented work culture in Case Study 5.4, "Personal Fouls," by Peter Golenbock. We could easily put North Carolina State's former basketball coach Jim Valvano in the place of the managers and company owners who feel the pressure of making a profit. Valvano's only goal was to get his basketball team to the Final Four of the NCAA playoffs. Actions like those of Valvano may have led Princeton University's Department of Athletics (1995) to include "A Message to Alumni" in the *Princeton Alumni Weekly*. This message cautions alumni about engaging in particular actions, such as cosigning loans or giving gifts, that "can render a student, and in some cases an entire team ineligible for intercollegiate competition" (29).

Opportunity Structure. Regardless of the work culture, one cannot engage in deviant behavior unless the means for participating in those deviant acts are available. Thus, work provides the *opportunity structure* in which the deviance can occur (Bryant, 1974). You can become an embezzler only if you have access to accounts from which you can steal money. You can become a physician addict only if you have the authority to write prescriptions for yourself.

Members of the Parking Meter Service Unit in New York City were accused of stealing from parking meters (Raab, 1993: A-1, B-4). Eight collectors had keys that could open all the parking meters in New York City, and they allegedly stole as much as $1,500 a day. Although it did not assure deviance, the fact that these employees had keys, that they were unsupervised, and that others had no way of knowing how much money was in each meter provided the opportunity structure in which this deviance could take place.

Stress. *Occupation-related stress* may also contribute to the propensity to commit deviant occupational behavior (Bryant, 1974). This stress can include boredom, overwork, a feeling of being unfairly treated, or other factors that may contribute to work alienation or dissatisfaction. For example, hours of unsupervised boredom lead a nightwatchman to discover that if he tilts the cigarette machine, coins fall out. He persists in this activity and tells himself that it makes up for his boredom. An overworked salesperson who has been making the kind of telephone, lunch, and dinner contacts with clients that the company encourages is asked 2 months later to hand in logs documenting this productive activity. The overworked salesperson has not kept good records, but spends a weekend creating 2 months worth of reports made to look like the required daily log. A loading dock worker, who feels as though he was treated unfairly by his foreman when the foreman "wrote up" the worker for being 3 minutes late to work, retaliates by lowering his productivity. When the foreman is looking, the dock worker is busily loading a truck; when the foreman turns away, the dock worker unloads freight from that same truck.

An interesting kind of deviance related to work stress involves the pace of work. Employers or coworkers often have norms about the pace at which work is completed. *Working to the rules* is when workers follow the rules and regulations of their company or industry to the letter. Although it would seem that an employee doing this would, in fact, be the perfect worker, this is not the case. Typically, employees work to the rules as a means of protest. One of the most well-known examples of working to the rules is when air traffic controllers follow the Federal Aviation Administration's regulations perfectly. The result is a slowdown. Following every safety rule to the letter instantly cuts air traffic by half or more. The airlines' goals of on-time service and passenger satisfaction are thwarted by a work-to-the-rules protest. For air traffic controllers, a slowdown helps point to difficulties in their work: too much stress, too many hours, or too little money. Any negotiations involved become loud and public as soon as the work-to-the-rules protest begins.

In Case Study 5.5, "How Police Justify the Use of Deadly Force," William Waegel describes the extreme effect of occupation-related stress on deviant behavior by one particular group. Police manuals state the formal rules about the conditions under which a police officer can fire his or her gun, but the police subculture develops a set of unwritten norms about the conditions under which lethal force is appropriate and acceptable.

Societal Influences

Conditions in the larger society may also contribute to deviant occupational behavior; consider technology. Technological advancements may provide the opportunity for many unanticipated deviant acts. An employee can fake electronic mail. Regardless of secret passwords, the operator of a corporate computer or a college computer network can read, intercept, or steal electronic mail. A malicious user could also introduce a computer virus that disables a corporation's entire billing system. On the one hand, technology may make some occupational deviance easier to track and trace. A computer system can be set to monitor and record the telephone calls of the corporate sales force as a quality check. Such monitoring could also uncover prearranged kickbacks and other unethical sales methods. If the most important resource of the future is the control of information, then technology gives greater power to both users and misusers of that information.

As we become a part of a global economy, the relative aspects of deviance may be even more difficult to define. While the informal norms of American executives may be well understood by other American executives, they may be misunderstood by their counterparts in Japan and vice versa. Whereas American executives who engaged in bribery in their transactions in this country would be labeled deviant and even criminal, executives who do not use "bribery" in foreign transactions may be labeled deviant by those in some other cultures.

In contrast, international quality standards, such as the best known ISO 9000, are bringing global uniformity to the quality of work, making it easier, for example, to compare the impact of occupational deviance on the process of manufacturing goods across cultures. To become registered as an ISO 9000 company, that company must be judged as meeting an international standard for a basic management system of quality assurance. This international standard was developed by the International Organization for Standards located in Geneva, Switzerland, which is composed of a consortium of 90 industrialized nations. As multinational corporations recognize high quality as the best route to higher profits, ISO 9000 registration has become increasingly desirable. With regard to manufactured goods, an ISO 9000 supplier company could assure buyers that the process by which their goods were produced meets an international quality standard.

To assure high-quality products, automobile manufacturers in Dearborn, Stuttgart, and Osaka have tried to increase worker satisfaction by involving them more in the process. One latent function of this involvement may be reduced acts of deviance. Ironically, the pace of change and the uniformity of work culture in the global economy are more evident in the factories where the goals are more obvious in the production of goods than in administrative and professional offices where subtlety is a part of the daily business of providing services.

Conclusion

In conclusion, although each individual makes his or her own decision about whether or not to participate in deviant occupational acts, that individual will most likely be feeling the pressure of the informal norms of coworkers and the work culture. Complying with the informal norms of coworkers may help a worker gain acceptance and increase solidarity among a group of coworkers. A worker's refusal to comply with the informal norms may leave that worker isolated, beaten, or worse. To change the norms of coworkers and the work culture, both the opportunity structure and the occupational stress would have to be removed to diminish the justification for the deviance. Reducing worker alienation to reduce the amount of deviant occupational behavior would require changing many aspects of the work environment and working conditions. Deviant occupational behavior will be reduced only when the conditions leading to the justification for occupational deviance change or when the chances of being caught and the consequences of being caught dramatically outweigh the benefits of engaging in the deviance.

REFERENCES AND SUGGESTED READINGS

Becker, Howard. 1966. *Outsiders: Studies in the Sociology of Deviance.* New York: Free Press.

Bryant, Clifton D. 1974. "A Conceptual Introduction." Pages 3–14 in *Deviant Behavior: Occupational and Organizational Bases,* edited by Clifton D. Bryant. Chicago: Rand McNally.

Clements, Richard Barrett. 1993. *Quality Manager's Complete Guide to ISO 9000.* Englewood Cliffs, NJ: Prentice-Hall.

Department of Athletics. 1995. "A Message to Alumni from the Department of Athletics." *Princeton Alumni Weekly* 95 (8): 29.

Ermann, David M., and Richard J. Lundman. 1992. *Corporate and Governmental Deviance.* New York: Oxford University Press.

Glueck, Sheldon, and Eleanor Glueck. 1950. *Unraveling Juvenile Delinquency.* New York: Commonwealth Fund.

Goring, Charles. 1913. *The English Convict.* London: His Majesty's Stationery Office.

Hills, Stuart L. (ed.). 1987. *Corporate Violence: Injury and Death for Profit.* Totowa, NJ: Rowman and Littlefield.

Jackall, Robert. 1988. *Moral Mazes: The World of Corporate Managers.* New York: Oxford University Press.

Jacobs, Patricia A., Muriel Brinton, and Marie M. Melville. 1965. "Aggressive Behavior, Mental Subnormality, and the XYY Male." *Nature* 208 (5017): 1351–1352.

Janofsky, Michael. 1993. "On Cigarettes, Health, and Lawyers." *The New York Times,* December 5: D-1, D-8.

Kohn, Howard. 1994. "Service with a Sneer." *The New York Times Magazine,* November 9.

Lemert, Edwin M. 1951. *Human Deviance, Social Problems, and Social Control.* New York: McGraw-Hill.

Lombroso-Ferrero, Gina. 1911. *Criminal Man.* Montclair, NJ: Patterson-Smith.

Merton, Robert K. 1968. *Social Theory and Social Structure.* New York: Free Press.

Owen, Bryn, and Peter Malkovich. 1995. *Understanding the Value of ISO 9000.* Knoxville, TN: SPC Press.

Raab, Selwyn. 1993. "20 in New York Anti-Theft Unit Accused of Stealing from Meters." *The New York Times*, December 10: A-1, B-4.

Sheldon, William H., Emil M. Hartl, and Eugene McDermott. 1949. *Varieties of Delinquent Youth.* New York: Harper.

Sutherland, Edwin. 1924. *Criminology.* Philadelphia: J. B. Lippincott.

Institutionalized Stealing Among Big-City Taxi-Drivers

Edmund W. Vaz

CASE STUDY QUESTIONS

1. What kinds of people are most likely to choose taxi driving as an occupation?

2. How are new drivers socialized to the group's occupational norms? What are those norms?

3. What forms of social control are used by those who are part of the subculture? Do any forms of social control outside the occupational subculture discourage taxi drivers from stealing?

4. What justifications do taxi drivers use to explain their deviant occupational behavior? Are those justifications reminiscent of any general theories of deviance? Where might taxi drivers fit into Merton's typology?

The world of the metropolitan taxi-driver is a way of life, a world of techniques, judgments, attitudes and relationships, and possesses its special ways of thinking, feeling and acting. It is a way of dealing with problems, defining situations and categorizing people. It generates its own social milieu garbed and distinguished by human overtones. It fosters its own customs and traditions, and furnishes its own rewards and

Source: Edmund W. Vaz's "Institutionalized Stealing Among Big-City Taxi-Cab Drivers" is reproduced from *The Sociology of Work,* ed. Audrey Wipper, Carleton University Press, 1994, with permission of the publisher.

heartaches. This is its ethos, the peculiar and colourful texture which is an intrinsic part of the occupation and an integral feature of its heritage. An arena of intimacy and collusion, it harbours its own secrets and trysts of which only the drivers are aware.

Some form of deviance (deception, guile, trickery, cutting corners, theft) is part and parcel of all kinds of work. However, the particular form that deviance takes depends largely on the special activities in which people engage, the roles that they occupy and the work they do, in addition to the norms that guide their conduct. Contrary to what people believe, deviance is seldom a solitary matter; nor is it rightly attributed to individual misbehaviour. The kind and form of deviance occurring almost always assumes shapes and patterns that betray its normative and institutionalized character. Among Montreal cabdrivers stealing is widespread and, like other forms of deviance, it is a firmly established, informal pattern of activity. The remainder of this [case study] will explore the normative and institutionalized features of stealing among these men.

Research

For over four years...the writer worked in Montreal as a part-time or full-time cabdriver. He worked for fleet owners (five to fifty cars) and small owners (one to five cars), and drove either "single" (24-hour period) or the day or night shift. This material was gathered on the job, talking in French and English with the other drivers, in the garage changing cars, at the corner restaurant after the morning rush, in a traffic jam shouting the "speed" to each other or simply waiting for a call with other drivers at a stand. Our informants comprised a "convenience sample" of between ninety-five and one hundred cab-drivers. Each level within the occupation was included in the sample. Information was obtained from the driver who worked permanently as well as the driver who merely drove weekends. The owner-driver was interviewed as well as the owner-driver who owned three or four cars. The writer interviewed the "bandit driver" (a driver who works for himself), and talked to drivers who drove for large or small companies. He also talked to company executives. Verbatim reports of all conversation were kept on the reverse side of waybill sheets. Personal experiences and impressions were similarly recorded. In addition, twenty formal interviews from the sample were conducted. Each interviews lasted approximately two hours, and was held either at the writer's home or at the home of the cab-driver.

Recent conversations with cab-drivers reveal that conditions have not much changed since this research was conducted. However, today many more drivers rent their cars (for a fixed price per shift or 24-hour period) rather than work for a 40 per cent commission of their total receipts.

Recruitment

The men who drive taxis have their roots in varied walks of life. Largerly, however, the occupation is a refuge for persons who are tradeless, who have nowhere to work or who seldom work with regularity. Without any skills, and with little ambition, these men drive taxis because usually they are certain of employment. Cab-driving functions as a work haven for the youthful unemployed, the transient, the feckless, the disillusioned and sometimes the undesirable (F. Zweig, 1952). Once employed, however, some decide to remain, a career is born, a role accepted and an identity develops. The unskilled become skilled, the jobless employed and the shiftless grow stable.

Unlike many occupations and professions in which a lengthy training period is required, taxi work makes no such demands upon its newcomers. Its occupational requirements are few, and the job of driving a cab is easily filled. Thus, the occupation finds within its ranks the flotsam and jetsam of urban life. Yet the elite of the work world, loosely termed professionals, occasionally must perform work other than that for which they were trained. Sometimes they select work where employment is certain, entrance requirements are negligible, and where social subterfuge is possible. Dentists, notaries, bank managers, sea captains and the like sometimes drive taxis. For these men cab-driving is temporary work—an occupational life-saver.

There are still others who are anxious to augment their weekly income by doing part-time work. For these men—the milkman, the student, the office clerk, the bus driver and the stevedore—taxi-driving holds a special attraction. Remuneration is surprisingly high and employment is usually assured. Others who enter the occupation often stem from occupations requiring similar kinds of skill.

Finally, for the immigrant newly arrived in the country, or for the worker who cannot obtain employment in his own field, or who, for one reason or another, has been relieved of his job, or who is waiting between jobs (for example, the painter or electrician), the need for immediate employment is often pressing. Taxi work helps meet the contingencies of these workers....

Drivers as a Social Group

The occupational experiences of the taxi-driver are not confined solely to the relationships that he has with his public. Although these contracts are important, the relationship with his employer and co-workers also shape his occupational behaviour.

Although taxi work precludes continuous interaction among drivers, they are nevertheless in frequent contact. They meet in the garage at the start and end of each shift, they meet on the stands and in the communal restaurant. The garage is the meeting place where the cabbie picks up his car, gasses up, changes cars, completes his shift and undergoes the strain of cashing-in to the boss. It is here that the good-natured give and take of occupational persiflage occurs. The daily experiences of the drivers (the jousts with the police, the drunk who wouldn't pay, the stupidity of non-taxi drivers, the out-of-town load) are relived and retold with the spontaneity, colour and emotion common to cab-drivers. The implicit jockeying for esteem is felt during these periods as each driver tries to outdo the other with a more adventurous tale. The clandestine thrust and parry of conversation is evident as the drivers inquire into, and partly determine the "speed" from one another.[1] The common experiences, the exchange of stories, the community of sentiment and emotional support offered by others plus their low occupational status relate the drivers to each other. By sharing the words, looks and gestures of his fellow workers the cab-driver enters into their experiences, by sharing their sentiments he acquires with them a common ground and enjoys a community of spirit and understanding. In this way drivers gradually acquire an image of themselves as belonging together, and the destiny of the individual driver becomes inseparably tied to that of other drivers.

Understandably there is considerably more interaction among drivers employed by the same boss, and there develop standards of behaviour and expectations of what constitutes right and wrong behaviour. These drivers come to expect certain forms of conduct from each other which help guide their own actions. It is these shared expectations that regulate work patterns among them. Under such conditions behaviour becomes largely removed from individual discretion. Adherence to group norms reaffirms and routinizes the collective uniformities of behaviour within a particular group of drivers.

Stealing as Expected Behavior

Within the occupation stealing is expected behaviour among drivers.[2] It is a normative part of the work and firmly rooted in the occupational folklore. Not only do drivers insist upon it from co-workers, but bosses expect it of their drivers. Both drivers and bosses joke about stealing; when a driver is entitled to "cigarettes and lunch" it becomes his right albeit an informal one. Drivers sometimes boast about the practice, and in cases where stealing is not practised bosses sometime become apprehensive.

Obs: Why is a certain amount of stealing O.K.?

Boss: Why? Well, if they [drivers] take their lunch and cigarettes it's O.K. You expect that. If they don't do it you know something is wrong. But don't take everything...

Obs: Why do they steal in taxi work?

Boss: They are tempted too much. There is no control, they are tempted too much. But if you don't steal the boss will still think that you steal. They figure that you steal off them. That's the business, that's the way they figure and they feel. You've got to do something.

Driver: The other night a guy comes in with his waybill and also an oil bill for 58 cents. He says, "What do I do with the oil bill? I don't want no coppers." So he takes his commission and leaves. He couldn't figure out what to do. He gypped himself. He should have taken his commission and then deducted 58 cents from the remainder. I told Harold [boss] when he came in. So Harold said, "He stole it from me anyway." Just to show you how dumb drivers can be.

The subject of stealing is usually treated discreetly between a boss and his drivers. A driver never admits to his boss that he steals, and a boss seldom accuses his drivers of stealing from him although he might joke about its practice. The reason is that the boss and driver define stealing in different terms. For the boss "two dollars" might be acceptable once the driver "brings me so much, you know what I mean." However, the driver's behaviour betrays a different definition of stealing. When drivers steal upwards of ten dollars a shift (on week-ends) this is attributable to more than mere luck.[3] The data exemplify this:

Obs: How much did you make for yourself?

Driver: Well…on two nights I made $31 and the next night I made $28.

Obs: How much did you turn in?

Driver: One night I gave him $19…the other night I gave him $20.

Driver: Last night I made $30, I cashed in $21. Saturday night I made $35 and I cashed in $21. I made $60 in two nights.

Obs: You know what the boss wants, eh?

Driver: Oh yes, I know the speed—about $12–15—that means I'm $5 over. So I make 40 per cent of what I cash, that's $8 plus $3–4, that's $12–13 and about $2 in tips.…

Obs: What do you usually give him? I'm starting to drive regularly at nights soon.

Driver: Well, if you drive seven nights a week I give him about $120–125–130. Sometimes a little less. You know you give him a decent amount. If you drive six nights I give him $105–110–115. He's satisfied with that. They know we steal, sure they know. I give them a good week-end and they are happy.

The norm of stealing among cab-drivers allows for a range of behaviour. This is evident in what the drivers say and also what they do on the job. Even drivers who did not abide by the norm knew what it was. The norm can be summarized in the following way:

1. A driver should not cash in much more than the speed otherwise he makes trouble for the other drivers.

2. A driver should not cash in much less than the speed otherwise he will be considered too "hungry." (This means that a driver must not steal too much.)

In effect, for the drivers there exists "the possibility of a second world alongside the manifest world, and the latter is decisively influenced by the former" (Simmel, 1950:330). This world of secrecy is evident from the clandestine remarks of the drivers (meeting in the garage) about the speed for a particular shift. Propinquity to the boss requires careful communication between drivers. Hushed tones between drivers working for the same boss reflect the need for secrecy in such matters. In the garage after the day shift the following brief conversation took place:

Obs: How much did you cash in?

Driver: Seize—$16

Obs: What did you make?

Driver: (Hushed tones) Vingt-deux—$22.

Knowledge of a driver's total receipts for a shift is concealed from the boss. The amount that a driver cashes in to his boss remains the property of the group, and helps strengthen the norm. This guarantees secrecy for the drivers, enables them to steal, yet satisfies the monetary demands set by the boss.[4]

Institutionalization of Stealing

Norms have their genesis in the social experiences of group life. The emergence of norms within a group depends largely on the interests and goals of its members. Among cab-drivers stealing is not an occupational peccadillo, but a learned practice originating from their work experiences. Homans suggests that no custom is self-sustaining, and the notion that obedience to a custom is automatic is false (1950:282). Conformity to a norm occurs and persists because there are people who will sanction those who violate the rule. Indeed, the sanction aspect—the application of sanctions for non-conformity—is a major dimension of the concept of institutionalization. Marion Levy writes as follows:

> A given normative pattern affecting human action in terms of a social system will be considered more or less well institutionalized to the degree to which conformity with the pattern is generally to be expected and to the degree to which failure to conform with the pattern is met by the moral indignation of those individuals who are involved in the system and who are aware of the failure...differences of degree relating to the second source of indeterminacy will be referred to as differences in the sanction aspects of the institution or its institutionalization (1952:104).

Although norm violation evokes the displeasure of drivers, the data illustrate that no single sanction is used regularly by a group of drivers against those who violate the norm. This is understandable since unity and cohesiveness vary among different groups of drivers, and the solidarity of a group is always vital in determining the sanctions employed. This is because members of a tightly knit group tend to respect the norms, customs and goals that they share.

The high rate of personnel turnover within the occupation weakens driver solidarity. General work conditions, for example, the mechanical condition and age of the car, plus a boss's attitudes toward his drivers strongly influence the turnover rate and cohesion among drivers of a particular employer. Yet stealing is so widespread among drivers that they are fully aware of group expectations, and realize the attitudes of other drivers toward deviants, and the deleterious effects of their actions on the group. The words "enemy" and "bug" directed toward drivers who violate the norm reflect their status in the eyes of the group.

Driver: You got to be smart in this business.

Obs: How?

Driver: I've made $28–29 when the other fellas have only made $13. But then you're a bug.

Obs: What do you mean?

Driver: Well, if you give the boss $29 while the others only give him $13 he will want to know what's going on. You make trouble, you are an enemy....

W.F. Whyte has shown the difficulties encountered whenever a novice is introduced to a group (1943:132). Unaware of group expectations the newcomer's acts are unexpected and disturbing. In the following excerpt experienced drivers condemn the actions of some new men. Cashing in more than the speed increases the boss' standards of judgment thereby decreasing the stealing potential for the other drivers. If the remaining drivers are still able to steal they are forced to steal less. The following brief conversation took place in the garage after a day shift:

Obs: How much did you make?

Driver: $8. I only worked this afternoon. What about you?

Obs: $16.

Driver: [Pointing towards a group of three drivers]. Seventeen, eighteen, nineteen. [He paused and then said angrily] God-damned fools, they are all new fellows. Eighteen! [Meaning $18]. That's crazy!

If newcomers are to conform to group expectations they must be socialized to role obligations and group standards, and if they trespass the norms they must be cautioned and censured. In this manner both the norms and the drivers' commitment to the norms will be strengthened. Our data reveal that the sanctions employed against offenders depend on the circumstances involved, and the solidarity of the particular group of drivers. Two kinds of sanction are used: verbal sanctions and physical violence.

Verbal sanctions: The verbal reprimand is one method used to generate obedience to group standards. The driver who cashes in too much money is cautioned to "smarten up." In this way the novice is introduced to the expected patterns of conduct.

Driver: The fella that was on my car last week, the night man. He used to hand him $30 and $25. I kept after him but he said no. And he kept on cashing in waybills like that. I told him to smarten up but he kept right on. He was crazy. They don't last long.

Name-calling is another method used against drivers who violate the norm. One owner, speaking of when he was a driver said, "No, I never stole, The drivers called me a fool...." Another driver said, "If you don't steal you're crazy." A stone's throw from name-calling is a more deadly weapon, the wisecrack. Though we have no data to substantiate this, the crushing force of the wisecrack at times likely contributes to bring drivers into line with group norms.

Physical Violence: Where a number of drivers comprise a strongly cohesive group, sanctions are apt to be more severe. Physical violence may be exercised against the offender. Although physical violence is seldom applied, it reflects the measures to which a group will resort in order to enforce its norms.

The following material reveals that both the threat of physical violence and violence itself are exercised against the deviant. In the first instance the driver is aware of the consequences of violating the norm and he conforms accordingly. The excerpt also exposes the action taken by the group against a driver who persistently violates group norms. Such evidence leaves little doubt regarding the institutionalization of stealing among these drivers.

Obs: Where did you first learn about stealing?

Driver: It depends how much the other guys made. If you make $30 you give him $18 or 20. I knew if I handed him too much the other guys would gang up on me.

Obs: How?

Driver: Well, up there it's all one clique. They are working day in and day out. They more or less keep together. They did it to one guy. The guy was honest and he was handing in everything that he made. He used to have a car of his own. So they ganged up on him and they told him that he better stop handing in everything that he took in. "We'll fix you."

Physical violence is an extreme measure within a range of regulatory controls exercised by the group against one of its recalcitrant members. The following datum reveals that violence has been used against an offender.

Obs: I heard the other day that some of the drivers at Jack's ganged up on one of the boys because he was turning in too much.

Driver: It's possible. There are some queer ones in this outfit. There wouldn't be any of that now because they are all working alone on the cars.

Obs: Driving single?

Driver: Yes, except [car no.] 316 and 528. You know about three years back they beat up a guy.

Obs: Who?

Driver: You know when Byron had her cars. The drivers beat up one fella because he was giving her too much. There are some queer ones in this outfit.

Learning to Steal

If a group is to persist for an appreciable period of time it is essential that its members learn the formal and informal role requirements. This socializing process makes persons into group members and prepares them for role occupancy. When he first joins the group the behaviour of the novice is unpredictable, naive, incongruous. Learning the role of cab-driver involves incorporating the various skills, attitudes and subtle nuances of behaviour that are unique to the role. It requires both experience on the job and instruction from others. This social enterprise occurs through group participation, and includes the passing on of techniques, attitudes and sentiments. It involves the telling of tales, the solving of problems, and experiencing common adventures behind the wheel. Older drivers provide an important source of instruction for the recruit. Gradually, the novice grows consistent in his actions, reflecting group expectations. This informal education is best illustrated in the advice which an experienced driver gives to the "cadet." In this case the new driver is taught how much to cash in.

Driver 1: Yesterday, before the cadet got the car, he asked me how much you can make. I told him you make $22 and cash in $15 and you have your tips. You got your commission and any graft you can make.

Driver 2: Graft! He probably thought graft was something to eat. It's no use handing him [boss] these big waybills.

Besides explicit instruction, the occupational recruit also learns while hustling on the street. In the garage mingling with the other drivers, at the street corner waiting for the light to change and the traffic to move, any place where taxis congregate, the new driver gradually, often imperceptibly, acquires the occupational veneer of his work role. In this way he acquires the appropriate attitudes, expressions, confidence and mannerisms besides learning the tricks of the trade. This socialization process is revealed in the following excerpts:

Obs: How do you know what to give him?

Driver: I ask the fellows. You hear the fellows talking in the garage and I give him the average....

Obs: What did you do the first day that you drove?

Driver: I think the first couple of times I gave in all that I made. After three or four times, when I found out what the other guys were turning in, and that he wasn't checking the meter, I began doing the same thing.

Obs: When did you begin handing in less money than you actually took in?

Driver: About two months after I began working.

Obs: Why didn't you start the first day?

Driver: I didn't have enough experience and I didn't make good waybills. I was only making little waybills and the others were making $10 and more so I had to give him everything.

Obs: How did you come to learn about it?

Driver: We would talk on the stands and we would ask each other how much we had made. We would decide on the stands how much to hand in. It depended on what the speed was $10–12–13.

Whenever drivers get together the speed for the shift is usually the first topic of conversation. The speed emerges while drivers are on the job, and this information is communicated quickly among them. A casual reference to the state of the work is sufficient to indicate the speed to a driver. The following example taken from my field notes typifies a conversation between two friends employed by the same owner.

As I was cruising slowly about Ben's tonight, Johnny called to me and stopped his car. I pulled alongside and the following conversation took place. It was 2:30 A.M.

Obs: How much have got you in?

Driver: $27. How much have you?

Obs: About the same.

Driver: How much would you charge to Laval des Rapides?

Obs: I don't even know where it is.

Driver: About three miles past Cartierville. I charged him $4.

Obs: That's O.K.

Driver: I think I f——myself. How much are you going to give him [the boss]?

Obs: I don't know, what about you?

Driver: $20.

Obs: Have you put your gas in yet?

Driver: Yeah. I put my bucks in already.

The question arises concerning employer control of drivers. Traditionally, control is exercised by checking the taxi meter at the start and end of each shift. This information reveals the mileage travelled by the car which, in turn, is calculated against the receipts cashed in by the driver. However, the vast majority of bosses do not check the meters. First, a boss who owns a large number of cabs finds it excessively time-consuming to do so; secondly, meters are often damaged which causes expense and trouble for the owner, and thirdly, bosses who check the meter find it difficult to hire drivers.

Ironically, stealing helps maintain harmonious relations between the drivers and their boss. The boss controls his drivers by requiring a minimum of $2 per gallon of gasoline consumed by the car. If a driver fails to achieve the necessary $2 per gallon prior to finishing his shift (for example, his receipts total $15 while the car has burned eight gallons of gasoline) he will purchase a gallon of gasoline with his own money. Since one gallon of gasoline costs approximately 50 cents and is equivalent to approximately $3 waybill receipts, the driver can now cash in $14 to the boss, steal 50 cents and yet satisfy the boss' expectations of $2 per gallon.[5]

However, if the driver has had a "good" day and achieved a high waybill (for exam-

ple, his receipts total $24 while the car has burned only eight gallons of gasoline) he may still purchase a gallon of gasoline for the car enabling him to steal even more than he has taken in above the speed. This, too, is learned on the job and is part of the recruit's education.

Obs: How do you know that your boss wants so much per gallon?

Driver: The fellas told me that he [boss] wants $2 per gallon.

Obs: Do you ever put gas in the car and pay for it from your own pocket?

Driver: Yes. Regularly.

Obs: When did you first do this?

Driver: About the same time that I didn't turn in all that I made. Of course I was more cautious at first.

Driver: I made $22 on Tuesday, $18 on Wednesday, $20 on Thursday. You see [showing me a little notebook] I keep account of what I take in.

Obs: Where do you make that kind of money?

Driver: I cruise, I never stop. I start at 5:30 in the morning and I never stop except for dinner. I go home and then I come out again. Some of the fellows eat on the cruise. I can't do that. Last week my net take was about $88. I wonder what he'd say if he knew.

Obs: Who's that?

Driver: Ike, the boss.

Obs: Oh, you mean you haven't been cashing in that amount?

Driver: Hell no, see here I keep account of what I take in and what I give him, here Thursday I took in $20 and I gave him $15.

Obs: But what about the gas?

Driver: Oh, I throw in a dollar's worth early in the morning. The other day I hit good and I threw in a little more but when I came to gas up there was only about a dollar's worth of gas taken. He didn't say a thing. You see today [it is raining] I've got in $19.25, well, I'm good for about $22–25.

On the other hand when a driver has enjoyed a "good" day he might keep a portion of his total receipts as insurance against the hazards of a slow day. He is now able to achieve the norm for both days which helps maintain his status in the boss's eyes and satisfy group expectations.

Obs: Have you ever worked for an owner?

Driver: Yes.

Obs: Have you ever given him less than you took in?

Driver: I have taken in more. I never gypped him. He was never unsatisfied. I've kept $5 for a bad day.

Obs: Bad day?

Driver: Yes, when I don't make very much, if I was too unlucky or couldn't hit. I have a fair idea of what he wants.

Obs: Does a lot of this go on?

Driver: Yes, definitely.

Obs: Why?

Driver: I know, I've been told. I think it's O.K. Everyone is entitled to a bad day. Go ahead and do it, we're not gypping him.

Homans has written that, "Once the norm is established it exerts a back-effect on the group. It may act as an incentive [in that] a man may try to bring his behaviour closer to the norm" (1950:126). The norm pulls the individual toward the expected behaviour of the group. To "make the speed" becomes imperative for the driver. Not only do his own actions behind the wheel partly determine the speed, but he also must achieve the speed for his shift. It becomes both cause and consequence of his work. The significance of achieving the speed is revealed from the following conversation:

Driver: I haven't had lunch yet.

Obs: Why?

Driver: I can't go to lunch yet. I haven't made a waybill yet.

Obs: Suppose you had $14 in by 1 o'clock, what would you do?

Driver: I would go home and have lunch and then come out after.

Obs: But now?

Driver: I can't now, I haven't got a waybill yet.

Here the driver is concerned with achieving a certain minimum amount of money—that is, the norm. His words, "I can't go to lunch yet I haven't made a waybill yet" illuminate the importance of his attaining the norm. Once the driver achieves a "waybill"—that is, the norm or speed, his behaviour is influenced by his own requirements rather than by those of the group and his employer. In this way the speed helps motivate the driver on the job.

Justification for Stealing

In the larger society stealing money is immoral, illegal and strongly condemned. Depending on the circumstances, resistance and punishment are brought to bear against the offender. Among taxi-drivers stealing on the job is not considered deviant behaviour. It is an integral part of the driver's role, and it is expected, condoned and enforced. In order to satisfy role obligations the cab-driver is expected to steal.

The cab-driver's legitimation for stealing is in terms of his work experiences. Occupational requirements help neutralize any moral compunction felt by the driver regarding other criteria by which stealing is evaluated. This is reflected in the institutionalization of stealing besides the moral impunity with which the drivers regard its practice.

Obs: How often do you steal?

Driver: Considering the cars I get and the reception I get with the waybill, I don't think I'm taking him for much. I'm giving him less than I actually earned.

Obs: Why?

Driver: I wouldn't make enough.

Obs: Do you think it is stealing?

Driver: It's never on my conscience. I've never taken 5 cents from somebody else. I earn that money when I'm out all night.

Obs: How much do you take?

Driver: I don't know because I don't keep track. I make about $28 and I give him $20–21. And I put gas in the car, I don't feel I'm gypping him. If anything goes wrong I've got to pay. When the lights went out I've got them fixed and I paid. If I left it up to the garage he'd start yapping and raising hell. Instead of this I take his money and pay anyhow.

The following example shows that the ideal of a "good" taxi-driver is someone who steals as part of his role obligations—a driver who "steals with a heart."

Obs: What is your conception of a good taxi-driver?

Driver: Somebody that stays on the job. That takes it easy on the car, doesn't drive too fast. If he breaks a spring he will take it easy, doesn't goose her in first, and steals a little bit.

Obs: What do you mean "steals a little bit?"

Driver: Well, if he takes in $19 he cashes in $16, and if he takes in $24 he cashes in $20—steals with a heart.

The justification that the individual offers for his action betrays the meaning which the conduct has for him. The cab-driver's definition of stealing is narrow, limited, and relates specifically to his work. By justifying his behaviour the driver mirrors the significance which he feels this practice has for him, and reflects his surrender to the new self-conception which requires incorporation of this value.

Obs: Do you think it's stealing?

Driver: It's not stealing if he gives him a certain amount one day and keeps some for the next day. If he spends the money, he makes it up.

Obs: Do you steal?

Driver: No. Just in the wintertime. Can't make enough now [summer].

Obs: Why do you steal?

Driver: If I give him what he wants it's O.K. Even if I make $100 I give him $35 and keep the rest.

Obs: That really isn't stealing then?

Driver: No. Not if I give him what he wants.

Driver: Sometimes it's not really stealing like you say. You're holding back. You hold back to keep your waybill steady. If in the summer say you make $12 you hold back $3. The next day you might make $5 so you add $3. It keeps things even. If you bring him $14 one day and $8 the next he'll start hollering you got to be even.

Some drivers feel that it is their implicit right to steal. As one driver remarked insightfully, "When [we] all do it it's no longer dishonest."

Obs: Do you steal?

Driver: Yes. Everybody does, don't they?

Obs: Do you think it's dishonest?

Driver: I suppose in the true sense of the word it is, but the mores keep changing. When all do it it's no longer dishonest.

Though the drivers' standards for judging stealing are not those of the larger society, the criteria they employ and the organization of their values are no less important. The potential amount that a driver can steal necessarily depends on his total receipts and the speed for his shift. If the driver has his own justification for stealing he also had his own definition of its abuse. If stealing is morally right in his terms, then, by the same token, it can be morally wrong. Stealing becomes morally reprehensible when it is flagrantly abused. The actual amount that the driver steals depends largely on his relationship with his employer. As one driver remarked, "You gotta take him with a heart." The driver tempers his actions with consideration for his boss; he feels that he must not steal everything. Although the greater his receipts for a shift the more he can steal, he nevertheless feels that he ought to cash in more to his boss. In his terms once the boss "is happy"[6] with the amount he cashes in the driver is morally innocent of any wrongdoing.

If the boss is a "good guy" yet a driver "takes him for everything he's got" then the driver is morally wrong. The standards by which the cab-driver evaluates the practice of stealing are diffuse (Parsons, 1949:190). It is his definition of, and feelings toward, his boss that govern how much he steals. The following data illustrate this clearly.

Obs: What is stealing in your opinion?

Driver: If the driver has no feelings towards the boss. He makes sure that the boss doesn't get much. You know you gotta take him with a heart—if it's there to take. If you make a big waybill and what you give the boss makes him unhappy, that's stealing. It's not stealing because 40% of that is your own anyway. You know it's a give and take affair.

Obs: Do you keep track of the number of loads you make each day?

Driver: I don't keep a waybill.

Obs: How do you know what to give him?

Driver: I give him his average as anybody else does. I figure out the gas and I figure out what will make him happy. If I haven't enough I take a few dollars off. As long as it keeps him happy. At the end of the week it evens up and maybe I'll have a few dollars over.

Obs: What do you think of stealing?

Driver: It depends who you work for.

Obs: What do you mean?

Driver: Well, if you work for a boss and he treats you nice you shouldn't steal from him. But if a boss, sometimes it is his mistake, doesn't pay you in full or makes you pay for a tire or something then you can't blame the guy for taking a meal and cigarettes from the boss. And he's working with a big responsibility. He's working trying to make the boss's living and his own living at the same time. Why shouldn't he take a 50-cent meal.

Obs: You really don't consider that stealing?

Driver: No.

Obs: What do you consider stealing?

Driver: If you make $10 load and you say $5 to the boss. Or if you tell him you put in $2 of gas in the tank and you really put in $4. That's stealing.

Conclusion

Varied practices of restricting production or of "putting on the brakes" are commonplace at all levels of the work world. Regardless of the formal rules and regulations that control workers on the job, an informal system of norms develops which governs the proper workload to be accomplished. Usually this refers to the refusal by workers to do as much work as their employers believe they can and ought to do (Hughes, 1952:425). Workers soon develop their own definitions of the proper levels of effort and product. In effect the informal norms help establish the limits regulating the quantity and quality of work to be completed. Thus we know that machine-shop workers systematically restrict quotas (Roy, 1952:427–442); workers in the Bank Wiring Observation Room of the Western Electric Company were guided by an informal code regulating their work output (Roethlisberger and Dickson, 1939); stealing is institutionalized among metropolitan taxi-drivers; policemen secretly smoke on the job and take their "breaks" in places hidden from public view; the kitchen staffs in restaurants and hotels often eat exceptionally well, and the wives of chefs and supermarket butchers serve the finest cuts of meat to their families. In sum, it is noteworthy that what appears unique to the occupation of the taxi-driver is, in fact, found in many other spheres of work.

NOTES

1. The "speed" refers to the average amount of money (receipts) the drivers have accumulated during a single shift. For example, when two drivers meet during a shift the immediate inquiry is, "What's the speed?" This asks how much money have you taken in? Knowing the speed enables a driver to judge his own receipts against the speed and establish whether he is above or below the average.

2. A driver's share of the total amount registered on the meter is 40 per cent. At the conclusion of each shift a driver is required to cash in to his boss all his receipts minus 40 per cent commission (if he is being paid on a daily basis); if he is being paid on a weekly basis the driver cashes in his total daily receipts to the boss. His weekly wage will be 40 per cent of the total amount he has cashed in during the week. Stealing is the practice of cashing in less than what is due the boss. For example, a driver might take in $18 for a shift yet he will cash in only $15 thereby stealing $3 for himself.

3. The notion of luck is felt to be in the nature of taxi work and pervades the occupation. The cab-driver performs his work hoping that he will be "in luck"; when he has a bad day luck helps him account for his failure which, in turn, helps him preserve his self-esteem. It also helps explain the success of his co-workers; it is not that one driver is more skilled or deserving than another, the explanation resides in the mysteries of luck.

4. Rather than control his drivers by checking the meters on his taxis a boss will demand that each driver cash in a minimum of $2 for every gallon of gasoline consumed by the car during a single shift. This is discussed more fully later in the paper.

5. The sums of money referred to in the data apply to wages and prices during 1950–55.

6. Roethlisberger and Dickson write that the external function of the Bank Wiring Observation Room Group was a "protective mechanism." They continue, "...their behaviour could be said to have been guided by the following rule: 'Let us behave in such a way as to give management the least opportunity of interfering with us'" (1939:525). It may be said that the drivers, by keeping the boss "happy" with the amount which they cash in, protect themselves from his interference. In this way they are able to steal and maintain their relations with their employer.

REFERENCES

Davis, Fred. "The Cabdriver and His Fare: Facets of a Fleeting Relationship." *American Journal of Sociology*, 65, no. 2 (September 1959), pp. 158–65.

Homans, George. *The Human Group*. New York: Harcourt, Brace and Co., 1950.

Hughes, Everett. "The Sociological Study of Work: An Editorial Forward." *American Journal of Sociology*, 57, no. 5 (March 1952), pp. 423–26.

Levy, Marion. *The Structure of Society*. New Jersey: Princeton University Press, 1952.

Mead, George Herbert. *Mind, Self and Society*. Chicago: University of Chicago Press, 1952.

Parsons, Talcott. *Essays in Sociological Theory: Pure and Applied*. Glencoe: The Free Press, 1949.

Roethlisberger, Fred J., and William J. Dickson. *Management and the Worker*. Cambridge, Mass: Harvard University Press, 1939.

Roy, Donald. "Quota Restriction and Gold-bricking in a Machine Shop," *American Journal of Sociology*, 57, no. 5 (March 1952), pp. 422–42.

Simmel, Georg. *The Sociology of Georg Simmel*. Kurt Wolfe, ed. Glencoe: The Free Press, 1950.

Sumner, William G. *Folkways*. Boston: Ginn and Co., 1906.

Westley, William. *Violence and the Police*. Amherst: MIT Press, 1970.

Whyte, William F. *Street Corner Society*. Chicago: University of Chicago Press, 1943.

Zweig, Ferdinand. *The British Worker*. Harmondsworth, Middlesex: Penguin Books, 1952.

The Portland Longshoreman
Work Culture

William W. Pilcher

CASE STUDY QUESTIONS

1. For a longshoreman, what constitutes stealing? How do the longshoremen learn the norms of pilfering?

2. Which of the sociological theories mentioned in this chapter help explain the pilfering behavior of longshoremen?

3. What do we learn about the relative aspects of deviance? Would the same behavior be looked on differently by outsiders?

4. To whom are these longshoremen committed—their customers, their employer, their coworkers, their families? How is their propensity to pilfer affected by those to whom they are committed?

5. What does this example tell us about the role of biology in occupational deviance?

When the longshoreman leaves his home and goes to his job, he enters a different world. The physical change is striking: the waterfront resembles nothing so much as a steel jungle. The apparent tangle of booms and rigging, the jumble of cargo piled on the dock, and the numbers of machines hauling cargo to and from the ship give the impression of vast confusion. Moreover, the language used to convey information concerning the work and cargo is largely incomprehensible to an outsider. This is typical of most industrial workplaces, but certain aspects of this environment are most atypical.

Skills

Loading a ship is a matter of placing various kinds of cargo of all different shapes and sizes into a ship having a rigid and unchangeable shape. The cargo is not designed to fit that shape and yet must be placed so that a minimum of space is lost. This problem is not improved by the fact that the cargo destined for different ports must be placed in the ship in a determined sequence so that when a particular lot of cargo is to be discharged it is not buried under a thousand tons of cargo meant to be removed in some subsequent port. The situation is never the same from one job to another and seldom the same from one hour to the next. Thus, the longshoremen's tasks are seldom boring or monotonous, although they are often hectic and exasperating.

The "tight stow"—placing cargo in the hold of the ship in such a manner that little space is left unfilled and the cargo will not

Source: Excerpt from *The Portland Longshoreman: A Dispersed Urban Community* by William W. Pilcher, copyright 1972 by Holt, Rinehart and Winston, Inc., reprinted by permission of the publisher.

shift with the heaving of the ship at sea—has long been the longshoreman's chief skill. This is not a skill that is learned in a few days but, like that of the top-hand on a cattle ranch, is learned over the course of years. The longshoremen take a great pride in this skill, and it is often said to a man who balks at a task or complains of its impossibility that "a good longshoreman can do anything." This is almost true in the sense that most of the men can perform almost any task involved in working cargo on and around the ships. The variety of these tasks and the number of small skills necessary to their performance is almost endless. Stowing sacks or canned goods would seem simple tasks and certainly are in comparison to many of the other tasks that longshoremen perform. But stowing these items so that they will not shift and fall, or so that the cases of canned goods will not chafe themselves into shreds with the vibration of the moving ship, requires the kind of knowledge that comes only with long experience.

The skill spectrum has shifted a great deal in recent years. More and more operating skills are needed and less and less of the older longshoremen's skills: that is, manual work techniques necessary to obtaining a tight stow and moving very large and heavy pieces of cargo. In addition to knowing these "tricks of the trade" for handling cargo in the hold of the ship or on the docks, longshoremen are expected to be able to operate a growing number of ever more complex hauling and hoisting equipment. A majority of men can operate many kinds and sizes of lift machines and many types of winches and cranes. Some men can operate nearly all of these machines.

Outsiders in the Workplace

The longshoremen are very possessive in their attitudes toward their workplace. Sailors, other dock and ship personnel, and ship repair crews are the only other cate-gories of people that belong in the workplace. These workers are treated in very much the same manner as longshoremen, but outsiders, such as stevedore company administrative personnel, are regarded as interlopers and often treated very rudely. The wearing of a suit and tie is the mark of an outsider and makes the person wearing them fair game for all sorts of practical jokes. One young man whose job was to check the amount of carbon monoxide in the air in the cargo hatches where machines were being used was left standing around on the deck of a ship for some time because no one, including the general foreman from the same company, would tell him how to enter the hatch. Many other forms of misdirection or nondirection of such persons are common, while men dressed in work clothes are generally treated in a helpful manner. Another sort of joke played on men wearing business suits by the winch drivers is to attempt to "drop the fall on him." This means operating the winch in such a manner that the victim will be struck by the slack portion of the wire rope used as a winch fall or runner. This wire is nearly always covered with extremely heavy, sticky grease and will so thoroughly stain a piece of cloth that expert professional cleaning is required to remove it.

Work Socialization

Longshoremen have a great deal of opportunity for socializing with one another in the work context because of the uneven pace of the work and the fact that they work in teams, called "gangs." Delays in getting cargo to and from the ship are common, which gives the longshoremen ample time to visit and gossip, one of their favorite pastimes. Not only do the longshoremen have plentiful opportunity to socialize with one another and thus cement relations with other members of the group, but these informal "caucuses" keep them well informed of current happenings around the waterfront.

Information about members of the group who are not present is exchanged among all of the men working on the job, and all of their virtues and faults are given ample consideration and are well-expounded. It is in this context that newcomers to the waterfront learn what forms of behavior are expected from them: from the criticism levelled against absent members of the longshore group as well as from the praise they may receive.

In this way new men are thoroughly indoctrinated by the older union men in approved union principles and work strategies, and it is apparent that they learn swiftly from this kind of instruction. The incentive to accept this indoctrination derives from the way in which B men gain A status. The A men form the group (the union membership) that makes the final decision as to whether or not any particular B man will be promoted to A status.

Enforcement of Norms

Among themselves and with other persons that they feel belong in the workplace the longshoremen maintain friendly and extremely informal relations. They resent any attempt on the part of a foreman or ship's officer to express social distance. Such an attitude will always elicit hostility on the part of the longshoremen. This hostility will invariably result in an attempt to "bring him down a few notches." The methods used to put an offender in his place vary with the person and the situation, but the method used to humble foremen is about the same at all times. Often the foreman will be "told off," in rather harsh terms, but this is not the end of the retaliation. The most effective and most common method, is to institute the "slowdown" in an attempt to make the foreman's work record look bad to the company. This method is also used when a foreman "chisels" the men out of time or mistreats the longshoremen in other ways. One fore-

man who was a constant offender became so consistently the target for the "slowdown" that he could obtain no employment with a stevedore company for months and was forced to fall back on unemployment compensation. Few foremen ever attempt to assume any role other than that of "one of the boys," and those who maintain themselves as part of the longshore in-group enjoy a good deal of popularity among the men and maintain good production records, because the longshoremen will usually give a break to a foreman who maintains his status as one of the men.

Conformity to group norms is obtained within the group of longshoremen in much the same manner as it is among foremen. The foremost offense that one longshoreman can deliver to another is to shirk his share of the work so that more work is shifted onto the other members of the work crew. Various techniques are used, from offering to fight to simply sitting down and making the offender do all of the work for a time. The most common method, however is to shift more work onto the victim by various means or by refusing to do more than their share of the work so that the offender comes to the attention of the foreman. "Finking" on a nonconforming longshoreman by telling the foreman of his misbehavior is not an approved form of obtaining conformity and, in fact, is considered a worse offense than not doing one's fair share of the work.

Another technique used to discipline a longshoreman who thus abuses his fellows is to embarrass him by showing up his misbehavior to the entire work crew and subjecting him to the ridicule of the entire longshore group. Longshoremen like to think of themselves as hard workers, and the reputation of being a loafer is not a happy one. In one incident, a cargo gang was stowing "Jap squares," huge timbers measuring two to four feet square. To turn one of these timbers with peaveys required the combined efforts of the entire hold crew of eight men.

One man was suspected of just "going through the motions" and making each of the other longshoremen expend additional energy to make up for his lack of effort. During the lunch break, the steel bolt that holds the cant hook onto the shaft was removed from the loafer's peavey, and a piece of soft wood was carved to the proper size and inserted in place of the bolt. The offender worked for two hours with the peavey and was exposed when one of the other men took the peavey and easily broke off the wooden pin by prying on the next timber to be stowed. This story was told for a considerable length of time in every longshore "bull session," and the offender is still reminded of his "wooden bolt" some ten years after the incident took place.

Pilfering

Pilfering of cargo is common to every waterfront in the world, and Portland is no exception, although the Portland longshoremen do not carry this activity to the extent of hauling away truckloads of cargo, as in some of the Eastern Ports. Generally they confine themselves to small objects that will fit in a pocket or inside their shirts or jackets without causing a noticeable bulge. Cargo is seldom stolen for sale, but rather for consumption or use by the longshoremen, their families, and friends. Most longshoremen do not consider pilfering cargo stealing, and men who are otherwise scrupulously honest will happily fill their pockets with whiskey or small merchandise. Few of the longshoremen would consider stealing from an individual, but a large company or corporation is not a person, and it seems to them that a few small items from a shipment that may exceed a thousand tons is not likely to cause deprivation to anyone. Baggage and other personal belongings are usually not pilfered, and the personal belongings of other longshoremen and the ship's crew are ordinarily quite safe from theft by longshoremen.

Stealing a worker's tools is thought to be the most reprehensible sort of misbehavior because like most workers, longshoremen regard a man's tools as his means for earning a living. On one occasion I witnessed, a carpenter's tools were stolen on a Dutch ship, apparently by a longshoreman. Rather than closing ranks and refusing even to discuss the matter as they normally do when one of them is accused of theft, all of the longshoremen aboard joined the carpenter in an attempt to find and recover his tools.

Liquor, transistor radios, and other relatively small and desirable objects are always subject to pilfering, and the longshoremen are more than ingenious in obtaining them. Moreover shipping companies have not always shown a great concern for the security of the cargo in their ships. More recently, however, competition has greatly increased the zeal with which these companies protect their cargo, bringing them into direct conflict with the established habits of the longshoremen. One of the more successful precautions employed to discourage the extensive pilfering of liquor was the practice of ships' mates of opening a case of liquor and distributing it to the longshoremen in the gang. This was fairly successful because the longshoremen felt that it was not really proper to steal from such a congenial fellow and the degree of intoxication produced made it much easier for the mate to observe their activities and stop any attempts to pilfer the cargo. More liquor was usually lost when the mate attempted to keep the longshoremen from getting any of it than when a small amount was distributed.

On one occasion, when a gang of longshoremen were discharging whiskey, under the watchful eyes of a mate who insisted that they were not going to steal any of the whiskey, it appeared that the longshoremen might fail in their attempts to steal it. However, when the last slingloads of whiskey were being loaded, the mate turned his back to one of the longshoremen just long enough for him to slip several pints under a piece of waterproof paper. Knowing that the mate would search the hatch before leaving, one of the longshoremen unzipped his fly and urinated on the paper. The mate did search the hatch, but the one place he did not look was under the waterproof paper. The urine, of course, had never touched the bottles.

Another method used to steal pure alcohol is also interesting in its ingenuity. The alcohol was shipped in steel drums which the shipping company obviously believed impervious to pilferage. This did present an obstacle to the longshoremen but not an insurmountable one. They waited until the alcohol was buried under six feet of other cargo, and then, one of the longshoremen, carrying a hammer and a two-by-four into which a large spike had been driven, slid down between the internal ribs of the ship. He drove the spike through the two by four and into the side of the steel drum a few inches from the top and then filled various containers that the other men passed down to him. When the hole in the barrel no longer gave forth alcohol, the spike was driven into the barrel a few inches below the original hole. One man, feeling limited by the size of container he could carry on his person, worked out a method for carrying a gallon at a time. He used clear half gallon jugs which he filled to the very top so that there would be no visible bubble of air at the neck and simply walked out of the dock with the apparently empty jugs in plain sight of the guards on the dock.

The tradition of pilfering is so well established that many longshoremen feel that they have a right to pilfer and resent attempts to stop them as unjust. That this is well recognized by the longshoremen themselves is evidenced by the actions of a longshoreman who shipped his personal automobile from Hawaii to the West Coast: he placed a note inside the windshield stating that the auto belonged to a longshore-man and member of the ILWU. The car was handled with special care and nothing was stolen from it. One longshoreman in the gang unloading the auto stated that this man "certainly knew his brothers."

It must, however, be stressed that pilfering is strictly part of longshore work behavior. There are out-and-out thieves among the longshoremen, and most of the men know who they are and do not trust them, but well-known "cargo inspectors" are often scrupulously honest in all other ways....

Longshore Subculture

The subculture of the Portland longshore group probably bears a greater resemblance to that of other Oregonians than to any other class of people in the country. Oregon forms a sort of cultural enclave even within the context of the Northwest due to its pattern of immigration, low population, and industrial structure; and the longshoremen would seem to form yet another enclave within the state-wide enclave. The longshoremen share many of the features of the "stable working class," but there are several differences in the accent placed on some features, and others lie completely outside the purvey of this class.

The extreme accent placed on physical courage and strength would seem unusual for an ordinary working class group, although it is not too dissimilar from that of the miners. This value on courage as well as the willingness to engage in physical aggression is probably related to the day-to-day need to face a good deal of physical danger in the workplace. It could be accounted for as a sort of survival of the frontier period; but there are men in the group who are relatively recent migrants from the East and Midwest, and they display the same values and behavior.

The occupational genealogies of the longshoremen are not what one would expect from blue-collar workers. If the longshoremen, loggers, and farmers are deleted from the list there are for the most part only businessman, professionals, semiprofessionals, and skilled workers. There are certain important similarities between these occupations: they involve certain sets of skills that are highly transferable. The persons having these skills are not obliged to live in one particular location or maintain an affiliation with any one business firm in order to earn a livelihood. To the contrary, such persons tend to be highly mobile. Another feature of the occupational histories of the longshore families is that they tend to present mirror images between the grandparent and grandchild generations. Again, this is only true if farmers are not included. This would seem to indicate a great deal of occupational mobility within certain specific types of occupations over time.

The depth of family involvement, making hunting and fishing trips into family affairs, and the very real stability of the longshoremen's families again seems unusual. This is very likely a reflection of the lack of some of the strains of typical blue-collar life deriving from the fear of the lay-off and deep financial problems rather than an intrinsic characteristic of the group. Another factor that contributes, to some unknown degree, to a stable family life is the great stability of residence and occupation. Most of the longshore families have deep local roots and few members of the longshore group ever leave the area or the industry for any length of time. Thus, kin networks are more extensive than they would otherwise be, and this again contributes to the stability of the group and the ability to engage in family affairs.

The deep value placed on individualism, personal independence, and freedom from a rigid work regime is one of the most striking features of the group. It is doubtful that this value has any relationship to any factors other than the old line American and Scandinavian ancestry of the overwhelming majority of the longshoremen, and that none of these men or their immediate ancestors have ever found it necessary to submit to the rigid way of life imposed by machine production and the assembly line. They are very aware that other workers must submit to these abhorrent conditions, but rather than feeling sympathy toward these workers, the longshoremen are much more likely to express contempt.

The extra-work economic activities of the longshoremen again do not fit within the framework of the "stable working class" subculture. Although the nature of this set of activities is quite different from that of other workers, the motivation for such economic strivings is even more at variance with the blue-collar norm. The agricultural portion of the economic activities of the group is not especially noteworthy since this seems to be common to the entire Northwest. Many of their other economic activities are also related to the nature of the area and its regional subculture. The motivation for engaging in extra-work economic activities may also be to some degree due to regional factors, but there is little doubt that it also differs sharply from the motivation of most blue-collar workers. The motivation is quite simply to contribute to the economic welfare of the longshoreman and his family, although there are a few men who seem totally engrossed in acquiring wealth as an end in itself. There is no concern with gaining social status or prestige, which is the usual reported motivation for blue-collar businessmen. But this may well be a false dichotomy, because the longshoremen tend to be native [born] Americans and nearly all of the reported cases of blue-collar workers seeking social status have dealt with groups of recent immigrant backgrounds, and immigrants are nearly always more concerned with social mobility than are native [born] Americans.

The longshoremen's attitudes toward race are unusual for any reported group of workers in that they are not deeply concerned with race *per se*....The tendency toward nepotism excluded everyone but longshoremen's kinsmen. In other words, it was not directed at blacks but at anyone who was not a member of the longshore group. The most important factor in the resistance to integration more recently has been the desire to protect their traditional recruitment procedures.

The forms of joking behavior reported in other industrial contexts neither resemble the longshore form, except in the vaguest manner, nor fit the original definition of joking behavior given by Radcliffe-Brown. Some form of "joking behavior" may be a common attribute of most social groups, but the extremely rough form of longshore joking behavior may be unique to longshoremen and a few other groups of roughneck workers such as loggers and construction workers. Certainly there is no mention of such behavior for either blue- or white-collar workers in the literature.

The most important of the longshoremen's values is the deeply felt need to manage their leisure time. And this ties them ever more tightly to the union and union affairs, for it is only the union that shelters them from the demands of the employers. This desire to tailor their work and leisure time to fit their personal requirements is not a feature of the longshore group that only came into being with the establishment of the union. It has been a factor on the waterfront since before 1922. The foremost aim of the waterfront employers in 1922 was to establish a "dependable" work force, and this goal, in the sense of maintaining a work force that would always show up for work on demand, was never fully realized. Even the "star men" occasionally failed to show up for work, and the employers were often forced to fall back on casual labor to fill the need for longshoremen. If this one feature of longshore life were removed, the rest of the way of life would soon disappear. It is this management of potential leisure time, combined with the right to "talk back," that the longshoremen refer to when they speak of "freedom and independence." Without this one essential feature, the longshoremen could no longer successfully manage their extra-work economic activities, and there would no longer be as great an incentive to engage in union affairs. Again, the avocations which require the ability to leave the job for extended periods of time would no longer be possible, and the role of the father as an almost omnipresent member of the nuclear family unit would be destroyed with possible detrimental consequences for the entire family structure. It is extremely doubtful that the present longshoremen could adjust to such a change in their way of life without extreme dislocations, and it is certain that any collective bargaining trend that appeared likely to deprive them of this one most salient feature of waterfront employment would lead to a strike.

The absolute necessity of balancing one's work and leisure time in a useful and productive manner is one of the most salient features of pre-industrial life. This feature has been preserved in the Portland longshore group because of the nature of the occupation and the union. In this respect, as in many ways, the Portland longshoremen may be said to represent an old, pre-factory, predominantly native [born] American substratum with a set of values and attitudes very much like those of the Anglo-Saxon elite of skilled workers that dominated the working-class hierarchy of the nineteenth century. This is not to say that they are not a completely modern, urbanized group in every other respect, but only that the set of values and attitudes detailed above, and some of their consequences, are related to and derive from the historical antecedents of the longshore group.

Crimes Against Health and Safety

Murder in the Workplace

Nancy Frank

CASE STUDY QUESTIONS

1. Which of the individual, workplace, and societal influences on occupational deviance apply to the situation described here?

2. Which of the general theories of deviance might lend insight into this incident?

3. Why did executives do nothing to improve the health and safety conditions?

4. How did the immigrant status of the employees influence their potential for exploitation?

Stefan Golab, a Polish immigrant, worked for Film Recovery Systems, Inc., a firm involved in recycling silver from used photographic plates. The recycling process used by Film Recovery involved soaking used X-ray plates in a cyanide solution. Golab and other workers in the Film Recovery plant "chipped the film, mixed the cyanide granules with water in the vats, stirred the chips in the potent mixture for three days with long rakes, scooped the spent—and cyanide soaked—film chips out of the vat with a giant vacuum cleaner, cleaned the tank in

Source: From *Crimes Against Health and Safety,* (pp. 21–26) by Nancy Frank, 1985, Albany: Harrow and Heston. Copyright 1985 by Harrow and Heston. Reprinted with permission.

preparation for the next load, and scraped the silver from the terminal plates on which it had been recovered" (Owens 1985, 31).

This recycling process is conducted safely by several firms across the country. Because of the dangers of cyanide, which is highly poisonous if swallowed, inhaled, or absorbed through the skin, workers must be protected with rubber gloves, boots, and aprons, respirators, and effective ventilation.

At the Film Recovery plant, however, these normal precautions were not taken. Workers were given only paper face masks and cloth gloves. Ventilation was so poor inside the plant that the air was thick with the odor of cyanide and a "yellowish haze" of cyanide fumes hung inside the plant (Nelson, 1985, 1). Workers frequently became ill, going outside the plant to vomit, and then returning to their work over the fuming cyanide vats.

On February 10, 1985, Stefan Golab staggered from the cyanide tank he was working over, stumbled to the adjacent locker room, and collapsed. Some of his fellow workers dragged him outside and called an ambulance. When the ambulance arrived back at the hospital, Golab was dead. An autopsy was performed to determine the cause of death. When the medical examiner made the first incision, a strong almond-like smell came out of the body, indicating cyanide poisoning. Subsequent blood tests revealed that Golab had a blood cyanide level of 3.45 micrograms per milliliter, a lethal dose.

The autopsy findings led to an eight month investigation, resulting in the indictment of five Film Recovery executives on charges of murder and the indictment of Film Recovery Systems, Inc., and two related corporations on charges of manslaughter. Under Illinois law, "A person who kills an individual without lawful justification commits murder if, in performing the acts which cause the death...He knows that such acts create a strong probability of death or great bodily harm to that individual or another..." The indictment became the first recorded case of an employer being charged with murder for the work related death of an employee.

The investigation of Film Recovery Systems and subsequent court testimony revealed a grim scenario. A Cook County Hospital study of Golab's fellow workers, which was undertaken following his death, found that "at least two-thirds of Film Recovery's workers suffered ten times a month or more from each of four major symptoms of cyanide intoxication—dizziness, the taste of bitter almonds in the mouth, headaches and nausea and vomiting" (Owens, 1985). When workers complained to the foreman and plant manager about feeling ill, they were told to "go outside so you can have some fresh air."

Many workers were not aware that they were working with cyanide. According to a former bookkeeper for Film Recovery, illegal aliens were chosen to work in the plant. Because they could not read English, they could not read the warning labels on the drums of cyanide. Several employees observed skull-and-crossbones markings being painted or burned off the drums. Because company managers had never informed workers of the hazards of working with the chemical, workers who did see the

skull-and-crossbones assumed that the chemical was dangerous only if it was swallowed. They did not know that it could be lethal if inhaled or absorbed through the skin.

At trial, the defense argued that conditions inside the plant were safe. Moreover, they argued, if it was unsafe, the defendants were not aware that it was unsafe. Finally, the defense argued that Golab died of causes unrelated to the plant conditions, challenging the medical examiner's findings and suggesting that perhaps Golab had eaten apple cores, and the cyanide in his blood came from the apple seeds. To corroborate the defendants' assertions that they did not believe that conditions in the plant were dangerous, defense counsel indicated that on several occasions the defendants had arranged to have family members work in the plant. The defense also noted that the plant had been given a "clean bill of health" by local and federal inspectors prior to Golab's death.

The failure of regulating agencies to discover the frightful conditions inside the Film Recovery plant is an unfortunate but interesting sidelight to this story. A federal OSHA inspector had visited the offices of Film Recovery, Inc., only two and one-half months before Golab collapsed from cyanide poisoning. The inspector never conducted an inspection of the plant, however, because of Reagan administration guidelines which prohibit inspectors from conducting on-site inspections unless an examination of company safety records reveals a poor accident record.

Although Film Recovery employees were frequently sent home to rest when they became too dizzy and nauseated to work, the company's records indicated little lost time. Consequently, the inspector did not conduct an inspection of the plant (Owens, 1985). In a subsequent inspection following Golab's death, OSHA issued two citations for lack of safety equipment and ultimately fined Film Recovery $2,425.

At the close of the trial, Judge Ronald J.D. Banks convicted three executives of murder and fourteen counts of reckless conduct, and convicted two corporations of involuntary manslaughter and fourteen counts of reckless conduct. In supporting his decision, Judge Banks found that

> …the conditions under which the workers in the plant performed their duties was [sic] totally unsafe. There was an insufficient amount of safety equipment on the premises. There were no safety instructions given to the workers. The workers were not adequately warned of the hazards and dangers of working with cyanide.

The judge also found that the three convicted defendants were "totally knowledgeable" of the hazards of cyanide. Judge Banks reiterated the evidence substantiating his finding that each of the three executives knew the dangers of cyanide and understood that their failure to provide proper protective equipment created a strong probability of death or great bodily harm. He continued:

> Steven O'Neil [defendant and president of Film Recovery] testified…, and I quote, "I was aware of all of the hazardous nature of cyanide." He knew hydrogen cyanide gas was present. He knew hydrogen cyanide gas, if inhaled, could be fatal.
>
> Charles Kirschbaum [defendant and plant manager] saw workers vomiting. He was given a Material Safety Data Sheet. He read the label, and he knew what it said. He said that he did not wear the same equipment the workers did because he did not do the same work as the workers, even though he testified to the contrary.
>
> Daniel Rodriguez [defendant and plant foreman] knew the workers got sick at the plant. He testified to that. He could read the label, and he read it many times.

Each of the three defendants was sentenced to twenty-five years in prison and each corporation was fined $10,000. (One of the original five indicted executives successfully fought extradition from Utah and another had the charges against him dismissed halfway through the trial.)

The central issue presented by this case is whether, as a matter of policy, it is desirable to equate the behaviors of the Film Recovery executives with murder and to punish it as such. Commentators have referred to the charge of murder in this case as unprecedented, scary, and wild. Some commentators, such as Ralph Nader and Christopher Stone, hailed the verdict as an appropriate application of the criminal law. Nader applauded the verdict, saying, "There was a courageous prosecutor and a prudent judge who applied the law to the facts, irrespective of the fact that the defendants had three-piece suits" (Gibson 1985, 2). Christopher Stone, an expert on corporate responsibility and corporate crime, commented, "I think this case will properly embolden prosecutors to bring corporate criminal cases, and other judges to stop looking the other way" (Gibson 1985, 1).

Others were more skeptical about the desirability of a murder conviction and expressed concern about how this verdict would change the traditional legal concept of murder. Richard Epstein, a University of Chicago Law School professor, noted, "One has had to show more than just knowledge of a risk of death, but also a hope or intent that the death would come to pass. Knowledge of risk has not been generally sufficient." He continued, commenting on the potential impact of the case, "There is the potential here, given the way most industrial accidents take place, that you'd have a credible shot of pursuing a murder case. It would present a very radical change, in nuance and practice, in the criminal law" (Gibson 1985, 2).

Perhaps the question should be put this way. Is there a difference between a murderer who exposed a person to risk of harm hoping that the person would die and a murderer who exposed a person to the same risk of harm, but hoped that no injury would occur? And what of the murderer who exposed a person to risk of harm, and simply did not care whether the person was injured or not? The latter depiction is closest to that made by Judge Banks above. He convicted the defendants of murder—murder by indifference.

Conclusion

Despite the success of Cook County prosecutors in the Film Recovery case, prosecuting crimes against health and safety under conventional criminal laws, such as homicide statutes, remains a rare event with doubtful prospects for success. The application of conventional statutes to behavior affecting health and safety is still a legal gamble in a very high stakes game. Although it can be argued that the criminal law serves as an added deterrent, relative to other available civil remedies, it is not clear whether the extra deterrent effect is proportional to the tremendous costs of prosecuting such cases. The more important effect is moral and symbolic. These symbolic values are not as clearly communicated through modern, specialized laws that deal with health and safety problems in technical terms. Though criminal penalties may attach to many of these specialized crimes against health and safety, the stigma associated with those charges is not the same as the stigma that attaches to a conviction for manslaughter, murder, or reckless homicide.

REFERENCES

Cullen, F. T., W. J. Maakestad, and G. Cavender 1984. The Ford Pinto Case and Beyond: Corporate Crime, Moral Boundaries, and the Criminal Sanction. In *Corporations as Criminals*, ed. E. Hochstedler. Beverly Hills, California: Sage Publications.

Dowie, M. 1977. Pinto Madness. *Mother Jones Magazine* (Sept–Oct), 18–24, 28–32.

Gibson, R. 1985. Illegal Aliens Picked for Cyanide Work, Bookkeeper Testifies. *Chicago Tribune*, April 24, 1985.

Maakestad, W. J. 1983. *State v. Ford Motor Co.:* Constitutional, Libertarian, and Moral Perspectives. *Saint Louis University Law Journal*, 27, 857–880.

Nelson, D. 1985. Foul Haze Veiled Factory Death. *The Daily Herald*, Palatine Inverness Edition. April 16, 1, 3.

Owens, P. 1985. Death of Worker Puts Factory Safety on Trial. *Newsday*. June 6, 1, 31.

Strobel, L. P. 1980. *Reckless Homicide? Ford's Pinto Trial*. South Bend, Indiana: And Books.

Personal Fouls

Peter Golenbock

CASE STUDY QUESTIONS

1. How can the concepts of rationalization, denial, and profit motive be applied to the basketball culture and the actions of the basketball coach?

2. Could Jim Valvano have done what he did in a vacuum?

3. Where does Valvano fall in Merton's typology of deviants?

4. How does the relative aspect of deviance come into play in this case? In whose eyes was Valvano deviant? What do we learn about the support he found for actions that others describe as illegal, unethical, or unprofessional?

5. What motivated Valvano to behave as he did? Is there any evidence that work culture, opportunity structure, and occupation-related stress played a role?

The Stakes

...[North Carolina State University basketball coach Jim Valvano] had a good reason for being so upset over the team's loss to Tampa. His players were messing up his grand plan for the season. As athletic director, one of Valvano's goals—and the goal of most athletic directors—was to mine the

Source: "Personal Fouls," Peter Golenbock from *Personal Fouls: The Broken Promises and Shattered Dreams of Big Money Basketball* (166–169, 34–46, 173–180), 1989, New York. Carroll & Graf Publishers, copyright 1989 by Carroll & Graf. Reprinted with permission.

gold at the end of the college basketball season: the $520,000 per team given to each of the four teams to reach the Final Four of the 1986-1987 NCAA national tournament.

He had said it often. "All that matters is getting to the Final Four. That is what I live for."

College basketball used to be about school spirit and cheering for the boys and beating the archrival, but with the age of television and now the superfund age of cable television, there is simply too much money being tossed around for any athletic director to ignore it.

Before TV, it used to be that all an athletic director had to do was field a representative team; you'd still draw full houses in your home arena. But with television doling out millions of dollars for the best teams to play on the tube, being representative is no longer good enough. Just as most high school players want the chance to be seen on national television, athletic directors want their teams to be seen on national television. There are two reasons. The first is that television visibility enhances recruiting tremendously. The second is that a team playing often on national TV stands to gain hundreds of thousands of dollars for its war chest. A team that makes it to the Final Four of the NCAA championship...well, there's riches in them there networks.

When Valvano composes his schedule, reportedly he is trying to figure out how his team can end the season with twenty wins out of the twenty-seven games it plays during the regular season. For with twenty wins, the team is guaranteed to get an invitation to the NCAA championships. If the team fails to win twenty games during the regular season, it can make up the difference in the Atlantic Coast Conference championships. If it wins seventeen games or less, to get to the NCAAs it must win the ACC championship outright, since the ACC winner automatically gets a bid to play in the national championships.

Valvano once explained his grand plan to John Simonds. According to Simonds, Valvano figured that in the ACC his team would probably lose twice to Carolina, once to Duke away, once to Georgia Tech away, and also to several of the national powers he routinely schedules in order to keep the Wolfpack on national television: Navy, Oklahoma, Louisville, Kansas, and DePaul. To win the magic twenty, the team had to win half of its tough games and roll over all of the pushovers including East Tennessee, Western Carolina, Duquesne, Asheville, Winthrop, Brooklyn College, Chicago State, and Tampa.

Losing to Tampa threatened his grand plan.

It is not easy to know how much money the N.C. State basketball team earns for the athletic department and for Valvano.

The athletic department budget comes solely from revenue-generating sports (basketball and football) and from donations to its Wolfpack Club, the alumni- and civic-sponsored group that funds scholarships and repairs facilities. Not a nickel of state funds goes to N.C. State athletics. Since the funding isn't public, the books are not open to the public.

While budget information is kept as secret as budgets for CIA covert missions, Valvano once discussed the subject with Andy Kennedy. He made it clear that basketball, not football, was N.C. State's meal ticket, the one sport that supported the rest of the athletic program.

"We used to have long layovers in the Atlanta airport," said Kennedy, "and sometimes Valvano would talk to us. I can remember that our football team had just gone eight, three, and one and played Virginia Tech in the Peach Bowl, the best record they ever had—ACC football stinks—but we were winning games and were ranked eighteenth in the country. And yet, with all of the fans we drew and the money we got from the bowl appearance, Valvano said we only cleared maybe five hundred ninety-five thousand dollars, because the football team has one hundred fifteen guys on scholarship, you have to feed them all, buy equipment for all of them, transport them to the games, and you can see it costs so much because of the sheer numbers.

"Well, there are fourteen of us on the basketball team. That same year Valvano said that on just our TV contract and our gate at Reynolds, we cleared over two-point-six million. We made five times more money with eight times fewer players."

And that doesn't include the torrent of money that comes pouring in from the 11,000 loyal members of the Wolfpack Club, which raises millions for N.C. State athletics.

The Wolfpack Club was founded in 1936, and it does the same thing similar organizations on college campuses all across America do—it funds scholarships for the athletes and does what it can to "promote and support the athletics program."

At the universities where such clubs don't exist, the donor gives the money to the college, and the college spends it where it needs it most. By giving to the Wolfpack Club—or whatever the local sports booster club may be—a donor can show unlimited generosity to athletics without being concerned that the money might go into the college treasury and be spent for other reasons—say, on education.

The Wolfpack Club has grown so large that there are thirteen full-time paid staff members who handle the operation, and another 400 volunteers who help solicit funds. The Wolfpack Club acts like any alumni fund. The difference is that the money going to an alumni fund provides chairs for visiting professors and scholarships for students. The purpose of the Wolfpack Club is to raise money for the athletic department only.

How much is raised? The guess is that it's in the millions.

When a member of the Athletics Council, the school watchdog over the athletic department, was asked whether it reviewed the Wolfpack Club budget, he said, "I can't remember the budget from the Wolfpack Club ever coming to us, because it's private, separate from the university. They raise the money and use it as they see fit."

The one piece of information that is public is Valvano's basic salary: That is public information because his salary is paid by the state of North Carolina as part of the funding for the college. He is paid $200,000 a year to be basketball coach and athletic director. He does, however, make much, much more than that.

He several times bragged to John Simonds, as though he couldn't quite believe it himself, "I make a million and a half dollars a year."

The biggest chunk of outside dough he gets is from Nike. Valvano makes his players wear Nike shoes and athletic wear during State's games at home and on the road. He gets paid $150,000 for them to serve as walking advertisements for Nike. They get free shoes and clothes.

In addition, Valvano gets money from his weekly hour-long TV show and his daily five-minute radio show, and he has earned revenue by becoming pitchman for Mountain Dew soft drink, Ronzoni, a health club, a bank, South Square Hyundai of Durham, and the public transportation system. He also signed a lucrative contract to give motivational speeches to employees of the North Carolina-based Hardee's hamburger chain at $4,500 per speech.

There's more. Valvano owns a summer basketball camp for 900 campers a summer (300 kids a week for three weeks) at $240 a head, and he gets most of those kids to pay $25 a pop to have their picture taken with him at the end of the week.

After he won the 1983 NCAA championship, he unveiled his own line of "Coach V" sportswear. Offering t-shirts, jogging suits, and color-coordinated sweater, shirt, and slack ensembles made of polyester, his label was carried throughout North Carolina at Belk department stores.

Valvano also has investments that are kept private under his JTV Enterprises. His magnificent home on Glasgow Road in the suburb of Cary is located in an ultra-exclusive section of town and is valued in the mid-six figures.

But like all college basketball coaches, Valvano lives on a tightrope. The money comes surging in only if his team keeps winning. In such an uncertain profession, a coach must keep up the pressure on his players not to let down, lest he end up like so many other former college coaches—even some of the best college coaches—teaching high school and coaching pimply-faced adolescents in the boondocks.

Losing to Tampa, then, meant more than just losing a ballgame to a bad team. It threatened a season he had worked hard to build. College basketball is no longer a sport. It has become a big multi-million-dollar business. It is the coaches who suffer the most under the strain of the pressure. It is no wonder coaches like Valvano are desperate to win.

Recruitment

Despite the dramatic, popular success of the North Carolina State basketball team, there were rumblings of dismay and disgust coming from a minority of faculty members and administrators whose emphasis was education first and sports second—educators who were concerned that the reputation of the university was being sullied by Coach Valvano's disregard of school standards in his recruitment of players.

If Valvano heard the criticism, he made it clear he didn't care. Valvano's goal, as it was at Iona, was to get his team to the Final Four, and past experience had taught him well that the only way to get there was to recruit the finest basketball talent the high schools had to offer. He demonstrated that he was determined to go after the best talent—regardless of academic ability or character.

In a speech in the spring of 1982, Valvano declared he would recruit as he saw fit and asserted that no one in the university had the power to stop him if they wanted to.

Stated Valvano, "We're not even really part of the school any more, anyway. I work for the N.C. State Athletic Association. That has nothing to do with the university. Our funding is totally independent. You think the chancellor is going to tell me what to do? Who to take into school or not to take into school? I doubt it."

Valvano's statement was cited on the editorial page of the New York *Times*, which asked, "How many scandals must erupt before the reputation of higher education, or at least of individual schools, is compromised?"

The first Valvano recruits who raised professors' eyebrows were two players from his first recruiting class, key members of the 1983 NCAA championships, Cozell McQueen and Lorenzo Charles, the former six feet ten inches, the other six feet eight inches, towering masses of muscle but highly suspect in terms of their suitability for a college curriculum.

McQueen, described as a "lovely guy" by friends, was functionally illiterate. On the day after the death of Maryland star Lenny Bias, Cozell sat with his roommate, trying to read the newspaper about Lenny. He asked his roommate the meaning of one word after another, getting stuck on so many words that finally his roommate took the newspaper and read the rest of the article to him. Cozell had loved Bias, a friend, and as the roommate read the account of Bias's accidental death from a drug overdose, Cozell cried.

Lorenzo Charles publicly embarrassed the university as a result of a lapse in social etiquette. The hulking giant was loitering in one of the university's public parking lots with a few of his friends when he noticed a Domino's pizza delivery boy taking two large pepperoni pizzas to one of the dorms. The talk around campus was that Lorenzo accosted the delivery boy and told him, "Hey, pal, give me those pizzas, or I'm going to beat the shit out of you." "Sure, man, just don't pound me," responded the deliveryman. Said Charles, "Give me those pizzas, you punk," and he took them and departed.

The delivery boy called the Raleigh police and based on his description—black and about as tall as a skyscraper—it wasn't difficult for the authorities to figure out the identity of the culprit.

In court, Charles was handed a ten-year suspended sentence and was ordered to perform 300 hours of community service.

Members of the North Carolina State administration and faculty were mortified that one of their students would gain national attention for the university in this manner.

Valvano tried to put a positive spin on Charles' behavior, declaring that the incident "may have turned his life around." Valvano cited Winston Churchill. "'Greatness,'" said Valvano, quoting Sir Winston, "'also brings on great responsibilities.' Lorenzo has learned that because he is an athlete, he must be responsible for his actions and, because he is an athlete, his actions will receive more attention."

He did not discuss his responsibility in bringing Charles to the university. If a coach recruits a player who has a high school reputation for avoiding the books and for hanging out with a bad crowd, no matter how tall or talented he is, trouble for the university lies right around the corner. Wasn't he concerned that Charles' behavior was a reflection on his win-at-all-costs philosophy?

Apparently not, because embarrassment was to repeat itself with the recruiting of another gigantic, talented academic Sahara by the name of Chris Washburn. Washburn, considered the single most promising high school athlete in the entire U.S. of A., stood six-foot-eleven and weighed 255 pounds as a high school senior. He was an unusually mobile athlete for a manchild of his size, cobralike on defense and able to dribble in traffic and dunk over his outmanned opponents, leading his first high school, Hickory, to a two-year record of 48 and 5, moving on to Fork Union Military Academy, where he led that team to a 22 and 5 record his junior year, and then finishing at Laurinburg Institute with an 18 and 2 record—a four-year record of eighty-eight victories and twelve losses.

Despite his switching from one school to another, the experts and scouts managed to keep up with him, as Washburn was named to the *Parade* magazine All American team for three consecutive years, only the fourth high school player in history to achieve that distinction. As a senior he averaged 30 points, 17 rebounds, and nine blocked shots a game, was named Co-Player of the Year, and was selected for the prestigious McDonald's All Star Team.

Chris Washburn knew at an early age he would go to college and ultimately to the pros—at age nine to be exact. That's when he got his first letter of college recruitment. From that time on, he was the target of hundreds of colleges, even though all along he displayed a marked lack of interest in doing any school work. He wasn't stupid or slow.

In fact, he had a sharp mind and at times displayed a charming wit. He simply refused to study. To him, learning was not related to his goal—playing professional basketball. Washburn reportedly had to leave Hickory High after his sophomore year because he failed driver education and phys ed during summer school, making him ineligible to play his junior year.

He moved on to Fork Union (Virginia) Military Academy, where he again performed dismally, and so again he changed alma maters, to Laurinburg (North Carolina) Institute, where questions were raised about his academic eligibility and where jaundiced eyes wondered who had bought him a new $10,000 Subaru.

Because Valvano had won the NCAA national championship, he could make Washburn a promise no other coach could make him: If you come to North Carolina State, you will start at center and you will have an opportunity to lead State to *another* national championship.

If anyone doubted Valvano could get any student he wished into N.C. state, those doubts were put to rest when Chris Washburn was accepted as a student. When he was admitted, rumors among concerned faculty members were rampant that a figure high in the school administration had ordered Washburn's admittance. Later it would be revealed in court that Washburn had scored but a 470 combined on his SATs! Concerned faculty members were appalled and embarrassed.

Washburn's lack of knowledge was appalling. At State, Washburn was getting tutored for a geography test. The tutor asked, "What is the country directly south of the United States?" Washburn thought a minute and said, "Canada." The tutor said, "No, they speak Spanish. Maybe that will help." Washburn responded, "Spain?"

When he was asked what country was directly north of the U.S., his answer was, "England?"

The NCAA looked into Washburn's recruitment. It, too, wondered whether Washburn's car had something to do with his choice of college, but it failed to turn up evidence of any violations.

Though Washburn and another of Valvano's prize recruits, Nate McMillan, a junior college All American transfer from Chowan Junior College in Murfreesburg, North Carolina, were joining Ernie Myers, Lorenzo Charles, and Cozell McQueen, Valvano knew that the inexperience of the team would probably keep it from reaching the Final Four in 1984. His big three from the Sloan era—Thurl Bailey, Sidney Lowe, and Derreck Whittenberg—had moved on, but Valvano was confident that from Washburn's sophomore season on, his recruiting efforts would be paying off. He was certain he'd get so many blue-chip high school All Americans to commit to him that the Wolfpack might be the next UCLA, winning the national championship year after year.

"For one year it will be a struggle; we'll be on hold," said Valvano just before Washburn's freshman year in November of 1983. "These young kids will develop and will be joined by some real great prospects. I think we'll be in the Top Ten for at least the next four years."

The problem for Jim Valvano was that Chris Washburn was a social deviant, and at almost seven feet and 260 pounds, he was a danger to Raleigh society. The catalyst that set him off, as the students around him well knew, was cocaine.

Early in his freshman year he strolled into one of the dormitories and rode the elevator to a girl's floor. The students who saw him said he looked "as high as a kite." He wandered into one of the girl's rooms, unplugged her telephone, and attempted to walk out with it.

The girl, who stood up to about his waist, went running up to him and screamed, "I don't care who you are, you'd better give me back my fucking phone or I'm going to have your ass in the slammer."

Washburn was so impressed with her moxie, he handed her back the phone.

A couple weeks later Washburn beat up a coed, was arrested, convicted, and placed on probation.

Despite his social difficulties, Washburn started at center when the basketball season began in November, and with his six-foot-eleven frame sandwiched between the six-foot-ten McQueen and the six-foot-eight Lorenzo Charles, the Wolfpack looked like an NBA team as it opened the season beating Houston by 12 in a rematch and then going on to win six of its first seven games. All he had to do was remain eligible, and N.C. State would have a real shot at another NCAA championship.

On December 18, 1984, Washburn visited the ground-floor room of William West, a sophomore football player with whom he had gone to school at Fork Union Military Academy. West lived down the hall from Washburn at the College Inn, the dormitory for North Carolina State's athletes. Washburn noticed West's five-piece stereo system and asked him how much it had cost. West replied, "About eight hundred dollars." Said Washburn, "Don't forget to take it home during Christmas vacation."

The next night, according to police, someone opened up the window to West's bedroom, climbed in, and removed a turntable, amplifier, tape deck, and two large stereo speakers. When West's roommate, Jeff Davis, returned about midnight, he saw that the stereo system was missing and noticed footprints the size of Bigfoot on the ledge outside the open window.

The roommate called the Raleigh police, not the North Carolina State campus police. Had he done the latter, Washburn might have avoided the trouble that was to follow, as the investigation might have remained internal. But because West called the Raleigh police, the incident was written into the night log, fair game for snoopy reporters.

When the Raleigh police arrived, they took a cast of the gigantic footprint on the windowsill and fingerprints from the room. The foot and fingerprints belonged to Washburn.

In a twenty-seven-minute interrogation, the nineteen-year-old Washburn at first denied knowledge of the theft. But police investigator D. A. Weingarten countered by calling him a liar. He told Washburn, "Chris, I'm telling you like it is. This is the real world now. Coach Valvano can't protect you." After Weingarten convinced Washburn he had enough evidence to prove his guilt, Washburn finally admitted he had taken the stereo, calling the episode "a stupid prank."

"I was going to give it back," Washburn said. "I was playing a joke on a friend."

But when asked where he had taken the stereo system, Washburn told Weingarten, "I took it to a guy in Durham. I can get it back."

On December 23, powerless to get Washburn out of his mess, Valvano suspended his star from the team for the rest of the season. Valvano made no mention of the burglary charges, saying only that Wash-burn had "personal problems" that made it inappropriate for him to continue on the team.

Valvano discussed the impact Washburn's loss would have upon his team.

"Before this happened," said Valvano, "we were a legitimate top ten team. Now we're mediocre. We're exactly back where we were last year." In discussing the year-long suspension, Valvano made himself seem the stern disciplinarian by saying, "I didn't do this to appease university or country officials. This was my decision.

"I could have waited until the January hearing and let him play all season. But I know Chris. I realize that he has yet to mature. He needs to understand where he is and where he's going. He needs to realize that he doesn't walk this earth alone, that his actions affect many other people. Chris needs to step back from the spotlight."

On January 8, 1985, Judge Narley Cashwell rejected a defense motion for dismissal, despite the contention that Washburn stole the stereo equipment in order to "play a joke" on West. He also refused to reduce charges from second-degree burglary—a felony—to something less. Washburn was facing a minimum sentence of fourteen years, with time off for good behavior. The possibility existed that Washburn would not only miss the season, but most of his prime as well.

The case went to trial, creating embarrassment for both Washburn and North Carolina State—including the revelation that Washburn had scored a dismally low combined total of 470 out of 1600 on his SATs (you are handed 400 points for signing your name). Washburn's attorney struck a deal with the prosecution. Washburn pleaded guilty to three misdemeanor charges and was sentenced by Wake County Superior Court Judge J. Milton Reid to forty-six hours in the local jail—to be served on the first anniversary of the theft—given a six-year suspended sentence, and placed on five years probation.

In return, Washburn agreed to the following conditions:

1. Pay $1,000 to the state's victims' compensation fund.
2. Undergo mental health counseling by a practitioner appointed by the court.
3. Undergo drug and alcohol therapy and thirty hours of confrontational therapy. (No mention was ever made of his drug habit throughout this entire episode, and even after he was ordered to undergo drug treatment, no one thought to ask why.)
4. Donate two hundred hours of his time to a center for mentally retarded children.

5. Perform one hundred hours of "heavy housecleaning tasks" at a home for persons on parole.

6. Do maintenance work for twenty hours for the Raleigh police department.

7. Surrender his driver's license for ninety days.

8. Allow himself to be subject to an ongoing search warrant "at reasonable times."

9. Avoid use or possession of illegal substances and stay away from other users.

10. Be gainfully employed the next two summer vacations.

11. Make a visit to the state prison.

Even without Washburn, the 1984–85 N.C. State basketball team was a powerhouse. Guards Ernie Myers and junior college transfer Spud Webb, a five-foot-seven-inch midget who could outrace anyone while dribbling a basketball, handled the ball, while seniors Lorenzo Charles and Cozell McQueen were joined by sophomore Bennie Bolton to give the team strength under the boards and a lot of scoring up front.

Valvano's Wolfpack finished the year 23 and 10, tying for the ACC regular-season title. The team lost in the second round of the ACC tournament to Carolina, but beat Nevada-Reno, Texas-El Paso, and Alabama before losing to St. John's in the finals of the Western Regionals of the NCAA.

Valvano's freshman recruits, moreover, were his finest class since his arrival on the N.C. State campus back in 1980.

With Cozell McQueen and Lorenzo Charles finishing their careers at State, Valvano badly needed athletes to team with Washburn, sophomore forward Bennie Bolton, and returning senior guard Ernie Myers, and he got them. Oh yes, he did.

Of the six youngsters coming to State, five were named high school All American

in one poll or another. All had been recruited by the cream of major basketball powers. Two, Charles Shackleford and Teviin Binns, stood six-foot-ten. Shackleford had been recruited by Maryland, Duke, North Carolina, Houston, Louisville, DePaul, and Kentucky. Binns, a Junior College All American from Midland Junior College, was reputed to be a scoring machine. He had been recruited by 150 major colleges. Walker Lambiotte, a six-foot-seven-inch guard with an uncanny shooting eye, was named the MVP of the prestigious McDonald's High School All Star Game and was rated among the top ten prospects in the nation.

Valvano, moreover, had induced Mike Giomi, the best rebounder on the Indiana University varsity, to come to State, after Giomi had been tossed off the Hoosier team for skipping too many classes. In high school, the six-foot-nine-inch Giomi had been named Ohio High School Player of the Year.

Not satisfied with adding two six-foot-tens and a six-foot-nine-inch tower, Valvano also convinced a former member of the Greek National Basketball Team, Panagiotis Fasoulas from Thessaloniki, Greece, to join the Wolfpack for the 1985–86 season.

It was a dazzling array of talent that Valvano managed to bring to Raleigh, and with his potential college All American Chris Washburn returning, the N.C. State campus was abuzz with talk of the possibility of another national championship.

The University Chancellor

Even before America discovered that Chris Washburn had been accepted into N.C. State after scoring only a 470 on his College Boards, the members of the State faculty who regarded Jim Valvano as a blemish on its academic reputation were conducting a study of N.C. State's admissions practices with regard to its athletes.

The Faculty Senate's investigation in 1984 disclosed that the administration had given Valvano and his coaches carte blanche to fill a certain number of spots at will.

"Basically speaking," said one of the faculty members who conducted the investigation, "the admissions process was a joke."

What was revealed was that the coaches themselves were acting as a separate admissions committee for the university. Valvano and his coaches were virtually admitting some athletes even *before* they took their SATs.

Said one of the investigators, "The coach went out and recruited a kid, announced in the newspaper that so-and-so had signed a letter of intent to attend the university, say on a basketball scholarship. That coach was tantamount to admitting that person to the university."

The report produced by the Faculty Senate revealed that the athletes admitted into the university had embarrassingly low SAT scores and extremely low high school grade point averages compared to the general student population.

None of this created a ripple of media attention until three-quarters of the way through the Faculty Senate investigation, when the Chris Washburn trial revealed his 470 SAT score. Then suddenly, to the chagrin of Chancellor Bruce Poulton and the athletic department, America's press began having a field day.

George Vescey of the New York *Times* interviewed N.C. State Assistant Vice Chancellor Hardy Berry, who said, "The history of American sports is tied in with education. Who can forget that Amos Alonzo Stagg helped give an identity to the University of Chicago, one of the great institutions in our country?"

Wrote Vescey, "The University of Chicago long ago divested itself of big-time sports, but somehow remains one of the finest schools in the country."

Hardy's boss was Bruce R. Poulton, the chancellor. What was Poulton's role in the admission of these academically deficient students? Did Poulton have the clout to order a player like Washburn into school? Was Poulton embarrassed over the Washburn revelations?

When the uproar subsided, little changed. The one significant outcome of the Faculty Senate report and the Washburn embarrassment was a recommendation to support the NCAA's Proposition 48, which called for any athlete who had less than a C average and less than a 700 on his College Boards to sit out his freshman year and hit the books instead. In itself, Proposition 48 was hard for the educators on the faculty to swallow because it was such a small step. The average nonathlete entered N.C. State with about a B-plus high school average and around 1100 combined on the SATs. Was it so much to ask a student athlete to come in with at least a C average and a paltry 700 on his College Boards? For many coaches around the country, it was, going back to the philosophy of so many high school basketball stars that studying was irrelevant to their lives. For those coaches, Proposition 48 was hard to swallow because potentially it could inhibit the participation of their recruits. But at State, the athletic department bowed to the pressure and publicly agreed to abide by Proposition 48 guidelines.

The Faculty Senate also recommended that the university admit students based upon their academic qualifications and not upon their athletic prowess. This dictum was ignored.

Another result of the activity of the Faculty Senate was the appointment of its chairman, Dr. Roger Clark, a professor in the field of architecture, as the faculty's representative to the Athletics Council for the 1985–86 academic year.

The NCAA requires that every college have an Athletics Council, a body comprised of a majority of faculty but including students and alumni, to oversee the athletic department and make it accountable to the university. The seven faculty members are selected by the school's chancellor, the three alumni by the alumni association, and the three students by the student body president.

Since he had just headed the Faculty Senate's study on academics, Dr. Clark assumed he would be given a spot on the council's Academic Policies Committee, the watchdog concerned with athletes' grades. He was not. Instead Dr. Clark was put on the committee overlooking the athletic facilities. After all, the veteran council members told him, he was an architect by trade and best suited to survey the athletic plant.

From the beginning Dr. Clark was viewed by the senior faculty members on the council as an outsider. Clark's intention had been to follow the mandate as set down by the NCAA, to be an overseer, to uphold the academic standards of the university with regard to athletics.

But he quickly realized that his fight to be a watchdog would be futile because, as he discovered, the majority of the council members had been provided with great seats to games, access to players, and access to Valvano. The real role of the Athletics Council, Dr. Clark discovered, was to act as an arm of the athletic department—a protector, apologist, and lobbyist.

When Clark attempted to pass the resolution "Athletes must go to class or they don't play," the Academic Policies Committee's chairman, Fred Smetana, a professor of mechanical engineering and a long-time member of the Athletics Council and supporter of Valvano, did not allow the resolution to come up for a vote by the full council.

Earlier, when both Clark and Smetana had been members of the Faculty Senate, that body had voted on a resolution declaring, "Students who come to the university ought to be qualified." Reportedly, the only faculty member on the Faculty Senate to vote against the resolution was Fred Smetana.

Council meetings were tightly controlled. Secrecy was stressed, as though national secrets, not collegiate athletics, were involved. The watchdogs, according to one council member, were kept in the dark about drug problems, and grade deficiencies were discussed in only the most general terms, as in "A swimmer is in academic trouble." The reason cited was a law designed to protect the privacy of the students from having their grades publicized.

The athletic budget, which at State comes solely from ticket sales, television revenues, and money donated by the Wolfpack Club, was revealed to the council members but kept secret from the public or press. At the yearly council meeting to discuss the budget, a copy would be distributed to each member, and at the end of the meeting it reportedly would be collected.

Said a council member, "The council would give its rubber stamp, and it would be passed."

For all but the most innocuous of noncontroversial topics, secrecy was called for. No other campus committee closed its meetings to the press. Moreover, the members of the Athletics Council routinely were warned by Chairman Richard Mochrie not to talk to reporters about what went on at the meetings. Again, one would have thought national security was at stake. Or that the athletic department was trying to hide something.

Council Chairman Mochrie, a professor of animal science, a nationally known official in the world of track and field, and a strong supporter of Valvano, often warned the other members that if the press had any questions about what went on at meetings, the proper procedure was to send the reporter to him.

When the student newspaper, the *Technician*, demanded that it be allowed to send a reporter to the council meetings, Chairman Mochrie was adamantly opposed.

In trying to justify the policy of secrecy, Mochrie told the paper, "I really think it's better in the long run. When you are batting things around, I can't see cluttering up the press with what's going on."

The council went so far as to solicit the opinion of the chief deputy attorney general of the State of North Carolina, who proclaimed that the Athletics Council was exempt from the state's Open Meeting Law "because it does not satisfy the law's definition of a public body."

Chairman Mochrie further justified the policy by citing his boss, saying, "Chancellor Poulton has asked that these meetings be closed."

When the reporter went to see Poulton, the chancellor told him, "If the majority of the committee wanted to open the meetings, I guess they could." Fat chance of that happening. He had appointed the members.

It was apparent to faculty members and students that under the Poulton administration, whatever Valvano and his athletic department wanted to do, they could do—and that if anyone dared buck Valvano, he would have to take on Poulton as well....

Grade Games

After the conclusion of the fall term final exams, Valvano reportedly told the players that "a few of them were in trouble academically," and he warned them not to say anything to the press about it.

He said, "Guys, I just want to emphasize that we are a team. Anything that happens to us, happens to us as a team, and when I say team, that includes the players, the coaches, and the managers. Everyone else is the outside world, and we don't need contact with them. Anything that happens to us as a team, stays as a team."

At practice Coach McLean told them, "I just want to remind you that it's against the law to talk about anybody else's grades, and if anybody asks you, tell them it isn't something you can talk about, that you don't know anything about it, and to talk to Coach V himself."

On most campuses, the less anyone knows about an athlete's grades, the better. Rarely are they a topic in the papers, because the information is limited to only a few people—the registrar, the coach, the player, the advisers—and since keeping a player eligible seems to be the highest priority at certain colleges, academic problems are tightly guarded secrets.

The public learned that three N.C. State basketball players were in academic trouble when a member of the Athletics Council, Dr. Keith Cassell, Dr. Roger Clark's replacement, revealed it to a student reporter from the *Technician*. He told the reporter three athletes had flunked out but were being readmitted under a special procedure.

Under that procedure, any student who flunked out could go before a university admissions committee to plead his case to be allowed back in, regardless of how poorly he had done the semester before.

If Dr. Cassell hadn't leaked the news to the press, Shack, Tev, and Kelsey could have gotten back into school without anyone even knowing they were in trouble. But Cassell's disclosure that more of Valvano's athletes weren't doing too hot academically created controversy as professors questioned whether everyday students had the same chance to be readmitted as the athletes did.

Where Jim Valvano has been most brilliant and innovative has been in the way he's been able to position himself before the public as an educator-coach. Whenever there is a scandal at another university concerning academics, Valvano is usually quick to say, "I wouldn't tolerate such behavior at N.C. State." In talking about education, he declares, "There is a commitment to academics in the N.C. State athletic department."

It's propaganda, nothing more. The reality is, Valvano's commitment to education is deplorable. During the eight years he has been at N.C. State, more of his players have been on academic probation than not.

The academic performance of Valvano's players has become a standing national joke among other coaches. Said Pat Williams, then general manager of the Philadelphia 76ers, in the *Sporting News*, "They had a big scandal at his place—three players found the library."

There is only one time a year that Valvano really has to sweat out a player's grades: the beginning of the school year, when the NCAA comes in and checks to make sure the athlete has passed twenty-four hours of classes the year before. (That translates to seven or eight different courses, depending upon how often the course meets each week.)

But another NCAA rule eases the burden. That rule states that a player cannot be suspended for the first twenty-four class hours of his career at the university. Hence, Valvano does not have to worry about freshmen their entire first year, and he doesn't have to worry about junior college transfers their first year—though they must have enough credits to pass by the end of summer school.

What the students must do is find a mix of courses from which they can attain an average grade of 2.0, or C. In other words, even if a player ends up failing a few courses, if he can find professors to give him off-setting Bs and As, then he can remain eligible for basketball. To accomplish this, the coaching staff closely monitors what courses their players sign up for.

To help keep the players eligible, a number of professors on campus, to one degree or another, aid the athletes in getting through. The academic advisers know who these professors are, and at the start of the semester, if a player is a serious academic risk, the academic advisers reportedly sit down with the player and say, "Based on your grade point average, these are the courses we think you should take." The player signs the class schedule and the adviser fills in the "right" classes for him.

Not all the players are handled this way—only those in danger of flunking out. The other players choose their own courses, but they, too, have a grapevine that informs them which professors are helpful and which ones dislike athletes. "If you get caught with the wrong professor," said one of the players, "you're in a lot of trouble."

Said one of the basketball players, "I say there are teachers at State and professors at State, two different kinds of categories. Professors really teach you and you can't get over on them. And then there are teachers who let you slide."

The players juggle schedules in search of their pet professors, though usually only one favorite can be assigned out of the four classes each player has to take.

According to one former professor, if you're not one of the professors under the spell of the basketball program, the basketball coaches lean on you hard if a basketball player is in your class and needs a good grade. "I saw it happen all the time," he said.

The course that every first-term freshman basketball player took was an offering called Leisure Alternatives. Said John Simonds, "Show up, and the basketball player usually gets an A. Every ballplayer takes this course. It's been a staple, even if the player had planned on becoming a chemical engineer."

There is one professor close to the athletic department who teaches a very technical, scientific course. To pass his course, ordinarily a knowledge of physics and higher mathematics is critical—but not if you're a basketball star. Among some members of the faculty, this professor is renowned for his generosity to the basketball players. When a fellow faculty member was asked why a PE major would take an honors level scientific course, his answer was, "To get a good grade." When asked, "Isn't this course too hard for your average basketball player?" his answer was, "Not in *his* course."

The faculty member added contemptuously, "[He] will give an athlete any grade that the athletic department thinks is important." Said another school official, "These players go through classes they don't have any business in, that they don't have any chance of passing, and somehow they get credit."

Said John Simonds, "One of the players told me he didn't even know he was in this professor's course until he looked at his report card and saw that he had taken it and gotten an A!"

The professors help out because, like so many other rabid fans at N.C. State, they love sports and feel it's their civic duty to help keep the players eligible. That they themselves are corrupting the educational process doesn't seem to bother them.

Said one of the players, "I had a teacher in speech communication. He was a sports fanatic. Me and Vinny del Negro was in the same class. All he would talk about was sports, and it was times when we could miss some days with no problem. You're on the team, and they know you be away a lot. There are teachers like that. Me and Vinny got a B."

Others players got good grades in that class, too.

John Simonds took a course with an English professor who boasted to him that despite the fact the Chris Washburn was virtually illiterate in English, the year before he had passed him anyway. "Washburn is a good addition to the university," the professor said by way of justification.

And there was the art history teacher who failed one of the players. The player

had missed the final exam, so the professor gave him an F. If the grade had remained, he would have been ineligible spring semester. Without the recorded F, his grade point average would have been high enough for him to play. To help out the basketball player, the professor agreed to give him an incomplete. The player was then eligible to play in the spring. The player ended up making up the exam, and he still got an F. But because a student need only concern himself with his grade point average at the beginning of the school year, when the NCAA comes around, that player was able to pass enough summer school courses to become eligible to play again the next year.

Summer school has been the savior of university athletic careers—and why so many of the players are on campus during the summer. Summer school classes are notoriously easier than regular semester courses. Also, during the summer there is another loophole: For the truly uneducatable, players can take correspondence courses, leaving a window of opportunity for someone else to aid in the at-home written exams.

With all of the available loopholes, any athlete could pass—if he did some work. But he had to do it. During a regular semester, even if he got an A from a teacher who loved basketball players, he still had three other courses to worry about. An A and three Fs translates to only a 1.25 grade point average. Most of the players who attended most of their classes and took most of their tests did pass, although their grade point averages still were not very high.

In fairness to them, it is very difficult for the best student athletes to find time to study, considering the amount of time spent practicing, going on long trips to play games as far away as Alaska, and thinking about playing.

Explained one of the players, "Say you're playing Loyola of Chicago on national television Sunday afternoon. You've got a big test Monday. What the hell are you going to be doing Sunday? You're not going to be studying. You're going to be thinking about the game. And after the game, the adrenaline is flowing. You have to get on a plane and get back at eleven-thirty at night, and get up for a seven o'clock class to take a test you haven't studied for. So it's tough."

For players like Shack, Tev, and Kelsey, who had counted their whole lives on becoming professional basketball players, it was difficult to study simply because they didn't possess the basic reading and writing skills. Teviin never did pass freshman English. More to the point, according to teammates, none of them really cared. Shackleford, especially, thought studying irrelevant to his life. Said an N.C. State student, "I'd hear someone say, 'I saw Shack going to class today.' Everyone would get excited and say, 'Wow!'" Said a teammate, "He didn't give a shit about it."

But other teammates were more sympathetic to their star center. They understood that in the basketball society that fosters a philosophy of b-ball first and only, studying was not what Shack was in school for.

"There are a lot of opportunities to play pro ball today," said one. "You can now make thirty thousand dollars a year playing in Germany. You can play in France, Italy, Venezuela, and in Israel. It isn't just the NBA. And that's solely what he's looking at."

Despite Shackleford's severe academic problems, all the players knew he would remain in school. Said a teammate, "Shack was The Man. If Shack was off the team, we were going to lose. Valvano would do that with all his star players. They would be on the team no matter what."

The loophole that allowed Shackleford to remain eligible—and Teviin Binns and Kelsey Weems as well—was the official readmission process. If a student flunked out at the end of the fall semester, he could go before the Academic Review Board and personally petition for readmission.

Each of the failing players went before the Academic Review Board. In addition, Valvano reportedly testified on their behalf that Chancellor Poulton had signed a contract with them giving his approval for them to play in exchange for their promise (1) to attend classes and (2) go to study hall.

At the Academic Review Board hearing, the players came one after the other. The members of the review board sat around a long table, asking questions like, "Do you think you can continue your education here?" "Are you capable of working toward a degree?" "Are you willing to be tutored and get academic assistance?"

Teviin Binns, one of the players who went through it, said, "All you have to say is, 'Yeah, yeah, yeah,' and they let you back in. After they finished asking their questions, I left, they discussed it, I came back in, and they told me their decision.

"They said, 'We're going to let you back in because you have the capability to maintain a passing record.'"

Teviin had had some concern as to whether he would be let back in, because he was not a star player and he also knew how negatively Valvano felt about him. According to Binns, a couple of years earlier, one of the basketball players, George McLain, who had been on the outs with Valvano, was denied readmission after going in front of the board. Teviin wondered whether Valvano would drop him the same way he had dropped McLain. At the same time, Teviin felt his chances of staying in school were good, because if he was dropped the press would be asking questions, something he knew Valvano wanted to avoid at all costs.

As for Shackleford, all the players knew Shack would be back. "Everybody knew Shack was going to make it," said Teviin. "Everybody knew that. And since Kelsey was Shack's homeboy, then nothing was going to happen to Kelsey either, 'cause they had their own apartment, so if they were taking care of Shack, they were taking care of Kelsey at the same time. 'Cause if Kelsey wouldn't have come back, then I think Kelsey would have told the papers what was going on with Shack."

Shackleford hadn't been worried, not for a moment. He told teammates, "Aw, nothing is going to happen. What are they going to do to me? They need me." And he was so right.

According to John Simonds, the white players—Vinny, Andy, Walker, and Giomi—couldn't believe that Shack, Teviin, and Kelsey were coming back to play after flunking out. Giomi was shocked most of all, because at the University of Indiana, where he had come from, that would have been unheard of. He told teammates he thought it morally wrong. To the white players, it was the "dumb niggies" getting away with murder again.

When news of the flunking players' readmission hit the school newspaper, the administration pulled the wagons into a circle. Chancellor Poulton was evasive. He said, "No one is eligible to represent N.C. State as an athlete unless I certify, or the Athletics Council certifies on my behalf, that [the students] are eligible." Which was true. What he didn't say was that if you were an athlete, you were much more likely to get certified.

Fred Smetana, representing the Athletic Council, told the student reporter that of the sixty-eight students readmitted to the university on appeal, only eight were members of revenue sports teams, as though that was somehow supposed to mean something.

The criticism of the smelly deal came both from educators and members of the student government. Said a member of the Student Senate, "All the athletes got back in, and then there were all those students who had tried hard and for some reason couldn't cut it, and only a small percentage of those got back in. It wasn't right. The chancellor wasn't going to go to bat for them."

"And what was even more ridiculous, the players had failed fall semester while playing a light schedule. They had had an entire semester to do well and to get ready for the real season. They were starting off the new term with a full ACC schedule and going all the way through March to the ACC tournament and possibly playing up through early April. How were they going to do that and carry any kind of academic load?"

Shack Gets a Baby-sitter

From the start of the second semester, Valvano apparently decided he wasn't going to take any more chances with sophomore Charles Shackleford's grades. After Shack had gotten this far, Valvano would have real trouble explaining things to the press and the public if Shack had to go before the Academic Review Board two semesters in a row, so he assigned Coach Stewart to be Shack's baby-sitter, to make sure he went to class and studied. Coach Stewart, however, wasn't up to the job. Shack was too slippery for him. Shack would go in the front door of the College Inn while Stewart waited for him, and then he'd sneak out a side entrance, wasting Steward's time and trying the coach's patience.

Valvano finally decided that in order to harness Shack, he would have to hire a full-timer who could stick to him like tar. Valvano could have chosen someone from the university tutoring program, but in keeping with his penchant for secrecy, he hired a man named Bruce Hatcher to be Shackleford's full-time personal tutor. Hatcher got paid good money, but who, the other players wondered, would want the job of having to baby-sit a six-foot-eleven twenty-year-old?

Hatcher told Simonds, "I was hired to make sure that Shack goes to class every day and that he goes to study hall every day and to make sure he doesn't get in trouble." The manager thought to himself, "Good luck to you."...

Captain Ahab

Before the Georgia Tech game Valvano was in a foul mood. The players had gone up to the court for the pregame workout, and he was sitting in the locker room with the other coaches and John Simonds, and he began talking about his problems. The losing was getting to him.

Valvano rambled, "I've got a bunch of guys who just can't play. Kelsey wants to play, but he's not good enough. Walker has completely let me down. He's washed up. He isn't any good. Andy hates me. Vinny keeps everyone else hating me. Shack isn't playing worth a shit. He doesn't care.

Teviins's mind is gone." And then suddenly Valvano began chuckling. He said, "In my twenty years of coaching, this is the wildest I have ever seen. I got kids who can't take care of themselves, who get in trouble grade-wise and in every other way."

He said, "One of these days, this is all going to come back and haunt me."

Then he repeated something he had said before: "I'm riding this big wave, and I'm going to fall off, and it's going to slap me."

He chuckled again and repeated himself. He said, "Sooner or later, that big wave is going to slap me. I just know it."

Postscript: Jim Valvano died of cancer at the age of 47 on April 28, 1993.

How Police Justify the Use of Deadly Force*

William B. Waegel

CASE STUDY QUESTIONS

1. How well do the various sociological perspectives on deviance apply to the use of deadly force?

2. With regard to the police and law enforcement, what is the acceptable goal and the acceptable means for achieving that goal? Is it possible for a police officer to be labeled deviant by another police officer? By whom are the actions of the police officers who use deadly force perceived to be deviant?

3. What are the influences of work culture, opportunity structure, and work-related stress on the police use of deadly force? How much belief do these officers have in the criminal justice system? How do retrospective accounts of shootings reflect the informal norms of the police subculture?

4. What evidence do we find for the idea that those who engage in deviant acts find ways to neutralize their guilt? What kinds of justifications does the police subculture offer for the use of deadly force? Are police justifications for the use of deadly force a cover for racism? Does use of deadly force stem from a desire to be macho?

5. Why do the norms differ from the rules? What does it mean that those responsible for enforcing the laws have their own informal norms about how to do their job?

*The author thanks an anonymous *Social Problems* reviewer for suggestions. Correspondence to: Department of Sociology, Villanova University, Villanova, PA 19085.

Source: © 1984 by the Society for the Study of Social Problems. Reprinted from *Social Problems* Vol. 32, No. 2 (December), 1984, pp. 144–155, by permission.

An average of 600 citizens are killed annually by police in the United State (Sherman, 1980:4). Fyfe (1981:381) estimates that in 1978 an additional 1,400 persons suffered serious injury from police shootings. The capacity to use force is the core of the police role and the unifying theme in police work (Bittner, 1970). Previous research in this area has directed relatively little attention to how police themselves view the use of lethal force against citizens.

Empirical studies have attempted to measure the extent of, and provide an explanation for, the use of lethal force by police. Sherman and Langworthy (1979:553) attributed 3.6 percent of all homicides to the police for the period 1971–1975. Kobler (1975:164) documents a consistent 5 to 1 ratio of police killing to police killed during the 1960s. More than half of those killed by police are members of minority groups (Sherman, 1980:11). A 1963 study of eight major cities found that the police homicide rate for blacks was nine times higher than for whites (Robin, 1963).

Police killings vary greatly between jurisdictions. For the period 1950–1960, the rates ranged from 1.4 deaths per 10,000 police officers in Boston to 63.4 deaths per

10,000 officers in Akron, Ohio (Robin, 1963). Kania and Mackey (1977) found that, for the years 1961–1970, police in Georgia had the highest rate of killing of 37.9 per one million residents, while police in Hawaii, New Hampshire, and Wisconsin killed slightly under three persons per one million residents.

The patterns revealed in survey research have provided the basis for efforts to explain police violence. Kania and Mackey's (1977) ecological study found a significant relationship between the rate of police homicide and the level of violent crime in the community. They suggest that police are predisposed to use violence against citizens in response to the level of violence they encounter in their working environment. Jacobs and Britt (1979), using the same data, found that police homicides were highest in states with the greatest economic inequality. Their findings challenge previous interpretations of police violence simply as a response to levels of violence in the community.

Some researchers have suggested that occupational stress may also be a factor in police killings. Research has shown that police suffer disproportionately from stress-related health problems (including gastrointestinal disorders and heart disease), alcoholism, marital and family problems, emotional disorders and suicide (Duncan, 1979:v). Blackmore (1978) argues that police hostility and aggression may also be related to occupational stress.

Another explanation, rooted in the sociology of occupations, emphasizes the influence of the work environment on attitudes, values, and behavior. Westley (1953:216) was the first to apply this perspective to police violence:

> The policeman uses violence illegally because such usage is seen as just, acceptable, and, at times, expected by his colleague group and because it constitutes an effective means for solving problems in obtaining status and self-esteem which policemen as policemen have in common.

The occupational environment of the police generates a collective emphasis on secrecy, an attempt to coerce respect from the public, and a legitimation of almost any means to accomplish an important arrest. In the everyday activities of policing, these values take precedence over legal responsibilities. Thus, in certain areas of police work— for example, the apprehension of an armed felon or the handling of a sex offender— the police justify excessive physical force as good, proper, and useful.

This paper examines police use of lethal force from a different perspective—that of the police themselves. Police departments have formal procedures to investigate cases in which police officers fire their weapons and incidents in which citizens are wounded or killed by officers. These procedures determine, after the fact, whether the shootings were legal and warranted, or illegal and unwarranted. Similarly, police training manuals and administrative guidelines attempt to specify the circumstances under which officers may, or should, draw and fire their weapons. Thus, a formal, bureaucratic set of procedures exists to evaluate, document, and explain police violence.

At another level, the occupational subculture of the police involves a set of understandings, beliefs, practices, and a language for talking about all problematic aspects of their work, including the shooting and killing of citizens. This perspective includes both prospective beliefs that influence the decisions of officers to use their weapons, and retrospective interpretations of events that have already occurred. The prospective beliefs might be called "techniques of neutralization" because they permit officers to violate both the general cultural prohibition against taking life and sometimes also the specific regulations of the police department and the law about the circumstances under which the police may use their weapons. The retrospective elements may be called "vocabularies of motives" or "accounts" (Mills, 1940; Scott and Lyman, 1968); they reveal the specific ways people either excuse or justify their actions when required to do so.

Any explanation of police violence must take into account how the police themselves account for and explain their use of weapons. This [case study] concentrates on the informal beliefs that permeate the police occupational subculture. It focuses on how the police themselves interpret and account for incidents in which they fire their weapons and wound or kill someone.

First, I describe the methods and data for my analysis. Second, I discuss procedures that formally govern this area of police behavior. Third, I look at prospective elements of the police subculture that guide the police in their use of weapons. Finally, I examine retrospective accounts of "incidents of police killing" that occurred during my research.

Data and Methods

The data for this [case study] come from two sources. First, I spent 10 months in 1976 and 1977 as a participant-observer in a police department in a city in the northeastern United States.[1] During my research, three police shootings occurred. The focus of my research was detective work. One of the citizens was shot by a detective, and I arranged to accompany that officer on his shift the day following the shooting. The other two shootings involved patrol officers. These incidents were widely discussed in the department at the time, and provided an opportunity to observe the police perspective on, and interpretation of, actual cases. In addition, I interviewed officers at length, discussing their use of firearms and past shooting incidents within the department. Quotations in this paper are taken from these interviews, unless otherwise attributed.

The second source of data is my analysis of 459 police shootings in Philadelphia between 1970 and 1978 (Waegel, 1984). This study employed accounts by police, witnesses, and surviving victims collected by the Philadelphia Public Interest Law Center (Jackson, 1979). The center's work is well respected by legal scholars, as indicated by its citation in a major appellate court decision (*Mattis v. Schnarr* 1976) on police use of lethal force.

Legal Rules, Formal Procedures, and Subcultural Understandings

Police use of firearms is formally governed by state laws and the policies and guidelines of particular police departments. Legal standards have been in transition since the early 1970s. The traditional common-law standard, the "fleeing felon rule," permits the use of deadly force to arrest any felony suspect. Since 1970, many states have departed from the traditional standard and restricted the use of deadly force only to incidents involving specific forcible felonies or to situations involving defense of life. In both of the jurisdictions I studied, statutory change departing from the fleeing felon standard occurred during the 1970s. Typical of the departmental guidelines are those provided in the Philadelphia Policeman's Manual:

> There are three instances in which a police officer may fire his revolver at another human. They are:
>
> 1. To protect his own life, when it is in imminent danger.
> 2. To protect the life of another.
> 3. In an effort to prevent the commission of certain violent felonies or to prevent the escape of a violent felon, but *only after all other means have been exhausted.*

Police use of firearms is embedded in a background of shared understandings developed out of occupational experiences and collegial discussions of past shooting incidents and their consequences. Shootings have a special prominence in the police subculture. They are the stuff of "real" police work as opposed to routine peace-keeping activities. That police are given guns and required to carry them 24 hours a day is a feature of the police world which has an importance that cannot be underestimated. The gun is a symbol which sets off the police and their work from other persons and occupations. Every police intervention takes place against an awareness of the ultimate power that can be brought to bear. When that power is used, the significance of the event extends beyond the particular incident. To shoot with state sanction is an experience virtually unique to police. It strikes at the heart of the police role, and is one of the matters around which subcultural solidarity is built. Shootings activate personal emotions, anxieties, sentiments, and recollections; all officers know that they may face the decision to shoot at any time. Tales of past shootings occupy a prominent position in the folklore of policing, frequently recounted to instruct new members and to reinforce the messages and injunctions they carry.

Every shooting of a citizen is subject to formal review. At the very least, police departments conduct internal inquiries. The officer is required to explain the grounds for the shooting in a written report. Beyond this, there may be an external review, either by prosecutors in conjunction with the departmental investigation or in the form of separate investigations by the public prosecutor or the coroner's office.

Central among the understandings police hold about shooting are that the review process is generally "friendly" and that the legal standards are sufficiently vague so that nearly all shootings can be interpreted to fit the legal criteria for justifiable police homicide. These understandings are grounded in accumulated knowledge about the review process and its outcomes.

That these views have an empirical basis is suggested in the literature on police use of lethal force. Kobler's (1975) study of 1,500 fatal police shootings found only three cases in which criminal punishment resulted. Harding and Fahey (1973) examined 85 fatal shootings by Chicago police during 1969 and 1970; in 11 of these, available information revealed *prima facie* cases for murder or manslaughter, but only one officer was charged and tried. Both studies discuss features of the formal review process that operate to produce very low rates of prosecution. Moreover, the vague character of formal standards and guidelines for using lethal force (e.g, "reasonable belief," "substantial risk," "only when all other means have been exhausted") has led Milton et al. (1977: 57) to observe that "their impact on the conduct of police officers is questionable."

Prospective Neutralizations

The occupational subculture of the police contains special beliefs and understanding about using firearms against citizens. Legal norms formally governing the use of deadly force may be rendered situationally ineffective through reference to shared understandings about justifications for infractions. Sykes and Matza (1957) examine such justifications as "techniques of neutralization" which precede deviant behavior and release the actor from conventional rules and prohibitions.

In the neutralization framework, violations are exceptions to otherwise accept rules. Accordingly, the justification for violation is usually specific to certain kinds of persons and circumstances or to the achievement of certain ends. The police officers I interviewed related their justifications to circumstances ('it's not wrong because of the special circumstances involved"), the characteristics of the victim ("it's not wrong because the person deserves it"), or the higher purpose achieved ("it's right because of the ends served"). While analytically distinguishable, these beliefs blend together, form packages of meaning, and constitute working formulas for the officer on the street. Only certain types of persons deserve violent treatment and then only under certain kinds of circumstances.

"I'd rather be judged by twelve than carried out by six"

A set of beliefs centering on the peculiar character and demands of police work generates a preparedness to "shoot first" in potentially dangerous situations. Many officers spoke of the uncertainty, anxiety, and danger they experience in their work—for example, while searching for an armed suspect and suddenly confronting a person in a dark alley. Such situations require split-second decisions which, if incorrect, can result in serious injury or death to the officer. One plainclothes officer, describing this type of circumstance in police work, remarked, "I'm not gonna get my ass shot by one of those scums while I'm trying to do my job."

Most police officers believed that mistakes are unavoidable due to the special nature of police work.[2] Past incidents in which an officer's hesitation resulted in injury or death to the officer or a colleague were prominent parts of the folklore of police work. A "war story" told to me on several different occasions involved a young officer who had hesitated in shooting and was killed at the scene of an armed robbery. The hesitation and fatal consequences were attributed to assumptions made by the officer because the first suspect to appear—and the one who shot the officer—was an attractive, white woman. Frequent recounting of such incidents and the lesson they carry crystallizes and cements a subcultural injunction: when dealing with certain kinds of persons and situations, be ready to shoot if you think you have to and worry about the paper work later. The conventional wisdom embodied in the saying "I'd rather be judged by twelve than carried out by six" is familiar to every urban police officer.

Some police shootings involve circumstances in which officers are afraid for their personal safety; a person may be confronted who suddenly turns toward an officer or is seen holding an object, and the officer spontaneously shoots. The nature of police work involves managing situations where persons make sudden or unexpected body movements—what police call "suggestive moves." Under these circumstances, police view shooting first as self-defense. However, this orientation is specific to certain territories and categories of people, and if the person encountered does not fit a stereotype connoting danger, officers may hesitate to shoot.

"What's another dead animal?"

Sykes and Matza (1957:668) describe the process by which members of certain groups are selected as deserving of abusive treatment:

> By a subtle alchemy the [actor] moves himself into the position of an avenger....The moral indignation of self and others may be neutralized by an insistence that the injury is not wrong in light of the circumstances....It is not really an injury; rather it is a form of rightful retaliation or punishment.

This neutralization technique, termed "denial of the victim," acts as a motivation. Regarding the other as a person who deserves victimization serves as a cue for action.

Police work commonly involves relying on minimal cues to assess the character and likely behavior of persons encountered. The police literature contains rich descriptions of the stereotyping schemes employed by officers and the differential treatment of citizens who fit these stereotypes (Bittner, 1967; Skolnick, 1967; Van Manaan, 1978). Stereotypes link different modes of police behavior to different categories of persons encountered (Waegel, 1981). Police commonly use negative stereotypes (e.g., "animals," "scrotes," "assholes") in dealing with persons displaying specific attitudes, behaviors, or characteristics such as race or type of dress. Persons so categorized are viewed as different in essential ways from respectable citizens; their imputed moral inferiority renders them deserving of harsh or abusive treatment. Police need only listen to sentiments frequently expressed within the wider culture to find support for their beliefs concerning rightful or deserved punishments. Public figures who call for the castration of rapists or the use of penal colonies or other repressive responses to crime may contribute to a moral climate favoring informal sanctions by police.

Blatant racism in the larger society also contributes to the moral climate. During the investigation of a particularly gruesome homicide involving minorities, a detective remarked to a colleague, "Maybe Hitler was right, he just had the wrong group." In urban areas where minorities are over-represented in serious crimes, many police interpret race as a major "cause" of crime. The general devaluation of minority groups by large segments of the wider culture nourishes beliefs about the propriety of harsh or abusive treatment.

Beliefs about minorities are reinforced by experiences which are unique to police, especially interaction with injured and angry crime victims. At crime scenes and during investigations, injured victims, friends, and bystanders sometimes advocated extra-legal treatment: "If you ever catch the guys who did this, you should kick their asses." Some victims urged the police to avenge their crimes. Out of their occupational experiences police develop working assumptions about categories of people. As one veteran, plainclothes officer said to me during a homicide investigation in which all the parties involved were lower-class blacks, "You've got to understand, these people are animals, and we're here to keep peace among the animals."

In another incident, both police officers accepted the idea that excessive force toward blacks fell within the zone of acceptable behavior. In the aftermath of a police shooting which I describe below, the shooter was approached by an officer from his former patrol platoon and asked what had happened. The officer described the circumstances, then concluded: "What was I supposed to do?" Without hesitation the patrol officer replied, "What's another dead nigger anyway?"

The belief that some persons, under certain circumstances, "deserve to be shot"—though strongly held by some segments of the urban police—is not sufficiently potent to neutralize the general cultural prohibition against unwarranted killing. This belief prepares the officer to shoot, and weakens external controls, but does not in itself allow the officer to shoot. But it combines with other beliefs about the police role and the circumstances under which shooting is desirable to form a frame of reference for when to shoot.

"Some of these guys want to hand out justice on the streets"

Occupational experiences generate cynicism among police toward the rule of law (Skolnick, 1967). They believe that justice is frequently thwarted. They "know" people are guilty but often go unpunished. As a result, police see themselves as unavoidably caught between two wrongs: it's wrong that criminals don't get what they deserve, and it's wrong to take justice into one's own hands. The dilemma is addressed by a subcultural injunction: sometimes a cop has to break the law to enforce the law. Accordingly, unlawful police conduct such as perjury is rendered acceptable among large segments of the police subculture by reference to the positive ends which motivate the behavior. Illegal police methods are not simply the lesser of two evils; rather, they become the means which ensure that offenders get what they deserve. So long as police methods are directed toward the end of dispensing just deserts, they fall within the police definition of acceptable behavior.

How far this definition extends and whether it includes legally unwarranted shootings varies. It may be influenced, for example, by exposure to atrocious, violent crimes. Police see the consequences of criminal behavior in ways which other segments of society seldom experience: mutilated, dismembered, decaying bodies, and victims who are battered, bloodied, and permanently disfigured and disabled. Officers who have seen the worst of what some people do to others have strong feelings that the offenders should be punished one way or another.

Veteran plainclothes officers in particular have strong feelings toward the perpetrators of violent crime. A detective described an incident in which he shot and killed a person in a robbery stakeout. Information obtained from an informant, a heroin addict facing multiple felony charges, indicated that a corner store would be robbed that night. Officers concealed themselves in a back room. The suspect entered, grabbed money from the cash register, and turned to run out of the store. By prearranged plan, the clerk dropped to the floor as an officer came out of the back room with a sawed-off shotgun. The officer yelled, "Halt," in order to make the suspect turn toward him. The officer then fired both barrels at close range. "People ask me how I feel about shooting somebody," he said. "After what I've seen people do to one another, it doesn't bother me a bit to shoot one of these people." Interviews with officers assigned to areas or police functions not involving regular experience with violent crime generally did not reveal the same level of animosity toward offenders.

During focused interviews and informal discussions about police shootings, the following sentiments and beliefs were expressed:

I no longer believe in the jury system after some of the cases I've seen. Twelve middle-class jurors judge an animal. We get a guy off the streets and within three or four days he's back committing more crimes. And those bastards in the federal courts, they sit back there in their robes on their benches and they don't understand the situation.

You know, the public wants us to do this [shoot] when we catch one of these people.

When we shoot somebody in one of these things [a robbery stake-out] we don't get any more of this type of robbery for a while.

The willingness to dispense justice on the streets was rooted in three widely shared beliefs: (1) Shooting a suspect dispenses a version of justice not commonly dispensed by the courts. (2) The public wants the police to shoot suspects when they are seen committing a crime. (3) Shooting suspects has a deterrent effect which benefits law-abiding citizens. When these beliefs converge with the perception of a suspect as the type of person who deserves to be shot, police are more likely to use their weapons. Popular sentiments about violent crime support such views. The return to the use of the death penalty, widely applauded by police, is taken as evidence of the true desires of the public for the harsh treatment of dangerous offenders. Influential politicians, appealing to law-and-order sentiments among their constituents, advocate get-tough, deterrence-based policies. The notion that the courts, through the exclusionary rule, the Miranda warning, and other rulings which limit police power, handcuff the police and thwart justice is not without considerable support in public opinion.

The media provide an important source of public images and understandings about the police and crime. Television super-cops such as Starsky and Hutch, and Kojak, and the movie character Dirty Harry routinely eliminate undesirables with their firearms. The continued popularity of such characters suggests a significant public appetite for this kind of police conduct.

Retrospective Accounts

Investigations of police shootings call for the construction of an account (Scott and Lyman, 1968). Accounts are socially approved vocabularies for reducing or relieving responsibility, or for neutralizing an act or its consequences when conduct is called into question. Accounts may be offered to explain one's own behavior or that of others. In occupations where mistakes are likely occurrences, members develop a collective rationale and build up collective defenses against the lay world (Hughes, 1971:318).

A shooting is perhaps the most dramatic event in policing. To the officer, it is the ultimate clash of good against evil. Subcultural sentiments are mobilized as officers seek out information and discuss, interpret, and evaluate the incident. Van Maanen (1980:153) notes that this talk among colleagues "also 'normalizes' a shooting, since it is only through discourse that a sense of typicality can emerge." Colleagues interpret the event by locating it within a familiar vocabulary of motives (Mills, 1940). As information is collected, accounts are fashioned which explain the incident as an instance of understandable and warranted conduct. In the police view, shootings are almost always justified, even though outsiders might disagree. Outsiders, police believe, do not fully understand the context of police work. This view is reflected, for example, in the almost universal resistance by police to civilian review boards or other mechanisms for external review of police conduct (Lundman, 1980:173).

How police retrospectively account for and explain their use of firearms is illustrated in the following three cases from my field research.

1. The police obtained a warrant to search the home of a person believed to be trafficking in illegal weapons. The resident was a middle-aged black man with no prior criminal record. The information, obtained from a juvenile informant facing serious charges, was entirely erroneous. Probable cause was fabricated in the application for a search warrant. Under the "no-knock" law, the officers kicked open the door with no prior warning. The first two officers to enter wore flak jackets and carried shotguns and were responsible for meeting any resistance. The resident was in the kitchen with three children, slicing vegetables for dinner. When the noise and commotion occurred at the front door, the man moved toward the front room holding an onion in one hand and a knife in the other. A plainclothes officer, entering behind the first two, saw a man with a knife moving forward and shot him with his handgun. The man was seriously but not critically wounded. His first statement was, "Somebody is gonna get sued over this."

   I had ridden with the officer who shot the man for three weeks earlier in the research period, and accompanied him on the shift following the shooting. He had already been interviewed by prosecutors and police investigators. Visibly upset by the incident and its potential consequences, the officer spent most of the shift simply driving around the city. On numerous occasions, he was approached by uniformed officers or stopped to talk with colleagues and was commended for the shooting. Twice he was told to "improve your aim next time." It was understood that the shooting was a mistake of a kind which had been made in the past and which any member might make in the future. The officer's account of the incident centered on placing it in an understandable context:

What could I do? I thought it was either him or me. You know all cops make mistakes. There's not a cop in here who hasn't made a mistake. I've got a split second to decide what a jury can take all week to decide.

A police department account of the incident that was made public assigned responsibility for the shooting to the juvenile informant, described both the resident and the officer as victims, and explained the finding of justifiable use of a firearm in terms of the rapid, unexpected, and confusing events at the scene.

2. Police were called to the residence of a 23-year-old Hispanic ex-Marine by reports that he was acting violently, breaking windows, and spraying family members with tear gas. Family members fled the house and the man locked himself inside, alone. The first two uniformed officers to arrive were told of the man's history of mental problems and of efforts to bring a relative to the scene who had been able to calm the man during previous outbursts. The officers agreed to wait. A white sergeant arrived minutes later and made a decision to enter the house. The door was broken in and the sergeant, gun drawn, entered the residence. He was followed at a distance by another officer, while the third remained outside arguing with and restraining family members. After several minutes of silence, a single shot was fired. The sergeant had climbed the stairs to the third floor, confronted the man who was holding a shotgun, and shot him once in the head.

   Controversy surrounded the incident, and a minister and leader of the Hispanic community described the shooting as a "brutal assassination." Although some officers confided to me privately that the sergeant used poor judgement in entering the house and was

attempting to "be a hero," the basic interpretation of the event was that the sergeant "had no choice" since he was confronted with a weapon. Colleague accounts placed responsibility on the victim for threatening the officer with a gun; regardless of other circumstances, when a suspect has a gun, shooting is seen as self-defense. Four separate investigations of the shooting were conducted: by the police department, the city prosecutor, the state attorney general, and the U.S. Attorney's office. Each produced a finding of justifiable homicide.

3. A young black man entered a fast-food restaurant and purchased a soda while holding a large knife in his hand. The man reportedly acted in a bizarre manner, although he paid for the soda and did not threaten anyone. Police were notified and a young white officer, working alone, was first to respond to the "man with a knife" radio call. As the officer approached the scene, he saw the man standing on the sidewalk with the knife still in hand. The officer stopped his car directly in front of the man, drew his revolver, and positioned himself behind the open door of the car with his gun pointed at the man. He shouted at the man to drop the knife. The man stopped but did not drop the knife, and the two were frozen in this position for a brief time. Apparently, the man then made a sudden movement and the officer fired six times. This incident generated relatively little controversy. Police are required to respond to situations involving armed and potentially dangerous persons. This event was seen as an instance of that class of situations where offenders place an officer's life in danger, and shooting first is viewed as a natural, understandable, and warranted response. My inquiries about the propriety of the officer's response or alterna-

tive ways of handling the encounter met with replies of "What was he supposed to do?"

Vocabularies of accounts become routinized within groups and subcultures. Conduct becomes explainable by locating it within such a routine account. When an officer explains a shooting by saying, "It happened so fast" or "I didn't have any choice," further explanation may not be required. Colleagues can fill in and flesh out the account using background understandings about the nature of policing and the use of force. What Rubinstein (1973) has called "cop's rules"—informal, subcultural understandings about acceptable methods of handling persons and situations—provide a common context of interpretation.

Routine ways of accounting for a shooting centered on deflecting responsibility to the conduct of the person shot or to special circumstances at the scene. Grounds for a shooting were commonly expressed in terms of the theme, "It was him or me." This justification was applicable to a wide range of situations, and was explicit or implicit in accounts of incidents whenever the victim was armed. In each of the three cases described above, accounts were fashioned around a kill-or-be-killed theme.

An important variant of this deflection of responsibility to the conduct of the person shot involves what police call a "suggestive move."[3] A suspect is confronted; the suspect makes a quick movement into a pocket or unexpectedly turns toward an officer holding an object; the officer shoots spontaneously only to learn later that the suspect was unarmed. One of the Philadelphia shootings I studied involved a young black man in the vicinity of a robbery scene who was ordered to stop and was shot when he turned toward the officers holding a shoe-horn in his hand. The anxiety associated with police functions such as area searches for armed felons and the sudden, unex-

pected movements persons sometimes make when confronted by police represent special circumstances which may generate a *belief* that shooting is in self-defense. Knowledge that accounts centering on suggestive moves have worked in the past suggests their applicability for explaining subsequent incidents.[4]

Most accounts, then, are fashioned to justify the conduct of the shooter; particular features of the situation permitted or required the officer to shoot. Ambiguities in the application of legal rules ("a reasonable belief that your life is in imminent danger") to particular situations provide fertile grounds for the construction of justifying accounts. The notorious reluctance of juries to convict police charged in shooting incidents (which, of course, police are well aware of) suggests a wider appreciation of this problematic quality of the rules governing the use of lethal force.

However, other shootings cannot reasonably be justified in terms of the kill-or-be-killed theme. Some shootings are mistakes. Here, accounts are fashioned as excuses, which acknowledge the error but mitigate or deny culpability. In the first case described above, the police department offered excuses based on the erroneous information provided by the juvenile informant. Had it not been for the juvenile's deceit, it was claimed, the shooting never would have occurred. Further, had the information been accurate and a large cache of weapons actually had been inside the residence, the police response probably would have been warranted. Such appeals to defeasibility (Scott and Lyman, 1968:48) are available as excuses because of general cultural understandings that incomplete or imperfect knowledge may diminish a person's responsibility for conduct.

The ultimate excuse, entailing a complete denial of responsibility, is the "accidental discharge." Probably only the shooter, and perhaps a partner or a few close colleagues, ever know whether this excuse is accurate or whether it is manufactured *post facto* because other reasonable grounds were not available. But accidental discharges do happen, generally in the context of a violent physical encounter where a suspect tries to take an officer's gun. The empirical frequency of this occurrence is not the issue. "War stories" about such incidents are part of the folklore of police work. An account centering on accidental discharge thus is available for situations where all else fails. It may be used for incidents where an officer lost control of his emotions, panicked, or for other reasons shot under legally unwarranted circumstances.

During an interview, a retired police officer described a case in which an accidental discharge account was fabricated to "cover up" an illegal shooting. An officer had shot and killed a man at point-blank range while the latter's hands were up. The exact motivation was unknown, but there had been a history of "bad blood" between the two. An account was contrived indicating that, as the officer was holding the man at gunpoint, the man lunged for the gun and grabbed the barrel pulling it toward him. This movement pulled the trigger against the officer's finger, causing the gun to discharge into the man's chest. The retired officer took a revolver, removed the bullets from it, and demonstrated to me the details around which the story was contrived. At the end of the demonstration, he rolled his eyes in an expression of disbelief. After a pause, he added, "But, the guy was a bad job anyway."

Of the 459 shootings I studied in Philadelphia, 22 were accounted for as accidents. Eight involved bystanders hit by stray bullets or ricochets. The remaining 14 were explained as accidental discharges. Ten were attributed to a struggle or other physical contact with a suspect which caused the discharge, three were said to have occurred during chases, and one while a suspect was being frisked.[5] In the most publicized of these cases, a 19-year-old black man was arrested for a traffic violation and taken to the police station. While handcuffed at the station, the man pushed an officer and fled. He was pursued, caught, and shot by a white officer while lying on the ground. The officer was charged with manslaughter, tried, and acquitted.

People change their accounts for different audiences; explanations are fashioned in ways calculated to earn audience acceptance. The background understandings which make colleagues receptive to certain accounts are unlikely to be shared by other audiences. It should be expected, then, that accounts given to colleagues may be quite different from official accounts provided in press releases. Indeed, the concerns and purposes of administrators frame the fashioning of official accounts. Van Maanen's (1980:150) examination of official reconstructions of shooting incidents suggests that administrators attempt to demonstrate (1) that the police presence at the scene was warranted; and (2) that selected facts of the case fit the legal justifications for the use of deadly force. What is released for public consumption, then, is an account "that is documented in a politically, culturally, and legally viable fashion" (Van Maanen, 1980:151). In large police departments, the process becomes routinized: accounts become reinterpreted and refashioned to fit common public understandings of when and why police must shoot. The clearest illustration is seen in stake-out shootings where a familiar and standard script is trotted out: the suspect, armed with a handgun, turned and pointed the gun at an officer; the suspect had a long criminal record.

Discussion

Formal rules, standards, and guidelines provide areas of uncertainty and therefore permit negotiation of the meaning of these formulations (Manning, 1978:78). Bittner

(1970:4) argues that this defeasible quality of formal rules provides the essential structure to the police role:

> While there may be a core of clarity about [their] application, this core is always and necessarily surrounded by uncertainty....No measure of effort will ever succeed in eliminating, or even in meaningfully curtailing, the area of discretionary freedom of the agent whose duty it is to fit rules to cases.

Formal prescriptions about the use of lethal force reflect political and cultural contradictions and accommodations regarding the sanctity of life and property and the protection and safety of citizens and enforcement agents. When police are sent out to do disagreeable and sometimes dangerous work, they carry with them latitude and flexibility in drawing the lines about acceptable methods. The law, as Matza (1964) has observed, contains the seeds of its own neutralization.

Police, then, operate within a wider context enabling them collectively to identify and negotiate particular instances in which the use of firearms are warranted as exceptions to the general rule. The police subculture contains interpretive schemes for addressing the practical problems of when to shoot first, who are the proper recipients of deadly force, and why and under what circumstances suspects deserve to be shot.

Against the background of general cultural and specific legal prohibitions against taking life, police assemble a sense of justification for their uses of lethal force. Particular incidents are accounted for by drawing on familiar subcultural understandings about "why these things happen." Common forms ("it was him or me," "the person made a suggestive move") locate responsibility outside the officer and within features of the event or the conduct of the suspect. In the retrospective interpretation of that frozen moment when the trigger was pulled, "it happened so fast" or "I was so scared I just

started shooting" or even "the scum deserved it" may ultimately become an accidental discharge. The infrequency of sanction and the often-heard cries of cover-up which inflame the issue may be understood as products of the official accounting work performed.

Finally, the defeasible quality of the formal rules governing police use of lethal force has important implications for the legal and political debate over when such force is warranted. The volatility of the issue and the identification of police shootings as factors in urban riots (President's Commission, 1967) have brought calls for more effective controls over police use of firearms. A favored political response has been the enactment of statutory change formally restricting circumstances under which firearms may be used. The efficacy of this response appears problematic. This paper suggests that such control efforts operate against a background of entrenched subcultural beliefs and justifications that are organizationally and politically nourished. The relevance of this nourishment is suggested by research which shows that changes in an administrative climate of tolerance or in the friendly nature of internal review procedures result in reductions in the number of police shootings (Fyfe, 1979; Reiss, 1980).

NOTES

1. For a discussion of the field role adopted by the author, the use of key informants, and other methodological issues involved in participant observation of the police, see Waegel (1979;1981).

2. Reiss (1971:278) found that some officers "even carry pistols and knives that they have confiscated while searching citizens; they carry them so they may be placed at a scene should it be necessary to establish a case of self-defense."

3. That accounts centering on suggestive moves are not specific to the department I studied but are a common way police explain shootings is suggested by the statement of the project director of a deadly force study funded by the Justice

Department. In a press interview, Arnold Binder recommended that "civilians should be advised of police training techniques so they do not inadvertently prompt a police shooting by acting in a way that a police officer would consider threatening.… [Citizens] must not behave in such easily misinterpreted ways as reaching rapidly into a pocket or into a glove compartment" (*Philadelphia Inquirer*, 1982).

4. During my fieldwork, a veteran plainclothes officer described how an account centering on a "suggestive move" by a suspect generally led to a departmental review board finding of justified firearms use: "All you have to do is say he reached into his pocket and you saw something in his hand. Then you have a reasonable *belief* the guy is armed and they can't do anything about it."

5. Fyfe (1979) reports a similar use of accidental discharge accounts of New York City police. Following the implementation of an administrative order banning warning shots, there was "a great and unexpected increase in reported accidental 'shots in the air' fired by police who 'tripped on curbs' while pursuing fleeing suspects" (Fyfe, 1979:313).

REFERENCES

Bittner, Egon
1967 "The police on skid row: A study of peace-keeping." *American Sociological Review* 32(5):699–715.

1970 *The Functions of the Police in Modern Society.* Washington, DC: U.S. Government Printing Office.

Blackmore, John
1978 "Are police allowed to have problems of their own?" *Police Magazine* 1(3): 47–55.

Duncan, Skip
1979 *Police Stress.* Washington, DC: U.S. Government Printing Office.

Fyfe, James J.
1979 "Administrative interventions or police shooting discretion: An empirical examination." *Journal of Criminal Justice* 7(4): 309–323.

Harding, Richard W. and Richard P. Fahey
1973 "Killings by Chicago police, 1969–1970: An empirical study." *Southern California Law Review* 46: 284–315.

Hughes, Everett C.
1971 "Mistakes at work." Pp. 316–325 in Everett C. Hughes (ed.), *The Sociological Eye.* Chicago: Aldine Atherton, Inc.

Jackson, Anthony
1979 *Deadly Force Report. Monograph.* Philadelphia: Philadelphia Public Interest Law Center.

Jacobs, David, and David Britt
1979 "Inequality and police use of deadly force: An empirical assessment of a conflict hypothesis." *Social Problems* 26(4): 403–412.

Kania, Richard, and Wade Mackey
1977 "Police violence as a function of community characteristics." *Criminology* 15(1): 27–48.

Kobler, Arthur
1975 "Police homicide in a democracy." *Journal of Social Issues* 31(1): 163–184.

Lundman, Richard J.
1980 *Police and Policing.* New York: Holt, Rinehart and Winston.

Manning, Peter K.
1978 "Rules, colleagues, and situationally justified actions." Pp. 71–90 in Peter K. Manning and John Van Maanen (eds.), *Policing: A View From the Streets.* Santa Monica, CA: Goodyear Press.

Matza, David
1964 *Delinquency and Drift.* New York: John Wiley and Sons.

Mills, C. Wright
1940 "Situated actions and vocabularies of motive." *American Sociological Review* 5: 904–913.

Milton, Catherine H., Jeanne W. Halleck, James Lardner, and Garry L. Abrecht
1977 *Police Use of Deadly Force.* Washington, DC: Police Foundation.

Philadelphia Inquirer
1982 "Gun courses for police criticized." February 26: sec, A, p. 9.

Philadelphia Police Department
1978 *Policeman's Manual.* Philadelphia, PA.

President's Commission on Law Enforcement and the Administration of Justice
1967 *Task Force Report: The Police.* Washington, DC: U.S. Government Printing Office.

Reiss, Albert
1971 *The Police and the Public.* New Haven, CT: Yale University Press.

1980 "Controlling police use of deadly force." *Annals of the American Academy of Political and Social Science* 552: 122–134.

Robin, Gerald
1963 "Justifiable homicide by police officers." *Journal of Criminal Law, Criminology and Police Science* 54(2): 225–231.

Rubinstein, Johnathan
1973 *City Police.* New York: Ballantine.

Scott, Marvin B., and Standord M. Lyman
1968 "Accounts." *American Sociological Review* 33(1): 46–62.

Sherman, Lawrence
1980 "Perspectives on police and violence." *Annals of the American Academy of Political and Social Science* 452: 1–12.

Sherman, Lawrence, and Robert Langworthy
1979 "Measuring homicide by police officers." *Journal of Criminal Law and Criminology* 70(4): 546–560.

Skolnick, Jerome
1967 *Justice Without Trial.* New York: Wiley.

Sykes, Gresham, and David Matza
1957 "Techniques of neutralization: A theory of delinquency." *American Sociological Review* 22(6): 664–670.

Van Maanen, John
1978 "The asshole." Pp. 221–238 in Peter K. Manning and John Van Maanen (eds.), *Policing: A View From the Street.* Santa Monica, CA: Goodyear Press.

1980 "Beyond account: The personal impact of police shootings." *The Annals of the American Academy of Political and Social Science* 452: 145–156.

Waegel, William B.
1979 "Routinization and typification in investigative police work." Unpublished Ph.D. dissertation, University of Delaware.

1981 "Case routinization in investigative police work." *Social Problems* 28(3): 263–275.

1984 "The use of lethal force by police: The effect of statutory change." *Crime and Delinquency* 30(1): 121–140.

Westley, William A.
1953 "Violence and the police." *American Journal of Sociology* 49(1): 34–41.

Case Cited
Mattis v. Schnarr, 547 F. 2d 1007, 1976.

6 | Combining Work and Family

A couple in Philadelphia has been married 2 years. One spouse is offered a wonderful job opportunity in a suburb of Chicago. The other has recently changed jobs in the Philadelphia area to take advantage of an equally wonderful job opportunity. After long discussions, they decide that he will live in Chicago and she will remain in Philadelphia. They decide to try a commuting relationship so that they can still spend time with one another.

A small group of women have gathered in a neighbor's front yard on a pleasant summer evening. Their conversation turns to discussions of how they each feel about their current child-care arrangements. One woman explains that although she is glad she decided to stay home with her children, she is frazzled at the end of each day. Another woman enjoys the home child care provided by a woman in the neighborhood, but complains that the woman occasionally has other obligations that interfere with a regular schedule of child care. She also talks of the difficulty she has getting her husband to help with the housework.

The third woman is afraid to say anything. Her children happily go to an on-site child-care center run by her employer. She and her husband share household tasks. She mows the lawn; he does the laundry. She takes the children to the child-care center more often than he does, but he usually makes the lunches for the kids. Any comments she makes will sound like boasting or whining to her frazzled peers. Nevertheless, both she and her husband feel that there are time constraints imposed on their family by work demands.

Many families fail to balance work and family in a way that satisfies everyone involved. These families may feel that their dilemmas and difficulties are a result of their individual situation. To better understand the many societal and organizational variables that affect the situations of the men and women described above, we must look at the structure of the relationship between work and family. We begin by looking at the history of the relationship between work and family.

Societal Changes

A number of economic and demographic shifts and changes have had a large impact on the relationship between family and work. If employers want to be able to hire their most qualified job applicants, they need to recognize the implications of societal changes and provide new benefits to meet the changing needs and desires of workers.

Economic Shifts

Although the media would have us believe that families in which both husbands and wives work are a relatively new phenomenon, this is not the case. A century ago, however, it is unlikely that a family would have discussed the tensions between work and family. Although both husband and wife worked hard, they did not leave the family property to do their work; they worked side by side on a farm. As soon as children were old enough, they took part in the work on the farm. Families who did not farm were likely to own small businesses, which often were located in or near the home. As soon as children were able, they worked in the family business. Entire families worked together in an agricultural economy. Farm families often worked from dawn to dusk just to sustain themselves, and everyone collapsed exhausted at the end of a day. If children had talents better used in another type of work, those talents went untapped. If the intense relationship with their family as a result of both working and playing together was undesirable to them, there was no escape.

Because the home and the workplace were typically co-located, many of the tensions between work and family that both adults and children now experience were eliminated. Men and women did not need to live in two different cities, look for affordable high-quality child care, or negotiate domestic tasks. As you read Case Study 6.1, Elise Boulding's "The Labor of U.S. Farm Women: A Knowledge Gap," you will find that the description from the early part of this century still holds in some respects but that these women's lives are also affected by current societal trends.

In the last century, our society shifted from an agricultural economy to a manufacturing economy and then to a service economy. These economic shifts led men and women to jobs in factories and companies, sometimes only minutes but often an hour or more from the family domicile. This separation of work and family led to many dilemmas for families.

Social and Demographic Trends

The most notable trend affecting work and family is that women's labor force participation has increased dramatically over the last several decades. Currently, 58.7 percent of women 16 years and over are a part of the labor force (U.S. Department of Labor, 1995b: Table A1-13). Over 60 million women and 71 million men are in the labor force (U.S. Department of Labor, 1995b: Table A-2). Despite the increase in labor force participation for all women, the most dramatic changes have occurred for married women and married women with children. The labor force participation rate of married women with children increased from 27.6 percent to 69.0 percent in the last 35 years. More than 55 percent of married women with children under 1 year of age are part of the labor force (U.S. Department of Labor, 1995c: Table 47). The labor force participation rate of divorced women, particularly those with children 6 to 17 years of age, has been high for the last several decades, now reaching nearly 85 percent, which is higher than the overall labor force participation rate for men (U.S. Department of Labor, 1995c: Table 15). More women than ever before are part of the labor force. That has many implications for the relationship between work and family, since women traditionally have been full-time caretakers of the children and the home.

A second trend is that individuals are more geographically mobile than ever before, often moving to take advantage of job opportunities. Sometimes geographic mobility means that couples, whether married or not, need to live in different places for job-related reasons. Commuter couples may live 300 or even 3,000 miles apart. They may see each other every weekend or every holiday. The couple may talk often on the telephone or choose to save their conversations for when they see each other in person. Case Study 6.2, "Commuter Marriage: Deciding to Commute," by Naomi Gerstel and Harriet Gross, considers what causes couples committed to both their marriages and their careers to make the decision to set up homes in two different locales. In addition, as a result of increased geographic mobility, workers with children are less likely to be living near the relatives who might have served as caregivers for their children.

Two demographic trends are increased life expectancy and a lower birth rate. Both men and women are living longer than ever before, and couples are having fewer children. Even women who stay home with their children devote fewer years to childbearing and childrearing. Women's interest in and need to work have increased the likelihood that women who are wives and mothers are a part of the labor force. Moreover, increased life expectancy and changing expectations about the years after retirement have caused grandparents in better health to devote their later years to activities of their choice rather than obligatory care of their grandchildren.

In addition, the increase of jobs in the service sector has resulted in more white-collar workers than in the past. The nature of white-collar work requires that they be at their place of work during "normal" working hours. This, of course, makes it impossible for white-collar workers to institute the two-shift child-care schedule of some blue-collar families. A couple engaged in blue-collar work might be able to choose among three shifts (morning, evening, and night) and arrange their work schedules so that one parent is always available to care for young children or provide after-school care for older children. White-collar workers are less likely to have that choice.

Another societal trend is the increased number of single-parent families. Single parents have even fewer choices than either white-collar or blue-collar two-parent families. For single-parent families, the heightened tensions between work and family, especially with regard to income and child-care issues, have brought needed media attention. The difficulty in balancing work schedules and family needs has also attracted more attention as high-powered, white-collar, dual-career couples confront work and family issues. Some dual-career couples in high-powered careers may find that their needs for child care far exceed the traditional 40-hour work week, further compounding child-care problems. This has brought additional media and corporate attention to child-care issues.

Although the relationship between work and family receives a lot of media attention, our society has not yet adapted to either dual-worker households or single-parent families. Few employers provide the family services or flexibility needed and desired by both their male and female employees to nurture their children.

Family Priorities and Preferences

Family priorities and preferences may have an impact on the choice to work, the choice of occupation, and the selection of an employer. When individuals consider family factors, they weigh them in different ways. Whereas one person may choose nursing because the demand is high in nearly every part of the country, another may choose farming because work and family are co-located. While early family experiences may affect the initial choice, individuals may choose employers on the basis of fringe benefits, such as health insurance, retirement contributions, or work scheduling flexibility. Consideration of such criteria by potential employees should encourage employers to examine their policies carefully.

Impact of Early Family Experiences

A family's position in the social stratification hierarchy is determined by the occupation and income of its adult members. The family of the elementary school custodian is located lower in the stratification hierarchy than the family of the school district's superintendent of schools. The social position of the family of the owner of five car dealerships is higher than that of the mechanic who fixes the Mercedes for his boss. The occupations of adult family members can determine the social position of the family and have a dramatic future effect on the social position of children as a result of influence on occupational aspirations and choice.

In addition, fathers' and mothers' choices about the relationship between work and family and children's perceptions of their parents' feelings about those choices can influence children's later choices. In Case Study 6.3, "Elizabeth: I Was Raised To Do Everything," by Michele Hoffnung, you will see how one woman made and implemented her decisions about work, marriage, and motherhood.

Job Security and Fringe Benefits

Men and women consider family in their choice of work, but sometimes in different ways. Because of the persistent stereotype of father as provider, some men feel a special obligation to choose a higher paying job when presented with a number of occupational options. They will not necessarily weigh the salary over everything else, but the income and security a job provides may play a greater role in their choice than it does for some women. As families have changed, however, with more women remaining single longer, becoming divorced, or finding themselves as the primary or single economic provider, women are more likely than before to make pay and job security their first priority.

Other women and men may choose jobs that give them geographic mobility so that they can relocate with a spouse or move to a place they have always dreamed of, knowing that they are highly employable. When looking at potential employers, some individuals want to be assured that the company they work for has relocation services that will help them and their spouse if they are transferred. These relocation services may not only cover relocation expenses, but also help in finding new housing for the family and a new job for a currently employed spouse.

Employees are increasingly interested in benefits that affect their families in the present and in the future. One immediate concern is that of health insurance. In this era of spiraling health costs, it is increasingly important that individuals have adequate medical coverage. Employees who can choose among job offers may sacrifice a higher salary for better health care benefits. Potential employees may be looking for health care coverage not only for themselves but also for children, a spouse, and other legal dependents. In New York City, heterosexual and homosexual domestic partners are using the new registry for unmarried couples to officially acknowledge their commitment to each other. The purpose is to provide these committed couples, a majority of whom are gay and lesbian, with the same rights accorded married couples. This has helped some couples secure the health insurance coverage available to other families and their dependents (Richardson, 1993). The Lotus Development Corporation began offering medical benefits to gay and lesbian employees in 1991 and joined the ranks of other companies such as Ben and Jerry's Ice Cream that provide such benefits (Noble, 1993b). Nevertheless, benefits offered by domestic partner plans are taxable because the Internal Revenue Service does not recognize such partners as official dependents. And residents of Austin, Texas, recently voted to repeal a law that gave city employees the possibility of extending their health insurance benefits to domestic partners (Rowland, 1994). Although many employers include health insurance among the fringe benefits they provide for their full-time employees, those working less than full-time and for smaller companies are less likely to receive health care benefits. For example, about 25 percent of those who work 25 to 34 hours a week have employer-provided health insurance compared to over 60 percent of those who work 35 hours a week or more. While 78 percent of men and 64 percent of women who work at companies with over 100 employees are insured through their employer, this is true for only 35 percent of men and 23 percent of women at companies with less than 25 employees. And 75 percent of the uninsured women are, in fact, employed (Noble, 1994b). Provision of adequate health care benefits was at the center of the reform of the health care system proposed by President Clinton.

Although health insurance is one of the more immediate concerns of workers, long-term retirement benefits are also of increasing interest. Retirement benefits that accrue to a worker's spouse and children are even more attractive. Some employers provide life insurance of one and a half times the employee's salary as an additional entice-ment. To retain such benefits, a worker might stay in a job that he or she might otherwise leave, or a worker may change jobs to obtain retirement benefits.

Care of Children and Other Dependents

Although the media occasionally reduce the cause of a dual-worker couple's need for child care to the fact that the mother works, it is more accurate to say that the need for child care arises from the fact that both father and mother work or that the single parent works. Some parents can take care of their children and aged relatives if their job provides the appropriate flexibility, while most will need to seek the help of others to deal with these responsibilities.

Time and Flexibility. Although pay and job security are top pri-orities for some, job flexibility is becoming a higher priority for oth-ers. Computer networks, electronic mail, voice mail, and fax machines provide some workers with the flexibility to do their work in a variety of locations, including their own home. This **telecom-muting** is one way individuals can combine work and family respon-sibilities. A vice president at Banker's Trust in New York City works in the office 3 days a week and out of her home 2 days a week. Telecommuting allows her to work with the bank accounts of those as far away as New Zealand. This vice president's productivity is higher than that of many of her colleagues who spend their entire week in their offices at Banker's Trust (Calem, 1993).

Others report choosing particular occupations because of the work schedule. Some women and men suggest that one of their many reasons for choosing teaching was so that they could be with their children after school and during the summer vacation months (Lortie, 1975). Women are more likely than men to work part-time and may choose occupations in which many part-time jobs are read-ily available. In addition, women and men with children may choose to be employed by organizations that offer a flexible schedule for full-time workers. For example, the National Treasury Employees Union, which acts as the collective bargaining agent for the U.S. Department of Health and Human Services, successfully negotiated for an Alternative Work Schedules program. The program offers two com-pressed work schedule options: four 10-hour days per week, or eight 9-hour days and one 8-hour day and one day off during each 2-week period. Employees can also now vary their starting and ending time from day to day as long as it is within an established time range. It is an employee's option to work and accumulate credit hours that can be used to take time off. This is similar to compensatory ("comp") time, but it is a right and is largely at the employee's discretion rather than that of the manager.

Couples may also be interested in jobs that offer shift work. Studies consistently show that although mothers still do more child care than fathers, it is often a shared responsibility. A U.S. Census Bureau survey found that 20 percent of preschool children are cared for by their fathers, the greatest increase in the last decade (Chira, 1993). As you read Case Study 6.4, "Beating Time/Making Time: The Impact of Work Scheduling on Men's Family Roles," by Jane Hood and Susan Golden, you will see the impact that work scheduling had on the lives of two families. Employment that offers job sharing so that two unrelated individuals can share a job may be appealing to some as a solution to their child-care difficulties. The schedule for two clerical workers sharing a job might be such that one woman works in the morning and the other works in the afternoon, providing their company with the services of a full-time clerical worker. This schedule may allow the two women to more easily balance their work and family responsibilities. The most liberal of these is offered by some colleges and universities. On occasion, a husband and wife in the same academic field may share one full-time teaching position. Couples may make this choice to both accommodate family needs and increase the time available to pursue research.

Some workers choose employers who can provide particular family-related benefits not because of their current needs, but rather because of anticipated family needs. A couple committed to having children might choose an employer who would provide maternity or paternity leave. Although a man may choose an organization even though there is no paternity leave, a woman may feel that she must choose an organization that at least provides a partially paid maternity leave.

Child-Care Arrangements. Some parents prefer full-time, on-site child care. The convenience, price, and possibility of visiting one's children during the work day have tremendous appeal. Where on-site child care is not available, a company may provide vouchers or a referral service for child care. Child-care centers are typically open from early morning to early evening. Some child-care centers offer a night shift that allows working parents to bring children to the center in the midafternoon and pick up their children after midnight, but this is relatively rare.

Working parents panic when a child is sick, when the usual child-care center is closed, or when the babysitter gets sick. Although coworkers and supervisors may tolerate a 3-year-old in the office once because of its novelty, a second time would be unacceptable. Goldman, Sachs and Company, a noted investment banking firm, opened an emergency child-care center on their premises in 1993 (Lawson, 1993). Emergency child-care centers are intended to provide care when the usual child-care arrangements break down. A number of large employers realized that when child-care arrangements break down, one parent is absent from work. Goldman, Sachs evaluated their situation and decided that it was more effective to provide free on-site emergency child care than to have parents losing work days. Other companies provide child-care workers who can go to the employees' home.

Ethnic background also may have an impact on child-care preferences. Researchers at Harvard's Graduate School of Education found that Hispanic families had a stronger preference for family-like care than black or white families. There are some mediating factors, however. Two-parent families and families with relatives living with them of any race are more likely to use family-like child care, and Hispanic families are more likely than black families to be two-parent households and to have relatives living with them (Chira, 1994: A-19). Perhaps, then, Hispanic families are using the child care that is both convenient and cost-effective—care by relatives who are willing to take on the responsibility. In addition, Hispanic families reported that they wanted their children in a situation where Spanish was spoken. Thus, cultural background plays an important role in child-care issues.

Children are not the only dependents who may need care. People are living longer than ever before, and the proportion of our population that is older rather than younger is increasing. Although many older people live independently until their death, some working couples may find themselves in the position of having to care for aging relatives. Some families opt for nursing home care, but for other families, this may not be the best choice. Most working couples cannot afford to curtail work to care for an aged parent. These families may choose an employer who either offers or assists with elder care or adult day care. When on-site care for either children or adults is not available, some organizations and corporations may provide relief from the burden of dependent care by offering subsidies or reimbursements.

Societal Comparisons. Because increasing numbers of women and men with children are in the work force, young children need all-day care and school-age children need after-school care. This points to the need for affordable, accessible, high-quality child care. In contrast to the United States, preschoolers in France attend full-day public preschool that is free and most parents want collective child care (Greenhouse, 1993). In Sweden, parents can care for young infants under the provisions of one of the most extensive parental leave policies in the world. Fathers and mothers are entitled to share a leave of 270 days at 90 percent of their regular pay (U.S. Department of Health and Human Services, 1985).

Compared to other industrialized nations, the United States is notably lagging in paid maternity and paternity leaves and lacking in high-quality care that is accessible to all. This leaves some workers individually negotiating with their employer for flexible schedules and family leave. Some men may take sick days rather than using their company's formal parental leave policy (Kimmel, 1993). Some employees fight for broader policy changes at their place of employment. Other white-collar workers feel, rightly or not, that opportunities for promotion may be jeopardized if they complain too loudly about the tensions between work and family schedules. They wonder if their employer will underestimate their commitment to their work and career.

Today, women and men are likely to take the benefit package and flexibility a company offers into account in making their job decisions. The benefit packages offered by employers may determine their chances of attracting their first-choice employees, particularly those who are seeking to accommodate the needs of their families. Employers who involve themselves in family issues will find that it is good business, that it is economically profitable. Two recent studies of the benefits of "family-friendly" or "family-supportive" corporate policies indicate that companies offering such policies could expect increased loyalty, higher job satisfaction, and lower turnover (Noble, 1993a).

Role Overload

Although basic financial benefits are important, workers with responsibility for their children or aging parents know that time is an important issue, too. Although both dual-worker and single-parent families experience daily role overload, dual-career workers experience an additional set of difficulties.

Career Obligations

Individuals pursuing careers typically find that the primary years for building their careers begin in their late twenties and continue through their thirties and early forties. These are typically the same years that couples begin to raise a family. In Case Study 6.3, by Michele Hoffnung, you will see how Elizabeth resolves some of these issues. As a result of concern about these career and family issues, business schools, such as the prestigious Wharton School of the University of Pennsylvania, have introduced work and family topics into their courses as a part of the required curriculum (Noble, 1994a).

One cause of the potential overload is the simultaneous building of both a career and a family in the same decade. The assumption that both can be built simultaneously seemed predicated on the notion that there is one person in a family pursuing a career and another supporting that career and taking care of family needs.

The Two-Person Career. Traditional gender roles are at the heart of the expectations associated with a two-person career. In the past, a man who was a top executive, president of a college, or even president of the United States could depend on his wife to be a full-time adjunct to his career. The executive wife kept up the social end of the career, hosting parties, remembering important dates, and spreading an aura of feminine good will around the rising leader. This is reminiscent of *emotional labor* (Hochschild, 1983) described earlier in this book. This emotional labor is expected, but nevertheless unpaid. Several members of one college community were alarmed when they learned that the next president of their college was married but that his wife would continue to teach at a college in the midwest, commuting to Pennsylvania on the weekends. Even James Buchanan, the only bachelor president of the United States, found it necessary to have his sister serve in the traditional role of First Lady.

In 1992, Hillary Rodham Clinton's career as an attorney caused some to doubt her ability to serve as First Lady. These traditional expectations obscure the full contributions of both husband and wife. The wife is usually the unofficial part of the political, corporate, or university hierarchy. She cannot get a bonus or merit increase for doing a great job in any particular year. These traditional expectations may cause corporate boards to overlook potential leaders who do not fit the mold: a married man who has a wife with a career of her own; a married woman who has a husband with a career of his own; a single man; a single woman; or a homosexual or lesbian couple.

The "Mommy Track." Several years ago, the possibility of a "mommy track" (Schwartz, 1989) at top law firms was a hot topic. The name itself, of course, reflects gender expectations. The idea was that women who chose to do so could pursue careers that did not require as much of them as of those who were pursuing the fast track toward partner. The downside for women or men who chose the "mommy track" was that they could not expect to be either promoted or paid the same way as others. The idea was criticized for many reasons (Ehrenreich and English, 1989). Some pointed out that the "mommy track" would be lower in prestige. Others said the mere existence of a "mommy track" that would be predominantly occupied by women would hurt the careers even of women who did not choose this track. All women would be regarded as lacking full commitment to their jobs and careers. Others were quick to point out that the "mommy track" label would further inhibit men from this track even though it might be compatible with their family life and interests outside work. Despite these criticisms, the idea of a "mommy track" pointed to the necessity of accommodating the reality that both women and men may want to have careers and to be involved in their children's lives.

Daily Obligations

Daily overload takes place as a couple or a single parent tries to juggle the demands of both work and family. The typical single parent needs to take care of all his or her family needs, including work responsibilities, children's needs, and the needs of a household. White-collar, dual-career couples may be able to diminish the impact of the overload by buying the services of others. A couple may choose to have their house cleaned, groceries delivered, and meals prepared by others. Nevertheless, the couple still needs to develop a division of labor within the household.

Case Study 6.5, "The Second Shift," by Arlie Hochschild with Anne Machung, describes the plight of working parents. More often than not, women complete their full day at work only to arrive home to the next shift, the second shift of child care and household tasks. Hochschild argues that this second shift stems from the traditional roles of women and men. Although society is adjusting to women's participation in the labor force, stereotypical images continue to influence the expectations of women and men at home. Couples often inadvertently expect women to continue in their traditional role as chief cook and child caregiver. Because women in dual-worker and dual-career families are working the same long, hard hours as men, they understandably expect their spouses to participate in the second shift. Many women complain, however, that their husbands do not take responsibility for the tasks.

In November of 1993, the United States Roman Catholic bishops wrote a letter entitled "Follow the Way of Love" as their official contribution to the International Year of the Family announced by the

United Nations for 1994. In this unanimously approved document, the bishops recognize the many difficulties caused by economic pressures and family problems. *The New York Times* describes the letter as "a message to families that tells husbands and wives to treat one another as equals and urges men to share fully in child rearing and household duties" (Steinfels, 1993). This was a ground-breaking statement given that the Catholic church has traditionally taken a more conservative stance on women's and men's roles in the economic and domestic spheres.

In the best situations, husbands and wives have worked out a division of labor that both are happy with. It may mean that they follow more traditional lines; she does more of the inside work, he does more of the outside work, and they share child-care responsibilities. Others forgo traditional roles. She likes being outside, so she mows the lawn. He likes to watch car racing, so he folds laundry while he watches. He works longer hours than she does, so he chooses the somewhat shorter but less desirable tasks to be responsible for such as changing the cat litter or cleaning old food out of the refrigerator. In Case Study 6.3, "Elizabeth," by Michele Hoffnung, consider how Walter and Elizabeth mutually support each other in their efforts to pursue careers, raise children, and run a household.

Historically, when work and home were separated, women were primarily responsible for the private sphere—taking care of the home and children—while men were primarily responsible for bringing in income from the outside. As more women enter the labor force, families and society must redistribute the tasks that formerly were the sole responsibility of women.

Legal Progress

Over the last several decades, a number of statutes have been passed that have an impact on the relationship between work and family. Title VII, the Civil Rights Act of 1964, made it illegal to discriminate on the basis of race, color, religion, sex, or national origin. In 1978, Congress passed the Pregnancy Discrimination Act related to Title VII. This made discrimination on the basis of conditions related to pregnancy illegal. Prior to this, employers could dismiss employees for becoming pregnant, regardless of the employee's own preferences concerning how long she planned to work and whether she planned to return to work after the birth of her child.

Although a number of state family leave acts have been on the books, the federally mandated Family and Medical Leave Act went into effect in 1993. This measure requires that employers with 50 or more employees grant up to 12 weeks of unpaid leave annually for the birth of a child or for adoption; for the care of a child, spouse, or parent with a serious health condition; or for the worker's own serious health condition that makes it impossible to perform a job. Employers covered by the law are required to maintain any pre-existing health coverage during the leave period and, once the leave period is concluded, to reinstate the employee to the same or an equivalent job. The employee must have worked for the employing organization for at least 12 months and at least 1,250 hours before applying for the leave. Strong supporters of the Family and Medical Leave Act regretted that the leave would typically be unpaid, making it economically unavailable for many workers. Others rejoice in the fact that even the unpaid leave is now available not as a benefit but as a right of employees, both men and women alike.

In addition, the current tax rules in the United States allow families to take a dependent care tax credit. Some employers also provide a dependent care plan that allows employees to receive some of their salary tax free to help defray dependent care expenses. The employee agrees to have the employer put aside a specified amount of his or her salary tax free for dependent care. The employee is then reimbursed from that tax-free account as he or she turns in monthly receipts for child care. The federally mandated limit on such reimbursements is $5,000 for two children. Such a plan provides substantial savings (Bernstein, 1993: 149). Without this plan, a family would have to earn $6,000 to $7,000 to have $5,000 after taxes to pay for dependent care. The complication for some families is that their dependent care provider is paid "under the table." The only way one can get a tax credit or be a part of a dependent care reimbursement plan is to be able to produce receipts for the care received. Whether the caregiver is an immigrant nanny or a neighborhood babysitter, if that individual is unwilling to declare that income and provide the family with a receipt, these tax programs are not useful. On the other hand, corporate or organizational child-care centers routinely provide receipts for money collected.

Despite the legal advancements and the possibility of employers offering the benefits mentioned above, many workers are employed by organizations that do not provide benefits that help with family responsibilities.

Conclusion

Both work and family life are important to a majority of women and men. A full-time homemaker may lament her lack of achievement outside the home, but men often talk about not spending enough time with their families, particularly their children. For both women and men to feel they have real choices about the balance between work and family, societal norms must continue to change. Although men are increasingly involved in the care of their children, societal norms still make it difficult for a man to feel that refusing a promotion or being a full-time househusband is an acceptable option.

The remedies needed to resolve some of the conflicts between work and family were not necessary when work and family were co-located on the farm. But now, flextime, flexplace, on-site day care, financial assistance for child care, extended maternity/paternity leave, and eldercare are all programs that would help reduce the tensions between work and family. We also need to change our values such that using these programs does not interfere with others' assumptions about an individual's commitment to his or her work.

Individual families experience the tensions between work and family, but the best solutions to these difficulties lie in the hands of employers and society. For work and family to mesh in a manageable way, employers must take care of families. Role overload is not a result of an individual's psychological inability to deal with work and family, but rather is a result of a lack of appropriate structures and support being available for families and workers. Implementing policies that help employees cope with their work and family responsibilities will increase workers' job satisfaction. Although implementation of such policies would help companies look socially responsible, the most significant result for companies is the increased productivity of their workers. That result should motivate companies to deal with family issues in this era of increasing competition.

REFERENCES AND SUGGESTED READINGS

Bernstein, Allen. 1993. *1994 Tax Guide for College Teachers.* Washington DC: Academic Information Service, Inc.

Calem, Robert E. 1993. "Working at Home, for Better or Worse." *The New York Times,* April 18: F-1, F-6.

Chira, Susan. 1993. "Census Data Show Rise in Child Care by Fathers." *The New York Times,* September 22: A-20.

Chira, Susan. 1994. "Hispanic Families Use Alternatives to Day Care, Study Finds." *The New York Times,* April 6: A19.

Crosby, Faye J. 1991. *Juggling.* New York: Free Press.

Ehrenreich, Barbara, and Deidre English. 1989. "Blowing the Whistle on the 'Mommy Track.'" *Ms.* 18 (July): 56.

Ferber, Marianne A., and Brigid O'Farrell, 1991. *Work and Family: Policies for a Changing Work Force.* Washington, DC: National Academy Press.

Fernandez, John P. 1990. *The Politics and Reality of Family Care in Corporate America.* Lexington, MA: Lexington Books.

Gerson, Kathleen. 1993. *No Man's Land: Men's Changing Commitments to Family and Work.* New York: Basic Books.

Greenhouse, Steven. 1993. "If the French Can Do It, Why Can't We?" *The New York Times Magazine,* November 14: 59–62.

Hochschild, Arlie. 1983. *The Managed Heart.* Berkeley: University of California.

Hochschild, Arlie, with Anne Machung. 1989. *The Second Shift.* New York: Viking.

Kimmel, Michael S. 1993. "What Do Men Want?" *Harvard Business Review* 71 (November–December): 50–63.

Lawson, Carol. 1993. "In Emergencies, These Children Commute to Work." *The New York Times,* April 22: C-1, C-8.

Lortie, Dan C. 1975. *Schoolteacher.* Chicago: University of Chicago.

Moen, Phyllis. 1992. *Women's Two Roles: A Contemporary Dilemma.* New York: Auburn House.

New York Times. 1994. "Children in Rural South Are Least Likely to Be Left Home Alone." May 22: A-28.

Noble, Barbara Presley. 1993a. "Making a Case for Family Programs." *The New York Times,* May 2: F-25.

Noble, Barbara Presley. 1993b. "A Quiet Liberation for Gay and Lesbian Employees." *The New York Times,* June 13: F-4.

Noble, Barbara Presley. 1994a. "Coming Soon: Get a Life 101." *The New York Times,* February 27: F-41.

Noble, Barbara Presley. 1994b. "Unhealthy Prospects for Women." *The New York Times,* May 22: F-23.

Richardson, Lynda. 1993. "Proud, Official Partners." *The New York Times,* August 1: B-37, B-38.

Rowland, Mary. 1994. "Hurdles for Unmarried Partners." *The New York Times,* May 22: F-15.

Ruddick, Sara, and Pamela Daniels. 1977. *Working It Out: 23 Women Writers, Artists, Scientists, and Scholars Talk About Their Lives and Work.* New York: Pantheon Books.

Schwartz, Felice N. 1989. "Management Women and the New Facts of Life." *Harvard Business Review* 67 (January–February): 65–76.

Steinfels, Peter. 1993. "U.S. Bishops Urge Men to Share in Work at Home." *The New York Times,* November 18: A-1, B-17.

Thompson, Linda, and Alexis Walker. 1989. "Gender in Families: Women and Men in Marriage, Work, and Parenthood." *Journal of Marriage and the Family* 51 (November): 845–871.

U.S. Department of Health and Human Services. 1985. *Social Security Programs Throughout the World.* Washington, DC: U.S. Government Printing Office.

U.S. Department of Labor. 1995a. *Employment and Earnings* 41 (January). Washington, DC: U.S. Bureau of Labor Statistics.

U.S. Department of Labor. 1995b. *Employment and Earnings* 42 (February). Washington, DC: U.S. Bureau of Labor Statistics.

U.S. Department of Labor. 1995c. *Marital and Family Characteristics of the Labor Force from the March 1994 Current Population Survey* (February). Washington, DC: U.S. Bureau of Labor Statistics.

Vogel, Lise. 1993. *Mothers on the Job: Maternity Policy in the U.S. Workplace.* New Brunswick, NJ: Rutgers University Press.

The Labor of U.S. Farm Women

A Knowledge Gap

Elise Boulding

CASE STUDY QUESTIONS

1. What are the differences between the farm wife, the woman farmer, and the farm housewife? How would each of these conceive of the relationship between their work and family roles?

2. To what extent are farm women expected to engage in social and civic activities? How do farm women feel about these expectations?

3. What is appealing about farm life to these women? What is unappealing?

4. How does the rhythm of the life cycle affect the degree of conflict between work and family roles?

Author's Note: I wish to thank the following persons for their help with this study: Mary Rainey, Director of Oklahoma State University's Family Study Center, and Sharon Nichols, her associate: Monica Porter of the Vermont Extension Service: Phyllis Worden, Assistant Director for Human Development of the Colorado Extension Service. Finally, I wish to thank my student research assistant, Elizabeth Pickar, who carried out follow-up interviews and direct observations of Vermont farm women.

Source: From *Sociology of Work and Occupations*, Vol. 7. No. 3, 1980, pp. 261–290. Reprinted by permission of Sage Publications, Inc.

In the third world, roughly 70% of the female population is involved with agriculture. In the United States it is less than 5%. The problems of the two groups of women are vastly different, yet in one respect they are the same. Both are seriously undercounted in the agricultural work force, and in both regions national agricultural policy systematically handicaps women in the performance of productive farm labor. At the world level, women are officially counted as roughly one-fifth the world's agricultural labor force, although field studies of rural women suggest they are more like 50% of that force, going as high as 80% in parts of Africa (Boulding, 1977). Quite rightly, most attention is currently focused on the potential role of third world women farmers in alleviating hunger crises in their own countries. In the process of modernization, women are often left with the most primitive tools, while technological advances are reserved for men....

The data used...comes from 27 women; the fourteen most complete of the Oklahoma interviews, twelve Vermont interviews, and only one Colorado interview.[1] Three additional solo women farmers were also interviewed (two of them from Colorado), and more intensive work will be done with this category in the future. Supplementary information from farm wife profiles in *Farm Wife*

News and from other farm journals has also been used....

What all these farms have in common is that they are family operations. Of the women, 16 are farmer's daughters, 21 of the husbands are farmer's sons. All but one of the 27 families have one or both families living nearby. There is much mutual aid in farm work as well as considerable social life among the relatives in the extended family. Local high school boys are hired for summer work on each farm. Most of the couples farm family land, although a few have bought or rented from the outside. Many rent land in addition to what they own, and the men engage in a variety of special operations with a brother, father, or uncle that make the farm bookkeeping a staggering proposition. (A venture with a sister would be described as with the sister's *husband*.) Modal education is 12 years, or high school completed. Eleven families have children under 12 at home, 10 have children over 12 at home, 2 have no children yet. Number of children ranges from 2 to 7, with 4 the modal number. Only 4 couples have no grown children available to help with chores. The major bias evident in this group of women, apart from their economic security, is that they are all more or less "happily" married and love farming and the farm way of life. They may represent the most married, least divorced, more childed, most hard-working, and most contented sector of American life: women of the successful small-farm family.

Women's Involvement in Family Farming

Work-Role Concepts and Farm Tasks

The 41-hour week calculated for farm tasks, added to the 58-hour week allotted to domestic tasks, makes for a 99-hour total work week (see Table 1). A little over 2 hours a day (averaged over a 7-day work week) for field and barn chores and kitchen garden seems skimpy given the large size of many kitchen gardens, but may be accurate for some farms, if considered as an average over the year. Bookkeeping, "gofer," and the veterinarian role seem to be realistically estimated according to my interviews. What is missing from the editors' list, which I have added, is the coordinating role enacted by so many farm women. They consult and advise with their husbands, relatives, and any hired help on hand. They transport equipment and supplies, as well as meals and snacks, transmit messages, and often mediate conflict to get the right person or equipment to where it is needed at the right time. (Just finding the right field can be a problem—lunch or equipment may be brought to one field when needed in another.)

Home tasks are more obvious. The one hour per week estimate for nursing, considering the small and large scrapes and bruises that occur on farms, is modest. I replaced the original 50-hour time allotment for child-care, which assumes child-care concurrently with all other tasks, with a 7-hour allotment giving one hour a day for undivided attention to children.[2] Since farm mothers teach skills to their children, and have from two to five children each, this is a reasonable estimate, averaged over the years that children are in the home. Farm women spend more time cooking than their urban counterparts, partly because they cook for relatives, neighbors, and extra hands at peak work-load times, partly because farm meals need to be heartier than urban meals, and partly because they preserve kitchen garden produce for winter use.

Farm and home tasks combined make a 14-hour work day, 7 days a week. In summer the work day stretches to 18 or 20 hours. Urban women with children spend 13.5 hours at work, whether or not employed (domestic work expands to fill work time) on week days, but have more leisure on

TABLE 1

Farm and Home Tasks for Farm Women Per Week[1]

Farm Tasks	Hours per Week	Home Tasks	Hours per Week
Field and barn chores	10	Nursing	1
Kitchen garden	6	Child-reading [4]	7 (50)
Bookkeeper	8	Decorator	1
"Gofer" [2]	7	Cook	14
Veterinarian	3	Maintenance and repair	2
Coordinator [3]	7	Routine housework	28
		Food Planning	3
		Food Buying	2
Total	**41**	**Total**	**58**

Total hours spent weekly on home and farm tasks:	99 hours
Daily average for farm tasks:	6 hours
Daily average for home tasks:	8 hours
Average working day:	14 hours

1. Adapted from *Farm Wife News,* May, 1979, center foldout.
2. "Go for": the errand-running, including replacing broken parts for machinery.
3. This job is added by E. Boulding.
4. This job is given 50 hours in *Farm Wife News,* but assumes child care concurrent with other activities.

weekends (Riandey, 1976). We might assign them a hypothetical 86-hour work week in contrast to the farm wife's 99-hour week. They do not ordinarily experience the seasonal overloads farm women do.

This time budget is an artificial construct. Not all farm women do all or even some of the farm tasks listed, although no farm wife can evade "gofer." How do farm women themselves distinguish among the different degrees of task involvement? A Missouri correspondent on *Farm Wife News* (June 1979) proposes a classification of farm women very close to the one developed for this study:

First there's the *farm wife*. She's involved with her husband in their business of farming, helping out as she can.

Secondly, there's the *woman farmer*. She's actually doing the farming, either as a single woman or widow, or because her husband works off the farm.

Finally, there's the *farm housewife*. She's a housewife who happens to live on a farm, but has little interest or involvement in the farm business.

The 27 women considered in the following discussion all qualify as *farm wives* by the above definition. None are *farm housewives*. The woman farmer will be described later.

Identifying the Farm Tasks

There are several problems associated with identifying the farm work women do. The first is its seasonal nature. For grain, vegetable, and fruit farms seasonal changes are major. For the dairy farmer the basic rhythm does not change so much from winter to summer, though there is the calving rhythm, and also some planting—harvesting rhythm. Since farm animals all breed, birthing seasons can be heavy 24-hour-day duty periods, and women seem to do most of the midwifing. All the women interviewed felt the peak season pressures of their farms. Some literally worked for 20-hour stretches at such times. By asking for seasonal descriptions of tasks, we obtained a reasonably complete list of major activities. Still, we assume that our informants underreported what they did. There are probably a number of activities that are taken for granted and therefore not mentioned. Our long-run strategy is to find out what farm women do by observing selected women for a day in each of the major seasons of the year, recording every activity.

Table 2 gives a rank ordering of farm tasks reported by our 27 informants. Almost all drive tractors and other heavy farm equipment. It is impossible to know how many hours they spend on the tractor. Six commented "only when necessary," but necessity could arise for substantial lengths of time. When sickness or disability hits any family in a neighborhood, other families contribute a member for emergency tractor work. The skill level of farm wives with heavy equipment is probably underestimated (it may well be to their self-interest interest to keep it underestimated!). Twenty-three of the 27 women have kitchen gardens, 3 jointly with a mother or other relative. Those who do not have kitchen gardens are usually too busy with field work and skip gardening and canning.

Bookkeeping is done by 20 of the 27. Some do computerized bookkeeping with the aid of the Extension Service, others follow simpler methods. All know how important this is, and sometimes complain that their husbands don't pay enough attention to financial matters. Yet they seem to underestimate their own skill and information level. Few think they know as much about the farm as their husbands, even though they process all the records. Feeding cattle and doing the recurring "gofer" are the other major tasks.[3]

Going out in a snowmobile to feed cattle during blizzards, not infrequent winter occurrences in ranch country, can take almost all of a working day. January and February are hard, physically demanding months for farm wives on cow-calf operations. One wife commented in *Hoard's Dairyman* of January 25, 1979, that "feeding 25 babies [newborn calves] on bottle outside in either a blizzard or in 20-below weather" was the chore her city sisters had the hardest time believing.

TABLE 2

Rank Ordering of Farm Tasks Reported by 27 Farm Wives

Frequency of Reporting	Task
25	Driving tractor, other heavy farm machinery (6 "only when necessary")
23	Kitchen garden (3 joint with another adult)
20	Bookkeeping
18	Feeding cattle
16	Harvesting
15	"Gofer"
11	Breeding, birthing, rearing animals
10	Milking (dairy)
9	Cleaning milking utensils (dairy)
9	Running message center, with or without CB
8	Cleaning dairy barn
8	Veterinarian
5	Poultry
5	Planting
4	Fencing
3	Sugaring
3	Reading farm journals for farm management information

"Gofer" is the glue that holds the modern farm together. When a piece of machinery breaks down, as it does frequently, parts must be replaced instantly, particularly at harvest time, and only the wife may drop everything in field or kitchen to do it. "We keep the roads hot getting parts" is the way one farm wife put it. The sense that she is the crisis person, the emergency specialist, always on call, induces both pride and frustration. Discussions about gofer brought to light one serious skill lack for farm women: insufficient knowledge about the machinery to bring back the right part, even when given "instructions." (Farm women commiserate with each other on the hopeless inadequacy of husbands' instructions in such cases.) It may take several trips to get the right part. Even when it is clear what is needed, gofer may take hours before a store is found with the necessary part in stock.

The term "breeding-birthing-rearing" is awkward, but conveys the range of tasks women assume associated with the *reproduction* of animals, as distinct from simply feeding livestock, and also as distinct from health care, or the veterinarian role. Next to midwifing itself, which is most onerous with cows and sheep, the feeding of baby animals in the first weeks or months is one of the heaviest animal-associated duties. In *Hoard's Dairyman* of January 25, 1979, one Indiana farm wife writes, "I have fed and cared for all the baby calves for their first three months. The number totals 1,600 calves. Sketching and filling out applications for registration takes time but are an important part of the total operation." Every physical task, it should be noted, has its record-keeping counterpart, and farm wives must be equally adept at both. As for milking, some wives do it all, some do half, working along with their husbands, some are available for emergency milking only, and some do none at all. It is one of the most confining of farm tasks because it must be done twice a day on a precise schedule. The average dairy farm in our group was milking 45 to 60 cows a day. Cleaning dairy barns and dairy equipment is a complex operation involving disassembling and assembling a lot of parts. It is heavy, tedious, and demanding.

The veterinarian work is enjoyed by some, not by others. Some wives dread castrating animals, others take it in stride. Treating the scours (diarrhea) becomes routine. (A "you know that you are married to a farmer when" joke: "when he asks if our baby is over the scours yet.") Fencing, mentioned by only four women, is probably done by all, but is so taken for granted that they do not think of it. Keeping fences in repair is a constant preoccupation wherever there are farm animals, and most wives are adept at handling barbed wire and fence post. Sugaring, whether done with ancient or modern equipment (it is done both ways in Vermont), is heavy work.

The last item in Table 2, reading farm journals for innovations to pass on to the husband, was mentioned only three times but represents a high degree of skill and involvement. Coordinating does not appear as a separate task because the women do not report it as such, although it is involved in running a message center....

The Woman Who Farms Alone

Women may farm alone because they have been widowed or because their husbands have been incapacitated by accident or illness. Women who farm because they love it and have nonfarmer husbands are more puzzling, as are the women who never marry and farm for the love of it. Yet all of these women gain respect and admiration, particularly if they are successful. It is an old tradition. Smuts, in his book *Women and Work in America*, recounts, "One observer reported in 1886 that women had taken up claims on public land in all parts of the West. 'All over the thinly settled portions of Dakota,' she wrote, 'women live alone in their own shack and garden patch'" (1959:

11; see also, Comstock, 1910). Today, 74,000 women own and manage farms in the United States (Joyce and Leadley, 1977: 8). What is surprising is that people keep being surprised that women can farm alone.

Successful women farmers prefer outdoors work to indoors work. If not taught by their own fathers, they may in childhood (like one woman rancher interviewed on the Western Slope) find a neighbor farmer who becomes a father figure and teaches them how to farm. A widowed woman may train a daughter or niece to take over the farm, as we found in Vermont. A fruit farmer on the Western Slope with an architect husband, having raised a family of four children, was experimenting with new approaches to dwarfing fruit trees so they would require less water in an arid region. Women farmers are not "female men." Rather they are persons with a highly developed sense of individuality and self-confidence, who also happen to love the land. Many farm wives also have these traits, but take on more domestic responsibilities than they might otherwise prefer because they also value family life and the relationship with husband and children. Farm wives and women farmers may be seen on a continuum, with the housewife who happens to live on a farm but is not involved with it all at one end, and the never-married woman farmer who lives for her farm at the other end. Life circumstances and temperament play a part in determining woman's place on the continuum, but the patriarchal social structure probably pushes more women toward the domestic side than would be there by choice.

Additional Occupations and Legal and Social Status of Farm Women

Additional Occupations

In the earlier discussion of the Work-Family Role System it was pointed out that farm women often had more than one work role.

The distinction was made between the farm maintenance work role and extra economic activities not directly related to the main work of the farm. These activities divide into (1) self-employment, entrepreneurial activities on the farm or in town, and (2) paid employment in town or on other farms.

We will begin with an examination of the more conventional off-farm work history of the wives. Because not enough time was spent questioning in this area, the work history is certainly underreported. One-third of the women work intermittently, bookkeeping for other farmers or for businesses in town, doing a range of secretarial and clerking functions, waitressing, or performing day labor on other farms or at packing houses in town. Some do professional work, like nursing, or directing a choir. This work is an aid to the farm cash flow. Whether a farm wife is working at any one time is partly a function of the farm's cash needs, partly a function of the availability of work. In fruit country, every adult woman has worked at the fruit packing sheds at some time in her life, if only in her teen years. While six women reported that they worked only before marriage, further questioning would likely reveal that some of these have done odd jobs since. Women are so used to doing a great variety of things that they may not distinguish between those which are paid and those—the majority—that are unpaid. Of 26 wives, 3 are working regularly at full-time jobs; 2 are teaching, and one is a nurse; 4 reported that they had recently stopped regular off-farm work (some of them had been working full time in town), in order to be able to do more farm work; 4 indicated no history of employment....

Off-farm employment is only a part of what farm women do beyond their regular farm tasks. Table 3 lists every type of "extra" economic activity performed by farm wives as found through interviewing and in the course of background reading for this study. ...Section I of the table lists on-farm individual enterprises. These are separate from the main farm production, but involve farm products. In every case the woman processes and then sells something grown on the farm (fruits, vegetables, wool, sheepskin, peanuts, and so on)....

Section II of Table 3 lists entrepreneurial enterprises which do not use farm products, and which may be conducted on or off the farm. Occupations range from music teacher, editor, auctioneer, dog-groomer, babysitter, and home craftsperson to proprietor of a specialty store in town. Section III includes the paid employment in town: teacher, school bus driver, postmistress, cook, clerical work, and day labor. Every one of the 27 women we interviewed did one or more of the activities listed in Table 3. Most of the activities are not included in occupational statistics....

Time allocations among the three sets of tasks—domestic, core farm work, and auxiliary enterprises— will vary from day to day and season to season. If we allow an average of 2 hours a day, or 14 hours a week for auxiliary tasks, we find that the farm wife spends, not 99 hours as estimated in Table 1, but 113 hours per week or 16 hours a day at her three-job work life.

Social and Civic Activities of Farm Women
As if her day were not already full enough, we must also take note of the social and civic activities of farm women. The high level of visiting, picnicking, and "day-tripping" within the extended family, the neighborhood get-togethers for folk dancing or cards, and the round of church activities, all belong to the traditional social patterns of rural life. These are rounded out by rodeos and county fairs at which a great deal of "showing" of prize animals and craft products is done by children and parents alike, and by frequent trips to town to watch school sports events of farm children. The farm wife is the chief organizer and provisioner for such events. Even at the peak of harvesting, a whole fam-

ily will leave the combine standing in the field to go to town to watch junior in a Little League game.

On top of these traditional activities comes an additional layer of voluntary organizations for women: in church, they lead the women's circle or teach Sunday School; they belong to a homemaker's club, to PTA; they serve as 4-H leaders, Scout leaders; they are active in the women's auxiliaries of the Farm Bureau and Young Farmers of America; they belong to relatively new women's organizations promoting farm products, such as the Cowbelles and Women for Fruitgrowing; they belong to local historical societies, to sororities, and to a host of women's clubs that are town-based but involve rural women. In addition, they attend Farm Bureau and Extension meetings and conferences on their own and with their husbands, and become involved in the politics of agricultural policy through local elections and state action.

They are "organization women," just like their sisters of the suburbs, only they do it on top of much longer working days....

Should the civic tasks be considered a fourth work role? The concept of community volunteer work as a career for women exists for suburbia, both as part-time and full-time careers. It is at least as appropriate to think of the civic work of farm women as a part-time career. This work produces the networks which make up the women's infrastructure of mutual aid so necessary to the survival of any community....

Why and How Women Stay in Farming
Are farm women superwomen? The farm woman's day seems staggering. First, there are the domestic tasks, which are more demanding than for urban households because the families are larger, and food, laundry, and physical support needs are greater; then the farm tasks, which become the equivalent of a second career; then the auxiliary enterprises, which in effect become

TABLE 3

Type of Economic Activity Outside Major Farm Enterprises Carried on by Farm Wives[a]

I. **Self-employed Using Farm Products (On-Farm Activities)**

Craft Shop
"Covered Wagon Drive-in" or farm restaurant
Raising sheep, dying, spinning wool, weaving, teaching all of foregoing
Specialty fruit mail order business
Specialty pecan mail order business
Roadside stand for fresh farm products
Selling processed farm products: juice, jellies, pickles, etc. by mail order, roadside stand, or
  through retail outlets in town
Greenhouse—selling plants from farmhouse and in town
Poultry enterprise
Sheepskin vest mail order business
Peanut craft products retailed in town
Maintain a tourist attraction (zoo, caves, gold mine, etc.)
Scheduling and organizing hay rides

II. **Self-employed, Not Using Farm Products (On or Off-Farm Activities)**

Licensed auctioneer
Dog-grooming business
Magazine editor
Quilt making
Doll-making
Macrame
Knitting
Sewing
Operating specialty shop in town (hairdressing salon, clothing store, etc.)
Babysitting
Rodeo musician
Choir director
Music teacher

III. **Employed by Outside Agency, Off the Farm**

School bus driver
Elementary or high school teacher
Postmistress
Cook for town restaurants, clubs, school cafeteria
Waitress
Part-time bookkeeper in town business or for state agency
Part-time secretary in town business or for state agency
Part-time clerk in town store
Fruit packing
Day labor on other farms

a. These activities are not counted among farm tasks listed in Table 2.

a third career; and finally the civic activities, which becomes the fourth career. (Social activities we count as recreation, even though women have administrative and maintenance responsibilities for recreational activities.) How can anyone do it? And why do they report such a sense of well-being? Our interviewees made it clear that they love their way of life. They feel sorry for city women.

One answer is that they do not do everything at once. My descriptions in this article have been somewhat misleading, because I have not emphasized the cyclic nature of farm activities. There are two cycles. One is the seasonal cycle, which means that farm women plan ahead to do certain things in winter, others in spring, summer, and fall. Many domestic tasks are simply ignored in peak outdoor seasons. Some women give up cooking, and feed harvest crews from the local fast food drive-in.

The other cycle is the life cycle. The years when there are babies have a different rhythm than the years when there is a growing band of child helpers on the farm. The years when children are adolescents are good years, because they become adults in helping with farm tasks. Women spend fewer hours a day in farm tasks during the years the children are young adults but still at home than they do before or after. Mothers of under-twelves have the greatest pressures, perhaps, yet also the greatest rewards, because these are the years when the family is always together. The great activity spate of women in their forties represents the takeoff phenomenon, familiar to students of the family life cycle, when women find they are still young, with an accumulated fund of vigor and ideas, and some margin of time to use them. Also it is in this decade of life that the farm enterprise is likely to be flourishing. The fruit of earlier labor begins to show.

What do women themselves say about the farming way of life? We asked them what they liked best, and what they like least, about farming. Togetherness with husband, having the husband around to father the children and be companion and work-partner to the wife, and experiencing family togetherness are the most valued things about farm life. Love of nature and love of independence, not being bossed around by others, are also highly valued, as is the sense of creating something for the future which will endure. Even harvest time, the time when women have to be three places at once for 18 to 20 hour days, is chosen by three as what they love best about farming. They love the excitement, the bustle. Work with animals is intrinsically enjoyable for many.

The list of what farm wives like least is much shorter. A few mention specific chores, such as cleaning milking utensils, or heavy lifting jobs, but the majority complain that they cannot get away. Cows have to be milked twice a day, all animals have to be fed daily, and emergencies like sick animals tend to occur whenever a family trip (rare enough at that) is planned. Planning is risky. Some are embarrassed that they always arrive at gatherings late and have to leave early because of chores. Others worry about getting rid of the barn smell in a hurry when they need to go to meetings or out on errands. The women pride themselves on their clothes and appearance when they are off the farm, and set high standards for their wardrobe, which may or may not be home-sewn. Some degree of worry about the future of the family farm and its long-run economic viability shows through in all the interviews, though only for two is it a major source of anxiety. This is a reflection of the farmer's economic and political status in the larger society, not of the experience with family farming as such. Two women give housework as their least-liked task—one can be sure they spend most of their time in the fields. The dislike of winter is an understandable choice for the two who give it, in that the interviews took place just after the worst winter in decades. Keeping cattle alive through blizzards is a physically awesome task, and one in which the women were strenuously involved.

Although rural-urban migration has been a major phenomenon of this century in the United States, none of these women ever suggested that they would like to leave the farm and move into town. Most of them could not imagine any other way of life. They know they work harder than city women, and are proud of the fact. Ultimately the pride rests in a feeling of independence, a feeling that survives all the constraints of farm life. The additional emphasis on the relationship with husband—the pleasure in companionship, the close working relationship, and the sharing of parenting—suggests that a study of the farm family from the rural rather than the urban perspective might bring new insights into the dynamics of contemporary family relationships. Since the focus here has been on women, husbands' activities have not been described. From the conversations with the women it is clear that most (not all) farm fathers spend a great deal of time with their children from very young ages, and give a relatively gender-free farmchore training to both daughters and sons, particularly in the under-twelve years....

We have seen that the work-family role system is more complex for farm women, with their two or more work roles added on to the family role, than for suburban women, who may have only family and volunteer role, or family and one additional work role.

Who is the better off, the farm wife with her 99- to 113-hour work week or the suburban employed wife with her 86-hour work week? The farm wives' economic and legal status and social recognition lag far behind the contribution they make. Farm women have always moved to the towns in larger numbers than farm men. In this study we have interviewed the women who intend to stay on the farm. The town-ward flow continues, however, because that is where the conventional social rewards are. Farm wives themselves are increasingly turning to the town for their auxiliary work role, entering the nonfarm labor force. When both husband and wife are part-time farmers, what happens to family farming? And to the way of life that goes with it?

Before this way of life disappears, it is important to study carefully the varied production roles of women on the family farm, and to make assessments of the costs and benefits of farm roles for women, as well as for the society at large. Current policies will continue to drive women off the farm. Only a major research effort will tell us how much we will lose thereby.

NOTES

1. Because the Colorado interviews were conducted for a different purpose, it was not possible to collect enough comparable information. A discussion of Western Slope farm women and the wives of farmer-miners will appear in Moen et al. (1980).

2. A European time-budget study shows employed women spending 0.7 hours a day on child care, homemakers 1.8 hours. I have chosen an intermediate figure for the farm wife (Riandey, 1976).

3. Field work as a generic task was rarely mentioned although it was clear that anyone who drove a tractor did a number of other kinds of field work. Had we been experienced interviewers of farm women, we would have been able to pick up a variety of field-related tasks that were not mentioned spontaneously.

REFERENCES

Boulding, E. (1977) "Women, bread and babies," chap. 5 in E. Boulding, *Women in the Twentieth Century World.* New York: Halsted Press (a Sage Publication book).

Blood, R. O., Jr. (1958) "The division of labor in the city and farm families." *J. of Marriage and Family* 20: 170–174.

Burchinal, L. G. (1961) "Correlates of marital satisfaction for rural married couples." *Rural Sociology* 26: 282–289.

Colvin, E. M. (1942) "Another women's land army?" *Independent Woman*, 21: 102–104.

Comstock, E. (1910) "The lady and the lord: some scientific and successful farmers of America." *Colliers* 45 (September): 20–21.

Dunne, F., R. Elliot, and A. Block (1978) "The design and evaluation of a high school curriculum meant to increase the career options of young rural women." Dartmouth College. (mimeo)

Gardner, B. (1972) *Eat Your Heart Out: Food Profiteering in America.* New York: Crown.

Horvath, J. (1975) "Exchange versus grant transactions in environmental models." *Amer. Econ. Rev.* (May).

Huffman, W. E. (1976) "The value of the productive time of farm wives: Iowa, North Carolina, and Oklahoma." *Amer. J. of Agricultural Economics* 58 (December): 836–841.

International Harvester Farm Forum (1975) "Sounding off on the role of women in farming." Editorial Research, Meredith Publishing Service.

Joyce, L. M. and S. M. Leadley (1977) *An Assessment of Research Needs of Women in the Rural United States: Literature Review and Annotated Bibliography,* A. E. and R. S. 127. University Park, PA: Agricultural Experiment Station, Pennsylvania State University.

Kohn, S. B. (1978) *Working Together: Women and Family of Southern Saskatchewan.* New York: Holt, Rinehart & Winston.

Knutson, M. and D. Schreiner (1975) "Income returns for working women by place of residence." *Oklahoma Agricultural Experiment Station, Current Farm Economics*: 39–49.

Landis, P. H. (1951) "Two generations of rural and urban women appraise marital happiness." *Washington Agricultural Experiment Station Bulletin 524* (March).

Leevy, J. R. (1940) "Contrasts in urban and rural family life." *Amer. Soc. Rev.* 5, 6: 948–953.

Moen, E., E. Boulding, J. Lilleydahl, and R. Palm (1980) *Women in and the Social Costs of Economic Development: Two United States Case Studies.* Boulder, CO: Westview Press.

OECD (1978) "Part-time farming in OECD farming." *Agricultural Policy Reports,* Paris: Author.

Nikolitch, R. (1972) *Size, Structure and Future Farms.* Ames, IA: Iowa State Univ. Press.

Pearson, J. (1979) "Note on female farmers." *Rural Sociology* 44, 1: 189–200.

Pimental, D. (1975) "World food, energy, man and environment," in W. Sewall (ed.) *Energy, Agriculture and Waste Management.* Ann Arbor, MI: Ann Arbor Science Publishers.

_____ (1973) "Food production and energy crisis." *Science* 182 (November 2): 443–449.

Pleck, J. (1977) "The work-family role system." *Social Problems* 84: 417–427.

Riandey, B. (1976) *Besoins et aspirations des familes et des jeunes. Analyses Complementaries, Tome III, Le Budget-Tempo des Mere de Famille.* Paris: Caisse Nationale des Allocations Familiales.

Salamon, S. and A. M. Kein (1979) "Land ownership and women's power in a Midwestern farming community." *J. of Marriage and Family* 41, 1: 109–119.

Sawer, B. J. (1973) "Predictors of the farm wife's involvement in general management and adoption decisions." *Rural Sociology* 38, 4: 412–425.

Sullerot, E. (1968) *Histoire et Sociologie du Travail Feminin.* Paris: Societe Nouvelle des Editions Gonthier.

Smuts, R. W. (1959) *Women and Work in America.* New York: Columbia Univ. Press.

U. S. Department of Commerce, Bureau of the Census (1975) "Farm population." *Current Population Reports* 46 (December): 27.

_____ (1968) "Census of agriculture, 1964: farm labor." *Special Report,* Volume 3, Washington, D.C.

Wilkening, E. A. and L. K. Bharadwaj (1968) "Aspirations and task involvement as related to decision-making among farm husbands and wives." *Rural Sociology* 33 (March): 30–45.

Commuter Marriage

Deciding to Commute

Naomi Gerstel and Harriet Gross

Because it is still a relatively rare choice, we might expect that a couple's decision to set up two homes would be a long and agonizing one. We might imagine them making lists, talking long into the night, consulting with friends and relatives. But this is not the case. Surprisingly, the commuters seem neither to have agonized over nor even to have seen their decisions as a matter of choice:

Source: From *Commuter Marriage: A Study of Work and Family,* (pp. 22, 36–49) by Naomi Gerstel and Harriet Gross, 1984, New York: Guilford Press. Copyright 1984 by Guilford Publications, Inc. Reprinted with permission.

It was not a decision. It was not one spot where one pulls oneself together and says "let's face up to it."

She fell into it. Not a conscious thing to do it.

No real discussion. It was the only logical thing to do.

The decision just grew on its own.

We talked about it very little before it began. I don't have a good deal of imagination and we didn't talk about it a great deal. It happened.

It was not really a decision. It was an evolution. There was nothing to talk about.

There is no reason to disbelieve these comments or even question how typical they are. Yet, they tell only a small part of the story. If the decision to commute is not itself difficult, it is only because it emerges out of a long series of earlier decisions, commitments, and experiences....

Husbands' Attitudes Toward Wives' Careers

While most of these wives, as well as their husbands, are deeply committed to their careers, they are, most emphatically, married and want to remain so. A husband's commitment to his own career is not equivalent to his willingness to support his wife's career. Yet, just such support on the part of the husband may be necessary for the maintenance of the wife's career and even their marriage. Research shows that the attitude of a woman's husband is a major factor in her willingness and even ability to work (Birnbaum, 1975; Weil, 1971). An examination of the attitudes of the commuter husbands suggests that they typically provide support for their wives' career involvements and often they even pressed for it. Thus, we should understand these men's attitudes as a factor in the decision to live apart.

Almost all of these husbands strongly supported their wives' professional activities. Only a very few opposed them, while the large majority (about 90%) were, or became over time, either "laissez-faire" or "demanding." The largest group of commuter husbands are "laissez-faire": They want a wife who does whatever she feels is appropriate. These "laissez-faire" husbands typically respond to questions concerning their current attitudes toward their wives working by saying:

I want her to do it only because she wants to, not because I want her to.

Who am I to tell her to work or not? She works because she wants to. That's okay by me. If she didn't want to, I suppose it would be okay by me as well.

These men do not assume that their wives will live through them or for them. Rather, these husbands believe their wives are individuals who can be expected to pursue their own interests.

Although we know of no national data that speak directly to this issue, we suspect that if these "laissez-faire" husbands are not a majority, they are at least not rare, especially among highly-educated men (see Lopata, 1980). They are not opposed to having a working wife, but neither do they exert pressure on their wives to continue their careers. Thus, they presumably have different expectations for men and women. For a

wife, work is a choice. The choice happens to be paid professional employment. For a husband, there is no alternative; it is still not considered legitimate in our society for men to drop out of the labor force.

It is in the second group, those whom we call "demanding," where we find husbands who seem exceptional. These husbands clearly expect their wives to be professionals and exert pressure on them to develop careers. They will accept no alternative. These men provide the clearest support, even impetus, for the commuter arrangement. Statements like the following were made by men in this group:

I like her to work. I've always encouraged her to work. It makes her more interesting to me. I couldn't even imagine not being with a professional woman. There is just no way the woman who is my wife could be a housewife. For me, that kind of marriage just wouldn't work.

I should tell you frankly, I don't think I'd ever be interested in a woman who wasn't a professional. I couldn't be.

These men, unlike the "laissez-faire" group, expect their wives to pursue careers. For them, an interesting wife is one who is professionally engaged. To this extent, these ideas of marriage presume an orientation more typically found among wives toward husbands, rather than the reverse. To both of them, then, employment is not a matter open to question; it is an essential element of an attractive identity.

The attitudes of the men in this "demanding" group can be seen even more clearly among those couples where the wife, at some point, expressed ambivalence toward her career. During periods of work-related frustration, the wives might veer toward the housewife role. If they did, they found little support from their husbands. For example, one woman felt some attraction to the traditional housewife image. She, herself, felt frustrated when she was not employed, but it was her own discontent coupled with her husband's demands that fully motivated her. She spoke of a period when she felt she should stay home and raise children. But her husband only became irritated with those wishes:

He would come home at dinner and I would mention something about the children and he was very resentful of the fact that all I had to talk about was the children. He kept after me and finally I decided he was right and I'd go back to work.

Her husband recounted the experience of her staying at home in much the same way:

The tensions in our marriage got very great and I eventually laid down the law. Maybe that's a little strong, but it was in that direction that she had to do something; either she had to go out to work or she had to go back to school. She had to get out of the house.

In this case, "getting out of the house" meant the wife had to set up a residence in a separate locale, commuting home on weekends.

These "demanding" husbands have identical expectations for both sexes. What makes a woman interesting is the same thing that makes any human interesting. "Demanding" husbands may feel as they do, in part, as a way of rationalizing their own high commitment to work. They want to put a great deal of time and energy into their own careers. If the wife became "only" a housewife, she might place greater demands on her husband. By contrast, the wife's deep involvement in her own career reduces the pressure on her husband. A wife's equal professional commitment legitimates the husband's extensive work involvement: She will understand, through her own experience, the pressure on her husband.

It may be that some of those in the "laissez-faire" group would have been more demanding if their wives had expressed a desire to remain housewives. But as they did

not, the husbands understood the situation to be one in which their wives should do what they wanted to do, and this happened to be professional work. Eventually that professional work came to prescribe the establishment of a commuter marriage.

Precipitating Conditions: Why Now?

These personal histories set the stage for the decision to commute. Those who finally set up two homes are typically ambitious, highly skilled women, most of whom are married to supportive or even "demanding" husbands. Their ambitions had been frustrated, often at no small cost. But their decisions to commute are not simply a matter of personal ambitions or personal frustrations alone. Structural and ideological conditions currently existing in American society interact with personal experiences to produce this voluntary decision to commute. These conditions help explain why commuting is a contemporary response and why these particular couples decided to commute. When these couples establish two separate homes, they are acting in the context of contemporary social conditions which both facilitate and force that choice.

Ideological Conditions: The Effect of Feminism

A major factor facilitating the decision to commute is an ideological commitment to equality between the sexes, especially in the occupational sphere. Only if a woman believes her aspirations are as legitimate as her husband's will she consider searching for a job in a separate location. If there is a supportive climate for this belief, such as the feminist movement presently provides, then a woman is more likely to engage in an open job search unbound by her husband's locale. The feminist movement has, in some measure, legitimated women's demand for individual freedom and personal growth.

Commuters, who are already committed to equalizing their job opportunities, may well be the ideological vanguard of women professionals…

Typical comments were:

It helped me stand up more and more.

It made me feel better about myself. It's like a rebirth having all these women say all those things. I do still feel some guilt, but less and less because there are so many people out there saying what you're doing is okay.

It helped me assert myself and be treated like an individual.

It made me realize my options are much broader. Made things easier for me.

It's had a tremendous effect. Instead of being like 10 or 15 years ago, I would have been a weird, strange person and now I am not a weird, strange person anymore. There's an acceptance of what I am doing. So it's easier to feel good about myself.

It has given credence to me in that it makes it easier to be who I am….

Changed objective conditions may have preceded these changes in ideology, but the new equality between the sexes facilitates such new social forms as commuter marriage.

Conditions of the Job Market

For many couples, the newly supportive ideological climate coincides with crises in their careers. These crises are not simply personal, but are linked, more generally, to tight job markets which reduce the opportunity to choose positions in specific locations. In this situation, when both spouses have high commitments to their careers, they may see no choice but to commute between a work residence and a home residence, spending some nights apart.

The specific market conditions that pressured a spouse into a decision to commute vary with the career stage of that spouse.

One group consisted of younger spouses, both in the early stages of their careers, who had trouble finding any job in their fields. A second group consisted of older couples in which the wife was in an early stage of her career—having put aside earlier career interests to raise children. In both these groups, individuals did not commute to find better jobs, but to avoid unemployment or severe underemployment. There was a third group, consisting of older spouses both in advanced stages of their careers, who faced crises of a different sort. For them, the issue was not avoiding unemployment, but maximizing career goals by accepting a better position, which was a logical career opportunity they preferred not to miss.

No Job Opportunities

There were several different situations in which jobs were not available for both spouses. In some cases, one spouse could only find work away from the area where the other was attending professional or graduate school. In other cases, both spouses were beginning careers at the same time and could only find acceptable employment at some distance from each other. Two journalists, for example, found themselves in such a situation. The wife tried working as a freelance reporter for a small, local newspaper. But they finally decided they both needed full-time work. Emphasizing the lack of personal choice in their decision to commute between jobs 300 miles apart, the wife said:

We tried to get full-time jobs near each other. Oh, did we try! Letters everyplace and phone calls to everyone. We sent applications all over the country together. Finally, we had to take these two jobs. It wasn't easy. We can't even talk about it now. Every now and then we try and one of us ends up crying and we give up and decide to keep on and see what happens.

As she went on to describe their move, she remarked, defensively but with much insight:

I think that when people focus on the internal dynamics of this, they miss the point. It's the economic climate not some quirk in our psyches or in our relationship.

As journalists sharing the same field, their situation was more difficult than most. However, other spouses in different fields also faced the same situation and tried "applying all over the place" so they might stay together in a single home. But they, too, could find nothing.

Finally, there were couples in which one spouse had a job, while the other, just beginning or renewing a career, could find no employment in the same location. In one such couple, the husband finished his degree before his wife finished hers. While writing her dissertation, they moved, with some excitement, near his new job. Upon finishing, she applied to every school in the area around their home. At first, finding nothing, she tried staying home. Finally, she "decided" they had to commute:

There was never any real discussion about it. It was the only logical thing to do. I mean, I had applied to over 100 schools in the area—from community colleges on up—and there just weren't any jobs. Graduate school is just not so much fun that you just go to it to do it. And I couldn't stay home any longer without a job. We both knew I had been wretchedly unhappy sitting at home.

All of these couples who were beginning careers had to commute to find any acceptable employment. Though in some cases they received more than one job offer, the choices did not include jobs in the same place for both spouses. As their comments illustrate, the situation then *demands* that they look elsewhere. As they put it, it was only "natural" or "logical" to do so. Most did not even think of themselves as having chosen to live apart; they could not sit down, discuss the possibilities, and choose between an intact nuclear structure or a commuter

structure. Rather, these couples saw no choice but to commute. Most saw it as a temporary adaptation. They hoped, by continuing to look for other positions and by establishing themselves in careers, that their situations would change and they would be able to share, once again, a single residence.

The "Best Job" Not Available

However, not all of the couples who did commute were unable to find two jobs in the same locale. In the second situation, where the couples were at a later stage in their careers, the spouses had been working for a period of time—most for many years—in the same location. They were both established and could have remained together in one home. Then, one of them was offered a "better" job—a job more attractive in terms of prestige, interest, security, or intellectual growth, as well as income—in a different location. In some cases, the new position involved a move within an organization; in other cases, a move from one employer to another. For this group as compared with both of the others (where at least one spouse was still in the initial stage of a career) how they got the job offer represented a crucial difference determining the choice to commute. Almost all of the spouses in this more-established group were sought out by employers.

For some, the job offer was a consequence of changes in the structure of the job market. Here, instead of a tightening job market which cut off options, affirmative action policies led to a widening job market as employers reached out for highly skilled women. Before the offer, these commuters had not actively pursued a position. But, since the offers were appealing career opportunities, they felt they could not turn them down.

The following case illustrates this situation. The husband was a therapist with an established practice. His wife had a job, but one dependent on periodic state funding. A prestigious organization approached her and offered her a stable, high level position. In explaining their approach, she said:

I was very fortunate to be a woman. I have to admit that. I will have to admit that they were hiring my potential and hiring a woman, but it was a situation I could grow into.

Because she had always followed her husband and minimized her own career, this potential "growth," the ability, finally, to maximize her career chances, led her to accept:

No other position offered such an attractive package. I really wanted something I could focus on, grow with, expand with. This offered prestige and a national orientation, a great deal of possible leverage, a great deal of challenge. If I hadn't accepted, I would never have had the opportunity to develop.

Her husband was not quite so excited about the change but, nonetheless, agreed that she should take the job:

She had worked her whole life. This is not a new thing, a commuter marriage that came out of nothing, or some kind of middle-aged doldrum from being chained to the stove. It was never a "sit down, think it out" decision. We talked about it, of course, but it just runs its natural flow. We both understood what it meant, that it wouldn't be easy. But it was just something she had to do.

Like other commuters, he felt that the establishment of two homes did not constitute a "decision" as we generally understand that term. Instead, the commuter arrangement grew from the way they had lived their lives and occurred at a time that did not speak so much to newly developed preferences as to a changing national climate.

However, it was not always women who responded to an employer's pursuits. In another, far less typical, case both the husband and wife had jobs in one location. Their situation was the reverse of most: She had tenure at a prestigious university, he was at a nearby community college where he felt frustrated. Having established a national reputation through his publications, he was approached by a much better university with an offer of tenure. Though accepting meant that he had to move far from their shared home, he could see no other choice:

I was very dissatisfied with my position and I had never intended it to be a permanent kind of thing. I was kind of dilly-dallying and didn't really know what to do. A tenure offer at such a good school was really hard to turn down. It was a very painful kind of thing. I felt deep down that I should get out of the other situation or I never would. So, I finally decided I had to move.

At the same time, his wife felt that she could not abandon her tenured position with no job in sight to replace it. But she fully supported her husband's need to move ahead in his career.

For all of these couples who could have remained in a single home work is clearly a dominant status. But, they, like commuters in the earlier stages of their careers, would have preferred to remain together. Not only are they willing to travel to their jobs, but back to their marital partners as well, investing a good deal of time, energy, and money in the process. Because they were in the latter stages of their careers, they have to commute if they are ever to attain the professional stature consistent with their aspirations and abilities. Both groups of commuters attempt to deal with the disjunction between the occupational and familial systems. Both groups respond to external pressures that, in concert with their personal predispositions, lead them to "choose" a commuter marriage.

What the Decision Indicates

As we have seen, by the time a particular position appears, commuting may well be a foregone conclusion. Commuters have developed a shared history in which professional involvement is important for both husband and wife. One spouse—typically the wife—is frustrated in this ambition. An egalitarian ideology legitimates the resolution of this frustration through a commuter marriage. At the same time, a bleak job market or changing job opportunities undermines the possibility of a wife remaining in the same locale as her husband. Thus, the job market, either the lack of any job or of the best job, pressures couples into the choice of a commuter marriage. In concert, these personal and societal factors promote the decision to commute and, at the same time, make the decision appear as though it were not a choice at all.

It is in this context that we can examine a number of factors that one might expect, at least at first glance, to promote the decision to live apart. First, we might expect couples, especially in an inflationary economy, to live apart for financial gain or even survival. This is not the case. Second, we might expect couples who set up two homes, while committed to their careers, are not deeply committed to their marriages. This, too, is an erroneous assumption. Let us look at each of these assumptions.

Work Is Not for a Wage

Commuters did not primarily accept job offers for financial gain. This fact can be demonstrated in two ways: Almost all commuters said that they would continue working even if it were not financially necessary; their actual behavior, as indicated by a cost–benefit analysis of commuting, supported this assertion.

To determine whether the separation of residences was undertaken for increases in revenue, we computed a financial cost–benefit analysis in the following manner. First, we subtracted each individual's salary before commuting from his or her salary while commuting. Second, we computed the yearly cost of commuting for each individual by adding the yearly cost of (1) the second residence, (2) phone calls to spouse, and (3) travel between homes. Third, we obtained the total cost or benefit of commuting by subtracting the yearly cost of commuting from the yearly change in income.

To analyze the data, we had to separate two groups of commuters. First, some commuters did not have any job before they established two residences. Of course, these individuals did make substantial gains in income by moving away from their spouses. However, their increases were far less than they would have been had they obtained the same salaries without commuting. If one subtracts each individual's yearly cost of commuting from his or her increase in salary (as described) the median income is at least $6110 below what it would have been if that job was in the same location as the spouse's.

It is among the second and larger group of commuters, who moved from one job to another, where the data show most clearly that commuting (and employment) is not undertaken for financial reasons. In this group, there were more reductions in individual income than increases (after commuting costs are subtracted from change in salary). Here commuting resulted in a median loss in family income of $1830. (The range of gains and losses was from +$6620 to –$9840.) Pursuing a particular job cost couples money.[1]

These figures would not surprise commuters. Most of the respondents in this study point to the financial drain of commuting as one of its greatest burdens. In many cases, expenditures they could previously support had to be foregone:

Some of the things we used to do, we can't do anymore, like taking expensive vacations. Everything we do is just to be together.

All kinds of money is just going down the drain that we might be using to travel together or enjoy ourselves. It's just a very expensive arrangement.

One man commented on the disadvantageous tax laws that are not even included in the above cost–benefit analysis:

> *I will say one of the real disadvantages of this is purely a financial one. On top of travel and living up here, are the very adverse tax laws whereby my two states of residence don't have reciprocal tax arrangements, so I end up paying taxes twice. So, I am paying for the privilege of commuting.*

We see from this analysis that most couples launch a commuter marriage to participate in careers which usually do not raise their standard of living. Though there may be gains in prestige, interest, "identity," and colleagueship, generally there is no gain in family income.

Marriage Retains Its Importance

We have suggested that work is a central life interest for both spouses in a commuter marriage. However, this does not mean they do not value their marriages. Rather, for individuals who are committed to their careers, the choice to commute in no sense means that they are not highly committed to their marriages. Because individuals value BOTH *career and marriage,* they may be forced to live apart from their spouses for some of the time.

Family and work are not independent of one another. Rather, satisfaction in one affects satisfaction in the other. Much research (Piotrkowski, 1979; Aldous et al., 1979) documents the negative marital consequences when a husband does not perform adequately in his job. The interdependence of the husband–worker roles partially explains such findings: if a man's performance in his job is adequate, he has, in some measure, fulfilled his family obligations. However, this fact alone does not explain the interdependence of family and work. Put

simply, an individual's self-esteem or happiness is the sum of performance and satisfaction in his or her various endeavors. Though some areas of life may be weighted more heavily than others, especially at different stages of family life and career, throughout life frustrations and gratifications in one affect behavior and sentiments in the other.

If the commuters had not chosen to live apart, and thereby gain satisfaction in their work, their marriages would have suffered. Throughout the interviews, their comments indicated awareness of the connections between these two spheres. Interestingly, their comments revealed two different perspectives. Some said that if they *themselves* were not satisfied with their careers, their marriages would suffer:

It was not just a career that led us to do this [commute]. A great deal has to do with how you see yourself and so on. It was very demoralizing for me to be there. And obviously, if I was going to be demoralized, in some way or the other, it was going to affect our relationship. I see a connection between the two and it is very hard to separate them.

It is important to realize that if I am unhappy in my job that I'll be unhappy in my marriage.

Simultaneously, they also suggested that if their *spouses* were happier in their work, they themselves would be happier in their marriages:

I want her to be successful. And I don't think there's any insincerity in my saying that. I think that she'll be a lot happier and I think she'll like me more as a result.

When he's feeling good about his work, he likes himself better and he likes everything better. That includes me. So it's just plain good sense to set up this arrangement [commuting].

Both sets of comments reflect a relatively new notion of marriage, a transformed "idea" of what marriage is and should be. That is, there is an unwillingness or inability to sacrifice oneself for the happiness of the marital unit. These spouses do not abide by the old image that supports models of marital "togetherness." Instead, marital satisfaction is predicated on individual work satisfaction.

The complementarity of work and family suggests that individuals need to perform well in both to be satisfied in either. However, the demands imposed by family and occupation are unequal. An individual who wants both a career and a marriage has more control over the latter. The employment system is relatively inflexible. Many employers still can, and do, require that employees follow prescribed patterns for output or amount of time on the job. In most cases, those hired are expected to spend much, if not all, of their time in the area near their jobs. In contrast, the structure of family is more susceptible to individual manipulation. Because family attachments are diffuse and emotional, they can be changed to allow concessions for work roles over which spouses have less control. If both spouses want careers as well as a marriage, adjustments have to be made in the more flexible—family—sphere rather than in the work sphere. Consequently, some couples are forced to set up two separate homes.

For commuters, such a choice does not imply that their marriages are unimportant or even that their careers are more important than their marriages. Instead, their willingness to expend a great deal of time, energy, and money commuting to their families (as well as to their jobs) highlights the value they place on their marriages.

In fact, most of these couples exhibit an intense commitment to maintaining the quality of their emotional relationships. They want to preserve this quality and are mindful of the threats that commuting imposes on it. One husband made this especially clear in discussing how annoyed he gets at imputations that there may be some-

thing wrong with his marriage if he is willing to endure separation. On the contrary, he argued:

Our relationship is like a potlatch. We're going through all this just because we want to keep what we have together.[2]

In general, these spouses provide descriptions of their marriages as emotionally valuable or significant to them. The premium they put on the relationship makes it worth their efforts to maintain it. They understand very well the significance of the relationship to their own individual well being and this recognition helps them choose and endure the challenges of commuting.

Clearly then, the choice to commute does not signal an unstable marriage or unstable individuals, unless commitment to a career itself is taken as a sign of instability. Rather, commuting is a response to an endemic condition of occupational life rooted in the social structure. As wives' lives change because of new values and behaviors, so, too, must the lives of their husbands change. Commuter marriage is better understood as a rational response to a societal disjunction than as a rejection of marriage....

NOTES

1. Of course, these figures only indicate that commuters were not working for a wage in the short-term. It might be argued that by commuting, they were investing in careers and consequently were likely to be increasing long-term returns. But, these figures were also computed without considering the higher rates of taxation that accompanied commuting: The costs of travel and a second home are rarely deductible. Some couples even paid taxes in two areas.

2. The term "potlatch" refers to the North American Indian custom which involves the purposeful destruction of property to express status and thereby "earn" leadership in the community by such conspicuous consumption (see Mauss, 1954).

REFERENCES

Aldous, J., Osmond, M., & Hicks, M. (1979) Men's work and men's families. In W. Burr, R. Hill, F. I. Nye, & I. Reiss (Eds.), *Contemporary theories and the family* (pp. 227–256). New York: Free Press.

Birnbaum, J. A. (1975). Life patterns and self-esteem in gifted family-oriented and committed career women. In M. Mednick, S. Tangr, & L. W. Hoffman (Eds.) *Women and motivation* (pp. 369–419). New York: Wiley.

Lopata, H. (1980). Spouses' contributions to each others' roles. In F. Pepitone-Rockwell (Ed.), *Dual-career couples* (pp. 111–141). Beverly Hills, CA: Sage.

Mauss, M. (1954). *The gift* Glencoe, IL: Free Press.

Piotrkowski, C. S. (1979). *Work and family system*. New York: Macmillan.

Weil, M. (1971). An analysis of the factors influencing married women's actual or planned work participation. In A. Theodore (Ed.), *The professional woman* (pp. 453–464). Cambridge, MA: Schenkman.

Elizabeth

I Was Raised to Do Everything

Michele Hoffnung

CASE STUDY QUESTIONS

1. How did Elizabeth's family situation when she was growing up affect her initial orientation toward and final decisions about work, marriage, and motherhood?

2. How did Elizabeth and Walter manage their interests in careers and children?

3. What kind of support systems were available for Elizabeth during pregnancy?

4. How do Walter and Elizabeth divide the obligations associated with running a family and a household?

5. How does Elizabeth feel about her choices regarding work and children?

...Elizabeth always wanted a career. She was raised by her widowed father and grew up expecting a full, many-roled life. She married while preparing for her career and established a conjugal relationship based upon a sharing of roles and respect for both partners' career goals. When she became a mother she continued her career commitment and her employment as well....

Elizabeth belies the stereotypical image of uncaring, preoccupied, career-oriented

Source: "Elizabeth: I Was Raised to Do Everything" by Michele Hoffnung is reprinted from *What's a Mother to Do?* by Michelle Hoffnung, by permission of Trilogy Books. Copyright © 1992 by Michele Hoffnung.

mother. She and her husband share strong family values. They spend a great of time with their children; their family is their recreation. They organize their work hours to ensure that one of them is with the children most of the time and utilize a regular babysitter three days a week.

Their relationship is mutual, supportive, and sharing. Neither values their career more than their family or their family more than their career; they delight in both of these aspects of their lives. By careful planning and role sharing they are able to reduce the stress and maximize their enjoyment of their multiple roles.

> I'm definitely sure I didn't want to be a mother when I was a little girl. I thought mothers did a lot of housework or died. I had very negative vibes about mothers per se. I never played with dolls; I had teddy bears who were always sick—probably working out all my fears—they were always bandaged up and in slings and things. I never played with dolls. I was given a doll by my long-suffering grandmother and I took the head off to see how it worked.

Elizabeth was raised by her father; her mother died of cancer when she was three and a half.

> We had a housekeeper for eight years and then his widowed sister moved in and was

with us from the time I was about eleven until I went to college. But actually, when I was in high school, she became rather ill, and it sort of ended up that we were taking care of her more than she was taking care of us. She left when I was in college; he has lived alone since then.

I think, like any other little girl in those days, I thought weddings were really neat, and swishing around in white dresses and all that was exciting. I also remember thinking that most of the women I knew had pretty dull lives. I didn't have a mother at home, so I didn't have a role model of anyone who was fulfilled doing the domestic business. The lady we had was marvelous, and she was a very affectionate, warm person, but she was also paid for doing it, and I think I knew that when I was very little. I don't ever remember thinking, "Gee, the life of wife and mother is what I want."

I think what I did yearn for was a close relationship. I realized that everybody else had that; after all, in those days nobody had a single parent. I think that when I would go over to other people's houses I rather liked the family idea; I sensed without ever having articulated it that my father didn't have a helpmate, didn't have another person in his life.

Elizabeth always expected to have a career as well as a relationship.

I think I wanted to be a writer as soon as I read *Little Women*. I think my father read it to me when I was six or seven. Ironically, I am a writer, although I'm not the kind of writer that I thought I would be when I was seven. I'm still very much into writing and research.

I think I was first allowed to babysit at about thirteen and I did that a lot in high school. I actually made, at the time, quite a bit of money. And then my first real salaried job was when I was seventeen; it was between my junior and senior years in high school. I worked in the catering department of a very large bakery and catering company. It was very much like working in a factory, and it was fun because I was earning mini-

mum wage, which at the time was eighty cents an hour! But it was also terribly boring work—I would do things like butter bread for eight hours, and I went nuts. I think that was one of the things that made me determined that I was going to get a profession: I had to do something to prevent this from becoming my career.

Her father expected a great deal from her, and she internalized these expectations.

When I was a girl, I was raised to do everything. I was raised to play the piano, to do well in school, to be a good athlete, to be a lady, to wear white gloves. I used to jokingly say that my father raised me to be a member of the junior league, a wife, a mother, and then if I wanted to be an academic, too, that was just fine. It never occurred to him that these things had to be choices. I think I spent high school and maybe part of my college and early professional years trying to do all things—making all the bread, being the perfect domestic one, in addition to being the best graduate student and all that. Pretty soon it dawned on me that you couldn't do all these things, that you had to make choices or else your health was going to crumble.

Elizabeth grew up in the midwest in a family of two. Her father was a manufacturer's agent who, although middle class, was always subject to the tensions of an uncertain income. He was also a very giving parent.

He is an extremely affectionate person, and he is one who has spent an awful lot of time with me. Sunday afternoons we always did something: we went to a museum, we went to concerts, we went for a walk around the park, or went hiking in the country if it was nice weather. I don't remember very many Sundays that we didn't do something. Saturdays we did a lot of errands—we did the grocery shopping and riding around after. He always got home early enough so that he was around; we ate dinner together. From the time when I was very small, he always ate dinner with me if he was home.

He did the shopping and lots of picking up stuff, but the housekeeper did the basic domestic work. He was a great breakfast cook because he had been a bachelor for a long time; he could make eggs and bacon and things like that. When the housekeeper left and my Aunt Miriam came and would occasionally get sick, he and I would sort of learn to cook together, beyond his earlier capabilities, because we got sick of eating the same foods all the time. I remember going to the bookstore and buying *Joy of Cooking* when I was eleven or twelve. We wanted gravy. We had a roast and we wanted to learn how to make gravy.

But he was not a demonstratively emotional person. I don't remember his saying things like "I love you"—it would have embarrassed him. He certainly showed it, and I certainly knew it. He read to me every night before I went to bed, gave lots of hugs and things like that, but I don't remember him saying in so many words, "I love you." It's something that I try to do with my own children because he didn't do it for me. I just feel it's too bad not to be able to verbalize it.

Elizabeth attended a private girls' school from seventh grade through high school, then went east to attend Smith College.

I had some notion that my mother had wanted to go to Smith, and, therefore, "I'm going to Smith for my mother." I don't know if that's really true. My father, of course, always dated Smithies, all the way through Dartmouth. I think I just had this feeling: "Carry on the family position." I think my father would have been very disappointed if I had said I wanted to stay home and go to school nearby. I think he very much wanted me to go away; I think he wanted me to go to Smith, as a matter of fact.

She spent her junior year abroad at a Canadian university and the summer between her junior and senior years in Europe.

She met Walter while touring Europe. They spent a casual afternoon together and did not even exchange last names. In the fall he looked her up at Smith and they started dating.

We went out together that year, my senior year, and I think that spring I was pretty serious about this guy. I was also very serious about my career. I remember our deciding very coldly and rationally that we didn't want to take on the first year of graduate school and the first year of marriage at the same time. And so we didn't; we got married a year after that.

Before starting to date each had applied to graduate school at Berkeley.

We both got in. God knows what would have happened if we hadn't, but we did. We went there unmarried, sort of unofficially engaged. We got officially engaged in November. We got married the next summer. My father was determined to roll out the wedding of the century, and he couldn't do it by himself, so I had to go back and do the mother-of-the-bride bit for myself and get myself married. He would never have been able to pull it off.

During the early years of their marriage, Elizabeth and Walter did their doctoral work and launched their careers.

Our relationship was very good; it was very academic. I think we had a lot of mutual interests, although we were not in the same field. No problems—just had a good time. We worked very hard; we didn't go out a lot and do a lot of socializing.

At the time of the interviews, Elizabeth was thirty-eight, Walter was forty, and their three children were eight, five, and two. Elizabeth was a college professor, Walter a research associate at a different university. They owned the comfortable home in which they lived.

They carefully planned the timing of their first child, who was born six years after they married.

We simply sat down and figured it out. He is a biologist after all and he knew the biological reasons for having children reasonably early. At that point we both had teaching experience, we had this house already, so we were settled. We were financially at the point where it would not be a drain to have a babysitter. We felt that I probably could finish my dissertation if I stopped teaching and had the child. I probably couldn't do the three things, but I could do the two. So it was really a calculation based on several variables.

When we were first married, we really didn't talk about having children. I think we just thought, "Someday we will probably have babies, but this is very much in the future." When we got to the point of five or so years of marriage, we simply thought, "It's about time; we don't want to be too much older; we don't want to wait too much longer." We had this myth that it would probably take us six or eight months, so we might as well start. It turned out that it didn't, but that's doctors' advice—don't race right in and assume you are going to get pregnant the next minute.

So it was a very calculated decision. In fact, one of my husband's running jokes, every time he sees one of these movies where women come fluttering in and throw their arms around their husbands and say, "Guess what, dear!" is, "You never did that. You always asked me two months ahead of time! Why don't we do these romantic things—roses, knitting booties!" It was not that way.

Elizabeth had few expectations and little support for her first pregnancy.

I wasn't around very many people having babies; my friends were all academics. I don't ever remember having a close pregnant friend. Those who were from college were always five thousand miles away and I sent them a silver spoon and that was it. I don't remember being afraid. I don't remember thinking anything much about it, except that this was a perfectly normal process and that I would probably do it—it wasn't a very great concern.

I remember the first visit to the obstetrician he started asking me things like, "Do you want to breastfeed?" And I had never thought about it, but said, "Well, sure, why not! This is the way one does it, or we wouldn't be here after ten thousand evolutions, so I think so." But I had never really read books, I never had sat down and planned these things out. I remember having seen a film in college, one of those awful old-fashioned childbirth films where they put a black band across the mother's eyes and then show you the obstetrician's eye view, and I remember thinking, "This is really sickening, and I don't want to watch, and I don't want to be very much involved in it." But I don't remember being afraid; I just remember thinking it was kind of yucky.

I did not want to use anesthetic because I had ether when I was eleven and it made me really sick, and it scared me to death. I think to any intellectual person, probably the thought of being put to sleep, you are afraid you are never going to wake up. Your identity is your mind; if somebody is going to put me to sleep, I'm just going to become a vegetable. So my feeling was, "I will go through anything other than be put to sleep."

Like many women committed to continuing their careers while embarking on motherhood, Elizabeth was glad to be expecting a child but not overjoyed with the experience of pregnancy. She had no models for being a pregnant college professor.

My first pregnancy was not uncomfortable— I taught right up until the end. I did not particularly enjoy being pregnant. I didn't hate it, but I wasn't the type to sit around contemplating my growing navel. I guess I found it in a faint way embarrassing because at that point nobody in academic life ever did this. I think it was a little uncomfortable to stand up and do things like give papers at meetings, or lecture to people, or teach, and colleagues tended not to mention it, even when I was practically ready to pop. I think I felt it was a little awkward. Maybe that's not true so much anymore.

I thought, "Okay, this is the way you get babies, I want babies." I didn't sit around glowing. I don't mean I hated it, but I think I was fairly neutral about it. I looked forward to having it over with. I didn't like the way I looked. I don't think it bothered me particularly, but I didn't go around jumping into maternity clothes in the sixth week, looking forward to saying "I'm pregnant." There wasn't anything I particularly liked about it. I disliked being fat, being ungainly, having trouble moving around a little bit. I'm not very comfortable that way. It's sort of like being five pounds overweight and wishing that you weren't.

I remember at one point, toward the end of the first pregnancy, thinking, "My goodness, I'll never be alone again," and being worried about that because I'd always enjoyed being alone a lot. I didn't like feeling that somehow I had been invaded and that I might never be really alone again. I think that was not true, in retrospect. I've been alone a lot; I don't think it changed very much, but I remember an afternoon's worth of subtly having this occur to me and thinking, "I wonder if I'm going to miss this."

Walter's involvement with the pregnancy was also down-to-earth.

I think he was very helpful, very matter-of-fact; he was interested but he didn't go wild. He read books, he went to Lamaze classes with me, but he wasn't romantically intrigued. I used to say, "Don't you want to feel a foot?" And he would say, "Yuck, no, not especially." On the other hand, he was very supportive. I think he was good for me because he didn't encourage me to wallow in it either, but if I felt like talking about it he didn't turn me off.

Her first pregnancy was very easy.

I think I had a couple of weeks of nausea with the first but not very much. That was much worse with my later pregnancies, as a matter of fact. I was just very lucky—I didn't have any backaches; I didn't have all the usual things that people complain about. Other than not feeling very good for a couple of weeks somewhere around the thir-

teenth or fourteenth week, I don't remember any discomfort. The first pregnancy was the most comfortable. I got increasingly nauseated, more so in the second one and more so in the third. I also, as everybody does I suppose, gained more weight with each one and had bigger babies with each one. And I was also that much older with each one, so who knows.

Elizabeth's low key attitude about her pregnancies did not carry over into the deliveries. She was well prepared, having taken Lamaze classes with Walter. All three deliveries were by natural childbirth.

I think, as every woman is, I was unsure. One never knows exactly what it is going to feel like, no matter how many films you watch or how much you read. I don't remember anything that I would really call fear. It was more apprehension and uncertainty. I was afraid of anesthetics, and still am, and I was determined that I wasn't going to take any—not because I wanted to be courageous but I think for two reasons: One, because I was really afraid of losing my mind, quite literally, and secondly because I've always been somebody who likes experiences, and I wanted to know what all this was about. I remember a friend who had a baby saying to me, "Oh, it was so comfortable, they put me to sleep and then I woke up and they told me I had a boy." I remember being really turned off and thinking, "My goodness, it's like having your appendix out, I don't want that. I want to be there. I want to know what it's like. I want to know that the baby's all right the minute that it's born. I want to know what it is. I don't want to be out of it."

The births were all very nice. In fact, I remember saying after the first one that delivery for me was really sort of redemption. I hadn't enjoyed the pregnancy much, had kind of tolerated it, but I really liked delivering babies. It was a lovely experience.

Elizabeth had no outside help after Rosa, her first child, was born, so she prolonged her hospital stay by a day. She came home four days after giving birth. Her hospital stay was only two days with each of the other children.

> After the second, my mother-in-law came for a little before and a week afterwards. And then my father came when Jesse was born. He and Walter divided everything right down the pipe. My father did the cooking and the dishes, and Walter did the kids and the laundry. He stayed for a week, and he loved it. He had a baby when fathers were kept away for about six weeks because they were germy and incompetent. He loved it. He came in to see Jesse the next morning, and Jesse was named after him and my father-in-law, so he was really thrilled with the whole thing. I don't think he'd seen such a tiny baby, certainly not to be able to hold it. He was marvelous and intrigued with the whole thing. I think he heartily enjoyed it.

> I remember being a bit more on sort of an emotional teeter-totter after the babies were born. I would either get the giggles, or, if something happened that was sad, it would sort of wipe me out. If academic pressure intensified, it would be that much more intense than it was normally. I had nothing like postpartum depression, just swings of emotion that I felt were hormonally caused. I could almost feel myself revving up when it was time to nurse the baby.

Elizabeth nursed all three of her children, for eight and one half, thirteen, and sixteen months respectively.

> I enjoyed breastfeeding. I thought that it was a lovely way to have sort of enforced leisure, especially with the second and third one when there was another one around wanting to be read to and all. It's a nice way of being sure that you have time for the newborn, and I thought that was good. I also just had a very strong sort of biological feeling about it, that this was a good system, that nature had intended it this way. The race had obviously evolved this way, and, if you could do it, it was very healthy. And I liked it. I thought it was easy. With Jesse [the youngest] if I had had to get up in the night

and warm a bottle, it would have done me in. It was all I could do to get up.

> I think, if anything, having a child made our marriage better. I don't think it did anything very radical to it, but what was really nice was seeing each other in a new role, that somebody you care about and someone you had a very good relationship with as a friend, as an intellectual companion, is suddenly someone you see as a father. It was nice. He has always been a very involved father, a very participating father, loves his children, likes to play with them, likes to be with them. I think that was obvious from the first five minutes, and it was just nice to see someone you care about in that new role. I don't remember ever feeling that it created tensions and all the things you read about. That just didn't happen.

Walter and Elizabeth were committed to both of their careers. As two professional people they planned to share family responsibilities and have outside help.

> I think we just assumed that we would hire a babysitter and that we would share a lot of the childcare. I don't remember feeling conflicted. I think initially we thought we would get someone who would come here, and then it just happened that the lady we got said she couldn't come here, but she could take the baby at her house, and that turned out to be an advantage because then we could work at home.

> Starting from eight or nine weeks, I did the same three-days-a-week thing. I have the babysitter three days a week, Monday, Wednesday, Friday, and then also work during naptimes the other days, and in the evenings. I have had the same babysitter for nine years, which must be some kind of modern miracle. She's two and a half blocks away; she is an Irish mother, fantastic, dedicated to the needs and interests of children. She had her own children very, very young. She is not a great deal older than I am, but when we first started with her, her youngest child was nine. She wanted to be home when the child came home for lunch, but she also needed some money. She has always

taken our infants at her house. We are an embarrassingly planned family, all exactly three years apart, so she had each child for three years and then, when they went to nursery school, she picked up with the next one.

Elizabeth was able to control the timing of her children exactly. Since her teaching commitments ran from September through May, she timed her babies for early June. This enabled her to be home the first eight or nine weeks without missing classes.

The first time we thought maybe in the next six months sometime we might want to have a baby, and it turned out that the minute we tried we did. After that we thought maybe we could do it that way the second and third time, and, as it happened, that was the case. So, by then we were sort of joking about it, saying why don't we have one on June 5th. Their birthdays are three years apart almost to the day.

When her family was complete she continued to control her fertility....

I had my tubes tied two years after Jesse was born. We both decided that we didn't want to do it right after Jesse, partly for practical reasons, since we understood it would be an added stay in the hospital, but also we both felt we didn't want to do it in the kind of postpartum feeling. We wanted to be really sure that we intended to do this. I talked it over with my doctor and he said it was better to wait until you really felt that you had handled all the awful contingencies that can happen and you're that much farther from having a newborn infant.

This careful planning was a consistent trait of Elizabeth and Walter's.

They already shared responsibility for household tasks before Rosa was born.

Years and years ago, before we ever had kids, we sat down and really talked about the whole housework business in a real time and motion way—my husband had his engineering degree. And we decided that we

would be very careful about things that had something to do with health or things that really bothered people: that if somebody had a real thing about a straight living room we would do the straight living room, but we would not do things that didn't pose a health risk and didn't bother us. We just decided that unmade beds did not bother either one of us and that we were not going to become slaves to the notion that you had to have a made bed to be a decent person. Basically nobody makes the beds, but the cleaning lady changes them once a week. Laundry we split. I do the clothes; Walt does the sheets and towels. He does the buttons; I do the sewing with a needle and thread. He does the buttons with one of those buttonnaire things.

In addition to household tasks, they also share financial responsibilities. Their joint earnings are between $55,000 and $64,000 a year, depending upon variability in book royalties. They live modestly, except for their children's private school tuitions. They rotate the task of paying the bills.

We are both natively very frugal. If there is any sort of unusually large expense we work it in, but we try not to do two of those kinds of things in a year. But I wouldn't say we budget in the same sense as friends of mine do, where they actually sit down and allocate every penny. We really lucked out on housing. We got this house when the housing prices were tolerable. We got very good rates for it, and we really don't have very heavy housing expenses, which is just a blessing.

Generally Walt pays the bills this year because he's home more. He kind of writes the checks as they come in. Neither of us can stand the idea of taking an evening out and doing it for the month, so we usually try to keep up with it as they come in. We always pay our own professional bills, things like fees for journal subscriptions, or the cap and gown I just had to rent. That kind of thing we do individually. Joint expenses for running the house and so on usually this year he does because he's home when the bills come in, and he can just sit down and write the check and send it off quickly.

This cooperative sharing of roles, in conjunction with careful scheduling, enables Elizabeth to continue to work full time after having children, with relatively little stress. She and her husband are equally responsible for picking up the children after school and babysitter and taking them to their various after-school activities.

Our attempt is to be quite fair with each other and to do it something like two days each, and then the fifth day we see who has got the biggest burden. It depends really upon whose needs are the greatest. We have been lucky this year that very seldom has anybody really had to give up something that really matters. And if it did, it was who announced first. Last Thursday we all had, ironically even the children all had, something we wanted to do. I had put in a claim about a month before that there was a seminar that I particularly wanted to attend and a person I had been invited to meet, so I just did it. My husband could have, I suppose, gotten an afternoon babysitter and gone to his, but it turned out that he decided that it was easier not to.

Elizabeth feels that her ability to work has improved by having children.

I think it organized us, at least me. My husband has always been pretty well-organized. Believe it or not, I think it made me a better thinker because I think it disciplined me. I realized, okay, you've got until three o'clock, or whatever, and you've got to get this amount done and thought through. I think before I tended to go up every possible little alleyway. I couldn't write a word until I read the last eighty-five things written on it. And I think I cut that out, I think I became a more efficient worker; I used my time better; I didn't fritter it away.

I also think there is something very joyous in the contrast between a child and academic work because academic work is selfish and narrowly focused. You can't be interrupted; it's not sociable. A child is just the opposite. A child is selfless, and broadly focused, and demanding, also very sociable, and you can play with them. When I got really sick of the dissertation, I had the baby. When I got sick of the baby, I had the dissertation. It was really a very nice balance.[1]

My husband has never been a nine-to-five person; I think that's why he likes academic work. He likes flexibility, and he is a very quick worker. He has always done a lot of things; he has always had a lot of hobbies and a lot of projects. We laugh that there was one scene that a friend of mine noticed; I didn't because he is like this all the time. She came in and the TV was on, my mother-in-law was visiting, and my husband was sitting at his desk holding the baby in one arm and sort of jostling her on his shoulder while writing an academic paper. Jeanne came in and said, "What are you doing?" and he said, "I'm writing such and such an article." And she said, "This is absurd! No one can work like this." But he can, he truly can. He can talk to his mother, hold the baby, have the TV going, and still think. Now, admittedly, he wasn't solving a differential equation, but he was doing something useful. He's like that—he's remarkable. I cannot do that, but he really can, so I honestly don't think having a child set him back.

I think he did feel that he wasn't the typical Yale assistant professor who worked ninety hours a week and went to the lab every night. I don't think he would have been without children and having children he's less inclined to do that. He's a family man. He was also an only child, and it's nice not to have only children. I think we like our family; we just like our family life.

Elizabeth puts neither career nor family first.

People who are basically housewives and mothers have often said, "What are your priorities? Now, don't you really put your children first, and don't you really feel that you put your professional life second and you really live for your children?" On the other hand, women who are basically career women have often said to me, "Don't you really find the children are just sort of an obstacle and your main goal is the career?" I keep resisting saying yes to either one of them because I really think that, aside from things like if a child becomes ill, I don't think there are fixed priorities. I think that the priorities shift from month to month and day to day. I remember when Aaron was going into first grade, right round the time that Jesse was born, he seemed to go through a period of being very nervous; he didn't want me out of his sight. He needed a lot of attention that particular summer that his sister didn't need and even a newborn baby didn't need. The baby could be lying on my lap and get all of his mothering while Aaron was getting a lot of personal attention. On the other hand, right now I've got that lovely stack of term papers to do. I will probably not take time to do something with a child that I would do three weeks from now when the semester is over. I think it's very important for anyone who takes on this multiple-roles business to realize that priorities shift. It's truly not that your career is more important, or really your children are. They're all very important, and they keep getting rearranged almost on a daily, certainly on a weekly basis.

Taking care of their two jobs, their three children, and their dog leaves Elizabeth and Walter very little free time.

What do you do with your spare time? The answer is, "What is that?" I would say basically an awful lot of things with the family. We usually try to do an outing at least every weekend. We cut out of the newspaper interesting things to do and have a file that we put them into, like maple syruping, apple picking, county fairs, zoos, things like that. We usually try to do one outing a weekend, sometimes more, but it depends on the season. We often do things with another family who have kids roughly the same age as ours. Sometimes it means them coming over for lunch and letting the kids play and having some adult conversation.

Neither of us plays any kind of sport regularly. We used to play tennis but we don't like to pay for babysitting to do it. I haven't been to a movie since Aaron was born, I don't think. Walt loves movies and he goes to movies a lot. I'm just not a media person. Sometimes he goes to matinees in the daytime, if he has time off, because I don't like to go. He used to have a great crony whose wife hated the movies too and the two of them went all the time but, sadly enough, they moved away.

We have a season subscription to Long Wharf Theater. We take advantage of a lot of free things at the university that come along. We occasionally go out to dinner with friends, though it's been a lot less often the last few years. It must be something about our lives suddenly that we're just so busy that the motivation for organizing a dinner party is not really there very often. As a matter of fact, I think I've had about five dinner parties this January, and they've all been on the spur of the moment, "We've got a refrigerator full of spaghetti sauce, come on over." They were lovely. I like them like that because you don't have to fuss for two days ahead of time. But I do like to entertain. I enjoy dinner parties. I love to cook and I would do it more often if I didn't mind spending the two days.

We get a babysitter and go out about once a month. As a matter of fact, we have never joined a babysitting pool because we don't go out often enough, and we've always been concerned about getting really boxed-in and losing evening work hours. In fact, we do it so seldom that our kids really complain when we do it; we keep telling them a lot of people go out twice a week, but they just aren't used to it.

I think we spend more time together than other people I know, and I value that. I sense that a lot of people that I know kind of want to get away from their children. They feel burdened. They are always looking for times to plan something when they don't have to be involved with the children. I don't feel that. I think we probably enjoy each other more than some married couples I know who seem to like to do a lot of things with other people, and sometimes you wonder if they are avoiding doing things together because they don't like to. In other words, I think we may value the old traditional notion of family life more than other people seem to. I think we have a tremendous sense of responsibility to one another and to the kids, and I think it's very mutual, which is what makes it work.

I feel very responsible for my husband's own satisfactions and happiness and professional fulfillment, and I think he does for me. When one of us has some kind of triumph—we publish a paper, or win an award, or get a book out—we celebrate as if it belonged to both of us, and we articulate this to each other. It's almost as if it's the same career and I'm just as thrilled when he gets something as I am when I get something, and I think vice versa. It's very mutual.

Elizabeth is very satisfied with her marriage, her family, her career. I asked her to project fifteen years into the future, when her youngest would be seventeen.

I don't expect to be doing anything all that radically different. I hope I'll have published some more books. I hope I still like the work I'm doing. I don't expect radical transformations. I'm ambitious academically—I hope people will have heard of me—I hope I have a lot of bibliography behind me. But as far as any major qualitative change, no. I hope I'm still married, but a little less harried. We won't have anyone who cries in bed anymore, I hope. At least Jesse now announces that he's "frying" in bed. He doesn't just cry, which is one advance, and it's "frying" because he can't say "C." So he says, "Mommy, come get me, I'm frying." Generally it's a nightmare.

She is extremely positive about the effect on her life of having children.

I would say it has been altogether positive. I think it's enriched my marriage because I've seen my husband in a new role, or a series of new roles, as a parent. On the practical level, it's made me more organized. I don't procrastinate as much as I used to. I have finally gotten the family which I did not have growing up, and I really like it.

I feel that I live very much in the present, and I don't plan ahead as much as I used to. I think I spent most of my twenties kind of "when I get my dissertation finished," "when I get the book out," "when I get this article written." In fact, I remember one time when we were in graduate school we had some kind of set-to and I accused my husband of really being unpleasant and he said, not altogether as a joke, "Oh, I'll be nice when I get my dissertation written." I think it was a joke; on the other hand, he was perfectly serious that there was going to come this utopian time when we wouldn't have pressures on us and everything would be very easy.

I think that we have realized that that time is never going to come. We're always going to be very pressured, we're always going to be busy, there are always going to be eighty-five more things to do than there is time in which to do them. And so I think we've learned not to say "someday we have to do that." I think that's what maturity means: coming to grips with the present and not always projecting into the future.

Yet, there are professional costs to her choices.

I went to a conference about four years ago and the topic that we discussed was "Can a feminist scholar who has multiple roles perform at the highest professional level?" That was a real toughy because then, four years ago, I kept insisting yes, damn it, I'm just as smart as anybody else. I think now I might modify that. If you're talking about becoming *the expert* in a field and putting out the sixty-hour weeks that you would have to do to achieve that, the answer is probably no. But I also think that's not a question for women, it's a question for people. I think the same thing is true for men. You read about people who are in high levels of government service who never see their families. I think that's a choice that people have to make: what kind of people they want to be. When I do commit myself to writing a book, writing a paper, doing a study, I try to do it at the highest professional level. I make sure that

that task is the best I can make of it. But as far as saying I have to get ten books out by the time I'm forty-five, no.

Elizabeth's approach to life is a wonderful example of good planning. She has the career she always wanted to have; she also has a fine family....She plans childcare arrangements, daily schedules, and housekeeping. Importantly, she does not do this alone. She and Walter have a relationship built upon mutual respect, egalitarian principles, and strong family values. Her middle-class background, her strong relationship with her father, and her high level of academic and professional achievement all contribute to her choices, and her choices clearly contribute to her happiness. She fully enjoys her combination of career and motherhood.

Beating Time/Making Time

The Impact of Work Scheduling on Men's Family Roles*

Jane Hood and Susan Golden

CASE STUDY QUESTIONS

1. What was the impetus for the change in family scheduling?

2. How did husband, wife, and children react to the change in scheduling?

3. What do we learn about the intricate connection between work and family roles, particularly in terms of scheduling?

4. What did James Mooney learn from taking on more of the child-care responsibilities in his family? How did his feelings about this change over time? Why do you think his feelings changed over time?

Men's work schedules are the revolving doors through which men leave and enter family relationships. Which and how many hours a man works help to determine not only the length and frequency of family interactions, but also their quality. This [case study] closely examines the impact of two men's work schedules on their family lives. The men were the same age, worked similar hours, and each had young children and

*We wish to thank Joseph Pleck and two anonymous reviewers for their helpful comments on earlier versions of this article.

Source: From *The Family Coordinator,* Vol. 28, No. 4 (October 1979). Reprinted with permission of the authors and The National Council on Family Relations.

earned similar incomes when interviewed....We find that for one, working an afternoon shift has unanticipated negative effects on his family relationships, while for the other, the same shift has an equally unintended positive effect. However, in the latter case, as the man becomes more involved in his family, work scheduling again becomes an issue....

Clearly, then the relationship between time and timing of a man's work and the quality of his family life is not a simple one. In the two case studies which follow, we illustrate how the impact of men's work schedules on families can vary depending on their wives' employment status, other family members' schedules, children's ages, and the priorities given to occupational and family roles. We also attempt to explain what it is about the work-family role system (Pleck, 1977) which forces one man into a vicious cycle of *beating time,* never having enough, and allows the other to find ways of *making time* even when he is working over 60 hours a week.

Case Studies

Methods
The concepts presented in this [case study] have been developed in the context of sev-

eral research projects. Jane Hood, a sociologist, studied the transition to a two-worker family. She used data from extensive taped discussions with sixteen middle and working class couples over a two year period.... The wives had returned to work up to five years before the first interview, after having been home full time for from two to twenty years. Susan Golden, a clinical psychologist, used interviews and methods of naturalistic observation in home, work and school settings to study the work-family interface in families with infants and pre-school children. The initial observational study of two contrasting families from urban and rural settings was extended to include data from short term preventive clinical work with fifteen families in a similar developmental stage in a pediatric setting. The names used in this article are pseudonyms.

John Williams: A Young Professional

This section...explores some of the ways in which the work hours and commitments of a young professional launching his career interact with family needs during the early child-rearing years. When Susan Golden observed the family, John and Deborah Williams were in their early thirties. John was a systems analyst, and Deborah had left her part-time job after the birth of their second child, planning to return in a few years. The children were 5 years and 5 months old at the time of the study.

John's description of his job centers on the theme of "time" and time use. He is disturbed that there is always more work to be done and not enough time. Accomplishments for him are measured in terms of production. At work, John is "beating time, buying time, selling time, losing time, fighting time." The images of aggressive procurement prevail. Time is the currency of management. His credibility and loyalty to the company are established by his willingness to put in more time for the company.

John feels he works between 40 and 60 hours a week for the sake of his family, but since there are only so many hours in the week, time "spent" in work is taken away from the family and vice-versa. When John's work drew him out of the family for prolonged periods of time, Deborah would find herself embroiled in a spiral of increasing conflict with 5 year old Seth. Tense and overloaded by the end of the day, she would greet John in an angry and demanding manner. John, in turn, would withdraw from her.

During a particular period of 4 weeks, John was managing a team of workers attempting to meet a difficult deadline. The project had had more problems than anticipated and they were behind schedule, having difficulty obtaining adequate computer time for their project. As a result, the team went onto a schedule of working from noon to past midnight, in effect, moving to the afternoon shift. John also commuted 45 minutes each way to work. Seth was in nursery school and arrived home after his father had left for work so that they kept missing each other. Deborah did not keep Seth home from school because she needed the break for herself, and John would only be able to spend one hour at most with Seth before he returned to work, if he had the energy to relate to him at all. John also worked throughout most of the weekends. John felt that this was difficult but that it was important for him to stay with his co-workers in order to sustain team support, as well as develop his own expertise.

During this time, Seth became increasingly provocative with his mother; every small issue became a battle, with resulting temper tantrums and tears. His mother's patience was wearing thin. Seth began to sleepwalk at night, carrying piles of paper around, finally falling asleep at the foot of his parents' bed curled up on his "papers." During the day, he would walk around carrying his "papers" and become very upset if anyone interfered with them. To Seth, the papers were the equivalent of the computer print-out his father always carried to and from work. At the same time, Seth also became more and more preoccupied with Spiderman and his special powers. Deborah said, "I feel as if Seth has turned the house into his own fantasy world. Spiderman is in every corner. Traps are everywhere." The living room was indeed strung from corner to corner with web-like string traps.

In an effort to get out of this uncomfortable power struggle with Seth, Deborah decided to ask Seth what was going on. After talking awhile, Seth broke down, crying, "I hate daddy, I hate daddy, where is he?" alternately hitting the pillow and attempting to hit his mother. Things began to make sense. Deborah had not connected Seth's anger at her to the changes in John's work schedule. The anger Seth felt towards his father for disappearing from the family was being displaced onto Deborah, who was bewildered by Seth's rage and in need of support from her absent husband. This was a crucial time in Seth's development when he needed increased distance from his mother and identification with his father. Seth has been doing well with this separation in nursery school. His attempts to be like his father are reflected in his frantic carrying of the "papers." However, this was not sufficient to help him sustain needed distance from his mother.

Shifts in the family's social network at this time left the family with few outside resources, all of which exacerbated the intensity of the troubled, reactive mother-son alignment. The extent of Seth's rage became more frightening for him the longer his father was gone from the family. Seth's school hours, combined with the availability of computer time at night meant that he did not see the reality of his father to temper his fantasies as this superhero reenacted the anger Seth felt towards his father by filling the house with traps and tricks. Deborah then became preoccupied with her relation-

ship with Seth rather than confront John with her anger.

At the same time, Seth's father was at work, trying to beat a deadline, and planning strategies, traps and tricks to procure more interesting work for his department. Moreover, the greater the tension and stress at home, the greater the distance between John and the family, the greater Deborah's hostility towards her husband, the more likely he is to distance himself from the family, feeling pushed into the role of outsider, completing the destructive spiral.

It would be all too easy to blame Seth's "behavior problem," Deborah's depression, or John's distancing rather than look at the work-family conflicts operating here. John says that he is working for his family and that work and family are separate. John explains that work is a "jungle" and home should be a comfortable nest. Despite John's wish for the separation of these two spheres, the frustrations of work are often inappropriately displaced onto the family. In addition, John's absence from his family has set off a chain of shifting alignments and reactions resulting in a home that is even less comfortable than work. While John has an ideological commitment to the importance of family life and would probably rate it as first priority on a survey questionaire, his 12–14 hour work days leave him without the energy to work out inter-personal issues within the family, or the awareness of the interdependence of events in work and family arenas. Moreover, on those days when John does get home and reinvests himself in the family, he is left with no time alone for himself.

In this case the strain created by the reallocation of John's work time was felt along the lines of stress already present, acting catalytically to intensify and shift problematic alignments in the family. It is as if the increased demands of a developing career can send ripple effects along the family "fault line," or point of weakness, resulting in shifts in the family structure which can have either constructive or destructive consequences for the family system.

John's dilemmas are not his alone, and the pressures he experiences in the dual role of worker and committed father are shared by many young fathers of this generation. The demands of these two roles are frequently in direct conflict with each other. Deborah has been considering returning to work. If she does this, the pressures on John for more role sharing will be even greater. They will have new areas of sharing but increased competition for resources within the family. Either way, the work-family issues are complex, and there is the potential for considerable growth as well as conflict.

James Mooney: A Day Shift Father

Although both rising young professionals and factory workers experience conflicts between work hours and family needs, both the nature of the conflicts and the timing of them differ. While John Williams' wife was home full time, hoping to return to part time work after the children were older, James Mooney's wife went back to work full-time when her youngest was 2. When Jane Hood interviewed them four years later, they had become co-providers and co-parents and were trying, in spite of inflexible work schedules, to make time to be together as a family.

In 1975, James Mooney was 30 and his wife, Jill, 27. They had two boys, Chuck, then 8, and Jimmy, 6. James had been working for the past 9 years as a diemaker in an auto plant and was earning $17,000 a year including overtime pay. Jill, after staying home full-time for 4 years, had gone back to work and had had a variety of unskilled jobs in the past 4 years. At the time, she was doing a routine clerical job in the finance office of a hospital and earning $7,000 a year, about 30% of their gross family income.

Jill remembers the early child rearing years as a nightmare. Their first son, Chuck, had arrived 9 months after their marriage, interrupting an extended honeymoon. Before that, James would take days off from work and borrow his brother's jeep so that they could go riding through the woods. The baby ended all of that, and James gradually withdrew to the basement with a set of model trains. Jimmy was born less than 2 years after Chuck, and Jill did the best she could with an infant and a very active toddler. However, by the time the youngest was 2, Jill had developed a bad case of eczema. "A nervous reaction," she told me. "Me and the children, we get along when they're older, but babies?" At age 19 and 21, neither Jill nor James was ready for "babies."

Jill's eczema got so bad that finally a doctor told her that she would have to get out of the house. Because he had less than 10 years seniority, James was still working the afternoon shift. This meant that Jill could leave the children with him while she worked from 7:00 a.m. to 3:30 p.m. A baby sitter could fill in for the hour between the time James left for work and Jill returned. Not only would she be getting out of the house, Jill reasoned, but also, she would be adding to the family income, and money was more important to her than it was to James.

James agreed to try the new arrangement, and suddenly found himself alone all day with a 2 year old and a 4 year old whom the doctors were now calling "hyperactive." Jill remembers that during this period, James frequently called her at work and complained about the children: "I finally told him to stop calling me at work or I'll just quit and stay home. We used to have a lot of arguments about this."

James did not remember it being as hard for him the first year as Jill had described, although he was ambivalent. "I was, kinda mixed emotions…kind of an economic deal …in our situation. I imagine, somebody with a doctor for a husband, it would be more or less something to do (for the wife to work)….It wasn't that much. You know, I helped out before. Just the first time I had them all to myself all day. It wasn't much of an adjustment. Diapers, I never could get used to that."

We will probably never know what really happened in the Mooney family during that first year, but, when interviewed 5 years later, James had just gotten back from a picnic lunch with Jill and the children at her work place. After the interview, he had an appointment to take Chuck to the doctor at 2:00 p.m. so that he could be back by 3:00 p.m. to let the baby sitter in before going to work. Although their work schedules make it difficult for James and Jill to spend as much time together as they would like, James feels that he is more fortunate than men whose wives do not work: "Yeah, I see situations like that, where the wife doesn't work. It seems the wife is 'the parent.' The father is always working. Whereas, the situation we have…I never really thought…it might be just the way the situation was out of necessity.…I was brought closer to my kids." In other words, although neither he nor Jill planned it that way, James became a psychological parent because he worked the afternoon shift and was home alone with the children while they were awake. Now, he says: "Some days you feel like knocking their heads together. I think it's good though. I'm thinking that later in life, when I get older, they'll be closer with me. And I like to be close to my kids. I think there's too many kids that are on their own nowadays. And when they get older, they get in trouble and the parents can't figure out why…and I figure it's because the parents weren't there when the kids needed them. Now, when they're young and everything, you should be developing their life." "Developing their life" is a responsibility that James takes so seriously that in the past year he has been going to P.T.A. conferences by himself, allowing *Jill* to remain at work.

Although James is delighted with the way things have worked out for him and his sons, he would like more time with Jill and more time together as a family. When interviewed, he was working 7 day, 66 hour weeks. He explained that it was mandatory and that if he didn't come in, he would be subject to reprimand and then a disciplinary layoff. He does not like having to leave Jill in the middle of a week-end afternoon to go to work when week-ends are the only time they have together. He does have the option of working days now, but hesitates to do this because of the child care problem they would have when the children are home from school in the summer.

While James would like to reduce his work commitment, Jill would like to increase hers. In between interviews, she had moved up a classification and had a job where, as she put it, she had to use her head. She would like to continue to advance, but that would mean working overtime and/or going to school, and further encroachments on the already too small amount of time she and James have as a couple. Thus, becoming a two-job family has had a positive effect on James' relationship with the children and has increased his role-sharing with Jill, but mandatory overtime and inflexible work-scheduling make it difficult for him to be with his family at the times they are free to be with him.

If the Mooneys could shape their work lives to fit their personal and family needs, James would work 30 to 40 hours a week on a flexible schedule which would allow him to adjust to both his children's needs and Jill's work hours. Jill would work and/or get additional training 40 to 50 hours per week, and would earn enough money to compensate for James' reduction in overtime pay. The family could also gain flexibility by developing a more widely based social support system. As it stands, they have few friends, partly because James is, as Jill describes him, "a loner," and partly because their time together is so valuable they don't want to share it with other people. This, however, makes them very dependent on each other. Given an emotional crisis in either of them or in the relationship, they have no outside resources to turn to. Although more flexible work scheduling would not in itself break the Mooney's isolation, it would provide them with more opportunities for doing this themselves.

Conclusions and Recommendations

The work/family conflicts experienced by John Williams and James Mooney are not isolated incidents in the lives of the two individuals, but examples of several of the ways work scheduling affects family life. This conclusion will underline some of the important similarities and differences in the two cases, the patterns that emerge from this comparison, and recommendations to family practitioners and policy-makers.

Unintended Consequences

In both cases, work schedule changes had unintended consequences for family roles and the quality of family interaction. In the first case, the choice of an afternoon shift had the unintended negative consequence of increasing the family's stress level and intensifying particular problematic relationships within the family. In the second case, a wife's return to work on the day shift had the equally unintended positive consequence of increasing the father's involvement in the family and investment in the father role. These changes then led him to consider negotiating a new work schedule which would allow him to live in accordance with his new priorities.

Work Schedules: Occupations and Class Differences

The range of work schedule options available, the overt and covert forces which shape the choices the men in these cases make, reflect differences in their social class and occupational prestige, as well as in the

structure of specific occupations. For example, working class men marry early and peak in earning capacity and on-the-job responsibility sooner than do professionals (Rubin, 1976; Aldous, 1969). They are also more likely to work predictable shift work schedules within a seniority system and be subject to explicit mandatory overtime requirements. The progression of shift work cycles is sometimes in conflict with the developmental needs of the children and other family members. For example, a shift worker who does not have enough seniority to move from the afternoon shift when his children are school age will see his children only on weekends, leaving his wife to resolve all their daily problems.

Professional men continue to add new occupational responsibilities in their 30's, becoming more focused on upward mobility, and less on leisure time. In contrast, skilled workers have gone as far as they can without becoming foremen, and must look to other areas of their lives for personal development in their 30's. In each occupational and class group, the peaking of work hour pressures for time, commitment, and involvement intersects differently with the changing developmental needs within the family.

Recommended Changes in the Work Force

For working class men such as James Mooney, the inflexibility of work organizations and the link between seniority and work shifts are major problems related to work scheduling. James needs changes in company policy which would allow him to work day shift during the school year, take time off if a child is sick, reduce his work week to forty hours or less, and abolish mandatory overtime. If James works fewer hours, Jill will need more opportunity for advancement on her job and a higher rate of pay. At present, occupational sex segregation keeps women such as Jill in jobs where they earn an average of 57% of what men do

(Levitin, Quinn, & Staines, 1970; Griffiths, 1976). Professionals such as John Williams need major changes in the formal and informal standards by which they are evaluated before they can freely choose to spend more time at home. In John's case, the nature of the task to be accomplished and the criterion for maintaining his professional reputation and credibility required that he work during the hours Seth was home. Moreover, by the time he got home after a 12–16 hour work day, he did not have the energy left to relate to Seth or other family members. Hence, men's values and ideals about work-family priorities are often not actualized under the pressure of conflicting expectations and pressures.

Family Issues

These work schedule problems also define, in part, the marital issues couples must negotiate. For example, if John Williams continues to commit as much of his time and energy to his work as he has, it will be increasingly difficult for Deborah to do anything but provide the support services necessary to keep the family going (Mortimer et al., 1978). Such a "two person career" can result in the spiral of anger, resentment, and distance described in the Williams family. While the increased demands of John's job may keep Deborah at home, the limitations of James Mooney's earning capacity sent Jill to work. James, in turn, seeks work schedule changes that will support and accommodate Jill's work requirements. In the process, James, who is not a feminist, has become a staunch supporter of role sharing, and John, ideologically egalitarian, has come to support a very unequal division of labor.

Shifts in work schedules are also reflected in realignments of family coalitions and changing patterns of closeness and distance both in and outside of the family. For John and Deborah Williams, this resulted in destructive rifts between Seth and both his parents, and between Deborah and John,

and the intensification of dysfunctional triangles in the family. James Mooney developed a closer relationship both with his children and his wife, but because of their complicated schedule, the family has become more isolated from neighborhood and friends.

Recommendations to Families and Family Counselors

We think that it is especially important that the effects each man's commitments and work schedule had on family interaction were unintended and unanticipated. As Renshaw (1976) has found in her consulting work with corporations, work-family problems often go undetected because of the tacit assumption that the two spheres are in fact as separate as John Williams wished they were….[I]t is especially important for family counselors to consider carefully the reciprocal relationship between work and family life. Problems experienced by many men within the family are often, in fact, work-family problems which cannot be adequately understood without considering the entire work-family role system.…

NOTES

1. Hood, J. *Becoming a two-job family*. Dissertation in preparation for the University of Michigan, Department of Sociology.

2. Lein, L., Durham, M. Pratt, M., Schudson, J., Thomas, R., & Weiss, H. *Final report: Work and family life* (National Institute of Education Project No. 3–3094). Wellesley, Massachusetts: Wellesley College Center for Research on Women, 1974.

REFERENCES

Aldous, J. Occupational characteristics and males' role performance in the family. *Journal of Marriage and the Family,* 1969, 31, 707–712.

Griffiths, M. Can we still afford occupational segregation? In M. Blaxall & B. Reagan (Eds.), *Women and the workplace: The implications of occu-*

pational segregation. Chicago: University of Chicago Press, 1976.

Levitin, T. E., Quinn, R. P., & Staines, G. L. A woman is 58% of a man on the American payroll. In C. Tavris (Ed.), *The female experience.* Del Mar, California: CRM Books, 1973.

Mortimer, J., Hall, R., & Hill, R. Husbands' occupational attributes as constraints on wives' employment. *Sociology of Work and Occupations,* 1978, 5, 285–313.

Pleck, J. The work-family role system. *Social Problems,* 1977, 24, 417–427.

Renshaw, J. An exploration of the dynamics of the overlapping worlds of work and family. *Family Process,* 1976, 15, 143–165.

Rubin, L. *Worlds of pain: Life in the working-class family.* New York: Basic, 1976.

The Second Shift

Arlie Hochschild and Anne Machung

CASE STUDY QUESTIONS

1. What is the significance of the reference to "the extra month a year"?

2. What is the cause of women's predominant role in the second shift? To what extent do societal norms affect the roles that women and men take in the second shift?

3. What troubles women about the second shift? Do their husbands recognize the difficulties of the second shift? To what extent do husbands participate in the second shift?

4. Why do family myths develop about how couples manage child care and household tasks?

5. What would need to change for the *second shift* to become less problematic?

She is not the same woman in each magazine advertisement, but she is the same idea. She has that working-mother look as she strides forward, briefcase in one hand, smiling child in the other. Literally and figuratively, she is moving ahead. Her hair, if long, tosses behind her; if it is short, it sweeps back at the sides, suggesting mobility and progress. There is nothing shy or passive about her. She is confident, active, "liberated." She wears a dark tailored suit, but with a silk bow or colorful frill that says, "I'm really feminine underneath." She has made it in a man's world without sacrificing her femininity. And she has done this on her own. By some personal miracle, this image suggests, she has managed to combine what 150 years of industrialization have split wide apart—child and job, frill and suit, female culture and male.

When I showed a photograph of a super-mom like this to the working mothers I talked to in the course of researching this book, many responded with an outright laugh. One daycare worker and mother of two, ages three and five, threw back her head: "Ha! They've got to be *kidding* about her. Look at me, hair a mess, nails jagged, twenty pounds overweight. Mornings, I'm getting my kids dressed, the dog fed, the lunches made, the shopping list done. That lady's got a maid." Even working mothers who did have maids couldn't imagine combining work and family in such a carefree way. "Do you know what a baby *does* to your life, the two o'clock feedings, the four o'clock feedings?" Another mother of two said: "They don't show it, but she's whistling"—she imitated a whistling woman, eyes to the sky—"so she can't hear the din." They envied the apparent ease of the woman with the flying hair, but she didn't remind them of anyone they knew.

The women I interviewed—lawyers, corporate executives, word processors, garment pattern cutters, daycare workers—and most of their husbands, too—felt differently about some issues: how right it is for a mother of young children to work a full-time job, or how much a husband should be responsible for the home. But they all agreed that it was hard to work two full-time jobs and raise young children.…

But I began with the measurable issue of time. Adding together the time it takes to do a paid job and to do housework and childcare, I averaged estimates from the major studies on time use done in the 1960s and 1970s, and discovered that women worked roughly fifteen hours longer each week than men. Over a year, they worked an *extra month of twenty-four-hour days a year*. Over a dozen years, it was an extra year of twenty-four-hour days. Most women without children spend much more time than men on housework; with children, they devote more time to both housework and childcare. Just as there is a wage gap between men and women in the workplace, there is a "leisure gap" between them at home. Most women work one shift at the office or factory and a "second shift" at home.

Studies show that working mothers have higher self-esteem and get less depressed than housewives, but compared to their husbands, they're more tired and get sick more often.…

Inside the Extra Month a Year

The women I interviewed seemed to be far more deeply torn between the demands of work and family than were their husbands. They talked with more animation and at greater length than their husbands about the abiding conflict between them. Busy as they were, women more often brightened at the idea of yet another interviewing session. They felt the second shift was *their* issue and most of their husbands agreed. When I telephoned one husband to arrange an interview with him, explaining that I wanted to ask him about how he managed work and family life, he replied genially, "Oh, this will *really* interest my *wife*."

It was a woman who first proposed to me the metaphor, borrowed from industrial life, of the "second shift." She strongly resisted the *idea* that homemaking was a "shift." Her family was her life and she didn't want it reduced to a job. But as she put it, "You're on duty at work. You come home, and you're on duty. Then you go back to work and you're on duty." After eight hours of adjusting insurance claims, she came home to put on the rice for dinner, care for her children, and wash laundry. Despite herself her home life *felt* like a second shift. That was the real story and that was the real problem.

Men who shared the load at home seemed just as pressed for time as their wives, and as torn between the demands of career and small children.…But the majority of men did not share the load at home. Some refused outright. Others refused more passively, often offering a loving shoulder to lean on, an understanding ear as their working wife faced the conflict they both saw as hers. At first it seemed to me that the problem of the second shift was hers. But I came to realize that those husbands who helped very little at home were often indirectly just as deeply affected as their wives by the need to do that work, through the resentment their wives feel toward them, and through their need to steel themselves against that resentment. Evan Holt, a warehouse furniture salesman, did very little housework and played with his four-year-old son, Joey, at his convenience. Juggling the demands of work with family at first seemed a problem for his wife. But Evan himself suffered enormously from the side effects of "her" problem. His wife did the second shift, but she resented it keenly, and half-consciously expressed her frustration and rage by losing interest in sex and becoming overly absorbed with Joey. One way or another, most men I talked with do suffer the severe repercussions of what I think is a transitional phase in American family life.

One reason women take a deeper interest than men in the problems of juggling work with family life is that even when husbands happily shared the hours of work, their wives felt more *responsible* for home and children. More women kept track of doctors' appointments and arranged for playmates to come over. More mothers than fathers worried about the tail on a child's Halloween costume or a birthday present for a school friend. They were more likely to think about their children while at work and to check in by phone with the baby-sitter.

Partly because of this, more women felt torn between one sense of urgency and another, between the need to soothe a child's fear of being left at daycare, and the need to show the boss she's "serious" at work. More women than men questioned how good they were as parents, or if they did not, they questioned why they weren't questioning it. More often than men, women alternated between living in their ambition and standing apart from it.

As masses of women have moved into the economy, families have been hit by a "speed-up" in work and family life. There is no more time in the day than there was when wives stayed home, but there is twice as much to get done. It is mainly women who absorb this "speed-up." Twenty percent of the men in my study shared housework equally. Seventy percent of men did a substantial amount (less than half but more than a third), and 10 percent did less than a third. Even when couples share more equitably in the work at home, women do two-thirds of the *daily* jobs at home, like cooking and cleaning up—jobs that fix them into a rigid routine. Most women cook dinner and most men change the oil in the family car. But, as one mother pointed out, dinner needs to be prepared every evening around six o'clock, whereas the car oil needs to be changed every six months, any day around that time, any time that day. Women do more childcare than men, and men repair more household appliances. A child needs to be tended daily while the repair of household appliances can often wait "until I have time." Men thus have more control over *when* they make their contributions than women do. They may be very busy with family chores but, like the executive who tells his secretary to "hold my calls," the man has more control over his time. The job of the working mother, like that of the secretary, is usually to "take the calls."

Another reason women may feel more strained than men is that women more often do two things at once—for example, write checks and return phone calls, vacuum and keep an eye on a three-year-old, fold laundry and think out the shopping list. Men more often cook dinner *or* take a child to the park. Indeed, women more often juggle three spheres—job, children, and housework—while most men juggle two—job and children. For women, two activities compete with their time with children, not just one.

Beyond doing more at home, women also devote *proportionately more* of their time at home to housework and proportionately less of it to childcare. Of all the time men spend working at home, more of it goes to childcare. That is, working wives spend relatively more time "mothering the house"; husbands spend more time "mothering" the children. Since most parents prefer to tend to their children than clean house, men do more of what they'd rather do. More men than women take their children on "fun" outings to the park, the zoo, the movies. Women spend more time on maintenance, feeding and bathing children, enjoyable activities to be sure, but often less leisurely or "special" than going to the zoo. Men also do fewer of the "undesirable" household chores: fewer men than women wash toilets and scrub the bathroom.

As a result, women tend to talk more intently about being overtired, sick, and "emotionally drained." Many women I could not tear away from the topic of sleep. They talked about how much they could "get by on"…six and a half, seven, seven and a half, less, more. They talked about who they knew who needed more or less. Some apologized for how much sleep they needed—"I'm afraid I need eight hours of sleep"—as if eight was "too much." They talked about the effect of a change in baby-sitter, the birth of a second child, or a business trip on their child's pattern of sleep. They talked about how to avoid fully waking up when a child called them at night, and how to get back to sleep. These women talked about sleep the way a hungry person talks about food.

All in all, if in this period of American history, the two-job family is suffering from a speed up of work and family life, working mothers are its primary victims. It is ironic, then, that often it falls to women to be the "time and motion expert" of family life. Watching inside homes, I noticed it was often the mother who rushed children, saying, "Hurry up! It's time to go," "Finish your cereal now," "You can do that later," "Let's go!" When a bath is crammed into a slot between 7:45 and 8:00 it was often the mother who called out, "Let's see who can take their bath the quickest!" Often a younger child will rush out, scurrying to be first in bed, while the older and wiser one stalls, resistant, sometimes resentful: "Mother is always rushing us." Sadly enough, women are more often the lightning rods for family aggressions aroused by the speed-up of work and family life. They are the "villains" in a process of which they are also the primary victims. More than the longer hours, the sleeplessness, and feeling torn, this is the saddest cost to women of the extra month a year.

Family Myths

As I watched couples in their own homes, I began to realize that couples sometimes develop "family myths"—versions of reality that obscure a core truth in order to manage a family tension. Evan and Nancy Holt managed an irresolvable conflict over the distribution of work at home through the myth that they now "shared it equally." Another couple unable to admit to the conflict came to believe "we aren't competing over who will take responsibility at home; we're just dreadfully busy with our careers." Yet another couple jointly believed that the husband was bound hand and foot to his career "because his work demanded it," while in fact his careerism covered the fact that they were avoiding each other. Not all couples need or have family myths. But when they do arise, I believe they often manage key tensions which are linked, by degrees, to the long hand of the stalled revolution.

After interviewing couples for a while, I got into the practice of offering families who wanted it my interpretations of how they fit into the broader picture I was seeing and what I perceived were their strategies for coping with the second shift. Couples were often relieved to discover they were not alone, and were encouraged to open up a dialogue about the inner and outer origins of their troubles.

Many couples…worked long hours at their jobs and their children were very young: in this way their lot was unusually hard. But in one crucial way they had it far easier than most two-job couples in America: most were middle class. Many also worked for a company that embraced progressive policies toward personnel, generous benefits and salaries. If *these* middle-class couples find it hard to juggle work and family life, many other two-job families across the nation—who earn less, work at less flexible, steady, or lucrative jobs, and rely on poorer daycare—are likely to find it much harder still…

How much had changed from 1976 to 1988? In practical terms, little: most women I interviewed in the late 1980s still do the lion's share of work at home, do most of the daily chores and take responsibility for running the home. But something was different, too. More couples *wanted* to share and imagined that they did. Dorothy Sims, a personnel director, summed up this new blend of idea and reality. She eagerly explained to me that she and her husband Dan "shared all the housework," and that they were "equally involved in raising their nine-month-old son Timothy." Her husband, a refrigerator salesman, applauded her career and "was more pleased than threatened by her high salary"; he urged her to develop such competencies as reading ocean maps, and calculating interest rates (which she'd so far "resisted learning") because these days "a woman should." But one evening at dinner, a telling episode occurred. Dorothy had handed Timothy to her husband while she served us a chicken dinner. Gradually, the baby began to doze on his father's lap. "When do you want me to put Timmy to bed?" Dan asked. A long silence followed during which it occurred to Dorothy—then, I think, to her husband—that this seemingly insignificant question hinted to me that it was *she*, not he, or "they," who usually decided such matters. Dorothy slipped me a glance, put her elbows on the table, and said to her husband in a slow, deliberate voice, "So, what do *we* think?"

When Dorothy and Dan described their "typical days," their picture of sharing grew even less convincing. Dorothy worked the same nine-hour day at the office as her husband. But she came home to fix dinner and to tend Timmy while Dan fit in a squash game three nights a week from six to seven (a good time for his squash partner). Dan read the newspaper more often and slept longer.

Compared to the early interviews, women in the later interviews seemed to speak more often in passing of relationships or marriages that had ended for some other reason but of which it "was also true" that he "didn't lift a finger at home." Or the extra month alone did it. One divorcee who typed part of this manuscript echoed this theme when she explained, "I was a potter and lived with a sculptor for eight years. I cooked, shopped, and cleaned because his art 'took him longer.' He said it was fair because he worked harder. But we both worked at home, and I could see that if anyone worked longer hours I did, because I earned less with my pots than he earned with his sculpture. That was *hard* to live with, and that's really why we ended."

Some women moved on to slightly more equitable arrangements in the early 1980s, doing a bit less of the second shift than the working mothers I talked to in the late 1970s. Comparing two national surveys of working couples, F. T. Juster found the male slice of the second shift rose from 20 percent in 1965 to 30 percent in 1981, and my study may be a local reflection of this slow national trend. But women like Dorothy Sims, who simply add to their extra month a year a new illusion that they aren't doing it, represent a sad alternative to the woman with the flying hair—the woman who doesn't think that's who she is.

7 | The Future

In this book, we explored a variety of topics related to work and occupations. We analyzed case studies using many different theories. In effect, we looked at what has been and what is. In this chapter, we look at a number of trends that will affect the future of work and occupations.

Technological innovation on work. Does technological innovation result in the deskilling or in the upgrading of jobs? How does technological change affect the occupational choices available to members of a given society?

Reengineering. Is the effort to achieve greater efficiency a good thing or not? What are the consequences for workers involved in reengineering?

Worker participation. Are self-directed work teams changing the relationship between workers and managers? Are they changing workers' relationship to their jobs and to one another?

As you will see, these trends overlap. Furthermore, the presence of some of these trends have been documented already. With others, you may want to decide whether the trend is even occurring. What you have read in previous chapters should also help you think about the possible short-term and long-term consequences of the trends.

Technological Innovation

The introduction of new technology often has a profound effect on work. Consider the materials handling industry, in which goods are moved from one warehouse to another and finally to a consumer outlet. In the earliest days, people unloaded freight cars and moved goods to warehouses. It took many people to unload the goods. Until the forklift was introduced, goods could be stored only as high as one person could reach with a ladder. The forklift allowed the workers to carry much more in one trip and to store even heavy goods 40 to 50 feet high. Anything from groceries to automotive parts that could be stored in boxes, bales, or buckets and put on a pallet could be stored on high shelves. Later, warehouses were further automated. Electric platforms on tracks allowed workers to more easily store and retrieve goods from high shelves. With the introduction of moving shelves, workers could stay in one place and move shelves to their location with the push of a button. Most recently, computerization and robotics have been introduced. Now, a worker scans a bar-coded request, and robots retrieve the needed goods. Today, a materials handler does not need to rely so much on physical strength. The job draws on completely different skills. Computers and electronics have similarly transformed nearly every occupation. Dance choreographers' imaginations have been unleashed with the option to manipulate figures and create dance phrases at the computer screen. CNN's "Talk Back Live" show receives immediate responses from viewers through electronic mail.

In the past, clothing store managers ordered new stock on the basis of guesses about how many items of what size would be bought in the coming weeks. Now, Wrangler jeans has provided laser scanners to local department stores across the nation so that Wrangler's headquarters in North Carolina can keep track of what is being sold (National Public Radio, 1994). Based on those actual figures rather than estimates of store managers, Wrangler ships jeans to restock the shelves. Thus, technology helps provide quick restocking of inventory and reduces the storage of excess inventory.

Technological innovation has been a boon to business, but it is not always beneficial to workers. Many sociologists, economists, managers, and union organizers note that technological innovation may lead to deskilling, in which a lower level of skills and training is required of workers in their jobs. On the individual level, if a worker's job is deskilled, he or she may find his or her job less interesting, challenging, and satisfying. Moreover, because the job requires less training and skills, the worker filling the position may be paid less than in the past.

The implications of upgrading, on the other hand, would be that those filling positions would need more training and skills than before. Workers can be retrained to fill the new, upgraded positions (although some will be laid off because they cannot be retrained). If the upgraded position is more interesting and challenging than the previous job, the worker is likely to be more satisfied than before.

The Deskilling Debate

The debate on the impact of technology on work, particularly the potential deskilling or upgrading, has been simmering for decades. In 1936, Charlie Chaplin's film *Modern Times* was an early reflection of the view that technology is dehumanizing. In the 1950s, a sociologist opined that industrial automation would reduce the skill level workers needed to new lows (Bright, 1958). It would also remove the responsibility for the quality of that work from the worker. The result would be not only deskilling, but also fewer opportunities for autonomy and less satisfaction.

This grim view of technology prevailed until 1973 when a well-known book by Daniel Bell, *The Coming of Post-Industrial Society,* was published. Bell's main argument was that the era of industrial society, dominated by the production of materials and manufacturing, was coming to an end and that the postindustrial society, dominated by provision of services, was on its way in. He argued that this economic shift would have far-reaching societal consequences. Contradicting the earlier view, Bell argued that the increasing use of technology would raise the skill level needed to function in the workplace.

It wasn't long before someone reasserted the negative view of the impact of technology. In *Labor and Monopoly Capital: The Degradation of Work in the Twentieth Century,* Harry Braverman (1974) argued that the potential automation of work was a powerful tool of managers that might result in more efficient production of goods. Braverman argued, however, that automation would downgrade the skills of the workers. Workers in deskilled jobs can more easily be replaced because new workers can be trained. Those filling deskilled jobs can be paid lower wages. These shifts not only would allow managers to take charge of the technology, but also would give them additional power over workers. This power would provide managers with additional incentives to introduce technological innovations.

In the mid-1970s, then, we have two well-known societal commentators, Braverman and Bell, espousing opposing views on the impact of technology on skilled work. The 1980s brought a third view: that technology and automation alone were not responsible for changing the required skill levels of workers (Spenner, 1983). The type of company, the corporate structure, the relationship between managers and workers, the organizational culture, and the societal structure also help determine whether a technological innovation will have a deskilling or upgrading effect. From this view, technological innovation affects some groups differently from others. In some work situations, automation may cause the deskilling of work for some while enhancing the skill requirements needed for others.

Variable Effects of Technological Innovation
One study of a General Motors plant found evidence that technological innovations have variable effects on workers (Milkman and

Pullman, 1991). Upgrading occurred for skilled workers such as machinists and pipefitters, who needed new skills and knowledge to maintain and manage new robots and lasers. However, with the introduction of technological innovations, deskilling occurred for production workers, such as those in the paint and body shops.

This variable effect occurred in the materials handling industry as well. The forklift operators developed some new skills when technology was introduced as did those operating the moving platforms. But now the materials handlers in the most up-to-date parts-ordering operations operate a fully automated order fulfillment system. All they have to do is to wave bar-code wands over coded forms and automated machinery does the work. The job requires little skill and not even the brute strength that materials handling originally required.

The effect of technological innovation on the skill level of jobs could be described as a U-shaped curve (Blauner, 1964). Automation initially increases the need for skills but ultimately results in decreased need for highly skilled workers. This is a general effect, however. We don't know whether the next technological innovation will result in deskilling or upgrading or both.

How then can we answer the question of the impact of technology in a broad way? We may want to consider the impact of technological innovation in different industries. Whereas the use of technology may increase the need for skills and training in one industry, it may decrease them in another. We may also want to consider the state of a particular company when the innovation was introduced. A company that has kept up with technological innovations in their industry may find that minor innovations lead to deskilling. Another company, on the cutting-edge, may find that increased use of technology leads to upgrading. Companies on the trailing edge of technology that replace outdated processing equipment may find that the innovations lead to upgrading for some workers and deskilling for others. In addition, the process by which automation is introduced to workers may also have a dramatic effect on their attitudes toward the new technology. In Case Study 7.1, "Smooth Sailing," Andy Cohen explores how one company successfully introduced automation to their sales force.

Much of the research and many of the perspectives on the deskilling controversy have focused on industrial jobs. Given the increased importance of work in service industries, particularly the increase in white-collar positions, what will the impact of technological innovation be? Moreover, what about the impact of technology on the work of those in the professions? Technology may allow those in the professions, such as law, to collect existing information more quickly than before. If one highly respected skill of the past was knowing how and where to find relevant legal cases, then one could argue that the work of lawyers has been deskilled. On the other hand, if lawyers are free to spend more of their time thinking about, rather than looking for, information, that could arguably be an upgrading of skills.

The deskilling hypothesis typically implies that deskilling has negative consequences for workers. Those negative consequences are often accompanied by gains in other areas, however, such as work that is less physically demanding or less hazardous. Furthermore, the technological advances that produce deskilling also increase productivity and make companies more competitive, thereby saving jobs. Should we then be against technological innovations, or are deskilling theorists merely cautioning us to recognize the potential negative consequences of the technology? How do we weigh the costs and benefits of an industry's increased productivity and potential deskilling compared to less productivity and potentially more satisfied workers? Personal and societal values affect our evaluation of those two possibilities. Decision makers in some developing countries may prefer to preserve jobs for a large and largely unskilled populace. In addition, some cultures simply do not consider "progress" and productivity as important as Westerners do.

In his book *Powershift,* Alvin Toffler (1990), a futurist, focuses on something he calls "the Fast and the Slow." He argues that the speed with which information, new ideas, decision making, capital, and transactions travel in some economies is much faster than that of other countries partially as a result of advanced technology. To this point in history, the lower cost of labor in developing nations has assured a link between the slow and the fast economies. But Toffler believes there will be an increasing wealth and power gap between the "fast" and "slow" societies. Paul Kennedy (1993), in his best-selling book *Preparing for the Twenty-First Century,* makes a similar argument in his discussion of winners and losers in the developing world. The global financial and communications revolution plays a large role in this drama. The electronic and informational gap may be lessened with the decreasing costs of telecommunication. But both Toffler and Kennedy express concern about increasing numbers of people in poverty and pockets of political instability that could lead to the threat of war and to an upset of the global system.

To better understand the impact of technology on jobs, we need more empirical studies of companies representing a wide variety of industries. We must evaluate factors other than technological advancement so that we know how much impact the technological innovation is having on needed job skills compared to the other factors, such as corporate structure or increased job specialization. We should also look at the impact of technological innovation cross-nationally if we are to weigh the effects of such factors as the societal values and type of economy. We will need to continue longitudinal studies so that we are not just capturing the effects of a particular innovation at a particular point in time. With longitudinal studies, we may be able to better discover the long-term impact of particular types of innovations as well as see the long-term effects of technological innovation more generally. Given these many questions, we cannot say for sure whether technological innovation will ultimately have the effect of deskilling or upgrading or some combination. In the meantime, however, college graduates seek jobs using the Internet, and a technological advancement as simple as voice mail, provided free of charge to homeless job seekers as part of programs in Seattle, Minneapolis, and New York, has led to gainful employment that allows these individuals to be productive members of society (Kleinfeld, 1995).

Reengineering

In a best-selling book, *Reengineering the Corporation: A Manifesto for Business Revolution*, Michael Hammer and James Champy (1993), highly paid consultants, advocate rethinking the way business tasks get done in a company. To them, **reengineering** means reevaluating whether each task is necessary and eliminating tasks that are not cost-effective in order to dramatically improve such critical measures of performance as cost, quality, service, and speed. Hammer and Champy say reengineering means asking, "If I were re-creating this company today, given what I know about current technology, what would it look like?" (31). The focus is on radically rethinking the processes that need to be done to keep business going.

Although Hammer and Champy (1993) examined a number of companies including Hallmark Cards, Aetna Life and Casualty, and Taco Bell to explain their ideas about reengineering, I will focus on only two of the companies described in their book. The first, the IBM Credit Corporation (36–39), provides financing for customers who are buying IBM products, such as computers, software, and services. In the past, when an IBM salesperson wanted to process a customer's request for financing, the request passed across the desks of five people, each responsible for a different part of the finance request process. Typically, this process took 6 days, which was long enough for a customer to find a better source of financing or to decide not to purchase the IBM product in question. A number of minor changes had been instituted over time. For example, one change allowed anyone who was a part of the process to know where in the process the finance request was; but, the logging of that information only increased the turnaround time. None of the changes made the difference that IBM needed.

One day, two managers walked a finance request through the five-step process and had each person in the process stop work and do whatever his or her job was to process the request. As soon as one step was completed, the managers walked the request to the next step. The two managers were surprised to learn that the entire process had taken only 90 minutes.

As a result of this experiment, IBM decided to radically rethink the way they did that process; that is, they decided to reengineer. Today, each person who processes a finance request takes care of the request from beginning to end. The redesign reduced the time required for the process to only 4 hours. Processing capacity increased a hundredfold from the pre-reengineering level.

Although IBM Credit thought it needed specialists to deal with every step of the process, it did not. IBM Credit had gone on the assumption that each finance request was unique and could therefore not be processed or considered in a typical way. By carefully evaluating the process, they discovered that most of the finance requests were typical cases. When particular finance requests vary from the norm, specialists can deal with the complexities.

Role of Computers

Although the desire for an upgraded computer system is not the impetus for reengineering in a company, the result typically is the installation of a new computer system. Computers allow the new generalists to have greater access to information. For example, one document can be in use at eight work stations simultaneously. Improvements in information technology often make reengineering highly profitable.

Hammer and Champy also look at Eastman Kodak (1993: 44–46) where the product development process used to take 70 weeks. Engineers often developed new products sequentially, with each group completing their step before the design could be passed on to the next group. In other situations, engineers would work at their drafting tables on part of the design, and at the end of the process, they would hope that the parts of the design could be integrated. More often than not, communication between groups was inadequate, and some groups would find themselves designing a part to integrate with another part that had been changed.

Reengineering of Kodak's new product development process put computers at the fulcrum. Product developers could work on their designs at their computers. The database would then collect the information from each engineer and integrate these designs into a coherent whole. The design engineers would always know what additional adjustments to make to keep the new product a working whole. This reengineering allowed Kodak to cut their redesign process time in half.

The Path to Higher Profit: Specialization or Reengineering?

Adam Smith's *Wealth of Nations* and Frederick Taylor's notion of scientific managment emphasized task specialization as the way to increase efficiency and profit (Hammer and Champy, 1993). Even today, for many businesses, specialization has developed into a means of achieving efficiency, predictability, and control over workers. In *The McDonaldization of Society*, George Ritzer (1993) describes how the principles of the fast-food restaurant have become the dominant mode of operation in all kinds of businesses, from croissanteries in Paris to dental clinics in Des Moines. Workers are trained to perform a limited number of specialized tasks in the name of efficiency. At the same time, to ensure a predictable product, much of the process is carefully controlled by technology or managers and dehumanized so that workers' individual skills and styles are neutralized. If Ritzer is right about the increasing "McDonaldization" of society, then specialization, deskilling, and control may have a larger influence on jobs than does reengineering.

On the other hand, Hammer and Champy (1993), strong advocates of reengineering, argue that we need to totally rethink the way we do business if we are to be effective in, to compete in, and to survive the forces of the changing global economy. In the past, models with well-defined organizational hierarchies and a great degree of specialization worked when labor was cheap and information was expensive. A company could be expanded easily by adding more workers to the hierarchy and more managers to supervise those workers. Workers could be quickly trained because the part of the process they were responsible for was relatively small. Specialization hinders business expansion today, however, because the business environment changes so rapidly. As more functions are added to the process, the problem of coordinating and holding together the tasks associated with the functions increases as tasks become more complex (Hammer and Champy 1993:16). Aspects of the current environment are also making the past methods of organization and coordination less efficient, most notable the rapidly changing and advanced technology; the growing connections between different nations and the global economy; and the higher expectations of customers regarding the choices that should be made available to them (11).

Effect of Reengineering on Jobs

The reengineering concept has been criticized as an excuse for shedding unwanted workers. For example, *Chemical Week,* the leading news journal of the chemical industry, in two articles on reengineering, acknowledges that job elimination is not the intent but often occurs. Streamlining processes usually requires radical changes. Most jobs are cut from lower and middle management, since those are most likely to hold together the rather disjointed and many-stepped processes that existed before reengineering. In the chemical industry, some of the natural job elimination that takes place is being taken care of through worker attrition and worker retraining. For those who do not fit these categories, "reengineering remains a euphemism for the cuts" (*Chemical Week,* 1993: 29). Sometimes reengineering projects fail as a result of not enough involvement from top-level managers (Hall, Rosenthal, and Wade, 1993). On the other hand, where the need for a particular process grows, such as that at IBM Credit, most employees remain and perform at a dramatically increased level of productivity. Moreover, one result of reengineering is often a more horizontal structure, one that is flatter and less hierarchical (*Business Week,* 1993). This means that more employees have potential decision-making power and control over their jobs. In Case Study 7.2, "Creativity at Work," Cheryl Harrison describes her dissatisfaction with the traditional pyramid or hierarchical structure of her graphics firm. She starts from ground zero and reengineers her firm so that the resulting organizational structure is a flatter circle that allows communication to flow more freely.

Some argue that reengineering is just the newest fad in business management. Others say it is not new and that companies have been undertaking reengineering for quite some time, but didn't use this catchy name for it. Critics say reengineering is just a new cover under which companies can downsize and lay off workers to save money. Hammer and Champy (1993) say reengineering is necessary for companies to remain competitive in the ever-changing marketplace. Only the future will tell us which view is most accurate.

Worker Participation

In general, **worker participation** is the power of workers to directly or indirectly influence management decision making (Tsiganou, 1991: 14). It takes a variety of forms.

In the early 1970s, quality-of-work-life programs were instituted in many U.S. corporations to battle the increasing alienation and low productivity of workers. Companies hoped that putting workers in Quality Circles, where they could discuss ways to improve the process and the product, and other similar programs would help workers feel more involved. Top executives also hoped they might better understand the causes of and possible solutions to workers' problems. Typically, the programs arranged workers in groups of 10 to 15 to meet in problem-solving sessions. The formal power of these groups was minimal because all solutions were, of course, overtly subject to management's approval.

New forms of worker participation have been in effect since the 1980s. Some corporations have organized workers into autonomous teams, often called self-directed work teams. Rather than having broad company decision-making power, self-directed work teams control the entire production process of a product or completion of a process. These teams are typically composed of 5 to 15 workers. The team plans, supervises, and performs the work. As a team, they, not management, decide the best way to get their work completed. The underlying idea is that when workers are a team they will work together, develop more innovative ideas, feel responsible for the whole process, feel empowered, and ultimately be more productive. By involving workers in decision making about their own work, companies also hope to gain more loyalty from their workers. At the broadest level, workers may hold decision-making positions on the Board of Directors or have ownership in the company. In most cases, however, worker participation means having input regarding one's own immediate work. In Case Study 7.3, "Management Ideology and Practice in Participative Plants," Louise Lamphere describes workers' feelings about the team structure at a silicon chip manufacturing company.

Forces Affecting Worker Participation

A number of forces influence the form of worker participation that an individual is likely to encounter in a particular workplace. They can vary by culture, industry, company, and manager.

First, a society's labor market conditions affect the extent and type of worker participation (Tsiganou, 1991). When the demand for labor is high, management is more likely to develop programs that encourage worker participation. These programs appear humanitarian and are attractive to prospective workers. Even in a time of recession, management may use worker participation as a tactic to try to increase productivity of the current workers by increasing worker satisfaction. In either case, the programs may help companies increase their cost-effectiveness. Certainly, increasing global competition encourages corporations to keep workers happy and thus highly productive.

Second, interest in worker participation rises with workers' increasing level of education (Tsiganou, 1991). Well-educated employees expect their work to be challenging and interesting. At the same time, corporations are seeing an increase in worker absenteeism and turnover. Workers' call for more challenging work and the corporate need for higher productivity dovetail to make both parties interested in worker participation programs.

Third, the quickly changing and competitive marketplace calls for a more flexible and participatory system (Tsiganou, 1991). New technology demands workers with upgraded skills and more educational training, and workers may need the flexibility and knowledge to be able to respond quickly and appropriately to changes in the marketplace. Workers who are expected to be well trained and flexible may demand more involvement in the decisions that affect their work.

Fourth, organized labor and the government play a role (Tsiganou, 1991). When organized labor or the government supports worker participation and gains power for workers, these gains are likely to be more substantial and sustained. On the other hand, organized labor often views the initiation of worker participation programs by management as an attempt to undermine the influence of unions on workers.

Fifth, at the industry or company level, businesses facing foreign competition and constantly introducing new products tend to have high employee involvement (Lawler, Mohrman, and Ledford, 1992). We would also expect to see worker participation schemes initiated in industries where the demand for labor is high, where highly educated workers are needed, and where new technology demands a highly flexible work structure.

Finally, corporate values and the values of the managers who are a part of the corporate structure affect interest in worker participation. Robert Jackall (1988), author of *Moral Mazes*, believes that for ambitious managers, "the real meaning of work...becomes...maintaining and furthering one's own position and career" (202). The impact of the current corporate culture, which emphasizes work success at nearly any cost, has a profound effect on corporate decision making as well as societal norms. Because of a manager's need to get results and to demonstrate and claim responsibility for successes, he or she may not have the patience to permit worker participation in decision making, or workers' contributions may go unrewarded. Either way, the potentially positive effects of worker participation are lost.

Support for and Resistance to Worker Participation

Self-directed work teams are not always introduced without incident (Stern, 1993). Some aspects of work formerly taken care of by supervisors and managers are put under the control of the work team. The managers may not, however, provide the resources the team needs to work effectively. Moreover, managers' reluctance to release control of decision making about the process can lead to turf battles between managers and the workers on the shop floor. In a dramatic move, the chairman of the Shelby Die Casting Company in Mississippi eliminated supervisors' jobs when he found that the former line workers who were African American could not get their white supervisors to listen to their team ideas (Stern, 1993: F-5). Moreover, diverse individuals put together as a team may not immediately warm to one another.

Another potential problem is the cyclical nature (Derber and Schwartz, 1983) of worker participation. As workers participate more in decision making, they gain in feelings of efficacy and self-confidence. This can lead them to then request even more decision-making power. Workers may eventually request decision-making power that exceeds what management wants to give them. The result is that management then begins to interfere with workers' decision-making power, and workers again end up feeling frustrated about issues of autonomy.

Although one would think that unions would offer their whole-hearted support to worker participation programs and self-directed work teams, this is not typically the case. When strict dividing lines existed between managers and those on the shop floor, unions could be more assured of worker support. In the past, unions have provided one of the few avenues for workers to formally influence management decision making that applied to workers, particularly when they were negotiating a collective bargaining agreement. The unions' gains have included rights associated with seniority and carefully refined job descriptions. Labor organizations have criticized the self-directed work team structure because it makes rights provided for in a collective bargaining agreement obsolete. The nonhierarchical structure of a self-directed work team removes seniority rights to prized jobs within a process, and workers are more likely to become generalists. Moreover, when companies institute self-directed work teams and workers control much of the immediate work environment, including the tasks they will do and the speed with which they will do them, these more satisfied workers may not feel a compelling need for union strength. Organized labor also has viewed the initiation of self-directed work teams and other participative programs as a management tactic to undermine potential union strength with the real goal of creating a nonunion shop.

Although many workers are less alienated than in the past, the potential cyclical nature of empowerment and later frustration could be enough to continue to give unions an important place in American work life. Although self-directed work teams give workers more power than before, that form of participation does not give workers the authority to fight a management decision. On the other hand, in some industries and companies, unions and management have together supported moves toward greater participation. For example, the United Auto Workers (UAW) has participated in General Motors (GM) in a number of formal ways. UAW and GM jointly initiated a quality-of-work-life program in 1973. UAW gained a seat on the Board of Directors of Chrysler in 1979. And UAW members currently participate on long-term national GM development and planning committees (Cornfield, 1987:347).

Employees also gain power when they buy the company. This can result from a potential plant closing, company benefits or gifts in the form of stock, employee takeovers, or the creation of a collective. The result is a new company organized around consensus decision making and jointly owned property (Ferguson, 1991; Woodworth, 1981). However, employee ownership does not necessarily guarantee workers' real power and participation (Zwerdling, 1980). Employee-owners are usually very interested in those aspects of work that affect them directly, such as wages, hours, and benefits; but they are often much less interested in the broad-based power that could be available to them (Hammer and Stern, 1980). This lack of interest appears to be related to the historical role of workers; they are more comfortable with the managers running the business. New enterprises that are organized as collectives are the most likely to have broad participation by workers because that was the philosophy from the inception of the new venture.

We are left with many questions about worker participation in the future. Where will the impetus come from for worker participation in the future? Will it come from managers, workers, organized labor, or the government? What kinds of participation do workers want? Will they want broad decision-making power or be content with power over their more immediate work conditions? Will such factors as gender, race, or social class affect the desire for work participation? What will the role of unions be in the future? Finally, how will the general level of worker participation in a society affect either the desire or demand for worker participation in specific workplaces?

Social Implications of Workplace Trends

A recent employment advertisement in a local newspaper may give us some clues about the future. A decade ago, Woodstream, a leading manufacturer of nontoxic pest control and small animal care products, would have advertised for a machine operator with very specific skills. Now, their ad reads:

> We are seeking individuals to join our team of flexible production operators on our second and third shifts. Qualified applicants will possess a high school diploma, an intense desire to learn, flexibility to perform in multiple work centers, a desire to participate in a team-oriented environment, strong interpersonal skills and a positive attitude, and an ability to problem solve and make decisions. (*Sunday News*, 1994; E-8)

This ad shows clear elements of both worker participation and reengineering, and undoubtedly technological innovation figures somehow in the company's changing needs.

In this chapter, we have examined the possible effects of technological innovation, reengineering, and worker participation on workers and the workplace. But, what specific impact can we expect these trends to have on the relationship between workers and managers? Two patterns of labor relations seem possible (Cornfield, 1987). The first possibility is that managers take greater control of some workers because of deskilling. The second is an increase in formal, labor–management cooperation. A multiplicity of forces will affect the evolving relationship between managers and workers, a relationship that can vary by company, industry, and society.

We should also think about the relationship of the three major topics in this chapter to the others topics discussed in previous chapters. For example, as a result of computer technology, some employees engage in leisure on the job as they contact friends through electronic mail or take a few moments to play a computer game. Technology also makes it possible to communicate with a traveling employee on a commercial airplane, a previously insulated environment. Some restaurants even provide special tables with modem hook-ups for their customers. If employees can always be reached, what are the consequences for conceptions of work and leisure time? Companies increasingly provide recreational facilities, Thanksgiving turkeys, birthday celebrations, and baby showers as a part of worker participation programs. While the provision of such gifts and leisure activities may cause us to deemphasize the dichotomy between work and leisure (Dandridge, 1988), companies may be intentionally co-opting the power of informal groups to increase commitment and loyalty to the company (Lamphere, 1985). Do technology and the provision of celebrations change our conception of the relationship between work and leisure?

In terms of other topics in this book, if reengineering becomes more accepted and is successful, what implications does that have for the range of occupational choices available for either workers new to the labor force or those wishing to change occupations? Will women and people of color be able to more easily enter the newer occupations compared to more established occupations? Similarly, what will be the effect of technological innovation and its potential deskilling or upgrading on occupational choice? Will technological innovation, reengineering, and worker participation flatten the social class hierarchy or further amplify differences between the higher and lower classes?

In addition, what implications might reengineering have for the process of occupational socialization? Will socialization require greater formal training for highly technical jobs or greater flexibility? Will reengineering result in a typically longer or shorter socialization process?

What will the effect of technological innovation, reengineering, and worker participation be on workers' feelings—alienation, satisfaction, or stress—and their commitment to the employing organization, coworkers, and their family? Which workers do you think will be most satisfied in the future—white-collar workers, blue-collar workers, managers, or executives? Which will be most alienated?

How will technological innovations affect the potential for deviance? Will there be more or less opportunity? Do you anticipate that the workers' cultures will support or discourage deviance? How will technological innovations affect the potential for monitoring performance? How will the monitoring itself affect workers?

What impact will the trends and controversies we have discussed have on the relationship between work and family? Our society currently pays lip service to the importance of family. Why then has the working world been relatively slow to adapt to the realities of working families? What aspects of society and organizations will need to change to accommodate the needs of the workers and their families? What factors will encourage companies and organizations to intervene constructively? What societal values must change for there to be a more compatible relationship between family and work? In Case Study 7.4, "Betty Foote: Autoworker," by Richard Feldman and Michael Betzold, a general assembler in a truck plant, discusses a variety of topics including worker participation, automation, and the relationship between work and family, and makes a plea for decent wages and humane work conditions for the future.

In a column published in the *New York Times,* entitled "Workers of the World, Get Smart," the U.S. Secretary of Labor described what he perceives as the long-term crisis in postindustrial society: a widening gap between the demand for workers with "problem-solving skills" and the demand for less-educated workers (Reich, 1993). He says, "How do we move a work force suited to one sort of economy quickly and smoothly into a world grown suddenly quite different?...Our greatest weakness has been the failure to invest adequately in our own learning. In the emerging global, high-tech economy, the development of our human resources will be the key means of creating wealth" (A-19). The success of both our own economy and the global economy depends on providing the resources to answer these questions adequately.

Conclusion

In this chapter, I raised many questions to get you thinking about the trends in work and occupations in an open-minded way. Although there are many unknowns in the future of work, we do know that the quickly changing nature of technology and the emergence of the global economy will have a great impact in the near future and perhaps for the long-term future.

One of the largest challenges of the future will be to find a way to make work both efficient and humane. The most positive outcome would be that work could be done more efficiently so that life will be more humane. If the same level of productivity took less time, more people could spend less time working and invest more in other aspects of life, including family, volunteer work, and other activities that contribute positively to our society. In the meantime, we will need to continue to watch the important changes and intervene when we want to and when we can. Whatever the changes, our working lives will continue to be affected by the people, organizations, and society around us.

REFERENCES AND SUGGESTED READINGS

Adler, Paul, ed. 1992. *Technology and the Future of Work.* New York: Oxford University Press.

Appelbaum, Eileen, and Rosemary Butt. 1994. *The New American Workplace.* Ithaca, NY: ILR Press.

Bachrach, Peter, and Aryeh Botwinick. 1992. *Power and Empowerment.* Philadelphia: Temple University Press.

Bell, Daniel. 1973. *The Coming of Post-Industrial Society.* New York: Basic Books.

Blauner, Robert. 1964. *Alienation and Freedom.* Chicago: University of Chicago Press.

Braverman, Harry. 1974. *Labor and Monopoly Capital: The Degradation of Work in the Twentieth Century.* New York: Monthly Review Press.

Bright, J. R. 1958. *Automation and Management.* Cambridge, MA: Harvard University Graduate School of Business Administration.

Burris, Beverly H. 1993. *Technocracy at Work.* Albany: State University of New York Press.

Business Week. 1993. "The Horizontal Corporation." December 20: 76–81.

Chemical Week. 1993. "Confronting the Challenge of Clean-Sheet Redesign." Novermber 24: 28–29.

Cornfield, Daniel. 1987. "Labor-Management Cooperation or Managerial Control." Pages 331–353 in *Workers, Managers, and Technological Change,* edited by Daniel Cornfield. New York: Plenum Press.

Dandridge, Thomas C. 1988. "Work Ceremonies: Why Integrate Work and Play?" Pages 251–259 in *Inside Organizations,* edited by Michael Owen Jones, Michael Dane Moore, and Richard Christopher Snyder. Newbury Park, CA: Sage.

Derber, Charles, and William Schwartz. 1983. "Toward a Theory of Worker Participation." *Sociological Inquiry* 53: 61–78.

Ferguson, Ann Arnett. 1991. "Managing Without Managers: Crisis and Resolution in a Collective Bakery" Pages 108–132 in *Ethnography Unbound: Power and Resistance in the Modern Metropolis,* edited by Michael Burawoy et al. Berkeley: University of California Press.

Halberstam, David. 1992. *The Next Century,* New York: Avon Books.

Hall, Gene, Jim Rosenthal, and Judy Wade. 1993. "How to Make Reengineering Really Work." *Harvard Business Review* 71 (November–December): 119–131.

Hammer, Michael, and James Champy. 1993. *Reengineering the Corporation: A Manifesto for Business Revolution.* New York: HarperCollins.

Hammer, Tove, and Robert N. Stern. 1980. "Decision-Making Policies and Worker Influence in Employee-Owned Firms." *Academy of Management Journal* 23 (March): 78–100.

Hartmann, Heidi I., Robert E. Kraut, and Louise A. Tilly. 1987. *Computer Chips and Paper Clips: Technology and Women's Employment.* Washington DC: National Academy Press.

Howard, Robert. 1985. *Brave New Workplace.* New York: Penguin Books.

Jackall, Robert. 1988. *Moral Mazes.* New York: Oxford University Press.

Juravich, Tom. 1985. *Chaos on the Shop Floor: A Worker's View of Quality, Productivity, and Management.* Philadelphia: Temple University Press.

Kennedy, Paul. 1993. *Preparing for the Twenty-First Century.* New York: Random House.

Kleinfeld, N. R. 1995. "For Homeless, Free Voice Mail on the Road Back." *The New York Times,* January 30: B-1, B-6.

Lamphere, Louise. 1985. "Bringing Family to Work: Women's Culture on the Shop Floor." *Feminist Studies* 11 (Fall): 519–540.

Lawler, Edward E., III. 1992. *Ultimate Advantage: Creating the High-Involvement Organization.* San Francisco: Jossey-Bass.

Lawler, Edward E., III, Susan Albers Mohrman, and Gerald Ledford, Jr. 1992. *Employee Involvement and Total Quality Management.* San Francisco: Jossey-Bass.

Milkman, Ruth, and Cydney Pullman. 1991. "Technological Change in an Auto Assembly Plant." *Work and Occupations* 18 (2): 123–147.

Morgan, Gareth. 1993. *Imaginization: The Art of Creative Management.* Newbury Park, CA: Sage.

Naisbitt, John, and Patricia Aburdene. 1990. *Megatrends.* New York: Morrow.

National Public Radio. 1994. "A Look at the Clothing Industry Today—Part 1." Morning Edition, December 19.

Reich, Robert B. 1993. "Workers of the World, Get Smart." *The New York Times.* July 20: A-19.

Ritzer, George. 1993. *The McDonaldization of Society.* Newbury Park, CA: Pine Forge Press.

Scott Morton, Michael S. 1991. *The Corporation of the 1990s: Information Technology and Organizational Transformation.* New York: Oxford University Press.

Spenner, Kenneth I. 1983. "Deciphering Prometheus: Temporal Change in the Skill Level of Work." *American Sociological Review* 48: 824–837.

Stern, Aimee L. 1993. "Managing by Team is Not Always as Easy as it Looks." *The New York Times,* July 18: F-5.

Sunday News, Lancaster, PA. 1994. "Classified Advertisements," June 5: E-8.

Toffler, Alvin. 1990. *Powershift: Knowledge, Wealth, and Violence at the Edge of the 21st Century.* New York: Bantam Books.

Tsiganou, Helen A. 1991. *Workers' Participative Schemes.* New York: Greenwood Press.

Woodworth, Warner. 1981. "Forms of Employee Ownership and Workers' Control." *Sociology of Work and Occupations* 8 (2): 195–200.

Zuboff, Shoshana. 1988. *In the Age of the Smart Machine.* New York: Basic Books.

Zwerdling, Daniel. 1980. *Workplace Democracy.* New York: Harper Colophon Books.

Smooth Sailing

Andy Cohen

CASE STUDY QUESTIONS

1. Does the way in which automation is introduced to the salespeople affect their attitudes about automation? To what extent is the reality of the impact of automation on individuals' jobs important relative to their attitude about that automation?
2. Will the work of these salespeople be enhanced or deskilled as a result of this automation? How much can we generalize from this case study to other jobs and other work environments?
3. Based on this case study, what advice would you give to those who want to introduce new automation or technology to others in a work organization?

Tani Marinovich was computer illiterate—and scared. This 30-year-old sales rep had been with her company, Carlson Wagonlit Travel, a Minneapolis–based travel agency, for three years. She felt comfortable with accounts. She was hitting her quota. And she was happy with her work environment. But her working climate was about to drastically change.

Carlson asked Marinovich to move out of her office and into her home. Her 36 sales and account management colleagues re-

Source: From *Sales and Marketing Management,* (March 1995), pp. 11–13, 16. Reprinted with permission of Sales and Marketing Management, Baldwin, NY.

ceived similar instructions. Equipped with a laptop, modem, and business phone line, Marinovich went to work out of her home and on the road. "It was a major change at first," Marinovich says. "I went from working with basically no technology to being fully dependent on it. It was a bit overwhelming."

But the move and the introduction of technology didn't come as a surprise to Marinovich. Carlson management ensured that its salespeople accepted the idea of sales force automation—and were motivated to use the system—before it was implemented. "[Management] took the time to teach everything to us," she says. "We had enough time to get used to the system. It took a year before I was comfortable with it, but my managers were patient with me."

Besides anxiety about her ability to learn the technology, Marinovich had other fears. How would she fit her whole office into her small one-bedroom apartment in Boston? Would she always bring her laptop with her on sales calls? What if it's too heavy to carry around? And, would she get lonely always working by herself? "Suddenly changing the work environment like we did made me have a lot of questions," she says. "But management sat down with us and answered our questions and fears long before we had to go out on our own. It made automation an easy transition for us."

Today, her view of automation has changed 180 degrees. "Now, I can't live without it," Marinovich says. "It makes me more efficient and saves me so much time. I don't know how I ever worked without it." Though she doesn't take her laptop wherever she goes, she constantly refers to it when on the phone with her travel agency clients. Also, she transfers data every morning, sends and receives e-mail from her managers and colleagues, and does product demonstrations in front of customers with her new technology.

Why did Marinovich and the sales force accept this automation project so quickly? Because Carlson had convinced its salespeople of the project's viability a year before they were moved out of their offices.

Where Carlson Wagonlit Travel went right, though, is precisely where many companies go wrong in implementing sales force automation: they don't speak to salespeople about their plans. Too often, while it's so caught up in creating an automation system, a company ignores its salespeople. Salespeople, then, never really learn about the system. Don't find out about its benefits. Don't view it as an important aspect of their jobs. Don't buy in to the idea of automation. And don't use it.

Looking to get salespeople on your side? Listen to them.

Salespeople Say...

A mistake in the beginning of the automation process can easily result in a zero return on the company's investment. "It's vital to first understand what problems your salespeople are having, and then design an automation system that solves those problems," says Paul Selden, president of the Sales Automation Association in Dearborn, Michigan. "If you give people the things that they've been asking for all along—rather than blindly giving them laptops and some software—then they will buy into the automation system, and they'll *want* to use it."

The key is to get salespeople involved in the process as early as possible. Find out what they think would make their job easier. How could they be more productive? Can the corporate office do anything differently to enhance their selling abilities? Do they have too much paperwork? An automation system that's designed with salespeople's input is likely to gain the approval of the sales force. And it will be used.

Cable & Wireless, Inc., a Vienna, Virginia-based long distance provider for small- and medium-size companies, attributes its success with automation to continuous meetings with the sales force.

At the beginning of 1993 the company's CEO and senior managers published their travel schedules so the sales force would know when they would be in their part of the country. "Our management engaged in real dialogue with salespeople," says Bill Coyne, executive vice president. "Not just presentations or speeches about the benefits of automation, but conversations that hit on exactly what the salespeople would want from an automation system, and what *they* felt would make their time more productive."

Management learned from its 450-person sales force that proposals took too long to create, too much paperwork was sent from corporate [headquarters], and lead tracking wasn't efficient enough. The company had the information it needed and could proceed with the creation of an automation system. "It's the salespeople's ideas at work in the system, so they will want to use it," Coyne says. "The last thing I want to do is spend a lot of money on something my salespeople haven't asked for."

What the company did spend money on (about $9,000 per salesperson) was applications that solve problems. It gave salespeople a program that reduced the time to generate a proposal (from three or four hours to about 10 minutes); an electronic marketing encyclopedia that allowed the corporate office to enter data without sending paper memos; and a lead tracking device that created synergy among the sales and marketing departments.

It's a system that the salespeople can relate to because it focuses on the problems that they pointed out to management. "We asked for these applications because they were things that would help us do our jobs better," says Ash Kumar, an Atlanta-based Cable & Wireless rep. "We bought into the technology because we knew the things we would receive would make our lives easier."

"If you appeal to the hopes of your salespeople by fulfilling things they want, then you will get buy-in," Selden says. He also points out that salespeople's fears should be addressed prior to implementation. Focus groups and surveys, can help determine what the sales force may be afraid of, or nervous about, in an automation system. Arguments such as "I'm not a typist," "I shouldn't have to do data entry," and "Some of my client information is private," need to be aired before automation is rolled out—and it must be explained that the system won't enhance these fears.

When Cable & Wireless management first started meeting with its sales force, worries about automation centered around time. "Our salespeople were nervous that they would be wasting time by entering data and reading information from the computer, rather than making sales calls," Coyne says. "But when we told them that the system would produce quicker proposals and less paperwork, their interest really piqued. They began to see that automation has a unique benefit to them—an individual win, because their personal productivity will be increased."

And salespeople have become more productive. Brett Harney, a Cleveland rep, points to the marketing encyclopedia feature. "It has increased my productivity considerably," he says. "It allows me to have customer, new business, and competitor information in one place. It makes me more efficient in front of the customer."

Plan Early and Slowly

By starting a year in advance, Carlson Wagonlit Travel built excitement and momentum for its automation project. "We knew that the first thing we had to do was make sure our salespeople understood the system," says Dwain Wall, vice president and general manager. "The system would be a failure if our sales force didn't accept it first."

The benefits were explained to reps: less paperwork, more time in front of customers, and improved communication. "At sales meetings, training sessions, and one-on-ones, management constantly talked about the advantages of automation, and kept salespeople abreast of where we were in the process," Wall says. "We always wanted to keep them updated so they would feel involved in the project."

Once the system was ready, Carlson didn't just give laptops to its sales reps and say "go." It took the slow, meticulous route in training the sales force. "Our salespeople, although their average age is only thirty-two, weren't very computer proficient," Wall says. "They were nervous, so we trained them in small groups and started with the basics."

For formal training, the sales force was broken up into groups of five to seven people, which participated in a day-long session. Simple things like how to turn a computer on and how to log in were the salespeople's introduction to automation.

Instructors constantly reinforced what they taught and stopped to make sure that all salespeople understood how to use the system. Another training session was held a month later so salespeople could have time to experience the system and come back with any questions.

Wall attributes the success of the system to the patient, deliberate approach that the company took implementing it. "If you don't start talking about automation early on in the process, then salespeople won't buy into the system—and ultimately won't use it," Wall says. "The slow process gives salespeople enough time to get excited about, and acquainted with, the automation system."

Automation Aftercare

Sales force automation is an ongoing process. The communication that occurs with salespeople prior to implementation has to continue afterward or they may lose the motivation to use the system.

For automation to be successful in an organization, it should become part of the everyday communication between management and the sales force. "Technology has to be embraced as a core part of a company's business practices," says Ken Dulaney, of the Gartner Group, a sales force automation consultancy in Stamford, Connecticut. "It has to be made as important a priority as anything else that's spoken about on an everyday basis."

Dulaney suggests organizations tie sales training to use of the automation system. "Salespeople will realize that technology is important to the company if it is always worked on and talked about at training sessions," he says. "A company should work on using technology as much as it works on presentations, cold calls, or sales strategies."

Besides informal discussions with salespeople about the progress of automation, Cable & Wireless has set up an advisory board. Consisting of two reps from each of five separate regions, technical staff, and support staff, the board meets every other month to discuss the evolution of the system. What is right, what is wrong, and what should be added to make the system as effective as possible. "It's important that we continue to have a voice in the automation process," says Harney, who is a member of the advisory board. "Reps will stay motivated to use the system if they know that their concerns are being heard."

At a recent board meeting, negative reactions to the proposal-generator application were aired. Reps weren't using it because it was too complicated and didn't offer a uniform picture of the company. The board made the complaints known, and now management is working to upgrade the application.

Also, putting certain features into an automation system will ensure that salespeople use it. Carlson Wagonlit Travel salespeople had to electronically report their sales once they were automated—the corporate office was not going to acknowledge sales reported on paper. In the beginning, "a couple reps weren't using the reporting system and came out with zero sales," says Wall. "They quickly learned to use their computers."

If features in the system appeal to the very nature of salespeople, then they're more likely to use it. "The technology an organization uses has to appeal to the primal motivations of sales reps—quota, commissions, and money," Dulaney says.

When Cable & Wireless sales reps turn on their computers, they immediately see their year-to-date commissions. Also, when they make a sale their commission is automatically tabulated, and their quota is updated. Tom Johnson, a Nashville-based Cable & Wireless rep, says, "The thing I'm concerned most with is making money. You can bet I'll use the system when I can immediately find out what my paycheck is going to say."

Creativity at Work

Cheryl Harrison

CASE STUDY QUESTIONS

1. What difficulties did the president of the graphics firm experience when the organizational structure was hierarchical? Who had and disseminated information in this structure?

2. What kind of structure did the president decide to move to? To what extent would you describe the changes in structure as reengineering? What kinds of assumptions did she make about how information would be controlled and disseminated? Did this new stucture better facilitate the sharing of information or not?

3. What kind of work environment do you think the author would recommend to those who want to enhance communication between individuals in an organization?

I went to work as an art director for an advertising agency right out of school. Six months later, the person I had replaced decided to rejoin the agency, and I was let go. The next day, I started my own graphics firm. That was in 1980. The business grew slowly, but steadily. In 1985, I was chosen San Francisco's Woman Entrepreneur of the Year by the Chamber of Commerce. By 1988,

as president and creative director of Harrison Design Group, I was at the top of a traditional pyramid structure that had evolved as the business grew to fourteen people. And I was miserable.

I had a couple of senior management people under me, then all the designers, below them the production staff, and then the administrative staff. But all roads led to me. And before long, I found that I was getting pretty frenetic. The structure didn't give me any time to work out important design decisions with my designers. It didn't allow me time to think or just to put things on the back burner. Rather than being proactive, I was reacting to problems. I had to react to things rather than thinking ahead and steering them in the right direction.

More and more, with this kind of organizational structure, I found communication breaking down. Clearly, participation in the creative process was stifled from the bottom up. The administrative staff couldn't possibly be creative in their jobs, because they didn't understand the context. They were isolated. Even the best designers were isolated, because they didn't understand the business side. They didn't necessarily have a hands-on feeling—if they went over budget or spent too many hours on a project, they had no idea what that really meant, what the consequences were. Some of the smallest decisions were ultimately left up to me.

I didn't have the solution, but I knew that things weren't working the way I wanted them to. Finally, I asked myself, Where is all this going? And my conclusion was that the business was only going to get bigger, only going to get more frenetic, and I just wasn't going to be able to handle it. It certainly wasn't going to be fun anymore. It was already pretty stressful. The creative product was suffering. We weren't rising to new levels. Clients started calling and saying, "Cheryl, we like working with you, but we haven't seen you in a long time. Where are you?" That was a signal for change.

I had no clue what the solution was. For the moment, I just stopped. I went to different consultants—even a financial consultant who had worked with a number of other design firms. I thought he might be able to suggest a different way to structure my business or something. I took the few available courses I could find. I talked with everybody I could. None said, "Cheryl, this is the answer."

I finally decided that the best way to regroup was to do it more or less from ground zero. So as people decided to leave the firm, I simply didn't hire replacements. Toward the end of this attrition process, I let one person go.

Shelli was very much a part of that major change effort, that transition period. She came in for a first interview at the office and said, "I realize that you have posted a position for an administrative employee with senior level experience, and I'm pretty much just out of school, but I'm still interested in the job." And I said, "I really need someone with a lot more experience. Because of what we need to do here and where we need to go, I'm not going to be able to do it alone. I'm going to do it with one other person who must have years of experience." She came back the next day for a second interview, and at the end of the interview, she said, "I really think you should give me a chance." That threw me completely. But I thought to myself, anyone who's this determined...So I said, "Why don't we try something for about two weeks, because I have someone going on vacation. You could fill in there."

She learned so fast and picked up things so beautifully that within days she was contributing to the office and coming up with new solutions. She just moved right ahead. She asked really good questions. She was very thoughtful, but she challenged the status quo. And she became one of the most fully dimensional employees that I've ever had. She understood the administrative functions. She saw their relationship to the business. She took that to the next step and said, "I'm enjoying working on the computer. Could I use it to do some design work?" She started learning the creative side. Then she asked if she could go on some printers' press checks. She learned all about printing from outside reps who serviced our account. She asked if she could take some evening classes. She embraced the computer, the technology, and encouraged me to buy more programs for the Mac. Sure, she came up against problems, but she found solutions. They didn't faze her. She didn't let herself get upset about them.

After about a year, there was a period when Shelli and I were the only people left, when we ran the entire office. What was fascinating was that the work load remained almost the same. And it occurred to me, "How did we go from fourteen people down to two people, and we're still handling so much business?"

Yes, we were more selective about the business we took on. We were careful about how we organized that business, how we organized our time. But the most shocking part of it all was how efficient just the two of us were.

By the middle of 1992—with Shelli as a prototype employee—we were handling almost the same volume of business with just *five* on staff as we had been with *fourteen* employees in 1988.

In retrospect, I believe that the traditional pyramid [hierarchical] organizational structure has failed us by pigeonholing responsibilities and capabilities and pinpointing exactly what someone's tasks should be during the day. This structure road map inevitably gets you demerits for not doing your job. And it's counterproductive to the creative process.

There was also a perplexing notion about information—somehow, I was the only one who had it, at the top. So I decided to build a centralized administrative system in which everyone would have access to all critical information, and everyone would contribute to the administration through whatever they were working on. From the process of conceptual design to project implementation, each designer in our group is now involved in the whole comprehensive notion of a project, not just an isolated element of it. The skills required to work in this way are different, but I feel that the results are far more successful.

In the past, one designer would take almost full responsibility for a particular client and a particular project, and my job was to keep each designer focused in the right direction. But now I feel that we all are taking responsibility for the joys and the disappointments, the good and the bad, the success or failure of each project. We all really feel that.

Today, I allow people to take on a lot more responsibility. Access to information and direct participation are the key—through the use of the computer, certainly, but also involving everyone much earlier on in the process. We work very collaboratively in the office to prepare for a client presentation so that everyone really knows what's going on. If the baton needs to be passed or the pendulum needs to swing—this person is now going to take a little more responsibility on this project and a little less responsibility over here—everybody's very comfortable doing that. And if someone's on vacation, no problem. We can handle it.

How did we get to this point? Let me reminisce.

The first computer in the office—an IBM clone—was like this black cloud, initially. It was *not* positively received in our creative environment.

What happened with that first computer experience—something that I realized years later—was that we became very detail oriented and very administratively oriented because we had a new tool available to track all these "business" things. But it started to detract from what we were in the business of doing, which was the creative product. The computer soon became all-consuming in its ability to take over administrative functions. It was such a challenge just to figure out how it was going to meet our wishes that we spent a lot of energy in that area—too much energy.

We broke this stranglehold with the introduction of the Macintosh as our right-hand creative tool, available to everyone. Fortunately, this time, it became a creative tool *first*, and *then* an administrative tool.

The designers can now relate to the complete creative, production, and implementation process by the unique nature of the Macintosh. Very early in the creative process, we put our design projects up on the computer. What followed was a fluid evolution of that design or that concept through to completion. Formerly, three or four different people worked to accomplish this same task. Now one person can carry a project through to completion. It's a very different type of person—one who has strong conceptual skills but also has implementation and management skills—who can envision how something would *really* be produced and how that design would successfully work once it was printed and implemented.

I think that the new organizational structure that is evolving—I see it as a flat circle—has a lot to do with one-on-one communications and access to information: information to determine what's important and what's not, what's possible and what's not, what the priorities, and project objectives are. It's core information—so that people can keep their own work, their own passion in the proper context.

I'm discovering that the best communication between people working in a collaborative environment is communication that's not really planned, when there's an informality in how people interact. To have people actually schedule meetings at various points in time is okay. But what seems to work best is when someone has an idea and I can just pop right over and we can look at it together—right then.

I try to create an atmosphere in which I make myself available to people as they need me. In a creative endeavor, it's hard to know when you're going to get to that critical point—at 1:00 P.M. or 3:15 P.M. or whenever. The way I'm trying to work is to say, "I'm going to be here from 1:00 to 5:00 this afternoon, so if you reach a point where we need to get together, anytime during that window is fine."

My approach is also to say, "Check in with me when you're at a point of needing to get away from an idea." It may not be complete, and it's fine if it's not yet perfect. In fact, I don't need to see the project when it's perfect. If it's perfect, then don't show it to me at all. When you need air space, when you've been so close to this thing that you just need to get some time away, do it. When you're thinking, "I need a new opinion, I need to bring this to another level, I need to figure out a way to look at this differently to

see whether I like it or don't like it, to see whether it's working," then I want people to come to me. But I come to them for the same reason. I need *them* sometimes more than they need me.

One thing I've learned during this transitional process is that the collaborative spirit of working out a problem together is heightened when nobody has to report to anyone. People are responsible for themselves. They have information, so they can find out what's going on. They don't have to waste time on typical office protocol. I don't have to scold anyone for being over budget or late for work. Everybody knows where things stand.

Within the structure of the office, I have been amazed to find out that people who thought that they were production-oriented ended up being great designers. People who came in with strong administrative skills ended up being some of the best conceptual thinkers. Suddenly, I found that when people who thought that they had very defined skills were given the opportunity to cross all parts of the process, they rose to the occasion and came up with ideas that offered a totally new, fresh perspective that contributed greatly to the end result. I call this structure the kinetic circle (see Figure 1).

Today, no one person's idea is any better than any other's. This is a big item. In the

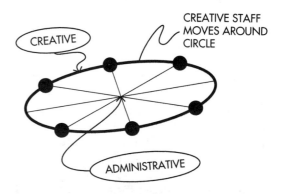

Figure 1. Diagram of the Kinetic Circle

former structure, I had the final say. People would wait to meet with me, and then what I said would go. It would frustrate the living daylights out of me. I'd say, "Why do you guys think that just because I said this or that, it's the way you necessarily have to go? It is not the case. Your idea is as good as mine." They wouldn't believe me.

However, in the kinetic-circle concept, people evolve their own ideas, bouncing them off me or, if I'm not there, if I'm out of town, doing it together, among themselves. There is no judgment of whether it's good, bad, or indifferent. Everybody knows that they can run something by a few other people in the office and then come to an even better decision.

Whether or not I agree with it in the end, I know that people thought it through to the best of their ability, that they used one another as a resource to get to the best point, and so I will always support them in their decision—unquestionably. And they know that. That's a very important notion. It's one of the biggest realizations that I've had—that I can trust people who work with me to come up with solutions equal to my own. It is a trust that is now very deep. It's a trust whereby I can walk away from something that I might have a lot of anxiety about and know that it's going to be taken care of. And that's an incredible feeling. It's an even more incredible feeling to come back and see how well something was solved—often much better than I could have done myself. It's an implicit trust—that I don't even need to question people's capability.

A lot of this is about freeing me up but also, in the process, freeing everyone up.

Now, when I hire someone new into the office, I like to give them a very big, multidimensional project. Typically, it involves design, a conceptual visual component, and client communication. It has management, production, and follow-through, requiring a whole spectrum of talents, tasks, and demands. It's a small enough project that, if some part doesn't go quite right, the patching up of some minor stumbling block is not going to be a problem. But what that project will tell me, and what it shows to the rest of the office, is how this person thinks—where they can run with something and where they hesitate, where they feel confident and where they flounder, where they're efficient and where they waste time. And I think that it's also a feedback mechanism for the new employee as well—sometimes very painful, because they're given so much responsibility so early.

I've met so many people who have said, "Cheryl, you're so lucky to be a creative person," and then in the same breath, they'll say, "I wish I were more creative." And I just feel like saying, "But you are!" I believe that every one of us has a huge creative potential. It's just that something happened when we were growing up, someone told us, "You don't know how to draw," or "You don't know how to write," or "You don't know how to play piano." And all of a sudden, we shut off that creative part of ourselves.

Our lives could be so much richer and so much more interesting if we just realized that we do have the capability to think differently—maybe to change the way we've done something, or to be a little bit more resourceful, or to find a different way of doing something. In our day-to-day lives, there are different options that may have even greater value that we're overlooking because we're used to doing it the same way. The greatest inventions and innovations often come from taking something that has existed in one area forever and putting it somewhere else. People say, "Isn't that just brilliant!" It's not necessarily that it was so brilliant or so unique. It was just that someone thought to look at it upside down and put it in a different context.

People have capabilities far beyond what they think they have. They are hired for a particular job but, given the opportunity, they end up being capable of so much more. They can contribute to the end result in areas no one, including themselves, ever believed they could.

Recently, I was thinking about the times when we've been in a crunch to design something, to create something from scratch, and we've had no boundaries. Actually, it's more difficult to create something when there are no walls, no boundaries whatsoever. Part of creative thinking is learning how to use the walls to guide you to a solution. People immediately look at the walls and don't look at the path created between the walls. Or they don't realize that they can reorient the walls. It has to do with observation of one's own thinking. In fact, walls and problems, issues and dilemmas, differing opinions, budget constraints, and other things that seem to get in the way can end up helping us to create the ideal solution.

It saddens me to think that many people in the workplace today really don't realize that they can move those walls. They do not believe that they can work with the people who are sitting right next to them, right across the desk from them, in the next office, or down the hall—or someone they meet in the elevator—that they can work with that person in some way just to run an idea by them, to get to the next level. Rather, people worry about what some other person will think.

Communication with co-workers can help all of us elevate a project to a new dimension. It doesn't matter what the person says. What matters is that they have a comment and they have an opinion. That opinion or observation, perfect or not, usually allows us to leverage yet another opinion on top of another. We would then, almost through a creative dialogue, evolve to a new, fresh approach. Whether or not we would evolve it into something that would ultimately work, who really cares at that point? In this dialogue, a solution evolves faster than if I just sat there alone and tried to stew in my own ideas.

As there are budget cuts across the board, as the economy sputters, as competition increases and the pace of change becomes exponential, we need to become more efficient in the workplace. We need to think more clearly. We can't be as wasteful. There's a sense of responsibility today. It's almost like caring for the ecology of the workplace, the balance of positive and negative. And I think that we have to be significantly more efficient with our own resources—ourselves, the people we work with, the things we work with—and more conscious of the waste that we might create in time and materials.

If we can find ways to inspire our human capabilities in the workplace, I think we might supersede what we ever thought we could do in many other aspects of our lives. And one way we might do this is by understanding how we think, how we create, how we problem solve, and how we can also work together with others.

The workplace has so much to offer, now more than ever before, because people are working together toward furthering common goals. Look at how much time we spend in the workplace today. With that dedication, there's an opportunity. With our enhanced relationships with co-workers, and better understanding of ourselves, we're all working to make a contribution to that entity, that company, that thing. And that entity, that thing, has a valued relationship to a greater world as well.

Management Ideology and Practice in Participative Plants

Louise Lamphere

1. How would you describe the team structure at the silicon chip plant?
2. To what extent did the team structure change relationships between supervisors and workers, trainers and workers, and between coworkers?
3. How do you think the workers at the plant feel about the team structure and their work at the plant? What are the factors that affect these workers' feelings?

During the early 1980s, as many American firms were enthusiastically adopting new forms of management derived from Japan, several new plants in Albuquerque...were experimenting with "participative management."...Such firms have a flat organizational structure with few levels between plant manager and shop floor workers, a mini-enterprise or team work structure, and a strong emphasis on egalitarianism in the way work and leisure areas are designed. There is usually a high commitment to

Source: "Management Ideology and Practice in Participative Plants," Louise Lamphere, Patricia Zavella, Felipe Gonzales, with Peter B. Evans from *Sunbelt Working Mothers: Reconciling Family and Factory,* 1993, pp. 138, 159–163. Permission granted by Cornell University Press.

employee stability, heavy emphasis on training, pay based on the attainment of "skill levels," and job enrichment whereby workers have some control over the organization of work....

Silicon Chip Manufacture and the Team Structure

...SystemsPlus, which manufactured silicon chips, had dispensed with assembly lines and traditional hierarchies to organize production around "teams."...[The company] espoused a participative management philosophy, and...instituted unusual shift schedules. SystemsPlus implemented a twelve-hour, three-and-a-half-day shift schedule...The restructuring of work, along with each firm's participative philosophy, obscured management's control system. ...The contradictions between management goals for productivity and workers' attempts to control their own work were less apparent. This in turn had implications for women's work practice and strategies for resistance. In contrast, the unusual shift schedules often sharpened the contradictions between women's work and family roles, as women had to rearrange child care and family responsibilities to fit schedules out of sync with the more usual nine-to-five, forty-hour work week....

SystemsPlus manufactured silicon chips that became parts of integrated circuits, a production process prior to and quite different from that of stuffing boards. The manufacture of wafers and cutting them into chips involved building the wafers from silicon and etching circuitry on them. Each wafer had 300 dies, and each die contained a separate circuit. The plant had several "fabs" (fabrication facilities) composed of "clean rooms" containing the complex machinery necessary to build the wafers. In the fab, workers had to wear special clothing and take special precautions to prevent wafers from becoming contaminated.

There were three departments in the fab that had opened in the Albuquerque plant in 1982: "masking," "diffusion," and "thin film." In the diffusion department, the wafers were constructed by layering oxide and nitrites. In masking, sectors of the wafer were blocked out and others etched with the circuits. In the thin film department, additional layers were built on.

At the time of our interviews the plant had only eighty-five employees, but by 1987 its labor force numbered 599: 43.1 percent women and 56.9 percent men. SystemsPlus was scheduled to run on a twenty-four-hour, seven-day-a-week schedule, but in 1982 only the day shifts were in operation. Shift A started on Sunday at 6:00 A.M. and continued to 6:00 P.M. on Sunday, Monday, and Tuesday and until noon on Wednesday. Shift B started at noon Wednesday, continued to 6:00 P.M., and resumed from 6:00 P.M. to 6:00 P.M. on Thursday, Friday, and Saturday. We interviewed Donna Garcia, a trainer responsible for teaching production jobs to new employees; she worked on shift B.

Within departments, production teams on each shift integrated employees from different supervisory and skill levels: each team had a supervisor, several engineers and technicians, and a number of operators. Since engineers and technicians were usu-ally men and assemblers were women, teams also brought males and females into the same work group. Team organization also emphasized job rotation among the assemblers and control over work scheduling. The plant manager told us that ideally a team would have six to eight assemblers, one for each task to be performed; if possible, each of these workers would be trained for all tasks within the team and would be able to switch off among them.[1] Each team was to have considerable autonomy and could often decide how to divide up its work.

The importance of job rotation was obvious in Donna's work experience. At the time of our interview she was working in the diffusion department and had learned eleven jobs there. Previously, she had mastered four jobs in masking. Donna described the rationale: "See, everybody is trained to run two different jobs. We run twelve hours a day, and this breaks up their day. Instead of being put on just one piece of equipment, and you're just there the rest of the day, you have a chance to get a little bit of variety."

In addition to job rotation, each team within a department met daily to plan production, a task often directed by an engineer but with the operators' participation.

> At 6:00 A.M. I have a meeting in the fab—we have what we call a team meeting. And this is the diffusion team; it's the supervisor of the operators, plus me and the other trainer, [and] the operators, the techs, and the engineers. We all get together, the supervisor lets us know what's in the area, what's priority, and asks the training department what we need for the day, what do you guys want to do? We say, "Well, we want to work on this product over here, so let us have all this product, and your operators can go off and do this other product over here."

The trainers carefully schedule which persons they will work with each day and how they will supervise and monitor their work.

Donna and her partner were training two new operators; the other workers in diffusion had completed training.

Donna was a particularly important person in the implementation of management's control system. She had responsibility not only for her trainees' output but also for quality control. Following a checklist of steps for each job, she instructed the workers and then graded them on their quality and quantity: "I have a master timing sheet in which I can get a grade for them; in other words, it's like a percentage. If they get three wrong out of thirty, I can give them a certain percentage. So that's their quality rating for the day." When they had learned the job, she then worked with each trainee to get the job done in a specified amount of time. The trainers used a learning curve for each operation and also kept a diary of what each person did during the twelve-hour shift. If one trainer monitored three individuals, and each was learning two different jobs, measuring their work and drawing up the charts could be a complex operation.

Once a week the trainers from all the teams had their own team meeting for two hours to discuss the progress of the workers they were supervising. Since we were unable to interview assemblers, we do not know what kinds of strategies and tactics grew up around the learning curves imposed on each job. Workers were being monitored very closely at the beginning of their training; however, the jobs were very complex, and it is possible that if trainers stressed quality rather than quotas, women workers did not feel at odds with a control system.

Donna's interview gives us some sense of how the team structure was used to change relationships between supervisors and workers, between trainers and workers, and between co-workers themselves. In team meetings, trainers could bring up any problems they had and suggest any improvements they wanted to make. An organizational development specialist gave the trainers exercises in role playing and conflict resolution. "Well, like our last team meeting…we had a deal on role playing and changing roles, and how communication is involved in that and how some people can only see one side of something, they don't really know all the facts. And why this other person is against them."

Each team, from management on down, also attended a "team concepts" seminar that lasted for three and a half days. "Some people, they don't really like to be involved. And they're the type of people who go to meetings and they don't say a word, you know, they never express themselves, but they are the ones who are having the problems.…In the year that I've been there, I can say that yes, it does work. We've matured, our team has matured a lot."

The trainers often solved problems within their group without going to the supervisors. For example, when one trainer was spending too much time away from the fab area, they wanted to encourage her to check more often on her trainees. But instead of criticizing the trainer directly, they suggested, "So and so in the fab, and they were asking for you." In that way, "we get the person to feel like, 'Well, maybe I should be in the fab more,'" Donna explained. In short, there seemed to be close monitoring of production, but the team structure was being implemented in a manner that produced more cooperative and less hierarchical relationships.

For working mothers, the SystemsPlus shift schedule had the single most important impact on the family. Aware that it might be an issue in recruiting a high-quality labor force, the firm had conducted a survey to find out whether enough people would be willing to work three and a half days on twelve-hour shifts. The results were positive; despite potential problems with family responsibilities, the plant manager thought the schedule would attract a different kind of employee, a younger population, and those who would be interested in a three-and-a-half-day weekend.

For some mothers, the shift schedule sharpened the contradictions between full-time mother and worker. Donna had had to make some adjustments, but she had been able to arrange a place at a day-care center for her three-year-old daughter only on Thursdays and Fridays (Donna's mother kept the child on Wednesday afternoons). Her husband's schedule as a facilitator at HealthTech was flexible enough so that he was able to drop the younger child off and pick her up, and to oversee the eight-year-old during nonschool hours. Thus, Donna had worked through the sharpened contradictions brought about by her unusual schedule.

> I like it. I like it. It's a hard adjustment to get used to when you first start out. And there's some problems involved that you wouldn't have normally in other jobs. One of them is day care, cause you go in at six. We have to be there by twenty to six in the morning, the trainers do; the operators have to be there at six. And the day cares aren't open at that time. And day cares usually close at 6:00 in the evening, and you don't get out of work until six, so that's a problem there. Another problem would be that [on second shift] you don't have a real weekend. That's an adjustment, also.

The job itself had a lot of positive benefits, including the pay. Since Donna worked a forty-two-hour week, she was paid time-and-a-half for the extra two hours. Averaged out, her earnings were about $7.00 an hour, a dollar or two over the wages earned by many other women we interviewed. She felt she was "very lucky" to get her job, rated it highly (a 1 or 2 on all items), and had never thought of quitting this position. "I like the people contact, I like working with people and teaching them. I get a lot of satisfaction out of it when they go through the job and they learn it and they demonstrate....It's like watching your kid graduate from high school or something. You're really proud of them because they know the job, and you know that you taught them right....So it's really satisfying work."

Donna was an enthusiastic employee who had made adjustments to the unorthodox shift schedule and who was happy with the high pay, benefits, and flexibility of her job. From her perspective, participative management was a success....

NOTE

1. This team structure is commonly used in automobile plants (Harley Shaiken, personal communication), but at SystemsPlus....there was more effort to transform relations between supervisors and workers in order to "debureaucratize control."

Betty Foote: Autoworker

Richard Feldman and Michael Betzold

CASE STUDY QUESTIONS

1. What is Betty Foote's attitude about employee involvement and worker participation? Why do you think she feels as she does?

2. How does she perceive the relationship between workers and management?

3. How important are issues and concerns about the relationship between work and family to Betty Foote? How responsive does she perceive the truck plant to be to issues and concerns about the relationship between work and family?

4. If Betty Foote were to recommend changes to the management of the truck plant, what recommendations would she make and what concerns would she be addressing with these recommendations? To what extent do her concerns represent those of other workers?

Born June 6, 1936, in Idlewild, Michigan
Hired June 15, 1976
General assembler

I love the people in the plants because they are so colorful. They are Richard Pryor- and Eddie Murphy-type people. They're really comical, and they can be uplifting.

Source: "Betty Foote: Autoworker," Richard Feldman and Michael Betzold from *End of the Line: Autoworkers and the American Dream*, 1988, pp. 198–206. Permission granted by Weidenfeld and Nicolson.

People in the auto plants are really honest inside the plant. Because we work close together, we talk about our lives and share our problems. We find out we all have similar concerns: house notes and marriages and neighborhoods and children and drugs. If I didn't hear about those concerns from people I work with, I would be like other black people who think their kids are the only ones doing bad things because that's what's reported in the newspapers. But it doesn't have anything to do with color. We're all just people, and we all have similar problems.

But when you get outside of the plant, there's a different attitude. We all make the same money, but the attitude still is: I don't really want you coming to live next door to me.

The supposed concern for workers' happiness now with the EI [employee involvement] program is a real joke. Ten years ago they didn't have EI, and they weren't talking about management-employee relationships. But all they are doing now is talking about it. It looks good on paper; but it is not effective, and they don't want it to be.

When you read that American autoworkers don't care, that is a lie. Workers' attitudes have changed; they want to see good products put out. And they want to call management's attention to any problems with the cars. But management is still the same. They don't care. You can tell them, "Look, this bolt doesn't fit in here," and they'll say, "Well, just put it in anyway." It embarrasses me to even tell them anything anymore because they look at me like: Well, so what? Just do it. We're just trying to get these cars out of here.

What's going on is no fault of the workers. American workers aren't shiftless. When you work in the plants, you understand why nobody wants to buy an American-made car. You see with your own eyes that all management wants is to get it out that door. You can't stop the line if there's a problem. Don't let anybody tell you that. If you stop the line, you're going to go right out on the street.

They showed us this movie about health and safety, and I learned a lot about some of the chemicals I work with. But what a joke! The film said that the rubber gloves I used when I was wiping cabs are not good enough because the solution leaks through and gets on your skin. Now suppose I had said, "Well, look, I cannot do this job because these rubber gloves are not the proper thing to use." They would have said, "Well, that's all we have. What you want us to do?" And if I'd called a union rep, he would have said, "Well, Betty, just use them tonight, and maybe tomorrow they'll have some more gloves."

Relations between workers and management haven't changed. The foremen are ridiculous. They really need to be retrained. They'll put you on a job, and they won't even show you the basics of the job. You have to ask another employee how to do it because the foremen don't know. But if I miss something, the foreman will say, "Well, baby, the inspector says that you missed that." Of course, I missed it. I don't even know what the hell I'm looking for. I'm just doing it by trial and error.

They shouldn't have any supervisors. Just let the employees run the department because at least they respect each other. The product would still get out, and you wouldn't get harassed by a dumb supervisor who makes unnecessary remarks and rules because he's trying to make you think he knows the job. An employee who works on a machine every day knows what he's doing. He doesn't need a supervisor to tell him.

When I first started at Wayne Assembly, there was a foreman who didn't want women in his department. He liked to shake his fingers in my face. I told him I didn't read sign language. I went to Labor Relations, and they came right down and told him to stop shaking his fingers in my face. There was no need for me to call a union rep.

In the paint booth when I started, we never saw our committeeman. I got into a little trouble because I got up at a meeting once and said our committeeman never came in the booth. They told me to keep my mouth shut. They still dislike me. I guess I talk too much. I tell the truth. I'm not going to lie, and if you don't know how to scheme and connive to get a problem solved in the plant, you're not going to get it solved.

I'm not sure if we need the union. It depends on how fair management is. Some small companies have good management. But the auto companies will lie and say one day they're not going to move the plant, and the next day the plant is closing up and shutting down. So I guess I'm happy the union's around.

The jobs haven't gotten harder over the years, but we have more work, and we're working faster. If they eliminate eighteen jobs off my line, the people who stay will be running to do the extra work. Me, I don't run. I'm too old to start that.

Nobody feels secure anymore because of robots. People are afraid their jobs will be eliminated. Automation means job elimination. That's the bottom line.

They're giving people an opportunity to go to school, so they can get trained to operate or repair the new machines. The classes are from 4 to 6 in the afternoon, so the day shift people can go to school after they get off and the night people have to come in two hours early. But you still have to work ten hours on top of going to school, and that's a big load. I tried to take some brushup classes in spelling and stuff like that, but I was nodding off all the time. I couldn't concentrate.

My dad and mom were born in Ohio, in a little town called Paulding, which had both white and black farmers. My older brothers and sisters were all born in Fort Wayne, Indiana. My dad used to go up north hunting and eventually decided to move up there, to a town called Idlewild. He was a builder and worked in a plant in Muskegon, about sixty miles away.

My mom died when I was 2. My dad remarried, to a really nice lady who wasn't much older than my oldest brother. He kind of raised her along with us. My dad didn't have any problem raising us. He could cook and wash and iron. He and my mom had six kids, plus he had one by my stepmom and she had two of her own.

At Christmas we had to go out in the woods and cut down our own tree. We couldn't afford tree lights, but we would make some flour paste, bring some construction paper home from school, and make little rings and decorate the tree. For a long time we didn't have electricity. We had kerosene lamps, and the lampshade cost a nickel. You had to guard it with your life when you cleaned it so it wouldn't break. A nickel was hard to come by.

We didn't have TV. We had to do our schoolwork before dark because my dad didn't want our eyes to be ruined reading by the kerosene lamp. At night we all sat in front of the radio and listened to school lessons they would broadcast. Everybody wanted to be top dog in school, so you studied.

Idlewild was a big resort for blacks. Count Basie, Della Reese, the Four Tops, all the big names used to perform there, and we got to know them all. We worked at the restaurants and the hotels they stayed at. I remember how the club owners would open up their drapes and put boxes on the outside so us kids could stand on them and watch the show.

We didn't even know what hope was. It wasn't acceptable. Anything that went against family values would cause you to be ostracized. If I had a girlfriend who got pregnant, I couldn't run around with her anymore. And if anyone got pregnant, she would get married.

I had big dreams because I met all these black lawyers, doctors, and politicians who were on vacation. They really helped me out later. The name Idlewild opened a lot of doors, because in any city there were people who had been to Idlewild.

When I got out of high school, I went to Chicago and got a job as a cashier at a clothing store. In 1961 I moved to Detroit, and the next year I married one of the businessmen I used to work for in Idlewild. He died four months later. My second marriage was another tragedy. He was a talented fellow, but he loved his liquor. I was no competition for the bottle, so we split up.

I moved back up north in 1968. By 1971 I had two daughters and was working for the school system as a librarian and a secretary, bringing home $126 every two weeks. I had a girlfriend in Detroit who told me the plants were hiring, so I came back down. A guy who was a hunting buddy of my dad got me a job at the truck plant.

At first the language at the plant frightened me. I had never been in an atmosphere like that, with all the joking. People called each other such bad names that I expected a fight any minute, every day. But there never was. They even would swear at the foreman and say, "Get out of here, motherfucker, I'm going to kick your ass," and he wouldn't get mad.

Some of the men were hard on me at first. They'd say things like "Oh, you're in nice shape for being an old lady." Or they might say, "We're going to take a leak." It took me a whole week to realize they weren't going to take a piss in front of me. They were just feeling me out.

I was going to quit after that first week. I was so tired. My hands were aching, and my whole body was a wreck. But when I got my first check, it was over $400 and I told myself, "Maybe I don't hurt as bad as I thought I did." The work didn't get any easier, but the money was decent, and I figured it would enable me to do some things I wanted to do, so I just hung in there, and now I've been there ten years.

The people at the plant are really good people, black and white, young and old. When my hands would hurt, someone would say, "Now, Betty, your hands are going to ache for a little while, but you'll get over it." Or they would say, "Betty, take a cigarette break, and we'll cover for you."

I painted with an air gun for three years, ten hours a day plus Saturdays, and all the time I had pain in my neck and shoulders and hands. They kept calling it tendonitis and giving me cortisone shots. But that didn't help. I finally found out that I had carpal tunnel syndrome and that any repetitious work, squeezing or pulling or pushing, would make it develop again.

Once I was properly diagnosed, they took me off the spray-painting job, and I worked with restrictions. I just floated around. For a few weeks I would wipe off cabs. Then I'd go out to the garage. I never had anything I could say was my job. I liked the variety, and I made friends in other departments.

I was laid off in 1980. For three years I was mostly laid off, but every year we would work for a few months. In 1983 I got permanently placed at Wayne Assembly and eventually got a job I could do without any pain: assembling brake lines.

I started coming in fifteen minutes early to build up some stock so I wouldn't have to do it the last hour. My foreman knew I was coming in early for my own benefit, but he told his bosses I had all this extra time, so they added an air gun to my job, despite my restriction. They said, "Either you do the job, or we don't have a job for you." So I did the job until I just couldn't hold the gun anymore. Then they sent me to the hospital, and the hospital told them my hands had become worse. But they wouldn't move me to another job. Finally, in 1984, I had an operation. After the operation they still didn't have a job that fit my restrictions. So they put me on medical leave.

To me being on medical is a form of punishment. They don't care that you hurt. They just want to keep you out on medical so long you'll do anything to come back. A lot of people on medical eventually go back and drop their restrictions.

I don't know whether I want to work anymore or not. Anything I do, my hands hurt. I can't even wring a cloth sometimes because they're so sore and swollen. My hands are always going to hurt.

Nobody in management really cares whether you are sick or not feeling well. They care more about the truck than they do about the person. In my opinion, the company doctors have ruined a lot of people's health. They tell you you can do the job no matter how sick you are.

When I started at the truck plant, I wasn't used to leaving my kids. Up north I would drop them off at school, go to my job, and pick them up after work. We were always together. But here I couldn't do that. I arranged for my next-door neighbor to watch to make sure they got off to school. A couple times I had to leave them in the house by themselves, and I worried all day long till I got back home. Those were the worst days of my life.

Finally I hired my neighbor. I bought food for her family and paid her $55 a week.

I took my kids over there after dinner, and she gave them baths and put their pajamas on. They would sleep there, and I would pick them up every day after I came home. I didn't like it, but what could I do? I had to get up at 4 A.M. and that was too early to get them up and take them to somebody else's house.

Other people in the plant had the same problems. Kids were getting themselves up and being left at home or being watched by neighbors. That's like breaking up your family. And for some people it really was the breakdown of their family.

When you work ten hours a day, you don't have time for your kids. When you get up, they're in bed, and when you come home, you're ready to go to bed. So on the weekends you let them have their way. You feel guilty, so you cater to them. I'd buy them pizza or fast food because that's what they wanted. Sometimes we would go downtown and stay at a nice hotel all weekend or go to Toronto and do whatever they wanted. They loved it.

A single parent who has to work can't get any help with child care. You cannot just go out in the streets and get a baby-sitter. You don't know who you're getting. But if I ask a child-care agency to send me a professional so my kids don't have to hang out in the streets, they won't do it because I make too much money, even though those are services I would pay for.

I can understand why kids get out of hand when parents have to work. It's because nobody wants to help you until it's too late. That's where the guns and things come in because your kids don't have any supervision while you're at work. And when you get home, you're so damn tired that you don't go in and search anybody's room.

In the plant they have women's lib mixed up. They think women want to be men. But we don't want to be men. We just want equal pay. We should all get paid the same because we are all autoworkers, but don't be ridiculous and pretend I can lift something I can't.

The women in the plant would like a law that they don't have to work more than forty hours. The men are the only ones who like ten-hour days. They're so geared to that check that a paycheck for eight hours would look ridiculous to them. I like the pay, too, but I want to be with my kids. The pay isn't worth it. Give me the eight hours, and let me go home and rest. Let me work some normal hours.

Working ten hours a day for years and years and years and years, and working every other Saturday, all you do is work and sleep. You're like a zombie. If your kids ask you something, you don't want any arguments, so you say yes to whatever they ask. Then, when they do it and you come to your right mind, you say, "God, did I tell you you could do that?" You're hardly even aware of what's happening with your kids.

When you talk to the union about working ten hours, they say, "Well, this is what the company and the UAW agreed to do." But I'm the one who works. Maybe I don't want to work that long.

To work ten hours, you have to be geeked up somehow. You have to be a really strong person not to take drugs. If you don't get on an inventive high, or a musical high, or do something to keep yourself happy at work, you are going to resort to drugs or booze or something.

We need shorter hours. Just have three shifts and let everybody get a little bit of money. Then you wouldn't have carpal tunnel syndromes and neck problems and back problems and all these health problems that people have. My doctor said ten hours is too long for anybody to work.

Glossary/Index

Career assessment survey, 51

Carnathan case, 116–117

Catholic church, stance on work/family roles, 357

Certification. *See* Credentialing

Champy, James, 412, 414

Chance, influence on occupational choice, 49, 79–85

Chaplin, Charlie, 408

Chemical Week (journal), 415

Child care, 2, 8, 50, 55, 345, 347–348, 359

    arrangements, 352–353

    in Europe and United States, 354

    men's role in, 394–400

    women's role in, 402–406

Children, 9

    occupational fantasies of, 48, 112

    socialization of, 49, 111

Chromosomes, deviance and, 277–278

Civilian labor force all employed and unemployed non-institutionalized civilians over 16 years of age, 7, 8

Civil Rights Act, 215, 357

Class system, in United States, 47, 421

Clinton, Bill, 350

Clinton, Hillary Rodham, 355

Coming of Post-Industrial Society, The (Bell), 409

Commuter marriage, 347, 373–381

Compensation, stress and, 205

Compensatory perspective, 5

Competition

    foreign, 417

    professional, 122

Computers, 128, 287, 351, 408, 413–414, 420. *See also* Technology

Conflict perspective on equality that argues that those who already have power and privilege in a society will try to keep them rather than share them with those who have less power and access

to the rewards offered by society, 47

Conforming environment, 51

Conformists, 279

Cosmetology, 116–117

Coworkers

    informal norms of, 279, 284, 287, 288–289

    relations with, 211–212, 436

Credentialing, 118–120, 123

Culture

    global economy and, 129–130, 201

    occupational deviance and, 288

    professional, 115

D

Danger, job related, 124, 130, 162–174, 205–206, 211–212

Day care. *See* Child care; Elder care

Death rates, occupation and, 2

Decision making, by workers, 416, 418, 419

Demographics, trends in, 347–348

Denial, of responsibility or injury, 282–283, 334–336

Denny's restaurants, racial discrimination and, 285

Dependent care plans, 358

Deprofessionalization the process by which occupations lose their standing as a profession, 121–123

Deskilling the process by which a job requires less skill from workers over time; often thought to be a consequence of technological innovation, 129, 407, 408–409, 412, 414, 420, 421

    consequences of, 409–411

    in industrial sector, 410–411

Developmental phases

    hierarchy of needs and, 200–201

    occupational choice and, 48–49

    women's alternative paths and, 102–109

Deviance behavior that violates important social norms or expectations biological explanations of, 277–278

categories of, 275–276

institutionalized, 291–301

sociological influences on, 282–301

technology and, 287–288, 421

Differential association a theory that argues that deviance results from learning norms and values from a group that supports breaking the norms, 278–279

Discouraged workers those who are interested in working, but who have not looked for work in the last 4 weeks because they have lost hope of finding a job, 10

Divorce, occupation and, 2

Dock work, 201, 203–204, 276, 287

Doctors. *See* Physicians

Downsizing, 6, 206, 415

Dual-career couples, 348, 354, 356, 378–381

Dualistic perspective, 5

E

Eastman Kodak, 413–414

Economic system, 47, 209, 212–213

changes in, 346–347, 409

impact of technology on, 411

Economy, globalization of, 14, 129–130, 201, 288, 414, 415, 422

Ectomorphs, 277

Education, 46, 47, 121

effect on worker participation, 417

opportunities for, 60

for professions, 118–120

social constraints and, 54, 57

Elder care, 353, 359

Electronic mail, 13, 287, 351, 408, 420

Emotional labor workers control their emotions in order to control the emotions of their customers or clients, 14, 129, 132–142

Empire Brush Company, 284

Employed those who, during the reference week, work at least an hour for pay or profit, who work 15 hours or more as unpaid workers in a family business, or who are temporarily absent from work, 7

Employee takeovers, 419

Endomorphs, 277

Engineering, 55, 56, 57

Environment, occupational, 1, 51–52, 124

hostile, 216

influence on workers' feelings, 202–207, 211

Equal Employment Opportunity Commission (EEOC), sexual harassment guidelines, 216

Equality, versus equity, 176–186

Establishment stage, 49

Ethics, code of, 115

Expert knowledge, routinization of, 121

F

Family

in agricultural economy, 346

as influence on women's occupational choices, 55

men's roles in, 394–400

work and, 345–359, 362–381, 383–393, 402–406, 421–422

Family and Medical Leave Act, 357–358

Fantasies, occupational, 45, 48, 50, 63–78

Farm workers, women as, 362–371

Feedback, 203, 204, 206

Femininity, as occupational type, 52, 86–100

Flexibility, in work schedules, 351–352

Flextime, 359

Flight attendants, 129, 283

"Follow the Way of Love" (letter), 356–357

Ford Co., 124

Formal learning, 112–113

Iron maiden role, 127
ISO 9000, 288

J

Jackall, Robert, 417
Job characteristics, formal, 202–203
Job loss, 206. *See also* Unemployment
Job security, 349
Job sharing, 352

K

Kanter, Rosabeth, 126
Koresh, David, 280

L

Labeling theory draws on the symbolic interactionist perspective while also recognizing the power of those who can label a behavior deviant, 280–282
Labor
    organized, effect on worker participation, 417
    relationship to management, 209–210
Labor and Monopoly Capital: The Degradation of Work in the Twentieth Century (Braverman), 409
Labor force typically refers to the civilian labor force only, but the total labor force actually includes members of the armed forces, 7–9, 10–12
Labor force participation rate the percent of employed and unemployed workers relative to the number of people in the noninstitutionalized population who are 16 years or older, 8, 9, 10–12
Labor market conditions, effect on worker participation, 416–417
Law/lawyers, 119, 121, 122, 123, 145, 153, 411
Laws, impact on work/family relationship, 357–358

Learning, formal and informal, 112–113
Leave acts, family, 357–358
Leisure nonwork activities chosen for their potential pleasure motivation
    characteristics of, 3–4
    impact of technology on, 421
    relationship to work, 4–5, 25–32
    social factors and, 6
    trends in, 6–7
Licensed practical nurses (LPNs), 118
Life expectancy, 2, 347, 348
Life insurance benefits, 350–351
Linder, Staffan, 7
Lombroso, Caesare, 277
Longshoremen, 275, 281, 303–309
Lotus Development Corporation, medical benefits offered by, 350

M

Maintenance stage, 49
Managed Heart, The (Hochschild), 129
Management practices, 207–212, 437–440
Managers, 421
    relationship with workers, 420, 441–442
    work teams and, 418, 419
Marx, Karl, 47, 209, 212
Mary Kay, 55, 86–100
Masculinity, as occupational type, 52
Maslow, Abraham, 200, 201, 202
Materials handling industry, impact of technology on, 407–408, 410
Maternity leave benefits, 352, 359
Mayo, Elton, 210
McDonaldization of Society, The (Ritzer), 122
Meaninglessness, 205
Medical school, 118, 120, 154–160
Men
    family roles of, 394–400
    gender expectations and, 55–56

Pink-collar occupations, 55
Pluralistic perspective, 5
Police officers, 275
  and use of deadly force, 330–341
  unwritten work norms of, 287
  women as, 176–186
Politics, occupation and, 2
Postindustrial society, 409, 422
Poultry workers, job satisfaction of, 240–250
Power, 409, 419. *See also* Status
Powershift (Toffler), 411
Pregnancy Discrimination Act, 357
Preparing for the Twenty-First Century (Kennedy), 411
Primary deviance deviant behavior that breaks the norms but is often temporarily or easily concealed, 281
Primary sector that part of the economy devoted to extracting from the land; includes farming, mining, and logging, 13
Privately held corporations, 124–126
Procter & Gamble, 125
Productivity, 202, 203, 204
  glass ceiling and, 215
  human relations model and, 210–211
  impact of technology on, 411
  reengineering and, 415
  scientific management and, 209, 210
  self-directed work teams and, 416, 417
  stress and, 206, 207
  worker satisfaction and, 199
Professionalization the process by which occupations gain their standing as a profession, 117–121
Professions, 113
  defining criteria for, 114–115
  legal applications, 115–117
Profit, 124, 201, 209, 285–286, 314–329

Proletariat in Marx's terms, those who have only their labor to sell, 47, 209, 212
Promotions
  glass ceiling effect and, 214, 215
  Mommy Track and, 356
Protegés, mentors and, 112–113
Publicly held corporations, 124–126

Q
Qualifications, 52
Quality Circles, 416
Quality-of-work-life programs, 416, 419

R
Race
  bias and, 214–215
  and child-care preferences, 353
  occupational choices and, 49, 54, 57, 58–59
  unemployed labor force and, 11–12
Railway workers, 25–32
Reality testing stage, 49
Rebels, 280
Reengineering reevaluating the structure of tasks and eliminating tasks that interfere with cost-effectiveness, 407, 412, 420
  computers and, 413–414
  effect on jobs, 415, 421
  profit motive and, 414–415
Reengineering the Corporation. A Manifesto for Business Revolution (Hammer and Champy), 412
Reference week the week when labor force participation information is collected, 8
Relationships
  with coworkers, 211–212
  and on-the-job stress, 206
Relocation services, 349–350
Responsibility, denial of, 282–283
Retirement benefits, 350–351
Retreatists, 280
Retrenchment, 6
Reverse socialization, 128

Rewards, 3, 17–24
  functional value of occupations and, 46–47, 50
  as immediate determinants of occupational choice, 53
  workers' feelings and, 202–204, 206
Risk. *See* Danger
Ritualists, 280
Ritzer, George, 414
Robotics, 408, 410
Role overload, 354–356, 359
Rules
  on-the-job, 206, 208
  violations of, 275–289

S

Safety hazards, 205–206, 310–313. *See also* Danger
Salary, 205, 213
  effects of deskilling on, 409
  as factor in job selection, 349
  and motivation, 209
Satisfaction good feelings about work, 199, 209, 240–250, 288, 411, 421
  expectations and, 202
  in family-friendly corporations, 354, 359
  and informal social interaction, 230–239
  and productivity, 199
  rewards and, 79–85, 204
  stress and, 207
Schor, Juliet, 6
Scientific management, 209–210, 414
Secondary deviance behavior that is labeled by others as deviant, 281
Secondary sector that part of the economy devoted to the production of manufactured goods, 14
Second shift taking care of household tasks and children after a full work day, 7, 356, 402–406
Seductress, as stereotypical role, 127

Self-actualization, 200, 201, 202
Service sector same as tertiary sector; that part of the economy devoted to the provision of services such as education, banking, and insurance, 13–14, 129, 130, 132–142
Sex segregation term used to describe the labor force and the large number of occupations that are filled predominantly by men or by women, 55
Sexual harassment unwelcome deliberate or repeated unsolicited sexual advances, verbal comments, gestures, or physical contact, 215–217
Shelby Die Casting Company, 418
Shift work, 352
Single-parent families, 348, 354, 356
Skill variety, 202
Sloan Management Review (journal), 129
Smith, Adam, 414
Social class, occupational position and, 1–2, 3, 6, 49, 54, 57, 60, 199, 349, 421
Social factors, occupational choice and, 49, 52–60
Socialization
  deviance and, 278–282
  gender and, 126–128, 176–186, 187–197
  process of, 111–113
  societal influences on, 128–130
  status and, 113–123
  workplace influences on, 123–128
Social Structural Model of Occupational Choice, 53
Socioeconomic organization, occupational choice and, 53
Sociological variables, 3, 6. *See also* Age; Gender; Race; Social class
Sociopsychological attributes, 53
Specialization, 122, 123, 209, 412, 414
Spillover perspective, 4